Medical Terminology *for* Insurance *and* Coding

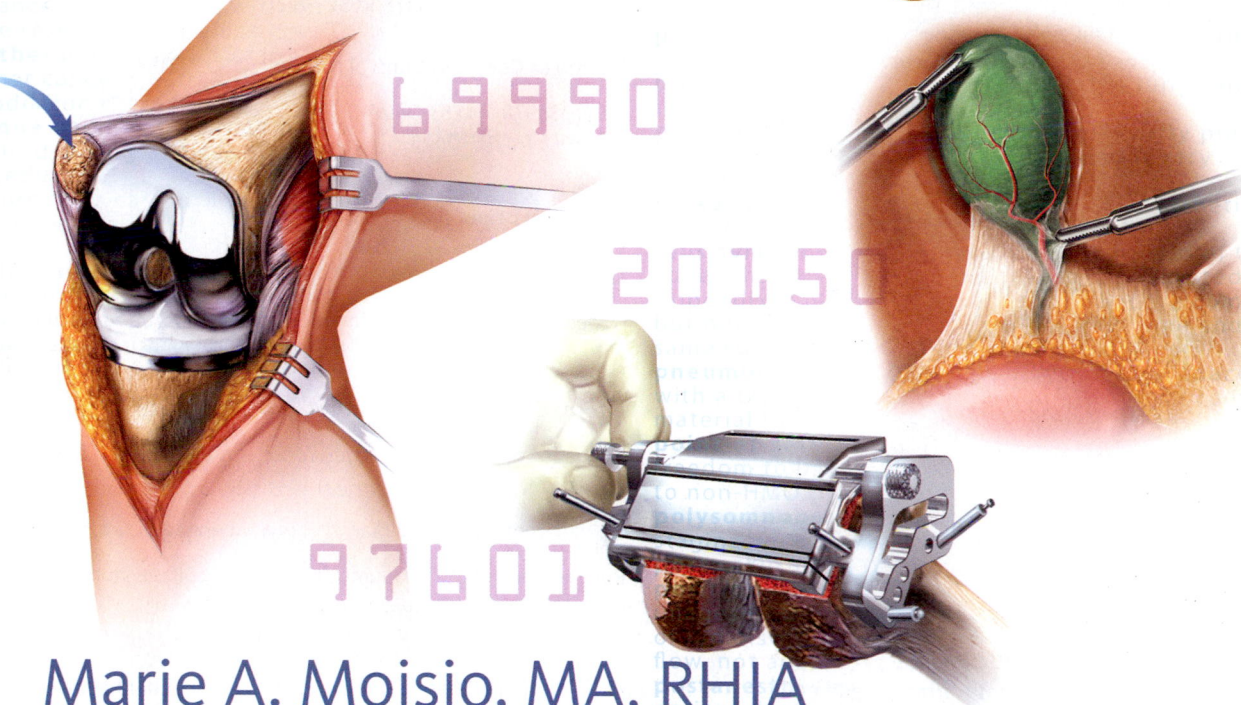

69990
20150
97601

Marie A. Moisio, MA, RHIA

Technical Collaborator
Judith E. Fields, CCS, CCS-P, CPC, CPC-H
Southeast Kentucky Community & Technical College
Coding Program Instructor
Harlan, Kentucky

DELMAR
CENGAGE Learning

Australia • Brazil • Japan • Korea • Mexico • Singapore • Spain • United Kingdom • United States

Medical Terminology for Insurance and Coding
Marie A. Moisio

Vice President, Career and Professional Editorial:
Dave Garza

Director of Learning Solutions:
Matthew Kane

Senior Acquisitions Editor:
Rhonda Dearborn

Managing Editor:
Marah Bellegarde

Product Manager:
Jadin Babin-Kavanaugh

Editorial Assistant:
Chiara Astriab

Vice President, Career and Professional
Marketing: Jennifer McAvey

Marketing Director:
Wendy Mapstone

Senior Marketing Manager:
Nancy Bradshaw

Marketing Coordinator:
Erica Ropitzky

Production Director:
Carolyn Miller

Production Manager:
Andrew Crouth

Content Project Manager:
Thomas Heffernan

Senior Art Director:
Jack Pendleton

2009 Current Procedural Terminology © 2008 American Medical Association. ALL RIGHTS RESERVED.

Library of Congress Control Number: 2009921851

ISBN-13: 978-1-4283-0426-0
ISBN-10: 1-4283-0426-6

Delmar
5 Maxwell Drive
Clifton Park, NY 12065-2919
USA

Cengage Learning is a leading provider of customized learning solutions with office locations around the globe, including Singapore, the United Kingdom, Australia, Mexico, Brazil, and Japan. Locate your local office at: **international.cengage.com/region**

Cengage Learning products are represented in Canada by Nelson Education, Ltd.

To learn more about Delmar, visit **www.cengage.com/delmar**

Purchase any of our products at your local college store or at our preferred online store **www.ichapters.com**

NOTICE TO THE READER

Printed in the United States of America
1 2 3 4 5 6 7 12 11 10

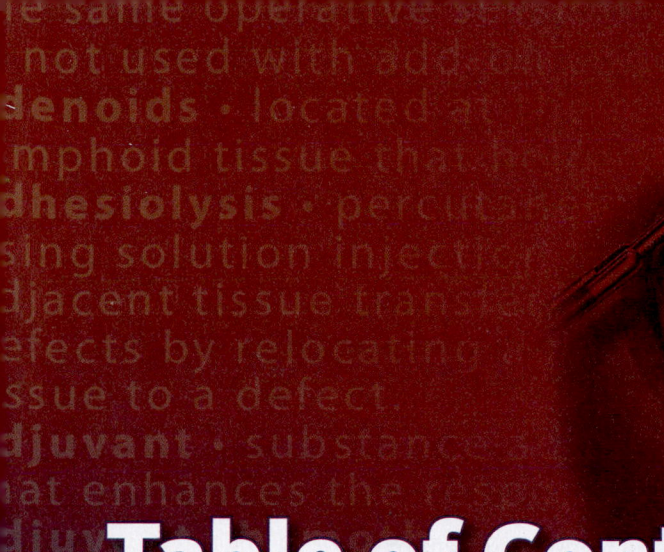

Table of Contents

CHAPTER 3
Introduction to Current Procedural Terminology (CPT) Coding   79

CHAPTER 4
Integumentary System   99

Preface

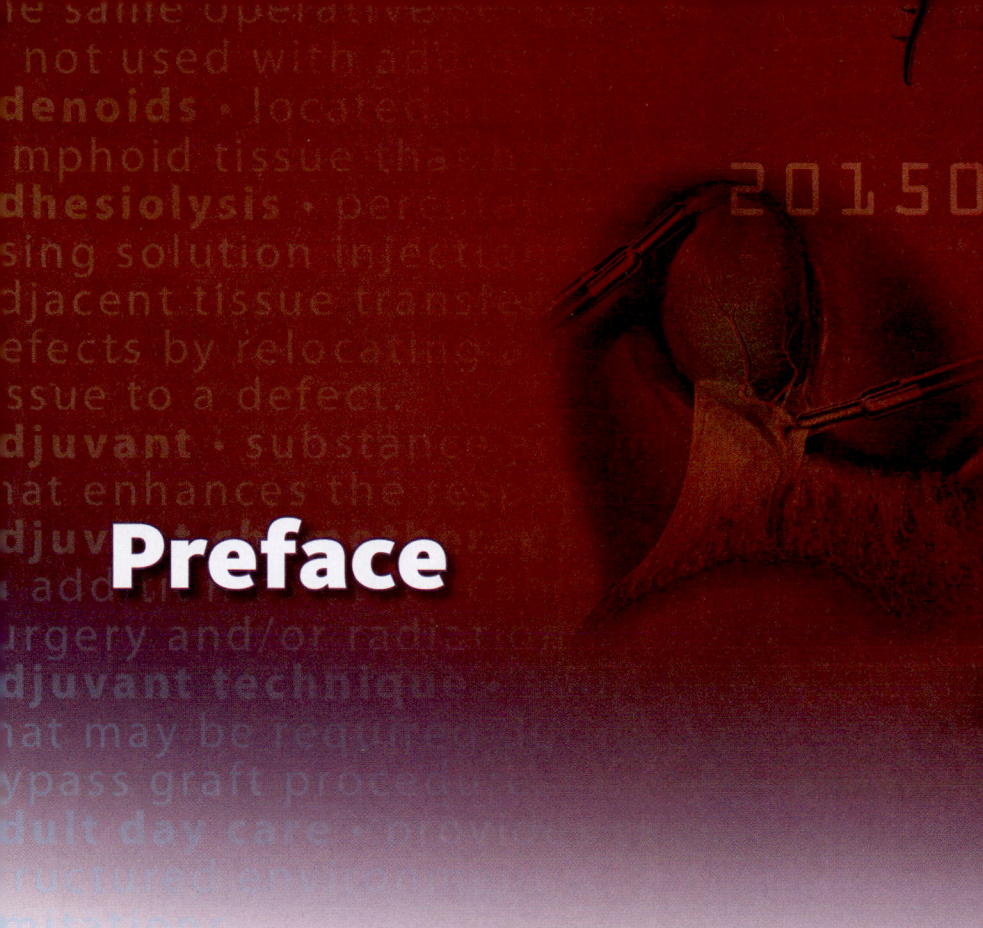

Medical terminology is the language of the health care industry. Accurate medical coding depends on a clear understanding of this language. *Medical Terminology for Insurance and Coding* provides students with the opportunity to work with medical terms within the context of medical coding. The text includes basic information related to medical terminology; *International Classification of Diseases, Ninth Revision, Clinical Modification* (ICD-9-CM) coding principles; and *Current Procedural Terminology* (CPT) coding principles.

The text is designed as a workbook for use in educational programs for medical assisting, medical coding, and health insurance billing. It can also be used for in-service training and professional development activities.

OBJECTIVES

The primary objective of this text is to provide students with a clear and concise understanding of the relationship between medical terminology and medical coding by:

- Introducing students to the foundations of medical terminology
- Introducing students to basic information related to medical coding
- Providing a variety of reinforcement exercises to enable students to learn medical terms and apply that knowledge to medical coding

FEATURES OF THE TEXT

Key features of this text are designed to encourage student success.

- Learning objectives identify expectations for each chapter.

- Medical reports provide an opportunity to learn medical terms in context and practice medical coding with realistic source documents.
- Numerous reinforcement exercises and end-of-chapter reviews measure student comprehension.
- Answers to some of the exercises are available in the back of the text to provide students with immediate feedback.

SUPPLEMENTS

The following supplements are available to facilitate the use of *Medical Terminology for Insurance and Coding* in the classroom.

Instructor's Manual

An Instructor's Manual is available for this textbook, and includes the following:

- **Section I: Suggestions for Course Development**—includes suggested classroom activities and lesson plans
- **Section II: Answer Key to Chapter Exercises and Reviews**—provides complete answer keys to all exercises
- **Section III: Final Examinations**—contains two sample exams and a final exam

Online Companion

The Online Companion Web site contains additional resources for both students and instructors. The site can be accessed by first going to **www.delmarlearning.com/companions**. Then select Allied Health from the left navigation menu, then scroll down to select the site for *Medical Terminology for Insurance and Coding*. To gain access to the password-protected side of the Online Companion site, see the print Instructor's Manual or contact your Delmar Sales Representative for the password.

Open Resources at the Online Companion

Anyone can access the following items without a password:

- Code updates to the textbook, as they become available

Password-Protected Resources at the Online Companion

For instructors only, the following items will be password-protected:

- Electronic version of the Instructor's Manual
- Code updates to answer keys as necessary

Thirty-Day Free Trial of EncoderPro™ CD-ROM

The EncoderPro™ CD-ROM included in the back of this textbook is a 30-day free trial version of Ingenix's powerful medical coding solution. The EncoderPro allows you to look up ICD-9-CM, CPT, and HCPCS Level II codes quickly and accurately. This software can be used to assign codes to any of the exercises in this textbook. If you are using this textbook in a classroom setting, please be sure to check with your instructor before installing the EncoderPro software, as the trial expires 30 days after installation.

REVIEWERS

The author and publisher would like to thank the following reviewers for their invaluable feedback on this product:

Michelle Cranney, MBA, RHIT, CCS-P, CPC
Program Director, Virginia College Online
Birmingham, Alabama

Deborah Fazio, CMAS, RMA
MBC Program Director, Sanford Brown College
Middleburg Heights, Ohio

Debra Tymcio, BA, RT(R)
Allied Health, Chair/Brown Mackie College
Akron, Ohio

Pam Ventgen, CMA, CCS-P, CPC
Professor, University of Alaska Anchorage
Anchorage, Alaska

Jan West-Boagni, BA
American Career College
Anaheim, California

Teresa Williamson, M.Ed, CMBS, MOS
Associate Professor, Chaffey College
Rancho Cucamonga, California

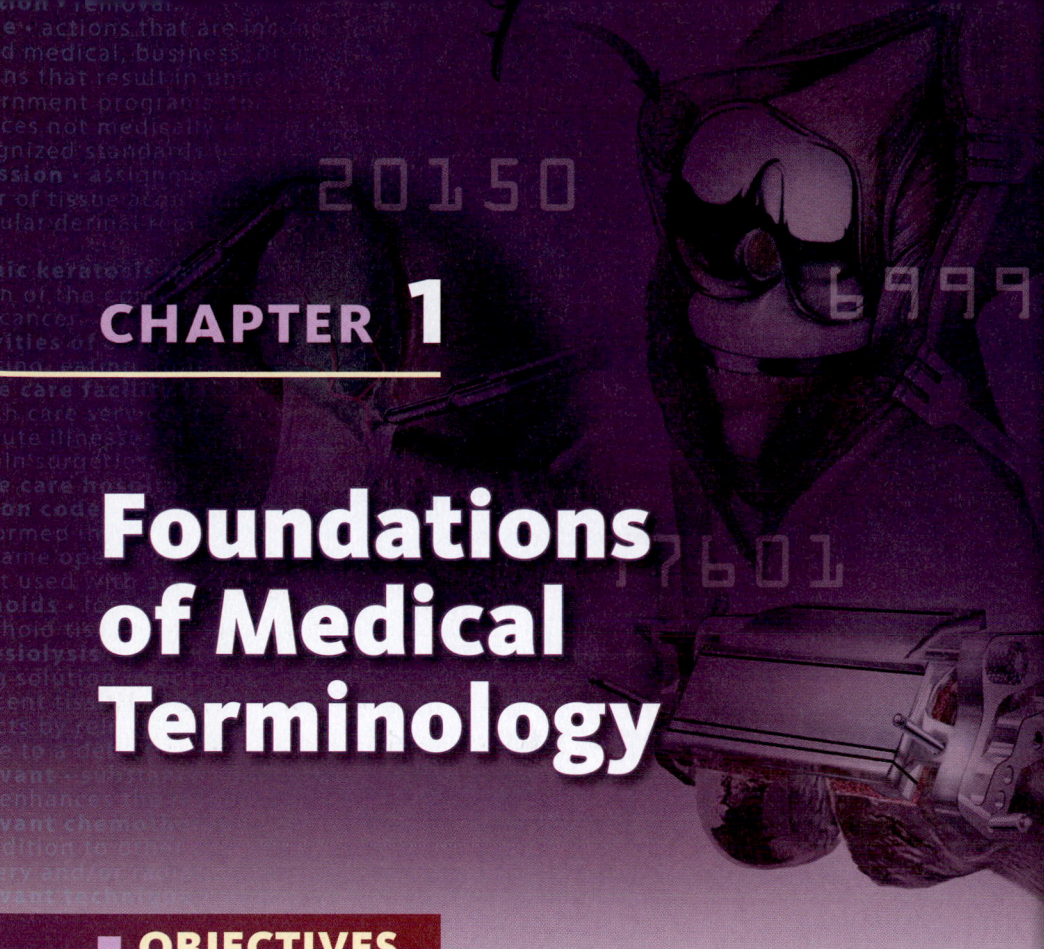

CHAPTER 1

Foundations of Medical Terminology

■ OBJECTIVES

At the completion of this chapter, the student should be able to:

1. Briefly define roots, prefixes, suffixes, combining forms, and combining vowels.
2. Combine roots and suffixes correctly.
3. Briefly define medical terms by recalling the meanings of roots, prefixes, and suffixes.
4. Describe the basic components of the body systems.
5. Accurately name, define, and spell body cavities, planes, quadrants, and regions.
6. Label the body cavities, regions, and quadrants.

■ OVERVIEW

Medical terminology is the language of the health care industry. Medical coders and billing specialists must acquire a working knowledge of this language. The first step toward this goal is to memorize the commonly used prefixes and suffixes. The prefixes and suffixes are combined with word roots to create medical terms. This chapter covers the following:

- Commonly used prefixes and suffixes
- Rules for combining roots, prefixes, and suffixes
- Pronunciation rules

continued

KEY TERMS

abdominal cavity
anatomical position
body directions
body planes
body quadrants
body regions
cell membrane
cells
chromosomes
combining form
combining vowel
connective tissue
coronal plane
cranial cavity
cytology
cytoplasm
deoxyribonucleic acid (DNA)
diaphragm
dorsal cavity
epigastric region
epithelial tissue
frontal plane
genes
horizontal plane
hypogastric region
left hypochondriac region
left iliac region
left inguinal region
left lower quadrant (LLQ)
left lumbar region
left upper quadrant (LUQ)
midsagittal plane
muscle tissue
nervous tissue
nucleus
organs
pelvic cavity
prefix
right hypochondriac region
right iliac region
right inguinal region
right lower quadrant (RLQ)
right lumbar region
right upper quadrant (RUQ)
root
sagittal plane
spinal cavity
suffix
systems
thoracic cavity
tissues
transverse plane
umbilical region
ventral cavity
viscera

- Analyzing medical terms
- Building medical terms

Exercises are designed to help you learn the commonly used prefixes and suffixes and their meanings.

The second step toward learning medical terminology is to master the terms related to the overall structure and organization of the body. These terms include the following:

- Structural organizational terms
- Body cavities
- Body planes
- Body quadrants and regions
- Directional terms

Exercises are designed to help you acquire a working knowledge of medical terms related to the body as a whole.

ROOTS

A **root** is the foundation of a medical term and usually identifies a body part, color, and sometimes a condition. Prefixes and suffixes combine with roots to create medical terms. Word roots have a **combining form** that is created when a root is combined with a vowel. The vowel, called a **combining vowel**, is usually an *o*, and occasionally an *e* or *i*. The combining forms of the roots used in this chapter are:

- arthr/o = joint
- cardi/o = heart
- dermat/o = skin
- gastr/o = stomach

The combining form of a root is used when joining roots with roots, or combining roots with suffixes that begin with a consonant. In this text, word roots are introduced with the appropriate body system. Roots that identify color are used in medical terms throughout the text. The combining forms for these roots are:

- cirrh/o = yellow
- cyan/o = blue; bluish
- eosin/o = rosy red; rosy
- erythr/o = red
- leuk/o = white
- melan/o = black
- xanth/o = yellow

PREFIXES

A **prefix** is a word part that is added to the beginning of a word root. In a list of word parts, prefixes are written with a hyphen after the prefix. Many prefixes in medical terms keep their English meaning, such as pre- (before), post- (after), and anti- (against).

Commonly used prefixes can be divided into four categories: general, negative, numerical, and problem or disease prefixes. Learn each group of prefixes and complete the exercises.

General Prefixes

General prefixes often refer to size, shape, direction, and location. The first set of general prefixes is listed in table 1-1. Examples of the prefixes in medical terms and regular words are intended to help you learn the prefixes.

Table 1-1 General Prefixes

PREFIX	MEANING	EXAMPLES
ab-	away from	**ab**normal = away from being normal
		abduct (ab-**DUCT**) = to move away from the body
ad-	to; toward	**ad**dendum = in addition to; added to
		adduct (ad-**DUCT**) = to move to or toward the body
ante-	before	**ante**room = a room or area before a larger room or area
		antefebrile (an-tee-**FEE**-brill) = before a fever
astr-	star	**astr**ology = study of the stars
		astrocyte (**ASS**-troh-sight) = star-shaped cell
auto-	self	**auto**biography = story written by yourself about your life
		autograft (**AH**-toh-graft) = surgical transplant of one's own tissue
brady-	slow	**brady**cardia (bray-dih-**KAR**-dee-ah) = slow heart rate

continued

Table 1-1 (*continued*) General Prefixes

PREFIX	MEANING	EXAMPLES
ect-	outside; outer	**ect**oderm (**EKT**-oh-derm) = outermost layer of the skin
en-	within; in	**en**trails = organs within or inside of a human or other animal
		entropia (en-**TROH**-pee-ah) = turning in of the eyes
endo-	within; inner	**endo**cardium (**en**-doh-**KAR**-dee-um) = within the heart; inner lining of the heart
epi-	above; upon	**epi**gastric (ep-ih-**GAS**-trik) = above the stomach
ex-	out; outer	**ex**it = to go out; passage/doorway used to go out
		excision (ek-**SIH**-zhun) = taking out; cutting away
hemi-	half	**hemi**sphere = half of a sphere
		hemiplegia (**heh**-mih-**PLEE**-jee-ah) = paralysis of one side (half) of the body
infra-	below; inferior	**infra**orbital (in-frah-**OR**-bih-tal) = below the eye socket
inter-	between; among	**inter**mission = time period between events or periods of activity
		intercellular (**in**-ter-**SELL**-yoo-lar) = between the cells
intra-	within	**intra**state = existing or occurring within a state
		intracellular (**in**-trah-**SELL**-yoo-lar) = within the cells
iso-	same; equal	**iso**metric (eye-soh-**MET**-rik) = having the same length or dimension

EXERCISE 1-1

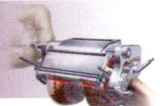

Circle the prefix in each term and write the definition of the prefix.

1. autoimmune _____ self _____
2. endocardium _____ within _____
3. abduction _____ away from _____
4. adduction _____ to; toward _____
5. intradermal _____ within _____
6. bradykinesia _____ slow _____
7. ectopic _____ outside _____
8. astrocyte _____ star _____
9. hemisphere _____ half _____
10. epigastric _____ above, upon _____

EXERCISE 1-2

Match the prefix in column 1 with the meaning in column 2.

COLUMN 1

_b_ 1. ab-

_c_ 2. ante-

_j_ 3. astr-

_h_ 4. auto-

_i_ 5. brady-

_k_ 6. ect-

_a_ 7. epi-

_d_ 8. infra-

_e_ 9. inter-

_f_ 10. intra-

_g_ 11. iso-

COLUMN 2

a. above; upon

b. away from

c. before

d. below; inferior

e. between

f. within; in

g. same; equal

h. self

i. slow

j. star

k. outside; out

EXERCISE 1-3

Write the prefix for each meaning.

1. above; upon _____ epi- _____
2. away from _____ ab- _____
3. before _____ ante- _____
4. below; inferior _____ infra- _____
5. between _____ inter- _____
6. half _____ hemi- _____
7. out; outer _____ ex- _____
8. outside; outer _____ ect- _____
9. same; equal _____ iso- _____
10. self _____ auto _____

continued

11. slow _____brady-_____
12. star _____astr-)_____

7. suprarenal _____above; over_____
8. multicellular _____many_____
9. retroflexion _____behind_____
10. postoperative _____after_____

The last set of general prefixes is listed in table 1-2. Learn the prefixes and complete the exercises.

EXERCISE 1-4
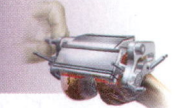

Circle the prefix in each term and write the definition of the prefix.

1. metamorphosis _____change_____
2. microscope _____small_____
3. semilunar _____half_____
4. tachycardia _____fast_____
5. substernal _____below; under_____
6. neoplasm _____new_____

EXERCISE 1-5
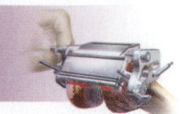

Match the prefix in column 1 with the meaning in column 2.

COLUMN 1		COLUMN 2
_c_	1. pan-	a. above; over; excess
_d_	2. para-	b. after
_d_	3. peri-	c. all
_a_	4. poly-	d. around; surrounding
_b_	5. post-	e. before; in front of

Table 1-2   General Prefixes

PREFIX	MEANING	EXAMPLES
macro-	large	**macro**cyte (**MAK**-roh-sight) = abnormally large red blood cell
meta-	change; after; beyond	**meta**plasia (met-ah-**PLAY**-zee-ah) = change from one type of growth to another
micro-	small	**micro**cyte (**MY**-kroh-sight) = abnormally small red blood cell
multi-	many	**multi**lobular (mul-tigh-**LOB**-yoo-lar) = having many lobes
neo-	new	**neo**plasm (**NEE**-oh-plazm) = new growth
pan-	all	**pan**carditis (**pan**-kar-**DIGH**-tiss) = inflammation of the entire heart
para-	near; beside	**para**nasal (**pair**-ah-**NAY**-sal) = near or beside the nose
peri-	around; surrounding	**peri**meter = boundary surrounding a specific location **peri**cardium (**pair**-ih-**KAR**-dee-um) = membrane around the heart
poly-	many	**poly**arthritis (**pall**-ee-ar-**THRIGH**-tiss) = inflammation of many joints
post-	after	**post**partum (post-**PAR**-tum) = after giving birth
pre-	before	**pre**natal (pre-**NAY**-tal) = before giving birth
retro-	behind; backward	**retro**spect = looking back at past events **retro**grade (**REH**-troh-grayd) = moving backward
semi-	half	**semi**lunar (sem-eye-**LOO**-nar) = half-moon shaped
sub-	below; under	**sub**hepatic (**sub**-heh-**PAT**-ik) = below or under the liver
super-	above; over; excess	**super**ior (soo-**PEER**-ee-or) = above or toward a higher place
supra-	above; on top of	**supra**spinal (**soo**-prah-**SPIGH**-nal) = above the spine
sym-	with; association	**sym**pathy = having an association with another's feelings **sym**biosis (sim-bee-**OH**-siss) = living with or in close association
syn-	together; with; union	**syn**chronize = to move or operate together or in unison **syn**ergistic (sin-er-**JISS**-tik) = related to working together
tachy-	fast	**tachy**cardia (**tak**-ih-**KAR**-dee-ah) = fast heart rate

_e_ 6. pre-   f. change

_f_ 7. meta-   g. many

_a_ 8. super-   h. near; beside

_j_ 9. sym-   i. together; with; union

_i_ 10. syn-   j. with; association

4. change _Meta-_

5. fast _tachy-_

6. half _semi-_

7. large _macro-_

8. near; beside _para-_

9. new _neo-_

10. together; with; union _syn-_

EXERCISE 1-6

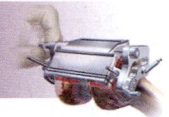

Write the prefix for each meaning.

1. above; on top of _supra-_

2. above; over; excess _super-_

3. behind; backward _retro-_

Negative, Numerical, and Disease Prefixes

Negative and numerical prefixes are self-explanatory. Problem or disease prefixes provide some information about an abnormal structure or function. Learn the prefixes in table 1-3 and complete the exercises.

Table 1-3 Negative, Numerical, and Disease Prefixes

NEGATIVE PREFIXES		
PREFIX	**MEANING**	**EXAMPLE**
a-; an-; ana-	no; not; without	**an**archy = without laws or government **an**algesia (**an**-al-**JEE**-zee-ah) = without pain; no sensation of pain
anti-	against	**anti**fungal (an-tigh-**FUNG**-al) = against fungus
contra-	against; opposite	**contra**ception (con-trah-**SEP**-shun) = against conception
non-	not	**non**functioning = does not function

NUMERICAL PREFIXES		
PREFIX	**MEANING**	**EXAMPLE**
bi-	two; double; both	**bi**lateral (bigh-**LAT**-er-al) = both sides; two sides
centi-	hundred; hundredth	**centi**meter (**SEN**-tih-**me**-ter) = one hundredth of a meter
dec-	ten	**dec**aliter (**DEK**-ah-**lee**-ter) = ten liters
milli-	one thousandth	**milli**liter (**MILL**-ih-**lee**-ter) = one thousandth of a liter
quadr-	four	**quadr**iplegia (**kwod**-rih-**PLEE**-jee-ah) = paralysis of all four limbs
tri-	three	**tri**cuspid (trigh-**KUSS**-pid) = having three flaps
uni-	one	**uni**lateral (yoo-nih-**LAT**-er-al) = one side

DISEASE AND PROBLEM PREFIXES		
PREFIX	**MEANING**	**EXAMPLE**
carcin-*	cancerous	**carcin**oma (kar-sin-**OH**-mah)
dys-	difficult; painful	**dys**uria (dis-**YOO**-ree-ah) = painful urination
hyper-	above; excessive	**hyper**thyroidism (**high**-per-**THIGH**-royd-izm) = excessive thyroid activity
hypo-	deficient; below	**hypo**thyroidism (**high**-poh-**THIGH**-royd-izm) = deficient thyroid activity
mal-	bad; poor; abnormal	**mal**absorption (mal-ab-**SORP**-shun) = abnormal absorption

*carcin/o = cancer is a word root.

EXERCISE 1-7

Circle the prefix in each term and write the definition of the prefix.

1. bicuspid _two-double_
2. antibiotic _against_
3. hypertension _above_
4. carcinoma _cancerous_
5. hypotension _below_
6. dyslexia _painful, difficult_
7. anaerobic _no, not, without_
8. malabsorption _bad, poor, abnormal_
9. contraindicated _against, opposite_
10. quadruplet _four_

EXERCISE 1-8

Write the prefix for each definition.

1. above; upon _epi-, supra-_
2. away from _ab-_
3. before _ante-, pre-_
4. below; inferior _sub-_
5. between _inter-_
6. half _hemi-_
7. out; outer _ex-, ect-_
8. outside; outer _ect-_
9. same; equal _iso-_
10. self _auto-_
11. slow _brady-_
12. star _astr-_
13. above; on top of _supra- (epi-, super-)_
14. above; over; excess _super-_
15. behind; backward _retro-_
16. change _meta-_
17. fast _tachy-_
18. half _hemi-_

19. large _macro-_
20. near; beside _para-_
21. new _neo-_
22. together; with; union _syn-_
23. above; excessive _hyper- (super-)_
24. against _anti-_
25. against; opposite _contra- (anti)_
26. bad; poor; abnormal _mal-_
27. cancerous _carcin-_
28. deficient; below _hypo-_
29. difficult; painful _dys-_
30. hundred; hundredth _centi-_
31. no; not; without _a-, an-, ana-_
32. not _a-, an-, ana-_
33. one _uni-_
34. one thousandth _milli-_
35. ten _dec-_
36. three _tri-_
37. two; double; both _bi-_

SUFFIXES

A **suffix** is a word part that is added to the end of the word root. Nearly all medical terms have a suffix. In a list of word parts, suffixes are written with a hyphen preceding the suffix. Suffixes indicate whether a medical term is a noun or an adjective. Remember that a noun identifies a person, place, animal, or thing; an adjective is a word that describes a noun. Examples of adjective suffixes include:

- -ac; -al; -ar; -ary = pertaining to; like
- -ic; -iac = pertaining to
- -oid = like; resembling

Suffixes can be divided into three categories: general suffixes, disease and abnormal condition suffixes, and treatment and procedure suffixes.

General Suffixes

General suffixes are used to describe general medical processes and functions. Learn the suffixes in table 1-4 and complete the exercises.

Table 1-4 General Suffixes

SUFFIX	MEANING	EXAMPLE
-ac; -al; -ar; -ary	pertaining to	cardiovascul**ar** (**kar**-dee-oh-**VASS**-kyoo-lar) = pertaining to the heart and vessels
-crine	to secrete	endo**crine** (**EN**-doh-krin) = to secrete into
-crit	to separate	hemato**crit** (hee-**MAT**-oh-krit) = to separate blood
-cyte	cell	leuko**cyte** (**LOO**-koh-sight) = white cell; white blood cell
-gen; -genesis; -genic	producing; forming	spermato**genesis** (sper-**mat**-oh-**JEN**-eh-siss) = producing sperm
-globin; -globulin	protein	hemo**globin** (**HEE**-mah-gloh-bin) = blood protein
-gram	record; picture	veno**gram** (**VEE**-noh-gram) = record or picture of the veins
-graph	instrument for recording	cardio**graph** (**KAR**-dee-oh-graf) = instrument that records heart activity
-graphy	process of recording	cardio**graphy** (**kar**-dee-**OG**-rah-fee) = recording the activity or a picture of the heart
-iac; -ic	pertaining to	card**iac** (**KAR**-dee-ak) = pertaining to the heart
-oid	like; resembling	ov**oid** (**OH**-voyd) = resembling an oval or an egg
-(o)logist	specialist	dermat**ologist** (**der**-mah-**TALL**-oh-jist) = skin specialist
-(o)logy	study of	dermat**ology** (**der**-mah-**TALL**-oh-jee) = study of the skin
-ous	pertaining to	muc**ous** (**MEW**-kuss) = pertaining to mucus
-pepsia	digestion	dys**pepsia** (diss-**PEP**-see-ah) = difficult or painful digestion
-phagia	eating; swallowing	a**phagia** (ah-**FAY**-jee-ah) = lack of the ability to swallow
-phonia	voice; sound	a**phonia** (ah-**FOH**-nee-ah) = lack of the ability to produce sound

EXERCISE 1-9

Circle the suffix in each term and write the definition of the suffix.

1. endo(crine) *to secrete*
2. patho(genic) *producing, forming*
3. gamma(globulins) *protein*
4. reno(gram) *record, picture*
5. echo(graph) *instrument for recording*
6. echocardio(graphy) *process of recording*
7. uro(logist) *specialist*
8. a(phonia) *voice; sound*
9. radio(logy) *study of*
10. erythro(cytes) *cell*

EXERCISE 1-10

Match the suffix in column 1 with the meaning in column 2.

COLUMN 1   **COLUMN 2**

h 1. -crine   a. cell
j 2. -crit   b. digestion
a 3. -cyte   c. eating; swallowing
l 4. -genesis; -genic   d. record; picture
g 5. -globin; -globulin   e. pertaining to
d 6. -gram   f. processing of recording
f 7. -graphy   g. protein
i 8. -(o)logist   h. secrete

continued

_e_ 9. -ous   i.   specialist
_b_ 10. -pepsia   j.   separate
_c_ 11. -phagia   k.   voice; sound
_k_ 12. -phonia   l.   producing

10. protein _-globin, -globulin_
11. record _-gram_
12. resembling; like _-iod_
13. specialist _-(o)logist_
14. study of _-ology_
15. to secrete _-crine_
16. to separate _-crit_
17. voice; sound _-phonia_

Learn the suffixes in table 1-5 and complete the exercises.

EXERCISE 1-11

Write the suffix for each definition.

1. cell _-cyte_
2. digestion _-pepsia_
3. eating; swallowing _-phagia_
4. instrument for recording _-graph_
5. pertaining to _-ac, -al, -ar, -ary, -ious, -iac, -ic_
6. pertaining to _''_
7. pertaining to _''_
8. process of recording _-graphy_
9. producing; forming _-gen, -genesis, -genic_

EXERCISE 1-12

Circle the suffix in each term and write the definition of the suffix.

1. oto(scope) _instrument for viewing_
2. hemato(poiesis) _formation_
3. cardio(version) _to turn_

Table 1-5   General Suffixes

SUFFIX	MEANING	EXAMPLE
-phoresis	carrying; transmission	electro**phoresis** (ee-**lek**-troh-for-**EE**-siss) = carrying or transmission of an electrical charge
-phoria	feeling; mental state	dys**phoria** (diss-**FOR**-ee-ah) = bad feeling
-pnea	breathing	dys**pnea** (disp-**NEE**-ah) = difficult breathing
-poiesis	formation	erythro**poiesis** (air-**rith**-roh-poy-**EE**-siss) = formation of red blood cells
-scope	instrument of viewing	micro**scope** (**MY**-kroh-scope) = instrument for viewing small objects
-scopy	process of viewing	arthro**scopy** (ar-**THROSS**-koh-pee) = viewing the joint(s)
-somnia	sleep	in**somnia** (in-**SOM**-nee-ah) = inability to sleep
-stasis	control; stop	hemo**stasis** (hee-moh-**STAY**-siss) = stopping blood flow
-therapy	treatment	chemo**therapy** (**kee**-moh-**THAIR**-ah-pee) = treatment using chemicals
-thorax	chest; pleural cavity	hemo**thorax** (hee-moh-**THOR**-acks) = blood in the pleural or chest cavity
-tocia	labor; birth	dys**tocia** (diss-**TOH**-see-ah) = abnormal labor
-tresia	opening	a**tresia** (ah-**TREE**-see-ah) = lack of a normal opening
-trophy	growth; development	dys**trophy** (**DISS**-troh-fee) = abnormal or bad growth
-tropin	nourish; develop; stimulate	somato**tropin** (**soh**-mat-oh-**TROH**-pin) = stimulates body growth
-version	to turn	retro**version** (**reh**-troh-**VER**-zhun) = to turn backward

4. atrophy _growth, development_
5. pneumothorax _chest, pleural cavity_
6. orthopnea _breathing_
7. euphoria _feeling, mental state_
8. endoscopy _process of viewing_
9. cryotherapy _treatment_

EXERCISE 1-13

Match the suffix in column 1 with the meaning in column 2.

COLUMN 1   **COLUMN 2**

_____ 1. -phoresis   a. breathing

_____ 2. -phoria   b. carrying; transmission

_____ 3. -pnea   c. control; stop

_____ 4. -poiesis   d. feeling; mental state

_____ 5. -scopy   e. formation

_____ 6. -somnia   f. labor; birth

_____ 7. -stasis   g. nourish; develop

_____ 8. -therapy   h. opening

_____ 9. -tocia   i. process of viewing

_____ 10. -tresia   j. sleep

_____ 11. -tropin   k. treatment

EXERCISE 1-14

Write the suffix for each meaning.

1. breathing _____
2. carrying; transmission _____
3. chest; pleural cavity _____
4. control; stop _____
5. feeling; mental state _____
6. formation _____
7. growth; development _____
8. instrument for viewing _____
9. labor; birth _____
10. nourish; develop; stimulate _____
11. opening _____
12. process of viewing _____
13. sleep _____
14. to turn _____
15. treatment _____

Disease and Abnormal Condition Suffixes

Disease and abnormal condition suffixes are used to identify what is wrong with a given body part. Learn the suffixes and meanings in table 1-6 and complete the exercises.

Table 1-6   Disease and Abnormal Condition Suffixes

SUFFIX	MEANING	EXAMPLE
-algia	pain	arth**ralgia** (ar-**THRAL**-jee-ah) = joint pain
-cele	hernia; herniation	recto**cele** (**REK**-toh-seel) = herniation into the rectum
-cytosis	condition of cells	leuko**cytosis** (**loo**-koh-sigh-**TOH**-siss) = condition of white blood cells (abnormal increase)
-dynia	pain	gastro**dynia** (**gass**-troh-**DIN**-ee-ah) = pain in the stomach
-emesis	vomiting	hemat**emesis** (hee-mah-**TEM**-ah-siss) = vomiting blood
-emia	blood condition	an**emia** (ah-**NEE**-mee-ah) = lack of quantity or quality of blood
-ia; -iasis	abnormal condition	lith**iasis** (lih-**THIGH**-ah-siss) = abnormal presence of stones
-itis	inflammation	gingiv**itis** (jin-jih-**VIGH**-tiss) = inflammation of gums
-lysis; -lytic	breakdown; destruction	hemo**lysis** (hee-**MALL**-oh-siss) = destruction of blood or red blood cells
-malacia	softening	osteo**malacia** (**oss**-tee-oh-mah-**LAY**-she-ah) = softening of bone
-megaly	enlargement	cardio**megaly** (**kar**-dee-oh-**MEG**-ah-lee) = enlarged heart
-oma	tumor	aden**oma** (ad-en-**OH**-mah) = tumor of the gland
-osis	abnormal condition	dermat**osis** (der-mah-**TOH**-siss) = abnormal skin condition

EXERCISE 1-15

Circle the suffix in each term and write the definition of the suffix.

1. melanoma _____
2. spherocytosis _____
3. bacteremia _____
4. hepatitis _____
5. chondromalacia _____
6. halitosis _____
7. cephalalgia _____
8. cystocele _____
9. nephromegaly _____
10. myodynia _____

EXERCISE 1-16

Write the suffix for each meaning.

1. blood condition _____
2. breakdown; destruction _____

3. abnormal condition _____
4. enlarged; enlargement _____
5. hernia; herniation _____
6. inflammation _____
7. pain _____
8. softening _____
9. tumor _____
10. vomiting _____

Review the suffixes in table 1-7 and complete the exercises.

EXERCISE 1-17

Circle the suffix in each term and write the definition of the suffix.

1. hemiparesis _____
2. menorrhagia _____
3. splenorrhexis _____
4. neutropenia _____
5. acrophobia _____
6. nephroptosis _____

Table 1-7 Disease and Abnormal Condition Suffixes

SUFFIX	MEANING	EXAMPLE
-paresis	slight paralysis	hemi**paresis** (**hem**-ee-pah-**REE**-siss) = slight paralysis of one side of the body
-pathy	disease	neuro**pathy** (noo-**ROP**-eh-thee) = disease of nerves
-penia	decreased number	leukocyto**penia** (**loo**-koh-sigh-toh-**PEE**-nee-ah) = decreased number of white cells (white blood cells)
-phobia	abnormal fear	arachno**phobia** (ah-**rak**-noh-**FOH**-bee-ah) = abnormal fear of spiders
-plegia	paralysis	quadri**plegia** (kwad-rih-**PLEE**-jee-ah) = paralysis of all four limbs
-ptosis	drooping; sagging; prolapse	nephro**ptosis** (**neff**-rop-**TOH**-siss) = drooping kidney
-ptysis	spitting up	hemo**ptysis** (hee-**MOP**-tih-siss) = spitting up blood
-(r)rhage; -(r)rhagia	bursting forth of blood	hemo**rrhage** (**HEM**-oh-rij) = bursting forth of blood
-(r)rhea	flow; discharge	rhino**rrhea** (**righ**-noh-**REE**-ah) = discharge from the nose; runny nose
-(r)rhexis	rupture	utero**rrhexis** (**yoo**-ter-oh-**RECKS**-siss) = rupture of the uterus
-sclerosis	hardening	arterio**sclerosis** (ar-**teer**-ee-oh-sklair-**OH**-siss) = hardening of the arteries
-spasm	contraction; twitching	cardio**spasm** (**KAR**-dee-oh-spasm) = twitching of the heart muscle
-stenosis	narrowing; tightening	arterio**stenosis** (ar-**teer**-ree-oh-sten-**OH**-siss) = narrowing of an artery

7. atherosclerosis _____

8. hemiplegia _____

9. neuropathy _____

10. otorrhea _____

_____ 13. -spasm   m. softening

_____ 14. -stenosis   n. spitting up

EXERCISE 1-18

Match the suffixes in column 1 with the meanings in column 2.

COLUMN 1

_____ 1. -malacia
_____ 2. -megaly
_____ 3. -osis
_____ 4. -paresis
_____ 5. -pathy
_____ 6. -phobia
_____ 7. -plegia
_____ 8. -ptosis
_____ 9. -ptysis
_____ 10. -(r)rhage
_____ 11. -(r)rhea
_____ 12. -sclerosis

COLUMN 2

a. abnormal condition
b. abnormal fear
c. bursting forth of blood
d. contraction; twitching
e. drooping; sagging; prolapse
f. disease
g. enlargement; enlarged
h. flow; discharge
i. hardening
j. narrowing; tightening
k. paralysis
l. slight paralysis

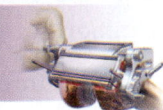

EXERCISE 1-19

Write the suffix for each meaning.

1. bursting forth of blood _____
2. decreased number _____
3. drooping; sagging _____
4. hernia _____
5. inflammation _____
6. mass; tumor _____
7. pain _____
8. rupture _____
9. slight paralysis _____
10. vomiting _____

Treatment and Procedure Suffixes

Treatment and procedure suffixes describe a variety of medical interventions such as the removal or repair of a body part or an organ. Review the suffixes in table 1-8 and complete the exercises.

Table 1-8   Treatment and Procedure Suffixes

SUFFIX	MEANING	EXAMPLE
-centesis	surgical puncture	thora**centesis** (**thor**-ah-sen-**TEE**-siss) = surgical puncture into the chest or thoracic cavity
-desis	binding together	arthro**desis** (ar-throh-**DEE**-siss) = binding together of joints
-ectasia; -ectasis	stretching; dilation	gastr**ectasia** (**gass**-trek-**TAY**-zee-ah) = stretching the stomach
-ectomy	surgical removal; excision	gastr**ectomy** (gass-**TREK**-toh-mee) = surgical removal of all or part of the stomach
-(o)stomy	create a new opening	colo**stomy** (koh-**LOSS**-toh-mee) = creating a new opening between the colon and abdominal wall
-(o)tomy	incision into	laparo**tomy** (**lap**-ah-**ROT**-oh-mee) = incision into the abdominal wall
-pexy	surgical fixation	utero**pexy** (**yoo**-ter-oh-**PEK**-see) = surgical fixation of the uterus
-plasty	surgical repair	rhino**plasty** (**RIGH**-noh-plass-tee) = surgical repair of the nose
-(r)rhaphy	suture	herniorr**rhaphy** (**her**-nee-**OR**-ah-fee) = suturing a hernia
-tripsy	crushing; friction	litho**tripsy** (**LITH**-oh-trip-see) = crushing of stones

EXERCISE 1-20

Circle the suffix in each medical term and write the definition.

1. arthrocentesis _surgical puncture_
2. splenectomy _excision surgical removal_
3. ileostomy _____
4. septoplasty _____
5. tracheotomy _____
6. colporrhaphy _suture_
7. orchidopexy _____
8. esophagectasia _streching_
9. bronchiectasis _____
10. chondrodesis _binding together_
11. arthrosclerosis _hardening_
12. cardiospasm _contraction_
13. lithotripsy _crushing_
14. ureterostenosis _narrowing_

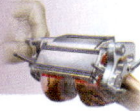

EXERCISE 1-21

Write the suffix for each meaning.

1. abnormal condition _____
2. abnormal fear _phobia_
3. binding together _desis_
4. blood condition _____
5. breakdown; destruction _____
6. breathing _pnea_
7. bursting forth of blood _rrhage_
8. carrying; transmission _phoresis_
9. cell _cyte_
10. chest; pleural cavity _thorax_
11. condition of cells _cyt_
12. contraction; twitching _spasm_
13. control; stop _____
14. create a new opening _ostomy_
15. crushing; friction _tripsy_
16. decreased number _penia_

17. digestion _pepsia_
18. disease _pathy_
19. drooping; sagging; prolapse _ptosis_
20. eating; swallowing _phagia_

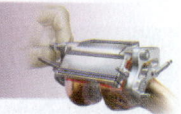

EXERCISE 1-22

Match the suffix in column 1 with the meaning in column 2.

COLUMN 1

- _o_ 1. -algia; -dynia
- _g_ 2. -cele
- _j_ 3. -graph
- _k_ 4. -graphy
- _i_ 5. -itis
- _a_ 6. -megaly
- _h_ 7. -(o)tomy
- _b_ 8. -phoria
- _d_ 9. -poiesis
- _c_ 10. -(r)rhea
- _f_ 11. -sclerosis
- _m_ 12. -stenosis
- _l_ 13. -tocia
- _n_ 14. -tresia
- _e_ 15. -trophy

COLUMN 2

a. enlarged; enlargement
b. feeling; mental state
c. flow; discharge
d. formation
e. growth; development
f. hardening
g. hernia; herniation
h. incision into
i. inflammation
j. instrument to record
k. process of recording
l. labor; birth
m. narrowing
n. opening
o. pain

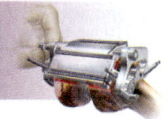

EXERCISE 1-23

Write the suffix for each meaning.

1. paralysis _____
2. pertaining to _____
3. process of recording _graphy_
4. process of viewing _scopy_
5. producing; forming _____
6. protein _globulin_
7. record _gram_
8. resembling; like _oid_
9. rupture _rrhexis_

10. sleep _insomia_

11. slight paralysis _____

12. softening _malacia_

13. specialist _ologist_

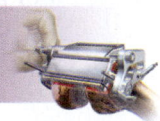

EXERCISE 1-24

Match the suffixes in column 1 with the meanings in column 2.

COLUMN 1		COLUMN 2	
e	1. -centesis	a.	drooping
i	2. -crine	b.	stretching; dilation
j	3. -crit	c.	study of
b	4. -ectasia; -ectasis	d.	surgical fixation
f	5. -ectomy	e.	surgical puncture
o	6. -emesis	f.	surgical removal; excision
c	7. -(o)logy	g.	surgical repair
m	8. -oma	h.	suture
d	9. -pexy	i.	to secrete
n	10. -phonia	j.	to separate
g	11. -plasty	k.	to turn
a	12. -ptosis	l.	treatment
h	13. -(r)rhaphy	m.	tumor
l	14. -therapy	n.	voice; sound
k	15. -version	o.	vomiting

COMBINING ROOTS, PREFIXES, AND SUFFIXES

Combining roots, prefixes, and suffixes is the basic way to create medical terms. Rules for combining the word parts are as follows:

1. *When combining more than one root in a medical term, the combining form of the root is usually used between the roots.*

   Example: **cardi**o**gastric** (**kar**-dee-oh-**GASS**-trik), pertaining to the heart and stomach.

2. *When combining a root with a suffix that begins with a consonant (any letter other than a, e, i, o, u, and y), the combining form of the root must be used to connect the suffix and root.*

   Example: **gastr**o**megaly** (gass-troh-**MEG**-ah-lee), enlarged stomach or enlargement of the stomach.

3. *When combining a root with a suffix that begins with a vowel, the combining form is not used.*

   Example: **gastrectomy** (gass-**TREK**-toh-mee), surgical removal of the stomach.

4. *There will always be some exceptions to these rules. When combining word roots and one of the roots begins with a vowel, the combining vowel is retained.*

   Example: **gastr**o**enterology** (**gass**-troh-en-ter-**ALL**-oh-jee), the study of the stomach and intestines. The root *gastr* means stomach and the root *enter* means intestine. To ease pronunciation of this term, the combining vowel *o* is retained with the root *gastr*.

PRONUNCIATION RULES

A comprehensive medical dictionary is the best reference for the pronunciation and definition of medical terms. There are some general guidelines that address pronunciation. Note that in this text, pronunciations are written phonetically (by sound) with the primary accented syllable in uppercase bold. Secondary accented syllables are in lowercase bold.

1. *Medical terms with two syllables are usually accented on the first syllable.*

   Example: gastric (**GASS**-trik), pertaining to the stomach.

2. *Medical terms with more than two syllables are usually accented on the third to last or next to last syllable.*

   Next to last example: gastritis (gass-**TRY**-tis), inflammation of the stomach.

continued

Third to last example: gastromegaly (gass-troh-**MEG**-ah-lee), enlarged stomach.

3. *The vowel in the accented syllable is pronounced with a long vowel sound when the syllable ends with the vowel.*

   Example: gastritis (gass-**TRY**-tis). The accented syllable *tri* is pronounced with the long *i* sound.

4. *The vowel in the accented syllable is pronounced with the short vowel sound when the syllable ends with a consonant.*

   Example: cardiomegaly (**kar**-dee-oh-**MEG**-ah-lee). The accented syllable *meg* is pronounced with the short *e* sound.

5. *There will always be exceptions to these rules.*

Singular and Plural Words

In the English language, singular words are often made plural by adding *s* or *es* to the word. Because medical terms are often derived from Latin, plural forms often follow Latin rules. This also happens with everyday words such as *alumni*, which is the plural of alumnus. Table 1-9 lists singular and plural endings for medical terms with examples.

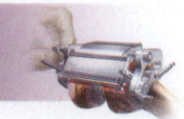

EXERCISE 1-25

Correctly combine each root with the suffix to form a medical term. You must decide whether or not to use the combining form.

	Root	Suffix	Term
Example:	arthr/o	-megaly	arthromegaly

	ROOT	SUFFIX	TERM
1.	arthr/o	-itis	*arthitis*
2.	arthr/o	-ectomy	*arthrectomy*
3.	arthr/o	-pathy	*arthropathy*
4.	dermat/o	-itis	*dermatitis*
5.	dermat/o	-pathy	*dermatopathy*
6.	gastr/o	-ic	*gastric*
7.	gastr/o	-ectomy	*gastrectomy*
8.	gastr/o	-megaly	*gastromegaly*
9.	cardi/o	-megaly	*cardiomegaly*
10.	cardi/o	-pathy	*cardiopathy*

Table 1-9   Singular and Plural Endings

SINGULAR ENDING	PLURAL ENDING	SINGULAR EXAMPLE	PLURAL EXAMPLE
-a	-ae	papill*a* (pah-**PILL**-lah) = a small nipple-shaped projection	papill*ae* (pah-**PILL**-ay)
-en	-ina	lum*en* (**LOO**-men) = cavity or channel of an organ or structure	lum*ina* (**LOO**-mih-nah)
-ex; -ix	-ices	ap*ex* (**AY**-pecks) = top; end; or tip of a structure	ap*ices* (**AY**-pih-seez)
-ies	-ietes	par*ies* (**PAIR**-ee-ess) = wall of an organ or cavity	par*ietes* (pah-**RIGH**-ih-teez)
-is	-es	diagnos*is* (digh-ag-**NOH**-sis) = name of a disease or condition	diagnos*es* (digh-ag-**NOH**-seez)
-is	-ides	epididym*is* (**ep**-ih-**DID**-ih-miss) = coiled duct of the testicle	epididym*ides* (**ep**-ih-dih-dih-**MY**-deez)
-nx	-nges	lary*nx* (**LAIR**-inx) = voice organ of the throat	lary*nges* (lah-**RIN**-jeez)
-on	-a	gangli*on* (**GANG**-lee-on) = knot or knotlike mass	gangli*a* (**GANG**-lee-ah)
-um	-a	atri*um* (**AY**-tree-um) = upper chamber of the heart	atri*a* (**AY**-tree-ah)
-us	-i	bronch*us* (**BRONG**-kus) = air passage of the respiratory system	bronch*i* (**BRONG**-ki)
-us	-era	visc*us* (**VISS**-kuss) = internal organ	visc*era* (**VISS**-eh-rah)
-us	-ora	corp*us* (**KOR**-pus) = body	corp*ora* (**KOR**-por-ah; kor-**POR**-ah)

EXERCISE 1-26

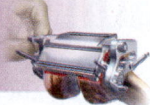

Write the plural form for the singular terms.

1. ampulla _____
2. fornix _____
3. foramen _____
4. ovum _____
5. phalanx _____
6. testis _____
7. thrombus _____

ANALYZING MEDICAL TERMS

Once you have mastered the meaning of roots, prefixes, and suffixes, you are able to analyze a medical term and arrive at a basic definition. This skill is very helpful for medical coding and insurance billing activities. To analyze a medical term, identify the root, prefix, and suffix and their meanings. To define the medical term, start with the meaning of the suffix, the prefix next, and the root last. Although a brief definition for many medical terms is possible, the best place to find the complete definition of all medical terms is in a medical dictionary. Practice analyzing medical terms by completing the following exercises.

EXERCISE 1-27

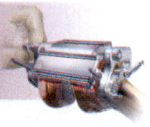

Analyze each medical term. Based on the meanings of the root, prefix, and suffix, write a brief definition for the term.

EXAMPLE: hemigastrectomy
ROOT: gastr, stomach
PREFIX: hemi-, half
SUFFIX: -ectomy, surgical removal
DEFINITION: surgical removal of half of the stomach

1. arthralgia
ROOT: _arthr/o_
PREFIX: _____
SUFFIX: _algia_
DEFINITION: _joint pain_

2. cardiomegaly
ROOT: _cardi/o_
PREFIX: _____
SUFFIX: _megaly_
DEFINITION: _enlargement of heart_

3. cardiopathy
ROOT: _cardi/o_
PREFIX: _____
SUFFIX: _pathy_
DEFINITION: _disease of heart_

4. dermatoplasty
ROOT: _dermat/o_
PREFIX: _____
SUFFIX: _plasty_
DEFINITION: _surgical repair of skin_

5. endocarditis
ROOT: _cardi/o_
PREFIX: _endo_
SUFFIX: _itis_
DEFINITION: _inflammation of inner lining of heart_

6. gastroplasty
ROOT: _gastr/o_
PREFIX: _____
SUFFIX: _plasty_
DEFINITION: _surgical repair of stomach_

7. hemigastroplasty
ROOT: _gastr/o_
PREFIX: _hemi_
SUFFIX: _plasty_
DEFINITION: _surgical repair half the stomach_

8. hepatomegaly
ROOT: _hepat/o_
PREFIX: _____
SUFFIX: _megaly_
DEFINITION: _enlargement of liver_

continued

9. hypogastric

ROOT: _gastr/o_

PREFIX: _hypo_

SUFFIX: _ic_

DEFINITION: _pertaining to below the stomach_

10. osteoarthritis

ROOT: _arthr/o oste/o_

PREFIX: _osteo_

SUFFIX: _itis_

DEFINITION: _inflammation of bones and joints_

11. osteopathy

ROOT: _oste/o_

PREFIX: _____

SUFFIX: _pathy_

DEFINITION: _bone disease_

12. pericarditis

ROOT: _cardi/o_

PREFIX: _peri_

SUFFIX: _itis_

DEFINITION: _inflammation around the heart_

13. polyarthritis

ROOT: _arthr/o_

PREFIX: _poly_

SUFFIX: _itis_

DEFINITION: _inflammation of many joints_

14. hepatitis

ROOT: _hepat/o_

PREFIX: _____

SUFFIX: _itis_

DEFINITION: _inflammation of liver_

15. dermatitis

ROOT: _dermat/o_

PREFIX: _____

SUFFIX: _itis_

DEFINITION: _inflammation of skin_

BUILDING MEDICAL TERMS

Knowing the meanings of roots, prefixes, and suffixes can help you build a medical term from its definition. Building medical terms from their definitions is an excellent way to develop mastery of roots, prefixes, and suffixes. This type of exercise also helps you develop a working knowledge of medical terminology.

EXERCISE 1-28

Read the definitions. Write the combining form of the root for the body part named in the definition. Write the prefix and the suffix for the meanings in the definition. Correctly combine the root, prefix, and suffix to create the term that matches the definition. Note: Not all terms have a prefix.

EXAMPLE:

DEFINITION: inflammation of the joints

ROOT: arthr/o, joint

PREFIX: none

SUFFIX: -itis, inflammation

MEDICAL TERM: arthritis

1. DEFINITION: disease of the heart

ROOT: _cardi/o_

PREFIX: _____

SUFFIX: _pathy_

MEDICAL TERM: _cardiopathy_

2. DEFINITION: surgical repair of the liver

ROOT: _hepat/o_

PREFIX: _____

SUFFIX: _plasty_

MEDICAL TERM: _hepatoplasty_

3. DEFINITION: stomach pain

ROOT: _gastr/o_

PREFIX: _a_

SUFFIX: _algia_

MEDICAL TERM: _gastralgia_

4. DEFINITION: skinlike; resembling skin
   ROOT: _dermat/o_
   PREFIX: _____
   SUFFIX: _iod_
   MEDICAL TERM: _dermetiod_

5. DEFINITION: pertaining to the area around the heart
   ROOT: _cardi/o_
   PREFIX: _peri_
   SUFFIX: _ac_
   MEDICAL TERM: _pericardiac_

6. DEFINITION: inflammation of bone
   ROOT: _oste/o_
   PREFIX: _____
   SUFFIX: _itis_
   MEDICAL TERM: _osteitis_

7. DEFINITION: surgical repair of the skin
   ROOT: _dermat/o_
   PREFIX: _____
   SUFFIX: _plasty_
   MEDICAL TERM: _dermaplasty_

8. DEFINITION: pain in many joints
   ROOT: _arthr/o_
   PREFIX: _poly_
   SUFFIX: _algia_
   MEDICAL TERM: _polyarthralgia_

9. DEFINITION: pertaining to under the liver
   ROOT: _hepat/o_
   PREFIX: _sub_
   SUFFIX: _ic_
   MEDICAL TERM: _subhepatic_

10. DEFINITION: enlarged heart
    ROOT: _cardi/o_
    PREFIX: _____
    SUFFIX: _megaly_
    MEDICAL TERM: _cardimegaly_

11. DEFINITION: pertaining to below the stomach
    ROOT: _gastr/o_
    PREFIX: _hypo_
    SUFFIX: _ic_
    MEDICAL TERM: _hypogastric_

12. DEFINITION: surgical repair of half of the stomach
    ROOT: _gastr/o_
    PREFIX: _hemi_
    SUFFIX: _plasty_
    MEDICAL TERM: _hemigastroplasty_

13. DEFINITION: inflammation of many joints
    ROOT: _arthr/o_
    PREFIX: _poly_
    SUFFIX: _itis_
    MEDICAL TERM: _polyarthritis_

14. DEFINITION: surgical removal of the stomach
    ROOT: _gastr/o_
    PREFIX: _____
    SUFFIX: _ectomy_
    MEDICAL TERM: _gastrectomy_

15. DEFINITION: inflammation within the heart
    ROOT: _cardi/o_
    PREFIX: _endo_
    SUFFIX: _itis_
    MEDICAL TERM: _endocarditis_

GENERAL BODY TERMINOLOGY

General body terminology applies to all body systems. The word roots associated with these terms are listed in table 1-10 with a combining vowel. Review the roots and complete the exercises that follow.

_mod 1

Table 1-10 General Body Word Roots

WORD ROOT/COMBINING FORM	MEANING
abdomin/o; lapar/o; ceil/o	abdomen
adip/o; lip/o	fat; fatty
anter/o	front
chondr/o	cartilage
crani/o	skull
cyt/o	cell
dors/o	back
gastr/o	stomach
hist/o	tissue
inguin/o	groin
later/o	side; away from the midline
lumb/o	loin
medi/o	middle
nucle/o	nucleus
pelv/i	pelvis
poster/o	back
proxim/o	near
spin/o	spine
thorac/o	chest
umbilic/o	navel
ventr/o	front side; belly
viscer/o	internal organs

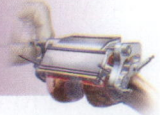

EXERCISE 1-30

Write the correct word root(s) for the following definitions.

1. abdomen _____
2. front _____
3. internal organs _____
4. navel _____
5. back _____
6. front side _____
7. side _____
8. near _____
9. nucleus _____
10. tissue _____
11. cartilage _____
12. stomach _____
13. loin _____
14. groin _____

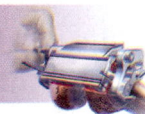

EXERCISE 1-29

Write the meaning of each word root.

1. cyt/o ___cell___
2. abdomin/o ___abdomen___
3. hist/o ___tissue___
4. later/o ___side away from the midline___
5. ventr/o ___front side - belly___
6. thorac/o ___chest___
7. pelv/i ___pelvis___
8. chondr/o ___cartilage___
9. gastr/o ___stomach___
10. lapar/o ___abdomen___

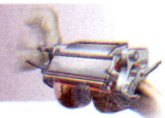

EXERCISE 1-31

Based on the meaning of the root and suffix, write a brief definition for each term.

1. abdominal ___pertaining to the abdomen___
2. cytology ___study of cell___
3. umbilical ___navel___
4. posterior ___back___
5. anterior ___front___
6. histology ___study of tissue___
7. ventral ___pertaining to belly___
8. proximal ___near___
9. adipose ___fat fatty___
10. spinal ___pertaining to spine___
11. cranial ___pertaining to skull___

STRUCTURAL ORGANIZATIONAL TERMS

Structures of the body are organized into four general categories: cells, tissues, organs, and systems.

- **Cells** are the foundation for all parts of the body.
- **Tissues** are composed of cells that come together to perform a function.
- **Organs** are made up of different types of tissue arranged together to perform a function.
- **Systems** include different organs that work together to perform the various functions of the body.

Cells

Human cells vary in size, shape, and function. The study of cells is called **cytology** (sigh-**TALL**-oh-jee). Figure 1-1 illustrates a human cell. The (1) **cell membrane** is the cell's outer covering. The membrane allows material to pass in and out of the cell so that the cell can receive oxygen and nutrients and release waste products. The cell's structures are housed in a gel-like substance called (2) **cytoplasm** (**SIGH**-toh-plazm). The (3) **nucleus** (**NOO**-klee-us) controls cellular functions and is made up of threadlike strands called **chromosomes** (**KROH**-moh-sohms). Chromosomes contain **deoxyribonucleic** (dee-**ocks**-ee-**righ**-boh-noo-**KLAY**-ik) **acid (DNA)**, which transmits genetic information. The chromosomes also have thousands of segments called **genes**, which are responsible for hereditary characteristics.

Tissues

Tissues are groups of cells working together to perform a specific function. There are four main types of tissue: connective, epithelial (**ep**-ih-**THEEL**-ee-al), muscle, and nervous.

Connective tissue functions as the name implies to connect or support other body tissue or structures. Connective tissue is classified into the following categories:

- Liquid—blood and lymph fluid
- Adipose—fat and fatty tissue
- Fibrous—tendons; ligaments
- Cartilage—nose; rings of the trachea
- Solid—bone

Epithelial tissue is found in the lining and covering of body cavities, glands, organs, and vessels. The skin is an example of epithelial tissue. The lining of the heart is another example of epithelial tissue.

Muscle tissue functions to produce movement in all parts of the body. Some movement, like walking, is normally under our control whereas other movement, like the movement of food through the small intestines, is not. There are three types of muscle tissue:

- Skeletal—attached to bone; moves the skeleton; voluntary muscle

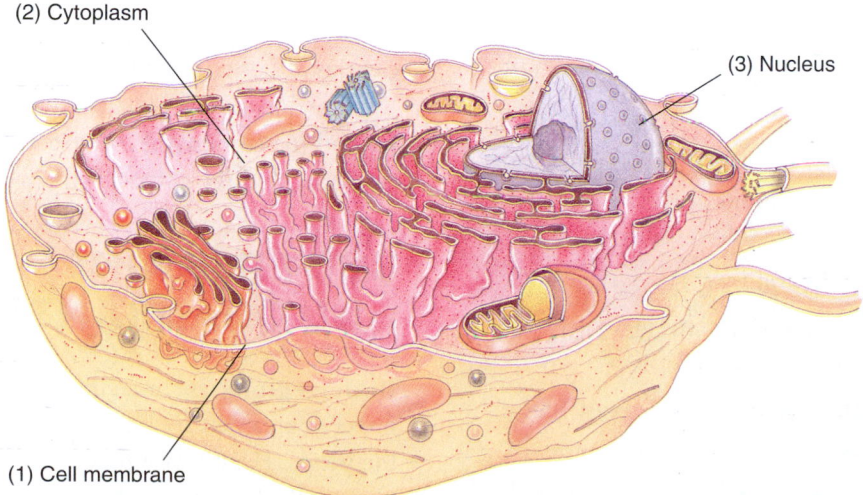

(2) Cytoplasm

(3) Nucleus

(1) Cell membrane

Figure 1-1 Human cell

- Smooth—located in the walls of hollow organs such as the stomach and intestines; produces movement in those organs; involuntary muscle
- Cardiac—makes up the muscular layer of the heart

Nervous tissue transmits information throughout the body that allows us to move, think, taste, see, and experience all functions associated with being alive. From blinking the eyes to solving the most complex mathematical equation, nervous tissue is ready to activate the body parts necessary to complete these activities.

Organs

Organs are groups of tissues working together to perform a specific function. Examples of organs are the heart, stomach, eyes, and skin. The internal organs of the body are known as the **viscera** (**VISS**-er-ah) or visceral organs.

Systems

Systems are groups of organs working together to perform the functions of the body. Each body system is discussed in a later chapter. Some of the organs in each system are listed here:

- Integumentary system—skin, hair, nails, glands
- Musculoskeletal system—muscles, bones, joints
- Cardiovascular system—heart, arteries, veins
- Blood/lymphatic system—blood, blood cells, lymph glands
- Respiratory system—lungs, trachea, bronchi
- Digestive system—mouth, throat, stomach, gallbladder, liver
- Urinary system—kidneys, ureters, urinary bladder
- Endocrine system—glands, hormones
- Male reproductive system—testes, penis, accessory organs
- Female reproductive system—ovaries, uterus, fallopian tubes
- Nervous system—nerves, brain, spinal cord
- Sensory system—eyes, ears, accessory organs

EXERCISE 1-32

Write a short answer for each question.

1. List and describe the four main types of body tissue.
2. What is the difference between smooth and skeletal muscle?
3. Name five types of connective tissue.
4. Name six body systems and three organs or structures that belong in each system.

BODY CAVITIES

Body cavities are hollow spaces that contain an orderly arrangement of internal organs. The main body cavities are the (1) **ventral cavity**, located on the front of the body, and the (2) **dorsal cavity**, located on the back of the body. Each main cavity is further subdivided and named for its specific location. Figure 1-2 illustrates the location and name of the body cavities.

The ventral cavity is divided into the (3) **thoracic** (thoh-**RASS**-ik) **cavity**, the (4) **abdominal cavity**, and the (5) **pelvic cavity**. The thoracic cavity, also called the chest cavity, houses the lungs, heart, aorta, esophagus, and trachea. The (6) **diaphragm** (**DIGH**-ah-fram), the chief muscle of respiration, separates the thoracic cavity from the abdominal cavity. The abdominal cavity houses the liver, gallbladder, spleen, stomach, pancreas, intestines, and kidneys. There is no specific structure that separates the abdominal cavity from the pelvic cavity. The pelvic cavity houses the urinary bladder and reproductive organs. The abdominal and pelvic cavities are often called the abdominopelvic cavity.

The dorsal cavity is divided into the (7) **cranial cavity** and the (8) **spinal cavity**. The cranial cavity houses the brain, and the spinal cavity houses the spinal cord.

BODY REGIONS AND QUADRANTS

Body regions are imaginary sections of the abdominopelvic area that are located between the diaphragm and the pelvis. Health care practitioners use these regions to identify the location of abdominal organs and to describe the location of pain. There are nine body regions that are illustrated in figure 1-3.

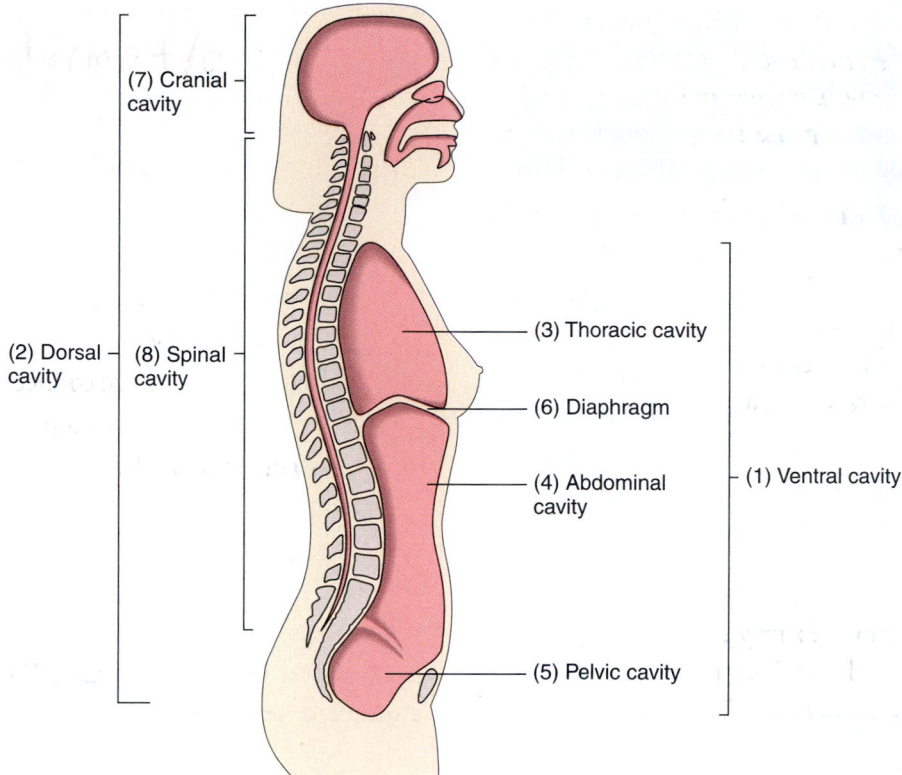

Figure 1-2   Body cavities

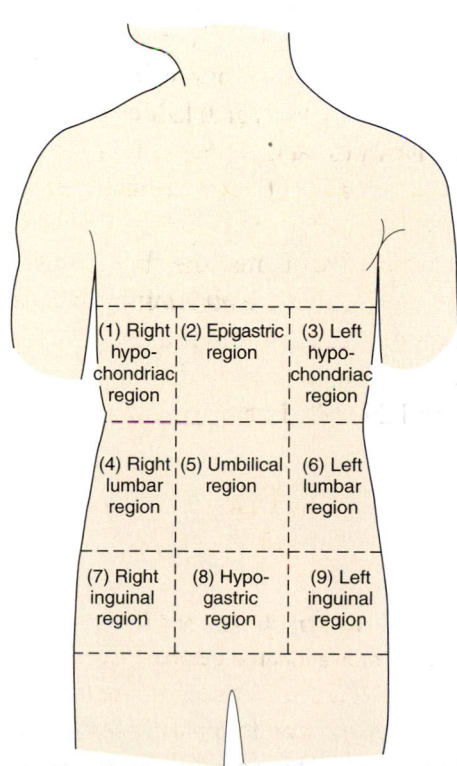

Figure 1-3   Body regions

1. **Right hypochondriac (high-poh-KON-dree-ak) region**. Located beneath the cartilage of the lower ribs in the upper right area of the abdomen.

2. **Epigastric (ep-ee-GASS-trik) region**. Located above the stomach and navel, between the right and left hypochondriac regions.

3. **Left hypochondriac region**. Located beneath the cartilage of the lower ribs in the upper left section of the abdomen.

4. **Right lumbar region**. Located directly below the right hypochondriac region.

5. **Umbilical region**. Located in the midsection of the abdomen at the level of the umbilicus or navel.

6. **Left lumbar region**. Located directly below the left hypochondriac region.

7. **Right inguinal (ING-gwih-nal) region**. Located directly below the right lumbar region. Also called the **right iliac region**.

continued

8. **Hypogastric region.** Located directly below the umbilical region.

9. **Left inguinal region.** Located directly below the left lumbar region. Also called the **left iliac region**.

Body quadrants are four imaginary areas of the abdomen that, like the body regions, provide reference points for locating abdominal organs and pain. The body quadrants are named based on their relationship to the umbilicus. Figure 1-4 illustrates the body quadrants.

The (1) **right upper quadrant (RUQ)** and the (2) **left upper quadrant (LUQ)** are above and to the right and left of the umbilicus. The (3) **right lower quadrant (RLQ)** and the (4) **left lower quadrant (LLQ)** are below and to the right and left of the umbilicus.

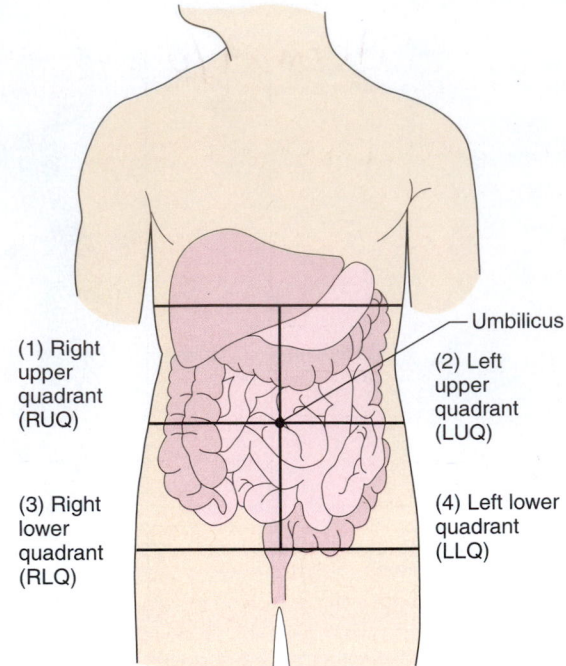

Umbilicus

(1) Right upper quadrant (RUQ)

(2) Left upper quadrant (LUQ)

(3) Right lower quadrant (RLQ)

(4) Left lower quadrant (LLQ)

Figure 1-4   Body quadrants

EXERCISE 1-33

Label the body cavities illustrated in figure 1-5.

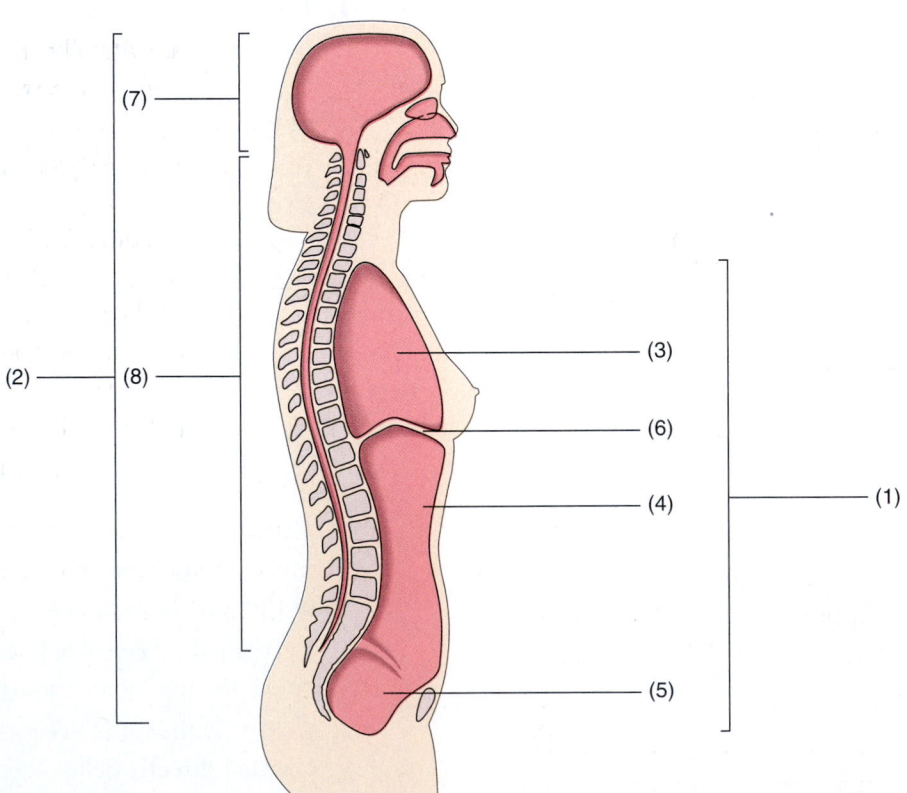

Figure 1-5

EXERCISE 1-34

Write the name of the body regions in figure 1-6 on the spaces provided.

1. _____
2. _____
3. _____
4. _____
5. _____
6. _____
7. _____
8. _____
9. _____

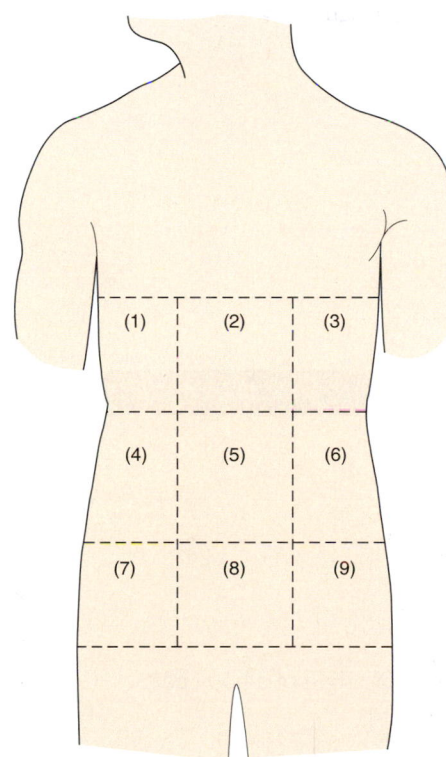

Figure 1-6

BODY PLANES

Body planes are imaginary slices, or cuts, that divide the body into right and left, front and back, and upper and lower segments. The body planes are illustrated in figure 1-7.

> 1. **Midsagittal** (mid-**SAJ**-ih-tal) **plane**. Divides the body, starting with the head and continuing through the pelvic area, into right and left halves. A **sagittal** (**SAJ**-ih-tal) **plane** is parallel to the midsagittal and divides the body into right and left segments.
> 2. **Frontal plane**. Divides the body, starting with the head and continuing through the legs and feet, into front and back segments; also called the **coronal** (koh-**ROH**-nal) **plane**.
> 3. **Transverse plane**. Divides the body into upper and lower segments, starting at any point along the body; also called the **horizontal plane**.

BODY DIRECTIONS

Body directions are literally the north, south, east, and west of medical terminology. The body directions provide health care professionals with a vocabulary that describes the location of body parts, incisions, diseases, and procedures.

Body directions are described in terms of a standard reference position of the body as a whole. This standard reference position is called the **anatomical position**. In the anatomical position, the body is viewed as erect or lying on its back, with the arms at the sides, and the palms, head, and feet facing forward. Commonly used directional terms are listed in table 1-11.

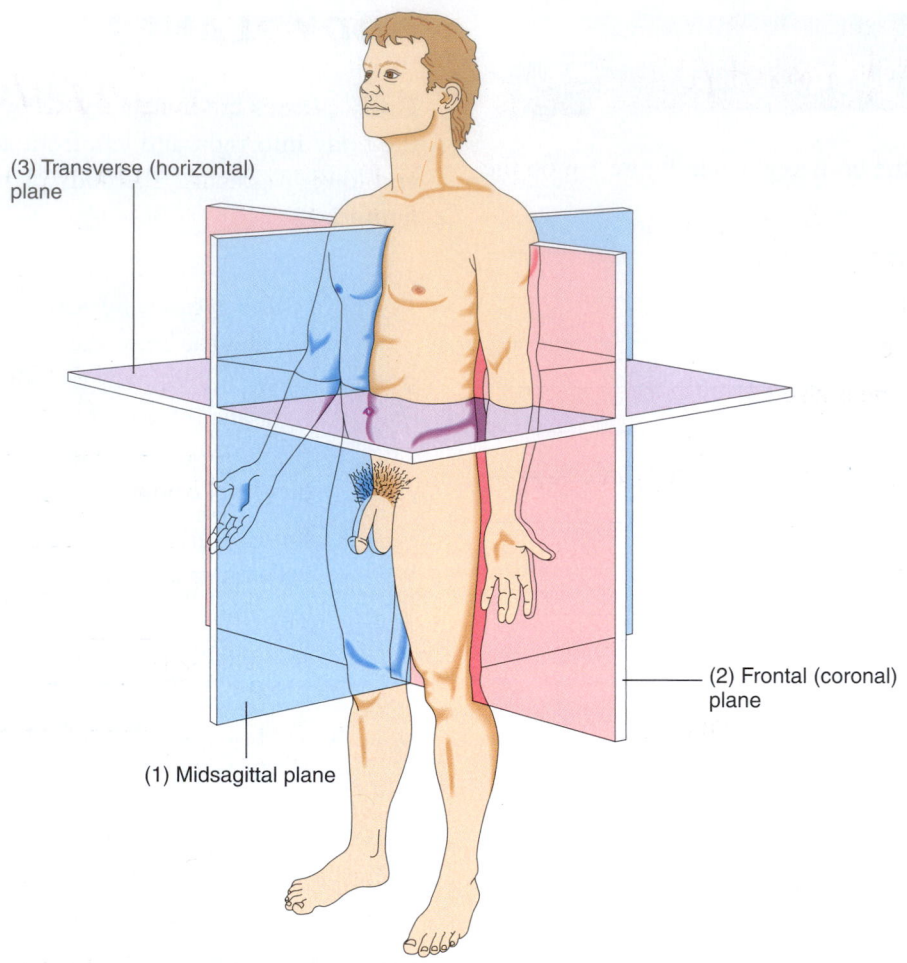

(3) Transverse (horizontal) plane

(2) Frontal (coronal) plane

(1) Midsagittal plane

Figure 1-7   Body planes

Table 1-11   Directional Terms

BODY DIRECTION	DEFINITION
Anterior	Toward the front; pertaining to the front
Anteroposterior (AP)	From the front to the back
Caudal	Downward; toward the tail
Cranial	Toward the head; pertaining to the head
Cephalad	Toward the head; pertaining to the head
Deep	Away from the surface
Distal	Away from the trunk; farthest from the point of origin of a body part
Dorsal	Toward the back; pertaining to the back
Inferior	Below; downward toward the feet
Lateral	To the side; away from the midline of the body
Medial	Toward the midline of the body; pertaining to the middle
Posterior	Toward the back; pertaining to the back of the body
Posteroanterior (PA)	From the back to the front; pertaining to the back and front
Prone	Face down; lying on the abdomen
Proximal	Toward the trunk of the body; nearest to the point of origin of the body part
Superficial	Near the surface; pertaining to the surface
Supine	Face up; lying on the back
Ventral	Toward the front; pertaining to the front side

EXERCISE 1-35

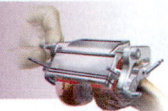

Fill in the blanks.

1. The _____ plane divides the body into right and left segments.

2. Horizontal plane is another name for the _____ plane.

3. Coronal plane is also known as the _____ plane.

4. The _____ plane divides the body into right and left halves.

5. A/an _____ wound is near the surface of the body.

6. The _____ position is best for examining the abdomen.

7. The knees are located in a/an _____ position from the ankles.

8. The _____ quadrant is above and to the left of the umbilicus.

9. The _____ region is directly above the umbilicus.

10. The _____ region is directly below the umbilicus.

EXERCISE 1-36

Write the directional term that has the opposite meaning of each listed directional term.

1. anterior _____

2. anteroposterior _____

3. caudal _____

4. distal _____

5. dorsal _____

6. lateral _____

7. prone _____

8. superficial _____

9. superior _____

10. ventral _____

EXERCISE 1-37

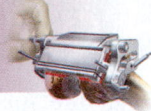

Write out each abbreviation with a brief definition for each term or phrase.

1. AP _____

   DEFINITION: _____

2. LLQ _____

   DEFINITION: _____

3. LUQ _____

   DEFINITION: _____

4. PA _____

   DEFINITION: _____

5. RLQ _____

   DEFINITION: _____

6. RUQ _____

   DEFINITION: _____

■ SUMMARY

Prefixes and suffixes are added to the beginning and end of word roots and change the meaning of medical terms. Prefixes can identify location, color, and number or amount. Suffixes identify a medical term as a noun or an adjective. Suffixes also represent diseases, conditions, and treatments. It is important to memorize the commonly used prefixes and suffixes because they make up many medical terms.

General body terminology includes words associated with the organization of the body from cells to body systems; the names of body cavities, planes, regions, and quadrants; and direction terms. The terms presented in this chapter are part of the foundation of the language of the health care industry.

■ CHAPTER REVIEW

Read the medical report. The italicized terms are listed after the report. Write the prefixes, suffixes, and their meanings. Look up the definition of the terms in a medical dictionary.

PATIENT NAME: MOISIO, SARA
PHYSICIAN NAME: Michael Cruchelow, M.D.

BRIEF HISTORY

The patient is a 28-year-old female who presents with gradual onset of upper right quadrant pain, vomiting, and (1) *diarrhea*. She was recently (2) *postpartum* and had a postpartum tubal ligation.

PHYSICAL EXAMINATION

Exam today revealed that she was (3) *afebrile*. She exhibited (4) *tachycardia* and massive (5) *hepatomegaly*. Pelvic exam revealed no cervical motion tenderness.

HOSPITAL COURSE

The patient was admitted for workup of her hepatomegaly. She was given (6) *intravenous* fluids for her dehydration and was started on iron for her (7) *anemia*. A liver biopsy revealed several (8) *hepatic* lesions and the tissue resembled neutrophils. (9) *Laparoscopy* was scheduled, a larger sample was taken, and frozen section was sent to the lab. The final (10) *pathology* report confirmed (11) *adenocarcinoma*. (12) *Oncology* was then consulted and a chemotherapy regimen was recommended. Further lab and x-ray report revealed (13) *hypoalbuminemia* and (14) *bilateral* pleural effusion, respectively. Pain control at home will be accomplished with a (15) *subcutaneous* morphine pump.

CASE 1

MEDICAL TERM	PREFIX/MEANING	SUFFIX/MEANING

1. diarrhea _____

   DEFINITION: _____

2. postpartum _____

   DEFINITION: _____

3. afebrile _____

   DEFINITION: _____

4. tachycardia _____

   DEFINITION: _____

5. hepatomegaly _____

   DEFINITION: _____

6. intravenous _____

   DEFINITION: _____

7. anemia _____

   DEFINITION: _____

8. hepatic _____

   DEFINITION: _____

9. laparoscopy _____

   DEFINITION: _____

10. pathology _____

    DEFINITION: _____

11. adenocarcinoma _____

    DEFINITION: _____

12. oncology _____

    DEFINITION: _____

13. hypoalbuminemia _____

    DEFINITION: _____

14. bilateral _____

    DEFINITION: _____

15. subcutaneous _____

    DEFINITION: _____

BODY CAVITIES, PLANES, AND REGIONS

Write the following medical terms next to their correct heading: abdominal cavity, coronal, cranial cavity, epigastric, frontal, horizontal, hypogastric, left hypochondriac, left inguinal, left lumbar, midsagittal, pelvic cavity, right hypochondriac, right inguinal, right lumbar, sagittal, spinal cavity, thoracic cavity, transverse, umbilical

16. Dorsal cavity _____

17. Plane(s) _____

18. Region(s) _____

19. Ventral cavity _____

NOTES:

CHAPTER 2

Introduction to ICD-9-CM Coding

■ OBJECTIVES

At the completion of this chapter, the student should be able to:

1. Explain the features of the three ICD-9-CM volumes.
2. Define all cross-reference and coding instruction terms.
3. Describe the difference between the first-listed diagnosis and the principal diagnosis.
4. Follow ICD-9-CM coding conventions for assigning diagnostic and procedure codes.
5. Accurately assign ICD-9-CM diagnoses and procedure codes.

■ OVERVIEW

There are two main coding systems used by all health care agencies and providers in the United States: (1) the *International Classification of Diseases, Ninth Revision, Clinical Modification* (ICD-9-CM) for medical diagnoses and procedures, and (2) *Current Procedural Terminology* (CPT) for physician and other provider services and procedures. The purpose of this chapter is to introduce the student to the basic principles of ICD-9-CM coding. Topics presented include the following:

- Unique characteristics and features of ICD-9-CM volumes 1, 2, and 3
- Coding conventions, such as special instructional notes, and the meaning of punctuation marks

KEY TERMS

benign
bilateral procedure
braces and double braces
carryover lines
category
closed biopsy
code also
code first [the] underlying
  condition
code, if applicable, any causal
  condition first
coding conventions
colons
connecting words
cooperating parties
E codes
encoder
encounter
etiology
exclusion notes
failed procedure
first degree, superficial
first-listed diagnosis
general notes
histological
inclusion notes
late effect
main terms
malignant
more specific subterms
NEC, not elsewhere classified
nonessential modifiers
NOS, not otherwise specified
omit code
open biopsy
open procedure
parentheses
pathology report
principal diagnosis
principal procedure
residual condition
second degree, partial thickness
section
see
see also
see category
see condition
sequencing
significant procedure
slanted square brackets
SOAP
square brackets
subcategories
subclassifications

continued

KEY TERMS *continued*

subterms	use additional code
third degree, full thickness	V codes
unspecified	visit

To meet the objectives of this chapter, you must have the ICD-9-CM volumes 1, 2, and 3 readily available as either the manual references or as an encoder. An **encoder** is an electronic version of the manual references.

INTERNATIONAL CLASSIFICATION OF DISEASES, NINTH REVISION, CLINICAL MODIFICATION (ICD-9-CM)

The *International Classification of Diseases, Ninth Revision, Clinical Modification* (ICD-9-CM) is the medical coding and classification system used in the United States to gather information about diseases and injuries. ICD-9-CM is scheduled to remain in effect until the United States adopts the *International Classification of Diseases, Tenth Revision, Clinical Modification.*

ICD-9-CM provides numerical codes for diagnoses, injuries, and procedures. The codes are contained in three volumes: Volume 1 is a numerical tabular list of disease and injury codes, volume 2 is an alphabetical index of diseases and injuries, and volume 3 is a combined numerical tabular list and alphabetical index of procedure codes. The ICD-9-CM diagnoses codes (volume 1) apply to all health care settings. The ICD-9-CM volume 3 procedure codes are used for inpatient hospital procedures.

The official version of ICD-9-CM is available on CD-ROM from the U.S. Government Printing Office in Washington, D.C. Code books and coding references are available from several commercial publishers. **Encoders**, electronic versions of the code books, are also available from commercial sources. Although each publisher may offer special editorial features, the codes are the same as those published in the official version. The official version of ICD-9-CM is the reference of choice for this text.

The ICD-9-CM is updated every year, and changes are effective October 1 of each year. There are four organizations that maintain and update ICD-9-CM. These organizations, called the **cooperating parties**, include the following:

- American Hospital Association (AHA)—maintains the ICD-9-CM central office to respond to coding questions; publishes the *Coding Clinic for ICD-9-CM,* the official resource for updated ICD-9-CM coding advice
- American Health Information Management Association (AHIMA)—provides training and certification for coding professionals
- Centers for Medicare and Medicaid Services (CMS)—maintains and updates ICD-9-CM volume 3, the procedure codes
- National Center for Health Statistics (NCHS)—maintains and updates the diagnosis portion of ICD-9-CM

The *ICD-9-CM Official Guidelines for Coding and Reporting* is an annual publication that contains updated guidelines for ICD-9-CM coding. This publication is produced by the CMS and the National Center for Health Care Statistics. The guidelines, a companion to the official version of ICD-9-CM, are available on the CMS Web site at http://www.cms.gov.

The *Coding Clinic for ICD-9-CM,* a quarterly publication of the AHA, includes the *ICD-9-CM Official Guidelines* and other coding advice from the cooperating parties. Medical coders and billing specialists rely on the *Coding Clinic* for updated information related to assigning ICD-9-CM codes.

The ICD-9-CM has specific guidelines called **coding conventions**. Coding conventions include instructional notes, abbreviations, cross-reference notes, punctuation marks, and specific meanings or usage of the words *and, with,* and *due to.* The main purposes of the coding conventions are (1) to standardize the way ICD-9-CM entries are organized, and (2) to provide specific directions for selecting codes. Medical coders and billing specialists must apply and follow the coding conventions when selecting or assigning ICD-9-CM codes.

VOLUME 1: TABULAR LIST OF DISEASES AND INJURIES

Volume 1, the *Tabular List of Diseases and Injuries,* is a numerical list of diseases and conditions that includes the following sections:

- Seventeen main chapters that classify diseases and injuries by body system or **etiology** (cause)
- Two supplementary classifications called "Classification of Factors Influencing Health Status and Contact with Health Services," commonly known as **V codes**; and "Classification of External Causes of Injury and Poisoning," commonly known as **E codes**
- Four appendices

Table 2-1 lists the 17 chapters and the range of codes covered in each chapter.

Each chapter in volume 1 is a numerical list of diseases and injuries organized by sections, categories, subcategories, and fifth-digit subclassifications. Section, category, and subcategories are illustrated in figure 2-1. Refer to the figure as you read the definition for these terms.

A **section** is a group of three-digit categories. A **category** is a three-digit code that represents a single disease or a group of closely related conditions. **Subcategories** consist of four digits and provide more information about the disease, such as the site, cause, or other characteristic. A period or decimal point precedes the fourth digit.

Subclassifications are represented by a fifth digit and allow for even more specific information about the disease. Fifth digits and their meaning are found at the beginning of a chapter, section, category code, and subcategory code. Figure 2-2 is an example of fifth-digit subclassification notations.

If the fourth and fifth digits are available they **must** be included on the insurance claim. Insurance carriers will deny payment for a claim that does not have the appropriate fourth or fifth digit.

Although most of the chapters in the *Tabular List* have self-explanatory titles, a brief description and explanation of chapters 11, 14, 15, 16, and 17 is presented in table 2-2.

Table 2-1 Tabular List Main Chapters

CHAPTER TITLE	CODE CATEGORIES
1. Infectious and Parasitic Diseases	001–139
2. Neoplasms	140–239
3. Endocrine, Nutritional, and Metabolic Diseases and Immunity Disorders	240–279
4. Diseases of Blood and Blood-Forming Organs	280–289
5. Mental Disorders	290–319
6. Diseases of the Nervous System and Sense Organs	320–389
7. Diseases of the Circulatory System	390–459
8. Diseases of the Respiratory System	460–519
9. Diseases of the Digestive System	520–579
10. Diseases of the Genitourinary System	580–629
11. Complications of Pregnancy, Childbirth, and the Puerperium	630–679
12. Diseases of Skin and Subcutaneous Tissue	680–709
13. Diseases of the Musculoskeletal System and Connective Tissue	710–739
14. Congenital Anomalies	740–759
15. Certain Conditions Originating in the Perinatal Period	760–779
16. Symptoms, Signs, and Ill-Defined Conditions	780–799
17. Injury and Poisoning	800–999

Diseases of Esophagus, Stomach, and Duodenum (530–538) ←→ **Section**
Category ←→ **531** Gastric ulcer
Subcategory ←→ **531.0** Gastric ulcer, acute, with hemorrhage
Subcategory ←→ **531.1** Gastric ulcer, acute, with perforation
Subcategory ←→ **531.2** Gastric ulcer, acute, with hemorrhage and perforation

Figure 2-1 Section, category, subcategory

LOCATION	DESCRIPTION
Chapter	Chapter 13. "Diseases of the Musculoskeletal System and Connective Tissue" (710–739)
	The following fifth-digit subclassification is used with categories 711–712, 715–716, 718–719, and 730:
	0 unspecified site; 1 shoulder region; 2 upper arm;
	3 forearm; 4 hand; 5 pelvic region and thigh;
	6 lower leg; 7 ankle and foot; 8 other specified sites; 9 multiple sites
Category	434 Occlusion of cerebral arteries
	The following fifth-digit subclassification is used with category 434:
	0 without mention of cerebral infarction; 1 with cerebral infarction
Subcategory	550.0 Inguinal hernia, with gangrene
	The following fifth-digit subclassifications apply to this subcategory:
	0 unilateral or unspecified (not specified as recurrent);
	1 unilateral or unspecified, recurrent; 2 bilateral (not specified as recurrent); 3 bilateral, recurrent

Figure 2-2 Examples of fifth-digit subclassifications

V Codes: Supplementary Classification of Factors Influencing Health Status and Contact with Health Services (V01–V89)

V codes are used to classify health care encounters that cover a range of services from an office visit for vaccinations to genetic screening for susceptibility to malignant neoplasms. V codes are most frequently assigned in health care settings such as physician offices, clinics, and outpatient departments. Figure 2-3 is an example of a V code category.

ICD-9-CM volume 2, the *Alphabetic Index,* is the key to locating the correct V code category. *Alphabetic Index* terms that lead to V code categories are listed in table 2-3. V code categories and titles are listed in table 2-4.

It is beyond the scope of this chapter to present comprehensive information about V codes. Review the *Tabular List* for the V code categories and codes associated with various health care encounters or services.

E Codes: The Supplementary Classification of External Causes of Injury and Poisoning (E800–E999)

E codes are used to classify environmental events, circumstances, and conditions that cause injury, poisoning, adverse effects, and other abnormal conditions.

Table 2-2   Tabular List Chapters 11, 14, 15, 16, and 17

CHAPTER 11: COMPLICATIONS OF PREGNANCY, CHILDBIRTH, AND THE PUERPERIUM (630–679)

Chapter 11 codes are only assigned to conditions that affect the mother, never to conditions that affect the newborn. These codes are used to classify conditions that affect the management of pregnancy, childbirth, and the **puerperium**. The puerperium is defined as the period of time that begins at the end of the third stage of labor and continues for six weeks.

CHAPTER 14: CONGENITAL ANOMALIES (740–759)

Chapter 14 codes are used to classify abnormal conditions that are **congenital**, which means "present at or since the time of birth." Although a congenital anomaly is present at birth, the condition may not manifest itself until later. Therefore, chapter 14 codes may be assigned to patients of any age. For example: A 16-year-old is recently diagnosed with polycystic kidney disease. This is a congenital condition and even though the individual is 16, the diagnosis is coded as a congenital anomaly.

CHAPTER 15: CERTAIN CONDITIONS ORIGINATING IN THE PERINATAL PERIOD (760–779)

Chapter 15 codes classify conditions associated with the **perinatal period**, which is defined as beginning before birth and lasting through the 28th day of life. Most perinatal conditions are resolved by time, treatment, or death. However, some conditions are diagnosed later in life. For example: A woman who is diagnosed with vaginal cancer discovers that her mother took the antinausea medication diethylstilbestrol (DES) while she was pregnant. Since intrauterine exposure to DES is a significant factor in the development of vaginal cancer, the code for DES exposure from chapter 15 may be assigned in addition to the code for vaginal cancer.

CHAPTER 16: SYMPTOMS, SIGNS, AND ILL-DEFINED CONDITIONS (780–799)

Chapter 16 includes medical codes for signs, symptoms, abnormal test results, and ill-defined conditions that cannot be classified or coded in another ICD-9-CM chapter. Chapter 16 codes should never be used when a more definitive diagnostic code is available.

CHAPTER 17: INJURY AND POISONING (800–999)

Chapter 17 codes apply to injuries, poisoning, burns, adverse effects caused by external factors, complications of trauma, and complications of surgical and medical care or treatment.

V Codes

PERSONS WITHOUT REPORTED DIAGNOSIS ENCOUNTERED DURING EXAMINATION AND INVESTIGATION OF INDIVIDUALS AND POPULATIONS (V70–V86)

V70   **General medical examination**

Use additional code(s) to identify any special screening examination(s) performed (V73.0–V82.9)

V70.0   **Routine general medical examination at a health care facility**

Health checkup

Excludes: *health checkup of infant or child (V20.2)*

pre-procedural general physical examination (V72.83)

V70.1   **General psychiatric examination, requested by the authority**

V70.2   **General psychiatric examination, other and unspecified**

V70.3   **Other medical examination for administrative purposes**

General medical examination for:

admission to old age home

adoption

camp

driving license

continued

Figure 2-3 V code examples

immigration and naturalization
insurance certification
marriage
prison
school admission
sports competition
Excludes: attendance for issue of medical certificates (V68.0)
pre-employment screening (V70.5)

V70.4   Examination for medicolegal reasons
Blood-alcohol tests
Blood-drug tests
Paternity testing
Excludes: examination and observation following:
accidents (V71.3, V71.4)
assault (V71.6)
rape (V71.5)

Figure 2-3 (*continued*)   V code examples

Table 2-3 Alphabetic Index Main Terms for V Codes

Admission (encounter)	Dialysis	Outcome of delivery
Aftercare	Donor	Pregnancy
Attention to	Examination	Problem
Boarder	Exposure	Prophylactic
Care (of)	Fitting (of)	Replacement by
Carrier (suspected) of	Follow-up	Resistance, resistant
Checking	Health	Screening
Contact	Healthy	Status
Contraception, contraceptive	History (personal) of	Supervision (of)
Convalescence	Maintenance	Test(s)
Counseling	Maladjustment	Therapy
Dependence	Newborn	Transplant, transplanted
	Observation	Vaccination

E codes provide data for research that is related to injuries and injury prevention, and are assigned in addition to a diagnostic code. E codes capture information about the following:

- Cause: How the injury or poisoning occurred (fall, flood, explosion)
- Intent: Why the injury or poisoning occurred (accident, assault, suicide attempt)
- Place: Where the injury or poisoning occurred (home, public building, workplace)

The use of E codes is sometimes optional, except for categories E930 through E949, "Drugs, Medicinal and Biological Substances Causing Adverse Effects in Therapeutic Use." A portion of this section is shown in figure 2-4. Review the figure and pay close attention to the inclusion and exclusion notes.

Some state laws require the use of E codes as in cases of firearms accidents, mass transport accidents, and other incidents related to public health and safety. In most coding references, the alphabetical index for E codes,

Table 2-4 V Code Categories and Titles

CATEGORIES	TITLES
V01–V06	Persons with Potential Health Hazards Related to Communicable Diseases
V07–V09	Persons with Need for Isolation, Other Potential Health Hazards, and Prophylactic Measures
V10–V19	Persons with Potential Health Hazards Related to Personal and Family History
V20–V29	Persons Encountering Health Services in Circumstances Related to Reproduction and Development
V30–V39	Liveborn Infants According to Type of Birth
V40–V49	Persons with a Condition Influencing Their Health Status
V50–V59	Persons Encountering Health Services for Specific Procedures and Aftercare
V60–V69	Persons Encountering Health Services in Other Circumstances
V70–V82	Persons with Reported Diagnosis Encountered during Examination and Investigation of Individuals and Populations
V83–V84	Genetics
V85	Body Mass Index
V86	Estrogen Receptor Status
V87	Other Specified Personal Exposure and History Presenting Hazards to Health
V88	Acquired Absence of Other Organs and Tissues
V89	Other Suspected Condition Not Found

E Codes

DRUGS, MEDICINAL AND BIOLOGICAL SUBSTANCES CAUSING ADVERSE EFFECTS IN THERAPEUTIC USE (E930–E949)

Includes: correct drug properly administered in therapeutic or prophylactic dosage, as the cause of any adverse effect including allergic or hypersensitivity reactions

Excludes: *accidental overdose of drug and wrong drug given or taken in error (E850.0–E858.9)*
accidents in the technique or administration of drug or biological substance such as accidental puncture during injection, or contamination of drug (E870.0–E876.9)
administration with suicidal or homicidal intent or intent to harm, or in circumstances classifiable to E980–E989 (E950.0–E950.5, E962.0, E980.0–E980.5)

See Alphabetic Index for more complete list of specific drugs to be classified under the fourth-digit subdivisions. The American Hospital Formulary numbers can be used to classify new drugs listed by the American Hospital Formulary Service (AHFS). See Appendix C.

E930 Antibiotics

Excludes: *that used as eye, ear, nose, and throat [ENT], and local anti-infectives (E946.0–E946.9)*

E930.0 Penicillin

Natural
Synthetic

Semisynthetic, such as:
ampicillin
cloxacillin
nafcillin
oxacillin

E930.1 Antifungal antibiotics

Amphotericin B
Griseofulvin

Hachimycin [trichomycin]
Nystatin

E930.2 Chloramphenicol group

Chloramphenicol

Thiamphenicol

Figure 2-4 E codes

called the "Index to External Causes," follows the "Table of Drugs and Chemicals Index."

Appendices

Volume 1, the *Tabular List*, includes four appendices:

- Appendix A, Morphology of Neoplasms (M codes). A list of optional codes that identify the **histological** (tissue) type and behavior of neoplasms. The first four digits represent the type of tissue, and the fifth digit represents the behavior of the neoplasm. M code fifth digits retain their meaning regardless of the histology code.
- Appendix C, Classification of Drugs by American Hospital Formulary Service (AHFS) List. A list of ICD-9-CM codes associated with AHFS categories of related drugs. For example, code 960.0 represents penicillins, code 964.2 represents anticoagulants, and code 962.3 represents insulins.
- Appendix D, Industrial Accidents According to Agency.
- Appendix E, List of Three-Digit Categories. A list of ICD-9-CM three-digit categories and their titles.

These appendices are a part of the official version of ICD-9-CM published by the U.S. Government Printing Office. Commercial ICD-9-CM coding references may include other appendices as well.

VOLUME 2: ALPHABETIC INDEX OF DISEASES AND INJURIES

Volume 2, the *Alphabetic Index of Diseases and Injuries,* often called the *Alphabetic Index* or simply the *Index,* is used to locate codes in volume 1, the *Tabular List.* Since the *Tabular List* has the full description of the codes in the *Index,* **codes must be verified by reviewing the full description in the *Tabular List*.** The *Index* is organized by the names of diseases or conditions. Specific sections of volume 2 include the following:

- Alphabetic Index to Diseases and Injuries
- Table of Drugs and Chemicals
- Alphabetic Index to External Causes of Injury and Poisoning (E codes)

Entries in the *Index* are organized by specific indentation patterns and alphabetization rules.

Indentation Patterns

Entries in the *Index* are classified as main terms, subterms, more specific subterms, and carryover lines. Each of these phrases has a specific and consistent indentation pattern. Figure 2-5 is an example of the indentation patterns. Refer to the figure as you read the explanations.

Main terms are diseases, conditions, or injuries such as appendicitis or fracture. Main terms are set

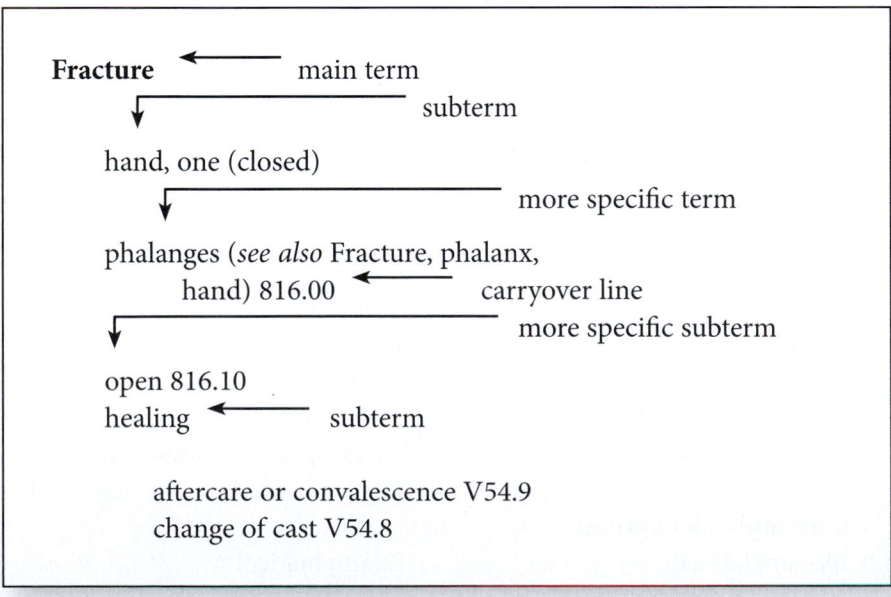

Figure 2-5 Alphabetic index indentation patterns

flush with the left margin, begin with a capital letter, and are printed in bold.

Subterms identify the site, type, or etiology for diseases, conditions, or injuries. Subterms are indented under a main term by one standard indentation, which is about two spaces. They begin with a lowercase letter and are printed in regular type.

More specific subterms are indented under a subterm by one standard indentation farther to the right as needed. More specific subterms are listed in alphabetical order, provide additional information related to subterms, and are printed in regular type.

Carryover lines are used when a complete entry does not fit on one line. Carryover lines are indented two standard indentations to avoid being confused with subterms and more specific subterms.

Identifying the main term in a diagnostic statement is the first step in locating a condition in the *Alphabetic Index*. Table 2-5 lists examples of various main terms.

Alphabetization Rules

The *Alphabetic Index* follows a letter-by-letter alphabetization format with the following exceptions:

- Subterms *with* or *without* are placed immediately after the main term.
- Subterms for numerical characters and words indicating numbers are listed in *numerical order*.

- Ignore single spaces or single hyphens between words.
- Ignore the final *s* in the possessive forms.

Figure 2-6 illustrates the exceptions to volume 2 alphabetization rules.

Alphabetic Index Tables

The *Alphabetic Index* has three tables that list the codes for hypertension, neoplasms, and drugs and chemicals with associated E codes. The indentation patterns and alphabetization rules for the tables are consistent with the rest of the *Index*.

Hypertension Table

Refer to figure 2-7 as you read about the features of the hypertension table.

After the main entry *Hypertension, hypertensive,* there are several terms in parentheses. These terms are **nonessential modifiers**, which means they do not affect code selection. The column headings **malignant**, **benign**, and **unspecified**, on the right-hand side of the table, are essential modifiers and do affect code selection. Malignant hypertension is uncontrolled and exhibits a diastolic pressure of 130 mmHg or greater and vascular damage. Benign hypertension is mild and under control. Unspecified hypertension means that there is no documentation to indicate if the hypertension is

Table 2-5 Alphabetic Index Main Terms

MAIN TERMS	DESCRIPTION
Anomaly	Congenital conditions, which are present at the time of birth, are listed alphabetically by anatomical site under the main term *Anomaly*.
Delivery	Conditions identified as *delivery complicated by* are listed alphabetically under the main term *Delivery*.
Disease, condition, injury	The name of the disease, condition, or injury is listed alphabetically in the *Index*.
Labor	Conditions that complicate or affect the progress of labor are listed alphabetically under the main term *Labor*.
Pregnancy	Conditions identified as *pregnancy complicated by* are listed alphabetically under the main term *Pregnancy*.
Puerperal	Conditions originating in the puerperium, the time period between the end of third-stage labor and six weeks, are listed alphabetically under the main term *Puerperium*.
Complications	Conditions originating as a complication of medical or surgical care are listed alphabetically under the main term *Complications*.
Late, effect of	Conditions that originate as a result of treatment for an illness or injury are listed alphabetically under the main term *Late, effect of.*

EXCEPTION	EXAMPLE
Ignore:	
S in the possessive form	**Addison's** anemia
Single hyphens within words	**Addison-Biermer** anemia
Single spaces between words	**Addison-Gull** disease
	Addisonian crisis
Numerical Order:	
Numerical characters and	**Paralysis, paralytic**
words indicating numbers	nerve . . .
	Third or oculomotor
	Fourth or trochlear
	Sixth or abducens
	Accessory (congenital)
	Chromosome(s) NEC 758.5
	13–15 . . .
	16–18 . . .
	21 or 22 . . .
With or **Without:**	
Immediately after the main	**Appendicitis** 541
term or related subterm	**with**
	perforation . . . 540.0
	with peritoneal abscess 540.1
	peritoneal abscess 540.1
	acute . . .
	amebic . . .

Figure 2-6 Exceptions to alphabetization rules

benign or malignant. In order to select a code from the *malignant* or *benign* column, the diagnostic statement must clearly state that the hypertension is either malignant or benign. When the diagnosis is stated simply as *hypertension,* the correct code is 401.9, *hypertension, unspecified.*

The first indentation under the main entry is the subterm *with* and indicates that another condition exists "with" the hypertension, but the relationship is not necessarily causal. The first indentation under *with* is *chronic kidney disease.* Under chronic kidney disease, the first indentation is *stage I through stage IV, or unspecified.* The codes for this condition are 403.00, 403.10, and 403.90. In order to select one of these codes for hypertension with chronic kidney disease, stage I through stage IV, or unspecified, the diagnostic

statement must include information about chronic kidney disease.

The second listing under *chronic kidney disease* is *stage V or end-stage renal disease.* In order to select a code from the list given, the diagnostic statement must include information about the severity (stage V or end-stage renal disease) of the chronic kidney disease.

The second indentation under *with* is *heart involvement (conditions classifiable to 429.0–429.3, 429.8, 429.9 due to hypertension) (see also* Hypertension, heart). In order to select codes 402.00, 402.10, or 402.90, the diagnosis must include a heart condition that falls into one of the codes listed with this indentation. The notation (*see also* Hypertension, heart) gives the coder another subterm that may be helpful in selecting the correct code.

HYPERTENSION, HYPERTENSIVE

	Malignant	Benign	Unspecified
Hypertension, hypertensive (arterial) (arteriolar) (crisis) (degeneration) (disease) (essential) (fluctuating) (idiopathic) (intermittent) (labile) (low renin) (orthostatic) (paroxysmall) (primary) (systemic) (uncontrolled) (vascular)...	401.0	401.1	401.9
with			
chronic kidney disease			
stage I through stage IV, or unspecified...	403.00	403.10	403.90
stage V or end stage renal disease...	403.01	403.11	403.91
heart involvement (conditions classifiable to 429.0–429.3, 429.8, 429.9 due to hypertension) (*see also* Hypertension, heart)...	402.00	402.10	402.90
with kidney involvement—*see* Hypertension, cardiorenal			
renal involvement (only conditions classifiable to 585, 586, 587) (excludes conditions classifiable to 584) (*see also* Hypertension, kidney)...	403.00	403.10	403.90
with heart involvement—*see* Hypertension, cardiorenal			
failure (and sclerosis) (*see also* Hypertension, kidney)...	403.01	403.11	403.91
sclerosis without failure (*see also* Hypertension, kidney)...	403.00	403.10	403.90
accelerated (*see also* Hypertension, by type, malignant)...	401.0	—	—
antepartum—*see* Hypertension, complicating pregnancy, childbirth, or the puerperium			
cardiorenal (disease)...	404.00	404.10	404.90
with			
chronic kidney disease			
stage I through stage IV, or unspecified...	404.00	404.10	404.90
and heart failure...	404.01	404.11	404.91
stage V or end stage renal disease...	404.02	404.12	404.92
and heart failure...	404.03▲	404.13▲	404.93 ▲
heart failure...	404.01▲	404.11▲	404.91 ▲
and chronic kidney disease...	404.01	404.11	404.91
stage I through stage IV or unspecified...	404.01	404.11	404.91
stage V or end stage renal disease...	404.03	404.13	404.93
cardiovascular disease (arteriosclerotic) (sclerotic)...	402.00	402.10	402.90
with			
heart failure...	402.01	402.11	402.91
renal involvement (conditions classifiable to 403) (*see also* Hypertension, cardiorenal)...	404.00	404.10	404.90
cardiovascular renal (disease) (sclerosis) (*see also* Hypertension, cardiorenal)...	404.00	404.10	404.90

Figure 2-7 Hypertension table

The first indentation under *heart involvement* is *with kidney involvement* (*see* Hypertension, cardiorenal). The coder must go to the subterm *cardiorenal* to continue coding. The entry *Hypertension, hypertensive, cardiorenal (disease)* provides a list of codes for hypertension with both heart and kidney involvement.

Neoplasm Table

The neoplasm table is an extensive *Alphabetic Index* entry that is used to code neoplasms according to the behavior of the tumor. The term *neoplasm* literally means "new growth," and not all neoplasms are malignant. A malignant neoplasm code can be assigned only when

the **pathology report** confirms the presence of a malignancy. *Never assign a malignant neoplasm code on the basis of a "suspected" or "rule out" diagnosis.*

Correct utilization of the neoplasm table depends on careful attention to the diagnostic statement, reading and following all instructional notes, and careful use of the *Alphabetic Index*. Figure 2-8 is a sample of the neoplasm table. Refer to the figure as you read about this table.

The neoplasm table provides codes for malignant, benign, uncertain behavior, and unspecified neoplasms. The table is arranged alphabetically by anatomical site. The codes listed with each site describe the behavior of

	Malignant				Uncertain	Unspecified
	Primary	Secondary	Ca in situ	Benign	Behavior	Nature
Neoplasm, neoplastic . . .	199.1	199.1	234.9	229.9	238.9	239.9

Notes—1. The list below gives the code numbers for neoplasms by anatomical site. For each site there are six possible code numbers according to whether the neoplasm in question is malignant, benign, in situ, of uncertain behavior, or of unspecified nature. The description of the neoplasm will often indicate which of the six columns is appropriate; e.g., malignant melanoma of skin, benign fibroadenoma of breast, carcinoma in situ of cervix uteri.

Where such descriptors are not present, the remainder of the Index should be consulted where guidance is given to the appropriate column for each morphological (histologic) variety listed; e.g., Mesonephroma—see Neoplasm, malignant; Embryoma—see also Neoplasm, uncertain behavior; Disease, Bowen's—see neoplasm, skin, in situ. However, the guidance in the Index can be overridden if one of the descriptors mentioned above is present; e.g., malignant adenoma of colon is coded to 153.9 and not to 211.3 as the adjective "malignant" overrides the Index entry "Adenoma—see also Neoplasm, benign."

2. Sites marked with the sign * (e.g., face NEC*) should be classified to malignant neoplasm of skin of these sites if the variety of neoplasm is a squamous cell carcinoma or an epidermal carcinoma; and to benign neoplasm of skin of these sites if the variety of neoplasm is a papilloma (any type).

abdomen, abdominal . . .	195.2	198.89	234.8	229.8	238.8	239.8
cavity . . .	195.2	198.89	234.8	229.8	238.8	239.8
organ . . .	195.2	198.89	234.8	229.8	238.8	239.8
viscera . . .	195.2	198.89	234.8	229.8	238.8	239.8
wall . . .	173.5	198.2	232.5	216.5	238.2	239.2
connective tissue . . .	171.5	198.89	—	215.5	238.1	239.2
abdominopelvic . . .	195.8	198.89	234.8	229.8	238.8	239.8
accessory sinus—*see* Neoplasm, sinus						
acoustic nerve . . .	192.0	198.4	—	225.1	237.9	239.7
acromion (process) . . .	170.4	198.5	—	213.4	238.0	239.2

Figure 2-8 Neoplasm table

the neoplasm. Malignant neoplasms are cancerous and are coded as follows:

- Primary, the site where the neoplasm originated.
- Secondary, the site to which the neoplasm has spread.
- In situ, the malignant cells have not spread.

Benign neoplasms are not cancerous and do not spread or invade other sites. Uncertain behavior describes a neoplasm that cannot be identified as benign or malignant. In these cases, the pathology or lab report is inconclusive and the pathologist is unable to make a definitive diagnosis. Unspecified is used when the documentation does not support a more specific code.

To use the neoplasm table, the coder first locates the diagnosis in the *Alphabetic Index*. The information in the *Alphabetic Index* directs the coder to the neoplasm table.

Table of Drugs and Chemicals

The table of drugs and chemicals is located after the last entry in the *Alphabetic Index*. Drugs and chemicals are listed in alphabetical order and include everything from antibiotics to zinc. This table enables the coder to select the appropriate poisoning code and associated E code. A sample of the table of drugs and chemicals is presented in figure 2-9. Refer to the figure as you read the explanation.

Poisoning is defined as a condition caused by drugs, medicines, and biological substances when taken improperly or not in accordance with physician orders.

Substance	Poisoning	Accident	External Cause (E-Code) Therapeutic Use	Suicide Attempt	Assault	Un-determined
1-propanol	980.3	E860.4	—	E950.9	E962.1	E980.9
2-propanol	980.2	E860.3	—	E950.9	E962.1	E980.9
2, 4-D (dichlorophenoxyacetic acid)	989.4	E863.5	—	E950.6	E962.1	E980.7
2, 4-toluene diisocyanate	983.0	E864.0	—	E950.7	E962.1	E980.6
2, 4, 5-T (trichlorophenoxyacetic acid)	989.2	E863.5	—	E950.6	E962.1	E980.7
14-hydroxydihydromorphinone	965.09	E850.2	E935.2	E950.0	E962.0	E980.0
A						
ABOB	961.7	E857	E931.7	E950.4	E962.0	E980.4
Abrus(seed)	988.2	E865.3	—	E950.9	E962.1	E980.9
Absinthe	980.0	E860.0	—	E950.9	E962.1	E980.9
beverage	980.0	E860.0	—	E950.9	E962.1	E980.9
Acenocoumarin, acenocoumarol	964.2	E858.2	E934.2	E950.4	E962.0	E980.4
Acepromazine	969.1	E853.0	E939.1	E950.3	E962.0	E980.3
Acetal	982.8	E862.4	—	E950.9	E962.1	E980.9
Acetaldehyde (vapor)	987.8	E869.8	—	E952.8	E962.2	E982.8
liquid	989.89	E866.8	—	E950.9	E962.1	E980.9
Acetaminophen	965.4	E850.4	E935.4	E950.0	E962.0	E980.0
Acetaminosalol	965.1	E850.3	E935.3	E950.0	E962.0	E980.0
Acetanilid(e)	965.4	E850.4	E935.4	E950.0	E962.0	E980.0
Acetarsol, acetarsone	961.1	E857	E931.1	E950.4	E962.0	E980.4
Acetazolamide	974.2	E858.5	E944.2	E950.4	E962.0	E980.4
Acetic						
acid	983.1	E864.1	—	E950.7	E962.1	E980.6
with sodium acetate (ointment)	976.3	E858.7	E946.3	E950.4	E962.0	E980.4
irrigating solution	974.5	E858.5	E944.5	E950.4	E962.0	E980.4
lotion	976.2	E858.7	E946.2	E950.4	E962.0	E980.4
anhydride	983.1	E864.1	—	E950.7	E962.1	E980.6

Figure 2-9 Table of drugs and chemicals

Examples of poisoning are taking or receiving the wrong medication in error, taking or receiving the wrong dose of the right medication in error, overdose, prescription drugs taken with alcohol, and mixing prescription drugs and over-the-counter medications without physician advice or consent.

The table of drugs and chemicals lists the names of the substances, the poisoning code for each substance, and five columns of E codes. The E code columns are labeled *accident, therapeutic use, suicide attempt, assault,* and *undetermined*. Unless the patient record clearly states otherwise, the E code is selected from the accident column. A poisoning code is never used in conjunction with an E code from the therapeutic use column.

Diagnostic statements can include other problems caused by the poisoning. For example: A child is treated for hives caused by ingesting her brother's psoriasis medication, triamcinolone. The diagnosis (hives) is coded as the reason for the visit. An additional code for the wrongful ingestion of triamcinolone as an accidental poisoning may also be assigned.

EXERCISE 2-1

Write a short answer for each question.

1. Name and describe the two main coding systems used in the United States. _____

2. List the purposes of ICD-9-CM coding conventions. _____

3. Describe the difference between ICD-9-CM volume 1 and volume 2. _____

4. Define the purpose of V codes. _____

5. Define the term *nonessential modifier*. _____
_____

6. Explain the purpose of the neoplasm table. _____

7. A/an _____ is an electronic version of coding books.

8. _____ classify external causes of injury and poisoning.

9. A/an _____ is a three-digit code representing a single disease or group of diseases.

10. In volume 2 (the *Index*), _____ are the names of diseases, conditions, or injuries.

ICD-9-CM CODING CONVENTIONS

Understanding and applying the ICD-9-CM coding conventions is necessary to accurately assign diagnostic codes. Coding conventions fall into five categories:

- Cross-references
- Instructional notes
- Connecting words
- Abbreviations
- Punctuation

Cross-References

ICD-9-CM cross-references, which are usually found in the *Alphabetic Index,* include *see, see also, see category,* and *see condition*. The cross-references direct the coder to look elsewhere before assigning a code.

- **See** is a mandatory direction. The coder must refer to the term that follows the word *see*.
- **See also** directs the coder to another entry in the *Alphabetic Index* when the entry under consideration doesn't provide the needed code. Basically, *see also* means "if you can't find the code you need here, check at this other location."
- **See category** is a mandatory direction and the coder must refer to a three-digit category code in the *Tabular List* (volume 1).
- **See condition** means that the coder is attempting to locate a code by using an adjective as the main term. *See condition* reminds the coder to use the condition or diagnosis as the main term.

Instructional Notes

Instructional notes provide information for accurate code selection. There are six types of instructional notes: general notes; inclusion notes; exclusion notes; use additional code; code first [the] underlying condition; and code, if applicable, any causal condition first.

General notes are found in all three ICD-9-CM volumes. In the *Alphabetic Index,* general notes are usually printed in italics and boxed. The most common application of general notes is to identify fifth-digit subclassifications in the *Tabular List* and *Alphabetic Index.* General notes are also used to clarify unique coding situations such as the difference between an open and closed fracture.

Inclusion notes are lists of conditions that are similar enough to be coded or classified by the same medical code. Inclusion notes are found at the beginning of a chapter and immediately following category, subcategory, and subclassification codes.

Exclusion notes are easy to identify, because the word *Excludes* is italicized and printed in a box. Exclusion notes are found immediately below the code to which the exclusion applies. A condition listed under the exclusion note cannot be coded or classified by the medical code that has the exclusion note. A code or range of codes for the excluded condition is also a part of the exclusion note.

Use additional code means that more than one code may be necessary to provide a complete picture of the patient's problem. For example, the code for vaginitis (616.10) directs the coder to "use additional code" to identify the organism that is the cause of the vaginitis. In order to use the additional code, the organism must be documented in the patient's record.

Code first [the] underlying condition indicates that the patient's condition is a manifestation of an underlying disease. This instruction applies to inpatient coding. When coding for an inpatient, the code for the underlying disease must be listed before the manifestation. For example, diabetic retinitis means that the inflammation of the retina is related to the patient's diabetes. The diabetes code must be listed first and the code for the retinitis is listed second. When coding for an outpatient or physician office visit, the first code listed is the code that applies to the reason for the office or outpatient visit.

Code, if applicable, any causal condition first means that the code with this note may be sequenced as the principal diagnosis when the causal condition is unknown or not applicable. If the causal condition is known, then the code for the causal condition should be sequenced as the principal or first-listed diagnosis.

Connecting Words

Connecting words are subterms listed primarily in the *Alphabetic Index* and indicate a relationship between

Pneumonia . . .
    with influenza, flu, or grippe 487.0
    adenoviral 480.0 . . .
    bacterial 482.9 . . .
    due to
        adenovirus 480.0 . . .
        Chlamydia, chlamydial 483.1 . . .
    in
        actinomycosis 039.1
        anthrax 022.1*[484.5]* . . .

Figure 2-10 Connecting words

the main term and other conditions or causes of disease. Commonly used connecting words include *associated with, complicated (by), due to, during, following, in, of, secondary to, with, with mention of,* and *without.* With the exception of *with* and *without,* connecting words are listed alphabetically under the main term. Figure 2-10 is an example of a main entry (pneumonia) and connecting words.

The phrase *due to* indicates a causal relationship between two conditions. In the example, pneumonia due to adenovirus means that the pneumonia is caused by an adenovirus.

The connecting words *with, associated with,* and *in* mean that both conditions must be present in order to use a specific code. To use code 487.0, pneumonia with influenza, flu, or grippe, both pneumonia and one of the other conditions must be documented. To use code 039.1, both pneumonia and actinomycosis must be documented.

The word *and* means "and/or" when it appears in the title of a code. For example, code 616.10 is vaginitis *and* vulvovaginitis, unspecified. This code can be assigned to either vaginitis or vulvovaginitis.

Abbreviations

The abbreviations **NEC, not elsewhere classified,** and **NOS, not otherwise specified,** are associated with the codes that include the fourth or fifth digits 8 and 9. These codes are known as residual subcategories. NEC, not elsewhere classified, means that the diagnosis or condition, no matter how specific, does not have a separate code. NOS, not otherwise specified, means the same thing as *unspecified*. This abbreviation is found only in the *Tabular List*. NOS codes should be used only when the diagnosis or the patient's medical record does not provide enough information to select a more specific code.

Punctuation

Punctuation marks such as parentheses ( ), slanted square brackets *[ ]*, square brackets [ ], colons :, section marks §, braces }, and double braces { } provide additional information for accurate coding. Some commercial ICD-9-CM publications do not use all punctuation marks. Table 2-6 lists the punctuation marks with an example. Refer to this table as you read about this coding convention.

Parentheses ( ) enclose nonessential modifiers that do *not* affect code selection. Parentheses also enclose cross-reference terms such as *see also,* which may affect code selection.

Square brackets [ ] are used to enclose synonyms, alternative wordings, abbreviations, and phrases related to a section, category, subcategory, or subclassification. Information in square brackets is not required as part of the diagnostic statement. Square brackets are also used to note fifth digits associated with a specific code.

Slanted square brackets *[ ]*, found only in the *Alphabetic Index,* enclose the manifestation code associated with an underlying condition. The underlying condition must be listed first, with the manifestation code listed second. For physician office coding, the reason for the office visit is listed first.

Colons : are used with inclusion and exclusion notes and are placed after the included or excluded condition. Additional descriptions are indented and listed beneath the included or excluded condition. The diagnosis must contain at least one of the descriptions in order to apply the inclusion or exclusion note.

Braces and double braces {, { } serve the same purpose as colons. They connect a list or series of descriptions or diagnostic terms with a common stem or with a main term. Braces are used in the *Tabular List* to reduce repetitive wording by connecting a series of terms on the left with a statement on the right. Some commercial ICD-9-CM coding references have dropped the use of braces. These publications rely on colons to connect terms and statements, or repeat the main statement with the series of terms.

Table 2-6 ICD-9-CM Punctuation Marks

PUNCTUATION MARK	EXAMPLE
Parentheses ( )	Enclose words that do not affect code assignment: Arteriosclerosis (obliterans) (senile)
Square brackets [ ]	Enclose information that does not affect code assignment: Arteriosclerotic heart disease [ASHD] Identify fifth digits associated with a specific code: 715.0 Osteoarthrosis, generalized [0,4,9]
Slanted square *[ ]* brackets	Enclose the manifestation code associated with an underlying condition: Anthrax, with pneumonia 022.1 *[484.5]* Pneumonia as the manifestation of the anthrax infection

Colons :	Identify required descriptions for exclusion and inclusion notes:
	 528.0 Stomatitis and mucositis (ulcerative)
	 Excludes: stomatitis:
	    acute necrotizing ulcerative (101)
	    aphthous (528.2.)

Section marks §	§662 Long labor Prolonged first stage

Braces
 { and double braces }
	528.4 Cysts
	   Dermoid cyst } of mouth
	   Epidermoid cyst

Section marks § are used in the official version of the ICD-9-CM to denote a footnote on the page.

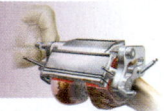

EXERCISE 2-2

Fill in the blank or write a short answer.

1. ICD-9-CM coding conventions _____ and _____ are mandatory cross-reference directions.
2. Briefly define the phrase *code first [the] underlying condition.*
3. Write out and define the abbreviation NEC.
4. The phrase _____ indicates a causal relationship between two conditions.
5. Write out and define the abbreviation NOS.

ICD-9-CM OFFICIAL GUIDELINES FOR CODING AND REPORTING

The *ICD-9-CM Official Guidelines for Coding and Reporting* provide coding and reporting instructions in situations where ICD-9-CM *does not* provide instructions. The ICD-9-CM coding conventions *take precedence over* the guidelines. It is beyond the scope of this text to review the entire content of the guidelines. The guidelines are available on the CMS Web site at http://www.cms.gov. Commercial ICD-9-CM publications and the *Coding Clinic* also include the guidelines. Some of the *ICD-9-CM Official Guidelines* are presented here.

Guidelines for Inpatient, Short-Term, Acute Care, and Long-Term Care Hospital Coding

Section II of the *ICD-9-CM Official Guidelines* gives instructions for selecting the **principal diagnosis**. The principal diagnosis is the condition established after study to be chiefly responsible for the patient's admission for care. The code for the principal diagnosis is listed first on the insurance claim. Guidelines A through J, *Section II: Selection of Principal Diagnosis,* are summarized here. ICD-9-CM coding conventions take precedence over these guidelines.

Guideline II.A. Codes for symptoms, signs, and ill-defined conditions

Codes for symptoms, signs, and ill-defined conditions (ICD-9-CM chapter 16) are **not** used as a principal diagnosis when a related definitive diagnosis has been established.

Guideline II.B. Two or more interrelated conditions, each potentially meeting the definition for principal diagnosis

When two or more interrelated conditions potentially meet the definition of principal diagnosis, either condition may be listed first, unless the circumstances of the admission, the therapy provided, or ICD-9-CM coding conventions indicate otherwise.

Guideline II.C. Two or more diagnoses that equally meet the definition for principal diagnosis

In the unusual instance when two or more diagnoses equally meet the criteria for principal diagnosis and ICD-9-CM coding conventions or other coding guidelines do not provide sequencing instructions, any one of the diagnoses may be sequenced first.

Guideline II.D. Two or more comparative or contrasting conditions

In the rare instance when two or more contrasting or comparative diagnoses are documented as "either/or" (or similar terminology), the diagnoses are coded as if confirmed and sequenced according to the circumstances of the admission. If no further determination can be made as to which diagnosis is principal, either diagnosis may be sequenced first.

Guideline II.E. Symptom or symptoms followed by contrasting/comparative diagnoses

When a symptom or symptoms are followed by contrasting or comparative diagnoses, the symptom or symptoms are coded and sequenced first. All contrasting or comparative diagnoses should be coded as secondary diagnoses.

Guideline II.F. Original treatment plan not carried out

The principal diagnosis is the condition after study that occasioned the admission to the hospital, even if the treatment may not have been carried out due to unforeseen circumstances.

Guideline II.G. Complications of surgery and other medical care

When the admission is for treatment of a complication resulting from surgery or other medical care, the complication code is sequenced as the principal diagnosis. When the complication is classified to categories 996 through 999, an additional code for the specific complication may be assigned.

Guideline II.H. Uncertain diagnosis

If the diagnosis documented at the time of discharge is qualified as *probable, suspected, questionable, possible, still to be ruled out,* or other similar terms indicating uncertainty, code the condition as if it existed or was established. The bases for these guidelines are the diagnostic workup, arrangements for further workup or observation, and initial therapeutic approach that correspond most closely with the established diagnosis. This guideline applies only to short-term, acute, or long-term care and psychiatric hospitals.

Guideline II.I. Admission from observation unit

1. Admission following medical observation: When a patient is admitted to an observation unit for a medical condition, which either worsens or does not improve, and is subsequently admitted as an inpatient of the same hospital for the same medical condition, the principal diagnosis would be the medical condition that led to the hospital admission.

2. Admission following postoperative observation: When a patient is admitted to an observation unit to monitor a condition (or complication) that develops following outpatient surgery, and then is subsequently admitted as an inpatient of the same hospital, hospitals should apply the Uniform Hospital Discharge Data Set (UHDDS) definition

of principal diagnosis as "that condition established after study to be chiefly responsible for occasioning the admission of the patient to the hospital for care."

Guideline II.J. Admission from outpatient surgery

When a patient receives surgery in the hospital's outpatient surgery department and is subsequently admitted for continuing inpatient care at the same hospital, the following guidelines should be followed in selecting the principal diagnosis for the inpatient admission:

- If the reason for the inpatient admission is a complication, assign the complication as the principal diagnosis.
- If no complication or other condition is documented as the reason for the inpatient admission, assign the reason for the outpatient surgery as the principal diagnosis.
- If the reason for the inpatient admission is another condition unrelated to the surgery, assign the unrelated condition as the principal diagnosis.

Diagnostic Coding and Reporting Guidelines for Outpatient Services

Diagnostic Coding and Reporting Guidelines for Outpatient Services are found in Section IV of the *ICD-9-CM Official Guidelines for Coding and Reporting.* Under the *Guidelines* the terms **encounter** and **visit** are used interchangeably to describe outpatient service contacts. In all cases, the reason for the encounter or visit is referred to as the **first-listed diagnosis**, although some practitioners may also use the term *primary diagnosis.* A summary of the outpatient services guidelines is presented here.

Guideline IV.A. Selection of first-listed condition

In the outpatient setting the term *first-listed diagnosis* is used in lieu of principal diagnosis. In determining the first-listed diagnosis, ICD-9-CM coding conventions as well as the general and disease-specific guidelines take precedence over the outpatient guidelines. Diagnoses often are not established at the time of the initial encounter/visit. It may take two or more visits before the diagnosis is confirmed. The most critical rule involves beginning the search for the correct code assignment through the *Alphabetic Index.* Never begin searching initially in the *Tabular List* as this will lead to coding errors.

1. Outpatient surgery: When a patient presents for outpatient surgery, code the reason for the surgery as the first-listed diagnosis (reason for the encounter), even if the surgery is not performed due to a contraindication.

2. Observation stay: When a patient is admitted for observation for a medical condition, assign a code for the medical condition as the first-listed diagnosis. When a patient presents for outpatient surgery and develops complications requiring admission for observation, code the reason for the surgery as the first reported (first-listed) diagnosis (reason for the encounter), followed by the codes for the complications as secondary diagnoses.

Guideline IV.B. Codes from 001.0 through V89.09

Appropriate ICD-9-CM codes, from 001.0 through V89.09, must be used to identify diagnoses, symptoms, problems, complaints, or other reason(s) for the encounter/visit.

Guideline IV.C. Accurate reporting of ICD-9-CM diagnosis codes

For accurate reporting of ICD-9-CM diagnosis codes, the documentation should describe the patient's condition, using terminology that includes specific diagnoses as well as symptoms, problems, or reasons for the encounter. There are ICD-9-CM codes to describe all of these.

Guideline IV.D. Selection of codes 001.0 through 999.9

These ICD-9-CM codes will frequently be used to describe the reason for the encounter.

Guideline IV.E. Codes that describe symptoms and signs

Codes that describe symptoms and signs, as opposed to diagnoses, are acceptable for report purposes when a diagnosis has not been established (confirmed) by the provider. ICD-9-CM volume 1, chapter 16, "Symptoms, Signs, and Ill-Defined Conditions," contains many but not all codes for symptoms.

Guideline IV.F. Encounters for circumstances other than disease or injury

ICD-9-CM V codes are used to report encounters for reasons other than disease or injury.

Guideline IV.G. Level of detail in coding

All ICD-9-CM codes must be assigned to the highest level of specificity based on the documentation in the patient's record. This means that a three-digit code must not be assigned when a four-digit code is available, and a four-digit code must not be assigned when a five-digit code is available.

Guideline IV.H. ICD-9-CM code for the diagnosis, condition, problem, or other reason for encounter/visit

List first the ICD-9-CM code for the diagnosis, condition, problem, or other reason for the encounter/visit shown in the medical record to be chiefly responsible for the services provided. List additional codes that describe any coexisting conditions. In some cases the first-listed diagnosis may be a symptom when a diagnosis has not been established (confirmed) by the physician.

Guideline IV.I. Uncertain diagnosis

Do not code diagnoses documented as *probable, suspected, questionable, rule out, working diagnosis, provisional,* or other similar terms indicating uncertainty. Rather, code the condition(s) to the highest degree of certainty for that encounter/visit, such as symptoms, signs, abnormal test results, or other reasons for the visit.

Guideline IV.J. Chronic diseases

Chronic diseases treated on an ongoing basis may be coded and reported as many times as the patient receives treatment and care for the condition(s).

Guideline IV.K. Code all documented conditions that coexist

Code all conditions that are documented, coexist at the time of the encounter/visit, and require treatment or affect the care of the patient. Do not code conditions that were previously treated and no longer exist. However, history codes (V10–V19) may be used as secondary codes if the historical condition or family history has an impact on current care or influences treatment.

Guideline IV.L. Patients receiving diagnostic services only

When a patient is seen for diagnostic services only during an encounter/visit, sequence first the diagnosis, condition, problem, or other reason for encounter/visit shown in the medical record to be chiefly responsible for the outpatient services provided during the encounter/visit. Codes for other diagnoses (e.g., chronic conditions) may be sequenced as additional codes.

For encounters for routine laboratory/radiology testing in the absence of any signs, symptoms, or associated diagnoses, assign V72.5 and V72.6. If routine testing is performed during the same encounter as a test to evaluate a sign, symptom, or diagnosis, it is appropriate to assign both the V code and the code describing the reason for the nonroutine test.

If outpatient encounters for diagnostic tests have been interpreted by a physician, and the final report is available at the time of coding, code any confirmed or definitive diagnosis(es) documented in the interpretation. Do not code related signs and symptoms as additional diagnoses.

Guideline IV.M. Patients receiving therapeutic services only

For patients receiving therapeutic services only during the encounter/visit, sequence first the diagnosis, condition, problem, or other reason for the encounter/visit shown in the medical record to be chiefly responsible for the outpatient services provided during the encounter/visit. Codes for other diagnoses (e.g., chronic conditions) may be sequenced as additional diagnoses.

The only exception to this rule is that when the primary reason for the admission/encounter is chemotherapy, radiation therapy, or rehabilitation, the appropriate V code for the service is listed first, and the diagnosis or problem for which the service is being performed is listed second.

Guideline IV.N. Patients receiving preoperative evaluation only

For patients receiving preoperative evaluation only, sequence first a code from category V72.8, *Other specified examinations,* to describe the preoperative consultations. Assign a code for the condition to describe the reason for the surgery as an additional diagnosis. Code also any findings related to the preoperative evaluation.

Guideline IV.O. Ambulatory surgery

For ambulatory surgery, code the diagnosis for which the surgery was performed. If the postoperative diagnosis is known to be different from the preoperative diagnosis at the time the diagnosis is confirmed, select the postoperative diagnosis for coding, since it is the most definitive.

Guideline IV.P. Routine outpatient prenatal visits

For routine outpatient prenatal visits when no complications are present, code V22.0, *Supervision of normal first pregnancy,* or V22.1, *Supervision of other normal pregnancy,* should be used as the principal diagnosis. These codes should not be used in conjunction with chapter 11, "Complications of Pregnancy, Childbirth, and the Puerperium," codes.

The coding conventions and coding guidelines are intended to ensure accurate and consistent assignment of medical codes. Although all of the conventions and guidelines are equally important, one coding rule actually supersedes all others: Code **only** the conditions, diagnoses, problems, and procedures that are **clearly** documented in the patient's medical record.

EXERCISE 2-3

Write a brief answer or fill in the blank(s) for each statement or question.

1. Define and compare the phrases *first-listed diagnosis* and *principal diagnosis.*

2. The _____ or _____ is listed first on the insurance claim.

3. _____ coding conventions take precedence over the *Official Guidelines for Coding and Reporting.*

4. The *ICD-9-CM Official Guidelines for Coding and Reporting* are available on the _____ Web site.

5. The _____, published quarterly, includes the *ICD-9-CM Official Guidelines for Coding and Reporting.*

ASSIGNING ICD-9-CM DIAGNOSTIC CODES

Accurate code assignment depends on three activities:

- Following the ICD-9-CM coding conventions and the *ICD-9-CM Official Guidelines for Coding and Reporting*
- Selecting diagnostic codes
- Sequencing diagnostic codes

The ICD-9-CM coding conventions and the *ICD-9-CM Official Guidelines* provide the coder with the "rules" of coding. The steps associated with selecting and sequencing diagnostic codes provide the coder with a procedure for implementing the conventions and guidelines.

Selecting the Diagnostic Code(s)

The procedure for selecting ICD-9-CM diagnostic codes is enumerated and discussed here:

1. Identify the main term(s) in the diagnostic statement. The main term is the condition or problem for which the patient seeks treatment. For example, the main term in urinary tract infection is *infection.*
2. Locate the main term in the *Alphabetic Index.*
3. Review the subterms listed under the main term to determine if an entry matches the additional information in the diagnostic statement.
4. Follow the mandatory cross-reference instructions. If there are no cross-references, note the code listed with the subterm entry.
5. **Check the code in the *Alphabetic Index* with the full description and any instructional notes in the *Tabular List.***
6. Follow all *Tabular List* inclusion, exclusion, and other instructional notes.
7. Assign the code(s) to the highest level of specificity; select a three-digit code only when no four-digit code is available; select a four-digit code only when no five-digit code is available; select a five-digit code when a fifth-digit subclassification is available.

Step 5 is bolded for a very important reason. The *Tabular List* provides a complete description of conditions included and excluded under a particular code, important instructional notes, and fifth-digit information. Do not assign codes directly from the *Alphabetic Index.*

Sequencing Diagnostic Codes

In order to ensure that the health care agency receives appropriate reimbursement for services rendered, diagnostic codes must be accurately listed on the insurance claim. Placing diagnostic codes in the correct order is called **sequencing**. For inpatient coding, the principal diagnosis is sequenced first. As mentioned earlier, the principal diagnosis is defined as the diagnosis determined after study to be the reason for the patient's admission to a hospital. For physician office and other ambulatory agency coding, the first-listed diagnosis is sequenced first.

Improper sequencing of diagnostic codes can lead to inadequate reimbursement for services rendered; denied or delayed reimbursement for services rendered; and, in a worst-case scenario, charges of fraud or abuse. Strict adherence to ICD-9-CM coding conventions and sequencing guidelines prevents these unpleasant outcomes.

MISCELLANEOUS CODING GUIDELINES

Miscellaneous coding guidelines cover conditions and problems related to late effects, burns, and HIV/AIDS.

Late Effects

A **late effect** is defined as the **residual condition** that remains after the acute phase of an illness or injury has been resolved. Residual conditions include problems like scar tissue as a result of severe burns or partial paralysis due to a stroke. Documentation of late effects may include wording such as *residual of, old, sequela of, late,* and *due to* or *following* a previous illness or injury. Late effect codes are located in the *Alphabetic Index* under the main term *Late* and the subterm *effect(s) (of).*

Late effects often require two codes, one for the residual condition that is currently affecting the patient and another for the original injury or illness. If the patient is being treated for the residual condition or late effect, the residual condition code is sequenced first. In some cases there is a combination code that includes the residual condition and the underlying cause. When the diagnostic statement does not include the residual condition, code only the cause of the late effect.

Burns

Codes from ICD-9-CM categories 940 through 949 apply to current unhealed burns with the exception of sunburn and friction burns. Sunburns are classified as dermatitis, and friction burns are classified as superficial injuries. Scars and contractures that remain after the burn is healed are coded as late effects.

Burn diagnoses require at least two codes, one for the location and degree of the burn, and another for the percentage of body surface affected. Burns are classified as **first degree** or **superficial**, such as a nonblistering sunburn; **second degree** or **partial thickness**, characterized by blistering; and **third degree** or **full thickness**, characterized by charred tissue.

Category 948, *Burns classified according to extent of body surface involved,* provides codes for burns that affect from less than 10% of the body surface to 90% or more of the body surface. Body surface percentages are estimated based on the "rule of nines," which assigns a percentage to specific areas of the body. Figure 2-11 illustrates the rule of nines. The percentages are adjusted for infants, children, and adults with large buttocks, abdomens, or thighs. The physician or other health care provider calculates the extent of the burn.

HIV/AIDS

HIV/AIDS conditions are coded to volume 1, chapter 1, "Infectious and Parasitic Diseases," and to volume 1, V codes. Chapter 1, category 042, *Human immunodeficiency virus (HIV) disease,* is used to code acquired immunodeficiency syndrome (AIDS), AIDS-like syndrome, AIDS-related complex (ARC), and symptomatic HIV infection. Specific conditions, such as Kaposi sarcoma, should also be coded. V codes that apply to HIV and AIDS conditions include:

- V08, *Asymptomatic human immunodeficiency virus infection*—the patient tests positive for HIV and displays no symptoms.
- V72.6, *Laboratory examination*—the patient's visit includes a lab test to rule out HIV infection.
- V73.89, *Other specified viral diseases*—patient exposure to HIV is unknown.
- V01.7, *Contact with or exposure to … other viral diseases*—the patient has been exposed to the AIDS virus.

The coding guidelines for reporting services rendered to patients who have conditions related to HIV and AIDS are as follows:

- Code only confirmed cases of HIV infection/illness. The provider's diagnostic statement that the patient is HIV positive or has an HIV-related disease is sufficient. When treating or evaluating an HIV-related illness, the principal or first-listed diagnosis code is 042. Codes related to other conditions or manifestations, such as Kaposi sarcoma, are listed as secondary conditions.

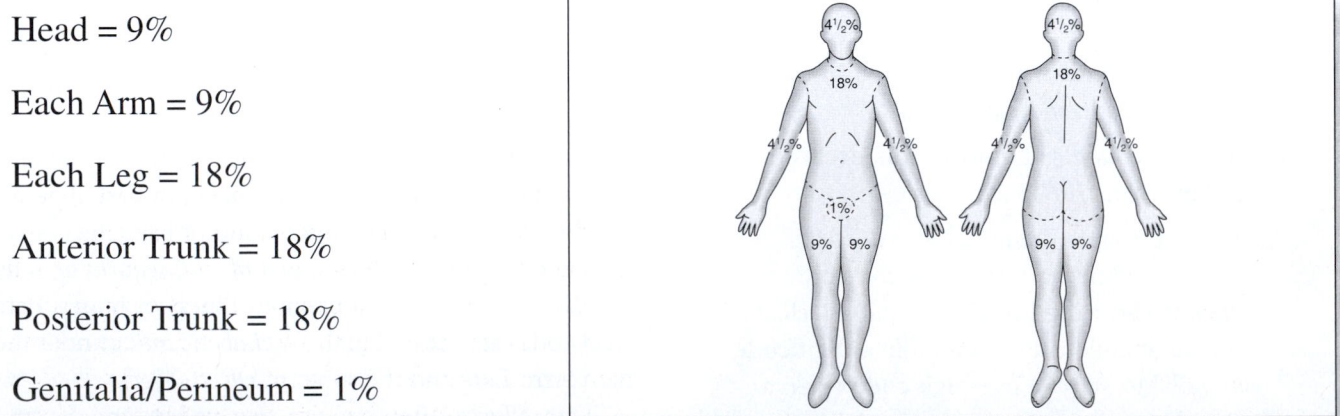

Head = 9%	
Each Arm = 9%	
Each Leg = 18%	
Anterior Trunk = 18%	
Posterior Trunk = 18%	
Genitalia/Perineum = 1%	

Figure 2-11 Rule of nines

- When treating or evaluating a condition unrelated to HIV-related illnesses, the reason for the visit is coded and listed as the principal or first-listed diagnosis. The HIV disease and related manifestations are sequenced as secondary diagnoses.
- V08, asymptomatic human immunodeficiency virus (HIV) is used when the patient's record states "HIV-positive," "known HIV," or "HIV test positive," or similar terminology. Do not use V08 if the documentation includes the terms "AIDS" or if the patient is being treated for an HIV-related illness.
- Code 795.71, inconclusive serologic test for human immunodeficiency virus (HIV) assigned when the blood test is inconclusive and there is no diagnosis or manifestation of HIV-related illness.

Because of the prejudicial nature of HIV- and AIDS-related diagnoses, the patient must sign an authorization for release of HIV status so that these codes can be included on the insurance claim.

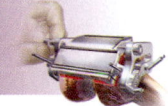

EXERCISE 2-4

Circle the main term in each diagnostic statement.

1. Acute gastric ulcer with hemorrhage
2. Hypertension due to constricted arteries
3. Third-degree burns over the right hand up to the wrist
4. Normal delivery, full-term infant
5. Cervical cancer, advanced

Briefly define each term.

6. sequencing _____
7. late effect _____
8. first-degree burns _____
9. second-degree burns _____
10 third-degree burns _____

VOLUME 3: TABULAR LIST AND ALPHABETIC INDEX OF PROCEDURES

ICD-9-CM volume 3, the *Tabular List and Alphabetic Index of Procedures,* is often called the *Procedure Codes.* The procedure codes in volume 3 are used to code and report services rendered during an inpatient or hospital episode of care. The organizational patterns, format, and conventions in volume 3 are nearly identical to those in volumes 1 and 2.

Volume 3 includes two main sections: (1) the alphabetic index to the tabular list of procedure codes, and (2) 17 chapters in the Tabular List of procedure codes.

Alphabetic Index

The Alphabetic Index is a listing of procedures, tests, operations, surgeries, and other therapies. The organization of the Alphabetic Index to procedures is very similar to the format of the *Alphabetic Index of Diseases and Injuries* (volume 2). Main terms are bolded and flush left. Main terms for the Alphabetic Index to procedures include the following:

- Eponyms, such as *Billroth II operation* (partial gastrectomy with gastrojejunostomy)
- Nouns, such as *examination, bypass, closure, operation, repair*
- Operations, such as diverticulectomy, gastrectomy, proctocolectomy
- Procedures or tests, such as amniocentesis, colonoscopy, scan
- Verbs, such as *repair, suture*

Subterms associated with main terms and other subterms are indented and listed in alphabetical order **except for** subterms that begin with the words *as, by,* and *with.* These words are known as *connecting words* and immediately follow a main term or subterm entry. Figure 2-12 is an example of an entry from the volume 3 Alphabetic Index.

Tabular List

The Tabular List in volume 3 contains 18 chapters. Table 2-7 lists the Tabular List chapters and code categories.

Procedure codes consist of 3 or 4 digits. Two digits precede the decimal point and one or two digits follow the decimal. A three-digit code cannot be used if a four-digit code is available. Inclusion and exclusion notes are an important part of the Tabular List. Figure 2-13 illustrates a Tabular List category entry.

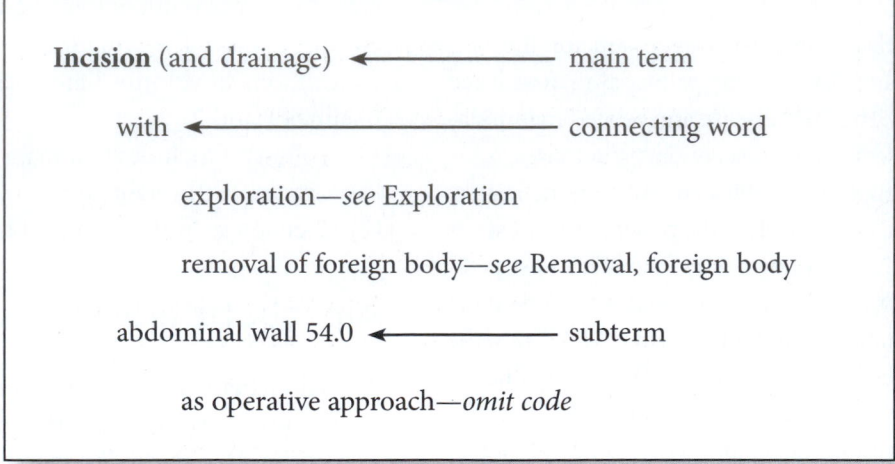

Figure 2-12 Volume 3 alphabetic index

Table 2-7 Volume 3 Tabular List Chapters and Code Categories

CHAPTER TITLES	CATEGORIES
0. Procedures and Interventions, Not Elsewhere Classified	00–00.9
1. Operations on the Nervous System	01–05
2. Operations on the Endocrine System	06–07
3. Operations on the Eye	08–16
3A. Other Miscellaneous Diagnostic and Therapeutic Procedures	17
4. Operations on the Ear	18–20
5. Operations on the Nose, Mouth, and Pharynx	21–29
6. Operations on the Respiratory System	30–34
7. Operations on the Cardiovascular System	35–39
8. Operations on the Hemic and Lymphatic System	40–41
9. Operations on the Digestive System	42–54
10. Operations on the Urinary System	55–59
11. Operations on the Male Genital Organs	60–64
12. Operations on the Female Genital Organs	65–71
13. Obstetrical Procedures	72–75
14. Operations on the Musculoskeletal System	76–84
15. Operations on the Integumentary System	85–86
16. Miscellaneous Diagnostic and Therapeutic Procedures	87–99

Volume 3 Coding Conventions

Most of the coding conventions discussed under volumes 1 and 2 also apply to volume 3. The exceptions are **code also**, **omit code**, and slanted brackets *[ ]*. *Code also* means more than one code is needed for a particular procedure. The *code also* instruction include a list of codes that are acceptable additional codes.

Omit code is found in both the Tabular List and Alphabetic Index of volume 3. This convention

describes situations when a procedure code is not assigned. *Omit code* usually applies to the following types of procedures:

- Closures of given procedures
- Exploratory procedures incidental to another procedure that is carried out

---

7. OPERATIONS ON THE CARDIOVASCULAR SYSTEM (35–39)

35   Operations on valves and septa of heart

Includes: sternotomy (median)

(transverse)   } as operative

thoracotomy   } approach

Code also cardiopulmonary bypass [extracorporeal circulation] [heart-lung machine] (39.61)

35.0   **Closed heart valvotomy**

Excludes: percutaneous (balloon) valvuloplasty (35.96)

35.00   **Closed heart valvotomy, unspecified valve**

35.01   **Closed heart valvotomy, aortic valve**

35.02   **Closed heart valvotomy, mitral valve**

35.03   **Closed heart valvotomy, pulmonary valve**

35.04   **Closed heart valvotomy, tricuspid valve**

Figure 2-13 Volume 3 tabular list entry

- Lysis of adhesions by blunt, digital, manual, or mechanical methods
- Usual surgical approaches of a given procedure

Slanted brackets *[ ]* are found in the Alphabetic Index of volume 3. Slanted brackets alert the medical coder that closely related procedures require two codes.

ASSIGNING ICD-9-CM PROCEDURE CODES

Accurate procedure code assignment depends on three activities:

- Identifying the principal procedure
- Selecting and sequencing procedure codes
- Following applicable ICD-9-CM coding conventions and all instructions noted in ICD-9-CM volume 3

As stated previously, ICD-9-CM procedure codes are used for coding and reporting inpatient or hospital episodes of care. The procedure codes must be supported by documentation in the patient's record.

Identifying the Principal Procedure

The **principal procedure** is defined as the procedure performed for definitive treatment rather than for diagnostic or exploratory purposes, or as the procedure performed to resolve a complication. If more than one procedure meets the definition of the principal procedure, the procedure most related to the *principal diagnosis(es)* is selected as the principal procedure.

Selecting and Sequencing Procedure Codes

Codes assigned to the principal procedure are always sequenced first. In addition to the principal procedure, other significant procedures are coded. A **significant procedure** is surgical in nature, carries a procedural and/or anesthetic risk, and requires specialized training. Codes for significant procedures are sequenced *after* the principal procedure code. The steps for selecting procedure codes are presented here:

1. Identify the main term in the procedure statement.
2. Locate the main term in the volume 3 Alphabetic Index.
3. Review the procedure statement for additional information about the main term.
4. Review the subterms listed under the main term to determine if any entry matches the additional information in the procedure statement.
5. Follow any cross-reference instructions, such as *code also*. If there are no cross-reference instructions, note the code listed with the applicable subterm entry.
6. **Check the code listed in the Alphabetic Index with the description in the Tabular List.**
7. Read and follow all inclusion, exclusion, and other instructional notes.
8. Assign the code(s) to the highest level of specificity by selecting a three-digit code only when no four-digit code is available.

Step 6 is bolded here for the same reason step 5 was bolded under diagnostic coding: **Never** code directly from the *Alphabetic Index*.

MISCELLANEOUS CODING GUIDELINES FOR PROCEDURES AND BIOPSIES

There are additional coding guidelines for the following situations: bilateral procedures; canceled, incomplete, or failed surgeries or procedures; and biopsies.

Bilateral Procedures

A **bilateral procedure** means the same procedure was performed on both sides of the body, such as a bilateral hernia repair. A hernia was repaired on the right and left side of the body. In some cases, there is a procedure code that addresses the bilateral nature of the procedure.

When a bilateral procedure code is not available, and the same procedure is done bilaterally during the same episode of care, the procedure code is listed twice.

Canceled, Incomplete, and Failed Procedures

When a scheduled surgery or procedure is not completed or is considered to have failed, codes are assigned to the level of service that was actually performed or completed. In these situations, the following general guidelines apply:

- An endoscopic operative approach is coded as an exploratory endoscopy of the site.
- An **open procedure**, defined as opening or entering a body cavity or space, is coded as an exploration of the anatomical site.
- When only an incision is made, code the incision of the anatomical site.
- A **failed procedure**, which is a procedure that did not achieve the desired result, is coded as a performed procedure.
- V codes related to the reason for the incomplete or canceled procedure may also be assigned.
- A surgery or procedure that is canceled before it begins is coded only to the appropriate V code related to the reason for canceling the surgery or procedure.

A careful review of the operative or procedure report provides information for accurate coding.

Biopsy Coding

When a biopsy is performed during an inpatient or hospital episode of care, codes from ICD-9-CM volume 3 are assigned. Biopsies are categorized as open or closed. An **open biopsy** is performed via an incision into an anatomical site or space, and tissue is taken for microscopic examination. A **closed biopsy** is performed without an incision. Tissue is taken percutaneously, endoscopically, by needle (often called *needle aspiration biopsy*), or by a bristle-type instrument called a brush (often called a *brush biopsy*). Figure 2-14 illustrates a biopsy entry in the Tabular List of volume 3.

15. OPERATIONS ON THE INTEGUMENTARY SYSTEM (85–86)

85   **Operations on the breast**

Includes: operations on the skin and subcutaneous tissue of:

breast   ⎫ female
previous mastectomy site ⎬ or male

revision of previous mastectomy site

85.1   **Diagnostic procedures on breast**

85.11   **Closed [percutaneous] [needle] biopsy of breast**

85.12   **Open biopsy of breast**

85.19   **Other diagnostic procedures on breast**

Excludes: *mammary ductogram (87.35)*

mammography NEC (87.37)

manual examination (89.36)

microscopic examination of specimen (91.61–91.69)

thermography (88.85)

ultrasonography (88.73)

xerography (87.36)

Figure 2-14 Volume 3 tabular list biopsy entry

General guidelines for coding biopsies include the following:

- Endoscopic biopsies may be assigned procedure codes that cover both the endoscopic procedure and the biopsy.
- When one code does not cover both the endoscopic procedure and the biopsy, the procedure and biopsy are coded separately. *The endoscopy is the principal procedure and is coded and sequenced first. The biopsy is coded and sequenced after the principal procedure.*
- When a biopsy is performed and immediately followed by a more extensive surgical procedure, *the surgical procedure is the principal procedure and is coded and sequenced first. The biopsy is coded and sequenced after the principal procedure.*

- An open biopsy is coded as such. Since an incision is implicit in an open biopsy, do not assign a separate code for the incision.

A careful review of the procedure report provides information for accurate biopsy coding.

EXERCISE 2-5

Fill in the blank.

1. ICD-9-CM volume 3 is commonly called the _____.

2. The _____ of volume 3 is an alphabetical list of procedures, tests, operations, surgeries, and therapies.

continued

3. The _____ of volume 3 has 17 chapters.

4. The coding convention _____ indicates that closely related procedures require two codes.

5. In volume 3, _____ are bolded and flush left.

Write out the abbreviations.

6. AHIMA

7. CMS

8. ICD-9-CM

9. NEC

10. NOS

MEDICAL REPORTS

Successful medical coders use the patient's medical or health record as the source document for accurate code assignment. The most frequently used medical reports include the history and physical examination, discharge summary, operative or procedure report, radiology report, laboratory report, pathology report, progress notes, consultation report, and autopsy report. Inpatient and ambulatory surgery health records may include all of these reports, whereas physician office, outpatient department, and emergency department reports may not. A sample of each type of report is included in the description and discussion of the report.

Every page of a medical report, either electronic or paper, must have appropriate patient identification. Patient identification always includes the following:

- Patient name—usually the last name, first name, and middle initial
- Date of birth (DOB)—often expressed in eight digits such as 12/15/1948
- Identification number—a unique number assigned to the patient at the time of the admission or encounter; may be called the *case number, medical record number, hospital number,* or *encounter number*
- Date of admission—date the patient was admitted to the hospital or entered the clinic, emergency department, or physician's office, often expressed in eight digits

Other identification information may include *sex (M/F), time of admission, unit or floor number,* and *room number.*

History and Physical Examination (H&P)

All health care facilities generate some type of history and physical examination for each patient. The history and physical examination documents information about the patient's medical, surgical, family, and social history and the physical examination performed by the physician, nurse practitioner, or physician assistant. The content of the history and physical examination depends on the condition of the patient, the reason for the health care encounter, and the type of health care facility. Table 2-8 lists the components of a history and physical examination with brief definitions. Figure 2-15 is a sample of a history and physical examination for a hospital inpatient.

In the medical office and clinic setting, the history and physical examination is often documented as a progress note using the SOAP format. The acronym SOAP stands for Subjective information, which is information that the individual relates to the health care professional; Objective information, which is information that the health care professional observes and records; Assessment, which is the health care professional's assessment of the individual's problem, condition, or diagnosis; and Plan, which is the health care professional's plan for treating the condition or obtaining additional information about the problem or condition. Figure 2-16 is an example of a history and physical examination in the SOAP format.

Diagnostic Imaging Report

Diagnostic imaging includes radiology, ultrasonography, nuclear medicine scans, computerized tomography (CT) scans, and magnetic resonance imaging (MRI) scans. Table 2-9 lists the components of a diagnostic imaging report with brief definitions. Figure 2-17 is an example of a radiology report.

The components of other types of imaging reports are essentially the same as shown in Figure 2-17. The name of the procedure indicates the type of diagnostic imaging performed.

Table 2-8 History and Physical Examination Components

COMPONENT	DEFINITION
PATIENT NAME	First name, last name, middle initial of the patient; may be entered in uppercase letters as last name, first name, middle initial
DATE OF BIRTH	Patient's date of birth; MM/DD/YYYY (12/15/1948)
HOSPITAL NUMBER	Unique number assigned at the time of admission; also called the case number, medical record number, or encounter number
DATE OF ADMISSION	Date the patient was admitted to the hospital; usually formatted as MM/DD/YYYY
ADMITTING PHYSICIAN	Name of the physician who admitted the patient to the hospital
ADMITTING DIAGNOSIS	Reason the patient was admitted to the hospital
CHIEF COMPLAINT	Condition, problem, or symptom as described by the patient; may also be the physician's admitting diagnosis
HISTORY OF PRESENT ILLNESS	Summary of the events that led to the decision to admit the patient to the hospital
PAST HISTORY	Summary of the patient's medical and surgical history and previous hospitalizations, as applicable
MEDICATIONS	List of current medications and allergies to specific medications; may also include other allergies such as eggs, strawberries, shellfish (Note: Other allergies may be listed in the medical history or as a separate heading in the H&P.)
SOCIAL HISTORY	Summary of the patient's occupation, marital status, recreational habits, smoking, or drinking
FAMILY HISTORY	Summary of family members' diseases, conditions, or age at time of death
REVIEW OF SYSTEMS	Information that the patient provides about various body systems
PHYSICAL EXAMINATION	Physician's (or other health care professional) assessment of various body systems
DIAGNOSTIC DATA	Clinical laboratory and diagnostic imaging tests such as blood tests and x-rays
ASSESSMENT	History and physical examination findings such as possible diagnoses or definitive diagnoses
PLAN	Plan of treatment for the conditions identified in the H&P
SIGNATURE BLOCK	Name of the health care practitioner who completed the H&P; electronic or manual signature; initials of the health care practitioner who dictated the report; initials of the individual who transcribed the report; date the report was dictated and transcribed, if applicable (D = dictated; T = transcribed)

HISTORY AND PHYSICAL EXAMINATION

PATIENT NAME: PUTUL BARUA
HOSPITAL NO.:   13579
ROOM NO.:   CCU-4
DATE OF ADMISSION: 01/07/_____
ADMITTING PHYSICIAN: Joshua Stephen Gatlin, MD, Pulmonology

Admitting Diagnoses
1. Rule out myocardial infarction.
2. History of tuberculosis.
3. Hemoptysis.
4. Status post embolectomy.

continued

Figure 2-15   History and physical examination

CHIEF COMPLAINT

Tightness in chest, shortness of breath, fast heart rate.

HISTORY OF PRESENT ILLNESS

Mr. Barua is a 42-year-old gentleman from Bangladesh who presents with chest tightness, shortness of breath, and a fast heart rate. Dr. Cecil Burnett, cardiology, is evaluating his heart condition. The patient has had the recent onset of hemoptysis. He was treated for tuberculosis in Bangladesh 15 years ago. This has prompted the concern of whether his treatment for tuberculosis was adequate or whether there is another cause for his hemoptysis. The duration of his tuberculosis treatment was apparently adequate, according to his wife, but no records are available. In addition, the patient had thrombosis of the axillary artery treated last year at Hillcrest. He had an embolectomy and has been on Coumadin since. INR is significantly elevated at 16. Nonetheless, because of the cavitary lesions that are seen in the right and left upper lobes, the possibility of tuberculosis has been raised. What history we have was obtained by my talking with his wife, Nupur, while having her translate for her husband from the Hindi language.

PAST HISTORY

Tuberculosis in the past. Embolectomy at Hillcrest last year.

SOCIAL HISTORY

Married with two daughters. Has been in the USA for ten years. Patient has no recent history of smoking; he smoked in the past, but the amount is unclear. He is a restaurant manager for the Marriott Hotel chain.

FAMILY HISTORY

No known family history of diabetes, heart disease, or cancer. Mother died of a stroke. Father was killed in an MVA in Bangladesh.

REVIEW OF SYSTEMS

Negative other than as stated in HPI.

PHYSICAL EXAMINATION

VITAL SIGNS are WNL. Apparently he has had no chills, night sweats, or fevers. Generalized malaise and a lack of energy have been the main concerns. HEART: Regular rate and rhythm with S1 and S2. No S3 or S4 are heard at this time. LUNGS: Bilateral rhonchi. No significant amphoric sounds are noted. ABDOMEN: Soft, nontender. No hepatosplenomegaly or masses are detected. RECTAL EXAM: Prostate smooth and firm. No stool is present for Hemoccult test.

DIAGNOSIS

Hemoptysis with history of tuberculosis.

PLAN

I have reviewed the chest x-rays available here and agree with the finding of bleb formation in the right and left upper lobes. Despite the fact that the patient has had a high INR, because of his history of tuberculosis and hemoptysis, I believe obtaining sputum for TB is very, very important. We should rule out any other endobronchial lesion as the cause for his bleeding. I have discussed this matter with the patient and his wife; I have told them that there is the possibility of observing the condition via x-rays and repeated tests of his sputum. They understand that this is an option; however, they have decided that because of the concern

continued

Figure 2-15 (continued) History and physical examination

regarding his repeated hemoptysis, they would consent to bronchoscopy. We will arrange for the patient to have a bronchoscopy done. He is off Coumadin. We will recheck the prothrombin time and INR tomorrow. Depending upon those results, we will proceed with bronchoscopy and further evaluation.

_____

Joshua Stephen Gatlin, MD

JSG: xx
D: 01/07/_____
T: 01/07/_____

C: Cecil Burnett, MD

Figure 2-15 (continued)   History and physical examination

OFFICE VISIT   06/20/YYYY

S   Elderly African-American male returns, after a two year hiatus, for follow-up of coronary artery disease and associated problems. Since triple coronary bypass surgery four years ago, he has had no chest discomfort. It should be noted that he had no chest discomfort during a markedly abnormal stress test performed just two weeks before the bypass surgery. He now reports intermittent dyspnea that occurs at rest, and spontaneously abates. He does not notice any discomfort on exertion, but he does report that his lifestyle is sedentary. He denies orthopnea, paroxysmal nocturnal dyspnea or edema. He has continued to follow-up with his internist, Dr. Gooddoc, for treatment of his dyslipidemia and hypertension. He is on Cholestin and Tenormin.

O   Patient is a mildly obese, African American male appearing his stated age, in no acute distress. Weight is 210. Height is 5'8". Pulse 16. BP 162/82, 172/82, and then 188/82 in the office. HEENT grossly unremarkable. Neck reveals normal jugular venous pressure, without hepatojugular reflux. Normal carotid pulses; no bruits present. Lungs are clear to A&P. Heart reveals regular rhythm, S1 and S2 are normal. There is no murmur, rub, click, or gallop. Cardiac apex is not palpable. No heaves or thrills are detected. Abdomen is soft, nontender, with normal bowel sounds, and no bruits. No organomegaly, including abdominal aorta, or masses noted. Extremities reveal a surgical scar in the right leg, presumably from saphenous venectomy. Femoral pulses are normal, without bruits. Dorsalis pedis and posterior tibial pulses are also normal. There is no cyanosis, clubbing, or edema. Neurological is grossly within normal limits.

A   1. Status post aortocoronary bypass surgery four years ago.
     2. Coronary artery disease. Today's abnormal EKG suggests, but does not prove, that an inferior myocardial infarction may have occurred sometime in the past. There is independent suggestion of this on stress-thallium test performed six months ago. Additionally, he still has symptoms of dyspnea.
     3. Hypertension.
     4. Hypercholesterolemia.

P   1. Patient was instructed to follow-up with Dr. Gooddoc for hypertension and dyslipidemia.
     2. Schedule treadmill stress test for next week.

Henry C. Cardiac, M.D.
Henry C. Cardiac, M.D.

Figure 2-16   SOAP history and physical examination

Table 2-9 Diagnostic Imaging Report Components

COMPONENT	DEFINITION
PROCEDURE	Name of the imaging procedure
DATE	Date of the procedure in MM/DD/YYYY format
DIAGNOSIS	Reason for the imaging procedure
CLINICAL INFORMATION	Report and interpretation of the information provided by the imaging
IMPRESSION	Diagnoses, findings, or assessment of the radiologist or physician who reads and interprets the image
SIGNATURE BLOCK	Name and signature of the radiologist; dictation and transcription dates and initials; names of the individuals who receive a copy of the report

RADIOLOGY REPORT

PATIENT NAME: MARIETTA MOSLEY
HOSPITAL NO.:   11446
X-RAY NO.:   03-2801
ADMITTING PHYSICIAN: John Youngblood, MD
PROCEDURE: LEFT HIP X-RAY.
DATE: 08/05/_____
PRIMARY DIAGNOSIS: Fractured left hip.
CLINICAL INFORMATION: Left hip pain. No known allergies.

Orthopedic device is noted transfixing the left femoral neck. I have no old films available for comparison. The left femoral neck region appears anatomically aligned. At the level of an orthopedic screw along the lateral aspect of the femoral neck, approximately at the level of the lesser trochanter, there is a radiolucent band consistent with a fracture of indeterminate age that shows probable nonunion. There is bilateral marginal sclerosis and moderate offset and angulation at this site.

Fairly exuberant callus formation is noted laterally along the femoral shaft.

IMPRESSION
1. No evidence for significant displacement at the femoral neck.
2. Probable nonunion of fracture transversely through the shaft of the femur at about the level of the lesser trochanter.

_____

Neil Nofsinger, MD

NN: xx
D: 08/05/_____
T: 08/05/_____

C: John Youngblood, MD

Figure 2-17   Radiology report

Operative or Procedure Report

An operative or procedure report is generated when an individual has surgery or undergoes a diagnostic procedure. Examples of diagnostic procedures include endoscopy, laparoscopy, and other invasive procedures that require some type of anesthesia. Table 2-10 lists the components of an operative report with brief definitions. Figure 2-18 is an example of an operative report.

The components of a procedure report are essentially the same as an operative report. Figure 2-19 is an example of a procedure report.

Table 2-10 Operative or Procedure Report Components

COMPONENT	DEFINITION
DATE	Date the surgery was performed; MM/DD/YYYY format
ADMITTING PHYSICIAN	Name of the admitting or attending physician
SURGEON	Name of the surgeon
ASSISTANT	Name of the physician or health care practitioner who assists the surgeon
PREOPERATIVE DIAGNOSIS	Diagnosis before the surgery is performed
POSTOPERATIVE DIAGNOSIS	Diagnosis after surgery is performed; the preoperative and postoperative diagnosis may not be the same
OPERATIVE PROCEDURE	Name of the surgery or procedure being performed
ANESTHESIA	Type of anesthesia, may include the name of the anesthesiologist and nurse anesthetist (Note: The type of anesthesia may also be included in the description of the surgery or procedure.)
PROCEDURE	Detailed description of the surgery that includes patient preparation and position; incisions; closure; sponge, instrument, and needle counts; blood loss; blood replacement (transfusion); condition of the patient after the surgery or procedure; tissue samples taken and sent to the pathology department
SIGNATURE BLOCK	Name and signature of the surgeon; dictation and transcription dates and initials; names of individuals who receive a copy of the report

OPERATIVE REPORT

PATIENT NAME: JANICE MCCLURE
HOSPITAL NO.:   11049
DATE OF SURGERY: 03/12/_____
ADMITTING PHYSICIAN: Kenneth Shaker, MD
SURGEON: Bernard Kester, MD
PREOPERATIVE DIAGNOSIS: Cholecystitis, cholelithiasis, choledocholithiasis.
POSTOPERATIVE DIAGNOSIS: Cholecystitis, cholelithiasis, choledocholithiasis.
OPERATIVE PROCEDURE: Cholecystectomy, intraoperative cholangiogram, common duct exploration, choledochoscopy, choledocholithotomy.
ANESTHESIA: General endotracheal.

PROCEDURE

After induction of general endotracheal anesthesia and the normal sterile preparation and draping, incision was made transversely in a skin crease. Fascia and rectus muscle were divided; the peritoneal cavity was entered. Exploration revealed the stomach and duodenum, small bowel, large bowel, pelvic organs, and liver

continued

Figure 2-18   Operative report

to be normal. A marked amount of edema and inflammation was present around the gallbladder and common bile duct; the anatomy was quite obscured.

Operative area was exposed. Dissection was done in a retrograde fashion. Cystic artery was doubly clamped and divided. A wide patch of the cystic duct was traced to its junction with the common duct. Gallbladder was excised. Operative cholangiogram with fluoroscopy was done to the cystic duct stump. This showed a floating common duct stone. We did have some expulsion of the dye into the duodenum.

Attempt was made initially to insert the choledochoscope into the cystic duct stump. I was unable to do this because of the large size of the scope. A Kocher clamp was placed, and the common duct was then exposed. Incision was made vertically and the edges tagged. Scope was passed and the stone identified in the common duct, snared with a stone basket, and removed. Following this, choledochoscopy up and down showed no other stones. Ampulla was identified.

I was able to pass a size four dilator easily into the duodenum. A size 16 T-tube was inserted and the common duct closed with interrupted 4-0 Vicryl suture. Cystic duct stump was transfixed with 4-0 Vicryl. The wound was irrigated with saline. Jackson-Pratt drain was placed and brought out through a separate stab wound. T-tube was brought out through a separate stab wound in a straight route.

Sponge, instrument, and needle counts were correct ×2. Closure of the peritoneum and fascia was done with running and interrupted 1-0 Novafil. Skin was closed with clips. The patient tolerated the procedure well and was transferred to PAR. Blood loss was minimal, and no transfusion was given. Intraoperative cultures were taken and sent to microbiology.

_____

Bernard Kester, MD

BK: xx
D: 03/15/_____
T: 03/15/_____

Figure 2-18 (_continued_) Operative report

RADIOLOGY—COLONOSCOPY PROCEDURE NOTE

PATIENT NAME: LEON MARKOWITZ
PCP: Ronald Reardon, DO
DATE OF BIRTH: April 1, _____
AGE: 59
SEX: Male
DATE OF PROCEDURE: June 12, _____
ENDOSCOPIST: Ken Miller, MD
TYPE OF PROCEDURE: Colonoscopy.

CONSENT

The benefits, risks, and alternatives to the procedure were discussed, and informed consent was obtained.

continued

Figure 2-19 Procedure report

ANESTHESIA

Local Xylocaine and Versed 1.5 mg.

INDICATIONS

This gentleman with severe iron deficiency anemia, a "big-time drinker" by history, has had an acute myocardial infarction and requires coronary artery bypass surgery. This upper and lower GI evaluation is being performed today to rule out the possibility of peptic ulcer disease, as he will need to be anticoagulated during the postoperative period. We will also rule out colonic neoplasia, as the patient presented initially with iron deficiency anemia.

FINDINGS

Patient was prepped and draped in the usual manner. The colonoscope was introduced with some diffi-culty, as the patient had many, many loops of bowel with excessive looping inside the belly. Finally, I managed to get to the ascending colon, and I was able to see the cecum. The cecum appeared quite mobile, and I was unable to fix and drop into the bottom itself. The valve was recognized, and the mucosa appeared essentially benign and intact. There was no bleeding. No blood was seen anywhere at that time. The ascending colon was essentially normal. The transverse colon was normal. The descending colon was normal.

In the sigmoid colon at about 20 cm, there was a small, sessile polyp measuring 3 mm to 4 mm in size. This was removed with a snare. There were a few scattered diverticula present. Multiple excisional biopsies were obtained. Photos were taken.

ASSESSMENT

1. A single sessile colon polyp in the sigmoid colon. 211.3
2. A few scattered benign diverticula in the colon.   562.1

NOTE

This was a somewhat difficult colonoscopic procedure. As far as the cecum, I am not completely sure, but it appeared essentially negative from what I could see from above. It was very mobile, and I had a hard time fixing the scope in the cecum. We will follow up on biopsy specimen results.

Ken Miller, MD
Gastroenterology

D: 06/12/_____
T: 06/12/_____

C: William Montfort, MD, Cardiac Surgery
Davis H. Cohen, MD, Hematology/Oncology

Figure 2-19 (*continued*)   Procedure report

Pathology Report

A pathology report is generated when an organ, tissue, or other substance or structure is removed from the patient and sent to the pathology or clinical laboratory department for further analysis. Table 2-11 lists the components of a pathology report. Figure 2-20 is an example of a pathology report.

A clinical laboratory report is generated when body fluids such as blood, urine, or sputum are analyzed. Figure 2-21 is an example of a blood chemistry test. Note that abnormal results are marked H for *high* and L for *low*. Figure 2-22 is an example of a routine urinalysis, a microscopic urine test, and a urine cytology test. Urine cytology tests are done to identify abnormal or malignant cells that slough off the lining of the bladder and are expelled in the urine.

Discharge Summary

A discharge summary is generated when an individual receives services as a hospital inpatient, in an ambulatory surgery center, or in an emergency department. The discharge summary is a recap of the events that led to the hospitalization, the treatment the patient received, the results of the treatment, and the follow-up

care the individual may need. Discharge summaries must include the following:

- Patient identification
- Admission and discharge dates
- Admitting diagnosis
- Discharge diagnosis
- Condition of the patient at the time of admission
- Hospital course
- Condition of the patient at the time of discharge
- Discharge instructions, medications, and follow-up appointments

Figure 2-23 is an example of a discharge summary that documents the required components as well as the name of the procedure, consultations, and complications that were part of the patient's episode of care.

Consultation Report

A consultation report is generated when one physician asks another physician to assess the patient, usually for a specific problem. Figure 2-24 is an example of a consultation report.

Table 2-11 Pathology Report Components

COMPONENT	DEFINITION
PATHOLOGY REPORT NO.	Identification number assigned in the pathology department
ADMITTING PHYSICIAN	Name of the admitting or attending physician
PREOPERATIVE DIAGNOSIS	Diagnosis before the surgery or procedure
POSTOPERATIVE DIAGNOSIS	Diagnosis after surgery is performed; the preoperative and postoperative diagnosis may not be the same
SPECIMEN SUBMITTED	Description of the specimen; may include the type of container
DATE RECEIVED	Date, and often time, the specimen was received in the pathology department
DATE REPORTED	Date the pathology report was completed or sent to the physician or surgeon
GROSS DESCRIPTION	Detailed description of the specimen as observed and measured without the use of microscopic or other analysis; includes the type of container and preservative substances
GROSS DIAGNOSIS	Diagnosis based on the gross description of the specimen
MICROSCOPIC DESCRIPTION	Detailed description of the specimen after microscopic and other analysis
MICROSCOPIC DIAGNOSIS	Diagnosis based on the microscopic description of the specimen
SIGNATURE BLOCK	Name and signature of the pathologist; dictation and transcription dates and initials; names of individuals who receive a copy of the report (Note: If the results of the gross and microscopic descriptions are available on different dates, both the gross and microscopic sections include a signature block.)

PATHOLOGY REPORT

PATIENT NAME: CARLOS LOPEZ
HOSPITAL NO.:   11546
PATHOLOGY REPORT NO.:   S-03-1745
ADMITTING PHYSICIAN: Nancy Lawrence, MD
PREOPERATIVE DIAGNOSIS: Enlarged prostate with bladder neck obstruction.
POSTOPERATIVE DIAGNOSIS: Enlarged prostate with bladder neck obstruction.
SPECIMEN SUBMITTED: Prostatic tissue.
DATE RECEIVED: 08/16/_____
DATE REPORTED: 08/17/_____

MACROSCOPIC EXAM

Specimen consists of 14.4 g of pink-tan, apparent prostatic tissue. Two cassettes are taken.

AG: xx
D: 08/16/_____
T: 08/16/_____

MICROSCOPIC EXAM

Multiple sections of the prostatic tissue reveal marked hyperplasia. The glands lie close together, but a fibrous stroma separates them. Corpora amylacea are present within numerous glands. Papillary epithelial hyperplasia is noted. Some of the ducts are dilated, and a periductal mononuclear cell infiltrate is noted.

PATHOLOGIC DIAGNOSIS

Benign glandular hyperplasia of the prostate.

_____

Angelo Garavalia, MD

AG: xx
D: 08/17/_____
T: 08/17/_____

C: Charles Mendez, MD

Figure 2-20   Pathology report

ACCESSION:	7285-GL1622		7285-GL1532	7284-GL1485		
COLLECTED:	10/12/97 11:20		10/12/97 04:10	10/11/97 22:35		

TEST	RESULTS	RESULTS	RESULTS	RESULTS	RESULTS	RANGE	UNITS
CHEMISTRY							
SODIUM		135 L	136			136–143	MMOL/L
POTASSIUM		3.6	3.6			3.6–5.0	MMOL/L
CHLORIDE		103	103			98–108	MMOL/L
TOT CO2		19 L	21 L			22–31	MMOL/L
ANION GAP		12.8	12.3			7.0–16.0	
GLUCOSE		108	112 H			70–110	MG/DL
BUN		24 H	20 H			7–18	MG/DL
CREATININE		1.6 H	1.6 H			0.5–1.2	MG/DL
BUN/CREA		15.0	12.5			12.0–20.0	
CALCIUM		8.8	9.5			8.5–10.5	MG/DL
PHOSPHORUS			3.2			2.5–4.5	MG/DL
T PROTEIN			5.8 L			6.5–8.0	G/DL
ALBUMIN			2.9 L			3.4–5.0	G/DL
A/G RATIO			1.0 L			1.1–2.3	
AST (SGOT)			13			13–35	U/L
ALK PHOSPHATASE			92			50–136	U/L
SPECIAL CHEM							
T4	9.6					4.5–11.5	MCG/DL
THYROID STIM. HOR	4.14					0.50–6.00	UIU/ML
VITAMIN B12	594					200–900	PG/ML
C3	137					86–184	MG/DL
C4	42					20–59	MG/DL
RHEUM FACTOR	<20					0–30	IU/ML

ACCESSION COMMENTS:

Figure 2-21 Blood chemistry

		Laboratory
Lab Ag Print		5Oct2007

Urinalysis. Tests AG	Reference Range		07:36
URINALYSIS, ROUTINE AG			MCR – RO
Source			VOID
Appearance	Normal		Normal
Osmolality	300–800	mosm/Kg	325
pH			6.6
Glucose	<25	mg/dL	2
Protein		mg/dL	5
Protein/Osmolality	<0.12	Ratio	0.15 *
Predicted 24h Protein		mg/24 h	158
Predicted Range		mg/24 h	50–498

		5Oct2007
Urinalysis Tests AG	Reference Range	07:36
URINE MICROSCOPY AG		MCR – RO
Microscopy	Normal	Normal

PATHOLOGY REPORTS

Pathology Reports

10/05/2007 Cytology Non-Gynecological   (PR07-87582)

SPECIMEN DESCRIPTION:

A. Urine Voided: Received 70cc of yellow urine

DIAGNOSIS

A. Urine Voided: Negative for malignancy.

Figure 2-22 Urine test report

DISCHARGE SUMMARY

PATIENT NAME: JOYCE MABRY
HOSPITAL NO.:   11709
ADMITTED: 02/18/_____
DISCHARGED: 02/24/_____
CONSULTATIONS: Tom Moore, MD, Hematology
PROCEDURES: Splenectomy.
COMPLICATIONS: None.

ADMITTING DIAGNOSIS

Elective splenectomy for idiopathic thrombocytopenic purpura and systemic lupus erythematosus.

continued

Figure 2-23 Discharge summary

HISTORY

The patient is a 21-year-old white woman who had noted excessive bruising since last June. She was diagnosed as having thrombocytopenic purpura. At the same time, the diagnosis of systemic lupus erythematosus was made. The patient continues with the bruising. The patient had been treated with steroids, prednisone 20 mg; however, the platelet count has remained low, less than 20,000. The patient was admitted for elective splenectomy.

DIAGNOSTIC DATA ON ADMISSION

Chest x-ray was negative. Electrocardiogram was normal. Sodium 138, potassium 5.2, chloride 104, CO_2 25, glucose 111. Urinalysis negative. Hemoglobin 14.8, hematocrit 43.5, white blood cell count 15,000, platelet count 17,000. PT 11.5, PTT 27.

HOSPITAL COURSE

The patient was taken to the operating room on February 19 where a splenectomy was performed. The patient's postoperative course was uncomplicated with the wound healing well. The platelet count was stable for the first three postoperative days. The patient was transfused intraoperatively with ten units of platelets and postoperatively with ten additional units of platelets. However, on the fourth postoperative day the platelet count had risen to 77,000, which was a significant increase.

The patient was discharged for followup in my office. She will also be seen by Dr. Moore, who will follow her SLE and ITP.

DISCHARGE DIAGNOSES

1. Idiopathic thrombocytopenic purpura.
2. Systemic lupus erythematosus.

DISCHARGE MEDICATIONS

1. Prednisone 20 mg q.d.
2. Percocet 1 to 2 p.o. q. 4 h. p.r.n.
3. Multivitamins, 1 in a.m. q.d.

_____

Carmen Garcia, MD

CD: xx
D: 02/25/_____
T: 02/26/_____

Figure 2-23 (continued)   Discharge summary

Death Summary

A death summary is generated when a patient expires during an inpatient episode of care. The content of a death summary is similar to a discharge summary except there is a detailed description of the events leading up to the death. Figure 2-25 is an example of a death summary.

Autopsy Report

An autopsy report is generated when the patient's representative gives consent, when a person dies under suspicious circumstances, or at the request of a medical examiner. Table 2-12 lists the components of an autopsy report with definitions. Figure 2-26 is an example of an abbreviated autopsy report.

REQUEST FOR CONSULTATION

PATIENT NAME: MARTY GIBBS
HOSPITAL NO.:   11532
CONSULTANT: Patrick O'Neill, MD, Plastic Surgery
REQUESTING PHYSICIAN: Diane Houston, MD, Internal
  Medicine
DATE: 11/25/_____

REASON FOR CONSULTATION
  Please evaluate extent of burn injuries.

BURNING AGENT
  Coals in fire pit.
  I have been asked to see this 5-year-old Caucasian male who appears in mild distress due to upper extremity burn after having fallen into hot coals in his backyard.
  Using the Lund Browder chart,[2] the severity of burn is first and second degree. The total body surface area burned includes right lower arm 3%, right hand 1%. The joints involved include the right elbow, right wrist, right hand.

TREATMENT PLAN
  Splinting right hand.
  Positioning: Elevation with splint on.
  Range of motion: Good mobility.
  Pressure therapy: Will follow for induration, for pressure fracture.

GOALS
1. Reduce risk of contractures of involved joints by positioning, splinting, and maintaining range of motion.
2. Reduce scar tissue formation by using Jobst bandages, pressure therapy, and splinting.
3. Obtain maximum mobility and strength of upper extremities.
4. Maximize independence in activities of daily living. Activity as tolerated.
5. Provide patient and family education regarding high-calorie, high-protein diet.

Thank you for asking me to see this delightful boy. I will follow him at the burn clinic in two weeks.

_____

Patrick O'Neill, MD

PO: xx
D: 11/25/_____
T: 11/28/_____

C: Diane Houston, MD

Figure 2-24   Consultation report

DEATH SUMMARY

PATIENT NAME: RUSSELL SYLER
HOSPITAL NO.:   11663
ADMITTED: 05/15/_____
DECEASED: 06/30/_____
CONSULTATIONS: Hematology/Oncology.
PROCEDURES: Abdominal ultrasound and insertion of Ommaya reservoir.

ADMITTING DIAGNOSES

1. Severe headache pain of two days' duration.
2. Non-Hodgkin lymphoma, large cell type.

FINAL DIAGNOSES

1. Polymicrobial sepsis.
2. Nodular, diffuse, histiocytic lymphoma of head and neck with metastases to central nervous system and liver.
3. Pancytopenia secondary to chemotherapy and sepsis.
4. Bilateral pneumonia.
5. Urinary tract infection due to *Candida* organisms.
6. Oral herpes simplex viral infection.

COURSE IN HOSPITAL

This 33-year-old black man was originally admitted in early April with the diagnosis of nasopharyngeal mixed, nodular, histiocytic, diffuse, large-cell, noncleaved lymphoma with extensive involvement of the paranasal, parapharyngeal, and nasopharyngeal areas with erosion into the left orbit and cribriform plate and possible abdominal involvement. The patient required a tracheostomy secondary to stridor, status post radiation therapy to the neck and face in early May. He was status post chemotherapy with Cytoxan, Adriamycin, vincristine, and prednisone every three weeks. His last chemotherapy had been administered one week prior to the current admission of May 15.

On admission the patient complained of intractable headache pain. He developed fever, chills, and sweats with nausea and vomiting, as well as decreased appetite for at least the past week. He also developed loose bowel movements on the day after admission. He had shortness of breath and a cough productive of yellow phlegm for the past week.

He had right upper quadrant and epigastric abdominal pain for the past week, not related to meals, with nausea and vomiting. He continued with positive frontal headache as well.

The patient's course deteriorated approximately one week into the hospital course with subsequent hypotension requiring dopamine for maintenance of blood pressure.

DIAGNOSTIC DATA

Blood cultures were positive for *Pseudomonas aeruginosa*. He was treated with tobramycin and penicillin G. As the sensitivity reports were returned from microbiology, vancomycin and Fortaz were added for better *Pseudomonas* coverage. Tobramycin was changed to amikacin when one of the patient's sputum cultures was positive for AFB, atypical, a slow grower, possible *Enterobacter* species.

continued

Figure 2-25 Death summary

Two days prior to death, antituberculous medications, including INH and rifampin, were added, as well as amphotericin B for possible systemic fungal infection after urine cultures were positive for *Candida*. He was treated with a five-day course of IV acyclovir for herpes simplex viral infection of the pharynx with resolution of the lesions.

The patient required multiple platelet transfusions as well as packed cells and occasional transfusions of fresh frozen plasma during his admission.

CAUSE OF DEATH

Secondary to circulatory collapse because of overwhelming sepsis, poor immune function, pancytopenia, and diffuse lymphomatous involvement. The patient's wife was notified of the grim prognosis and decided to make the patient "do not resuscitate" status.

The patient was pronounced dead on June 30, _____, at 4:12 a.m. Permission for autopsy was requested, but the family refused.

_____

Anthony Zanotti, MD

AZ: xx
D: 07/03/_____
T: 07/05/_____

Figure 2-25 (continued)   Death summary

Table 2-12 Autopsy Report Components

COMPONENT	DEFINITION
AUTOPSY NO.	Identification number assigned in the pathology department; may also be called the *necropsy number*
ADMITTING PHYSICIAN	Name of the admitting or attending physician
PATHOLOGIST	Name of the pathologist who conducted the autopsy
DATE OF DEATH	Date that death occurred; MM/DD/YYYY format
DATE OF AUTOPSY	Date the autopsy was performed; MM/DD/YYYY format
FINAL ANATOMICAL DIAGNOSIS	A list of diagnosis(es) based on the gross and microscopic examination of organs, tissues, fluids, and other body structures
GROSS DESCRIPTION	Description of the position, appearance, weight, size, and other physical characteristics of organs, tissues, and other body structures
EXTERNAL EXAMINATION	Description of the observations and measurements of the body
INCISIONS AND EVISCERATION	Description of how the body was opened and the organs removed
SUBCUTANEOUS TISSUE AND MUSCLES	Description of the condition of the subcutaneous tissue and muscles
PERITONEAL CAVITY	Description of the peritoneal cavity; location of the organs; presence of fluid or adhesions; condition of the diaphragm
MEDIASTINUM	Condition of the mediastinum and thymus gland

continued

Table 2-12 (_continued_)   Autopsy Report Components

COMPONENT	DEFINITION
PLEURAL CAVITY	Description of the pleural cavity and related organs or tissue
PERICARDIAL CAVITY	Condition of the pericardial cavity and related organs or tissue
HEART	Description of the size, weight, position, and appearance of the external surface of the heart; description and condition of the internal structures of the heart
GREAT VESSELS	Description of the internal and external condition of the aorta, pulmonary vessels, renal artery, and associated structures
THYROID	Description of the size, shape, color, consistency, and condition of the thyroid gland
PARATHYROID GLANDS	Description of the size, shape, color, consistency, and condition of the parathyroid glands
LARYNX AND TRACHEA	Description of the size, shape, color, consistency, and condition of the larynx and trachea
LUNGS AND BRONCHI	Description of the size, shape, color, consistency, and condition of the lungs, bronchi, hilum, and smaller arteries of the lungs
GASTROINTESTINAL TRACT	Description of the size, shape, color, consistency, and condition of the internal and external structures of the gastrointestinal tract that includes the stomach, small intestine, large intestine, appendix, omentum, arteries, veins, and fat
LIVER	Description of the weight, size, shape, color, consistency, and internal and external condition of the liver, portal vein, and portal artery
GALLBLADDER	Description of the location, shape, size, and internal and external condition of the gallbladder and bile ducts
PANCREAS	Description of the internal and external condition of the pancreas, pancreatic duct, and blood vessels
SPLEEN	Description of the weight, size, shape, and internal and external condition of the spleen
ADRENAL GLANDS	Description of the size, shape, consistency, position, and internal and external condition of the adrenal glands
KIDNEYS	Description of the size, weight, and location of the right and left kidney; the condition of the internal and external structures of the kidneys
URETERS AND BLADDER	Description of the internal and external condition of the ureters and urinary bladder
GENITAL ORGANS	Description of the size, shape, and location of the organs of the pelvic cavity such as the prostate, uterus, ovaries, and fallopian tubes; description of the size, shape, and condition of the testes, penis, and other external genitalia
LYMPH NODES	Description of the larger lymph nodes
BONES AND JOINTS	Description of the condition of the bones and joints
CRANIAL CAVITY	Description of the condition of the skull and meninges
BRAIN	Description of the weight, size, shape, and internal and external condition of the brain and its structures
MICROSCOPIC DESCRIPTION	Documentation of information about organs, tissue, cells, fluids, and other substances that underwent clinical laboratory, chemical, or microscopic analysis
SIGNATURE BLOCK	Name and signature of the pathologist who conducted the autopsy; dictation and transcription dates and initials; names of individuals who receive a copy of the report

AUTOPSY REPORT

PATIENT NAME: KENNEDY, ELOISE
MEDICAL RECORD NUMBER: 15-15-15
AUTOPSY NO: 1600
ADMITTING PHYSICIAN: Roger Wellhouse, MD
PATHOLOGIST: Shana Ostwald, MD
DATE OF DEATH: 10/06/20xx
DATE OF AUTOPSY: 10/07/20xx

FINAL ANATOMIC DIAGNOSES

1. Coronary atherosclerosis.
2. Acute myocardial infarction, left ventricle, atrial walls, and septum.
3. Cerebral, pulmonary, and visceral congestion with edema.
4. Ascites.
5. Bilateral pleural effusion.
6. Centrilobular congestion, liver.
7. Early bronchopneumonia, right.
8. Tuberculous granulomata, upper left lobe
9. Apoplexy, uterus.
10. Polycystic ovaries.
11. Fibrocystic disease, breasts.

GROSS EXAMINATION

EXTERNAL EXAMINATION

The body is that of a well-nourished, well-developed Caucasian female who appears the stated age of 45 years. The body measures 165 cm. The lips are purple-blue. Fingernail beds are pale gray. Hair is brown. The eyes have been donated as well as the bones of the lower limbs and iliac crest. The anterior chest wall displays CPR marks. Rigor and lividity are moderate.

LUNGS: Left weighs 900 g. Right weighs 840 g. Parenchyma is semicrepitant to noncrepitant and reddish gray. The left lower part of the upper lobe displays gray-white soft granulomata measuring up to 0.5 cm. The hilar nodes are dark gray-tan. Bronchi contain thick grayish translucent mucus. The mucosa is reddish gray. Pulmonary arteries display no thromboemboli.

HEART weighs 390 g. Valve casts are semitranslucent and pliable. The left anterior descending coronary artery displays focal thickening of its wall by atheromatous plaque with approximately 20% narrowing of the lumen. The aortic valve measures 6.7 cm in circumferences, mitral 11 cm, pulmonic 8 cm, and tricuspid 11.5 cm. The left ventricular wall is 1.5 cm in thickness, the right 0.5 cm. There are no mural thrombi. Cut sections of the myocardium of the left ventricular wall and septum display a superficial zone 0.4 cm in average thickness of pale gray-brown coloration. The deeper myocardium is pale to dark red-gray. Coronary arteries display no thrombi. The aorta displays a thin, elastic wall.

SPLEEN weighs 225 g. The capsule is thin, bluish gray. The cut surface displays soft, dark red pulp and inapparent follicles.

LIVER weighs 1950 g. The capsule is thin, red-brown. The liver parenchyma is semifriable, red-brown.

KIDNEYS: Left weighs 210 g. Right weighs 200 g. The capsules strip easily from a smooth pink-gray cortical surface. The medulla is pink-gray. Pelvic calyceal mucosa is smooth and ureters are patent.

continued

Figure 2-26   Autopsy report

FEMALE GENITAL TRACT: The inner endometrial cavity and the inner portions of the myometrium are dark purplish red. The endocervical canal is lined by pale gray-tan tissue. The ovaries display multiple small cortical cysts.

BRAIN: Skull displays no evidence of fracture. The brain is markedly edematous. The circle of Willis is patent. There is no evidence of conization. Sulci and gyri are of normal configuration. The pia-arachnoid are semitranslucent, pink-gray-tan. The dura is pearly gray-white, and the brain is fixed. Sections display no gross pathologic change.

MICROSCOPIC DESCRIPTION

HEART: Coronary arteries display moderate to marked thickening of the walls by atheromatous plaque. Myocardium in multiple sections displays increased eosinophilia and waviness with edema and hemorrhage. Multiple areas display scars within papillary muscles. The epicardium displays infiltrates of small numbers of lymphocytes.

LUNGS: A large granuloma is noted in sections of the left lung, upper lobe, with central caseation and Langhans-type giant cells at the periphery. Lung parenchyma is congested with hemosiderin-laden macrophages noted in multiple alveoli. Rare polymorphs are seen. The latter are noted in sections of the right lung. Trachea and mainstem bronchi are lined by partially denuded epithelium. Bronchial mucous glands are hyperplastic. One area displays exudates of fibrin-meshed polymorphs within a bronchus, in the section of the right lung, with denuded epithelium and infiltrates of small numbers of polymorphs and lymphocytes involving the mucosa.

FEMALE GENITAL TRACT: A small cyst is noted in sections of the cervix. The myometrium displays congestion and hemorrhage within the inner half. Ovaries display multiple follicular cysts. A corpus luteum is noted in sections of the left ovary. A polyp is noted composed of slightly dilated and coiled glands in a moderately cellular stroma. This is noted both within the endometrial cavity and attached to the endometrium. Fallopian tubes display regular architecture. A paratubal cyst lined by flat and sticky walls of the epithelium is noted in sections of the right ovary.

BRAIN: Meningeal congestion with psammoma bodies noted in sections of the pia-arachnoid and dura.

ADDENDUM

Special stains for acid-fast and fungal elements display the presence of acid-fast bacilli within the granulomata noted in sections of the left lung, upper lobe.

SIGNATURE BLOCK

Figure 2-26 (*continued*)   Autopsy report

■ SUMMARY

This chapter includes an introduction to the *International Classification of Diseases, Ninth Revision, Clinical Modification* (ICD-9-CM). Health statistics and reimbursement for services rendered depend on accurate coding and sequencing of medical diagnoses and procedures. ICD-9-CM coding conventions, the *Official Guidelines for Coding and Reporting*, and the *Coding Clinic* ensure that medical coders have accurate and up-to-date coding advice. The ICD-9-CM coding conventions take precedence over other coding guidelines. Inappropriate or inaccurate coding can result in rejected insurance claims, inadequate reimbursement, and in the worst case, charges of fraud or abuse. Medical reports are the source documents for accurate code assignment.

■ CHAPTER REVIEW

Short Answer

Write the coding convention that best fits the description.

1. Direct the billing specialist or medical coder to look elsewhere _____

2. A list of conditions that are coded to the same ICD-9-CM code _____

3. A list of conditions not covered by a specific ICD-9-CM code _____

4. Placing diagnostic codes in the correct order _____

5. Enclose nonessential modifiers _____

6. Enclose a manifestation code _____

Fill in the Blank

7. A/an _____ procedure indicates that the procedure was done and the desired result was not achieved.

8. The ___ procedure is performed for definitive treatment rather than for diagnostic or exploratory purposes.

9. The reason for an encounter or visit to a health care provider is called the _____ diagnosis.

10. The condition, after study, that is responsible for the admission to the hospital is called the _____ diagnosis.

■ ICD-9-CM CODING PRACTICE SETS

The purpose of these coding exercises is to give you an opportunity to practice using the ICD-9-CM coding manuals. Always check the codes you select with the description in the *Tabular List* (volume 1). Coding exercises that are based on medical reports are included in the body system chapters.

Write the main term for each diagnostic statement. Assign the correct ICD-9-CM code(s) for each diagnosis.

1. Chest pain, unspecified

   MAIN TERM: _____

   CODE: _____

2. Diarrhea, unspecified

   MAIN TERM: _____

   CODE: _____

3. Gastroenteritis due to *Salmonella*

   MAIN TERM: _____

   CODE: _____

4. Hyperthyroidism

   MAIN TERM: _____

   CODE: _____

5. Rheumatoid arthritis

   MAIN TERM: _____

   CODE: _____

6. Classic migraine headache

   MAIN TERM: _____

   CODE: _____

7. External hemorrhoids

   MAIN TERM: _____

   CODE: _____

8. Orthostatic hypotension

   MAIN TERM: _____

   CODE: _____

9. Purulent bronchitis

   MAIN TERM: _____

   CODE: _____

10. Bleeding gastric ulcer

    MAIN TERM: _____

    CODE: _____

11. Reflux esophagitis

    MAIN TERM: _____

    CODE: _____

12. Urinary tract infection

    MAIN TERM: _____

    CODE: _____

13. Premenstrual syndrome

    MAIN TERM: _____

    CODE: _____

14. Ulcerative stomatitis

    MAIN TERM: _____

    CODE: _____

15. Acute gastroenteritis

    MAIN TERM: _____

    CODE: _____

Write the main term for each procedural statement. Provide the correct ICD-9-CM code(s) for each procedure.

16. Cholecystectomy, open

    MAIN TERM: _____

    CODE: _____

17. Bilateral total knee replacement of both knee joints

    MAIN TERM: _____

    CODE: _____

18. Proximal gastrectomy

    MAIN TERM: _____

    CODE: _____

19. Total abdominal hysterectomy

    MAIN TERM: _____

    CODE: _____

20. Vaginal hysterectomy

    MAIN TERM: _____

    CODE: _____

21. Bilateral repair of direct inguinal hernia

    MAIN TERM: _____

    CODE: _____

22. Unilateral simple mastectomy

    MAIN TERM: _____

    CODE: _____

23. Tonsillectomy and adenoidectomy

    MAIN TERM: _____

    CODE: _____

24. Laparoscopic appendectomy

    MAIN TERM: _____

    CODE: _____

25. Face lift

    MAIN TERM: _____

    CODE: _____

NOTES:

NOTES:

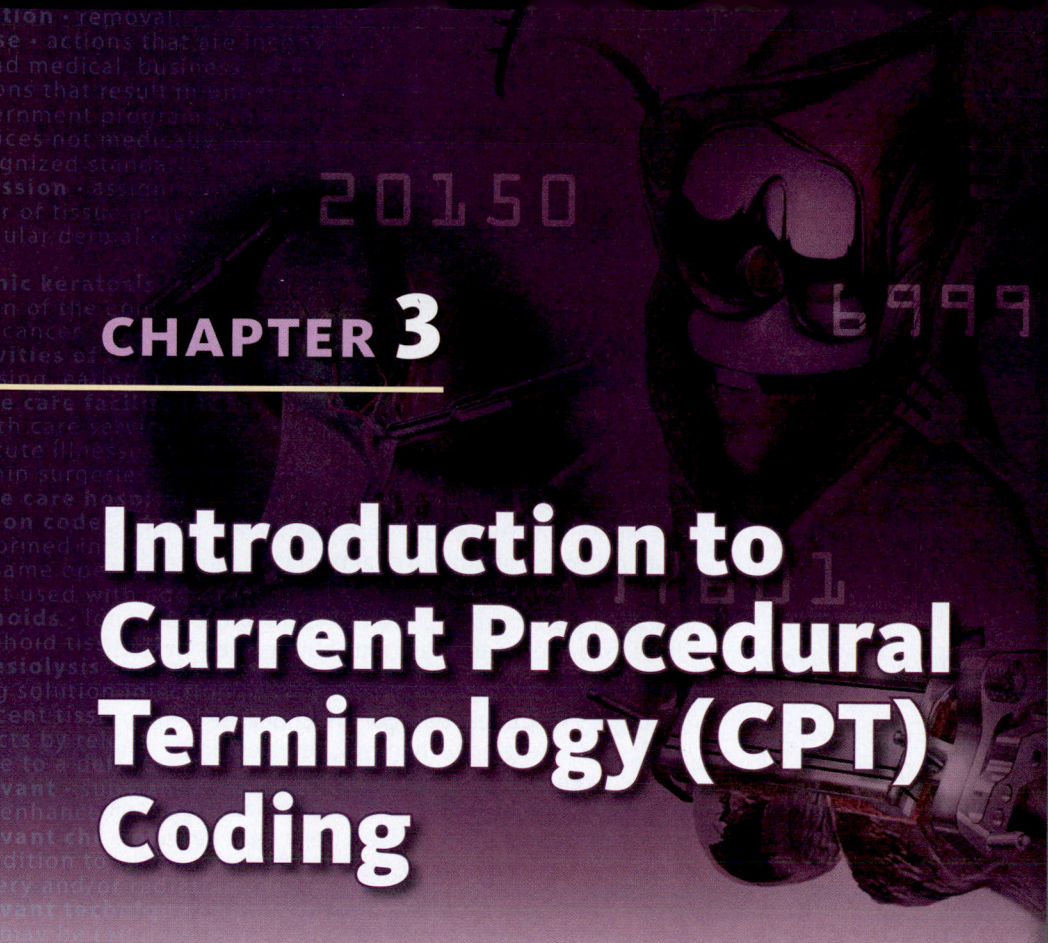

CHAPTER 3

Introduction to Current Procedural Terminology (CPT) Coding

■ OBJECTIVES

At the completion of this chapter, the student should be able to:

1. Identify the six main sections of the *Current Procedural Terminology* coding manual.
2. Explain the difference between the ICD-9-CM, CPT, and HCPCS coding systems.
3. Define the CPT coding conventions and cross-reference terms.
4. Discuss the purpose of CPT modifiers.
5. Accurately assign CPT and HCPCS codes.

■ OVERVIEW

Current Procedural Terminology **(CPT)** and the *Healthcare Common Procedure Coding System* **(HCPCS)** are used to code the treatment a patient receives at a physician or provider's office, at an **ambulatory surgery center (ASC)**, or as a hospital outpatient. CPT is updated and published by the American Medical Association. HCPCS was developed and is maintained by the **Centers for Medicare and Medicaid Services (CMS)**, which is a division of the **U.S. Department of Health and Human Services (HHS)**.

CPT and HCPCS codes are used in conjunction with ICD-9-CM diagnosis codes to communicate patient services to insurance carriers (also called fiscal

KEY TERMS

add-on code
ambulatory surgery center (ASC)
anesthesia add-on codes
bullet
Centers for Medicare and Medicaid Services (CMS)
circle
circled bullet
Current Procedural Terminology (CPT)
durable medical equipment (DME)
facing triangles
global surgery concept
Healthcare Common Procedure Coding System (HCPCS)
instructional notes
key components
level II codes
main terms
moderate sedation
modifier
modifier -51
modifying terms
national codes
null zero, universal no code
physical status modifier
plus sign
qualifying circumstances
section guidelines
see
see also
semicolon
separate procedures
surgical package
triangle
unbundling
U.S. Department of Health and Human Services (HHS)

intermediaries) and various government and regulatory agencies. Both diagnoses and procedure codes are used to determine provider reimbursement. The documentation in the patient's medical record must clearly support *all* codes.

This chapter is an *introduction* to CPT and HCPCS coding conventions and applications and is not intended to be a comprehensive presentation of either system.

CURRENT PROCEDURAL TERMINOLOGY

The American Medical Association developed *Current Procedural Terminology* (CPT) to provide a uniform language to accurately describe physician and provider services. The first edition was published in 1966, and over the years CPT has been revised and expanded. CPT is the accepted coding system for nearly all provider services in ambulatory or outpatient settings and for some provider services related to hospital and long-term care. CPT is updated annually in the fall and the revisions become effective on January 1. CPT codes answer this question: What did the provider do for the patient's problems?

CPT Components

The CPT manual consists of an introduction, six main sections or chapters, a list of category II codes, a list of category III codes, 13 appendices, and an alphabetic index. Table 3-1 lists CPT components with a brief description.

CPT Main Sections

The CPT main sections have guidelines that provide additional information unique to that section. Each main section has a range of five-digit codes related to that section. Table 3-2 lists the main sections and range of codes for each section.

CPT Appendices

The CPT appendices are a quick reference to CPT modifiers; added, deleted, and revised codes; clinical examples of various CPT codes; and other summary information. Table 3-3 lists the appendices with a brief description.

Table 3-1   CPT Components and Descriptions

Introduction. The introduction includes instructions for using the CPT manual, definitions of terms, anatomical illustrations, procedural illustrations, and roots, prefixes, and suffixes for medical terms.

Main Sections. CPT main sections include guidelines for each section, a range of codes for the section, and definitions of selected terms or illustrations of selected services.

Category II Codes. Category II codes are supplemental tracking codes that can be used for performance measurement. These codes are intended to facilitate data collection about the quality of care rendered by coding certain services and test results that support nationally established performance measures and that have an evidence base as contributing to quality patient care. *The use of these codes is optional.*

Category III Codes. Category III codes are temporary codes for emerging technology, services, and procedures that have not yet been assigned a category I CPT code. If a category III code is available for a specific technology, service, or procedure, *it must be used instead of a category I unlisted code.* Category III codes consist of four numeric characters and one alpha character as the fifth character.

Appendices. CPT appendices provide a quick reference for modifier descriptions; clinical examples of evaluation and management (E/M) codes; summaries of CPT code changes, deletions, and additions; CPT add-on codes; CPT codes exempt from modifier -51; CPT codes exempt from modifier -63; CPT codes that include moderate (conscious) sedation; an alphabetic index of performance measures; genetic testing code modifiers; electrodiagnostic medicine codes; product pending Food and Drug Administration (FDA) approval codes; vascular families; and a crosswalk to deleted CPT codes.

Alphabetic Index. The CPT alphabetic index is the key to locating codes in the main sections. The index is organized by main terms that include the type of procedure or service; by the organ or anatomical site; by the condition such as *fracture;* or by synonyms, eponyms, and abbreviations, such as EEG and Pomeroy's operation.

Table 3-2   CPT Main Sections

MAIN SECTION	CODE RANGE
Evaluation and Management (E/M) Services	99201–99499
Anesthesia	00100–01999; 99100–99150
Surgery	10021–69990
Radiology	70010–79999
Pathology and Laboratory	80047–89356
Medicine	90281–99199; 99500–99607

Table 3-3 Appendices with Descriptions

Appendix A: Modifiers—A list of modifiers that may be added to a five-digit code; modifiers are used to explain any unique circumstances about the services rendered.
Appendix B: Summary of Additions, Deletions, and Revisions—A summarization of the CPT codes that have been added, deleted, or revised.
Appendix C: Clinical Examples—Clinical examples of services for various E/M codes.
Appendix D: Summary of CPT Add-on Codes—A list of add-on codes, which are CPT codes that are used in conjunction with another CPT code.
Appendix E: Summary of CPT Codes Exempt from Modifier -51—A list of codes that may not be used with modifier -51.
Appendix F: Summary of CPT Codes Exempt from Modifier -63—A list of codes that may not be used with modifier -63.
Appendix G: Summary of CPT Codes that Include Moderate (Conscious) Sedation—A list of CPT procedure codes that include moderate (conscious) sedation as part of the procedure.
Appendix H: Alphabetic Index of Performance Measures by Clinical Condition or Topic—A list of treatment or performance services by clinical condition.
Appendix I: Genetic Testing Code Modifiers—A list of modifiers that apply to molecular laboratory procedures related to genetic testing.
Appendix J: Electrodiagnostic Medicine Listing of Sensory, Motor, and Mixed Nerves—A list of codes that apply to each sensory, motor, and mixed nerve. Each nerve constitutes one unit of service. These codes are used to enhance accurate reporting of codes 95900, 95903, and 95904.
Appendix K: Product Pending FDA Approval—A list of codes for some vaccine products that are pending Food and Drug Administration (FDA) approval.
Appendix L: Vascular Families—A summary of the branches of vascular families when the starting point of intravascular catheterization is the aorta.
Appendix M: Crosswalk to Deleted CPT Codes—A summary of deleted CPT codes that have been crosswalked to new or revised CPT codes.

CPT Alphabetic Index

The CPT alphabetic index is organized by **main terms**, also called main entries. Main terms are followed by a series of indented terms, called **modifying terms**, that affect code selection. There are four types of main terms:

- Procedure or service—laparoscopy, repair, cast
- Organ or anatomical site—heart, skin, thyroid gland
- Condition—fracture, ectopic pregnancy, pressure ulcer (decubitus)
- Synonyms, eponyms, and abbreviations—EEG, Caldwell-Luc procedure, Pomeroy's operation

Fracture

Ankle

    Bimalleolar 27808–27814

    Closed 27816–27818

    Lateral 27786–27814, 27792

Femur

    Closed Treatment . . . 27230, 27238–27240,
                        27246, 27267–27268,
                        27500–27503, 27508,
                        27510, 27516–27517

    with Manipulation 27232

    without Manipulation 27267

Figure 3-1 CPT alphabetic index with modifying terms

Figure 3-1 illustrates a CPT alphabetic index entry with the main term *fracture.* Note that the main term fracture has several modifying terms.

CPT codes from the alphabetic index must be verified in the appropriate CPT section or subsection. For example, CPT code 27238, *intertrochanteric fracture of the femur, closed treatment,* must be verified in the Musculoskeletal subsection. As with ICD-9-CM codes, CPT codes are **never** assigned from the alphabetic index.

CPT Section Guidelines and Instructional Notes

CPT has extensive **section guidelines** and **instructional notes** that provide additional information for accurate coding. Section guidelines are clearly labeled at the beginning of each main section. The guidelines can be brief, as with the Anesthesia guidelines, or extensive, as with the Evaluation and Management (E/M) guidelines.

Instructional notes are located at the beginning of a CPT heading and before or after

COMPONENTS OF A SERVICE OR PROCEDURE

Instructional notes under **Esophagus, Endoscopy** in the digestive system surgery codes direct the coder to select the code based on anatomical site, and surgical endoscopy always includes the diagnostic endoscopy.

DEFINITIONS OF TERMS AND CODES

The instructional notes under the **Vestibule of Mouth** heading in the digestive surgery codes describe the **vestibule** as "the part of the oral cavity outside the dentoalveolar structures; [including] the mucosal and submucosal tissue of lips and cheeks."

ADDITIONAL CODE ASSIGNMENT

The instructional notes under **Repair, Hernioplasty, Herniorrhaphy, Herniotomy** in the digestive surgery codes direct the billing specialist or coder to use an additional code for the repair of strangulated organs or structures.

Figure 3-2   Instructional notes/CPT headings

codes. These notes provide information about the following:

- Components of a service or procedure
- Definitions of terms and codes
- Directions for additional code assignment
- Additional, alternative, or deleted codes, and other general information

Figure 3-2 is an example of the notes located at the beginning of a CPT heading. Examples of instructional notes before or after CPT codes are listed in table 3-4.

CPT Coding Conventions

CPT coding conventions include symbols and cross-references. The symbols are semicolons (;), bullets (•) and triangles (▲), facing triangles (▶◀), plus signs (+), circles (○), circled bullets (☉), null zero or universal no code (Ø), and the symbol that flags *FDA approval pending*. The cross-references are *see* and *see also*.

Table 3-4   CPT Before and After Instructional Notes

ALTERNATIVE CODES
The note (For excision of pilonidal cyst, see 11770–11772) located under code 10081, *incision and drainage of pilonidal cyst; complicated*, directs the coder to the correct codes for "excision" of a pilonidal cyst.

ADDITIONAL CODES
The note (List 41114 in addition to code 41112 or 41113) located under code 41114, *excision of lesion of tongue with closure; with local tongue flap*, indicates that code 41114 is an additional code for codes 41112, *excision of lesion of tongue with closure; anterior two-thirds*, and 41113, *excision of lesion of tongue with closure; posterior one-third*.

Semicolon

The **semicolon** (;) is used to identify the common part or main entry for indented modifying terms or descriptions. When several codes and descriptions refer to a specific procedure or have a shared beginning description, a semicolon follows the shared portion. Figure 3-3 is an example of CPT semicolon use.

In Figure 3-3, *colonoscopy, flexible, proximal to splenic flexure* is the common description shared by codes 45378 through 45382. Therefore, the full description for CPT code 45380 is *colonoscopy, flexible, proximal to splenic flexure; with biopsy, single or multiple*.

Bullets and Triangles

A **bullet** (•) placed before a CPT code identifies the code as a new code. A **triangle** (▲) placed before a code identifies a revision in the narrative description of the code.

Endoscopy

☉45378	Colonoscopy, flexible, proximal to splenic flexure; diagnostic, with or without collection of specimen(s) by brushing or washing, with or without colon decompression (separate procedure)
☉45379	with removal of foreign body
☉45380	with biopsy, single or multiple . . .
☉45382	with control of bleeding . . .

Figure 3-3   Semicolon use

Facing Triangles

Facing triangles (►◄) are used to set off new or revised information in the CPT guidelines at the beginning of each main section and throughout the CPT manual.

Plus Sign

The **plus sign** (+), which is placed in front of a five-digit CPT code, identifies an **add-on code**. Add-on codes are defined as CPT codes that must be used with a related procedure code. In addition to the plus sign, the narrative description of add-on codes includes instructional notes as reminders that the codes must be used with another code. Figure 3-4 is an example of the plus sign and add-on codes.

Circle

A **circle** (○) is placed before a CPT code to indicate that the code has been reinstated or recycled.

Circled Bullet

A **circled bullet** (⊙) is placed before a CPT code to indicate that the service or procedure includes the use

of **moderate sedation**. Moderate sedation, formerly called conscious sedation, is defined as the use of sedatives or pain relievers to minimize pain and discomfort without causing complete unconsciousness. Patients under moderate sedation are usually able to respond to verbal cues and communicate discomfort during the procedure. According to CPT coding guidelines, the physician who performs a procedure that includes moderate sedation should *not* submit a separate claim for the moderate sedation. When anesthesia services, including moderate sedation, are performed by someone other than the physician performing the procedure, the anesthesia code should be reported. Refer to figure 3-3 for an example of circled bullets.

Null Zero or Universal No Code

The **null zero** or **universal no code** (Ø) identifies CPT codes that may not be used with **modifier -51**. Modifier -51 is used when multiple procedures are performed by the same provider during a single encounter. A CPT **modifier** is a two-digit number that is added to the five-digit CPT code or a five-digit number that is reported in addition to the CPT code. The modifier provides additional information about the procedure.

See and See Also

The cross-references *see* and *see also* are found in CPT's main sections and alphabetic index. These references tell the billing specialist or medical coder to look at other CPT codes or sections.

Surgery Section/Integumentary Subsection (10021-19499)

Excision—Debridement

11000	Debridement of extensive eczematous or infected skin: up to 10% of body surface
+11001	each additional 10% of body surface (List separately in addition to code for primary procedure) (Use 11001 in conjunction with 11000)

Dr. Romero debrides the eczema from 30% of Loretta's body surface, which includes her trunk and legs. Code 11000 is selected to show that 10% of [the] body surface was debrided. Code 11001 is selected twice to indicate that an additional 20% of [the] body surface was debrided. Three codes, 11000, 11001, and 11001, are used to accurately indicate what Dr. Romero did for his patient.

Figure 3-4 Plus sign and add-on code example

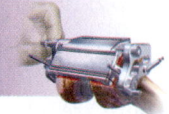

EXERCISE 3-1

Fill in the blank.

1. A/an _____ is used to identify the main entry for indented modifying terms or descriptions.

2. A new CPT code is identified by a/an _____ placed in front of the code.

3. Revised CPT code descriptions have a/an _____ placed in front of the code.

4. _____ are used to set off new or revised information in CPT guidelines and main sections.

5. Add-on CPT codes are identified by a/an _____ placed in front of the code.

continued

6. A/an _____ placed before a CPT code means that moderate sedation is included in the procedure.

7. The _____ identifies CPT codes that may not be used with modifier -51.

8. A/an _____ is a two-digit number that is added to the CPT code.

Evaluation and Management (E/M) Section (99201–99499)

The E/M section codes include the following provider services: office or other outpatient services; hospital services; consultations; emergency department services; critical care services; nursing facility services; domiciliary, rest home, or custodial care services; prolonged services; preventive medicine services; and newborn and neonatal care services. E/M codes capture information about medical services, as opposed to surgical services. As the name implies, evaluation and management codes are used to report physician or provider activities associated with evaluating an individual's health status and managing or implementing a plan of care related to that status. Evaluation and management services range from a routine sports physical to planning and implementing care for critically ill or injured individuals. There are several pages of E/M guidelines that include the following:

- Definitions of commonly used terms
- Categories and subcategories of services
- Instructions for selecting a level of E/M service

Since this information is available in the CPT manual, it is not repeated in this text.

E/M Categories

There are 22 categories of E/M codes. Each category has specific guidelines that describe the type of services that fall into the category. Table 3-5 lists the E/M categories and range of codes.

Additional information about E/M categories and their guidelines is available in the CPT manual.

E/M Codes and Levels of Service

Most E/M categories and subcategories have several codes that represent different levels of service. Levels of service are related to the nature of the patient's problem or problems and the complexity of the provider's evaluation. The CPT manual describes seven

Table 3-5 E/M Categories and Code Ranges

CATEGORY	RANGE OF CODES
Office or Other Outpatient Services	99201–99215
Hospital Observation Services	99217–99220
Hospital Inpatient Services	99221–99239
Consultations	99241–99255
Emergency Department Services	99281–99288
Critical Care Services	99291–99292
Nursing Facility Services	99304–99318
Domiciliary, Rest Home (e.g., Boarding Home), or Custodial Care Services	99324–99337
Domiciliary, Rest Home (e.g., Assisted Living Facility), or Home Care Plan Oversight Services	99339–99340
Home Services	99341–99350
Prolonged Services	99354–99359
Physician Standby Services	99360
Case Management Services	99363–99368
Care Plan Oversight Services	99374–99380
Preventive Medicine Services	99381–99397
Counseling Risk Factor Reduction and Behavior Change Intervention	99401–99429
Non-Face-to-Face Physician Services	99441–99444
Special Evaluation and Management Services (Basic Life and/or Disability Evaluation Services; Work Related or Medical Disability Evaluation Services)	99450, 99455, 99456
Newborn Care Services	99460–99465
Inpatient Neonatal Intensive Care Services and Pediatric and Neonatal Critical Care Services	99466–99480
Other Evaluation and Management Services	99499

components that contribute to E/M levels of service. Of these seven components, E/M guidelines identify three **key components** that are required for most E/M codes. The key components are history, examination, and medical decision making. Table 3-6 lists all seven components with a brief description.

There are specific documentation requirements associated with E/M codes. E/M codes that reflect a higher level of service require more documentation in each of the three key components. A complete description of the documentation requirements for E/M levels of service codes is available in the E/M section guidelines of the CPT manual.

Table 3-6   Components of E/M Codes

History—A chronological review of the individual's past medical and surgical history, family history, and social history, and a review of one or more body systems. E/M codes that reflect a higher level of service require a more comprehensive history.

Examination—A physical examination of the individual that includes one or more body systems. E/M codes that reflect a higher level of service require an examination of more body systems.

Medical Decision Making—The complexity of establishing a diagnosis or selecting a management option based on the number of possible diagnoses; the amount of medical information obtained, reviewed, and analyzed; and the risks of complications or death. E/M codes that reflect a higher level of service require an increased complexity of medical decision making.

Counseling—A discussion with the individual about diagnoses, treatment, options, risks and benefits, follow-up, risk factor reduction, and compliance with treatment plans.

Coordination of Care—Activities related to ordering, referring, and discussing the patient's treatment with other providers, agencies, and the patient.

Nature of Presenting Problem—The level of severity or complexity of the individual's problem, disease, condition, illness, injury, symptom, or complaints; ranges from minimal severity to high severity.

Time—The number of minutes a provider spends with the individual; the number of minutes the provider spends reviewing tests, records, and other patient-related information.

Selecting E/M Codes

Selecting or assigning E/M codes is usually the responsibility of the physician or health care provider. In the physician office setting, the E/M codes are often pre-printed on the encounter form. The physician checks or circles the E/M code that accurately reflects the level of service rendered.

In some situations medical coders are expected to select the appropriate E/M code. Evaluation and management codes are listed in the CPT alphabetic index by type of service. For example, office visit codes are listed under *office and/or other outpatient services,* consultations are listed under *consultation,* hospital visits are listed under *hospital services,* and so forth. Once a code is located in the alphabetic index, the medical coder refers to the E/M section for a complete description of the code. The code description includes the documentation requirements for the specific code.

The medical coder must carefully compare the documentation in the medical record with the requirements for the E/M code. The medical coder must select the code that is supported by the documentation. References that help guide the coder to the correct E/M code include (1) the section and subsection guidelines for E/M codes; (2) appendix C of the CPT manual, which lists clinical examples of E/M codes; and (3) *CPT Assistant,* a monthly publication of the American Medical Association that provides practical advice from coding specialists.

E/M Modifiers

Although most modifiers apply to surgery or procedure codes, there are four modifiers that are used with E/M codes. Table 3-7 provides descriptions and examples of these modifiers.

Table 3-7   E/M Modifiers

-24 UNRELATED EVALUATION AND MANAGEMENT SERVICE BY THE SAME PHYSICIAN [PROVIDER] DURING A POSTOPERATIVE PERIOD
Modifier -24 is used to identify an E/M service that is unrelated to the original procedure that was rendered to the patient during the postoperative period of the original procedure. *Example: During a routine postoperative office visit following gallbladder surgery, the patient states he has noticed bright red blood in his stool. The physician performs a rectal exam and prescribes a topical medication for the patient's hemorrhoids.*
-25 SIGNIFICANT, SEPARATELY IDENTIFIABLE EVALUATION AND MANAGEMENT SERVICE BY THE SAME PHYSICIAN ON THE SAME DAY OF THE PROCEDURE OR OTHER SERVICE
Modifier -25 is used to identify that an E/M service was performed on the same day of a procedure, and the E/M service was above and beyond the usual preoperative or postoperative care. The E/M service may be prompted by the condition that necessitated the procedure. As such, different diagnoses are not required for reporting the E/M services on the same day. *Example: Following gallbladder surgery, the surgeon visits the patient in the recovery room. The patient has a respiratory attack, and the physician performs an emergency tracheotomy.*
-57 DECISION FOR SURGERY
Modifier -57 is used to identify that an E/M service resulted in the initial decision to perform surgery. *Example: During a new patient office visit for a sore throat, the physician discovers that the seven-year-old patient has had strep throat six times in the past six months. Today's rapid strep test is positive. The patient is scheduled for a tonsillectomy.*

E/M modifiers tell the insurance carrier or fiscal intermediary why a particular service is being submitted for reimbursement.

Anesthesia Section

Anesthesia is defined as the pharmacological suppression of nerve function that is administered by a general, regional, or local method. The CPT codes for anesthesia (00100–01999) are used to report the administration of anesthesia by an anesthesiologist or nurse anesthetist who is supervised by an anesthesiologist. Anesthesia codes include the following services:

- General, regional, and local anesthesia
- Other support services during the procedure that are deemed necessary by the anesthesiologist
- Preoperative and postoperative visits by the anesthesiologist
- Care during the procedure
- Monitoring of vital signs
- Administration of blood or any other fluid

Anesthesia codes are organized primarily by anatomical site and are located in the alphabetic index under the main term *anesthesia*. Anesthesia category codes are listed in table 3-8.

Moderate sedation, with or without analgesia, is reported using codes 99143–99145, and 99148–99150 in CPT's Medicine section. Moderate sedation codes are flagged as add-on codes. Unusual forms of monitoring, such as intra-arterial, central venous, and Swan-Ganz, are not included in the anesthesia codes and are coded separately.

Anesthesia Modifiers

Anesthesia services are reported with a five-digit CPT code plus the addition of a **physical status modifier** that addresses the overall health status of the patient. Table 3-9 lists the modifiers and their meanings.

In addition to the physical status modifiers, other CPT modifiers apply to anesthesia codes. Table 3-10 provides descriptions and examples of these modifiers.

Table 3-8 Anesthesia Categories

ANESTHESIA CATEGORY	CPT CODE RANGE
Head	00100–00222
Neck	00300–00352
Thorax (Chest Wall and Shoulder Girdle)	00400–00474
Intrathoracic	00500–00580
Spine and Spinal Cord	00600–00670
Upper Abdomen	00700–00797
Lower Abdomen	00800–00882
Perineum	00902–00952
Pelvis (Except Hip)	01112–01190
Upper Leg (Except Knee)	01200–01274
Knee and Popliteal Area	01320–01444
Lower Leg (Below Knee, Ankle, and Foot)	01462–01522
Shoulder and Axilla	01610–01682
Upper Arm and Elbow	01710–01782
Forearm, Wrist, and Hand	01810–01860
Radiological Procedures	01916–01936
Burn Excisions or Debridement	01951–01953
Obstetrics	01958–01969
Other Procedures	01990–01999

Table 3-9 Anesthesia Physical Status Modifiers

ANESTHESIA MODIFIER	DESCRIPTION
P1	Normal healthy patient
P2	Patient with mild systemic disease
P3	Patient with severe systemic disease
P4	Patient with severe systemic disease that is a constant threat to life
P5	A moribund patient who is not expected to survive without the operation
P6	A declared brain-dead patient whose organs are being removed for donor purposes

Anesthesia Add-On Codes

Anesthesia add-on codes are used to describe additional information that affects anesthesia delivery such as anesthesia during burn excisions or debridement that covers more than 9% of the total body surface. There are specific **qualifying circumstances** that also require anesthesia add-on codes. Qualifying circumstances are

Table 3-10   Anesthesia Modifiers

-23 UNUSUAL ANESTHESIA

Modifier -23 is used to identify situations in which general anesthesia is administered during a procedure that is usually done with no anesthesia or with local anesthesia.

Example: A six-year-old patient is seen in the emergency department because she pushed a pebble into her left nostril. Although the pebble can be reached with a snare, the child is so agitated it is necessary to use a general anesthetic to remove the pebble.

-51 MULTIPLE PROCEDURES

Modifier -51 is used to identify situations in which multiple anesthesia services were provided on the same day or during the same operative episode.

Example: Within 12 hours after surgery for a total hip replacement, the patient develops "trash foot syndrome" and is taken to the operating room to have a blood clot removed from her external iliac artery.

-53 DISCONTINUED PROCEDURE

Modifier -53 is used to identify situations in which the physician elects to terminate or discontinue a procedure because of the risk to the patient's health. Do not use this modifier when the procedure is canceled before the patient is prepped for the procedure or anesthesia is started.

Example: During the first 10 minutes of surgery under general anesthetic, Mr. Lawrence's blood pressure "bottoms out" and the surgeon decides to close immediately and reschedule the surgery.

very difficult situations that significantly affect the anesthesia service. The circumstances include extraordinary condition of the patient, notable operative conditions, and unusual risk factors. Add-on codes are not reported alone but in addition to the selected anesthesia CPT code. Table 3-11 lists the add-on codes and their qualifying circumstances.

Table 3-11   Qualifying Circumstances for Anesthesia Add-On Codes

ADD-ON CODE	QUALIFYING CIRCUMSTANCES
+99100	Anesthesia for patients of extreme age (i.e., under one year or over seventy years)
+99116	Anesthesia complicated by utilization of total body hypothermia
+99135	Anesthesia complicated by utilization of controlled hypotension
+99140	Anesthesia complicated by emergency conditions (specify the emergency conditions)

For purposes of the anesthesia add-on codes, an emergency exists when a delay in treatment would lead to a significant increase in the threat to the patient's life or body part.

Anesthesia Code Selection and Reporting

CPT codes from the Anesthesia section must be reported on all Medicare insurance claims. Some insurance carriers require anesthesia services to be reported with the applicable surgery code. When a physician provides the anesthesia for a surgery that he or she performs, the appropriate codes from the Surgery section are selected and modifier -47, *anesthesia by surgeon,* is added to the surgery CPT code.

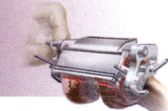

EXERCISE 3-2

Write a brief answer for each statement or question.

1. Briefly discuss the purpose of E/M codes. _____
2. List and describe the three key components for most E/M codes. _____
3. Explain the meaning of modifier -57, *decision for surgery.* _____
4. Briefly describe the type of information found in the E/M guidelines. _____
5. List three references for E/M coding that are available to the medical coder. _____
6. List three types of services included in CPT anesthesia codes. _____

Fill in the blank.

7. Anesthesia _____ modifiers refer to the overall health of the patient.
8. Anesthesia _____ codes are used to describe circumstances that significantly affect the anesthesia service.
9. Under the main term *anesthesia,* anesthesia codes are organized by _____.

Surgery Section

The CPT Surgery section defines surgical procedures in the broadest possible sense of the term, from heart

Table 3-12 Surgery Subsections

SURGERY SUBSECTION	CODE RANGE
General and Integumentary System	10021–19499
Musculoskeletal System	20000–29999
Respiratory System	30000–32999
Cardiovascular System; Hemic and Lymphatic Systems	33010–39599
Digestive System	40490–49999
Urinary System	50010–53899
Male/Female Genital System	54000–55980 (Male)
	56405–59899 (Female)
Endocrine System	60000–60699
Nervous System	61000–64999
Ocular/Auditory System	65091–68899 (Eye and Ocular Adnexa)
	69000–69990 (Auditory System)

- Administration of local infiltration, metacarpal/digital block, or topical anesthesia
- Following the decision for surgery, one related evaluation and management encounter on the date of surgery or the day immediately before surgery
- Immediate postoperative care, such as dictating operative notes or talking with the family and other physicians
- Writing orders
- Evaluating the patient in the postanesthesia recovery area
- Typical postoperative follow-up care

transplant to cystoscopy. The Surgery section has ten subsections that are organized by body system. Table 3-12 lists the Surgery subsections and range of codes for each subsection.

Surgical and procedure codes are listed in the CPT alphabetic index by the specific name of the procedure (e.g., cystoscopy); the type of procedure (incision, excision, repair, removal); or anatomical site. The medical coder or insurance billing specialist first checks the alphabetic index for a given surgery or procedure. Once the code or range of codes is identified, go to the appropriate surgical category or subcategory and select the CPT code that is supported by the information in the patient's medical record.

Assigning surgical codes is influenced by factors such as the surgical package and global surgery concept, the separate procedure guidelines, CPT modifiers, and ambulatory surgery center modifiers.

Surgical Package

A **surgical package** is defined as the services that are included in a surgical intervention and procedure. Reimbursement for the actual surgery or procedure is counted as reimbursement for the included services. According to CPT guidelines, a surgical package includes the following services:

Physician or provider services that are not included in the surgical package are coded and submitted with the insurance claim. Examples of included services are cast removal, suture removal, and routine postoperative office follow-up. Examples of services that are not included in a surgical package are follow-up office visits for surgical complications, excessive inpatient postoperative hospital visits, and any services that relate to another disease that may exist during the postoperative period.

The CPT definition of a surgical package may not apply to all insurance carriers. Under Medicare, the surgical package is called a **global surgery concept** and the included services are divided into two categories: major surgeries and minor or endoscopic procedures. Table 3-13 lists the services for major and minor surgeries or procedures.

Services that are part of a surgical package or global surgery concept cannot be billed individually. This practice is called **unbundling** and constitutes fraud. Unbundling results in additional reimbursement to the provider for services that are intended to be covered by one payment. *Never* unbundle services that are included in a surgical package.

Separate Procedures

The CPT procedures or services identified as **separate procedures** are usually carried out as a component of another more comprehensive procedure and under that circumstance cannot be billed separately. The separate procedure designation tells the medical coder that if the procedure is *not* done as a component of another more comprehensive procedure, the procedure may be billed

Table 3-13 Medicare Global Surgery Concept

MAJOR SURGICAL PROCEDURES	MINOR AND ENDOSCOPIC PROCEDURES
1. Preoperative services provided one day prior to the day of surgery, except when the preoperative service resulted in the initial decision to perform the surgery, or when the service provided by the same physician during a preoperative period is unrelated to the original procedure	1. Preoperative services provided one day prior to the day of surgery, except when the preoperative service resulted in the initial decision to perform the surgery, or when the service provided by the same physician during a preoperative period is unrelated to the original procedure
2. The actual surgical procedure	2. The actual procedure
3. Postoperative services provided within *90 days* of the surgical procedure, except when the service is unrelated to the surgical procedure	3. Postoperative services provided within *10 days* of the procedure, except when the service is unrelated to the surgical procedure
4. Postoperative services that do not require a return to the operating room, such as dressing changes and care of the operative incision; removal of sutures, staples, wires, lines, tubes, drains, casts, and splints; urinary catheter care; and care of other postoperative tubes and intravenous lines	

as a separate procedure. When a procedure is billed as a separate procedure, the medical coder adds modifier -59 to the procedure code.

Modifiers

Surgery modifiers are used to communicate the following additional information about a given procedure:

- A service or procedure has both a professional and a technical component.
- A service or procedure was performed by more than one physician or in more than one location.
- A service or procedure has been increased or reduced.
- Only part of a service was performed.
- An adjunctive service was performed.
- A bilateral procedure was performed.
- A service or procedure was provided more than once.
- Unusual events occurred.

Modifiers are expressed as either a two-digit or a five-digit number, depending on the preference of the third-party payer. A five-digit modifier always begins with 099, and it is the last two digits that distinguish one modifier from another. A hyphen precedes a two-digit modifier. Therefore, modifier -47 and 09947,

anesthesia by surgeon, indicates that the surgeon provided regional or general anesthesia for a surgical procedure. Table 3-14 lists the modifiers that are used with surgery codes.

Ambulatory Surgery Center Modifiers

Several CPT modifiers are approved for use with procedures provided in ambulatory surgery centers and hospital outpatient departments. Table 3-15 lists the CPT modifiers that apply to ambulatory surgery centers and hospital outpatient departments.

Except for modifier -27, the descriptions of the modifiers are in table 3-14 and in CPT's appendix A. For hospital outpatient reporting purposes, modifier -27 may be used to report separate and distinct evaluation and management encounters or services performed in multiple outpatient hospital settings on the same day. Modifier -27 is *not* to be used for services provided by the *same* physician on the *same* date.

Radiology Section (70010–79999)

Radiology procedures are also known as diagnostic imaging procedures. The radiologist's services are called the professional component, and the radiology technician's services are known as the technical component. The professional component includes supervising the service, reading and interpreting the results, and documenting the interpretation in a report. When the

Table 3-14 Surgical Code Modifiers with Descriptions

-22 Increased Procedural Services—The service provided is greater than the service usually associated with a specific procedure.

-26 Professional Component—The provider/physician delivers the professional component only of a given procedure or service.

-32 Mandated Service—The service or consultation is provided because a third party (e.g., insurance carrier, regulatory agency) requires it.

-47 Anesthesia by Surgeon—The surgeon provided the regional or general (not local) anesthesia for a surgical procedure.

-50 Bilateral Procedure—Bilateral procedures are performed during the same operative episode. Do not use this modifier when there is a procedure code that identifies a procedure as bilateral.

-51 Multiple Procedures—Multiple procedures are performed at the same session by the same provider. The primary procedure or service is reported as listed; additional procedures or services are identified by adding this modifier to the code. Do not use this modifier for E/M services, physical medicine and rehabilitation, or provision of supplies, such as vaccines.

-52 Reduced Services—Part of the procedure or service is reduced or eliminated at the discretion of the physician; applies to inpatient procedures or services.

-53 Discontinued Procedure—The procedure is discontinued because of the risk to the patient's well-being; not to be used if an elective procedure is canceled prior to surgical preparation or induction of anesthesia; applies to inpatient procedures or services.

-54 Surgical Care Only—One physician performs the procedure only; a different physician provides the preoperative and postoperative care.

-55 Postoperative Management Only—The physician provides postoperative services only.

-56 Preoperative Management Only—The physician provides preoperative services only.

-57 Decision for Surgery—The evaluation and management service results in the initial decision to perform surgery.

-58 Staged or Related Procedure or Service by the Same Physician During the Postoperative Period—Performance of a procedure or service during the postoperative period was planned or anticipated (staged); was more extensive than the original procedure; therapy following a surgical procedure is necessary. Treating problems that require a return to the operating or procedure room (e.g., unanticipated clinical condition) is covered by modifier -78.

-59 Distinct Procedural Service—A procedure or service that is distinct from the original service is provided on the same day as the original service; usually a different procedure, operative site, or organ; separate incision or excision; or separate lesion or injury. Do not use this modifier if another modifier is more applicable to the situation. This modifier does not apply to E/M services.

-62 Two Surgeons—Two surgeons are required to perform the procedure; both surgeons must report the service with modifier -62; does not apply to assistant surgeon(s) (see modifier -80).

-63 Procedures Performed on Infants Less than 4 Kilograms—Applies to procedures performed on neonates and infants up to a present body weight of 4 kilograms.

-66 Surgical Team—Procedure is performed by a surgical team; applies to very complex procedures such as organ transplants.

-76 Repeat Procedure or Service by Same Physician—Identifies that a procedure or service was repeated subsequent to the original procedure or service.

-77 Repeat Procedure by Another Physician—The procedure or service is repeated by a physician different from the one who performed the original procedure.

-78 Unplanned Return to the Operating/Procedure Room by the Same Physician Following the Initial Procedure for a Related Procedure During the Postoperative Period—An unplanned procedure related to the original procedure's postoperative period requires the use of an operating or procedure room. Does not apply to repeating the original procedure or service (see modifier -76).

-79 Unrelated Procedure or Service by the Same Physician During the Postoperative Period—A procedure or service that is unrelated to the original procedure is performed during the original procedure's postoperative period.

-80 Assistant Surgeon—The physician who assists a surgeon during a particular procedure reports the procedure with modifier -80; the operating surgeon does not use modifier -80.

-81 Minimum Assistant Surgeon—The physician who provided minimal assistance to the operating surgeon reports the procedure with modifier -81; the operating surgeon does not use modifier -81.

-82 Assistant Surgeon (when a qualified resident surgeon is not available)—Applies primarily to teaching hospitals where surgical residents are often the assistant surgeon; when a surgical resident is not available, another physician may assist the operating surgeon; the operating surgeon does not use modifier -82.

continued

Table 3-14 (*continued*) Surgical Code Modifiers with Descriptions

-90 Reference (Outside) Laboratory—Identifies that laboratory procedures/tests were performed by a lab outside the control of the reporting physician.

-91 Repeat Clinical Diagnostic Laboratory Test—Identifies the need to repeat a lab test on the same day that the original test is done; used when multiple test results are necessary to establish a diagnosis; do not use modifier -91 when a test is repeated due to specimen or equipment problems or when the test itself requires multiple results.

-92 Alternative Laboratory Platform Testing—Identifies that laboratory testing is being performed using a kit or transportable instrument that wholly or in part consists of a single-use, disposable analytical chamber; test may be transported to the location of the patient for immediate testing at that site; location of the testing does not in itself determine the use of modifier -92.

-99 Multiple Modifiers—Alerts insurance carriers that more than one modifier is being submitted on a claim; many insurance carriers have a limit on the number of modifiers that are reported.

Table 3-15 Ambulatory Surgery Center Modifiers

-25 Significant, Separately Identifiable Evaluation and Management Service by the Same Physician on the Same Day of the Procedure or Other Service

-27 Multiple Outpatient Hospital E/M Encounters on the Same Date

-50 Bilateral Procedure

-52 Reduced Services

-58 Staged or Related Procedure or Service by the Same Physician During the Postoperative Period

-59 Distinct Procedural Service

-73 Discontinued Outpatient Hospital/Ambulatory Surgery Center (ASC) Procedure Prior to Administration of Anesthesia

-74 Discontinued Outpatient Hospital/Ambulatory Surgery Center (ASC) Procedure After Administration of Anesthesia

-76 Repeat Procedure or Service by Same Physician

-77 Repeat Procedure by Another Physician

-78 Unplanned Return to the Operating/Procedure Room by the Same Physician Following Initial Procedure for a Related Procedure During the Postoperative Period

-79 Unrelated Procedure or Service by the Same Physician During the Postoperative Period

-91 Repeat Clinical Diagnostic Laboratory Test

Table 3-16 Radiology Subsections and Code Ranges

RADIOLOGY SUBSECTIONS	CODE RANGE
Diagnostic Radiology (Diagnostic Imaging)	70010–76499
Diagnostic Ultrasound	76506–76999
Radiologic Guidance; Fluoroscopic Guidance; Computed Tomography Guidance; Magnetic Imaging Guidance; Other Radiologic Guidance	77001–77032
Breast Mammography	77051–77059
Bone/Joint Studies	77071–77084
Radiation Oncology	77261–77799
Nuclear Medicine (Diagnostic)	78000–78999
Nuclear Medicine (Therapeutic)	79005–79999

Radiology section codes are organized by type of imaging, such as radiography, ultrasonography, and nuclear medicine, and by anatomical site. Radiology subsections include instructional notes that contribute to coding accuracy. Table 3–16 lists the radiology subsections and the code ranges.

Pathology and Laboratory Section (80047–89356)

The Pathology and Laboratory section of CPT includes services by a physician or by technicians under the responsible supervision of a physician. This section includes codes for services and procedures that range from a straightforward urinalysis to the more complex cytogenetic studies. Table 3-17 lists the categories of pathology and laboratory services and code ranges.

radiologist interprets and documents the results of a radiographic procedure, modifier -26, *professional component,* is added to the procedure code. The technical component includes doing the diagnostic imaging, and the expenses for the supplies and equipment. A radiologist may perform both the professional and technical components.

Table 3-17 Pathology and Laboratory Services and Code Ranges

PATHOLOGY/LABORATORY SUBSECTIONS	CODE RANGE
Organ or Disease Oriented Panels	80047–80076
Drug Testing	80100–80103
Therapeutic Drug Assays	80150–80299
Evocative/Suppression Testing	80400–80440
Consultations (Clinical Pathology)	80500, 80502
Urinalysis	81000–81099
Chemistry	82000–84999
Hematology and Coagulation	85002–85999
Immunology	86000–86804
Tissue Typing	86805–86849
Transfusion Medicine	86850–86999
Microbiology	87001–87999
Anatomic Pathology	88000–88099
Cytopathology	88104–88199
Cytogenetic Studies	88230–88299
Surgical Pathology	88300–88399
In Vivo (e.g. Transcutaneous) Laboratory Procedures	88720–88741
Other Procedures	89049–89240
Reproductive Medicine Procedures	89250–89356

CPT coding conventions discussed earlier in the chapter apply to the Pathology and Laboratory section as well. One CPT modifier is unique to this section. Modifier -90, *reference (outside) laboratory,* is used to indicate that another party besides the reporting physician performed the actual laboratory procedure.

Medicine Section (90281–99607)

The Medicine section includes a range of medical services and procedures, from routine childhood vaccinations to renal dialysis. Table 3-18 lists and briefly describes the categories of medical services and procedures.

Medicine codes are listed in the CPT alphabetic index by type of service and anatomical site. For example, heart catheterization is indexed under *catheterization, cardiac, left heart, right heart,* and *heart, catheterization.* When a physician or provider renders more than one service on the same day or during the same office or other outpatient visit, each service is coded and submitted for reimbursement.

EXERCISE 3-3

Write a short answer for the statements.

1. List three services that are included in CPT's definition of a surgical package. _____

2. List three services that are included in Medicare's global surgical concept. _____

3. Describe the differences between a surgical package and the global surgical concept. _____

4. List two ways to locate medicine codes in the CPT alphabetic index. _____

Fill in the blank.

5. The radiologist's services during a radiology procedure are called the _____.

6. According to Medicare guidelines, a/an _____ is defined as the range of services that is included in a surgical intervention.

7. _____ is defined as submitting claims for services that are a part of a surgical package.

8. A/an _____ is usually part of a more comprehensive service, but under some conditions may be billed separately.

9. Routine childhood vaccinations are assigned codes from CPT's _____ section.

10. _____ is a type of anesthesia that may be assigned a code from CPT's Medicine section.

HEALTHCARE COMMON PROCEDURE CODING SYSTEM (HCPCS)

The information presented here is a brief introduction to the *Healthcare Common Procedure Coding System* (HCPCS), which was developed by the Centers for Medicare and Medicaid Services (CMS). This system is also known as **level II codes** and the **national codes**. Initially developed for Medicare, HCPCS codes also apply to commercial insurance companies. In fact, some insurance carriers require the use of HCPCS codes rather than certain CPT codes. Bulletins provided by Medicare and private insurance carriers alert the agency to the mandated HCPCS codes. The national codes are used to report physician and nonphysician

Table 3-18 Medicine Subsections with Descriptions

Immune Globulins (90281–90399): Codes apply only to the immune globulin product and are reported with the administration code.

Immunization Administration for Vaccines/Toxoids (90465–90474): Codes apply to the administration of the product and are reported with the correct vaccine or toxoid code.

Vaccines, Toxoids (90476–90749): Codes apply to vaccine or toxoid products only.

Psychiatry (90801–90899): Codes apply to several psychotherapy modalities in various health care settings.

Biofeedback (90901, 90911): Codes apply to biofeedback training.

Dialysis (90935–90999): Codes apply to end-stage renal disease services, hemodialysis, and miscellaneous dialysis procedures.

Gastroenterology (91000–91299): Codes apply to tests related to esophageal and gastric motility, and gastric secretions.

Ophthalmology (92002–92499): Codes apply to ophthalmology services including supplies.

Special Otorhinolaryngologic Services (92502–92700): Codes apply to services related to hearing, swallowing, and laryngeal functioning.

Cardiovascular (92950–93799): Codes apply to therapeutic and diagnostic tests of the heart and blood vessels.

Noninvasive Vascular Diagnostic Studies (93875–93990): Codes apply to Doppler studies and other noninvasive tests of arteries and veins.

Pulmonary (94002–94799): Codes apply to ventilation management and pulmonary and respiratory function tests.

Allergy and Clinical Immunology (95004–95199): Codes apply to allergy tests and allergy immunotherapy.

Endocrinology (95250, 95291): Codes apply to ambulatory, continuous glucose monitoring of interstitial tissue fluid using a subcutaneous sensor.

Neurology and Neuromuscular Procedures (95803–96020): Codes apply to nerve and muscle function tests, sleep testing, electroencephalography, electromyography, neurostimulator analysis-programming, motion analysis, and functional brain mapping.

Medical Genetics and Genetic Counseling Services (96040): This code applies to genetic counseling services provided by trained genetic counselors.

Central Nervous System Assessments/Tests (96101–96125): Codes apply to neurocognitive, mental status, and speech testing.

Health and Behavior Assessment/Intervention (96150–96155): Codes apply to assessments related to biopsychosocial factors of physical health problems.

Hydration, Therapeutic, Prophylactic, Diagnostic Injections and Infusions, and Chemotherapy and Other Highly Complex Drug or Highly Complex Biologic Agent Administration (96360–96549): Codes apply to a range of services from intravenous hydration to chemotherapy injection in the subarachnoid or intraventricular space via a subcutaneous reservoir.

Photodynamic Therapy (96567, 96570–96571): Codes apply to the application of light to destroy lesions.

Special Dermatological Procedures (96900–96999): Codes apply to dermatology services not covered elsewhere.

Physical Medicine and Rehabilitation (97001–97799): Codes apply to services related to physical therapy, occupational therapy, tests and measurements, and other services associated with rehabilitation medicine.

Medical Nutrition Therapy (97802–97804): Codes apply to assessment and intervention related to nutrition.

Acupuncture (97810–97814): Codes apply to acupuncture with or without electrical stimulation.

Osteopathic Manipulative Treatment (98925–98929): Codes apply to services provided by an osteopathic physician.

Chiropractic Manipulative Treatment (98940–98943): Codes apply to services provided by a chiropractor.

Education and Training for Patient Self-Management (98960–98962): Codes apply to education and training prescribed by a physician and provided by a qualified nonphysician health care professional. The purpose of the education and training is to teach the patient (or caregiver) how to effectively self-manage a disease or condition.

Non-Face-to-Face Nonphysician Services (98966–98969): Codes apply to services provided by a qualified health care professional via the telephone or online.

Special Services, Procedures, and Reports (99000–99091): Codes apply to services not covered elsewhere, such as handling a specimen for transfer, hospital-mandated on-call service, services provided outside of regularly scheduled office hours or on holidays, travel to escort a patient, and other miscellaneous services.

Qualifying Circumstances for Anesthesia (99100–99140): Codes apply to anesthesia services complicated by the patient's age or other unusual circumstances.

Moderate (Conscious) Sedation (99143–99150): Codes apply to the administration and monitoring of moderate sedation that is used during procedures that require the patient to be able to respond to stimulation.

Other Services and Procedures (99170–99199): Codes apply to unique services such as anogenital examination of a child for suspected trauma, ipecac administration for emesis and continued observation, hypothermia, and therapeutic phlebotomy.

Home Health Procedures/Services (99500–99602): Codes apply to services rendered in the patient's home by a nonphysician health care professional.

Medication Therapy Management Services (99605–99607): Codes apply to services provided by a pharmacist and that are related to the patient's medication regimen.

services, such as ambulance services, chiropractic services, dental procedures, drugs and medications, and **durable medical equipment (DME)**. Complete listings of HCPCS codes may be purchased from the U.S. Government Printing Office, the local Medicare insurance carrier, or commercial publishers. The American Dental Association has copyrighted the "D codes," which are the HCPCS codes that apply to dental services. A list of D codes must be purchased from the American Dental Association.

HCPCS Level II: National Codes

Level II HCPCS codes are five-digit alphanumeric characters, beginning with a letter and ending with four numbers. Table 3-19 lists the HCPCS sections and descriptions.

Table 3-19 HCPCS Sections and Descriptions

SECTION	DESCRIPTION
A codes	Transportation Services, Including Ambulance, Medical and Surgical Supplies, Administrative, Miscellaneous, and Investigational Services
B codes	Enteral and Parenteral Therapy
C codes	Temporary Codes for Use with Outpatient Prospective Payment System
D codes	Dental Procedures
E codes	Durable Medical Equipment (DME) (e.g., wheelchair)
G codes	Procedures/Professional Services (Temporary)
H codes	Alcohol and Drug Abuse Treatment Services
J codes	Drugs Administered, Other than Oral Method, Chemotherapy Drugs
K codes	Temporary (Codes Assigned to Durable Medical Equipment Regional Carriers)
L codes	Orthotic Procedures, Prosthetic Procedures
M codes	Medical Services
P codes	Pathology and Laboratory Services
Q codes	Miscellaneous Services (Temporary Codes)
R codes	Diagnostic Radiology Services
S codes	Temporary National Codes (Non-Medicare)
T codes	Established for State Medicaid Agencies
V codes	Vision Services, Hearing Services

HCPCS Level II Modifiers

In addition to the alphanumeric codes, HCPCS uses modifiers that provide further information about services provided to the patient. For Medicare claims, HCPCS level II modifiers may be used with either HCPCS or CPT codes. Private insurance carriers may also allow level II modifiers to be combined with CPT codes. Modifiers do not change the basic definition of the service/procedure and are used to describe the following types of information:

- The service was provided by an anesthesiologist.
- The service was performed by a nonphysician health care professional (clinical psychologist, nurse practitioner, physician assistant).
- The service was provided as part of a specific government program.
- Equipment was purchased or rented.
- Single or multiple patients were seen during nursing home visits.

There are literally hundreds of modifiers, and they are updated as needed. Table 3-20 lists HCPCS modifiers for services or treatment.

Table 3-20 HCPCS Modifiers for Services/Treatment

MODIFIER	DESCRIPTION
-AA	Anesthesia services furnished by anesthesiologist
-AH	Clinical psychologist
-AJ	Clinical social worker
-AS	Physician assistant, nurse practitioner, or clinical nurse specialist for assistant at surgery
-E1	Eyelid, upper left
-F1	Left hand, second digit
-F5	Right hand, thumb
-LC	Left circumflex coronary artery
-LT	Left side
-NU	New equipment
-RC	Right coronary artery
-RT	Right side
-TD	Registered nurse
-T1	Left foot, second digit
-T5	Right foot, great toe

Transportation modifiers consist of two characters; the first character identifies the point of origin and the second character identifies the destination. Table 3-21 lists HCPCS transportation modifiers.

Table 3-21 HCPCS Transportation Modifiers

MODIFIER	DESCRIPTION
D	Diagnostic or therapeutic site other than *P* or *H* when these are used as origin codes
E	Residential, domiciliary, custodial facility (excepted skilled nursing facility)
G	Hospital-based dialysis facility
H	Hospital
I	Site of transfer (e.g., airport or helicopter pad) between modes of ambulance transport
J	Nonhospital-based dialysis facility
N	Skilled nursing facility (SNF)
P	Physician office (includes HMO nonhospital facility, clinic)
R	Residence
S	Scene of accident or acute event
X	*Destination Code Only.* Intermediate stop at physician's office (includes nonhospital facility or clinic) en route to the hospital

SUMMARY

Current Procedural Terminology (CPT) is the accepted coding system for provider services in ambulatory or outpatient settings. Each CPT section has guidelines and instructions that give medical coders information necessary for accurate code selection. CPT coding conventions further clarify the selection of a specific code. CPT modifiers represent special circumstances and are reported with the main CPT code.

The *Healthcare Common Procedure Coding System* (HCPCS) is published and maintained by the Centers for Medicare and Medicaid Services. HCPCS includes level I codes, which are the CPT codes, and level II codes, called the national codes. HCPCS level II codes are used to report services such as drugs, chiropractic services, and durable medical equipment.

Insurance carriers, the government, and regulatory agencies closely monitor ICD-9-CM, CPT, and HCPCS codes for accuracy. Medical coders and insurance billing specialists must be certain that any codes included on an insurance claim are clearly supported by the documentation in the patient's medical record.

CHAPTER REVIEW

Write out the abbreviations.

1. CPT

2. ASC

3. HCPCS

4. CMS

5. E/M

Fill in the blank.

6. _____ are used to set off new or revised information in the CPT manual.

7. Add-on codes are identified by a/an _____.

8. A/an _____ indicates that a procedure code includes the use of conscious sedation.

9. Physical status modifiers are associated with _____ codes.

10. Transportation modifiers are associated with _____ codes.

■ CPT CODING EXERCISES

The purpose of the coding exercises is to give you an opportunity to practice using the CPT manual. Always check the codes you find in the alphabetic index with the full description in the appropriate CPT section, subsection, or category.

Write the main term for each procedural statement. Assign the correct CPT code for each procedure.

1. Abdominal hysterectomy

    MAIN TERM: _____

    CODE: _____

2. Throat culture, bacterial

    MAIN TERM: _____

    CODE: _____

3. Cesarean section only

    MAIN TERM: _____

    CODE: _____

4. Appendectomy for an abscessed, ruptured appendix

    MAIN TERM: _____

    CODE: _____

5. Percutaneous needle biopsy of the liver

    MAIN TERM: _____

    CODE: _____

6. Complete thyroidectomy

    MAIN TERM: _____

    CODE: _____

7. Superficial dermabrasion for tattoo removal

    MAIN TERM: _____

    CODE: _____

8. Amputation of the foot, midtarsal

    MAIN TERM: _____

    CODE: _____

9. Simple excision of a nasal polyp

    MAIN TERM: _____

    CODE: _____

10. Removal of impacted cerumen (earwax) one or both ears

    MAIN TERM: _____

    CODE: _____

11. Chest x-ray, frontal and lateral views

    MAIN TERM: _____

    CODE: _____

12. Urine pregnancy test

    MAIN TERM: _____

    CODE: _____

13. Autopsy (necropsy), gross and microscopic examination

    MAIN TERM: _____

    CODE: _____

14. Bone density study, forearm

    MAIN TERM: _____

    CODE: _____

15. Primary tonsillectomy (patient is 10 years old)

    MAIN TERM: _____

    CODE: _____

16. Vaginal hysterectomy, 225 gram uterus

    MAIN TERM: _____

    CODE: _____

17. Unilateral simple mastectomy, complete

    MAIN TERM: _____

    CODE: _____

18. Tonsillectomy and adenoidectomy, patient is 10 years old

    MAIN TERM: _____

    CODE: _____

19. Colonoscopy with biopsy

    MAIN TERM: _____

    CODE: _____

20. Repair of initial incisional hernia, reducible

    MAIN TERM: _____

    CODE: _____

21. Excision, 0.5 cm benign lesion on the right forearm

    MAIN TERM: _____

    CODE: _____

22. Excision, malignant lesion, top of left foot, 0.8 cm

    MAIN TERM: _____

    CODE: _____

23. Excision of a portion of the mandible due to a bone abscess

    MAIN TERM: _____

    CODE: _____

24. Drainage of an abscess on the fourth digit, left hand; simple

    MAIN TERM: _____

    CODE: _____

25. Arthroscopy of the right knee for removal of foreign body

    MAIN TERM: _____

    CODE: _____

26. Removal of a foreign body (penny), intranasal; physician's office

    MAIN TERM: _____

    CODE: _____

27. Circumcision of a newborn, clamp method

    MAIN TERM: _____

    CODE: _____

28. Eye exam; intermediate, new patient

    MAIN TERM: _____

    CODE: _____

29. First-trimester ultrasound of the uterus, transabdominal approach; single gestation

    MAIN TERM: _____

    CODE: _____

30. Drug screening; multiple (illegal) drugs

    MAIN TERM: _____

    CODE: _____

NOTES:

CHAPTER 4

Integumentary System

■ OBJECTIVES

At the completion of this chapter, the student should be able to:

1. Learn the word roots associated with the integumentary system.
2. Label the basic structures of the integumentary system.
3. Discuss the functions of the integumentary system.
4. Accurately spell and define integumentary system terminology.
5. Accurately assign medical codes to integumentary diagnoses and procedures.

■ OVERVIEW

The integumentary system is made up of the skin, hair, nails, and glands. The structures of the integumentary system function together for the following purposes: (1) to provide a protective covering for the entire body; (2) to produce sweat, which cools the body, and oil, which lubricates the body; and (3) to receive sensory information associated with pain, temperature, pressure, and touch. The medical specialty of the integumentary system is **dermatology** and physician specialists are **dermatologists**.

INTEGUMENTARY SYSTEM ROOTS, PREFIXES, AND SUFFIXES

Roots, prefixes, and suffixes associated with the integumentary system are listed in table 4-1. Review the word roots and complete the exercises.

Table 4-1 Integumentary System Roots, Prefixes, and Suffixes

ROOT/COMBINING FORM	MEANING
cut/o; cutane/o	skin
derm/o; dermat/o	skin
hidr/o	sweat
kerat/o	horny tissue; hard
melan/o	black
myc/o	fungus
onych/o; ungu/o	nail
pachy/o	thick
pil/o	hair
rhytid/o	wrinkles
seb/o	sebum
squam/o	scale
sud/o; sudor/o	sweat
trich/o	hair
xer/o	dry

PREFIX	MEANING
hypo-	beneath; below
intra-	within
para-	around; beside
per-	through

SUFFIX	MEANING
-ectomy	excision; surgical removal
-malacia	softening
-oma	tumor; swelling
-phagia	eating
-plasty	surgical repair
-(r)rhea	flow; excessive discharge
-tome	cutting instrument

EXERCISE 4-1

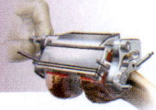

Write the root, prefix, suffix, and their meaning. Based on the meanings, write a brief definition for each term.

1. Melanocyte

   ROOT: _____ MEANING: _____

   SUFFIX: _____ MEANING: _____

   BRIEF DEFINITION: _____

2. Squamous

   ROOT: _____ MEANING: _____

   SUFFIX: _____ MEANING: _____

   BRIEF DEFINITION: _____

3. Keratome

   ROOT: _____ MEANING: _____

   SUFFIX: _____ MEANING: _____

   BRIEF DEFINITION: _____

4. Dermatologist

   ROOT: _____ MEANING: _____

   SUFFIX: _____ MEANING: _____

   BRIEF DEFINITION: _____

5. Dermatology

   ROOT: _____ MEANING: _____

   BRIEF DEFINITION: _____

6. Subcutaneous

   ROOT: _____ MEANING: _____

   PREFIX: _____ MEANING: _____

   SUFFIX: _____ MEANING: _____

   BRIEF DEFINITION: _____

7. Epidermal

   ROOT: _____ MEANING: _____

   PREFIX: _____ MEANING: _____

   SUFFIX: _____ MEANING: _____

   BRIEF DEFINITION: _____

8. Percutaneous

   ROOT: _____ MEANING: _____

   PREFIX: _____ MEANING: _____

   SUFFIX: _____ MEANING: _____

   BRIEF DEFINITION: _____

9. Hypodermic

   ROOT: _____ MEANING: _____

   PREFIX: _____ MEANING: _____

   SUFFIX: _____ MEANING: _____

   BRIEF DEFINITION: _____

10. Intradermal

   ROOT: _____ MEANING: _____

   PREFIX: _____ MEANING: _____

   SUFFIX: _____ MEANING: _____

   BRIEF DEFINITION: _____

STRUCTURES OF THE INTEGUMENTARY SYSTEM

The major structures of the integumentary system include the skin, glands, hair, and nails. The skin provides a protective covering for the body and aids in the identification of sensations such as heat, cold, pain, and touch. The glands produce sweat to help cool the body and oil to lubricate the skin. Nails provide protection for the tips of the fingers and toes.

Skin and Glands

The skin is the largest organ of the body and has two distinct layers: the (1) **epidermis** (**ep**-ih-**DERM**-is), the outermost layer of the skin, and the (2) **dermis** (**DERM**-is), the middle or inner layer of the skin. A third layer, the (3) **subcutaneous** (**sub**-kyoo-**TAYN**-ee-us) **tissue**, is closely attached to the dermis. Refer to figure 4-1 as you read about the layers and glands of the skin.

The epidermis has about five layers called **strata** (**STRAH**-tah). The singular form is **stratum** (**STRAH**-tum). The outermost layer of the epidermis is the **stratum corneum** (**STRAH**-tum **KOR**-nee-um) made up of flat, horny cells that are constantly shed. These cells die and are filled with **keratin** (**KAIR**-ah-tin), a hard,

water-repellent protein. The keratin-filled cells waterproof the body and create a first line of defense for the body. The **stratum basale** (**STRAH**-tum **BAY**-sall), also called the basal layer, is another layer of the epidermis. New cells are continuously being reproduced in the basal layer, pushing older cells toward the outermost surface of the skin. The basal layer also contains **melanocytes** (meh-**LAN**-oh-sites) that provide skin color and some protection from the ultraviolet rays of the sun.

The dermis contains blood vessels, sensory nerve endings, oil and sweat glands, and hair follicles. The dermis is often called the "living" tissue of the skin. (4) **Sebaceous** (seh-**BAY**-shus) **glands** secrete **sebum** (**SEE**-bum), or oil, into hair follicles. Sweat glands, also called (5) **sudoriferous** (**soo**-dor-**IF**-er-us) **glands**, emerge through pores to the surface of the skin.

Although the subcutaneous tissue is not a layer of skin per se, it is closely associated with the dermal layer of the skin. The subcutaneous layer is made up of (3) **adipose** (**ADD**-ih-pohs), fatty tissue, and connective tissue. This layer provides insulation and protection for deeper body structures.

Hair and Nails

Hair is defined as a meshwork of cells that contain the protein keratin. Hair originates from the (1) **hair follicles**

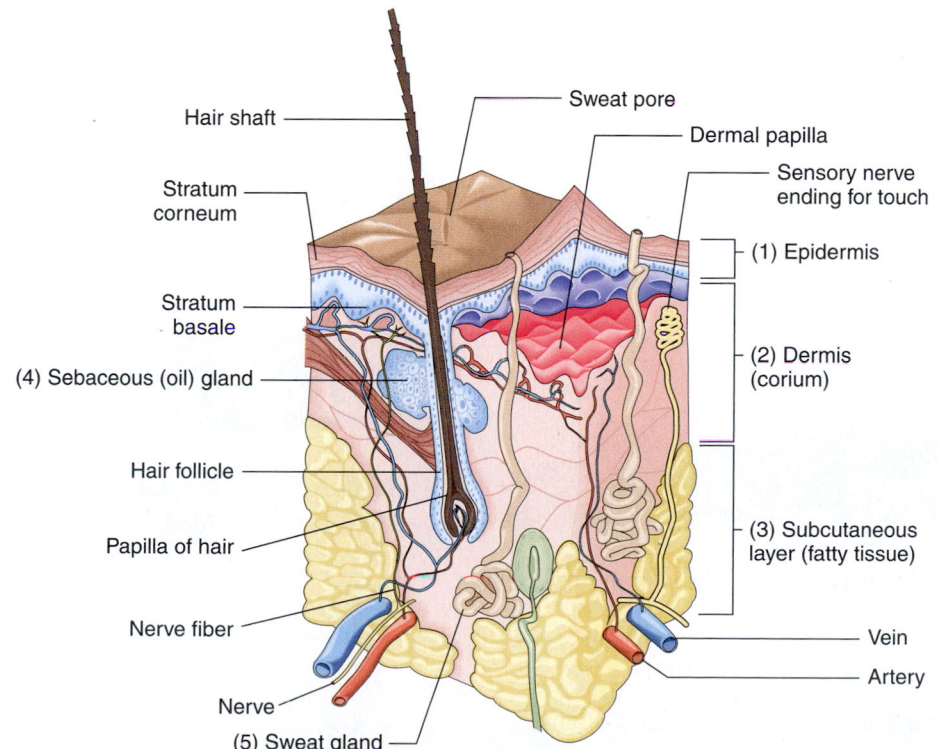

Figure 4-1 Layers and structures of the skin

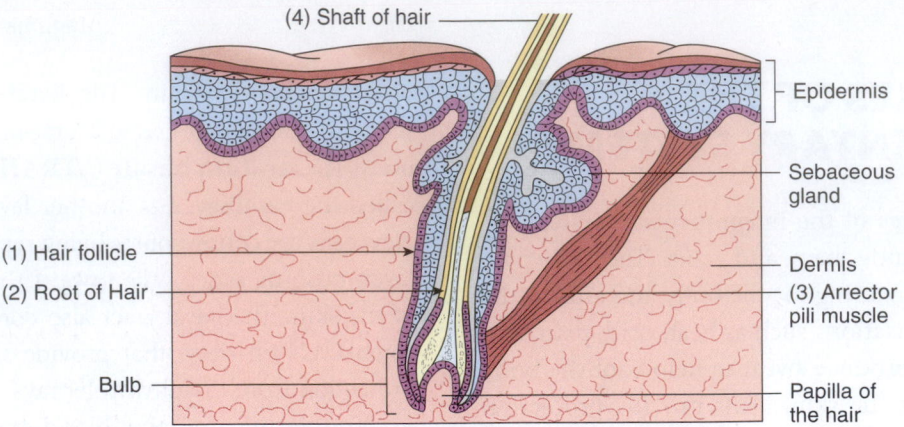

Figure 4-2   Major structures of hair

(**FAH**-lih-kuls), which are located in the dermis of the skin. The (2) **hair root** is embedded in the hair follicle. The (3) **arrector pili** muscle provides support for hair follicles. The (4) **hair shaft** is the visible portion of the hair. The hair shaft is actually dead tissue and does not have nerve endings or a blood supply, which is why it does not hurt when your hair is cut. Figure 4-2 illustrates the major structures of hair.

Fingernails and toenails are also made up of keratin and originate in the epidermis. Although both hair and nails contain keratin, nails are arranged as flat, hard, plate-like coverings located at the ends of toes and fingers. Nails consist of the (1) **nail plate**, also called the nail body; the (2) **lunula** (**LOO**-noo-lah), a pale or white half-moon-shaped area at the base of the nail plate; and the (3) **cuticle**, a narrow band of epidermal skin at the base and sides of the nail plate. Figure 4-3 highlights nail structures.

_____	3. dermis	c. produces sweat
_____	4. epidermis	d. flat, platelike coverings
_____	5. follicle	e. outermost skin layer
_____	6. hair	f. contains hair root
_____	7. lunula	g. provides skin color
_____	8. melanin	h. meshwork of cells with protein
_____	9. nail	i. area at the base of the nail
_____	10. sebaceous gland	j. band of skin around the nail plate
_____	11. sweat gland	k. provides support to the hair follicle

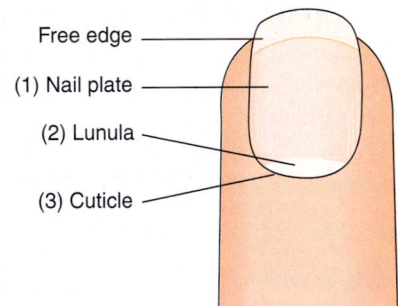

Figure 4-3   Structures of nails

EXERCISE 4-2

Match the structures in column 1 with the definitions in column 2.

COLUMN 1

_____   1. arrector pili

_____   2. cuticle

COLUMN 2

a. secretes sebum

b. "living" skin tissue

EXERCISE 4-3

Write the name of the skin structures shown in figure 4-4 on the spaces provided.

1. _____

2. _____

3. _____

4. _____

5. _____

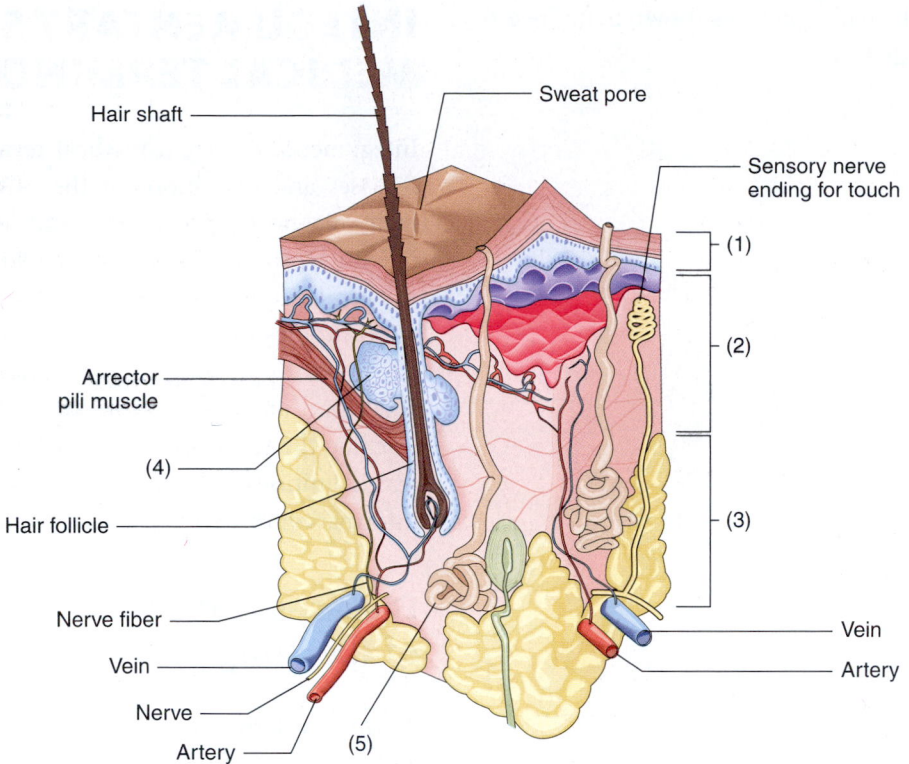

Figure 4-4   Label/name the structures of the skin

Write the name of the hair structures shown in figure 4-5 on the spaces provided.

6. _____

7. _____

8. _____

9. _____

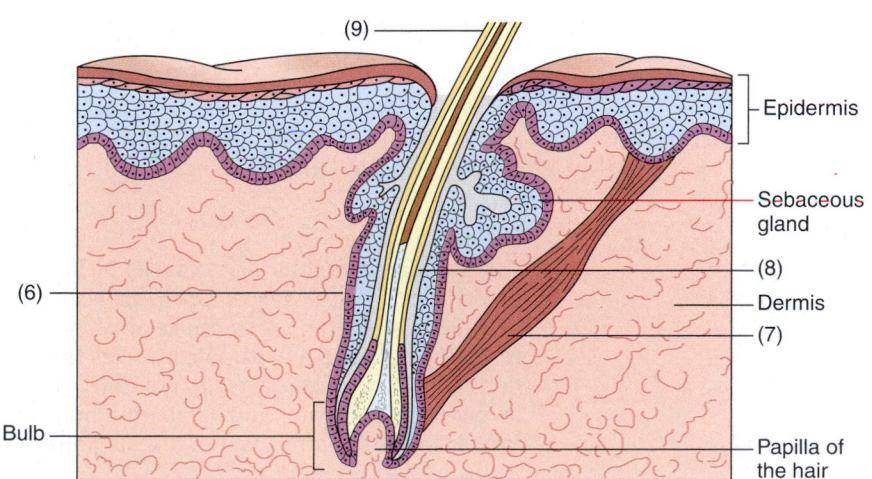

Figure 4-5   Label/name the structures of hair

continued

Write the name of the nail structures shown in figure 4-6 on the spaces provided.

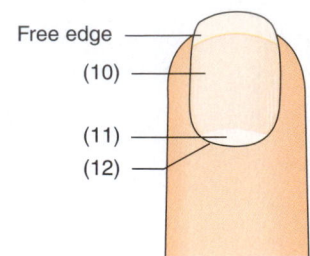

Free edge

(10)

(11)

(12)

Figure 4-6 Label/name the structures of nails

10. _____

11. _____

12. _____

INTEGUMENTARY SYSTEM MEDICAL TERMINOLOGY

Integumentary system medical terms are organized by diseases and conditions of the skin, glands, hair, and nails; diagnostic procedures and laboratory tests; and operative procedures. There are two categories of medical terminology exercises: (1) those designed to provide opportunities to learn the terms; and (2) those designed to provide opportunities to accurately assign diagnosis, procedure, and operative procedure codes. Exercises for learning the terms immediately follow the lists of terms and definitions. Coding exercises are available after the information related to medical coding.

Diseases and Conditions of the Integumentary System

The medical terms in table 4-2 are signs, symptoms, diseases, and conditions of the skin, glands, hair, and nails. Review the meaning of these terms and complete the exercises.

Table 4-2   Integumentary System Signs, Symptoms, Diseases, and Conditions

TERM WITH PRONUNCIATION	DEFINITION
abrasion (uh-**BRAY**-zhun)	scraping away of the skin; a scrape
acne, acne vulgaris (**AK**-nee vull-**GAIR**-is)	inflammatory disease of the sebaceous glands and hair follicles characterized by papules, pustules, and comedones
actinic keratosis (ak-**TIN**-ik **kair**-ah-**TOH**-sis)	precancerous skin condition related to excessive sunlight exposure
albinism (al-**BYN**-ism)	a congenital hereditary condition characterized by a lack of skin pigmentation
alopecia (**al**-oh-**PEE**-she-ah)	partial or complete loss of hair; also called baldness
anhidrosis (**an**-high-**DROH**-sis) an- = without, lack of hidr/o = sweat -osis = condition	a condition of sweat glands characterized by inadequate sweat production or an inability to produce sweat
bulla (**BOO**-lah)	a large blister
basal cell carcinoma (**BAY**-zal sell **kar**-sin-OH-mah) carcin- = cancer -oma = tumor	cancerous tumor of the basal cell layer of the epidermis occurring most often on areas exposed to the sun
burns	skin and subcutaneous injury caused by flame, heat, chemicals, gas, radiation, or electricity; *first-degree* or *superficial burn*, redness and swelling of the epidermis as in a sunburn; *second-degree* or *partial-thickness burn*, blistering, pink to red color, sensitive and painful, involves the epidermis and upper layers of the dermis as in quick contact with hot objects; *third-degree* or *full-thickness burn*, involves the epidermis and full dermis, may include subcutaneous and muscle tissue, appears charred, wet or dry, sunken, with a dry crust
callus (**CAL**-us)	a common thickening of the epidermis at the site of external pressure or friction
carbuncle (**KAR**-bung-kal)	skin infection characterized by a cluster of boils

continued

Table 4-2 (*continued*) Integumentary System Signs, Symptoms, Diseases, and Conditions

TERM WITH PRONUNCIATION	DEFINITION
cellulitis (**sell**-yoo-**LIGH**-tis)	acute infection of the skin and subcutaneous tissue characterized by heat, redness, pain, and swelling
cicatrix (**SIH**-kah-triks; or sih-**KAY**-triks)	a scar left by a healed wound
comedo (**KOM**-ee-doh)	acne lesion due to an accumulation of keratin and sebum in the opening of a hair follicle; *closed comedo,* a whitehead; *open comedo,* a blackhead
contusion (kon-**TOO**-zhun)	an injury characterized by pain, swelling, and discoloration of the skin without a break in the skin; a bruise
cyanosis (**sigh**-ah-**NOH**-sis) cyan/o = blue -osis = condition	bluish discoloration of the skin; may be a symptom of a lack of oxygen in the blood
dermatitis (**der**-mah-**TIGH**-tis) dermat/o = skin -itis = inflammation	inflammation of the skin; *contact dermatitis,* caused by contact with an irritant
diaphoresis (**digh**-ah-for-**EE**-sis)	excessive excretion of sweat due to increased body temperature, physical activity, heat exposure, and mental or emotional stress
ecchymosis (eh-kee-**MOH**-sis)	superficial discoloration caused by blood in the tissue; a bruise
eczema (**EGGS**-ih-mah)	inflammatory skin disorder characterized by redness, itching, vesicles, weeping, oozing, and crusting
edema (eh-**DEE**-mah)	abnormal swelling of tissue
erythema (**air**-ih-**THEE**-mah)	redness of the skin such as blushing or a mild sunburn
excoriation (**eks**-kor-ee-**AY**-shun)	an injury to the surface of the skin; a scratch
fissure (**FIH**-shur)	cracklike sore or groove in the skin
furuncle (**FIR**-ung-kal)	an inflamed hair follicle; a boil

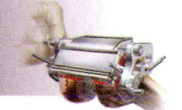

EXERCISE 4-4

Circle the term that best fits the definition or description.

1. a scrape — *contusion* or *abrasion*
2. large blister — *bulla* or *ecchymosis*
3. inflammation of the sebaceous glands — *acne vulgaris* or *actinic keratosis*
4. a scar left by a healed wound — *callus* or *cicatrix*
5. a bruise — *cyanosis* or *contusion*
6. a scratch — *abrasion* or *excoriation*
7. a boil — *furuncle* or *carbuncle*
8. redness of the skin — *diaphoresis* or *erythema*
9. inflammation of the skin and subcutaneous tissue — *dermatitis* or *cellulitis*

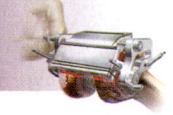

EXERCISE 4-5

Replace the italicized phrase with the correct medical term.

1. Roland was diagnosed with a/an *hereditary lack of skin pigmentation.*
2. Mr. Basu's *bluish discoloration of the skin* was caused by a lung disease.
3. Peter went to a dermatologist because he had a/an *cluster of boils.*
4. One should never squeeze a/an *blackhead.*
5. Rosita had a/an *inflamed hair follicle* that caused her discomfort.
6. When Moses meets new people he experiences *excessive sweating.*

continued

7. The podiatrist removed the *thickened epidermis* from LaQueesha's heel.

8. *Inflammation of the skin* may be caused by touching poison ivy.

9. *Baldness* can affect men and women.

10. Reducing salt intake may help alleviate *abnormal swelling of tissue*.

11. The *inability to produce sweat* may affect body temperature.

EXERCISE 4-6

Write a short answer.

1. Briefly describe the difference between *basal cell carcinoma* and *actinic keratosis*.

2. List and describe the three levels of *burns*.

3. Name the medical terms that mean *bruise*.

4. What are the characteristics of *eczema*?

Review the medical terms in table 4-3 and complete the exercises.

Table 4-3 Integumentary System Signs, Symptoms, Diseases, and Conditions

hemangioma (**heem**-an-jee-**OH**-mah) hem/o = blood angi/o = vessel -oma = tumor	a benign reddish purple tumor of blood vessels on the surface of the skin
herpes simplex (**HER**-peez **SIM**-plex)	a viral infection that usually occurs on the skin near the lips; also called a fever blister or a cold sore
herpes varicella (**HER**-peez var-ih-**SELL**-ah)	a highly contagious viral infection usually seen in children; commonly called chickenpox
herpes zoster (**HER**-peez **ZOSS**-ter)	a viral infection characterized by painful skin eruptions that follow a nerve path; commonly called shingles
hirsutism (**HUR**-soot-izm)	excessive body hair in a male distribution pattern, occurring in women
impetigo (im-peh-**TIGH**-goh)	highly contagious bacterial superficial skin infection characterized by vesicles and pustules
jaundice (**JAWN**-dis)	yellow discoloration of the skin
Kaposi sarcoma (**KAP**-oh-see sar-**KOH**-mah) sarc/o = flesh -oma = tumor	a cancerous growth that begins as soft, purple-brown papules on the feet and gradually spreads throughout the skin
keloid (**KEE**-loyd)	abnormally large, raised, or thickened scar
laceration (lass-er-**AY**-shun)	a tear or cut in the skin
lesion (**LEE**-zhun)	any damage to the skin and tissues caused by trauma or disease
lichen planus (**LIGH**-ken **PLAY**-nus)	a chronic skin condition characterized by itching and small, flat, purplish papules and patches that exhibit gray lines
macule (**MAK**-yool)	small, flat discoloration of the skin
malignant melanoma (mah-**LIG**-nant **mell**-ah-**NOH**-mah)	cancerous skin tumor originating from the melanocytes of a mole, freckles, or pigmented skin; skin cancer
nevus (pl. nevi) (**NEE**-vus; pl. **NEE**-vigh)	pigmented area present at birth; mole, birthmark
onychomalacia (**on**-ee-koh-mah-**LAY**-shee-ah) onych/o = nail -malacia = softening	softening of the nails
onychomycosis (**on**-ee-koh-my-**KOH**-sis) onych/o = nail myc/o = fungus -osis = condition	fungal infection of the nails

continued

Table 4-3 (*continued*) Integumentary System Signs, Symptoms, Diseases, and Conditions

pachyderma (pack-ee-**DER**-mah) pachy- = thickening derma/o = skin -a = noun ending	thickening of the skin
pallor (**PAL**-or)	paleness
papule (**PAP**-yool)	small, solid, raised lesion of the skin; commonly called a pimple
paronychia (par-oh-**NIK**-ee-ah) para- = around, near, beside onych/o = nail -ia = condition	inflammation of the fold of skin surrounding the fingernails
pediculosis (peh-**dik**-yoo-**LOH**-sis)	lice infestation associated with the skin and hair
petechia (pl. petechiae) (peh-**TEE**-kee-ah; pl. peh-**TEE**-kee-ee)	pinpoint bleeding of the skin
pilonidal cyst (**pigh**-loh-**NIGH**-dal)	a closed sac containing hair located in the sacrococcygeal (sacrum and coccyx of the spinal column) area; if it becomes acutely infected it must be drained and removed
plantar warts (**PLAN**-tar)	benign, circumscribed, elevated skin lesions caused by the human papilloma virus; occur either singly or in clusters on the soles of the feet
pressure ulcer	open lesion of the skin characterized by a breakdown of the skin and underlying tissue due to constant pressure to bony prominences under the skin and an inadequate blood supply to the affected area; also called pressure sore or decubitus ulcer

EXERCISE 4-7

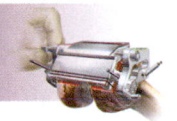

Circle the term that best fits the definition or description.

1. a tear or cut in the skin   *lesion* or *laceration*

2. small, flat discoloration of the skin   *macule* or *papule*

3. skin cancer   *malignant melanoma* or *Kaposi sarcoma*

4. chickenpox   *herpes zoster* or *herpes varicella*

5. yellow discoloration of the skin   *pallor* or *jaundice*

6. cold sore, fever blister   *herpes simplex* or *herpes zoster*

7. pinpoint bleeding in the skin   *hemangioma* or *petechia*

8. benign lesion caused by the human papilloma virus   *plantar wart* or *papule*

9. lice infestation   *impetigo* or *pediculosis*

10. highly contagious bacterial superficial skin infection   *impetigo* or *pediculosis*

EXERCISE 4-8

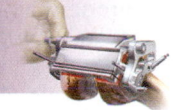

Replace the italicized phrase with the correct medical term.

1. Roger was born with a/an *birthmark*.

2. Marusha was disappointed to hear that *shingles* can reoccur.

3. Mrs. Washington was concerned about her son's *paleness*.

4. *Decubitus ulcers* may be a problem for individuals who are confined to bed.

5. Betty's dermatologist examined a large *pimple* on her left cheek.

6. A/an *raised or thickened scar* may be the result of a deep laceration.

7. Myroslav went to a dermatologist to have several *moles* removed from his chest.

8. A hormone imbalance may cause *body hair in a male pattern on a woman*.

EXERCISE 4-9

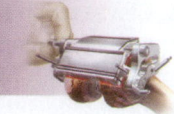

Write the medical term for each definition.

1. inflammation of the fold of skin surrounding the fingernails _____

2. a benign reddish purple tumor of blood vessels _____

3. thickening of the skin _____

4. fungal infection of the nails _____

5. softening of the nails _____

6. small, flat, purplish papules and patches with gray lines _____

7. sac containing hair located in the sacrococcygeal area _____

Review the medical terms in table 4-4 and complete the exercises.

Table 4-4 Integumentary System Signs, Symptoms, Diseases, and Conditions

TERM WITH PRONUNCIATION	DEFINITION
pruritus (proo-**RIGH**-tis)	severe itching
psoriasis (soh-**RIGH**-ah-sis)	chronic skin condition characterized by dry, silvery scales covering red lesions
purpura (**PER**-pyoo-rah)	large bruises under the skin associated with hemorrhages into tissue
pustule (**PUST**-yool)	circumscribed elevation of the skin containing pus
pyoderma (**pigh**-oh-**DERM**-ah)	any purulent (producing or containing pus) skin disease
pyoderma gangrenosum (**pigh**-oh-**DERM**-ah **gang**-reh-**NOH**-sum)	a purulent skin lesion characterized by irregular, blue-red ulcerations; the edges of the lesions are often painful
scabies (**SKAY**-beez)	a skin infection caused by infestation of the itch mite
scleroderma (sklair-oh-**DER**-mah) sclero- = hardening derm/o = skin -a = noun ending	hardening of the skin
sebaceous cyst (she-**BAY**-shush)	a cyst composed of sebum and epithelial debris that forms in the duct of a sebaceous gland; also called an epidermoid cyst
seborrhea (seb-oh-**REE**-ah) seb/o = sebum -(r)rhea = flow, discharge	excessive discharge of sebum, the oil produced by sebaceous glands
seborrheic dermatitis (seb-oh-**REE**-ik derm-ah-**TIGH**-tis) seb/o = sebum -(r)rhea = flow, discharge -ic = pertaining to dermat/o = skin -itis = inflammation	an inflammatory condition in areas where the oil glands are most prevalent, such as the scalp, sides of the nose, and area behind the ears; characterized by redness of the skin and greasy, yellowish crusting or scales; a common form occurs in infants and is called cradle cap
seborrheic keratosis (seb-oh-**REE**-ik kair-ah-**TOH**-sis) seb/o = sebum -(r)rhea = flow, discharge -ic = pertaining to kerat/o = hard, horny -osis = condition	a brown or waxy yellow wartlike lesion, loosely attached to the surface of the skin; also called senile warts
skin tag	a small brownish or flesh-colored outgrowth of skin; occurs frequently on the neck; also called cutaneous papilloma
squamous cell carcinoma (**SKWAY**-mus sell **kar**-sin-**OH**-mah) squam/o = scale -ous = like, pertaining to carcin- = cancer -oma = tumor	cancer of the squamous or scalelike cells of the skin; the lesions appear as a firm, flesh-colored or red papule, may have a crusted appearance, and may bleed or become ulcerated

continued

Table 4-4 (continued) Integumentary System Signs, Symptoms, Diseases, and Conditions

TERM WITH PRONUNCIATION	DEFINITION
tinea (**TIN**-ee-ah)	fungal infection of the skin; ringworm
tinea capitis (**TIN**-ee-ah **KAP**-ih-tiss)	fungal infection of the scalp
tinea corporis (**TIN**-ee-ah **KOR**-por-is)	fungal infection of the body
tinea cruris (**TIN**-ee-ah **KROO**-ris)	fungal infection of the groin; jock itch
tinea pedis (**TIN**-ee-ah **PEE**-dis)	fungal infection of the foot; athlete's foot
urticaria (**er**-tih-**KAY**-ree-ah)	skin eruption of wheals; hives
verruca (ver-**ROO**-kah)	elevated skin lesion caused by the human papilloma virus; a wart; a common wart is called *verruca vulgaris*
vesicle (**VESS**-ih-kul)	a small skin elevation filled with clear liquid; a blister
vitiligo (**vih**-tih-**LIGH**-goh)	skin condition characterized by irregular white patches of skin that are totally lacking pigmentation due to the destruction of melanocytes
wheal (**WHEEL**)	transient, round itchy elevation of the skin; one hive
xeroderma (**zee**-roh-**DERM**-ah) xer/o = dry derm/o = skin -a = noun ending	a chronic condition characterized by rough, dry skin

EXERCISE 4-10
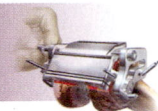

Circle the term that best fits the definition or description.

1. skin infection caused by the itch mite — *scabies* or *tinea*
2. cradle cap — *seborrheic keratosis* or *seborrheic dermatitis*
3. severe itching — *psoriasis* or *pruritus*
4. large bruises under the skin — *purpura* or *vitiligo*
5. wart — *urticaria* or *verruca*
6. one hive — *wheal* or *pustule*
7. jock itch — *tinea cruris* or *tinea corporis*
8. fungal infection of the head — *tinea corporis* or *tinea capitis*
9. a blister — *pustule* or *vesicle*

EXERCISE 4-11
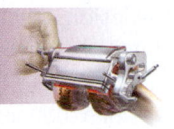

Replace the italicized phrase with the correct medical term.

1. Chi developed *athlete's foot* after using the shower at the public swimming pool.

2. Mr. Cholovek was diagnosed with *cancer of the scalelike cells of the skin.*

3. Julie was concerned about the *irregular white patches* of the skin on her hands.

4. *Hives* may be caused by a food allergy.

5. A/an *fungal infection of the body* may be treated with a topical medication.

6. *Small brownish outgrowths of skin* are often removed with little or no discomfort.

7. Marie's *purulent and irregular skin ulceration* was treated with prednisone injections.

EXERCISE 4-12
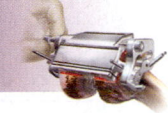

Write the medical term for each definition.

1. chronic condition of rough, dry skin _____

2. excessive discharge of sebum _____

3. chronic skin condition with dry, silvery scales _____

4. hardening of the skin _____

5. senile warts _____

continued

6. circumscribed elevation of the skin containing pus _____

7. a cyst composed of sebum and epithelial debris _____

8. any purulent skin disease _____

Integumentary System Operative and Diagnostic Procedure and Treatment Terms

Review the operative and diagnostic procedure and treatment terms in table 4-5 and complete the exercises.

Table 4-5 Integumentary System Operative and Diagnostic Procedure and Treatment Terms

TERM WITH PRONUNCIATION	DEFINITION
Botox injection (Botox is a registered trade name for botulinum toxin)	a nonsurgical cosmetic procedure during which a minute dose of botulinum toxin is injected into forehead creases, frown lines, and crow's feet (wrinkles at the corner of the eyes) to temporarily reduce or eliminate wrinkles; the toxin blocks nerve impulses, temporarily paralyzing the facial muscles associated with wrinkles; botulinum toxin is one of the most poisonous naturally occurring substances in the world
collagen injection (**KALL**-ah-jen)	a procedure used in cosmetic surgery during which the protein collagen is injected into the lips or other facial areas
cryosurgery (**krigh**-oh-**SER**-jer-ee)	use of extreme cold to freeze and destroy unwanted tissue
debridement (dah-**BREED**-mon)	removal of debris and dead, damaged, and necrotic tissue from a wound to prevent infection and promote healing
dermabrasion (derm-ah-**BRAY**-zhun)	removal of skin blemishes, wrinkles, scars, and tattoos, using mechanical or chemical methods
dermatome (**DER**-mah-tohm) dermat/o = skin -tome = instrument for cutting	an instrument for cutting skin
dermatoplasty (der-**MAT**-oh-**plass**-tee) dermat/o = skin -plasty = surgical repair	surgical repair of the skin; skin transplant
electrodesiccation (ee-**lek**-troh-**dess**-ih-**KAY**-shun)	destruction of tissue by burning or drying the tissue with an electric current; primarily used to destroy superficial growths such as warts, but may also be used on deeper tissue
incision and drainage (I & D)	procedure to remove the contents of a cyst; the cyst is incised (cut into) and the contents are drained or suctioned away
liposuction (**LIP**-oh-suck-shun) lip/o = fat	removal of subcutaneous fat (adipose) tissue by aspiration through a suction instrument to alter body contours
Mohs surgery (**MOHZ**)	surgical procedure for removing malignant skin growths in mapped layers that involves the removal of the visible and root portions of the malignancy
rhytidectomy (**rit**-ih-**DEK**-toh-mee) rhytid/o = wrinkles -ectomy = surgical removal; excision	excision or removal of excess skin for the elimination of wrinkles; also called a face-lift
rhytidoplasty (**RIT**-ih-doh-**plass**-tee) rhytid/o = wrinkles -plasty = surgical repair	tightening of facial skin to remove wrinkles and make the skin appear firm and smooth
skin biopsy	removal of a small piece of tissue from skin lesions for microscopic examination; *excisional biopsy,* removal of the complete tumor or lesion; *incisional biopsy,* removal of a portion of the lesion; *punch biopsy,* removal of a small specimen of the lesion; *shave biopsy,* removal of portions of a raised lesion with a scalpel or razor blade
skin graft	procedure of placing healthy skin (donor tissue) on a lesion or site (recipient site) that is unable to regenerate skin, as in third-degree (full-thickness) burns; *autografting,* donor tissue is taken from one part of the body and placed on another part of the body of the same individual; *homografting* or *allografting,* the donor tissue is taken from a cadaver; *heterograft* or *xenograft,* the donor tissue is obtained from an animal

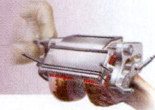

EXERCISE 4-13

Write the medical term for each definition.

1. surgical repair of the skin; skin transplant _____
2. an instrument for cutting skin _____
3. excision or removal of excess skin; face-lift _____
4. use of extreme cold to freeze and destroy unwanted tissue _____
5. removal of skin blemishes using mechanical or chemical methods _____
6. tightening of facial skin to remove wrinkles _____
7. removal of debris and dead, damaged, and necrotic tissue from a wound _____
8. destruction of tissue by burning or drying with an electric current _____
9. removal of malignant skin growths in mapped layers _____

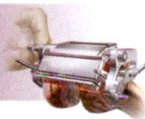

EXERCISE 4-14

Write a short answer for each question.

1. What is the difference between Botox and collagen injections?
2. Briefly define the three types of skin grafting.
   a. autografting
   b. homografting (allografting)
   c. heterograft (xenograft)
3. What is the difference between an *excisional biopsy* and an *incisional biopsy*?
4. What is the purpose of liposuction?
5. Write out the abbreviation I & D and include a brief description of the procedure.

ABBREVIATIONS

Integumentary system abbreviations are listed in table 4-6. Practice writing out the abbreviations with a brief definition for each phrase or term.

Table 4-6 Abbreviations

ABBREVIATION	MEANING
Bx; bx	biopsy
decub.	decubitus ulcer
ID	intradermal
I & D	incision and drainage
SC; subQ	subcutaneous

INTEGUMENTARY SYSTEM MEDICAL CODING

To successfully complete the exercises in this section, the ICD-9-CM volumes 1, 2, and 3, and the CPT (Current Procedural Terminology) coding reference must be readily available. The information in this section is presented as follows:

- An introduction to ICD-9-CM, chapter 12, "Diseases of the Skin and Subcutaneous Tissue"
- ICD-9-CM diagnostic coding exercises
- A summary of ICD-9-CM coding conventions that apply to integumentary procedures
- ICD-9-CM procedure coding exercises
- A summary of the CPT Integumentary System coding guidelines
- CPT coding exercises

Students are *strongly* encouraged to review the information at the beginning of the ICD-9-CM and CPT coding references. Commercial publishers include instructions on how to use the reference, the ICD-9-CM official coding conventions, additional conventions used by the publisher, and the ICD-9-CM Official Guidelines for

Coding and Reporting. Some publishers include the three ICD-9-CM volumes in one book and put the *Alphabetic Index* (volume 2) at the beginning of the reference.

The *Introduction* to CPT includes detailed instructions for using this code book, an index to the illustrations throughout the book, and anatomical illustrations of the major structures of the body systems.

ICD-9-CM Volume 1, Chapter 12, Diseases of the Skin and Subcutaneous Tissue (680–709)

Integumentary system diseases are coded to ICD-9-CM chapter 12, "Diseases of the Skin and Subcutaneous Tissue." This chapter includes the following major sections:

- **Infections of Skin and Subcutaneous Tissue (680–686).** The codes in this section include infections related to carbuncles and furuncles, cellulitis, abscesses, impetigo, pilonidal cyst, and other local infections of the skin and subcutaneous tissue.

  NOTE: The *exclusion note* at the beginning of this section tells the coder that certain infections of the skin such as herpes and viral warts are coded to chapter 1, "Infectious and Parasitic Diseases."

- **Other Inflammatory Conditions of Skin and Subcutaneous Tissue (690–698).** The codes in this section are related to dermatitis, erythematous conditions, psoriasis, lichen, and pruritus.

- **Other Diseases of the Skin and Subcutaneous Tissue (700–709).** The codes in this section are related to corns, calluses, keratosis, and disorders of the nails, hair, and glands.

Several *exclusion notes* direct the coder to other chapters in ICD-9-CM such as congenital conditions, carcinoma in situ (cancer confined to one site), and some conditions related to the ear, eyelid, lips, mouth, and internal structures of the nose. Injuries to the skin such as abrasions, burns, excoriations, and lacerations are coded to chapter 17, "Injuries and Poisonings."

EXERCISE 4-15

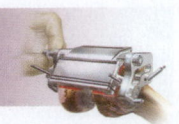

Write a brief definition for each diagnosis. Identify the main term in the diagnostic statement and assign the correct ICD-9-CM code(s).

1. Dermatitis due to contact with silver necklace _____

   DEFINITION: _____

   MAIN TERM: _____

   ICD-9-CM CODE: _____

2. Full-thickness burn of the cheek with partial loss

   DEFINITION: _____

   MAIN TERM: _____

   ICD-9-CM CODE: _____

3. Abscessed pilonidal cyst

   DEFINITION: _____

   MAIN TERM: _____

   ICD-9-CM CODE: _____

4. Actinic keratosis due to excessive exposure to sunlight

   DEFINITION: _____

   MAIN TERM: _____

   ICD-9-CM CODE: _____

5. Pyoderma gangrenosum, left lower leg

   DEFINITION: _____

   MAIN TERM: _____

   ICD-9-CM CODE: _____

6. Necrotic carbuncle of the axilla

   DEFINITION: _____

   MAIN TERM: _____

   ICD-9-CM CODE: _____

7. Pustular eczema, both hands

   DEFINITION: _____

   MAIN TERM: _____

   ICD-9-CM CODE: _____

8. Onychomalacia, left thumb

   DEFINITION: _____

   MAIN TERM: _____

   ICD-9-CM CODE: _____

9. Onychomycosis due to microsporum infection

   DEFINITION: _____

   MAIN TERM: _____

   ICD-9-CM CODE: _____

10. Three-inch laceration of the right forearm

   DEFINITION: _____

   MAIN TERM: _____

   ICD-9-CM CODE: _____

11. Pediculosis (head lice)

   DEFINITION: _____

   MAIN TERM: _____

   ICD-9-CM CODE: _____

12. Plantar warts, sole of left foot

   DEFINITION: _____

   MAIN TERM: _____

   ICD-9-CM CODE: _____

13. Senile warts, neck and chest

   DEFINITION: _____

   MAIN TERM: _____

   ICD-9-CM CODE: _____

14. Acne vulgaris

   DEFINITION: _____

   MAIN TERM: _____

   ICD-9-CM CODE: _____

15. Basal cell carcinoma, right cheek, primary site

   DEFINITION: _____

   MAIN TERM: _____

   ICD-9-CM CODE: _____

16. Malignant melanoma, external nose, primary site

   DEFINITION: _____

   MAIN TERM: _____

   ICD-9-CM CODE: _____

17. Sebaceous cyst of the scalp

   DEFINITION: _____

   MAIN TERM: _____

   ICD-9-CM CODE: _____

18. Pressure ulcer, third stage, right buttock

   DEFINITION: _____

   MAIN TERM: _____

   ICD-9-CM CODE: _____

19. Athlete's foot

   DEFINITION: _____

   MAIN TERM: _____

   ICD-9-CM CODE: _____

20. Vitiligo, fingers of both hands

   DEFINITION: _____

   MAIN TERM: _____

   ICD-9-CM CODE: _____

21. Febrile alopecia

   DEFINITION: _____

   MAIN TERM: _____

   ICD-9-CM CODE: _____

22. Hirsutism, acquired

   DEFINITION: _____

   MAIN TERM: _____

   ICD-9-CM CODE: _____

23. Herpes zoster (shingles)

   DEFINITION: _____

   MAIN TERM: _____

   ICD-9-CM CODE: _____

24. Thermogenic anhidrosis

   DEFINITION: _____

   MAIN TERM: _____

   ICD-9-CM CODE: _____

25. Psoriasis, elbows and knees

   DEFINITION: _____

   MAIN TERM: _____

   ICD-9-CM CODE: _____

ICD-9-CM Volume 3, Chapter 15, Operations on the Integumentary System (85–86)

Integumentary system operations and some therapeutic treatments are coded to ICD-9-CM volume 3, chapter 15 "Operations on the Integumentary System." The major categories in this chapter include the following:

- **Operations on the breast (85).** The breasts are actually an appendage of the skin and function as milk glands. Procedures related to the breast are presented in chapter 11, "Female Reproductive System," of this text.

- **Operations on the skin and subcutaneous tissue (86).** Codes in this category include incision, excision, destruction, skin grafting, and other repair and reconstruction of the skin and subcutaneous tissue.

Codes related to destruction of the skin and subcutaneous tissue are listed in the volume 3 index under the main term *destruction*. Other main terms for integumentary system procedures may include *closure, drainage, excision, incision,* and *removal.*

Volume 3, chapter 16, "Miscellaneous Diagnostic and Therapeutic Procedures" (87–99) also has codes that apply to the integumentary system. Codes related to microscopic examination of specimens taken from skin and subcutaneous tissue, hypodermal and subdermal injections, and ultraviolet light therapy may apply to diagnostic and therapeutic procedures of the integumentary system.

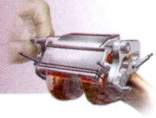

EXERCISE 4-16

Write a brief definition for each operative, treatment, and diagnostic procedure term. Identify the main term and assign the ICD-9-CM code(s).

1. Cryosurgery to remove three nevi

   DEFINITION: _____

   MAIN TERM: _____

   ICD-9-CM CODE(S): _____

2. Rhytidectomy, facial

   DEFINITION: _____

   MAIN TERM: _____

   ICD-9-CM CODE(S): _____

3. Incision and drainage of a sebaceous cyst

   DEFINITION: _____

   MAIN TERM: _____

   ICD-9-CM CODE(S): _____

4. Liposuction of the arms

   DEFINITION: _____

   MAIN TERM: _____

   ICD-9-CM CODE(S): _____

5. Mohs surgery

   DEFINITION: _____

   MAIN TERM: _____

   ICD-9-CM CODE(S): _____

6. Laser dermabrasion of facial scars

   DEFINITION: _____

   MAIN TERM: _____

   ICD-9-CM CODE(S): _____

7. Electrodesiccation of three warts, left hand

   DEFINITION: _____

   MAIN TERM: _____

   ICD-9-CM CODE(S): _____

8. Excisional debridement of a burn wound

   DEFINITION: _____

   MAIN TERM: _____

   ICD-9-CM CODE(S): _____

9. Skin graft (autografting) of the hand, full thickness

   DEFINITION: _____

   MAIN TERM: _____

   ICD-9-CM CODE(S): _____

10. Biopsy of a suspicious mole, left arm

    DEFINITION: _____

    MAIN TERM: _____

    ICD-9-CM CODE(S): _____

Current Procedural Terminology (CPT) Integumentary System Codes (10021–19499)

CPT integumentary system codes are located in the Surgery section and in the Medicine section. The Surgery guidelines provide important information for all subsections of the Surgery section. Review the guidelines in the CPT manual and in chapter 3 of this text. There are additional and extensive instructional notes throughout the Integumentary System subsection of the Surgery section. The Integumentary System subsection includes these major categories:

- **Skin, Subcutaneous and Accessory Structures (10040–11646).** Codes in this category cover procedures like incision and drainage, excision and debridement, paring or cutting, removal of skin tags, shaving of epidermal or dermal lesions, excision of benign lesions, and excision of malignant lesions.

- **Nails (11719–11765).** Codes in this category include various procedures related to fingernails and toenails.

- **Repair (Closure) (12001–16036).** This category is extensive and includes codes for three types of repair: (1) *simple repair,* the wound is superficial involving the epidermis, dermis, or subcutaneous tissue with minimal involvement of deeper structures, and requires a one-layer closure; (2) *intermediate repair,* the wound includes all of the elements of simple repair, requires closure of one or more of the deeper layers of subcutaneous and nonmuscle fascia, or single-layer closure of heavily contaminated wounds with extensive cleaning or removal of particulate matter; and (3) *complex repair,* includes repair of wounds requiring more than layered closure such as scar revision, debridement, and other extensive repair procedures. The coder *must* read and follow the instructional notes to ensure accurate code selection. Other subcategories in this category include adjacent tissue transfer or rearrangement, free skin grafts, flaps (skin and/or deep tissue), pressure ulcers (decubitus ulcers), and burns.

- **Destruction (17000–17999).** Codes in this category cover procedures related to the destruction of benign or premalignant lesions, destruction of malignant lesions, and Mohs surgery. The instructional notes describe the types of destruction included in this category, and list procedures that are coded to other categories or sections.

- **Breast (19000–19499).** Since the breasts are actually an appendage of the skin, CPT codes related to the breasts are included in the Integumentary System subsection of the Surgery section. Coding exercises related to the breast are covered in chapter 11 of this text.

Integumentary procedures are also coded to the Medicine section. Allergy testing (95004–95056), active wound care management (97597–97606), and special dermatological procedures (96900–96999) have codes related to the integumentary system.

EXERCISE 4-17

Identify the main term and assign the correct CPT code(s) for each procedure.

1. Cryosurgery to remove three nevi
   MAIN TERM: _____
   CPT CODE(S): _____

2. Rhytidectomy of the cheek, chin, and neck
   MAIN TERM: _____
   CPT CODE(S): _____

3. Incision and drainage of a sebaceous cyst
   MAIN TERM: _____
   CPT CODE(S): _____

4. Liposuction of the arms
   MAIN TERM: _____
   CPT CODE(S): _____

5. Mohs surgery, four specimens, left arm
   MAIN TERM: _____
   CPT CODE(S): _____

continued

6. Superficial dermabrasion, tattoo removal left forearm

   MAIN TERM: _____

   CPT CODE(S): _____

7. Electrodesiccation of three warts, left hand

   MAIN TERM: _____

   CPT CODE(S): _____

8. Debridement of a burn wound, without anesthesia, left lower extremity

   MAIN TERM: _____

   CPT CODE(S): _____

9. Skin graft (autografting) of the hand, full thickness, 18 sq cm

   MAIN TERM: _____

   CPT CODE(S): _____

10. Biopsy of a suspicious mole, left arm

    MAIN TERM: _____

    CPT CODE(S): _____

11. Incision and drainage, pilonidal cyst, simple

    MAIN TERM: _____

    CPT CODE(S): _____

12. Removal of 25 skin tags, neck and upper chest

    MAIN TERM: _____

    CPT CODE(S): _____

13. Excision of a sacral pressure ulcer, primary suture

    MAIN TERM: _____

    CPT CODE(S): _____

14. Total facial dermabrasion, acne scarring

    MAIN TERM: _____

    CPT CODE(S): _____

■ SUMMARY

This chapter covered medical terms related to the integumentary system, which includes the skin, glands, hair, and nails. Integumentary system diagnoses and procedures were identified and defined. Integumentary system diseases and conditions are coded to ICD-9-CM volume 1, chapter 12, "Diseases of the Skin and Subcutaneous Tissue" and chapter 17, "Injuries and Poisonings." Integumentary procedures are coded to ICD-9-CM volume 3, chapter 7, "Operations on the Integumentary System" and chapter 16, "Miscellaneous Diagnostic and Therapeutic Procedures."

Current Procedural Terminology (CPT) integumentary procedure codes are found in the CPT Surgery section, Integumentary System subsection, and the Medicine section.

■ CHAPTER REVIEW

Read each medical note. Write the diagnosis(es) and identify the main term in the diagnostic statement. Assign the ICD-9-CM diagnostic code(s).

CASE 1

Roberto was seen in the office for dermatitis and pruritus that bothers him and keeps him awake most of the night. A prescription for each problem was called in to his local pharmacy. He will try the ointments for three days. He was instructed to call back in three days if there is no improvement.

DIAGNOSIS(ES): _____

MAIN TERM(S): _____

ICD-9-CM DIAGNOSIS CODE(S): _____

CASE 2

Marianne is a 21-year-old female who is seen today for follow-up for psoriasis. The topical medication prescribed last month is working fine, as long as she applies it at least twice a day. A new prescription was written and she will schedule a follow-up in two months.

DIAGNOSIS(ES): _____

MAIN TERM(S): _____

ICD-9-CM DIAGNOSIS CODE(S): _____

CASE 3

Ricardo presents with an infected wound of the forearm. He states he obtained a superficial laceration about a "week or so ago" when he was "goofing around" with his friend. Culture of the wound was positive for staphylococcus. He received appropriate antibiotic therapy for cellulitis and will return in three days.

DIAGNOSIS(ES): _____

MAIN TERM(S): _____

ICD-9-CM DIAGNOSIS CODE(S): _____

CASE 4

Henry is seen as a consult to assess a rather large keloid scar on his abdomen. He was traveling in remote areas of South America and sustained a rather serious laceration. Medical care was limited and although the wound healed, he is very unhappy with "this huge scar." Options were discussed for scar reduction. He decided to study the risks and benefits and call within one week with his final decision.

DIAGNOSIS(ES): _____

MAIN TERM(S): _____

ICD-9-CM DIAGNOSIS CODE(S): _____

CASE 5

Betsy is a pleasant 10-year-old child who is seen today for assessment of the blisters and bullae that appear on her face and neck. At first her mother thought she was "coming down with chickenpox." The ruptured blisters subsequently present as crusty, yellow lesions. On physical examination of the lesions, impetigo is the presumed diagnosis. We will try a topical ointment for five days. If there is no improvement within that time, an oral antibiotic is necessary. Her mother was instructed to call in a progress report in three days.

DIAGNOSIS(ES): _____

MAIN TERM(S): _____

ICD-9-CM DIAGNOSIS CODE(S): _____

CASE 6

TaWanda is home from college and presents with dermatitis-type lesions scattered over her entire body. She had been using an over-the-counter anti-itching preparation until she arrived at home. She denies ingesting anything unusual, coming in contact with poison ivy, or a past history of a similar outbreak. She stated that she ran out of her own laundry detergent and borrowed some from a friend in her dorm. According to her, this is the "only thing" that is different from her usual activities. She was advised to wash all of her clothing in her regular detergent, as this appears to be a case of contact dermatitis due to detergents. If the dermatitis doesn't clear up in five days, we will move forward with allergy testing.

DIAGNOSIS(ES): _____

MAIN TERM(S): _____

ICD-9-CM DIAGNOSIS CODE(S): _____

CASE 7

Elmer Mattson is seen today for assessment of a pigmented, ulcerative lesion on his forehead. On visual examination, the provisional diagnosis is actinic keratosis.

DIAGNOSIS(ES): _____

MAIN TERM(S): _____

ICD-9-CM DIAGNOSIS CODE(S): _____

CASE 8

Nhu is a 55-year-old male who presents with a skin fissure located on the back of the right leg, behind the knee. A small amount of exudate was cultured and is positive for streptococcus. He left with a sample of a topical bacteriostat and will call in three days if there is no improvement.

DIAGNOSIS(ES): _____

MAIN TERM(S): _____

ICD-9-CM DIAGNOSIS CODE(S): _____

CASE 9

John was admitted to Bell Hospital with cellulitis of the left lower leg due to a scratch which became infected. He received Claforan and bed rest. The lesion is improved. He is discharged today on Keflex 250 mg q.i.d. to be taken orally for the next four days. An office visit follow-up is scheduled a week from today.

DIAGNOSIS(ES): _____

MAIN TERM(S): _____

ICD-9-CM DIAGNOSIS CODE(S): _____

Read the procedure note, operative report, and discharge summary excerpts. Write the diagnosis(es) and the ICD-9-CM diagnosis(es) code. Write the name of the procedure and the main term. Assign the ICD-9-CM procedure code(s).

CASE 10

PREOPERATIVE DIAGNOSIS: Full-thickness burn of the left lower leg from the knee to the ankle.

POSTOPERATIVE DIAGNOSIS: Full-thickness burn of the left lower leg from the knee to the ankle.

OPERATION: Extensive excision and debridement of the burn, left lower leg. Application of split-thickness skin graft. Total area of the graft is 2000 sq cm.

PROCEDURE: Adequate general anesthesia was achieved and the patient was placed in the supine position. The burn wound was totally excised, including excision of the muscle, for a full-thickness excision. The wound was irrigated. A skin graft was taken from the patient's upper thigh. The graft was meshed and applied to the burn wound, with satisfactory coverage. A pressure dressing was applied to the graft, and the donor site was appropriately dressed. The leg was immobilized in a splint. Sponge and needle count correct times two. The patient tolerated the procedure well and was sent to the recovery room in satisfactory condition. Estimated blood loss was 200 cc.

DIAGNOSIS: _____

ICD-9-CM CODE: _____

PROCEDURE(S): _____

MAIN TERM(S): _____

ICD-9-CM PROCEDURE CODE(S): _____

CASE 11

PREOPERATIVE DIAGNOSIS: 4.1 cm infected sebaceous cyst, back; 2.5 cm infected sebaceous cyst, posterior neck.

POSTOPERATIVE DIAGNOSIS: 4.1 cm infected sebaceous cyst, back; 2.5 cm infected sebaceous cyst, posterior neck.

OFFICE SURGERY: Excision, 4.1 cm benign cyst, back. Excision, 2.5 cm benign cyst, neck.

DETAILS: The patient was placed in the prone position and the back and posterior neck were prepared with Betadine scrub and solution. Sterile towels were applied in the usual fashion, and 0.25% Marcaine was injected subcutaneously in a linear fashion transversely over each of the cysts. The lower cyst on the back was excised and the cavity was irrigated with copious amounts of Marcaine solutions. The skin edges were loosely reapproximated throughout with 3-0 nylon suture. Following this, Marcaine was injected around the superior cyst on the neck and the cyst was completely excised. The wound was irrigated with Marcaine and packed with iodoform, and sterile dressings were applied. The patient was released with written and verbal instructions, as well as Tylenol #3 for pain. She will return in three days for packing removal.

DIAGNOSIS: _____

ICD-9-CM CODE: _____

PROCEDURE(S): _____

MAIN TERM(S): _____

ICD-9-CM PROCEDURE CODE(S): _____

CASE 12

PREOPERATIVE DIAGNOSIS: Basal cell carcinoma, right upper anterior cheek and left forearm.

POSTOPERATIVE DIAGNOSIS: Basal cell carcinoma, right upper anterior cheek and left forearm.

PROCEDURE: Wide excision of basal cell carcinoma right upper cheek and left forearm.

DESCRIPTION: The patient was sedated (moderate sedation) with 2 mg of Versed administered intravenously. The lesion on the right upper anterior cheek was very near the nose and lower eyelid. It was 2 cm in diameter, indurated, and had a shiny surface. The lesion on the left forearm measured 4 × 2 cm in size and exhibited a shiny central portion. It was quite scarred and had raised nodules around the periphery. The patient was prepped and draped in the usual fashion. The lesions were delineated in an elliptical fashion and anesthetized with equal parts of 1% lidocaine and 0.25% Marcaine. Both lesions were excised and sent to pathology for frozen section analysis. Both were reported as basal cell carcinoma. The margins were clear and both lesions completely excised. Closure of the cheek wound was accomplished with interrupted 5-0 Dexon in the subcuticular layer. The skin was closed with running interlocked 6-0 black silk. The wound on the forearm was closed with interrupted 5-0 Vicryl in the subcuticular layer and a running suture of 4-0 monofilament nylon on the skin. The patient left the operating room in good condition. She will be seen in the office in one week.

DIAGNOSIS: _____

ICD-9-CM CODE: _____

PROCEDURE(S): _____

MAIN TERM(S): _____

ICD-9-CM PROCEDURE CODE(S): _____

CASE 13

PREOPERATIVE DIAGNOSIS: Status post burns to chest and abdomen, with keloid formation. Tissue expanders were placed and inflated at the time of the initial surgery and skin grafts.

POSTOPERATIVE DIAGNOSIS: Status post burns to the chest and abdomen, with keloid formation. Tissue expanders were placed and inflated at the time of the initial surgery and skin grafts.

OPERATION: 1. Removal of five (5) tissue expanders. 2. Excision of keloids with flap closure of resultant defects, 41 cm total length, with the chest keloid measuring 19 cm and the abdominal keloid measuring 22 cm.

ANESTHESIA: General, nasotracheal intubation.

DIAGNOSIS: _____

ICD-9-CM CODE: _____

PROCEDURE(S): _____

MAIN TERM(S): _____

ICD-9-CM PROCEDURE CODE(S): _____

CASE 14

PREOPERATIVE DIAGNOSIS: Ingrown toenail with cellulitis, medial right great toe.

POSTOPERATIVE DIAGNOSIS: Ingrown toenail with cellulitis, medial right great toe.

INDICATIONS: There is a one-month history of pain, swelling, and erythema of the medial aspect of the right great toenail with ingrown symptoms. Conservative treatment has been unsuccessful.

PROCEDURE: Avulsion (removal) of the medial aspect of the nail plate of the great right toenail with ablation of the nail bed with phenol.

DESCRIPTION: The nail was anesthetized with approximately 4 cc of 1% lidocaine. After satisfactory anesthesia was obtained, the nail was grasped with a needle driver and the medial aspect of the nail was removed from the nail bed and was pulled out from the ingrown area. After clipping off the nail, the nail bed was treated with phenol for approximately 10 seconds. A Neosporin dressing was applied. The patient tolerated the procedure well and was advised to change the dressing once a day for three days. Activities as usual and as tolerated.

DIAGNOSIS: _____

ICD-9-CM CODE: _____

PROCEDURE(S): _____

MAIN TERM(S): _____

ICD-9-CM PROCEDURE CODE(S): _____

Using the same excerpts from previous cases, assign the CPT code(s) to the procedure(s).

CASE 15

PREOPERATIVE DIAGNOSIS: Full-thickness burn of the left lower leg from the knee to the ankle.

POSTOPERATIVE DIAGNOSIS: Full-thickness burn of the left lower leg from the knee to the ankle.

OPERATION: Extensive excision and debridement of the burn, left lower leg. Application of split-thickness skin graft. Total area of the graft is 2000 sq cm.

PROCEDURE: Adequate general anesthesia was achieved and the patient was placed in the supine position. The burn wound was totally excised, including excision of the muscle, for a full-thickness excision. The wound was irrigated. A skin graft was taken from the patient's upper thigh. The graft was meshed and applied to the burn wound, with satisfactory coverage. A pressure dressing was applied to the graft, and the donor site was appropriately dressed. The leg was immobilized in a splint. Sponge and needle count correct ×2. The patient tolerated the procedure well and was sent to the recovery room in satisfactory condition. Estimated blood loss was 200 cc.

PROCEDURE(S): _____

MAIN TERM(S): _____

CPT PROCEDURE CODE(S): _____

CASE 16

PREOPERATIVE DIAGNOSIS: 4.1 cm infected sebaceous cyst, back; 2.5 cm infected sebaceous cyst, posterior neck.

POSTOPERATIVE DIAGNOSIS: 4.1 cm infected sebaceous cyst, back; 2.5 cm infected sebaceous cyst, posterior neck.

OFFICE SURGERY: Excision, 4.1 cm benign cyst, back. Excision, 2.5 cm benign cyst, neck.

DETAILS: The patient was placed in the prone position and the back and posterior neck were prepared with Betadine scrub and solution. Sterile towels were applied in the usual fashion, and 0.25% Marcaine was injected subcutaneously in a linear fashion transversely over each of the cysts. The lower cyst on the back was excised and the cavity was irrigated with copious amounts of Marcaine solutions. The skin edges were loosely reapproximated throughout with 3-0 nylon suture. Following this, Marcaine was injected around the superior cyst on the neck and the cyst was completely excised. The wound was irrigated with Marcaine and packed with iodoform, and sterile dressings were applied. The patient was released with verbal and written instructions, as well as Tylenol #3 for pain. She will return in three days for packing removal.

PROCEDURE(S): _____

MAIN TERM(S): _____

CPT PROCEDURE CODE(S): _____

CASE 17

PREOPERATIVE DIAGNOSIS: Basal cell carcinoma, right upper anterior cheek and left forearm.

POSTOPERATIVE DIAGNOSIS: Basal cell carcinoma, right upper anterior cheek and left forearm.

PROCEDURE: Wide excision of basal cell carcinoma right upper cheek and left forearm.

DESCRIPTION: The patient was sedated (moderate sedation) with 2 mg of Versed administered intravenously. The lesion on the right upper anterior cheek was very near the nose and lower eyelid. It was 2 cm in diameter, indurated, and had a shiny surface. The lesion on the left forearm measured 4×2 cm in size and exhibited a shiny central portion. It was quite scarred and had raised nodules around the periphery. The patient was prepped and draped in the usual fashion. The lesions were delineated in an elliptical fashion and anesthetized with equal parts of 1% lidocaine and 0.25% Marcaine. Both lesions were excised and sent to pathology for frozen section analysis. Both were reported as basal cell carcinoma. The margins were clear and both lesions completely excised.

Closure of the cheek wound was accomplished with interrupted 5-0 Dexon in the subcuticular layer. The skin was closed with running interlocked 6-0 black silk. The wound on the forearm was closed with interrupted 5-0 Vicryl in the subcuticular layer and a running suture of 4-0 monofilament nylon on the skin. The patient left the operating room in good condition. She will be seen in the office in one week.

PROCEDURE(S): _____

MAIN TERM(S): _____

CPT PROCEDURE CODE(S): _____

CASE 18

PREOPERATIVE DIAGNOSIS: Status post burns to chest and abdomen, with keloid formation. Tissue expanders were placed and inflated at the time of the initial surgery and skin grafts.

POSTOPERATIVE DIAGNOSIS: Status post burns to the chest and abdomen, with keloid formation. Tissue expanders were placed and inflated at the time of the initial surgery and skin grafts.

OPERATION: 1. Removal of five (5) tissue expanders. 2. Excision of keloids with flap closure of resultant defects, 41 cm total length, with the chest keloid measuring 19 cm and the abdominal keloid measuring 22 cm.

ANESTHESIA: General, nasotracheal intubation.

PROCEDURE(S): _____

MAIN TERM(S): _____

CPT PROCEDURE CODE(S): _____

CASE 19

PREOPERATIVE DIAGNOSIS: Ingrown toenail with cellulitis, medial right great toe.

POSTOPERATIVE DIAGNOSIS: Ingrown toenail with cellulitis, medial right great toe.

INDICATIONS: There is a one-month history of pain, swelling, and erythema of the medial aspect of the right great toenail with ingrown symptoms. Conservative treatment has been unsuccessful.

PROCEDURE: Avulsion (removal) of the medial aspect of the nail plate of the great right toenail with ablation of the nail bed with phenol.

DESCRIPTION: The nail was anesthetized with approximately 4 cc of 1% lidocaine. After satisfactory anesthesia was obtained, the nail was grasped with a needle driver and the medial aspect of the nail was removed from the nail bed and was pulled out from the ingrown area. After clipping off the nail, the nail bed was treated with phenol for approximately 10 seconds. A Neosporin dressing was applied. The patient tolerated the procedure well and was advised to change the dressing once a day for three days. Activities as usual and as tolerated.

PROCEDURE(S): _____

MAIN TERM(S): _____

CPT PROCEDURE CODE(S): _____

MEDICAL TERMINOLOGY CHALLENGE

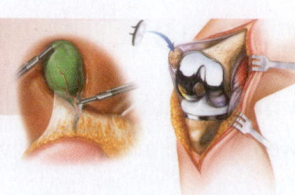

Write a brief definition for each medical term. Use a medical dictionary as necessary.

1. ablation _____

2. allergy testing _____

3. antibiotic _____

4. bacteriostat _____

5. conscious sedation _____

6. frozen section _____

7. general anesthesia _____

8. indurated _____

9. lidocaine _____

10. medial _____

11. nasotracheal _____

12. intubation _____

13. nodules _____

14. pathology _____

15. pigmented _____

16. prone _____

17. staphylococcus _____

18. sterile _____

19. subcuticular _____

20. superficial _____

NOTES:

_____ _____

_____ _____

_____ _____

_____ _____

_____ _____

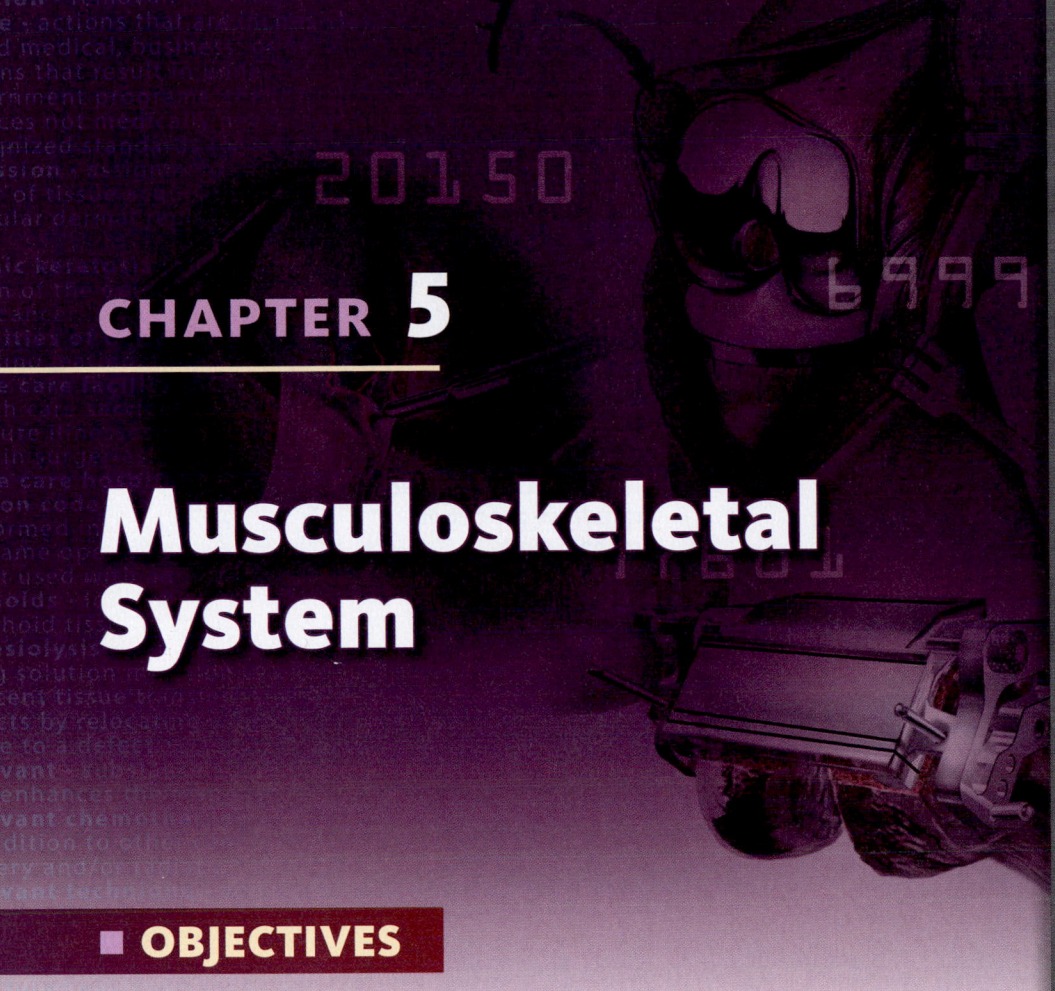

CHAPTER **5**

Musculoskeletal System

■ OBJECTIVES

At the completion of this chapter, the student should be able to:

1. Learn the word roots associated with the musculoskeletal system.
2. Label the basic structures of the musculoskeletal system.
3. Discuss the functions of the musculoskeletal system.
4. Accurately spell and define musculoskeletal system terminology.
5. Accurately assign medical codes to musculoskeletal diagnoses and procedures.

■ OVERVIEW

The musculoskeletal system is made up of muscles, fascia, ligaments, bones, joints, and tendons. The structures of this system function together for the following purposes: (1) to permit movement; (2) to provide a supporting framework for the body; (3) to protect the internal organs from injury; (4) to serve as a storage location for minerals such as calcium and phosphorus; and (5) to play a role in blood cell formation.

The medical specialty related to the musculoskeletal system is **orthopedics** and the physician specialist is an **orthopedist**. Chiropractic is a health care specialty that focuses on manipulation of the spinal column for therapeutic purposes. Practitioners are called chiropractors. After completing two years of premedical studies and four years of training in an approved chiropractic school, practitioners are awarded the degree of doctor of chiropractic.

KEY TERMS

abduction
acetabulum
acromion
adduction
anterior cruciate ligament
articular cartilage
articulation
bursa
calcaneus
cardiac muscle
carpals
cartilaginous joint
cervical vertebrae
clavicle
coccyx
compact bone
condyle
cranium
crest
diaphysis
distal epiphysis
epiphyseal line
fascia
femur
fibrous joint
fibula
fibular collateral ligament
fissure
foramen
fossa
frontal bone
head
humerus
ilium
intervertebral disk
ischium
joint capsule
lamina
lateral meniscus
ligament
lumbar vertebrae
mandible
maxilla
medial meniscus
menisci
metacarpal
metatarsal
occipital bone
orthopedics
orthopedist
osteoblast
osteocyte
parietal bone

continued

KEY TERMS continued

patella
periosteum
phalanges
posterior cruciate ligament
proximal epiphysis
pubis
radius
red bone marrow
ribs
sacrum
scapula
sinus
skeletal muscle
smooth muscle
spine
spinous process
sternum
striated muscle
symphysis pubis

synovial cavity
synovial fluid
synovial joint
synovial membrane
talus
tarsal
temporal bone
tendon
thoracic vertebrae
tibia
tibial collateral ligament
transverse processes
trochanter
ulna
vertebrae
vertebral arch
vertebral body
vertebral foramen
xiphoid process
yellow bone marrow
zygomatic bone

MUSCULOSKELETAL SYSTEM ROOTS, PREFIXES, AND SUFFIXES

Roots, prefixes, and suffixes associated with the musculoskeletal system are listed in table 5-1. Review the word elements and complete the exercises.

EXERCISE 5-1

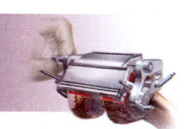

Write the root, prefix, suffix, and their meaning. Based on the meanings, write a brief definition for each term.

1. Osteocyte

    ROOT: _____ MEANING: _____

    SUFFIX: _____ MEANING: _____

    BRIEF DEFINITION: _____

2. Pectoral

    ROOT: _____ MEANING: _____

    SUFFIX: _____ MEANING: _____

    BRIEF DEFINITION: _____

3. Clavicular

    ROOT: _____ MEANING: _____

    SUFFIX: _____ MEANING: _____

    BRIEF DEFINITION: _____

4. Laminectomy

    ROOT: _____ MEANING: _____

    SUFFIX: _____ MEANING: _____

    BRIEF DEFINITION: _____

5. Osteomalacia

    ROOT: _____ MEANING: _____

    SUFFIX: _____ MEANING: _____

    BRIEF DEFINITION: _____

6. Craniotomy

    ROOT: _____ MEANING: _____

    SUFFIX: _____ MEANING: _____

    BRIEF DEFINITION: _____

7. Costovertebral

    ROOT: _____ MEANING: _____

    SUFFIX: _____ MEANING: _____

    BRIEF DEFINITION: _____

8. Arthritis

    ROOT: _____ MEANING: _____

    SUFFIX: _____ MEANING: _____

    BRIEF DEFINITION: _____

continued

Table 5-1 Musculoskeletal System Roots, Prefixes, and Suffixes

WORD ROOT/ COMBINING FORM	MEANING
ankyl/o	stiff; mobile
arthr/o	joint
articul/o	joint
burs/o	bursa
bucc/o	cheek
carp/o	wrist bones
chondr/o	cartilage
clavicul/o	clavicle; collarbone
coccyg/o	coccyx; tailbone
cost/o	rib
crani/o	skull
electr/o	electricity
fasci/o	band of fibrous tissue
femor/o	femur; thighbone
fibr/o	fiber
fibul/o	fibula; outer lower leg bone
humer/o	humerus; upper arm bone
ili/o	ilium; pelvic bone, upper section
ischi/o	ischium; pelvic bone, lower section
kyph/o	outward curvature of the spine; pertaining to a hump
lamin/o	lamina
ligament/o	ligament
lord/o	forward curvature of the spine; swayback
lumb/o	lower back
mandibul/o	mandible; lower jawbone
maxill/o	maxilla; upper jawbone
metacarp/o	hand bones
metatars/o	foot bones
myel/o	bone marrow
my/o	muscle
orth/o	straight
oste/o	bone

WORD ROOT/ COMBINING FORM	MEANING
patell/o	patella; kneecap
pect/o; pector/o	chest
ped/o	foot
pelv/i	pelvis
phalang/o	finger and toe bones
pubi/o; pub/o	pubis; pelvic bone, anterior section
radi/o	radius; outer lower arm bone
sacr/o	sacrum
scapula/o	scapula; shoulder blade
scoli/o	lateral curvature of the spine; crooked; bent
spondyl/o	vertebra
stern/o	sternum; breastbone
tars/o	ankle bones
ten/o; tendin/o	tendon
vertebr/o	vertebra

PREFIX	MEANING
brady-	slow
dys-	abnormal; difficult
intra-	within
poly-	many
sub-	below; under
supra-	above

SUFFIX	MEANING
-algia	pain
-asthenia	without feeling or sensation
-dynia	pain
-kinesia	movement
-lysis	destruction, breakdown
-oma	tumor
-tonia	muscle tone
-trophy	growth; development

9. Cranial

ROOT: _____ MEANING: _____

SUFFIX: _____ MEANING: _____

BRIEF DEFINITION: _____

10. Femoral

ROOT: _____ MEANING: _____

SUFFIX: _____ MEANING: _____

BRIEF DEFINITION: _____

11. Intercostal

ROOT: _____ MEANING: _____

SUFFIX: _____ MEANING: _____

BRIEF DEFINITION: _____

12. Humeral

ROOT: _____ MEANING: _____

SUFFIX: _____ MEANING: _____

BRIEF DEFINITION: _____

13. Lumbosacral

ROOT: _____ MEANING: _____

SUFFIX: _____ MEANING: _____

BRIEF DEFINITION: _____

14. Substernal

ROOT: _____ MEANING: _____

PREFIX: _____ MEANING: _____

SUFFIX: _____ MEANING: _____

BRIEF DEFINITION: _____

15. Submandibular

ROOT: _____ MEANING: _____

PREFIX: _____ MEANING: _____

SUFFIX: _____ MEANING: _____

BRIEF DEFINITION: _____

16. Submaxillary

ROOT: _____ MEANING: _____

PREFIX: _____ MEANING: _____

SUFFIX: _____ MEANING: _____

BRIEF DEFINITION: _____

17. Supraclavicular

ROOT: _____ MEANING: _____

PREFIX: _____ MEANING: _____

SUFFIX: _____ MEANING: _____

BRIEF DEFINITION: _____

18. Ischiopubic

ROOT: _____ MEANING: _____

SUFFIX: _____ MEANING: _____

BRIEF DEFINITION: _____

19. Intervertebral

ROOT: _____ MEANING: _____

PREFIX: _____ MEANING: _____

SUFFIX: _____ MEANING: _____

BRIEF DEFINITION: _____

20. Polyarthritis

ROOT: _____ MEANING: _____

PREFIX: _____ MEANING: _____

SUFFIX: _____ MEANING: _____

BRIEF DEFINITION: _____

21. Subarticular

ROOT: _____ MEANING: _____

PREFIX: _____ MEANING: _____

SUFFIX: _____ MEANING: _____

BRIEF DEFINITION: _____

22. Myalgia

ROOT: _____ MEANING: _____

SUFFIX: _____ MEANING: _____

BRIEF DEFINITION: _____

23. Suprapatellar

ROOT: _____ MEANING: _____

PREFIX: _____ MEANING: _____

SUFFIX: _____ MEANING: _____

BRIEF DEFINITION: _____

24. Dyskinesia

PREFIX: _____ MEANING: _____

SUFFIX: _____ MEANING: _____

BRIEF DEFINITION: _____

STRUCTURES OF THE MUSCULOSKELETAL SYSTEM

The major structures of the musculoskeletal system include muscles, fascia, ligaments, bones, joints, and tendons. Figure 5-1 illustrates some of the major muscles of the body, showing both anterior and posterior views.

The body has more than 600 muscles and many tendons. Table 5-2 lists and describes some of the more commonly known muscles and one tendon. The numbers in parentheses correspond to the enumerated muscles in figure 5-1. Refer to the figure as you read the description of the selected muscles.

Muscles

Muscles are actually groups of muscle cells called *fibers*. The body contains three types of muscles: **skeletal muscle**, **smooth muscle**, and **cardiac muscle**. Skeletal muscles, also known as **striated** (**STRIGH**-ay-ted) **muscles** or voluntary muscles, are usually attached to bones. Muscles of the face, eye, tongue, and pharynx do not attach to bones. The term *striated* refers to the striped appearance of skeletal muscles when viewed under a microscope.

Skeletal muscles are voluntary because the individual must make a conscious choice to move them. Smooth muscles, also known as involuntary muscles, are located in the walls of organs such as blood vessels, glands, intestines, stomach, and parts of the respiratory system. Smooth muscles are not under the voluntary control of the individual.

Cardiac muscles form the walls of the heart, are striated in appearance, and are classified as involuntary muscles. These tough muscles are arranged in branching fiber bundles and are able to withstand a great deal of stress. Figure 5-2 illustrates the three types of muscles.

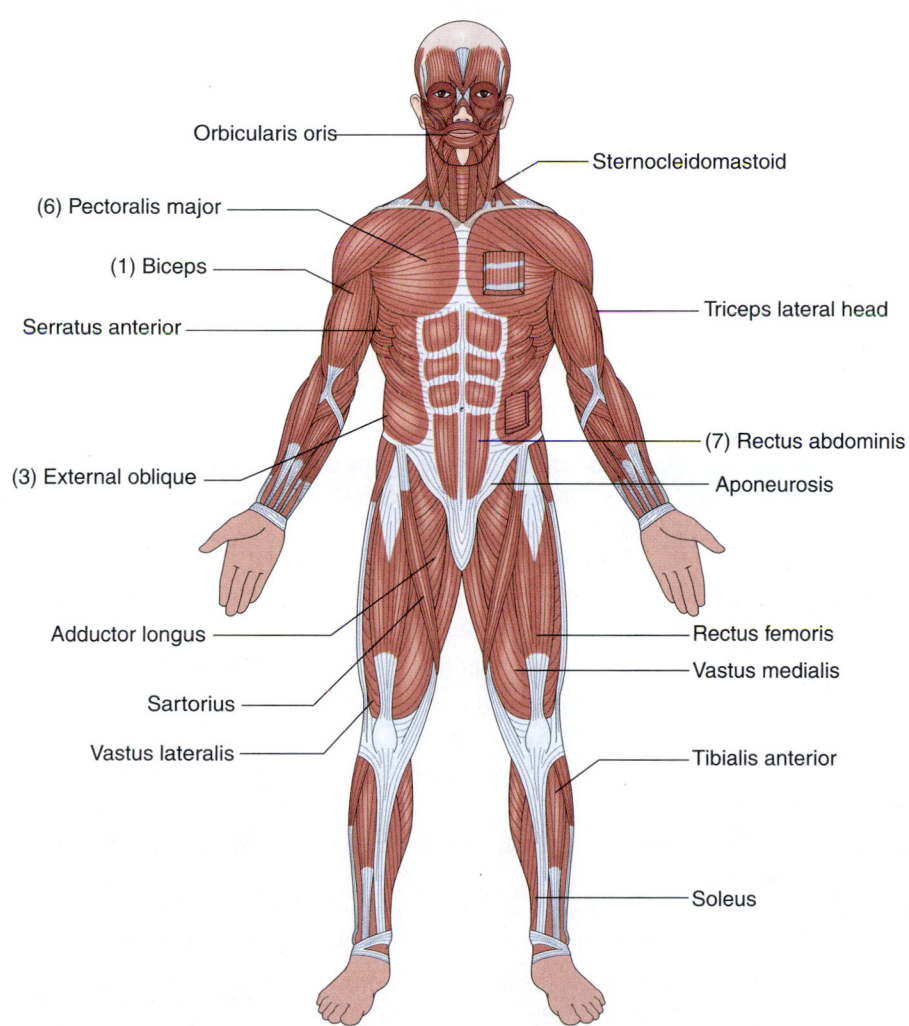

Figure 5-1 Muscles of the body (anterior)

continued

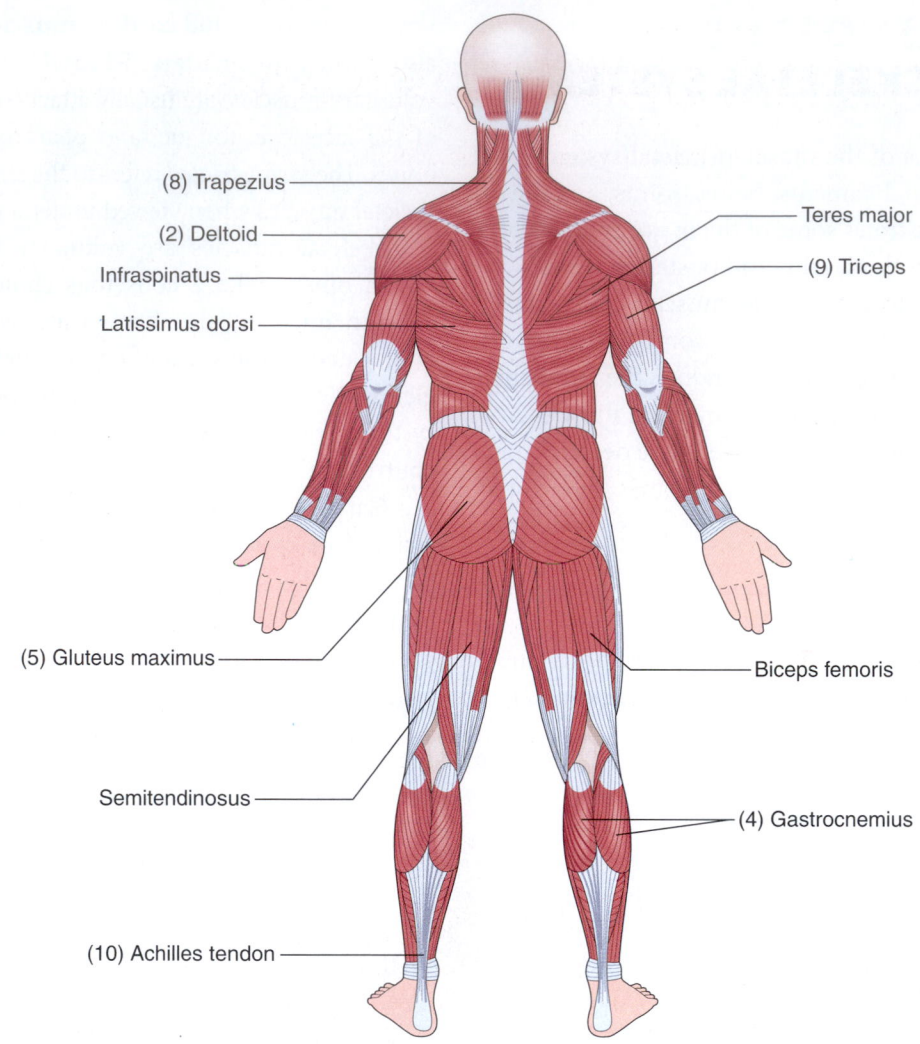

(8) Trapezius

Teres major

(2) Deltoid

(9) Triceps

Infraspinatus

Latissimus dorsi

(5) Gluteus maximus

Biceps femoris

Semitendinosus

(4) Gastrocnemius

(10) Achilles tendon

Figure 5-1 (continued) Muscles of the body (posterior)

Table 5-2 Muscles and Tendon

MUSCLE/TENDON	DESCRIPTION
biceps (1) (**BIGH**-seps)	located on the anterior surface of the humerus; movements include bending and extending the arms
buccinator (**BUCK**-sin-ay-tor) bucc/o = cheek	cheek muscle; movements include sucking, whistling, blowing, and smiling
deltoid (2) (**DELL**-toyd)	covers the shoulder joint; common site for medication injections
external oblique (3)	muscles of the sides of the upper body; movements include turning or twisting the upper body
gastrocnemius (4) (**gass**-trok-**NEE**-mee-us)	calf muscle; movements include pointing toes and standing on tiptoe
gluteus maximus (5) (**GLOO**-tee-us **MACKS**-ih-mus)	buttock muscle; moves the thigh (you sit on your gluteus maximus)
hamstring muscles	located on the posterior part of the thigh; a group of three individual muscles; movements include flexing or bending the thigh, kneeling
masseter (mass-**SEE**-ter)	located at the angle of the jaw; movements include biting and chewing, mastication

continued

Table 5-2 (*continued*)   Muscles and Tendon

MUSCLE/TENDON	DESCRIPTION
pectoralis major (6) (peck-toh-**RAY**-lis)	chest muscle; large, fan-shaped muscle that crosses the upper part of the chest; moves the arms; commonly called *pecs*
quadriceps femoris (**KWAHD**-rih-seps **FEM**-or-iss)	anterior thigh muscle; a group of four individual muscles; movements include extending the thigh, kicking; commonly called *quads*
rectus abdominis (7) (**RECK**-tus ab-**DOM**-in-iss)	abdominal muscles; commonly called *abs*; movements include raising the upper body
sternomastoid; sternocleidomastoid (stir-noh-**MASS**-toyd, stir-noh-**KLIGH**-doh-mass-toyd) stern/o = sternum	extends from the sternum up the side of the neck to the mastoid process; moves the head and neck
temporal (**TEMP**-or-al) muscle	located above and near the ear; movements include biting and chewing
tibialis anterior (tib-ee-**AY**-lis)	located on the front lower part of the leg; movements include pulling the foot toward the leg and walking on the heels of the foot
trapezius (8) (trah-**PEE**-zee-us)	triangular-shaped muscle that extends across the back of the shoulder and back of the neck; connects to the clavicle and scapula; moves the shoulders
triceps (9) (**TRIGH**-seps)	located on the posterior surface of the humerus; movements include bending and extending the arms
Achilles tendon (10) (ah-**KILL**-eez)	tendon that attaches the gastrocnemius muscle to the calcaneus

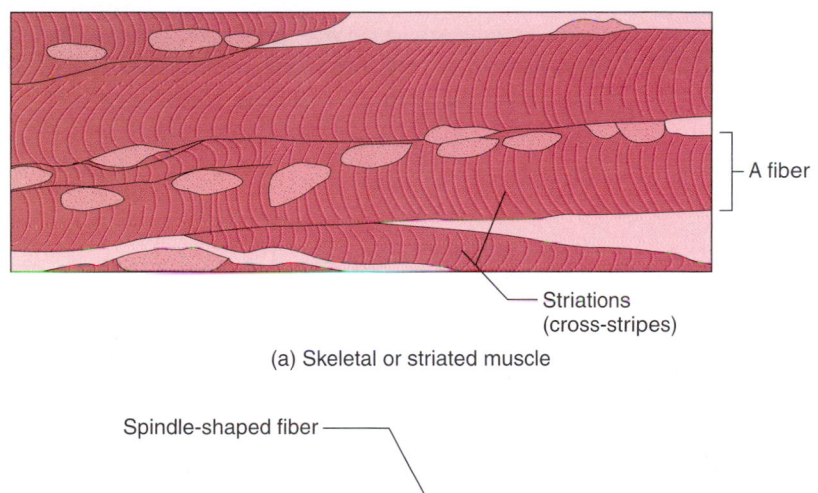

(a) Skeletal or striated muscle

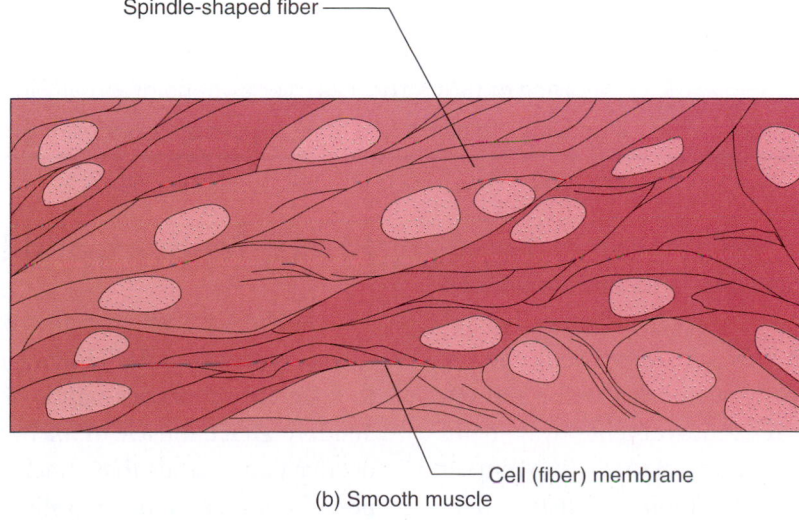

(b) Smooth muscle

Figure 5-2   Three types of muscles

continued

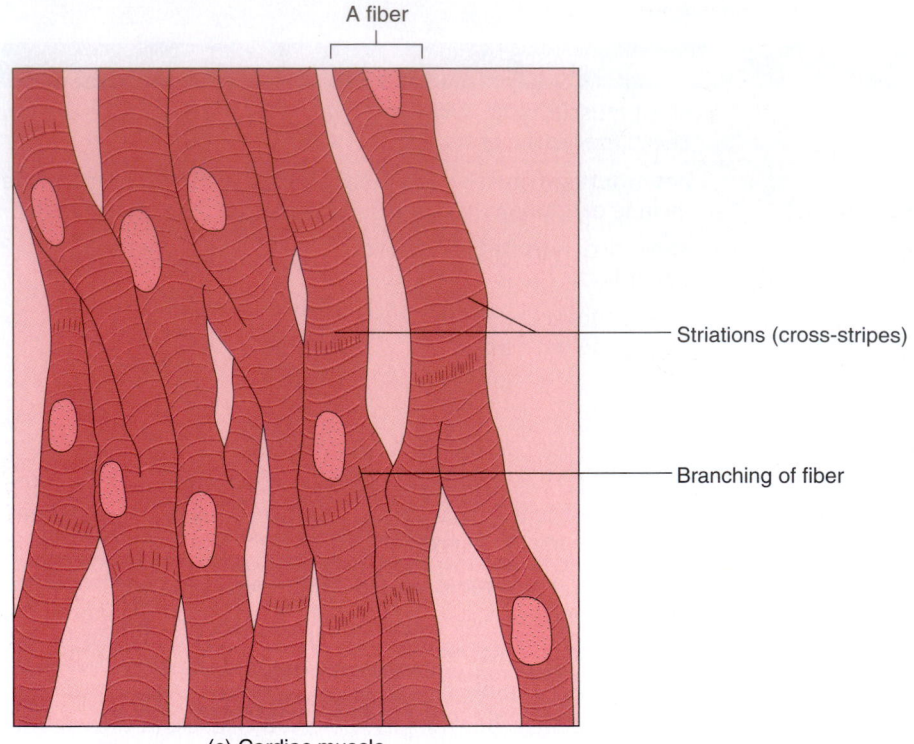

A fiber

Striations (cross-stripes)

Branching of fiber

(c) Cardiac muscle

Figure 5-2 (*continued*)   Three types of muscles

Table 5-3   Movement Terms

MOVEMENT	MEANING
abduction (ab-**DUCK**-shun)	movement away from the midline of the body
adduction (ad-**DUCK**-shun)	movement toward the midline of the body
circumduction (**sir**-kum-**DUCK**-shun)	movement in a circular motion
dorsiflexion (**dor**-see-**FLEX**-shun)	moving the foot upward toward the leg
extension (ecks-**TEN**-shun)	straightening motion; movement to increase the angle between bones
flexion (**FLEK**-shun)	bending motion; movement to decrease the angle between bones
plantar flexion (**PLAN**-tar **FLEK**-shun)	moving the foot in a downward position away from the leg; pointing the toes downward
pronation (proh-**NAY**-shun)	moving the palm face down or toward the back; palms down
rotation (roh-**TAY**-shun)	moving or turning on an axis or pivot point, usually in a left-to-right motion
supination (**soo**-pih-**NAY**-shun)	moving the palms face up or toward the front; palms up

Body movement is accomplished by extending and flexing various muscles and muscle groups. When one muscle, or set of muscles, flexes, the opposing muscle or set extends and movement occurs. Medical terms related to movement can be paired. For example, **abduction** is movement away from the midline and body, and **adduction** is movement toward the midline and body. Table 5-3 lists movement terms.

Fascia, Tendons, and Ligaments

Muscle fibers are held together by fibrous connective tissue called **fascia** (**FASH**-ee-ah). Muscle fascia extends to form strong fibrous bands of tissue called **tendons**. Tendons attach muscle to the bone. **Ligaments** are connective tissue bands that attach bones to bones and support the joints. Figure 5-3 illustrates a muscle, tendon, and ligament.

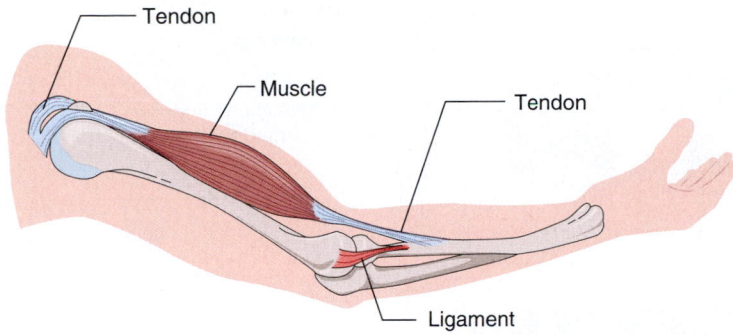

Figure 5-3 Muscle, tendon, and ligament

EXERCISE 5-2

Write the name of the muscle for each description.

1. abs
2. buttock muscle
3. calf muscle
4. cheek muscle
5. chest muscle
6. mastication or chewing muscle
7. tendon associated with the heel
8. located on the anterior surface of the humerus
9. movements include flexing the thigh and bending the knee
10. pecs
11. quads
12. moves the shoulders
13. posterior surface of the humerus
14. moves the head and neck
15. pulls the foot toward the leg (walking on the heels)

EXERCISE 5-3

Write the term that describes the "paired" or opposite movement of the listed term.

1. adduction _____
2. dorsiflexion _____
3. extension _____
4. pronation _____

EXERCISE 5-4

Label the muscle structures shown in figure 5-4. Write your answers in the spaces provided.

1. _____
2. _____
3. _____
4. _____
5. _____

Bones

The bones of the musculoskeletal system provide places for muscle attachments, protect the internal organs, store calcium and phosphorus, and play a role in blood cell production. An immature bone cell is an **osteoblast** (**OSS**-tee-oh-blast), and a mature bone cell is an **osteocyte** (**OSS**-tee-oh-sight).

Bones are often classified by their shape. According to this classification method, there are five types of bones: long, short, flat, irregular, and sesamoid. Table 5-4 gives a brief description and a few examples of each type of bone. The structures of long bones have specific functions. Refer to figure 5-5 as you read the description of the structures.

The shaft of a long bone is called the (1) **diaphysis** (digh-**AFF**-ih-sis). The (2) **proximal epiphysis** (eh-**PIFF**-ih-sis) is the upper end of a long bone, and the (2) **distal epiphysis** is the lower end. The (3) **epiphyseal** (**ep**-ih-**FIZZ**-ee-al) **line** or plate is a layer of cartilage between the diaphysis and epiphysis where bone growth occurs. The (4) **periosteum** (**pair**-ee-**OSS**-tee-um) is a white membrane that covers the shaft of a long bone.

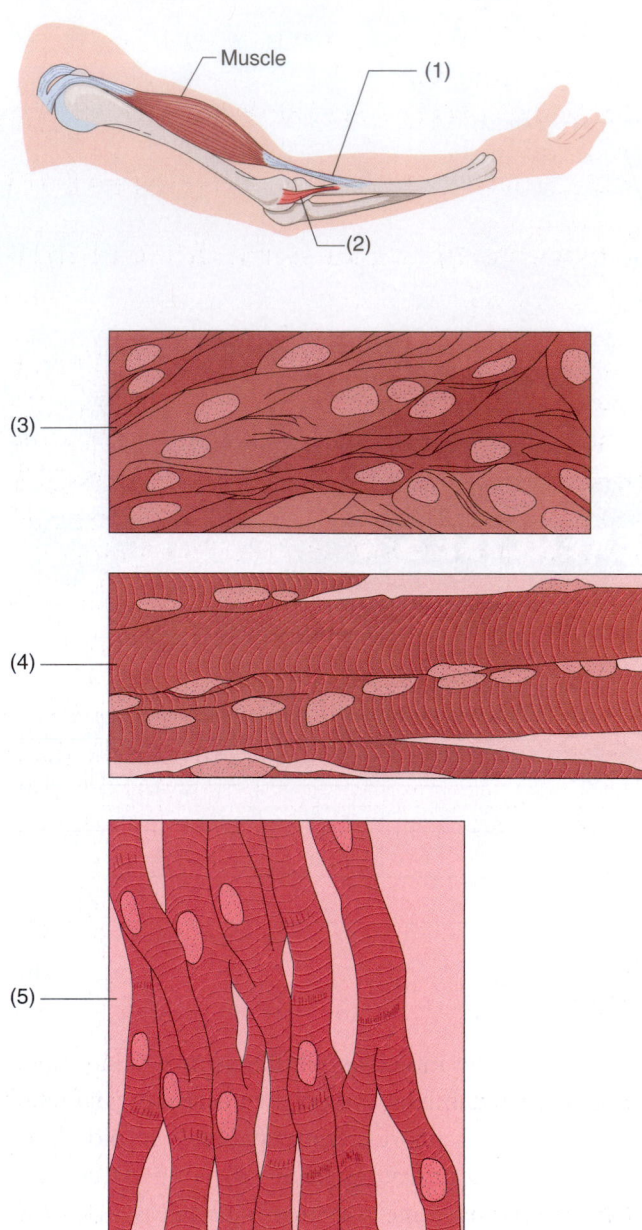

Figure 5-4 Muscle structures

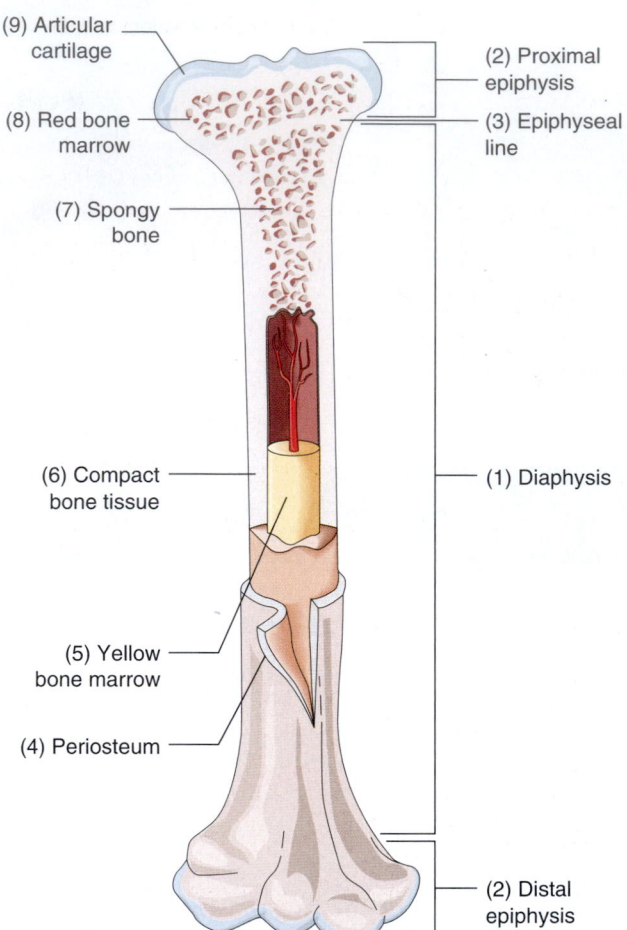

Figure 5-5 Structures of long bone

Other long bone structures include (5) **yellow bone marrow**, which stores fat; (6) **compact bone**, the hard, outer shell of the bone; (7) spongy or cancellous bone that contains the (8) **red bone marrow** that produces red blood cells; and the (9) **articular** (ar-**TIK**-yoo-lar) **cartilage**, a thin layer of cartilage that covers the ends of long bones and the surface of the joints.

Bone Processes and Depressions

In addition to their shape, bones have markings called processes and depressions. Bone processes, also known as projections, help form joints and serve as attachment points for muscles and tendons. Examples of bone processes include the following:

- **Condyle** (**KON**-dill)—round knuckle-like projection
- **Crest**—prominent ridge along the border of a bone

Table 5-4 Type of Bones

TYPE OF BONE	DESCRIPTION	EXAMPLES
Long bones	Longer than wide	Femur, radius, ulna, tibia, fibula, phalanges
Short bones	Nearly as long as wide	Carpals, tarsals
Flat bones	Broad, thin, flat	Sternum, ribs, scapula
Irregular bones	Various sizes	Vertebrae, facial bones
Sesamoid bones	Irregular, round	Patella

- **Head**—large, rounded end of a long bone set off from the shaft of the bone by a neck
- **Spine**—sharp projection from the surface of a bone
- **Trochanter** (troh-**KAN**-ter)—large, somewhat rounded projections near the neck of the femur

Bone depressions are holes or indentations that allow nerves and blood vessels to pass through or into the bones. Examples of bone depressions include the following:

- **Fissure**—groove or slitlike opening
- **Foramen** (for-**AY**-men)—hole or opening in a bone
- **Fossa** (**FOSS**-ah)—indentation in the surface of a bone
- **Sinus**—air space or opening in the bones of the skull

Bone processes and depressions are noted on the bone illustrations in this chapter.

Bones of the Head, Shoulders, Chest, Arms, and Hands

The bones of the head are collectively called the **cranium**. The cranial bones protect the brain, eyes, and inner structures of the ears. Cranial bones are illustrated in figure 5-6. Note the mastoid process of the temporal bone.

The (1) **frontal bone** forms the forehead and part of the bony protection for the eyes. Just behind the frontal bone are the (2) **parietal** (pah-**RIGH**-eh-tal) **bones**, one on each side of the head. These bones form the top and upper sides of the cranium. A single (3) **occipital** (ok-**SIP**-ih-tal) **bone** forms the back of the head and the base of the skull. The (4) **temporal** (**TEM**-por-al) **bones**, one on each side of the head, form the lower sides and part of the base of the skull.

The facial bones of the cranium are the (5) **mandible**, the lower jawbone and the only cranial bone that moves; the (6) **maxilla** or upper jawbone; and the (7) **zygomatic** (**zigh**-goh-**MAT**-ik) **bones**, one on each side of the face, which form the cheekbones and the outer part of the bony protection for the eyes.

The bones of the shoulders, chest, arms, and hands are illustrated in figure 5-7.

The bones of the shoulder are the (1) **clavicle**, commonly called the collarbone, and the (2) **scapula**, commonly called the shoulder blade. A section of the scapula, the (3) **acromion** (ah-**KROH**-mee-on) process, joins with the clavicle to create the highest point of the shoulder.

The bones of the chest or thorax are the (4) **sternum**, commonly called the breastbone, and the (5) **ribs**. The **xiphoid** (**ZIGH**-foyd) **process** is a projection at the lower end of the sternum.

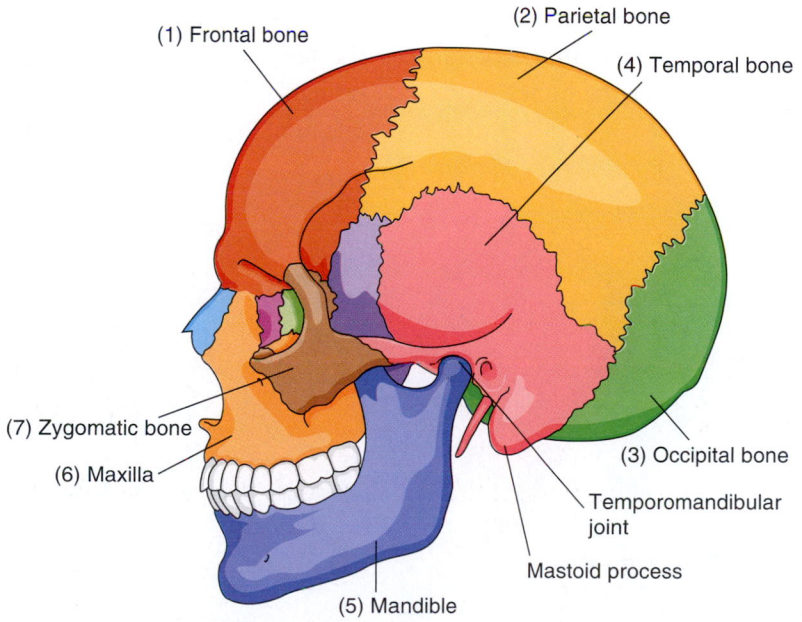

Figure 5-6 Cranial bones

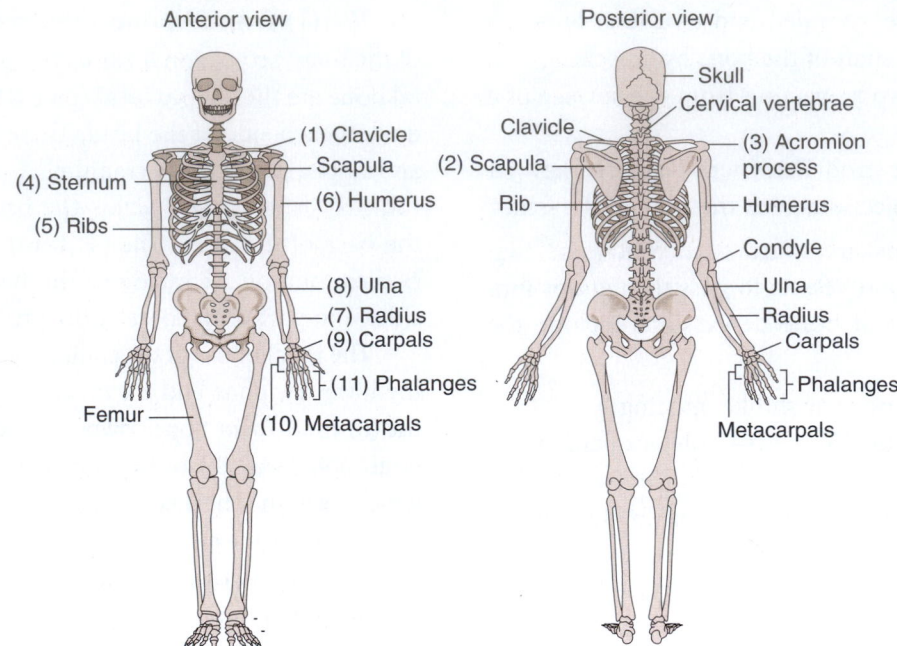

Figure 5-7 Shoulder, chest, arms, and hand bones

The bones of the arms are the (6) **humerus**, the upper arm bone, and the lower arm bones that include the (7) **radius**, the lateral bone of the lower arm, and the (8) **ulna**, the medial bone of the lower arm. The bones of the hands are the (9) **carpals**, wrist bones; the (10) **metacarpals**, bones of the palm; and the (11) **phalanges**, finger bones.

Bones of the Hips, Pelvis, Legs, and Feet

The bones of the hips and pelvis are formed by three fused bones and two sections of the vertebral column. Refer to figure 5-8 as you learn about the bones of the hips and pelvis.

The (1) **ilium** (**ILL**-ee-um), the largest of the three pelvic bones, is broad and flat. It is a good source of red bone marrow. The ilium is commonly called the hipbone. The (2) **ischium** (**ISH**-ee-um) is the lowest and strongest section of the pelvic bones. This is the bone you sit on. The (3) **pubis** (**PYOO**-biss) is the anterior segment of the pelvic bones. The two bones of the pubis meet in the front and are connected by a cartilage joint called the (4) **symphysis** (**SIM**-fih-siss) **pubis**.

Other structures of the hips and pelvis are the (5) **acetabulum** (**ass**-eh-**TAB**-yoo-lum), the socket for the femur; the (6) **coccyx** (**KOCK**-sicks), commonly called the tailbone; and the (7) **sacrum** (**SAY**-krum), a large triangular bone that is the fourth segment of the vertebral column. The (8) iliac crest is the upper ridge of the ilium.

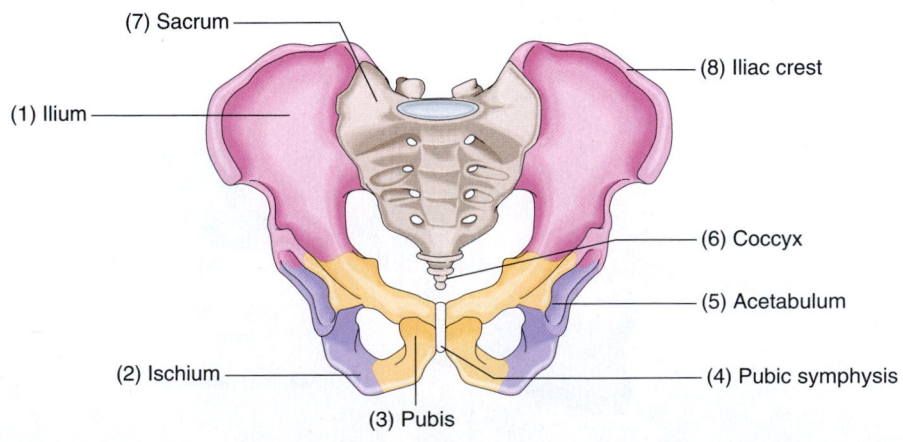

Figure 5-8 Hip and pelvis bones

The bones of the legs and feet are collectively known as the bones of the lower extremities. These bones are shown in figure 5-9. Refer to the figure as you learn about the bones.

The (1) **femur**, commonly called the thighbone, is the heaviest, longest, and strongest bone in the body. It consists of a rounded head that fits into the acetabulum to form the hip joint, a neck, and a shaft. The inset in figure 5-9 illustrates the head, neck, and greater trochanter (troh-**KAN**-ter) of the femur. The (2) **patella** (pah-**TELL**-ah), commonly called the kneecap, is a large sesamoid bone that protects the knee joint. The two lower leg bones are the (3) **tibia** (**TIB**-ee-ah), the larger of the two bones, and the (4) **fibula** (**FIB**-yoo-lah), a slender non-weight-bearing bone.

The bones of the ankle and foot bear the full weight of our bodies every time we walk, skip, run, or jump.

The bones of the ankle are called the (5) **tarsals** (**TAR**-sals), which include several small bones and a few larger ones. The largest ankle bone is the (6) **calcaneus** (kal-**KAY**-nee-us), commonly called the heel bone. The **talus** (**TAL**-us), located just above the calcaneus, joins with the tibia and fibula to form the ankle joint. The bones of the foot are called the (7) **metatarsals** (**met-ah-TAR**-sals). The bones of the toes, like the finger bones, are called (8) phalanges.

Bones of the Vertebral/Spinal Column

The bones of the vertebral column literally provide each of us with a "back-bone." The vertebral column protects the spinal cord and consists of 24 **vertebrae** (**VER**-teh-bray), the sacrum, and coccyx. Figure 5-10 illustrates the bones of the spinal column.

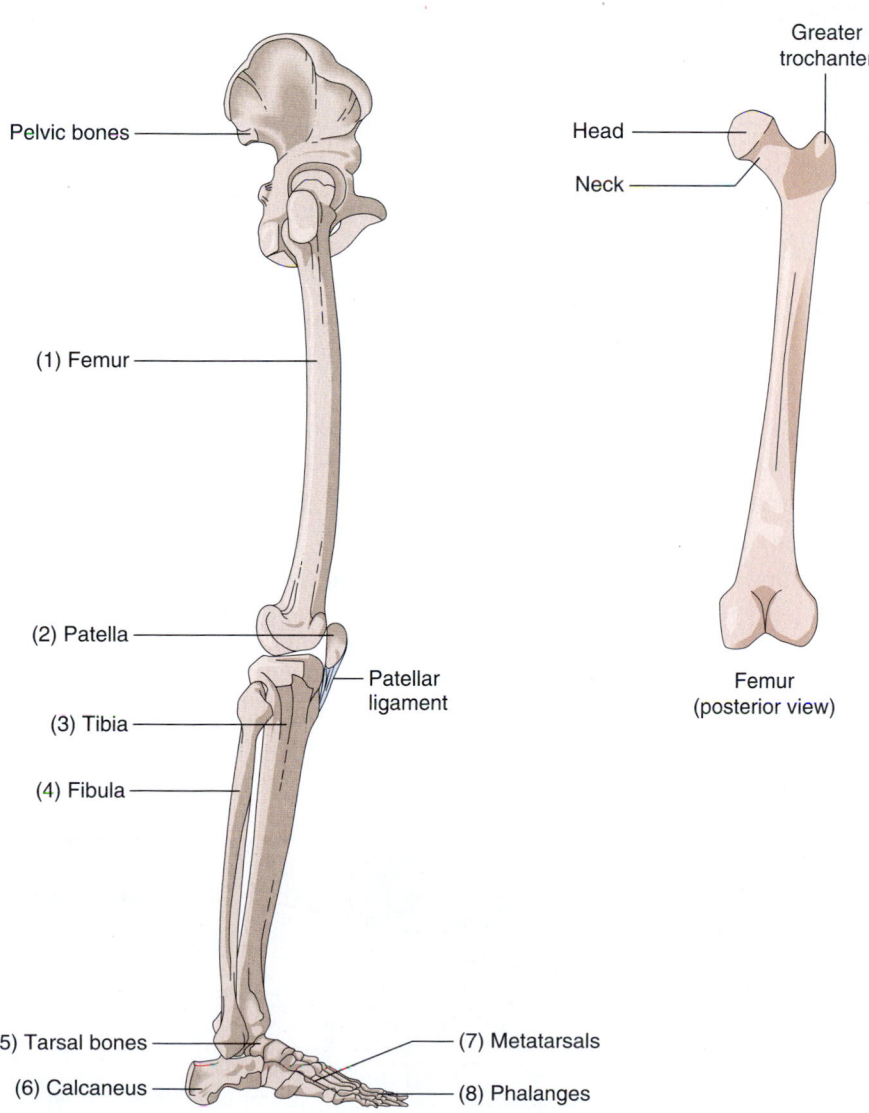

Figure 5-9 Leg and foot bones

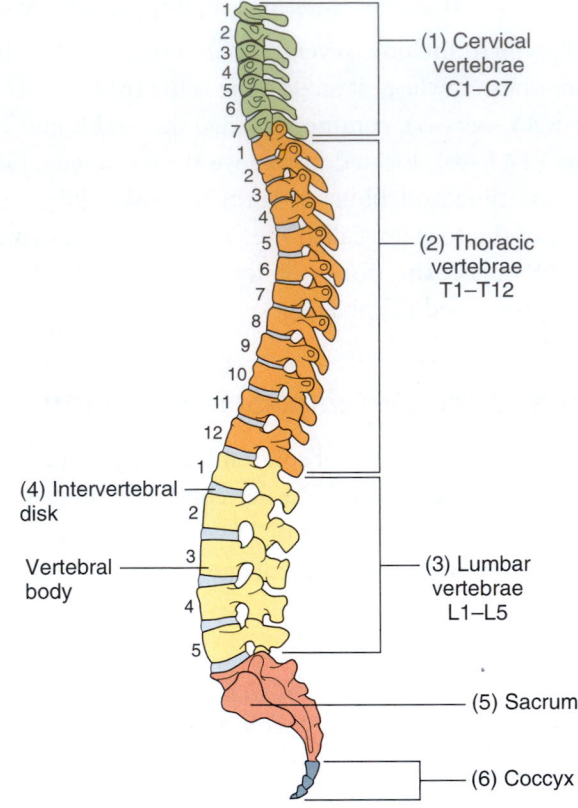

Figure 5-10 Spinal column bones

24 vertebrae. The disks are made of cartilage and prevent the vertebrae from rubbing against each other.

The last two segments of the spine are the (5) sacrum and the (6) coccyx. The adult sacrum is a single, triangular-shaped bone that results from the fusion of the five individual sacral bones during childhood. The adult coccyx is also a single bone that results from the fusion of four individual coccygeal bones. The basic structures of an individual vertebra are illustrated in figure 5-11.

The anterior portion of the vertebra is the (1) **vertebral body**, the weight-bearing segment of the vertebral column. The (2) **vertebral foramen** is a large opening that serves as a passageway for the spinal cord. The posterior portion of a vertebra is called the (3) **vertebral arch**. Three bony processes extend from the vertebral arch; the (4) **spinous process** projects from the midline of the vertebral arch, and the (5) **transverse processes** project from both sides of the vertebral arch. The area between the right and left transverse process is called the (6) **lamina** (**LAM**-ih-nah). The spinous and transverse processes serve as points of attachment for muscles and ligaments.

Joints

The area where two or more bones meet is called a joint or an **articulation** (ar-**tik**-yoo-**LAY**-shun). Joints are classified by the type of movement they allow. **Fibrous** (**FIGH**-brus) **joints** are nonmovable and are located between the cranial bones. **Cartilaginous** (**kar**-tih-**LAJ**-in-us) **joints** allow limited movement. The pubic symphysis of the pelvis is an example of a cartilaginous joint. The pubic symphysis allows the pelvic bones to expand during childbirth. Figure 5-12 illustrates fibrous and cartilaginous joints.

The vertebrae of the spinal column are divided into three distinct sections: cervical, thoracic, and lumbar. The first seven vertebrae are the (1) **cervical vertebrae**, abbreviated as C1 through C7. The next twelve vertebrae are the (2) **thoracic vertebrae**, abbreviated as T1 through T12. The thoracic vertebrae provide the posterior attachments for the ribs. The next five vertebrae are the (3) **lumbar vertebrae**, abbreviated as L1 through L5. An (4) **intervertebral disk** sits between each of the

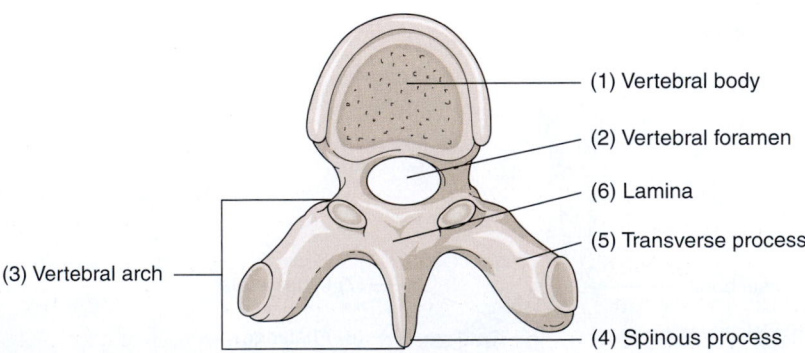

Figure 5-11 Structures of a vertebra

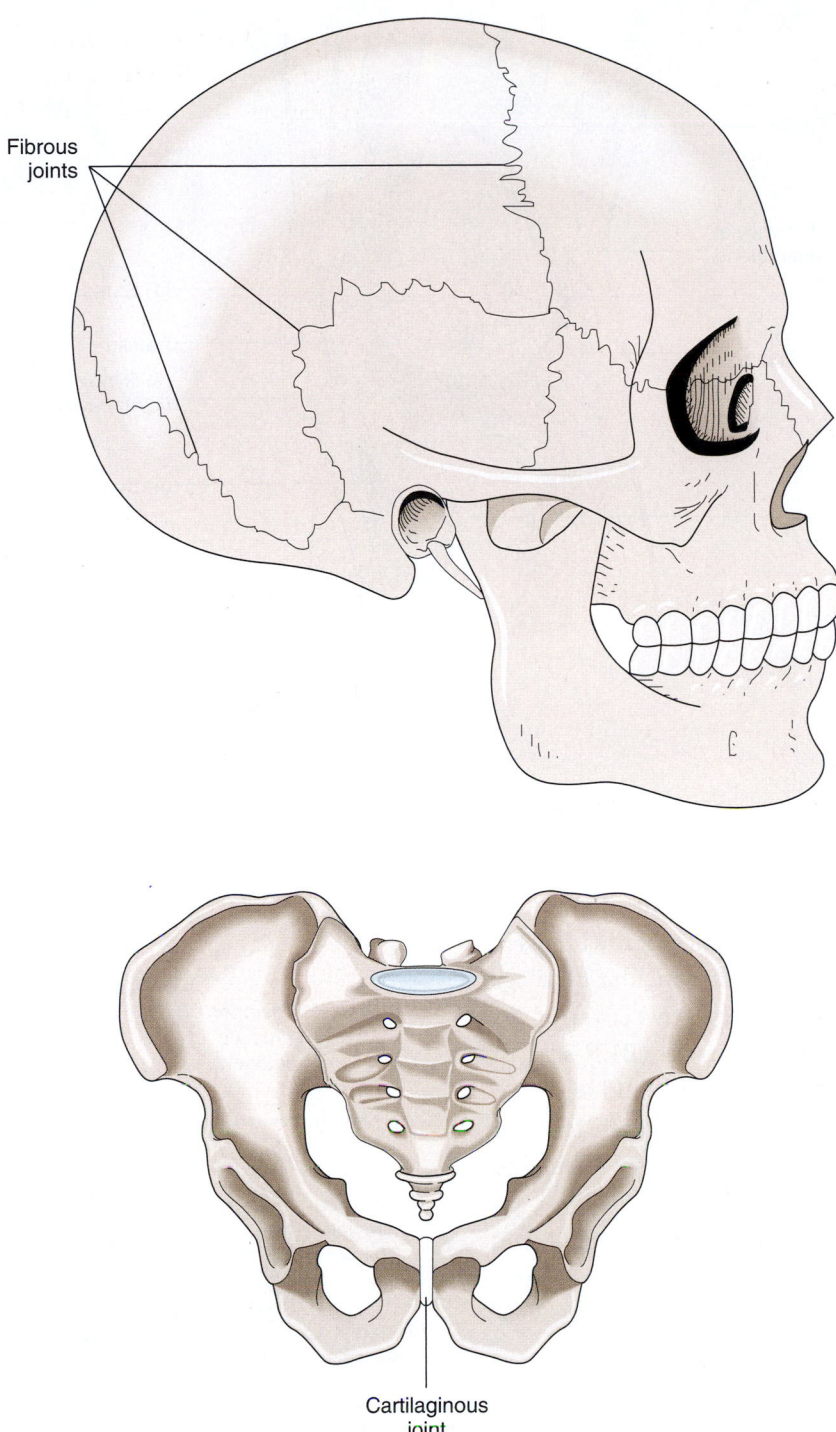

Figure 5-12 Fibrous and cartilaginous joints

Synovial (sin-**OH**-vee-al) **joints** are freely movable. They include ball-and-socket joints that permit movement in a wide range of directions and hinge joints that move in one direction. The hip and shoulder joints are ball-and-socket joints. The elbow and knee joints are hinge joints. Synovial joints have several structures.

Refer to figure 5-13 as you read the description of the components of a synovial joint.

A synovial joint is enclosed within a **joint capsule** made up of ligaments. The (1) **synovial membrane** lines the capsule and secretes a lubricating fluid called **synovial fluid**. This fluid circulates in the

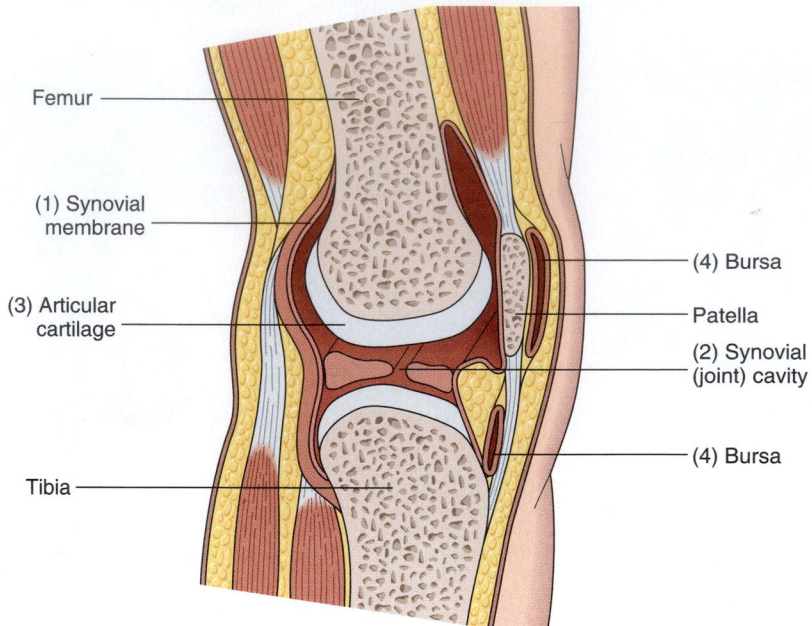

Figure 5-13   Synovial joint

(2) **synovial cavity**, the space between the bones, and allows the joint to move freely. The ends of the bones in a synovial joint are covered with (3) articular cartilage (ar-**TIK**-yoo-lar **KAR**-tih-laj), a protective covering for the bones. Fibrous sacs, called (4) **bursae** (**BER**-see), or bursa (singular), are filled with synovial fluid and provide a cushion for the friction points between tendons and bone. Bursae are located in the elbow, knee, and shoulder joints.

The knee is the most complex synovial joint and provides a good example of ligaments and **menisci** (meh-**NISS**-kigh). Figure 5-14 illustrates the major ligaments and menisci of the knee joint.

The (1) **posterior cruciate** (**KROOH**-she-it) **ligament (PCL)** prevents the femur from sliding anteriorly on the tibia; and the (6) **anterior cruciate ligament (ACL)** prevents the femur from sliding posteriorly on the tibia. The (2) **lateral meniscus** and the (5) **medial meniscus** keep the femur and tibia from rubbing against each other. The (3) **fibular collateral ligament** and the (4) **tibial collateral ligament**, along with the other ligaments of the knee, hold the knee joint in place.

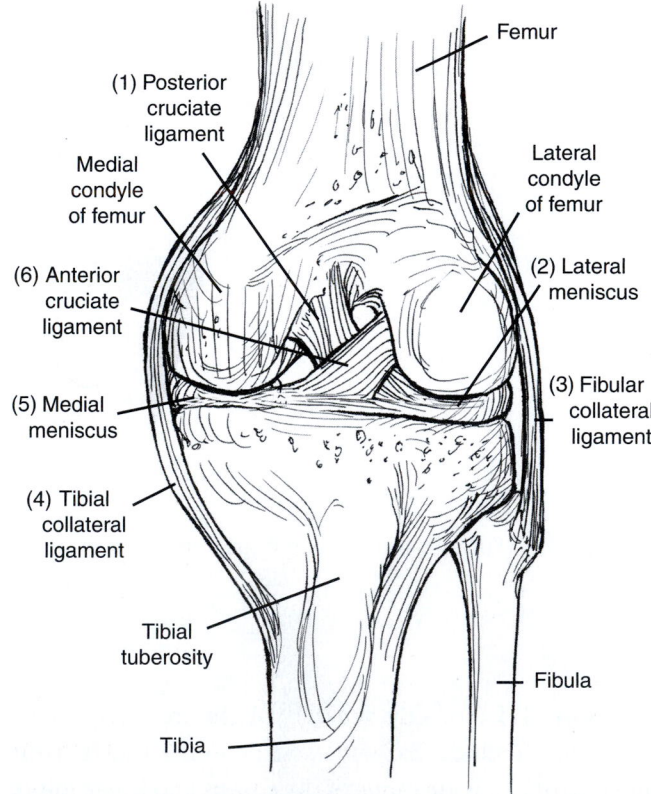

Figure 5-14   Ligaments and menisci of the knee joint

EXERCISE 5-5

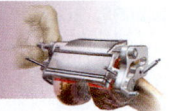

Write the musculoskeletal term for each definition.

1. ankle bone(s) _____
2. kneecap _____
3. heel _____
4. thighbone _____
5. finger and toe bones _____
6. non-weight-bearing lower leg bone _____
7. larger lower leg bone _____
8. slightly movable joint _____
9. lubricating fluid in a joint _____
10. nonmovable joint _____
11. projection at the end of the sternum _____
12. slightly movable joint _____
13. palm bones _____
14. foot bones _____
15. wrist bones _____
16. large bony projection of the thighbone _____
17. indentation in the surface of a bone _____
18. large, rounded knuckle-like projection _____

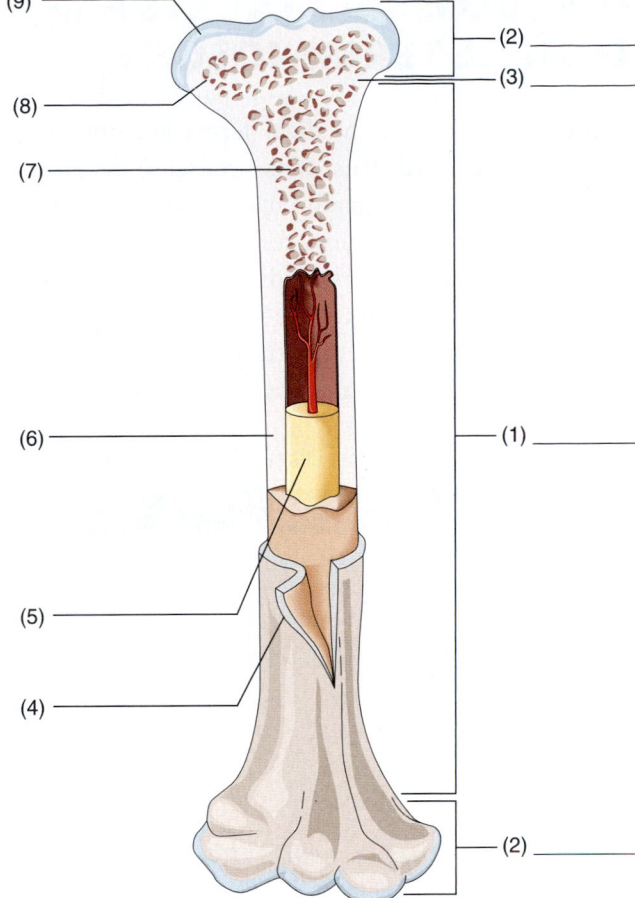

Figure 5-15   Long bone

EXERCISE 5-6

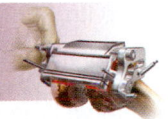

Write the name of the structures of a long bone that are labeled in figure 5-15.

1. _____
2. _____
3. _____
4. _____
5. _____
6. _____
7. _____
8. _____
9. _____

EXERCISE 5-7

Write the names of the following bones next to the correct skeletal structure: calcaneus, carpals, clavicle, coccyx, frontal bone, fibula, humerus, ilium, ischium, metacarpals, metatarsals, occipital bone, parietal bones, phalanges, pubis, radius, ribs, scapula, sternum, temporal bones, tibia, ulna.

1. Cranium: _____
2. Shoulders and chest: _____
3. Arms and hands: _____
4. Legs and feet: _____
5. Hips and pelvis: _____

MUSCULOSKELETAL SYSTEM MEDICAL TERMINOLOGY

Musculoskeletal system medical terms are organized by diseases and conditions of the muscles; diagnostic procedures, operations, treatments, and laboratory tests of the muscles; diseases and conditions of the bones and joints; and diagnostic procedures, operations, treatments, and laboratory tests of the bones and joints. There are two categories of medical terminology exercises: (1) those designed to provide opportunities to learn the terms; and (2) those designed to provide opportunities to accurately assign diagnostic or procedure codes. Exercises for learning the terms immediately follow the lists of terms and definitions. Medical coding exercises are available after all terms have been presented.

Diseases and Conditions of the Muscles

The medical terms in table 5-5 are signs, symptoms, and diseases or conditions related to muscles. Review the meaning of these terms and complete the exercises.

Table 5-5   Signs, Symptoms, Diseases, and Conditions of Muscle

TERM WITH PRONUNCIATION	DEFINITION
atrophy (**AT**-troh-fee) a- = without -trophy = growth; development	wasting or decrease in size of an organ or tissue
bradykinesia (**brad**-ee-kih-**NEE**-see-ah) brady- = slow -kinesia = movement	extremely slow movement
carpal tunnel syndrome	inflammation and swelling of the tendons and median nerve that pass under the carpal ligament; also called repetitive stress syndrome or disease
Charcot-Marie-Tooth disease (shar-**KOO**)	hereditary condition characterized by progressive degeneration of the muscles of the lower leg, specifically those associated with the fibula
contraction (con-**TRACK**-shun)	shortening or tightening of a muscle
contracture (kon-**TRAK**-cher)	abnormal and often permanent flexion at a joint caused by atrophy and shortening of muscle fibers
dermatomyositis (der-**mat**-oh-**my**-oh-**SIGH**-tis) dermat/o = skin my/o = muscle-itis = inflammation	connective tissue disease characterized by the destruction of muscle tissue and pruritic inflammation of the skin
dyskinesia (**diss**-kih-**NEE**-see-ah) dys- = abnormal; difficult -kinesia = movement	abnormal or difficult movement
dystonia (diss-**TOH**-nee-ah) dys- = abnormal; difficult -tonia = muscle tone	abnormal muscle tone; prolonged muscle contractions
dystrophy (**DISS**-troh-fee) dys- = abnormal; difficult -trophy = growth; development	abnormal development
fibroma (fih-BROH-mah) fibr/o = fiber -oma = tumor	tumor of connective tissue
fibromyalgia (FM) (**figh**-broh-my-**AL**-jee-ah) fibr/o = fiber my/o = muscle -algia = pain	chronic pain illness characterized by widespread muscular aches, pains, and stiffness
ganglion (**GANG**-lee-on)	cystic tumor of a tendon
hyperkinesia (**high**-per-kih-**NEE**-see-ah) hyper- = excessive; increase -kinesia = movement	increased muscular movement and physical activity

continued

Table 5-5 (*continued*)   Signs, Symptoms, Diseases, and Conditions of Muscle

TERM WITH PRONUNCIATION	DEFINITION
hypertrophy (high-**PER**-troh-fee) hyper- = excessive; increase -trophy = growth; development	increased growth or development of an organ tissue not related to a tumor
leiomyofibroma (**ligh**-oh-**my**-oh-fih-**BROH**-mah) leiomy/o = smooth muscle fibr/o = fiber -oma = tumor	benign tumor of smooth muscle and fibrous connective tissue
loose body	a fragment of solid tissue in a body cavity or joint; *joint mouse,* a type of loose body associated with the knee; *rice body,* a type of loose body that resembles grains of rice
muscular dystrophy (MD) (**MUSS**-kyoo-lar **DIS**-troh-fee)	progressive weakness and degeneration of muscle fiber; genetically transmitted; one of the most common types of MD is *Duchenne muscular dystrophy*
myalgia (my-**AL**-jee-ah) my/o = muscle -algia = pain	muscle pain
myasthenia (my-ass-**THEE**-nee-ah) my/o = muscle -asthenia = without feeling or sensation	muscle weakness and abnormal fatigue
myasthenia gravis (my-ass-**THEE**-nee-ah **GRAV**-is) my/o = muscle -asthenia = without feeling or sensation	serious, generalized muscle weakness and abnormal fatigue without atrophy
myositis (my-oh-**SIGH**-tis) my/o = muscle -itis = inflammation	inflammation of muscle tissue
polymyositis (**pall**-ee-**my**-oh-**SIGH**-tis) poly- = many my/o = muscle -itis = inflammation	chronic, progressive inflammation of skeletal muscles with muscle weakness and atrophy
rhabdomyolysis (**rab**-doh-**my**-oh-**LIGH**-sis) rhabdomy/o = skeletal muscle -lysis = destruction; breakdown	hereditary or acquired condition characterized by the destruction of skeletal muscle fibers and the release of muscle cell contents into the bloodstream
rhabdomyosarcoma (**rab**-doh-**my**-oh-sar-**KOH**-mah) rhabdomy/o = skeletal muscle sarc/o = flesh -oma = tumor	highly malignant neoplasm or tumor of the skeletal muscle
tendinitis, tenditis (ten-din-**EYE**-tis, ten-**DIGH**-tis) tendin/o, ten/o = tendon -itis = inflammation	inflammation of a tendon
tenodynia (ten-oh-**DIN**-ee-ah) ten/o = tendon -dynia = pain	tendon pain
tenosynovitis (**ten**-oh-**sin**-oh-**VIGH**-tis) ten/o = tendon synov/o = synovial membrane; synovial -itis = inflammation	inflammation of a tendon sheath
torticollis (tor-tih-**KALL**-lis)	shortening of the muscles on one side of the neck; wryneck
Werdnig-Hoffmann disease	genetic disorder characterized by progressive atrophy of skeletal muscles; also known as familial spinal muscle atrophy and floppy infant syndrome

EXERCISE 5-8

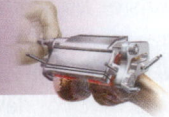

Circle the medical term that best fits the description.

1. abnormal growth and development — *atrophy* or *dystrophy*
2. prolonged muscle contractions — *dystonia* or *dyskinesia*
3. cystic tumor of a tendon — *fibroma* or *ganglion*
4. increased muscular movement — *hyperkinesia* or *bradykinesia*
5. shortening or tightening of a muscle — *contraction* or *contracture*
6. extremely slow movement — *hyperkinesia* or *bradykinesia*
7. tumor of connective tissue — *ganglion* or *fibroma*
8. abnormal or difficult movement — *dyskinesia* or *dystrophy*
9. increased growth or development — *atrophy* or *hypertrophy*
10. benign tumor of smooth muscle and fibrous tissue — *leiomyofibroma* or *Charcot-Marie-Tooth disease*

EXERCISE 5-9

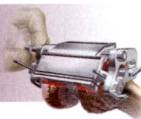

Match the terms in column 1 with the definitions in column 2.

COLUMN 1

a. atrophy
b. carpal tunnel syndrome
c. Charcot-Marie-Tooth disease
d. contracture

e. fibromyalgia
f. muscular dystrophy
g. myalgia
h. myasthenia
i. myasthenia gravis
j. rhabdomyosarcoma
k. sprain
l. torticollis

COLUMN 2

1. abnormal flexion; atrophied, shortened muscle fibers _____
2. chronic condition; widespread muscle aches, pains, and stiffness _____
3. degeneration of the muscles of the lower leg _____
4. malignant neoplasm of skeletal muscle _____
5. muscle pain _____
6. muscle weakness and abnormal fatigue _____
7. progressive weakness and degeneration of muscle fiber _____
8. repetitive stress syndrome _____
9. serious, generalized muscle weakness and abnormal fatigue _____
10. shortening of the neck muscles on one side of the neck _____
11. wrenching or twisting of the ligaments of a joint _____
12. wasting of an organ or tissue _____

EXERCISE 5-10

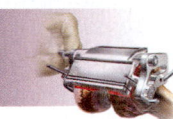

Write the medical term for each definition.

1. destruction and inflammation of muscle tissue and skin _____
2. inflammation of muscle tissue _____
3. chronic, progressive inflammation of skeletal muscle _____
4. destruction of skeletal muscle fibers, hereditary or acquired _____
5. inflammation of a tendon _____
6. tendon pain _____
7. inflammation of a tendon sheath _____
8. familial spinal muscle atrophy; floppy infant syndrome _____

Diagnostic Procedures, Operations, Treatments, and Laboratory Tests of the Muscles

Review the pronunciation and definition of the diagnostic procedures, operations, treatments, and laboratory tests in table 5-6 and complete the exercises.

Table 5-6   Diagnostic Procedures, Operations, Treatments, and Laboratory Tests of Muscle

TERM WITH PRONUNCIATION	DEFINITION
aspartate aminotransferase (AST)	laboratory test that measures blood levels of the enzyme associated with muscular dystrophy; also called serum glutamic oxaloacetic transaminase (SGOT)
creatine kinase (CK)	laboratory test that measures blood levels of the enzyme associated with muscular dystrophy; also called creatine phosphokinase (CPK)
electromyogram (ee-**lek**-troh-**MY**-oh-gram) electr/o = electricity my/o = muscle -gram = graphic record	graphic record of muscle contraction as a result of electrical stimulation
electromyography (EMG) (ee-**lek**-troh-my-**OG**-rah-fee) electr/o = electricity my/o = muscle -graphy = process of recording	process of recording muscle contraction when receiving electrical stimulation
fasciectomy fasci/o = fascia -ectomy = surgical removal	surgical removal or excision of muscle fascia
fasciotomy (fash-ee-**OTT**-oh-mee) fasci/o = fascia -(o)tomy = incision into	surgical incision and division into muscle fascia
ganglionectomy (**gang**-lee-on-**ECK**-toh-mee) -ectomy = surgical removal	excision of a ganglion
myoplasty (**MY**-oh-plass-tee) my/o = muscle -plasty = surgical repair	surgical repair or plastic surgery of muscle tissue
myorrhaphy (my-**OR**-ah-fee) my/o = muscle -(r)rhaphy = suture; suturing	suture of muscle tissue or a muscle wound
tenomyoplasty (ten-oh-**MY**-oh-plass-tee) ten/o = tendon my/o = muscle -plasty = surgical repair	surgical repair of muscles and tendons
tenorrhaphy (ten-**OR**-ah-fee) ten/o = tendon -(r)rhaphy = suture, suturing	suturing of a tendon
tenosynovectomy (**ten**-oh-**sin**-oh-**VEK**-toh-mee) tenosynov/o = tendon sheath -ectomy = surgical removal	surgical removal of a tendon sheath

EXERCISE 5-11

Write the medical term for each definition.

1. excision of a ganglion _____
2. graphic record of muscle contractions _____
3. incision and division into fascia _____
4. surgical repair of muscles and tendons _____
5. surgical removal of a tendon sheath _____

EXERCISE 5-12

Write a brief definition for each term.

1. AST _____
2. CK, CPK _____
3. myorrhaphy _____
4. myoplasty _____
5. tenorrhaphy _____

Diseases and Conditions of Bones and Joints

The medical terms in table 5-7 are signs, symptoms, and diseases or conditions related to bones and joints. Review the meaning of these terms and complete the exercises.

Table 5-7   Signs, Symptoms, Diseases, and Conditions of Bones and Joints

TERM WITH PRONUNCIATION	DEFINITION
ankylosing spondylitis (**ank**-ih-**LOH**-sing spon-dih-**LIGH**-tiss) ankyl/o = stiff spondyl/o = spinal column -itis = inflammation	inflammation of one or more vertebrae characterized by joint stiffness or immobility; rheumatoid arthritis of the spine
ankylosis (ank-ih-**LOH**-sis) ankyl/o = stiff -osis = condition	immobility of a joint
arthralgia (ar-**THRAL**-jee-ah) arthr/o = joint -algia = pain	joint pain
arthritis (ar-**THRIGH**-tis) arthr/o = joint -itis = inflammation	inflammation of a joint
arthrochondritis (**ar**-throh-kon-**DRIGH**-tis) arthr/o = joint chondr/o = joint -itis = inflammation	inflammation of an articular cartilage
Baker cyst	accumulation of synovial fluid in the knee joint
bucket handle tear	tear around the rim of the medial meniscus
bunion	inflammation and enlargement of the bursa of the joint of the great (big) toe; also known as hallux valgus
bursitis (ber-**SIGH**-tis) burs/o = bursa -itis = inflammation	inflammation of the bursa
chondromalacia (**kon**-droh-mah-**LAY**-she-ah) chondr/o = cartilage -malacia = softening	softening of cartilage
crepitation (crep-ih-**TAY**-shun)	crackling or clicking sound present during joint movement
cruciate (**KROO**-shee-it) ligament tear	tear usually associated with the anterior cruciate ligament (ACL) of the knee; often a result of an athletic injury
dislocation (diss-loh-**KAY**-shun)	temporary displacement of a bone from its joint
Ewing sarcoma sarc/o = flesh -oma = tumor	malignant bone tumor that usually develops in the long bones; may involve the entire shaft of a long bone
fibrous dysplasia (**FIGH**-brus dis-**PLAY**-zhah) fibr/o = fiber; fibrous tissue -ous = pertaining to dys- = abnormal; difficult -plasia = growth or development	a cystic bone lesion associated with abnormal bone development during childhood; lesions commonly stop growing at puberty; also called *Albright syndrome*
fracture (Figure 5-16 illustrates five types of fractures.)	sudden breaking of a bone; broken bone

continued

Table 5-7 (*continued*)   Signs, Symptoms, Diseases, and Conditions of Bones and Joints

TERM WITH PRONUNCIATION	DEFINITION
fracture, Colles	fracture of the distal end of the radius, just above the wrist
fracture, comminuted	fracture in which the bone is broken or splintered into pieces
fracture, greenstick	fracture in which the bone is partially bent and partially broken; incomplete fracture
fracture, impacted	fracture in which the bone is broken and wedged into the interior of another bone
fracture, open	fracture in which the bone is broken and bone fragments protrude through the skin; compound fracture
genu valgum	deformity of the knees characterized by the knees coming together when the legs are straightened; commonly called *knock-knees*
genu varum	deformity of the knees, femur, and tibia characterized by an outward curvature of the femur and tibia; commonly called *bow-leg* and *bandy-leg*
gout	acute arthritis characterized by inflammation of the first joint of the great toe
hammer toe	acquired or congenital deformity of the toe as a result of abnormal positioning of the interphalangeal joints of the toe; also called *claw toe* and *mallet toe*
herniated disk (**HER**-nee-ay-ted disk)	rupture of the intervertebral disk, which protrudes between the vertebrae and puts pressure on the spinal nerve root; also known as *herniated nucleus pulposus*; commonly called a *slipped disk*

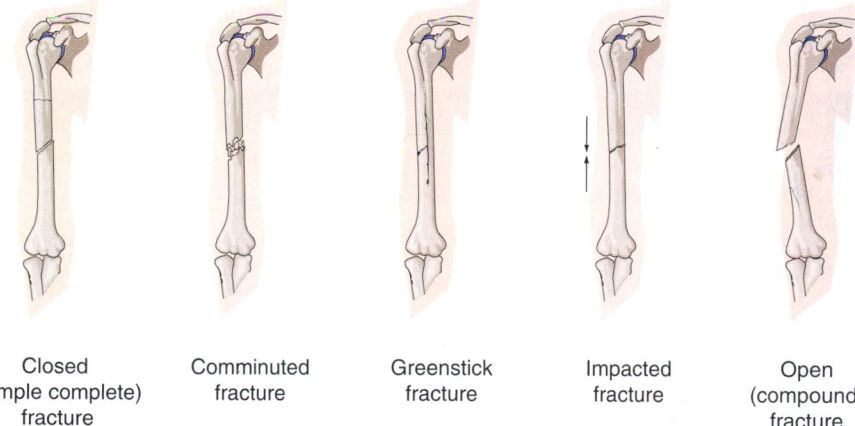

Closed (simple complete) fracture   Comminuted fracture   Greenstick fracture   Impacted fracture   Open (compound) fracture

Figure 5-16   Five types of fracture

EXERCISE 5-13

Circle the medical term that best fits the description.

1. temporary displacement of a bone from its joint — *subluxation* or *dislocation*

2. knock-knees — *genu valgum* or *genu varum*

3. fracture of the distal end of the radius — *greenstick* or *Colles*

4. incomplete fracture — *closed* or *greenstick*

5. compound fracture — *impacted* or *open*

6. crackling during joint movement — *crepitation* or *ankylosis*

EXERCISE 5-14

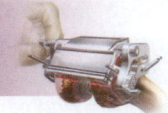

Write a brief definition for each term.

1. arthralgia _____

2. arthritis _____

3. bursitis _____

4. arthrochondritis _____

5. chondromalacia _____

6. fracture _____

7. ankylosing spondylitis _____

EXERCISE 5-15

Match the terms in column 1 with the definitions in column 2.

COLUMN 1

a. Baker cyst

b. bucket handle tear

c. bunion

d. cruciate ligament tear

e. Ewing sarcoma

f. fibrous dysplasia

g. genu varum

h. gout

i. hammer toe

j. herniated disk

COLUMN 2

1. acquired or congenital deformity of the joints of the toe _____

2. acute arthritis of the first joint of the great toe _____

3. bow-leg; bandy-leg _____

4. cystic bone lesion _____

5. excessive fluid in the knee joint _____

6. inflammation of the bursa of the great toe _____

7. injury associated with the ACL _____

8. malignant bone tumor of long bones _____

9. ruptured intervertebral disk _____

10. tear around the rim of the medial meniscus _____

The medical terms in table 5-8 are signs, symptoms, and diseases or conditions related to bones and joints. Review the meaning of these terms and complete the exercises.

Table 5-8 Signs, Symptoms, Diseases, or Conditions of Bones and Joints

TERM WITH PRONUNCIATION	DEFINITION
kyphosis (kigh-**FOH**-sis) kyph/o = pertaining to a hump -osis = abnormal condition	outward curvature of the upper sections of the spinal column; humpback (figure 5-17)
lordosis (lor-**DOH**-sis) lord/o = swayback -osis = abnormal condition	forward curvature of the lower sections, usually the lumbar section, of the spinal column; swayback (figure 5-18)
multiple myeloma (my-eh-**LOH**-mah) myel/o = bone marrow -oma = tumor	a malignant neoplasm originating from the bone marrow that disrupts bone marrow functions, destroys osseous tissue, especially in flat bones
osteitis (oss-tee-**EYE**-tis) oste/o = bone -itis = inflammation	inflammation of the bone
osteochondritis (**oss**-tee-oh-kon-**DRIGH**-tis) oste/o = bone chondr/o = cartilage -itis = inflammation	inflammation of bone and cartilage
osteofibroma (**oss**-tee-oh-fih-**BROH**-mah) oste/o = bone fibr/o = fibrous tissue -oma = tumor	tumor of bony and fibrous tissue
osteogenesis imperfecta (OI) (**oss**-tee-oh-**JEN**-ih-sis im-per-**FECK**-tah)	genetic and congenital condition involving defective development of connective tissue and characterized by abnormally brittle and fragile bones

continued

Table 5-8 (*continued*)   Signs, Symptoms, Diseases, or Conditions of Bones and Joints

TERM WITH PRONUNCIATION	DEFINITION
osteomalacia (**oss**-tee-oh-mah-**LAY**-she-ah) oste/o = bone -malacia = softening	softening of the bone
osteomyelitis (**oss**-tee-oh-**my**-eh-**LIGH**-tis) oste/o = bone myel/o = bone marrow -itis = inflammation	inflammation of the bone and bone marrow
osteoporosis (**oss**-tee-oh-poh-**ROH**-sis) oste/o = bone -porosis = porous condition	decreased bone density or loss of bone mass
osteosarcoma (**oss**-tee-oh-(spread) to the sar-**KOH**-mah) oste/o = bone sarc/o = flesh -oma = tumor	highly malignant bone tumor with a tendency to metastasize lungs; often found in the knee; also called *osteogenic sarcoma*
Paget disease of the bone	chronic bone disease of the adult skeleton characterized by hyperactivity of bone cells and the replacement of bone with a softened, enlarged osseous structure
plantar fasciitis (**PLAN**-tar excessive fash-ee-**EYE**-tis) fasci/o = fascia -itis = inflammation	pain and inflammation of the fascia of the sole of the foot due to stretching or pulling of the plantar fascia
rheumatoid arthritis (RA) (**ROO**-mah-toyd ar-**THRIGH**-tis) arthr/o = joint -itis = inflammation	chronic, systemic inflammatory disease of the joints, especially the joints of the hands and feet
scoliosis (**skoh**-lee-**OH**-sis) scoli/o = crooked, bent -osis = abnormal condition	abnormal lateral curvature of the spine (figure 5-19)
spondylitis (spon-dih-**LIGH**-tiss) spondyl/o = spinal column, vertebra -itis = inflammation	inflammation of one or more vertebrae
spur	bony growth arising from the surface of the bone
subluxation (sub-luks-**AY**-shun)	incomplete dislocation of a bone from its joint

continued

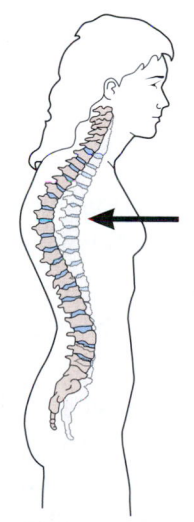

Figure 5-17   Kyphosis

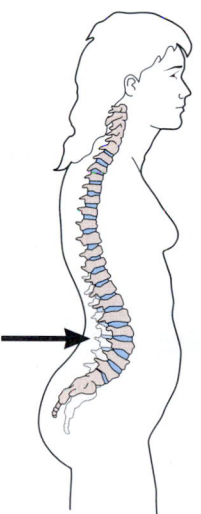

Figure 5-18   Lordosis

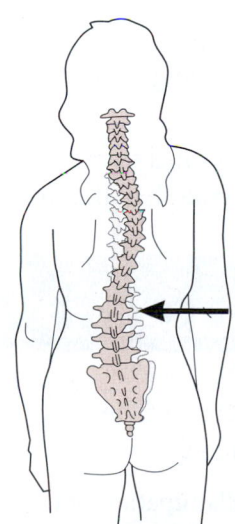

Figure 5-19   Scoliosis

Table 5-8 (*continued*) Signs, Symptoms, Diseases, or Conditions of Bones and Joints

TERM WITH PRONUNCIATION	DEFINITION
systemic lupus erythematosus (SLE) (**LOO**-pus air-**rith**-eh-mah-**TOH**-sis)	autoimmune disease that affects a number of organs and systems; musculoskeletal system involvement includes arthralgia, polyarthritis, joint weakness, tendon contracture, and joint erosion
talipes (**TAL**-ih-peez)	congenital deformity characterized by an abnormal alignment of the bones of the feet; commonly called clubfoot
temporomandibular joint syndrome (TMJ) tempor/o = temporal bone mandibul/o = mandible -ar = pertaining to	mandibular dysfunction due to a defective or dislocated temporomandibular joint characterized by pain, headaches, clicking of the joint during movement, and limitation of jaw movement; may also be caused by an abnormality of the fifth cranial nerve
torn meniscus (meh-**NISS**-cus)	tear in the crescent-shaped cartilage (meniscus) located in the knee joint; the *lateral* and *medial menisci* are between the femoral and tibial bones
torn rotator cuff	tear of the tendons of the four muscles that encircle the shoulder joint and hold the head of the humerus in position; the muscles are responsible for the strength and stability of the shoulder joint; the tendons associated with these muscles, and an overall connective tissue sheath, make up the *rotator cuff*

EXERCISE 5-16

Circle the medical term that best fits the description.

1. outward curvature of the spine — *lordosis* or *kyphosis*

2. chronic bone disease, adult skeleton — *SLE* or *Paget*

3. forward curvature of the spine — *lordosis* or *kyphosis*

4. malignant bone tumor — *osteogenesis imperfecta* or *osteosarcoma*

5. softening of bone — *osteomalacia* or *osteoporosis*

6. abnormal lateral curvature of the spine — *spondylitis* or *scoliosis*

EXERCISE 5-17

Write the name of the medical term for each definition or abbreviation.

1. inflammation of the bone _____

2. inflammation of the bone and bone marrow _____

3. inflammation of one or more vertebrae _____

4. decreased bone density _____

5. inflammation of bone and cartilage _____

6. tumor of bone and fibrous tissue _____

7. bony growth arising from the surface of a bone _____

8. RA _____

EXERCISE 5-18

Match the terms in column 1 with the definitions in column 2.

COLUMN 1	COLUMN 2
a. multiple myeloma	1. autoimmune disease; arthralgia, polyarthritis _____
b. osteogenesis imperfecta	2. clubfoot _____
c. plantar fasciitis	3. genetic condition; abnormally brittle and fragile bones _____
d. subluxation	4. incomplete dislocation of a bone _____

e. SLE

f. talipes

g. TMJ

h. torn meniscus

i. torn rotator cuff

5. limited jaw movement; defective or dislocated joint _____

6. malignant neoplasm arising from bone marrow _____

7. pain and inflammation in the sole of the foot _____

8. tear of the tendons in the shoulder joint _____

9. torn cartilage of the knee joint _____

Diagnostic Procedures, Operations, Treatments, and Laboratory Tests of the Bones and Joints

Review the pronunciation and definition of the diagnostic procedures, operations, treatments, and laboratory tests in table 5-9 and complete the exercises.

Table 5-9 Diagnostic Procedures, Operations, Treatments, and Laboratory Tests of Bones and Joints

TERM WITH PRONUNCIATION	DEFINITION
anterior cruciate ligament repair	repair or replacement of the anterior cruciate ligament
antinuclear antibody (ANA)	blood test that screens for systemic lupus erythematosus (SLE)
arthrocentesis (**ar**-throh-sen-**TEE**-sis) arthr/o = joint -centesis = surgical puncture to withdraw fluid	surgical puncture of a joint to withdraw fluid
arthroclasis (ar-throh-**CLAY**-sis) arthr/o = joint -clasis = therapeutic or surgical breaking	therapeutic breaking of a joint or adhesions of a joint
arthrodesis (ar-throh-**DEE**-sis) arthr/o = joint -desis = surgical fixation	surgical fixation, binding, or immobilization of a joint
arthrogram (**AR**-throh-gram) arthr/o = joint -gram = picture or record of a joint	x-ray picture of a joint
arthrography (ar-**THROG**-rah-fee) arthr/o = joint -graphy = process of recording	process of obtaining a radiograph of the internal structures of a joint aided by the injection of a contrast medium
arthroplasty (**AR**-throh-plass-tee) arthr/o = joint -plasty = surgical repair	surgical repair of a joint
arthroscopy (ar-**THROSS**-koh-pee) arthr/o = joint -scopy = process of viewing; visualization	visualization of the internal structures of a joint using an endoscope
arthrotomy (ar-**THROT**-oh-mee) arthr/o = joint -tomy = incision into	incision into a joint
bone marrow aspiration (ass-per-**AY**-shun)	removing a sample of bone marrow using an aspiration needle
bone scan	nuclear medicine diagnostic imaging procedure that allows visualization of bone structures; a radioisotope is injected intravenously
bunionectomy (bun-yun-**ECK**-toh-mee) -ectomy = surgical removal	surgical removal of a bunion
bursectomy (ber-**SEK**-toh-mee) burs/o = bursa -ectomy = surgical removal	surgical removal of a bursa
bursotomy (ber-**SOT**-oh-mee) burs/o = bursa -tomy = incision into	incision into a bursa

continued

Table 5-9 (*continued*) Diagnostic Procedures, Operations, Treatments, and Laboratory Tests of Bones and Joints

TERM WITH PRONUNCIATION	DEFINITION
closed reduction	process of aligning fractured bones through manual manipulation or traction without making an incision into the skin
craniotomy (kray-nee-**OT**-oh-mee) crani/o = skull -tomy = incision into	incision into the cranium or bones of the skull
diskectomy (disk-**EK**-toh-mee) -ectomy = surgical removal	surgical removal of a herniated intervertebral disk
dual-energy x-ray absorptiometry (DEXA) (**ab**-sorp-she-**AH**-meh-tree)	noninvasive x-ray procedure that measures bone density
dual-photon absorptiometry (**FOH**-ton **ab**-sorp-she-**AH**-meh-tree)	noninvasive procedure using a small amount of radiation to measure bone density
laminectomy (lam-in-**EK**-toh-mee) lamin/o = lamina -ectomy = surgical removal	surgical removal of the posterior arch of the vertebra
open reduction	surgical alignment of fractured bones
open reduction and internal fixation (ORIF)	surgical alignment of fractured bones using screws, pins, wires, or nails to maintain bone alignment (figure 5-20)
osteoclasis (**oss**-tee-oh-**KLAY**-sis) oste/o = bone -clasis = surgical fracture	surgical fracture of a bone
osteoplasty (**OSS**-tee-oh-**plass**-tee) oste/o = bone -plasty = surgical repair	surgical repair of a bone
osteotomy (oss-tee-**OT**-oh-mee) oste/o = bone -tomy = incision into	incision into a bone
spinal fusion	permanent joining of two or more vertebrae
synovectomy (sin-oh-**VEK**-toh-mee) -ectomy = surgical removal	surgical removal of a synovial membrane
total hip replacement (THR)	surgical replacement of the head of the femur and the acetabulum with synthetic components (figure 5-21)

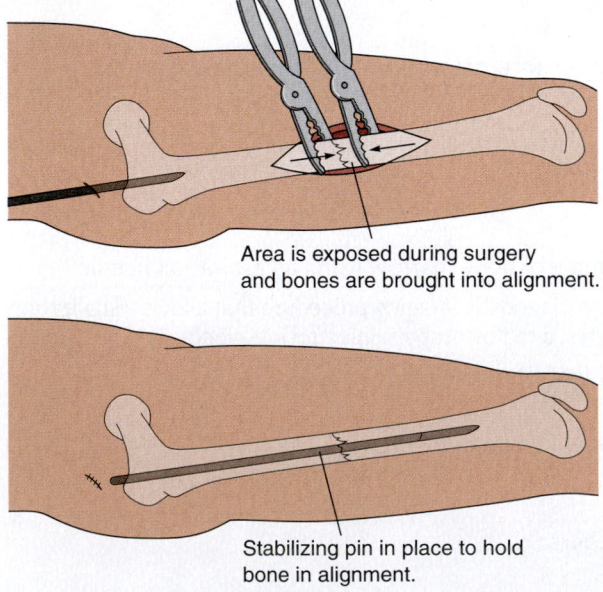

Area is exposed during surgery and bones are brought into alignment.

Stabilizing pin in place to hold bone in alignment.

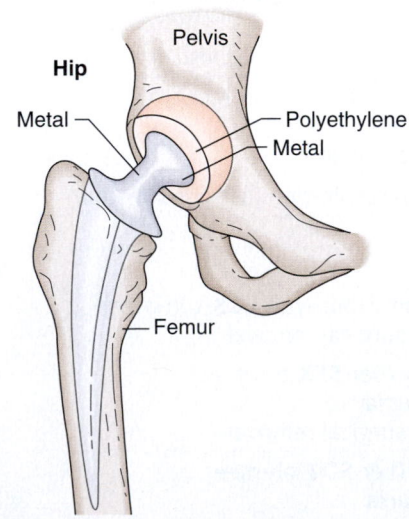

Figure 5-20 Open reduction and internal fixation

Figure 5-21 Total hip replacement

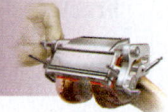

EXERCISE 5-19

Place a *D* next to the diagnostic tests. Place a *P* next to the treatment procedures.

1. antinuclear antibody _____
2. arthrodesis _____
3. arthrography _____
4. closed reduction _____
5. DEXA _____
6. osteoclasis _____
7. THR _____
8. ORIF _____
9. bone scan _____

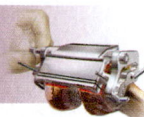

EXERCISE 5-20

Write the medical term for each definition.

1. surgical puncture of a joint to withdraw fluid _____
2. removal of a synovial membrane _____
3. incision into a bone _____
4. therapeutic breaking of a joint _____
5. viewing a joint with an endoscope _____
6. removal of a bunion _____
7. surgical repair of a joint _____
8. surgical alignment of fractured bones _____
9. removal of the posterior arch of a vertebra _____

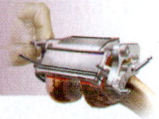

EXERCISE 5-21

Write a brief definition for each medical term.

1. craniotomy _____
2. osteoplasty _____
3. bone marrow aspiration _____
4. arthrotomy _____
5. bone scan _____

6. bursotomy _____
7. arthrogram _____
8. diskectomy _____
9. spinal fusion _____

ABBREVIATIONS

Musculoskeletal system abbreviations are listed in table 5-10. Practice writing out the abbreviations with a brief definition for each phrase or term.

MUSCULOSKELETAL SYSTEM MEDICAL CODING

To successfully complete the exercises in this section, the ICD-9-CM volumes 1, 2, and 3, and the CPT (Current Procedural Terminology) coding references must be readily available. The information in this section is presented as follows:

- An introduction to ICD-9-CM, chapter 13, "Diseases of the Musculoskeletal System and Connective Tissue"
- ICD-9-CM diagnostic coding exercises
- A summary of ICD-9-CM volume 3 coding conventions that apply to musculoskeletal procedures

Table 5-10 Musculoskeletal System Abbreviations

ABBREVIATION	MEANING
ANA	antinuclear antibody
C1–C7	cervical vertebrae, 1 through 7
DEXA	dual-energy x-ray absorptiometry
DTR	deep tendon reflex
EMG	electromyography
FM	fibromyalgia
fx	fracture
L1–L5	lumbar vertebrae, 1 through 5
MD	muscular dystrophy
ORIF	open reduction and internal fixation
RA	rheumatoid arthritis
SLE	systemic lupus erythematosus
T1–T12	thoracic vertebrae, 1 through 12
THR	total hip replacement
TMJ	temporomandibular joint

- ICD-9-CM procedure coding exercises
- A summary of the CPT Musculoskeletal System coding guidelines
- CPT coding exercises

Students are *strongly* encouraged to review the information at the beginning of the ICD-9-CM and CPT coding references. Commercial publishers include instructions on how to use the reference, the ICD-9-CM official coding conventions, additional conventions used by the publisher, and the ICD-9-CM Official Guidelines for Coding and Reporting. Some publishers include the three ICD-9-CM volumes in one book and put the *Alphabetic Index* (volume 2) at the beginning of the reference.

The *Introduction* to CPT includes detailed instructions for using this code book, an index to the illustrations throughout the book, and anatomical illustrations of the major structures of body systems.

ICD-9-CM Volume 1, Chapter 13, Diseases of the Musculoskeletal System (710–739)

Musculoskeletal system diseases are coded to ICD-9-CM chapter 13, "Diseases of the Musculoskeletal System." This chapter includes the following major sections:

- **Arthropathies and Related Disorders (710–719).** Codes in this section cover diffuse diseases of connective tissue, joints, and cartilage.

- **Dorsopathies (720–724).** Codes in this category cover a variety of diseases and conditions related to the spine and intervertebral disks.

- **Rheumatism (725–729).** Codes in this section include inflammatory conditions of muscles, tendons, ligaments, bursae, and other soft tissue.

- **Osteopathies, Chondropathies, and Acquired Musculoskeletal Deformities (730–739).** Codes in these categories include diseases of the bones, cartilage, and muscle deformities.

Several of the categories have extensive fifth-digit instructional notes, and *includes* and *excludes* notes.

Fractures are coded to ICD-9-CM volume 1, chapter 17, "Injury and Poisoning." The following sections are related to fractures:

- **Fractures of the Skull (800–804).** The fifth-digit instruction notes are used to identify whether injury caused a loss of consciousness.

- **Fractures of the Neck and Trunk (805–809).** The fifth-digit instruction notes are used to identify fractures of the vertebral column when there is no mention of spinal cord injury. This section also includes codes for fractures of the ribs, sternum, larynx, trachea, and pelvis.

- **Fractures of Upper Limb (810–819).** Codes in this section cover fractures of all bones associated with the arms, hands, clavicle, and scapula. Nearly all the codes in this section require fifth digits.

- **Fractures of Lower Limb (820–829).** Codes in this section cover fractures and dislocations of all bones associated with the legs and feet. Nearly all the codes in this section require fifth digits.

- **Dislocations (830–839).** Codes in this section cover dislocations of all areas of the musculoskeletal system. Fifth digits are used to identify the joint or body part that is dislocated. Nearly all the codes in this section require fifth digits.

Sprains and strains of joints and adjacent muscles, tendons, and ligaments are also coded to chapter 17, "Injury and Poisonings." Sections 840–848 contain codes for conditions such as sprains or strains of the upper extremities, lower extremities, back, and other ill-defined sprains and strains.

Conditions related to the musculoskeletal system may also be coded to the following chapters in volume 1: chapter 14, "Congenital Anomalies"; chapter 16, "Symptoms, Signs, and Ill-Defined Conditions"; and chapter 2, "Neoplasms."

Several conditions listed with musculoskeletal diseases and conditions are coded to chapter 8, "Diseases of the Nervous System and Sense Organs." The conditions include, and may not be limited to, carpal tunnel syndrome, muscular dystrophy, myasthenia, myasthenia gravis, and Werdnig-Hoffmann disease.

EXERCISE 5-22

Write a brief definition for each diagnosis. Identify the main term in the diagnostic statement and assign the correct ICD-9-CM code(s).

1. Disuse muscular atrophy

   DEFINITION: _____

   MAIN TERM: _____

   ICD-9-CM CODE(S): _____

2. Fibromyalgia

   DEFINITION: _____

   MAIN TERM: _____

   ICD-9-CM CODE(S): _____

3. Systemic lupus erythematosus

   DEFINITION: _____

   MAIN TERM: _____

   ICD-9-CM CODE(S): _____

4. Plantar fasciitis

   DEFINITION: _____

   MAIN TERM: _____

   ICD-9-CM CODE(S): _____

5. Rheumatoid arthritis, hands and feet

   DEFINITION: _____

   MAIN TERM: _____

   ICD-9-CM CODE(S): _____

6. Ankylosing spondylitis

   DEFINITION: _____

   MAIN TERM: _____

   ICD-9-CM CODE(S): _____

7. Baker cyst, left knee

   DEFINITION: _____

   MAIN TERM: _____

   ICD-9-CM CODE(S): _____

8. Old bucket handle tear, medial meniscus

   DEFINITION: _____

   MAIN TERM: _____

   ICD-9-CM CODE(S): _____

9. Acute osteomyelitis of the pelvis and thigh

   DEFINITION: _____

   MAIN TERM: _____

   ICD-9-CM CODE(S): _____

10. Genu varum, acquired

    DEFINITION: _____

    MAIN TERM: _____

    ICD-9-CM CODE(S): _____

11. Bunion, great toe, left foot

    DEFINITION: _____

    MAIN TERM: _____

    ICD-9-CM CODE(S): _____

12. Contracture, joints of the fourth and fifth fingers, right hand

    DEFINITION: _____

    MAIN TERM: _____

    ICD-9-CM CODE(S): _____

13. Fibrous dysplasia, left femur

    DEFINITION: _____

    MAIN TERM: _____

    ICD-9-CM CODE(S): _____

14. Acute polymyositis

    DEFINITION: _____

    MAIN TERM: _____

    ICD-9-CM CODE(S): _____

15. Torticollis

    DEFINITION: _____

    MAIN TERM: _____

    ICD-9-CM CODE(S): _____

16. Recurrent dislocation of the shoulder

    DEFINITION: _____

    MAIN TERM: _____

    ICD-9-CM CODE(S): _____

17. Chondromalacia, tibial plateau

    DEFINITION: _____

    MAIN TERM: _____

    ICD-9-CM CODE(S): _____

continued

18. Greenstick fracture, shaft, left fibula

    DEFINITION: _____

    MAIN TERM: _____

    ICD-9-CM CODE(S): _____

19. Pathological fracture, closed, femoral neck

    DEFINITION: _____

    MAIN TERM: _____

    ICD-9-CM CODE(S): _____

20. Postmenopausal osteoporosis

    DEFINITION: _____

    MAIN TERM: _____

    ICD-9-CM CODE(S): _____

21. Paget bone disease

    DEFINITION: _____

    MAIN TERM: _____

    ICD-9-CM CODE(S): _____

22. Subluxation of the patella, closed

    DEFINITION: _____

    MAIN TERM: _____

    ICD-9-CM CODE(S): _____

23. Bone spur, calcaneus

    DEFINITION: _____

    MAIN TERM: _____

    ICD-9-CM CODE(S): _____

24. Multiple myeloma

    DEFINITION: _____

    MAIN TERM: _____

    ICD-9-CM CODE(S): _____

25. Herniated disk, between L3 and L4

    DEFINITION: _____

    MAIN TERM: _____

    ICD-9-CM CODE(S): _____

26. Idiopathic rhabdomyolysis

    DEFINITION: _____

    MAIN TERM: _____

    ICD-9-CM CODE(S): _____

27. Rice bodies, ankle and foot

    DEFINITION: _____

    MAIN TERM: _____

    ICD-9-CM CODE(S): _____

28. Ewing sarcoma, humerus

    DEFINITION: _____

    MAIN TERM: _____

    ICD-9-CM CODE(S): _____

29. Fibrous ankylosis, elbow

    DEFINITION: _____

    MAIN TERM: _____

    ICD-9-CM CODE(S): _____

30. Calcific tendinitis, right shoulder

    DEFINITION: _____

    MAIN TERM: _____

    ICD-9-CM CODE(S): _____

ICD-9-CM Volume 3, Chapter 14, Operations on the Musculoskeletal System (76–84)

Musculoskeletal system operations and some therapeutic treatments are coded to ICD-9-CM volume 3, chapter 14, "Operations on the Musculoskeletal System." This chapter includes these major categories:

- **Operations on facial bones and joints (76).** Codes in this category include incision, excision, reconstruction, reduction, and biopsy of the facial bones and joints.
- **Incision, excision, and divisions of other bones (77).** Codes in this category cover all bones, except for the facial bones.
- **Other operations on bones, except facial bones (78).** Codes in this category cover procedures like bone grafts, internal fixation, removal of implanted devices, and miscellaneous procedures.

continued

- **Reduction of fracture and dislocation (79).** Codes in this category include open and closed reductions of fractures and dislocations, with and without internal fixation devices.

- **Incision and excision of joint structures (80).** Codes in this category cover procedures related to joints, intervertebral disks, and synovial membranes.

- **Repair and plastic operations on joint structures (81).** Codes in this category include fusion, refusion, joint repair, joint replacement, procedures on the spine, and repair of joints of the hand, fingers, and wrist.

- **Operations on muscle, tendon, and fascia of hand (82).** Codes in this category cover all procedures on the hand and related structures.

- **Operations on muscle, tendon, fascia, and bursa, except hand (83).** Codes in this category cover all parts of the body, except the hand.

- **Other procedures on musculoskeletal system (84).** Codes in this category include amputation, disarticulation, reattachment, prosthetic limbs, and implantation, application, revision, or replacement of internal and external fixation devices.

All codes in this chapter have four digits. The fourth digit gives additional information about the location of the procedure and the type of procedure, such as amputation, insertion, and removal.

Volume 3, chapter 16, "Miscellaneous Diagnostic and Therapeutic Procedures" (87–99) also contains codes that apply to the musculoskeletal system. Physical therapy, skeletal traction, application of casts and splints, and osteopathic manipulative treatments are examples of diagnostic tests and procedures related to the musculoskeletal system.

Operations and procedures related to the cranial (skull) bones are coded to volume 3, chapter 1, "Operations on the Nervous System." These codes cover procedures like craniotomy, excision of lesions of the skull, and cranial bone grafts.

EXERCISE 5-23

Write a brief definition for each operative, treatment, or diagnostic procedure term. Identify the main term in the statement and assign the correct ICD-9-CM code(s).

1. Electromyography, left lower limb
   DEFINITION: _____
   MAIN TERM: _____
   ICD-9-CM CODE(S): _____

2. Fasciotomy, muscles of the forearm
   DEFINITION: _____
   MAIN TERM: _____
   ICD-9-CM CODE(S): _____

3. Anterior cruciate ligament repair
   DEFINITION: _____
   MAIN TERM: _____
   ICD-9-CM CODE(S): _____

4. Bunionectomy and insertion of prosthesis, right great toe
   DEFINITION: _____
   MAIN TERM: _____
   ICD-9-CM CODE(S): _____

5. Bursectomy, right elbow
   DEFINITION: _____
   MAIN TERM: _____
   ICD-9-CM CODE(S): _____

6. Needle core stem cell bone marrow aspiration, iliac crest
   DEFINITION: _____
   MAIN TERM: _____
   ICD-9-CM CODE(S): _____

7. Closed reduction, simple fracture of the tibia
   DEFINITION: _____
   MAIN TERM: _____
   ICD-9-CM CODE(S): _____

continued

8. Open reduction, internal fixation, crushed calcaneus

   DEFINITION: _____

   MAIN TERM: _____

   ICD-9-CM CODE(S): _____

9. DEXA scan, left femur

   DEFINITION: _____

   MAIN TERM: _____

   ICD-9-CM CODE(S): _____

10. Craniotomy, to relieve intracranial pressure

    DEFINITION: _____

    MAIN TERM: _____

    ICD-9-CM CODE(S): _____

11. Total hip replacement, right hip

    DEFINITION: _____

    MAIN TERM: _____

    ICD-9-CM CODE(S): _____

12. Laminectomy with removal of a herniated disk, fusion of third and fourth lumbar vertebra

    DEFINITION: _____

    MAIN TERM: _____

    ICD-9-CM CODE(S): _____

13. Open reduction, impacted fracture of the femur

    DEFINITION: _____

    MAIN TERM: _____

    ICD-9-CM CODE(S): _____

14. Full skeleton bone scan (radioisotope), rule out multiple myeloma

    DEFINITION: _____

    MAIN TERM: _____

    ICD-9-CM CODE(S): _____

15. Arthroscopic removal of the lateral meniscus

    DEFINITION: _____

    MAIN TERM: _____

    ICD-9-CM CODE(S): _____

16. Excision of a ganglion, left wrist

    DEFINITION: _____

    MAIN TERM: _____

    ICD-9-CM CODE(S): _____

17. Arthrodesis and repair of the toe, hammer to repair

    DEFINITION: _____

    MAIN TERM: _____

    ICD-9-CM CODE(S): _____

18. Myoplasty, left hand

    DEFINITION: _____

    MAIN TERM: _____

    ICD-9-CM CODE(S): _____

19. Arthrocentesis, right knee to withdraw fluid in Baker cyst

    DEFINITION: _____

    MAIN TERM: _____

    ICD-9-CM CODE(S): _____

20. Osteoclasis, radius, right arm

    DEFINITION: _____

    MAIN TERM: _____

    ICD-9-CM CODE(S): _____

21. Amputation of the thumb

    DEFINITION: _____

    MAIN TERM: _____

    ICD-9-CM CODE(S): _____

Current Procedural Terminology (CPT) Musculoskeletal System Codes (20000–29999)

CPT musculoskeletal system codes are located in the Surgery, Radiology, and Medicine sections. The Surgery guidelines provide important information for all of the Surgery subsections. Review the guidelines in the CPT manual and in chapter 3 of this text. There are additional and extensive instructional notes in the Musculoskeletal System subsection of the Surgery section. The Musculoskeletal System subsection includes these major categories:

- **General (20000–20999).** Codes in this category cover exploration of wounds caused by trauma (i.e., gunshot and stab wounds), excision and incision of musculoskeletal tissue, application of fixation systems or devices, replantation, and grafts or implants.

- **Head (21010–21499).** Codes in this category cover procedures of the skull, facial bones, and temporomandibular joint.

- **Neck (Soft Tissue) and Thorax (21501–21899).** Codes in this category cover incisions, excisions, repair, revision, reconstruction, fractures, and dislocations of the neck and thorax.

- **Back and Flank (21920–21935).** Codes in this category cover excisions on the soft tissue of the back and flank.

- **Spine (Vertebral Column) (22010–22899).** Codes in this category cover incisions, excisions, osteotomy, fractures, dislocations, manipulation, embolization, injection, arthrodesis, correction of spine deformities, spinal fusions, and application or insertion of spinal prosthetic devices. The instructional notes at the beginning of this section give examples of several procedure and coding scenarios.

- **Shoulder (23000–23929).** Codes in this category cover procedures of the clavicle, scapula, humerus head and neck, sternoclavicular joint, acromioclavicular joint, and shoulder joint.

- **Humerus and Elbow (23930–24999).** Codes in this category cover procedures of the humerus, the olecranon process, and head and neck of the radius.

- **Forearm and Wrist (25000–25999).** Codes in this category cover procedures of the radius, ulna, and carpal bones and joints.

- **Hand and Fingers (26010–26989).** Codes in this category cover procedures of the hand and fingers ranging from drainage of an abscess to amputation.

- **Pelvis and Hip Joint (26990–27299).** Codes in this category cover procedures of the pelvis, hip joint, and head and neck of the femur.

- **Femur and Knee Joint (27301–27599).** Codes in this category cover procedures of the femur, structures of the knee joint, and the tibial plateaus.

- **Leg (Tibia and Fibula) and Ankle Joint (27600–27899).** Codes in this category cover procedures of the tibia, fibula, and ankle joint such as fractures, dislocations, manipulation, and amputation.

- **Foot and Toes (28001–28899).** Codes in this category cover procedures of the foot and toes such as bunion correction, fractures, dislocations, arthrodesis, and amputation.

- **Application of Casts and Strapping (29000–29799).** Codes in this category cover the application of casts, strapping, and splints.

- **Endoscopy/Arthroscopy (29800–29999).** Codes in this category cover arthroscopic surgical and diagnostic procedures. The instruction note at the beginning of the section reminds the coder that when a diagnostic arthroscopy becomes the surgical approach, only the surgical arthroscopy is coded.

Musculoskeletal diagnostic imaging procedures are coded to the Radiology section. Some of the categories related to the musculoskeletal system include the following:

- **Diagnostic Radiology (Diagnostic Imaging) (70010–73725).** Codes in this category include radiography of the head, neck, chest, spine, pelvis, upper extremities, and lower extremities. Magnetic resonance imaging (MRI) and computerized tomography (CT) scans are included in this section.

- **Nuclear Medicine: Musculoskeletal System (78300–78399).** Codes in this category cover bone scans and bone density studies.

Musculoskeletal diagnostic procedures and therapeutic treatments are also coded to the Medicine section. Some of the categories related to the musculoskeletal system include the following:

- **Muscle and Range of Motion Testing (95831–95857).** Codes in this category include manual evaluation of muscular movement and range of motion.

- **Electromyography and Nerve Conduction Tests (95860–95904).** Codes in this category include testing muscle movement as it is affected by nerve impulse conduction.

- **Physical Medicine and Rehabilitation (97001–97546).** Codes in this category include physical therapy assessment, application of any physical agent that produces a therapeutic change to biological tissue.

- **Osteopathic Manipulative Treatment (98925–98929).** Codes in this category are selected based on the number of body regions treated by osteopathic manipulative treatment.

- **Chiropractic Manipulative Treatment (98940–98943).** Codes in this category are selected based on the number of body regions treated by chiropractic manipulative treatment.

EXERCISE 5-24

Identify the main term in each statement. Assign the correct CPT code(s).

1. Needle electromyography, one extremity

   MAIN TERM: _____

   CPT CODE(S): _____

2. Myoplasty of the flexor muscle of the forearm

   MAIN TERM: _____

   CPT CODE(S): _____

3. Primary ganglionectomy of the wrist

   MAIN TERM: _____

   CPT CODE(S): _____

4. Tenosynovectomy, flexor tendon of the right palm

   MAIN TERM: _____

   CPT CODE(S): _____

5. Radical fasciectomy, plantar fascia

   MAIN TERM: _____

   CPT CODE(S): _____

6. Arthrodesis of the shoulder joint

   MAIN TERM: _____

   CPT CODE(S): _____

7. Anterior cruciate ligament repair, primary

   MAIN TERM: _____

   CPT CODE(S): _____

8. Repair of the medial meniscus, arthroscopic

   MAIN TERM: _____

   CPT CODE(S): _____

9. Closed reduction and manipulation of Colles fracture

   MAIN TERM: _____

   CPT CODE(S): _____

10. Open reduction, internal fixation, proximal fibula, left leg

    MAIN TERM: _____

    CPT CODE(S): _____

11. Femoral neck osteoplasty, open treatment

    MAIN TERM: _____

    CPT CODE(S): _____

12. Total hip replacement

    MAIN TERM: _____

    CPT CODE(S): _____

13. Full body bone scan, rule out multiple myeloma

    MAIN TERM: _____

    CPT CODE(S): _____

14. Aspiration, knee bursa

    MAIN TERM: _____

    CPT CODE(S): _____

15. Thoracic osteotomy including diskectomy, single vertebral segment

    MAIN TERM: _____

    CPT CODE(S): _____

■ SUMMARY

This chapter covered medical terms related to the musculoskeletal system, which includes muscles, bones, tendons, ligaments, and joints. Musculoskeletal diagnoses and procedures were identified and defined. Musculoskeletal diseases and conditions are coded to ICD-9-CM volume 1, chapter 13, "Diseases of the Musculoskeletal System." Fractures are coded to chapter 17, "Injury and Poisoning." Other chapters that have codes relating to musculoskeletal conditions are chapter 2, "Neoplasms"; chapter 14, "Congenital Anomalies"; and chapter 16,

"Signs, Symptoms, and Ill-Defined Conditions." Musculoskeletal procedures are coded to ICD-9-CM volume 3, chapter 14, "Operations of the Musculoskeletal System." Operations and procedures related to the cranium are coded to chapter 1, "Operations on the Nervous System." Chapter 16, "Miscellaneous Diagnostic and Therapeutic Procedures," also includes codes that apply to the musculoskeletal system.

Current Procedural Terminology (CPT) musculoskeletal procedures codes are found in the CPT Surgery subsection Musculoskeletal System (20000–29999), and in the Radiology and Medicine sections.

■ CHAPTER REVIEW

Read each medical note. Write the diagnosis(es) and the main term. Assign the ICD-9-CM diagnosis codes.

CASE 1

DISCHARGE DIAGNOSIS: Compression fracture, C-5.

PROCEDURE(S) PERFORMED: Anterior cervical diskectomy.

BRIEF HISTORY: This 27-year-old male fell 12 feet from a ladder. He complained of pain radiating to the occipital region of the skull. Cervical x-rays were suspicious for a compression fracture at the level of C-5. A myelogram and CT scan of the cervical spine confirmed the fracture.

DISPOSITION: The patient was discharged home on the third postoperative day. He will wear a cervical collar at all times and will be seen at the orthopedic clinic in two weeks.

DIAGNOSIS(ES): _____

MAIN TERM(S): _____

ICD-9-CM DIAGNOSIS CODE(S): _____

CASE 2

Mr. Mattson is a 55-year-old healthy appearing individual who is seen today for a follow-up evaluation of fibrous dysplasia involving the femur, left leg. The diagnosis was originally identified at age 15. At that time he underwent bone replacement surgery with minimal results. He has had regular evaluations, at least every three years, since that time. X-ray today reveals an ovoid lesion in the femur, left leg approximately 6 × 3 cm. Compared to the x-ray taken three years ago, the lesion has not changed. In fact, there has been no change since age 21. Based on this evaluation, Mr. Mattson's fibrous dysplasia is quiescent. He was advised to continue with his current level of activity. He was instructed to refrain from activities that increase the risk of fracture.

DIAGNOSIS(ES): _____

MAIN TERM(S): _____

ICD-9-CM DIAGNOSIS CODE(S): _____

CASE 3

Mr. Rosachovich presents today with swelling, warmth, redness, and extreme tenderness of the right great toe. He noticed the warmth, redness, and "some tenderness" a few days ago. Yesterday, the tenderness became almost unbearable. The skin in the area is warm, shiny, and has a red-purplish appearance. Given his history, he appears to be experiencing an episode of gout. He will start a course of anti-inflammatory medication today and should see a noticeable improvement within 48 hours. He was instructed to call the office the day after tomorrow to report if he is getting relief with this course of treatment.

DIAGNOSIS(ES): _____

MAIN TERM(S): _____

ICD-9-CM DIAGNOSIS CODE(S): _____

CASE 4

The patient is seen today for evaluation of the latest course of treatment for rheumatoid arthritis. She states that "there is some improvement," related to pain, but her hands "still feel like stones." Ambulation is still very difficult, and her husband must help her in the morning until she "gets moving around." We discussed the possibility of knee-joint replacement. She is hesitant at this time. She was provided with additional information about joint replacement and advised to give this option serious consideration. Medications were adjusted. She will schedule another appointment within three months or sooner if necessary.

DIAGNOSIS(ES): _____

MAIN TERM(S): _____

ICD-9-CM DIAGNOSIS CODE(S): _____

CASE 5

Barbara Loonsfoot is seen in the office today for heel pain. X-ray today reveals an inferior calcaneal spur that extends forward horizontally toward the plantar fascia. During the examination, pressure was applied along the entire inner border of the fascia with the ankle in dorsiflexion. Ms. Loonsfoot indicated that on a scale of 1 to 10, pain during examination was "about an 8." The diagnosis is plantar fasciitis. A steroid injection was administered. She is to call the office tomorrow to report if there is any improvement.

DIAGNOSIS(ES): _____

MAIN TERM(S): _____

ICD-9-CM DIAGNOSIS CODE(S): _____

CASE 6

Martina Wallace is seen for a review of her recent lab work. For the past three months she has had complaints of achy pain, tenderness, and stiffness of muscles, tendons, and ligamental areas, especially in the neck and thighs. During her first visit, a complete physical examination was conducted. Osteoarthritis, rheumatoid arthritis, and psychogenic muscle pain and spasm were ruled out. She continued to exhibit anxiety, fatigue, restless sleep patterns, and irritable bowel syndrome. Chronic fatigue syndrome has also been ruled out. Based on the recent lab results, there is no evidence of Lyme disease. The best diagnosis is fibromyalgia. Considerable time was spent discussing the syndrome and outlining treatment options. Martina appeared relieved to "finally have a name for this problem." She is to return in three months or sooner if necessary.

DIAGNOSIS(ES): _____

MAIN TERM(S): _____

ICD-9-CM DIAGNOSIS CODE(S): _____

CASE 7

Ms. Ming is a new patient who recently moved to this city. Her medical records, which were sent by her previous internist, have been reviewed. Two months ago she began describing pain and stiffness in the neck, shoulder, and pelvis. She denies any permanent weakness, but states that she feels "really stiff" after periods of inactivity, like watching a movie. There is no evident joint swelling or other signs or symptoms of rheumatoid arthritis. An EMG done one month ago was normal, with no pathological findings. Her most recent lab work was faxed to us today. Most notable is the elevated ESR. Enzyme tests are within normal limits. Clinical laboratory data and an extensive physical examination here and by her previous internist most certainly rule out rheumatoid arthritis and polymyositis. All findings were explained to Ms. Ming, including the fact that we would be treating her condition as polymyalgia rheumatica. She will be started on oral prednisone 15 mg/day. She will start prednisone today and call the office on Wednesday with an update of her symptoms.

DIAGNOSIS(ES): _____

MAIN TERM(S): _____

ICD-9-CM DIAGNOSIS CODE(S): _____

CASE 8

Alex Obydynev is seen for evaluation of muscle weakness, tenderness and pain, and a rash. He states that he really noticed these symptoms when he started having a hard time raising his arms over his shoulder. At first he thought he had "overdone it" while working on a home remodeling project. He applied his usual OTC remedies, without relief. In fact, he states that now he has a hard time climbing stairs and getting up out of his recliner. A comprehensive medical history and physical examination were completed, and a full lab workup was ordered. Until all lab results are received, we will treat this as polymyositis. Mr. Obydynev is to restrict his activities until test results are available. He is started on a course of prednisone 40 mg/day, antacids, and potassium supplements.

DIAGNOSIS(ES): _____

MAIN TERM(S): _____

ICD-9-CM DIAGNOSIS CODE(S): _____

Read the procedure note, operative report, or discharge summary excerpts. Write the diagnosis and its ICD-9-CM code. Write the name of the procedure and the main term. Assign the ICD-9-CM procedure code(s).

CASE 9

PREOPERATIVE DIAGNOSIS: Lateral recess syndrome at L4–L5, right.

POSTOPERATIVE DIAGNOSIS: Herniated disk at L4–L5, right.

OPERATIVE PROCEDURE: Lumbar laminectomy and excision of disk at L4–L5 on the right.

ANESTHESIA: General endotracheal plus Marcaine with epinephrine.

PROCEDURE: The patient was placed under general anesthesia, prepped and draped in the usual sterile fashion, and placed in the prone position. A midline incision centered over the L4–L5 was made and carried down to the fascia. Marcaine 0.25% with epinephrine was injected and the fascia was incised alongside the L4 spinous process and the muscle stripped off laterally. A portion of the lamina of L4 was removed. The disk herniation between L4–L5 was removed using curettes and rongeurs. The wound was irrigated with Kantrex. Closure was done with 2-0 Vicryl in the fascia and subcutaneous tissue. Then 4-0 undyed Vicryl was used as a subcuticular stitch. Dressing was applied. Sponge and needle count was correct ×2. The patient tolerated the procedure without incident.

DIAGNOSIS: _____

ICD-9-CM DIAGNOSIS CODE: _____

PROCEDURE(S): _____

MAIN TERM(S): _____

ICD-9-CM PROCEDURE CODE(S): _____

CASE 10

ADMITTING DIAGNOSIS: Bilateral hallux valgus.

DISCHARGE DIAGNOSIS: Bilateral hallux valgus, corrected.

CONSULTATIONS: None.

PROCEDURES: Bilateral correction of hallux valgus with osteotomy.

COMPLICATIONS: None.

HOSPITAL COURSE: This 15-year-old young man was admitted for scheduled surgery as listed above. On admission all labs were normal. Preoperative chest film was normal. The patient responded to anesthesia uneventfully. His postoperative course was unremarkable as he remained stable and afebrile. Physical therapy was initiated during hospitalization. The therapist taught the patient to use crutches, including on stairs and at curbs.

DISCHARGE INSTRUCTIONS: He was discharged on postoperative day five in improved condition to be seen in the office for a dressing check in one week. He was given Tylenol #3 p.r.n. pain. Diet regular. Activities: Crutches, no weight bearing. Keep lower limb iced and elevated as much as possible. Patient voiced understanding of the plan as described. Both he and his parents agreed to the plan and scheduled follow-up.

DIAGNOSIS: _____

ICD-9-CM DIAGNOSIS CODE: _____

PROCEDURE(S): _____

MAIN TERM(S): _____

ICD-9-CM PROCEDURE CODE(S): _____

CASE 11

PREOPERATIVE DIAGNOSIS: Right intertrochanteric femoral fracture.

POSTOPERATIVE DIAGNOSIS: Right intertrochanteric femoral fracture.

OPERATIVE PROCEDURE: Open reduction, internal fixation of right intertrochanteric fracture with DePuy sliding screw.

PROCEDURE: The patient was taken to the operating room and administered general endotracheal anesthesia with prominences well padded. A straight lateral approach to the proximal femur was made. Dissection was carried through the skin and subcutaneous tissue. Hemostasis was obtained with electrocautery. The fascia lata was divided in line with the skin incision. The lateral aspect of the proximal femur was revealed, and the tissue was retracted with Bennett and Hohmann retractors without complication. An 85-mm sliding screw was inserted across the fracture site into the head and neck without complication. A four-hole 135-degree side plate was then attached. We slid it over the DePuy sliding screw and attached it to the proximal femur using a Lowman turkey-claw clamp. With fixation in place, AP and lateral fluoroscopic images throughout the fracture site and hardware position confirmed good reduction and good placement of the hardware. All screws were tightened with a screwdriver. The Lowman was removed as was all hardware. The wound was copiously irrigated and the wound was closed.

The patient tolerated the procedure well. There were no complications. Blood loss was negligible. Needle and sponge counts were correct ×2.

DIAGNOSIS: _____

ICD-9-CM DIAGNOSIS CODE: _____

PROCEDURE(S): _____

MAIN TERM(S): _____

ICD-9-CM PROCEDURE CODE(S): _____

CASE 12

PREOPERATIVE DIAGNOSIS: Torn left medial meniscus.

POSTOPERATIVE DIAGNOSIS: Torn left medial meniscus.

OPERATIVE PROCEDURE: Arthroscopic partial medial meniscectomy.

PROCEDURE: The patient was brought into the operating room, placed under general anesthesia, and prepped and draped in the usual sterile manner. A standard three-portal approach was used to access the operative site. No chondromalacia changes were noted in all three compartments. Both the anterior cruciate ligament and lateral meniscus were intact. The anterior portion of the medial meniscus had a flap tear that was removed. Instruments were withdrawn. The wound was closed and dressing applied. Blood loss was minimal. All counts were correct ×2. The patient tolerated the procedure well and was taken to the recovery room in good condition.

DIAGNOSIS: _____

ICD-9-CM DIAGNOSIS CODE: _____

PROCEDURE(S): _____

MAIN TERM(S): _____

ICD-9-CM PROCEDURE CODE(S): _____

CASE 13

PREOPERATIVE DIAGNOSIS: Osteoarthritis, acromioclavicular joint, right.

POSTOPERATIVE DIAGNOSIS: Osteoarthritis, acromioclavicular joint, right.

OPERATIVE PROCEDURE: Mumford procedure, right shoulder, distal clavicle.

PROCEDURE: The patient was brought to the operating room and placed under general anesthesia, prepped and draped in the usual fashion, and placed in the lounge chair position. The right shoulder was scrubbed in the usual sterile manner. The incision was made to the distal clavicle and retractors were placed. The distal end of the clavicle was removed. The wound was irrigated and injected with Marcaine and epinephrine. The wound was closed and sterile dressings applied. Blood loss was negligible. Sponge and needle counts were correct ×2. The patient was sent to the recovery room in good condition.

DIAGNOSIS: _____

ICD-9-CM DIAGNOSIS CODE: _____

PROCEDURE(S): _____

MAIN TERM(S): _____

ICD-9-CM PROCEDURE CODE(S): _____

Using the same excerpts in the previous exercises, assign the CPT codes to the procedures.

CASE 14

PREOPERATIVE DIAGNOSIS: Lateral recess syndrome at L4–L5, right.

POSTOPERATIVE DIAGNOSIS: Herniated disk at L4–L5, right.

OPERATIVE PROCEDURE: Lumbar laminectomy and excision of disk at L4–L5 on the right.

ANESTHESIA: General endotracheal plus Marcaine with epinephrine.

PROCEDURE: The patient was placed under general anesthesia, prepped and draped in the usual sterile fashion, and placed in the prone position. A midline incision centered over the L4–L5 was made and carried down to the fascia. Marcaine 0.25% with epinephrine was injected and the fascia was incised alongside the L4 spinous process and the muscle stripped off laterally. A portion of the lamina of L4 was removed. The disk herniation between L4–L5 was removed using curettes and rongeurs. The wound was irrigated with Kantrex. Closure was done with 2-0 Vicryl in the fascia and subcutaneous tissue. Then 4-0 undyed Vicryl was used as a subcuticular stitch. Dressing was applied. Sponge and needle count was correct ×2. The patient tolerated the procedure without incident.

PROCEDURE(S): _____

MAIN TERM(S): _____

CPT CODE(S): _____

CASE 15

ADMITTING DIAGNOSIS: Bilateral hallux valgus.

DISCHARGE DIAGNOSIS: Bilateral hallux valgus, corrected.

CONSULTATIONS: None.

PROCEDURES: Bilateral correction of hallux valgus with osteotomy.

COMPLICATIONS: None.

HOSPITAL COURSE: This 15-year-old young man was admitted for scheduled surgery as listed above. On admission all labs were normal. Preoperative chest film was normal. The patient responded to anesthesia uneventfully. His postoperative course was unremarkable as he remained stable and afebrile. Physical therapy was initiated during hospitalization. The therapist taught the patient to use crutches, including on stairs and at curbs.

DISCHARGE INSTRUCTIONS: He was discharged on postoperative day five in improved condition to be seen in the office for a dressing check in one week. He was given Tylenol #3 p.r.n. pain. Diet regular. Activities: Crutches, no weight bearing. Keep lower limb iced and elevated as much as possible. Patient voiced understanding of the plan as described. Both he and his parents agreed to the plan and scheduled follow-up.

PROCEDURE(S): _____

MAIN TERM(S): _____

CPT CODE(S): _____

CASE 16

PREOPERATIVE DIAGNOSIS: Right intertrochanteric femoral fracture.

POSTOPERATIVE DIAGNOSIS: Right intertrochanteric femoral fracture.

OPERATIVE PROCEDURE: Open reduction, internal fixation of right intertrochanteric fracture with DePuy sliding screw.

PROCEDURE: The patient was taken to the operating room and administered general endotracheal anesthesia with prominences well padded. A straight lateral approach to the proximal femur was made. Dissection was carried through the skin and subcutaneous tissue. Hemostasis was obtained with electrocautery. The fascia lata was divided in line with the skin incision. The lateral aspect of the proximal femur was revealed, and the tissue was retracted with Bennett and Hohmann retractors without complication. An 85-mm sliding screw was inserted across the fracture site into the head and neck without complication. A four-hole 135-degree side plate was then attached. We slid it over the DePuy sliding screw and attached it to the proximal femur using a Lowman turkey-claw clamp. With fixation in place, AP and lateral fluoroscopic images throughout the fracture site and hardware position confirmed good reduction and good placement of the hardware. All screws were tightened with a screwdriver. The Lowman was removed as was all hardware. The wound was copiously irrigated and the wound was closed. The patient tolerated the procedure well. There were no complications. Blood loss was negligible. Needle and sponge counts were correct ×2.

PROCEDURE(S): _____

MAIN TERM(S): _____

CPT CODE(S): _____

CASE 17

PREOPERATIVE DIAGNOSIS: Torn left medial meniscus.

POSTOPERATIVE DIAGNOSIS: Torn left medial meniscus.

OPERATIVE PROCEDURE: Arthroscopic partial medial meniscectomy.

PROCEDURE: The patient was brought into the operating room, placed under general anesthesia, and prepped and draped in the usual sterile manner. A standard three-portal approach was used to access the operative site. No chondromalacia changes were noted in all three compartments. Both the anterior cruciate ligament and lateral meniscus were intact. The anterior portion of the medial meniscus had a flap tear that was removed. Instruments were withdrawn. The wound was closed and dressing applied. Blood loss was minimal. All counts were correct ✕2. The patient tolerated the procedure well and was taken to the recovery room in good condition.

PROCEDURE(S): _____

MAIN TERM(S): _____

CPT CODE(S): _____

CASE 18

PREOPERATIVE DIAGNOSIS: Osteoarthritis, acromioclavicular joint, right.

POSTOPERATIVE DIAGNOSIS: Osteoarthritis, acromioclavicular joint, right.

OPERATIVE PROCEDURE: Mumford procedure, right shoulder, distal clavicle.

PROCEDURE: The patient was brought to the operating room and placed under general anesthesia, prepped and draped in the usual fashion, and placed in the lounge chair position. The right shoulder was scrubbed in the usual sterile manner. The incision was made to the distal clavicle and retractors were placed. The distal end of the clavicle was removed. The wound was irrigated and injected with Marcaine and epinephrine. The wound was closed and sterile dressings applied. Blood loss was negligible. Sponge and needle counts were correct ✕2. The patient was sent to the recovery room in good condition.

PROCEDURE(S): _____

MAIN TERM(S): _____

CPT CODE(S): _____

MEDICAL TERMINOLOGY CHALLENGE

Write a brief definition for each medical term. Use a medical dictionary as necessary.

Mr. Crucheltow is a 40-year-old man. He is brought to surgery for an (1) *arthroplasty* of the right shoulder, repair of (2) *tibial* nonunion, and (3) *iliac crest* bone graft. The patient underwent general endotracheal anesthesia without difficulty. We turned our attention to the (4) *proximal* humerus and noted there was a good fit. The (5) *rotator cuff* was reattached and there was excellent stability and range of motion. In the lower extremity we prepped and draped the limb in the normal sterile (6) *orthopedic* manner. The incision was carried over the (7) *anterolateral* aspect of the leg down to the level of the fracture. A listhtype plate was inserted in (8) *submuscular* fashion and the fracture was stabilized.

1. _____

2. _____

3. _____

4. _____

5. _____

6. _____

7. _____

8. _____

NOTES:

NOTES:

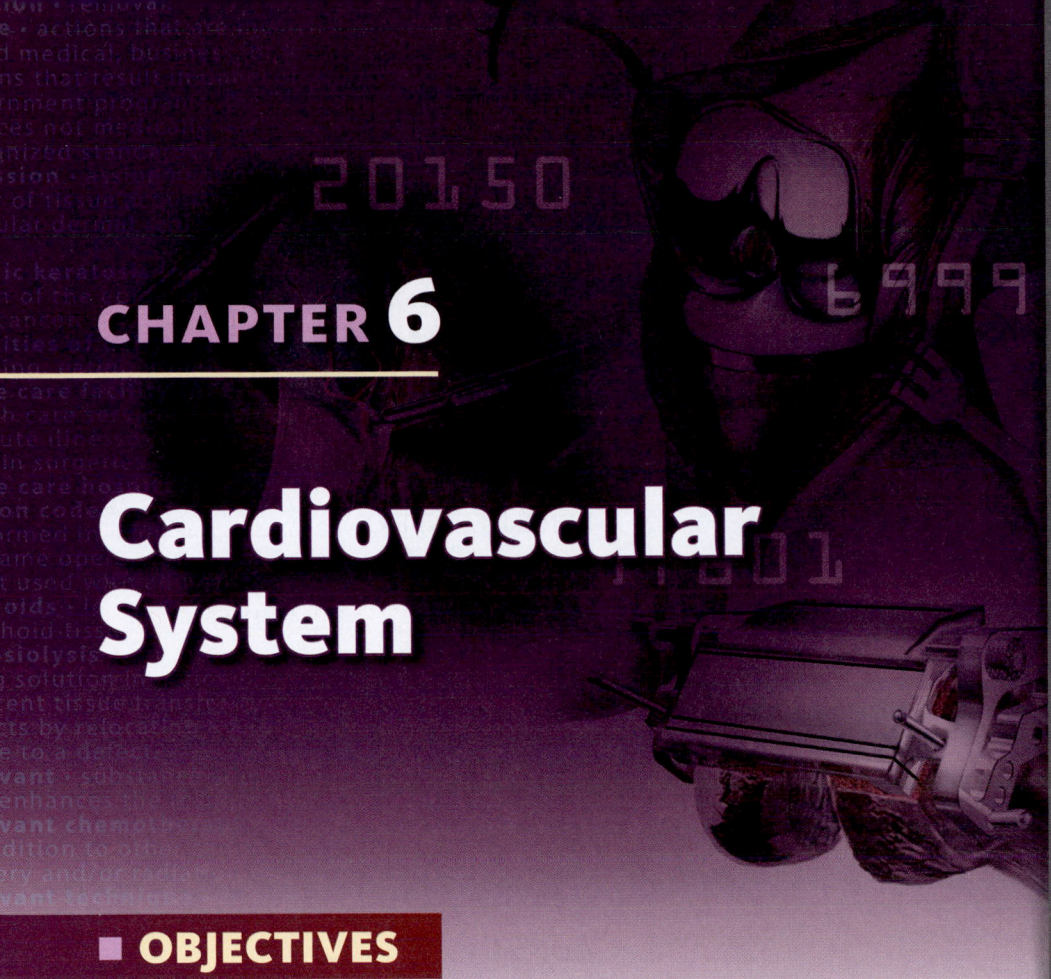

CHAPTER **6**

Cardiovascular System

■ OBJECTIVES

At the completion of this chapter, the student should be able to:

1. Learn the word roots associated with the cardiovascular system.
2. Label the basic structures of the cardiovascular system.
3. Discuss the functions of the cardiovascular system.
4. Accurately spell and define cardiovascular system terminology.
5. Accurately assign medical codes to cardiovascular diagnoses and procedures.

■ OVERVIEW

The cardiovascular system is made up of the heart and blood vessels. The blood vessels include arteries, arterioles, veins, venules, and capillaries. The structures of the system function together for the following purposes: (1) to pump blood to the tissues and cells of the body, (2) to distribute oxygen and nutrients to tissues and cells, and (3) to remove carbon dioxide and other waste products from the tissues and cells.

The medical specialty related to the cardiovascular system is **cardiology** (kar-dee-**ALL**-oh-jee), and the physician specialist is a **cardiologist** (kar-dee-**ALL**-oh-jist). A **cardiovascular surgeon** specializes in surgical interventions of the heart and blood vessels.

KEY TERMS

aorta
aortic valve
artery
arteriole
atrioventricular bundle
atrioventricular node; AV node
atria; atrium
bicuspid valve
blood pressure (BP)
bundle branches
bundle of His
capillary
cardiologist
cardiology
cardiovascular surgeon
circulation
circumflex artery
deep veins
diastolic pressure
endocardium
endothelium
epicardium
heart
inferior vena cava
left anterior descending artery (LADA)
left coronary artery (LCA)
lumen
mediastinum
mitral valve
myocardium
oxygenated
pericardial cavity
pericardial fluid
pericardium
posterior descending artery
pulmonary arteries
pulmonary circulation
pulmonary valve
pulmonary veins
right coronary artery (RCA)
septum
sinoatrial node; SA node
sphygmomanometer
superficial veins
superior vena cava
systemic circulation
systolic pressure
tricuspid valve
tunic
tunica adventitia
tunica externa
tunica intima
tunica media
vein
ventricle
venule

CARDIOVASCULAR SYSTEM ROOTS, PREFIXES, AND SUFFIXES

Roots, prefixes, and suffixes associated with the cardiovascular system are listed in table 6-1. Review the word roots and complete the exercises that follow.

Table 6-1 Cardiovascular System Roots, Prefixes, and Suffixes

ROOT/COMBINING FORM	MEANING
aneurysm/o	aneurysm
angi/o	vessel
arter/o; arteri/o	artery
arteriol/o	arteriole
ather/o	fatty, yellowish plaque
cardi/o	heart
coron/o	heart; heart vessel; coronary vessel
ech/o	sound
electr/o	electric; electricity
end/o	within; inner
ischi/o	deficiency; blockage
my/o	muscle
phleb/o	vein
sphygm/o	pulse
steth/o	chest
thromb/o	clot
ven/o	vein
ventricul/o	ventricle

PREFIX	MEANING
brady-	slow
poly-	many
tachy-	fast

SUFFIX	MEANING
-graph	instrument to record
-graphy	process of recording
-gram	record; picture
-megaly	large; enlarged
-pathy	disease
-sclerosis	hardening
-stenosis	narrowing; narrow

EXERCISE 6-1

Write the root, prefix, suffix, and their meaning. Based on the meanings, write a brief definition for each term.

1. Cardiologist
   ROOT: _____ MEANING: _____
   SUFFIX: _____ MEANING: _____
   BRIEF DEFINITION: _____

2. Myocardium
   ROOT: _____ MEANING: _____
   SUFFIX: _____ MEANING: _____
   BRIEF DEFINITION: _____

3. Angiography
   ROOT: _____ MEANING: _____
   SUFFIX: _____ MEANING: _____
   BRIEF DEFINITION: _____

4. Endocarditis
   ROOT: _____ MEANING: _____
   PREFIX: _____ MEANING: _____
   SUFFIX: _____ MEANING: _____
   BRIEF DEFINITION: _____

5. Electrocardiography
   ROOT: _____ MEANING: _____
   PREFIX: _____ MEANING: _____
   SUFFIX: _____ MEANING: _____
   BRIEF DEFINITION: _____

6. Coronary
   ROOT: _____ MEANING: _____
   SUFFIX: _____ MEANING: _____
   BRIEF DEFINITION: _____

7. Cardiomegaly
   ROOT: _____ MEANING: _____
   SUFFIX: _____ MEANING: _____
   BRIEF DEFINITION: _____

8. Tachycardia
   ROOT: _____ MEANING: _____
   PREFIX: _____ MEANING: _____
   BRIEF DEFINITION: _____

9. Bradycardia

ROOT: _____ MEANING: _____

PREFIX: _____ MEANING: _____

BRIEF DEFINITION: _____

10. Phlebitis

ROOT: _____ MEANING: _____

SUFFIX: _____ MEANING: _____

BRIEF DEFINITION: _____

11. Cardiology

ROOT: _____ MEANING: _____

SUFFIX: _____ MEANING: _____

BRIEF DEFINITION: _____

12. Echocardiography

ROOT: _____ MEANING: _____

PREFIX: _____ MEANING: _____

SUFFIX: _____ MEANING: _____

BRIEF DEFINITION: _____

13. Aneurysmectomy

ROOT: _____ MEANING: _____

SUFFIX: _____ MEANING: _____

BRIEF DEFINITION: _____

14. Arteriosclerosis

ROOT: _____ MEANING: _____

SUFFIX: _____ MEANING: _____

BRIEF DEFINITION: _____

15. Stethoscope

ROOT: _____ MEANING: _____

SUFFIX: _____ MEANING: _____

BRIEF DEFINITION: _____

STRUCTURES OF THE CARDIOVASCULAR SYSTEM

The major structures of the cardiovascular system are the heart, great vessels, coronary vessels, and peripheral blood vessels. Coronary vessels and great vessels are attached to the heart. The peripheral blood vessels are distributed to every living cell in the body.

Heart, Great Vessels, and Coronary Vessels

The **heart** is a four-chambered pump about the size of a fist and located in the **mediastinum** (**mee**-dee-ah-**STIGH**-num), which is the space between the lungs. The heart is encased in a membrane sac, the **pericardium** (pair-ih-KAR-dee-um). The pericardium is a double-folded membrane that covers the heart and lines the mediastinum. The space between the folds is called the **pericardial cavity** and is filled with **pericardial fluid**. Figure 6-1 illustrates the heart chambers, heart wall, and great vessels. Refer to this figure as you learn about these structures.

The right and left upper chambers of the heart are the (1) **atria** (**atrium**, singular). The right and left lower chambers of the heart are the (2) **ventricles**. The right and left sides of the heart are separated by a wall called a (3) **septum**. The heart wall has three layers of tissue: (4) the **epicardium** (**ep**-ih-**KAR**-dee-um) is the outer layer; (5) the **myocardium** (my-oh-**KAR**-dee-um) is the thick, muscle layer; and (6) the **endocardium** (en-doh-**KAR**-dee-um) is the inner layer. The heart valves arise from the endocardium.

The great vessels include the (7) **superior vena cava** (**VEE**-nah **KAY-vah**), which means large vein; (8) **aorta**; (9) **pulmonary arteries**; (10) **pulmonary veins**; and (11) **inferior vena cava**. The venae cavae collect blood from all parts of the body, the aorta sends blood out of the heart, and the pulmonary arteries and veins shuttle blood between the heart and the lungs.

The blood that moves through the heart chambers does not provide vascularization to the heart itself. Coronary arteries bring oxygen and nutrients to heart tissue, and coronary veins move waste products away from heart tissue. Figure 6-2 illustrates coronary vessels. Refer to this figure as you learn about these vessels.

The major coronary vessels are the (1) **right coronary artery (RCA)**; **posterior descending artery**, which is a branch of the RCA that circles to the back of the heart; (2) **left coronary artery (LCA)**; (3) **circumflex artery**, which is one branch of the LCA; and (4) **left anterior descending artery (LADA)**, which is another branch of the LCA. The right coronary artery delivers blood to the right atrium and ventricle, and the posterior descending artery

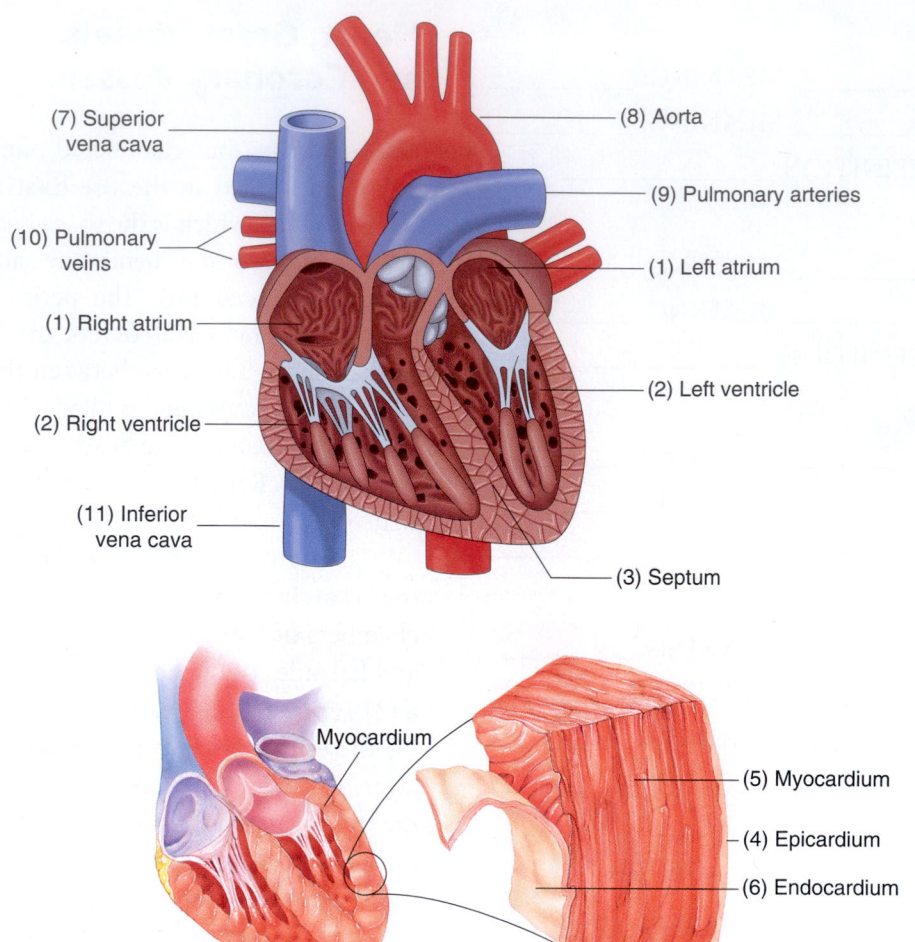

Figure 6-1 Heart, great vessels, heart wall

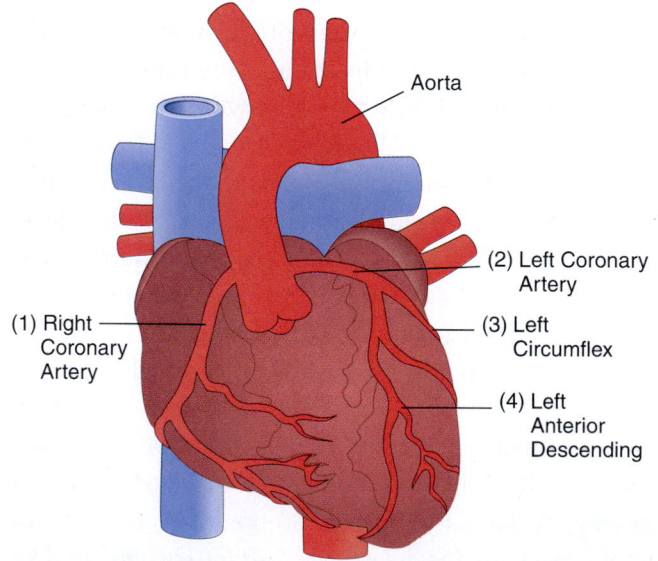

Figure 6-2 Coronary arteries

supplies the bottom of the left ventricle and the back of the septum. The left anterior descending artery brings blood to the front and bottom of the left ventricle and to the front of the septum. The circumflex

artery supplies the left atrium and the back of the left ventricle.

Electrical System of the Heart

The pumping action of the heart is controlled by a complex electrical system. The heart's electrical system consists of specialized cardiac muscle tissue that generates the electric impulses, which cause the heart to contract. Figure 6-3 illustrates the key structures of the heart's electrical system. Refer to this figure as you read about the heart's electrical system.

The (1) **sinoatrial** (**sigh**-noh-**AY**-tree-al) **node (SA node)** is located in the right atrium. The sinoatrial node is often called the pacemaker because it starts the electrical impulse. The (2) **atrioventricular** (**ay**-tree-oh-ven-**TRIK**-yoo-lar) **node (AV node)** is located between the right atrium and right ventricle. The AV node carries the impulse to the (3) **atrioventricular bundle**. The atrioventricular bundle, also called the **bundle of His**, is located in the septum between the atria and the ventricles.

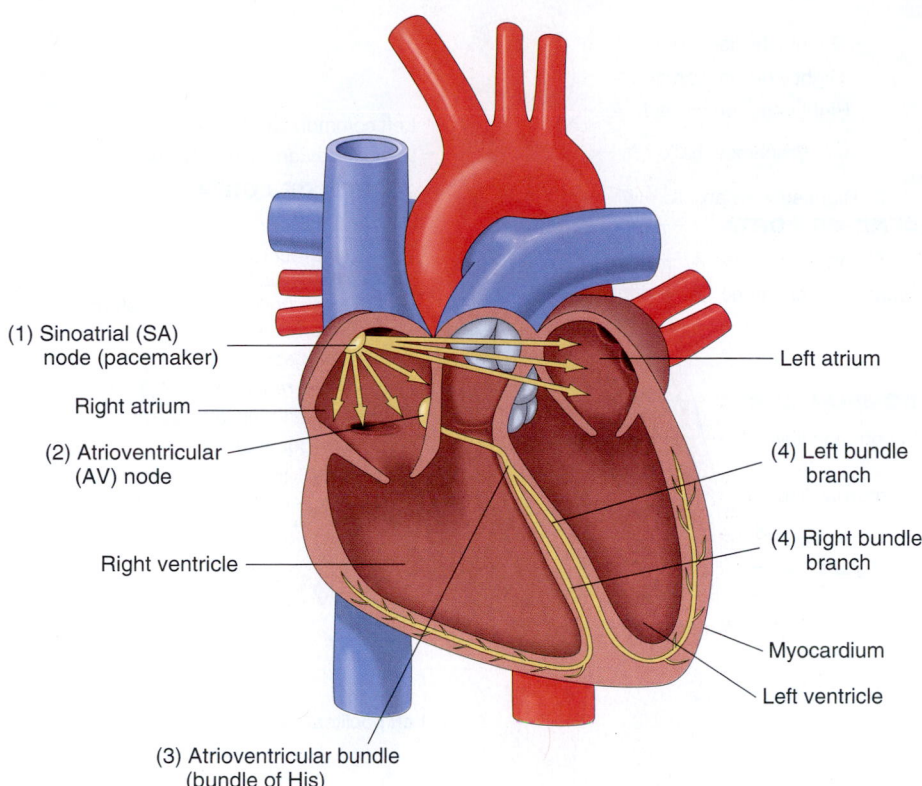

Figure 6-3 Electrical system of the heart

Labels on figure:
- (1) Sinoatrial (SA) node (pacemaker)
- Right atrium
- (2) Atrioventricular (AV) node
- Right ventricle
- (3) Atrioventricular bundle (bundle of His)
- Left atrium
- (4) Left bundle branch
- (4) Right bundle branch
- Myocardium
- Left ventricle

The atrioventricular bundle divides into the right and left (4) **bundle branches**, which are located in the septum between the ventricles. The bundle branches carry the electrical impulse to the right and left ventricles. The bundle branches cause the ventricles to contract, which pushes blood out of the heart.

Peripheral Blood Vessels

The peripheral blood vessels carry blood to and from every living cell in the body. The blood vessels include arteries, arterioles, capillaries, venules, and veins. **Arteries** carry blood away from the right and left ventricles of the heart. Figure 6-4 illustrates the location of the larger arteries. Specific sections of the aorta are highlighted in bold.

The walls of an artery consist of three layers called **tunics**. Figure 6-5 illustrates an arterial wall.

The outer tunic, called the (1) **tunica externa** (**TOO**-nih-kah eks-**TER**-nah) or **tunica adventitia** (**ad**-ven-**TISH**-ee-ah), consists of connective tissue and attaches the artery to surrounding tissue. The middle and thickest tunic, called the (2) **tunica media**, consists of smooth muscle and elastic fibers. The smooth muscle and elastic fibers allow the (3) **lumen** (**LOO**-men) to

contract and relax. The lumen is the tubular cavity of arteries and veins. The inner tunic, called the (4) **tunica intima** (**IN**-tih-mah), consists of a lining called the **endothelium** (**en**-doh-**THEE**-lee-um). The endothelium must be smooth so that blood can flow freely throughout the body.

Arteries grow progressively smaller until they become **arterioles** (ar-**TEER**-ee-olz). Arterioles grow progressively smaller until they become **capillaries** (**KAP**-ih-lair-eez). Capillaries are one cell thick, deliver oxygen and nutrients to the cells, and allow carbon dioxide and waste products from the cells to enter **venules**. Venules are the smallest veins.

Veins have the same three layers as arteries. However, the tunica externa is the thickest layer, there is less muscle tissue in the tunica media, and the tunica intima is thinner. The lumen of veins is larger than that of arteries. Veins are equipped with valves that help keep blood flowing toward the venae cavae. Figure 6-6 illustrates some of the major veins. The superior and inferior vena cava are highlighted in bold.

Superficial veins are located near the surface of the body just below the skin. **Deep veins** are located closer to arteries and often have the same name. Note in figures 6-4 and 6-6 the location of the right brachial

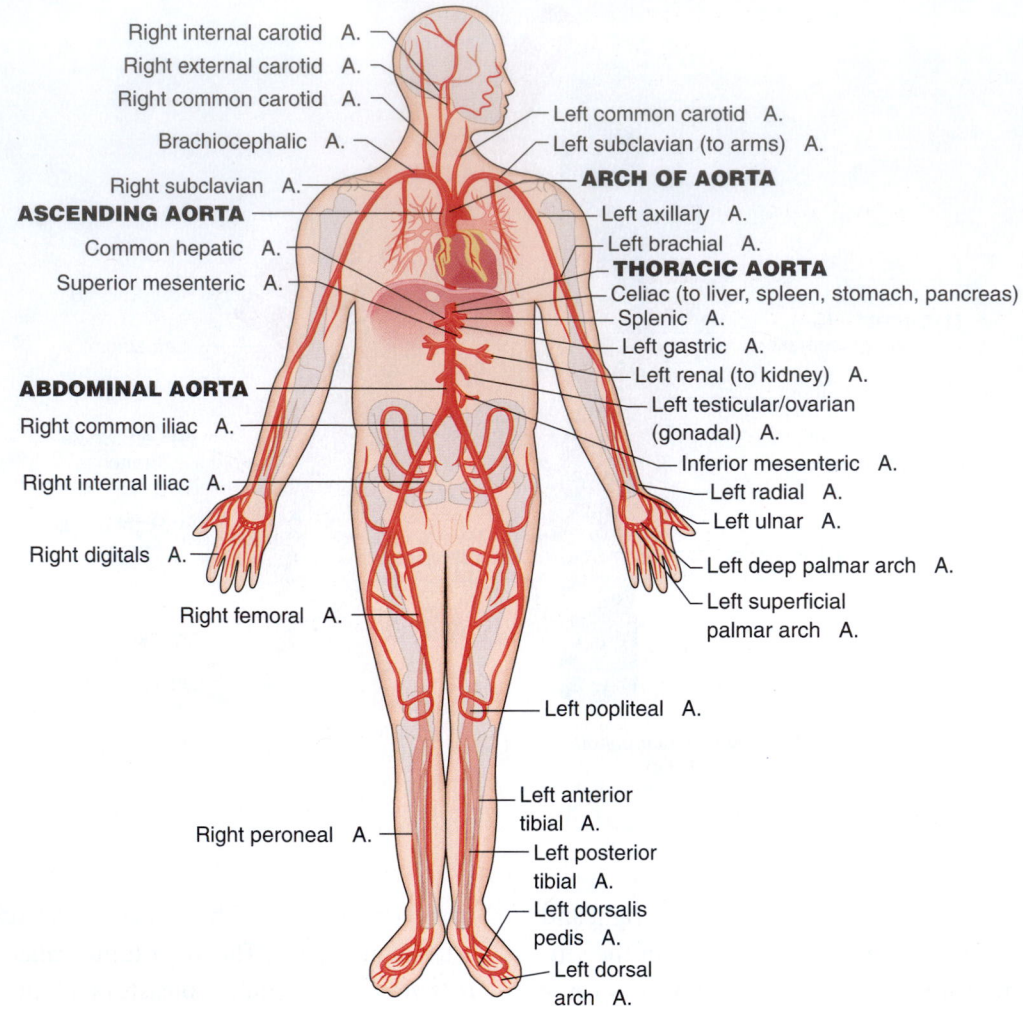

Right internal carotid A.
Right external carotid A.
Right common carotid A.
Brachiocephalic A.
Right subclavian A.
ASCENDING AORTA
Common hepatic A.
Superior mesenteric A.
ABDOMINAL AORTA
Right common iliac A.
Right internal iliac A.
Right digitals A.
Right femoral A.
Right peroneal A.

Left common carotid A.
Left subclavian (to arms) A.
ARCH OF AORTA
Left axillary A.
Left brachial A.
THORACIC AORTA
Celiac (to liver, spleen, stomach, pancreas)
Splenic A.
Left gastric A.
Left renal (to kidney) A.
Left testicular/ovarian (gonadal) A.
Inferior mesenteric A.
Left radial A.
Left ulnar A.
Left deep palmar arch A.
Left superficial palmar arch A.
Left popliteal A.
Left anterior tibial A.
Left posterior tibial A.
Left dorsalis pedis A.
Left dorsal arch A.

Figure 6-4 Major arteries

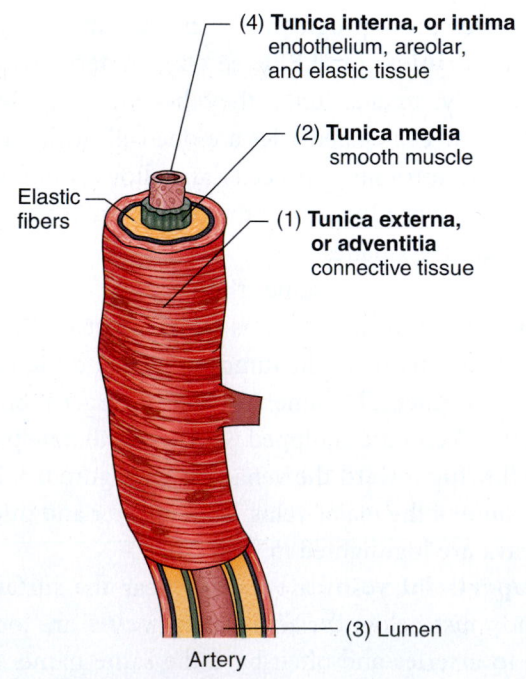

(4) **Tunica interna, or intima** endothelium, areolar, and elastic tissue

(2) **Tunica media** smooth muscle

Elastic fibers

(1) **Tunica externa, or adventitia** connective tissue

(3) Lumen

Artery

Figure 6-5 Arterial wall

artery and right brachial vein, the right common iliac artery and right common iliac vein, and the right femoral artery and right femoral vein.

Circulation

Circulation is the movement of blood throughout the entire body. Oxygen- and nutrient-rich blood must be delivered to every living cell. With the exception of the pulmonary arteries, arteries transport oxygen and nutrient-rich blood. Waste-filled blood must be removed from every living cell. With the exception of the pulmonary veins, veins transport waste-filled blood. During circulation, the lungs, liver, and kidneys also play an important role in filtering waste products from the blood.

This chapter covers **systemic circulation**, which is the circulation between the heart and the rest of the body, and **pulmonary circulation**, which is the

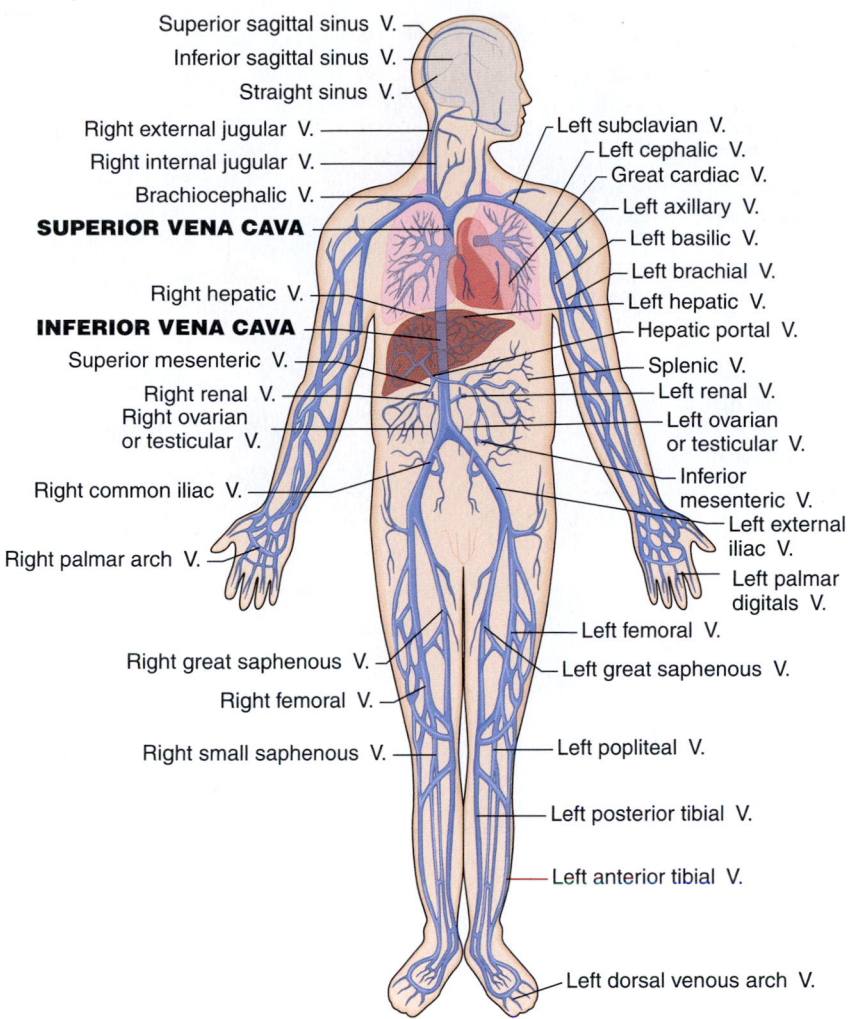

Figure 6-6 Major veins

circulation between the heart and the lungs. Figure 6-7 illustrates the heart and great vessels as they relate to circulation. Refer to this figure as you read about circulation.

- The (1) superior and (2) inferior vena cava collect the waste-filled blood and deposit it into the right atrium.

- The right atrium contracts and pushes the waste-filled blood through the (3) **tricuspid valve** into the right ventricle.

- The right ventricle contracts and pushes the waste-filled blood through the (4) **pulmonary valve** into the right and left (5) pulmonary arteries. The pulmonary arteries lead to the lungs.

- In the lungs, carbon dioxide and other waste products are removed from the blood, and the blood picks up oxygen and becomes **oxygenated** (**OCKS**-ih-jeh-**nay**-ted).

- The (6) pulmonary veins deliver the oxygenated blood to the left atrium.

- The left atrium contracts and pushes blood through the (7) **bicuspid valve** into the left ventricle. The bicuspid valve is also called the **mitral valve**.

- The left ventricle contracts and pushes blood through the (8) **aortic valve** into the (9) aorta.

- The aorta branches and divides into arteries and blood is distributed to all parts of the body.

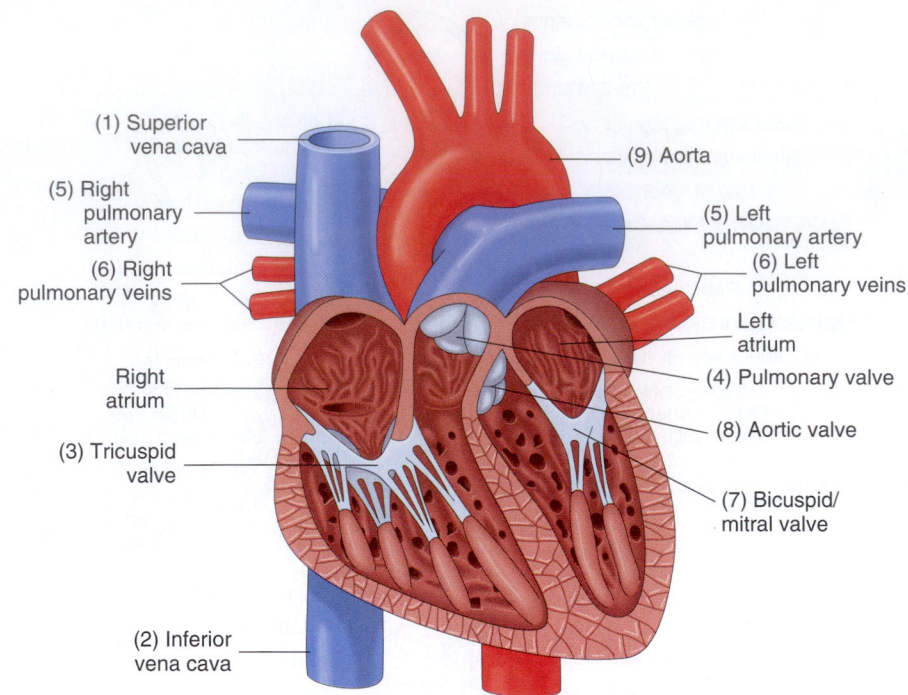

Figure 6-7 Circulation through the heart

The right and left atria contract at the same time sending blood into both ventricles. The right and left ventricles contract at the same time sending blood to the pulmonary arteries and aorta.

Blood Pressure

Blood pressure (BP) is defined as the pressure that circulating blood exerts on the walls of arteries, veins, and the chambers of the heart. A routine blood pressure check identifies the pressure exerted on arterial walls. The instrument used to measure this pressure is a **sphygmomanometer** (**sfig**-moh-man-**AH**-meh-ter), commonly called a blood pressure cuff. Blood pressure is expressed as two measurements: (1) **systolic** (sis-**TALL**-ik) **pressure**, and (2) **diastolic** (**digh**-ah-**STALL**-ik) **pressure**. Systolic pressure is defined as arterial wall pressure during heart muscle contraction. Diastolic pressure is defined as arterial wall pressure during heart muscle relaxation, or rest period. Systole (**SISS**-toh-lee) is the period of time during ventricular contraction. Diastole (digh-**ASS**-toh-lee) is the period of time when the ventricles relax between contractions. Therefore, systolic pressure is expected to be higher than diastolic pressure.

Blood pressure measurements are recorded as millimeters (mm) of mercury (Hg). The systolic pressure is noted first and the diastolic pressure is noted second, as in 120/80 mmHg. In this example, the systolic pressure is 120 and the diastolic pressure is 80. Many factors such as age, gender, weight, physical health, and emotional state might affect a blood pressure reading. In general, a normal systolic pressure ranges from 90 to less than 140 mmHg, and a normal diastolic pressure ranges from 50 to less than 90 mmHg.

EXERCISE 6-2

Write out the abbreviations and a brief definition of the term.

1. AV node _____
   DEFINITION: _____

2. BP _____
   DEFINITION: _____

3. Hg _____
   DEFINITION: _____

4. LADA _____
   DEFINITION: _____

5. LCA _____
   DEFINITION: _____

6. mm _____
   DEFINITION: _____

7. RCA _____

   DEFINITION: _____

8. SA node _____

   DEFINITION: _____

EXERCISE 6-3

Label the structures of the heart in figure 6-8. Write your answers on the spaces provided.

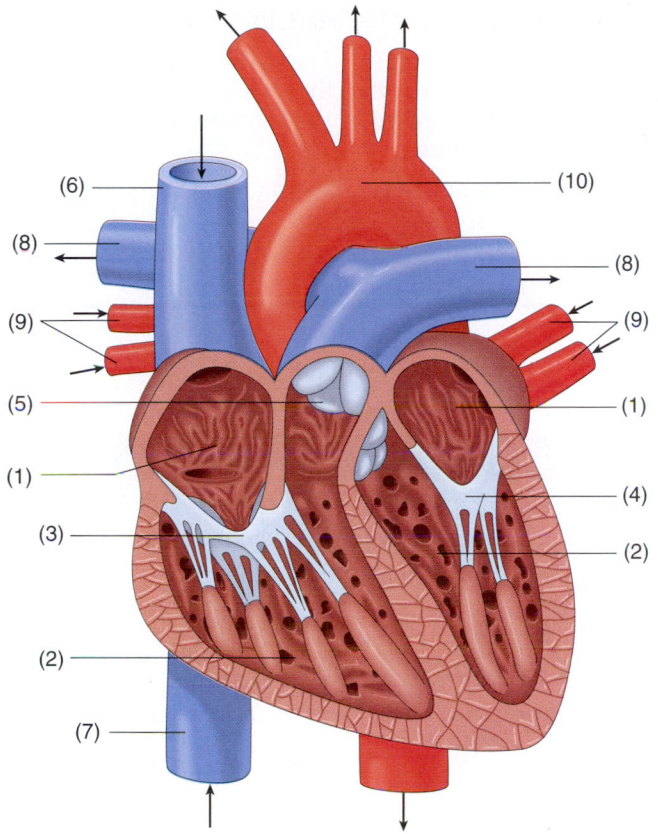

Figure 6-8 Structures of the heart

1. _____
2. _____
3. _____
4. _____
5. _____
6. _____
7. _____
8. _____
9. _____
10. _____

CARDIOVASCULAR SYSTEM MEDICAL TERMINOLOGY

Cardiovascular medical terms are organized by diseases and conditions of the heart and great vessels; diseases and conditions of the peripheral blood vessels; and diagnostic and treatment procedures, and laboratory tests. There are two categories of medical terminology exercises: (1) those designed to provide opportunities to learn the terms, and (2) those designed to provide opportunities to accurately assign diagnostic or procedure codes. Exercises for learning the terms immediately follow the lists of terms and definitions. Medical coding exercises are available after all terms have been presented.

Diseases and Conditions of the Heart and Great Vessels

The medical terms in table 6-2 are signs or symptoms of diseases or conditions related to the heart and great vessels. Review the meaning of these terms and complete the exercise.

EXERCISE 6-4

Circle the medical term that best fits the description.

1. rapid, uncoordinated ventricular contractions — *flutter* or *fibrillation*

2. throbbing and fluttering reported by the patient — *palpitation* or *flutter*

3. unusually fast, regular heart rate — *fibrillation* or *flutter*

4. abnormal heart rate over 100 beats/minute — *tachycardia* or *palpitation*

5. any irregular heartbeat — *bradycardia* or *arrhythmia*

The medical terms in table 6-3 are diseases and conditions of the heart and great vessels. Review the meaning of these terms and complete the exercises.

Table 6-2 Signs, Symptoms, Diseases, and Conditions of the Heart and Great Vessels

TERM WITH PRONUNCIATION	DEFINITION
arrhythmia (ah-**RITH**-mee-ah)	any irregular heartbeat
bradycardia (**brad**-ih-**KAR**-dee-ah) brady- = slow cardi/o = heart -ia = condition	slow heart rate characterized by ventricular contraction of less than 60 beats/minute
fibrillation (fib-rih-**LAY**-shun)	rapid and uncoordinated contractions of the atria or ventricles
flutter	an usually fast, regular heart rate (up to 350 beats/minute)
ischemia (iss-**KEE**-mee-ah) isch/o = deficiency, blockage -emia = blood	deficient or decreased blood supply to a body part
palpitation (pal-pih-**TAY**-shun)	abnormally rapid throbbing or fluttering of the heart, usually felt and reported by the individual or patient
pitting edema	abnormal swelling of the skin of the extremities that, when pressed firmly, maintains the depression or dimpling caused by the pressure; often associated with congestive heart disease
tachycardia (tak-ih-**KAR**-dee-ah) cardi/o = heart tachy- = fast -a = noun ending	abnormally rapid heartbeat, usually defined as more than 100 beats/minute

Table 6-3 Diseases and Conditions of the Heart and Great Vessels

TERM WITH PRONUNCIATION	DEFINITION
abdominal aortic aneurysm (AAA) (**AN**-yoo-rizm)	dilation or bulging of the abdominal aorta
angina pectoris (**AN**-jin-ah *or* an-**JIGH**-nah **PECK**-tor-is); *stable angina pectoris* is often controlled with medication; *unstable angina pectoris,* also called preinfarction angina, is progressive and occurs spontaneously	severe pain and constriction around the heart; caused by a lack of oxygen to the myocardium; commonly called chest pain
aortic stenosis	abnormal narrowing of the aorta
arteriosclerotic heart disease (ASHD) (ar-**tee**-ree-oh-skleh-**RAH**-tic) arteri/o = artery -sclerosis = hardening -ic = pertaining to	heart disease caused by hardening of the arteries
atrioventricular canal defect (**ay**-tree-oh-ven-**TRIK**-yoo-lar) atri/o = atrium ventricul/o = ventricle -ar = pertaining to	a congenital condition characterized by a large hole in the center of the heart between the atria and ventricles; the tricuspid and bicuspid valves are absent; one single valve is present
atrial septal defect (ASD)	a congenital condition characterized by an opening between the right and left atria
bundle branch block (BBB)	interruption or blockage of the electrical impulse to the right or left bundle branch of the ventricles of the heart
cardiac arrest	a sudden and immediate cessation of the pumping action of the heart
cardiac tamponade (tam-poh-**NAYD**)	compression of the heart due to an accumulation of fluid or blood in the pericardial sac
cardiomegaly (**kar**-dee-oh-**MEG**-ah-lee) cardi/o = heart -megaly = enlarged; enlargement	enlargement of the heart; enlarged heart

continued

TERM WITH PRONUNCIATION	DEFINITION
cardiomyopathy (**kar**-dee-oh-my-**OP**-ah-thee) cardi/o = heart my/o = muscle -pathy = disease	any disease that affects the structure and function of heart muscle; cardio-myopathy may be a primary disease, or it may be secondary to an underlying disease, such as diabetes mellitus
coarctation (koh-ark-**TAY**-shun) of the aorta	congenital condition characterized by the narrowing of a segment of the aorta
congestive (kon-**JESS**-tiv) heart failure (CHF)	a condition characterized by impaired cardiac pumping resulting in an inadequate ejection of blood from the ventricles of the heart; CHF develops over a period of time
endocarditis (**en**-doh-kar-**DIGH**-tis) end/o = within; inner cardi/o = heart -itis = inflammation	inflammation of the inner layer of the heart wall (endocardium)
hypertensive heart disease (HHD)	heart disease caused by long-term high blood pressure (hypertension)
mitral valve prolapse (**MY**-tral valve **PROH**-laps)	protrusion of one or both flaps of the mitral (bicuspid) valve into the left atrium
mitral valve stenosis (**MY**-tral valve sten-**OH**-sis)	narrowing or obstruction of the leaflets of the mitral valve due to scarring or adhesions
myocardial infarction (MI) (my-oh-**KAR**-dee-al in-**FARK**-shun) my/o = muscle cardi/o = heart -al = pertaining to	death of heart muscle due to a lack of oxygen caused by an insufficient blood supply from the coronary arteries; heart attack
myocarditis (**my**-oh-kar-**DIGH**-tiss) my/o = muscle cardi/o = heart -itis = inflammation	inflammation of the muscle layer of the heart
paroxysmal atrial tachycardia (PAT) (pair-ok-**SIZ**-mal atrial tak-ih-**KAR**-dee-ah) tachy- = fast cardi/o = heart -a = a noun ending	rapid atrial contractions that begin and end suddenly; usually from 150 to 240 beats/minute
patent ductus arteriosus (**PAY**-tent **DUK**-tus **ar**-tee-ree-**OH**-sis)	a congenital condition characterized by an opening between the main pulmonary artery and the aorta
pericarditis (**pair**-ih-kar-**DIGH**-tis) peri- = around; surrounding cardi/o = heart -itis = inflammation	inflammation of the pericardium, the membrane that surrounds the heart
premature atrial contraction (PAC)	an irregular heart rhythm characterized by atrial contractions occurring before the expected time
premature ventricular contraction (PVC)	an irregular heart rhythm characterized by ventricular contractions occurring before the expected time
rheumatic (roo-**MAT**-ik) heart disease (RHD)	a manifestation of rheumatic fever characterized by endocarditis that often results in damage to the heart valves
sick sinus syndrome (SSS)	a group of signs and symptoms that indicate that the sinoatrial node is not functioning properly; the condition is characterized by bradycardia or tachycardia
ventricular tachycardia (ven-**TRIK**-yoo-lar tak-ih-**KAR**-dee-ah) ventricul/o = ventricle -ar = pertaining to cardi/o = heart tachy- = fast -a = noun ending	abnormally rapid ventricular contractions, usually between 150 and 200 beats/minute

EXERCISE 6-5

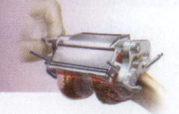

Replace the italicized phrase or abbreviation with the correct medical term.

1. Nitroglycerin might relieve *severe pain and constriction around the heart.*

2. The child was born with a/an *abnormal narrowing of the aorta.*

3. Rashel was scheduled for surgery to correct a/an *large hole between her atria and ventricles.*

4. The cause of death was listed as *a sudden and immediate cessation of the pumping action of the heart.*

5. Obesity is often a contributing factor to a/an *enlarged heart.*

6. A/an *inflammation of the inner layer of the heart wall* might lead to heart valve disease.

7. Immediate medical care can reduce the effects of a *heart attack.*

8. Monroe was scheduled for a pacemaker insertion to treat his diagnosis of *SSS.*

EXERCISE 6-6

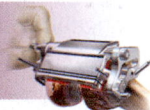

Circle the medical term that best fits the description.

1. an opening between the right and left atria — *ASD* or *atrioventricular canal defect*

2. heart compression due to pericardial fluid or blood — *cardiac tamponade* or *angina pectoris*

3. heart muscle death; heart attack — *cardiac arrest* or *myocardial infarction*

4. an opening between the pulmonary artery and the aorta — *patent ductus arteriosus* or *ASD*

5. protrusion of one or both flaps of the bicuspid valve — *mitral valve stenosis* or *mitral valve prolapse*

6. inflammation of heart muscle — *cardiomyopathy* or *myocarditis*

EXERCISE 6-7

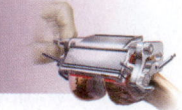

Write out the abbreviation and a brief definition for the condition.

1. BBB _____

   DEFINITION: _____

2. CHF _____

   DEFINITION: _____

3. HHD _____

   DEFINITION: _____

4. PAT _____

   DEFINITION: _____

5. PAC _____

   DEFINITION: _____

6. PVC _____

   DEFINITION: _____

7. RHD _____

   DEFINITION: _____

8. ASHD _____

   DEFINITION: _____

9. AAA _____

   DEFINITION: _____

Diseases and Conditions of the Coronary and Peripheral Blood Vessels

The medical terms in table 6-4 are signs, symptoms, diseases, or conditions related to the coronary and peripheral blood vessels. Review the meaning of these terms and complete the exercises.

Table 6-4 Signs, Symptoms, Diseases, and Conditions of Coronary and Peripheral Blood Vessels

TERM WITH PRONUNCIATION	DEFINITION
aneurysm (**AN**-yoo-rizm)	localized dilation or ballooning of an artery at a weak point in the vessel wall; there are three types of aneurysms: *dissecting,* between the out and middle layer of the arterial wall; *fusiform,* affects the entire circumference of the artery; and *saccular,* a smaller, saclike arterial protrusion (figure 6-9)
angiocarditis (**an**-jee-oh-kar-**DIGH**-tis) angi/o = vessel cardi/o = heart -itis = inflammation	inflammation of the coronary blood vessels
angiospasm (**AN**-jee-oh-spazm) angi/o = vessel -spasm = involuntary contraction	abnormal contraction of the blood vessels, primarily the arteries
arteriosclerosis (ar-**tee**-ree-oh-skleh-**ROH**-sis) arteri/o = artery -sclerosis = hardening	hardening of the arteries
atherosclerosis (**ath**-eh-roh-skleh-**ROH**-sis) ather/o = fat -sclerosis = hardening	hardening and narrowing of the arteries due to deposits of fat and other debris along arterial walls (figure 6-10)
bruits (broo-**EEZ**)	abnormal blowing sounds or murmurs heard while listening to the blood flow through the arteries, usually the carotid arteries
coronary artery disease (CAD)	any abnormal condition of the arteries of the heart
coronary occlusion	an obstruction of any one of the coronary arteries
coronary thrombosis (throm-**BOH**-sis) thromb/o = clot -osis = condition of	presence of a blood clot in a coronary artery
deep vein thrombosis (DVT)	presence of a blood clot in a deep vein; often located in the iliac or femoral vein (figure 6-11)

continued

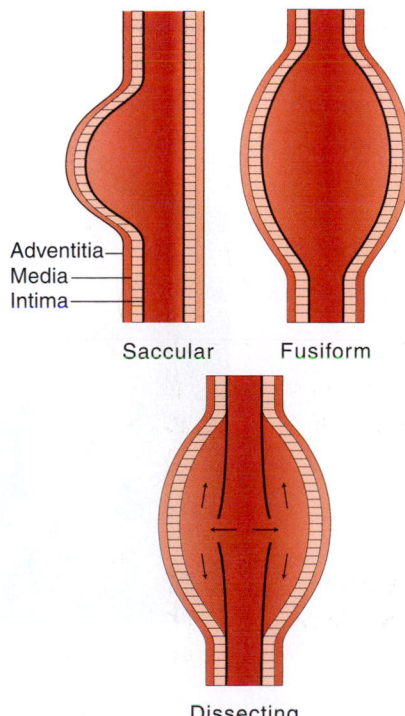

Figure 6-9 Three types of aneurysm

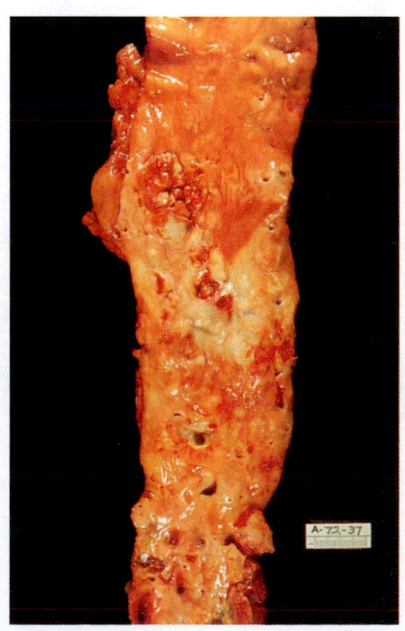

Figure 6-10 Atherosclerosis in the aorta

Table 6-4 (*continued*)   Signs, Symptoms, Diseases, and Conditions of Coronary and Peripheral Blood Vessels

TERM WITH PRONUNCIATION	DEFINITION
hypertension	elevated blood pressure due to increased pressure on arterial walls
hypotension	abnormally low blood pressure due to decreased pressure on arterial walls
occlusion (oh-**KLOO**-zhun)	a blockage in a vessel, cavity, or other passage of the body; usually associated with the arteries
phlebitis (fleh-**BIGH**-tis) phleb/o = vein -itis = inflammation of	inflammation of a vein
polyarteritis (**pall**-ee-ar-teh-**RIGH**-tis) poly- = many arteri/o = artery -itis = inflammation	inflammation of the medium and small arteries
temporal arteritis (TA) arter/o = artery -itis = inflammation	a chronic inflammatory disease of large blood vessels, especially the carotid artery and its branches; also called *giant cell arteritis* and *cranial arteritis*
polymyalgia rheumatica (PMR) poly- = many my/o = muscle -algia = pain	an inflammatory disease of the large arteries that is closely associated with temporal arteritis; primarily affects the muscles; characterized by severe pain and stiffness of the neck and pectoral and pelvic girdles
thrombophlebitis (**throm**-boh-fleh-**BIGH**-tis) thromb/o = clot phleb/o = vein -itis = inflammation	inflammation of a vein in the presence of a blood clot
varicose (**VAIR**-ih-kohs) veins	enlarged, twisted, and often dilated veins most commonly located in the superficial veins of the legs; also found in the veins of the esophagus (figure 6-12)
vasoconstriction (**vay**-zoh-con-**STRIK**-shun) vas/o = vessel -constriction = narrowing	constriction or narrowing of the diameter of a blood vessel

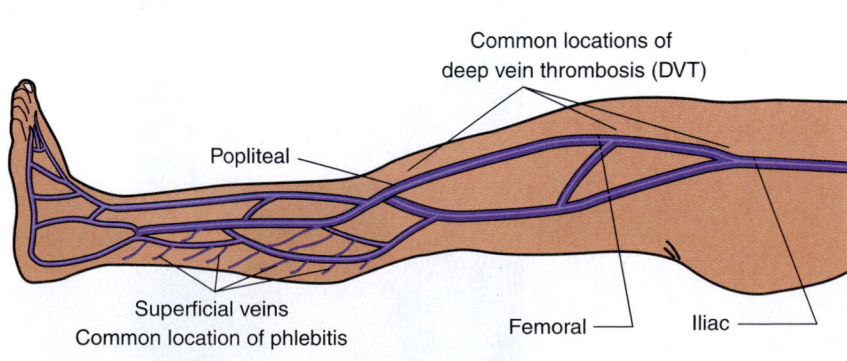

Figure 6-11 Deep vein thrombosis

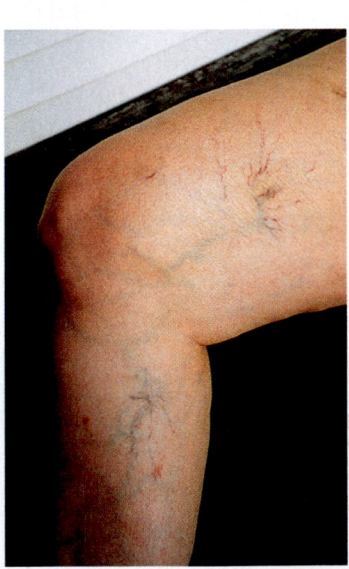

Figure 6-12 Varicose veins

EXERCISE 6-8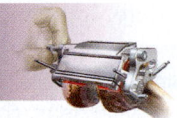

Replace the italicized phrase or abbreviation with the correct medical term.

1. The *ballooning artery* required immediate surgical intervention. _____

2. Marta's leg cramps and severe aching was due to *DVT*. _____

3. Dr. Washington heard *abnormal blowing sounds* during his assessment of my carotid arteries. _____

4. *CAD* may be related to an individual's personal habits. _____

5. *Elevated blood pressure* is often controlled with medication. _____

6. *Enlarged, twisted veins* respond to both surgical and nonsurgical treatments. _____

7. Eleanor was told that the "warm spot" on her leg was *an inflammation of a vein.* _____

8. A superficial *inflammation of a vein in the presence of a blood clot* often causes the vein to be very sensitive to pressure. _____

EXERCISE 6-9

Write a brief definition for each term.

1. angiocarditis _____
2. angiospasm _____
3. arteriosclerosis _____
4. atherosclerosis _____
5. coronary occlusion _____
6. coronary thrombosis _____
7. hypotension _____
8. vasoconstriction _____

Cardiovascular System Diagnostic, Procedure, and Treatment Terms

The medical terms in table 6-5 are diagnostic, procedure, and treatment terms related to the heart. Review the terms and complete the exercises.

Table 6-5 Cardiovascular System Diagnostic, Procedure, Treatment, and Laboratory Terms

TERM WITH PRONUNCIATION	DEFINITION
cardiac catheterization (**KAR**-dee-ak **kath**-eh-ter-ih-**ZAY**-shun)	a diagnostic procedure during which a catheter is guided into the heart through a blood vessel for the purpose of injecting a contrast medium to view and image the heart chambers and coronary arteries; also called left heart catheterization (Note: Cardiac catheterization may also be used as the procedural approach for coronary angioplasty.)
cardiac enzyme (**EN**-zighm) blood test(s)	clinical laboratory blood tests that measure the level of cardiac enzymes in the blood; abnormally increased enzyme levels indicate heart muscle damage associated with myocardial infarction (MI)
cardiopulmonary bypass (**kar**-dee-oh-**PULL**-mon-air-ee) cardi/o = heart pulmon/o = lungs -ary = pertaining to	a procedure used during heart surgery in which the blood is diverted from the heart and lungs and cycled through a machine and returned directly to the aorta; also called *extracorporeal circulation*
cardiopulmonary resuscitation (CPR) (**kar**-dee-oh-**PULL**-mon-air-ee ree-**suss**-ih-**TAY**-shun) cardi/o = heart pulmon/o = lungs -ary = pertaining to	a procedure for life support consisting of artificial respiration and manual external cardiac compression
coronary artery bypass graft (CABG)	a surgical procedure that requires implanting a piece of vein onto the heart to bypass a blockage in a coronary artery and to improve blood flow to the heart; mammary vessels (veins) and saphenous vessels (veins) from the leg are often used for the bypass; synthetic graft material may also be used; the procedure is commonly called bypass surgery (figure 6-13)

continued

Table 6-5 (*continued*)   Cardiovascular System Diagnostic, Procedure, Treatment, and Laboratory Terms

TERM WITH PRONUNCIATION	DEFINITION
cardioversion (**kar**-dee-oh-**VER**-zhun)	restoration of normal heart rhythm by delivering synchronized electric shocks through paddles placed on the chest
defibrillation (dee-**fib**-rih-**LAY**-shun)	a technique used to interrupt ventricular fibrillation and restore a normal heart rhythm by delivering electric shocks to specific areas around the heart
echocardiogram (**ek**-oh-**KAR**-dee-oh-gram) echo- = sound cardi/o = heart -gram = record	graphic record of an ultrasound visualization of the heart
echocardiography (**ek**-oh-**kar**-dee-**OG**-rah-fee) echo- = sound cardi/o = heart -graphy = process of recording	ultrasound diagnostic procedure for the purpose of evaluating and recording the structures and motion of the heart
electrocardiogram (EKG, ECG) (ee-**lek**-troh-**KAR**-dee-oh-gram) electr/o = electricity cardi/o = heart -gram = record	graphic record of the electrical activity and contractions of the heart (figure 6-14)
electrocardiography (ee-**lek**-troh-**kar**-dee-**OG**-rah-fee) electr/o = electricity cardi/o = heart -graphy = process of recording	process of recording the electrical activity and contractions of the heart
exercise stress test	a method of assessing cardiac functioning or heart irregularities using controlled amounts of physical activity such as walking on a treadmill; an EKG is usually done throughout the testing
Holter monitoring; Holter electrocardiography	a diagnostic test that continuously records the electrical activity of the heart over an extended time period to identify suspected cardiac rhythm disorders that may occur during daily activities; the individual wears a portable EKG device and keeps a diary of all activities during the test period
multigated acquisition (MUGA) scan	a nuclear medicine study of heart function while the heart is in motion; records images of the heart chambers, the pumping action of the ventricles, heart muscle damage, ventricular wall abnormalities, and abnormal movement of blood between the chambers of the heart; the images are viewed as a motion picture; a tracer (radioactive substance) is used to enhance the images

continued

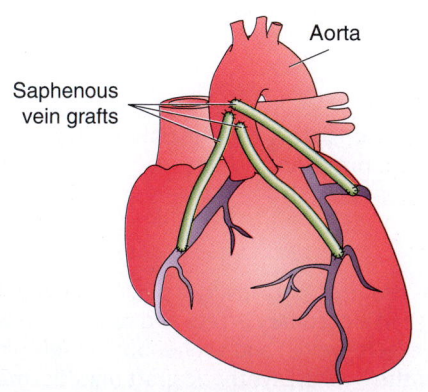

Figure 6-13 Coronary artery bypass graft (CABG)

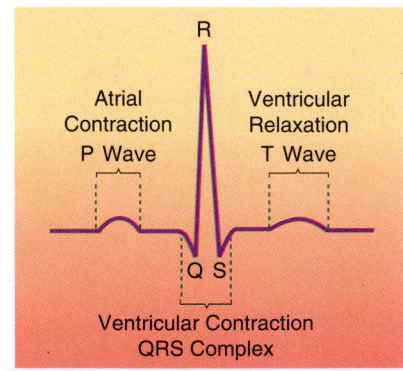

Figure 6-14 Electrocardiogram showing the contraction and relaxation of the heart

Table 6-5 (*continued*) Cardiovascular System Diagnostic, Procedure, Treatment, and Laboratory Terms

TERM WITH PRONUNCIATION	DEFINITION
percutaneous transluminal coronary angioplasty (PTCA) (per-kyoo-**TAY**-nee-us trans-**LOO**-min-al **KOR**-oh-nair-ee **AN**-jee-oh-**plass**-tee)	surgical repair of an obstructed coronary artery by inserting a balloon at the end of a catheter into the artery, inflating the balloon, flattening the fatty deposits on the arterial wall, and stretching or increasing the diameter of the artery; a prosthetic device called a *stent* may be placed in the artery to keep it open; PTCA may be done during a cardiac catheterization (figure 6-15)
thallium (**THAL**-ee-um) stress test	a nuclear medicine imaging test that shows how well blood flows to the heart muscle during exercise; usually done at the same time as a stress test; the first images are taken shortly after the exercise (stress) test and again after the patient has rested for 2–3 hours
transesophageal echocardiography (TEE) (**trans**-eh-soff-ah-**JEE**-al **ek**-oh-**kar**-dee-**OG**-rah-fee) trans- = through esophag/o = esophagus -al = pertaining to	a diagnostic procedure that uses both endoscopic and ultrasonic techniques in a process of viewing the structures of the heart; an endoscope is inserted into the esophagus and an ultrasound transducer records images of the heart; a local anesthetic agent is applied to the throat and intravenous sedation may be administered
(**VAL**-vyoo-loh-**plass**-tee) valv/o = valve -plasty = surgical repair	surgical repair of a heart valve

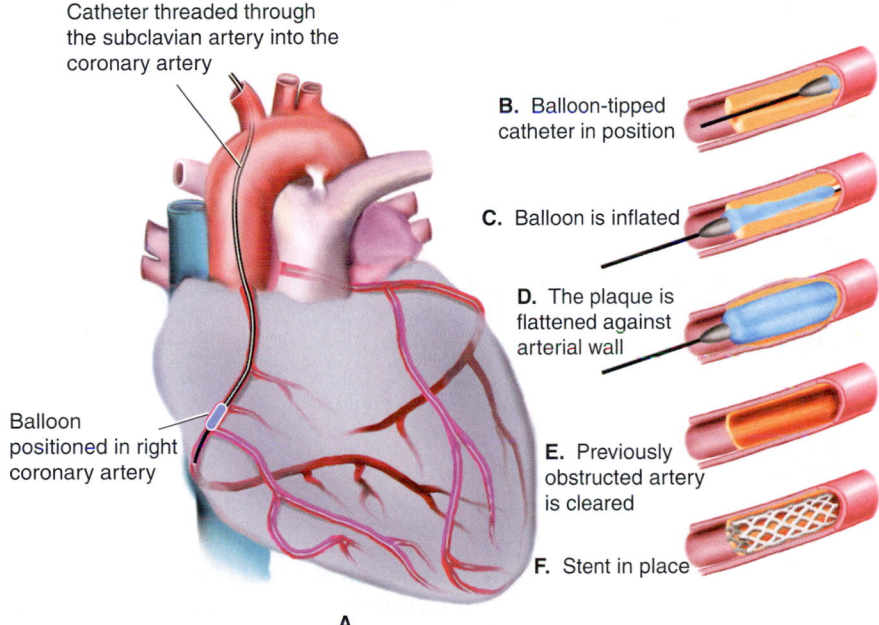

Catheter threaded through the subclavian artery into the coronary artery

Balloon positioned in right coronary artery

B. Balloon-tipped catheter in position

C. Balloon is inflated

D. The plaque is flattened against arterial wall

E. Previously obstructed artery is cleared

F. Stent in place

A.

Figure 6-15 Percutaneous transluminal coronary angioplasty with stent placement

EXERCISE 6-10

Write out the abbreviation and a brief definition of the test or procedure.

1. CPR _____

   DEFINITION: _____

2. CABG _____

   DEFINITION: _____

3. EKG, ECG _____

   DEFINITION: _____

4. PTCA _____

   DEFINITION: _____

5. TEE _____

   DEFINITION: _____

EXERCISE 6-11

Place a check mark after the procedure(s) done to restore normal heart rhythm.

1. CPR _____
2. electrocardiography _____
3. echocardiography _____
4. defibrillation _____
5. Holter electrocardiography _____
6. cardioversion _____

EXERCISE 6-12

Place a *D* next to the diagnostic tests. Place a *P* next to the surgical procedures.

1. valvoplasty _____
2. TEE _____

3. thallium stress test _____
4. PTCA _____
5. EKG _____
6. cardioversion _____
7. CABG _____
8. cardiac enzyme blood tests _____
9. cardiac catheterization _____
10. MUGA scan _____

The medical terms in table 6-6 are diagnostic, procedure, and treatment terms related to blood vessels. Review the terms and complete the exercise.

Table 6-6 Diagnostic, Procedure, and Treatment Terms of Blood Vessels

TERM WITH PRONUNCIATION	DEFINITION
anastomosis (ah-**nas**-toh-**MOH**-sis) ana- = without stom/o = mouth, opening -osis =condition	surgical connection of two vessels (or other tubular structures); a vascular anastomosis is performed to bypass an aneurysm or an occluded vessel or segment of a vessel
aneurysmectomy (**an**-yoo-rizm-**EK**-toh-mee) aneurysm/o = aneurysm -ectomy = surgical removal	surgical removal of an aneurysm
angiography (an-jee-**OG**-rah-fee) angi/o = vessel -graphy = process of recording	process of recording an image of blood vessels using a contrast medium to enhance the visualization of the location and internal structures of the vessels
arteriogram (ar-**TEER**-ree-oh-gram) arteri/o = artery -gram = record	an x-ray of an artery (figure 6-16)
arteriography (ar-**teer**-ee-**OG**-rah-fee) arteri/o = artery -graphy = process of recording	process of recording an image of an artery using a contrast medium to enhance the visualization of the location and structure of the artery
endarterectomy (**end**-ar-ter-**EK**-toh-mee) end/o = within arteri/o = artery -ectomy = surgical removal	surgical removal of the lining of an artery that is occluded due to fatty deposits, sometimes called plaque; the carotid artery is a common site for endarterectomy (figure 6-17)

continued

Table 6-6 (*continued*)   Diagnostic, Procedure, and Treatment Terms of Blood Vessels

TERM WITH PRONUNCIATION	DEFINITION
Doppler ultrasonography (**DOPP**-ler **ull**-trah-son-**OG**-rah-fee) The four types of Doppler ultrasonography: (1) *pulse wave Doppler (PW Doppler)* or *continuous wave Doppler (CW Doppler)*, can be done at the bedside with portable equipment; (2) *duplex Doppler*, produces a picture of a blood vessel and surrounding organs; (3) *color Doppler*, colors are overlaid on the image of the blood vessel; (4) *power Doppler*, highly sensitive, used to evaluate blood flow through vessels within solid organs	process of recording images of sound waves as blood flows through blood vessels to detect blood clots and blocked or narrowed blood vessels
ligation and stripping	a treatment for varicose veins that includes tying off (ligation) and removal (stripping) of the vein

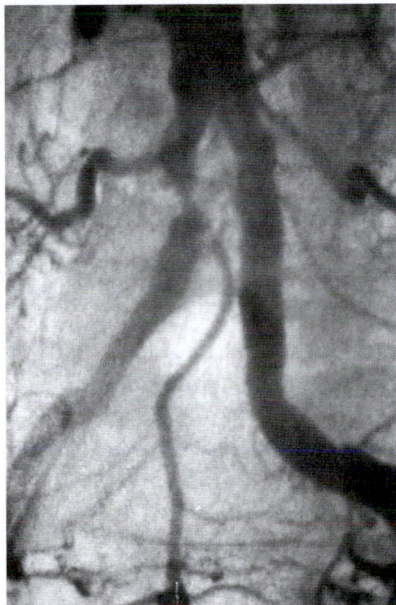

Figure 6-16 Iliac arteriogram

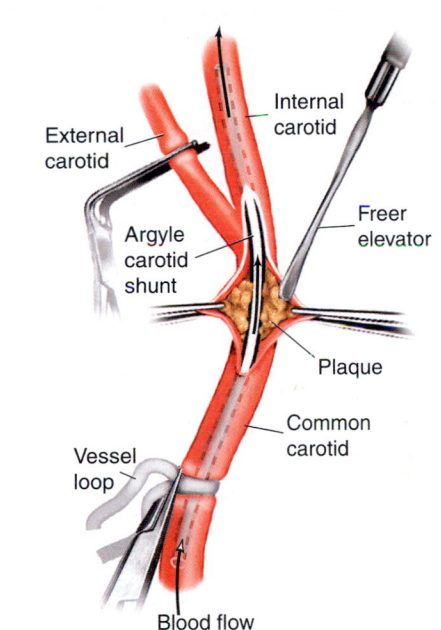

External carotid

Internal carotid

Freer elevator

Argyle carotid shunt

Plaque

Common carotid

Vessel loop

Blood flow

Figure 6-17 Carotid endarterectomy

EXERCISE 6-13

Write a brief definition for each term or phrase.

1. arteriogram _____

2. arteriography _____

3. anastomosis _____

4. duplex Doppler _____

5. endarterectomy _____

6. angiography _____

7. power Doppler _____

ABBREVIATIONS

Cardiovascular system abbreviations are listed in table 6-7. Practice writing out the abbreviations with a brief definition for each phrase or term.

Table 6-7 Cardiovascular Abbreviations

ABBREVIATION	MEANING
AAA	abdominal aortic aneurysm
ASD	atrial septal defect
ASHD	arteriosclerotic heart disease
AV node	atrioventricular node
BBB	bundle branch block
BP	blood pressure
CABG	coronary artery bypass graft
CAD	coronary artery disease
CHF	congestive heart failure
CPR	cardiopulmonary resuscitation
CW Doppler	continuous wave Doppler
EKG, ECG	electrocardiogram
DVT	deep vein thrombosis
HHD	hypertensive heart disease
LADA	left anterior descending artery
LCA	left coronary artery
MI	myocardial infarction
MUGA scan	multigated acquisition scan
PAC	premature atrial contraction
PAT	paroxysmal atrial tachycardia
PMR	polymyalgia rheumatic
PTCA	percutaneous transluminal coronary angioplasty
PVC	premature ventricular contraction
PW Doppler	pulse wave Doppler
RCA	right coronary artery
RHD	rheumatic heart disease
SA node	sinoatrial node
SSS	sick sinus syndrome
TA	temporal arteritis
TEE	transesophageal echocardiography

CARDIOVASCULAR SYSTEM MEDICAL CODING

To successfully complete the exercises in this section, the ICD-9-CM volumes 1, 2, and 3, and the CPT (Current Procedural Terminology) coding references must be readily available. The information in this section is presented as follows:

- An introduction to ICD-9-CM, chapter 7, "Diseases of the Circulatory System"
- ICD-9-CM diagnostic coding exercises
- A summary of ICD-9-CM volume 3 coding conventions that apply to cardiovascular procedures
- ICD-9-CM procedure coding exercises
- A summary of the CPT Cardiovascular System coding guidelines
- CPT coding exercises

Students are *strongly* encouraged to review the information at the beginning of the ICD-9-CM and CPT coding references. Commercial publishers include instructions on how to use the reference, the ICD-9-CM official coding conventions, additional conventions used by the publisher, and the *ICD-9-CM Official Guidelines for Coding and Reporting.* Some publishers include the three ICD-9-CM volumes in one book and put the *Alphabetic Index* (volume 2) at the beginning of the reference.

The *Introduction* to CPT includes detailed instructions for the using this code book, an index to the illustrations throughout the book, and anatomical illustrations of the major structures of body systems.

ICD-9-CM Volume 2, Chapter 7, Diseases of the Circulatory System (390–459)

Cardiovascular system diseases are coded to ICD-9-CM, chapter 7, "Diseases of the Circulatory System." This chapter includes the following major categories:

- **Acute Rheumatic Fever (390–392).** With the exception of code 390, *rheumatic fever without mention of heart involvement,* the codes in this category apply to heart conditions that are associated with an acute episode of rheumatic fever.
- **Chronic Rheumatic Heart Disease (393–398).** Codes in this category apply to chronic heart conditions associated with rheumatic fever.

- **Hypertensive Disease (401–405).** Codes in this category apply to hypertension and hypertensive heart disease, hypertensive chronic kidney disease, and hypertensive heart and chronic kidney disease.
- **Ischemic Heart Disease (410–414).** Codes in this category range from acute myocardial infarction to heart aneurysms.
- **Disease of Pulmonary Circulation (415–417).** Codes in this category apply to conditions related to the pulmonary vessels and heart conditions associated with pulmonary conditions.
- **Other Forms of Heart Disease (420–429).** Codes in this category cover heart conditions ranging from pericarditis to conduction disorders, various arrhythmias, and ill-defined conditions and complications of heart disease.
- **Cerebrovascular Disease (430–438).** Codes in this category apply to the conditions associated with the vessels of the head and neck. (Note: Since this textbook chapter covers the heart and blood vessels, diseases and conditions in this ICD-9-CM category are appropriate here.)
- **Diseases of Arteries, Arterioles, and Capillaries (440–449).** Codes in this category apply to conditions associated with the peripheral arterial system that include atherosclerosis of native arteries and grafted arteries, arterial embolisms, and arterial thrombi (blood clots).
- **Diseases of Veins and Lymphatics, and Other Diseases of the Circulatory System (451–459).** Codes in this category apply to conditions associated with veins and lymph vessels. For purposes of this textbook chapter, exercises that use codes from this category will be limited to conditions related to the veins.

Several of the categories have instructional notes that describe fifth-digit requirements. Figure 6-18 is an example of fifth-digit instructional notes.

Coding hypertension diagnoses can be frustrating and complicated. Remember that the *documentation in the patient's medical record must support the ICD-9-CM*

---

410 Acute myocardial infarction

. . .

The following fifth-digit subclassification is for use with category 410:

0 Episode of care unspecified
Use when the source document does not contain sufficient information for the assignment of fifth-digit 1 or 2.

1 Initial episode of care
Use fifth-digit 1 to designate the first episode of care (regardless of facility site) for a newly diagnosed myocardial infarction; the fifth-digit 1 is assigned regardless of the number of times a patient may be transferred during the initial episode of care.

2 Subsequent episode of care
Use fifth-digit 2 to designate an episode of care, following the initial episode of care, when the patient is admitted for further observation, evaluation, or treatment for a myocardial infarction that has received initial treatment but is still less than 8 weeks old.

Figure 6-18 Fifth-digit instructional notes

code. The hypertension table in the *Alphabetic Index* provides instructions for assigning fourth and fifth digits to codes in categories 403 and 404. The Official Coding Guidelines, provided by the Centers for Medicare and Medicaid Services and the National Center for Health Statistics, give specific instructions for coding hypertension with heart disease and hypertensive kidney disease. To code a heart disease to category 402, *Hypertensive heart disease,* the diagnosis must include a clear statement that the heart disease is caused by or due to hypertension; or the diagnosis must include the term *hypertensive.* To code hypertensive kidney disease, ICD-9-CM coding conventions presume a causal relationship between hypertension and renal failure. When the diagnosis states renal failure with hypertension it is coded to category 403, *Hypertensive kidney disease.* When both hypertensive heart and hypertensive kidney disease are part of the diagnosis, use category 404, *Hypertensive heart and kidney disease.*

EXERCISE 6-14

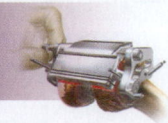

Write a brief definition for each diagnosis. Identify the main term in the diagnostic statement and assign the correct ICD-9-CM code(s).

1. Aortic stenosis, calcified

    DEFINITION: _____

    MAIN TERM: _____

    ICD-9-CM CODE(S): _____

2. Arteriosclerotic heart disease

    DEFINITION: _____

    MAIN TERM: _____

    ICD-9-CM CODE(S): _____

3. Atherosclerosis of the aorta

    DEFINITION: _____

    MAIN TERM: _____

    ICD-9-CM CODE(S): _____

4. Atrial fibrillation

    DEFINITION: _____

    MAIN TERM: _____

    ICD-9-CM CODE(S): _____

5. Bilateral thrombosis of carotid artery

    DEFINITION: _____

    MAIN TERM: _____

    ICD-9-CM CODE(S): _____

6. Left and right bundle branch block

    DEFINITION: _____

    MAIN TERM: _____

    ICD-9-CM CODE(S): _____

7. Cardiac arrest

    DEFINITION: _____

    MAIN TERM: _____

    ICD-9-CM CODE(S): _____

8. Cardiac tamponade

    DEFINITION: _____

    MAIN TERM: _____

    ICD-9-CM CODE(S): _____

9. Cardiomegaly due to congestive heart failure

    DEFINITION: _____

    MAIN TERM: _____

    ICD-9-CM CODE(S): _____

10. Congestive heart failure

    DEFINITION: _____

    MAIN TERM: _____

    ICD-9-CM CODE(S): _____

11. Coronary artery disease

    DEFINITION: _____

    MAIN TERM: _____

    ICD-9-CM CODE(S): _____

12. Dissecting aneurysm of the thoracic aorta

    DEFINITION: _____

    MAIN TERM: _____

    ICD-9-CM CODE(S): _____

13. Hypertensive cardiovascular disease, malignant

    DEFINITION: _____

    MAIN TERM: _____

    ICD-9-CM CODE(S): _____

14. Infected varicose vein, ulcerated, lower left leg

    DEFINITION: _____

    MAIN TERM: _____

    ICD-9-CM CODE(S): _____

15. Mitral valve stenosis with regurgitation

    DEFINITION: _____

    MAIN TERM: _____

    ICD-9-CM CODE(S): _____

16. Occlusion of the iliac artery

    DEFINITION: _____

    MAIN TERM: _____

    ICD-9-CM CODE(S): _____

17. Orthostatic hypotension

    DEFINITION: _____

    MAIN TERM: _____

    ICD-9-CM CODE(S): _____

18. Paroxysmal ventricular tachycardia

    DEFINITION: _____

    MAIN TERM: _____

    ICD-9-CM CODE(S): _____

19. Polyarteritis

    DEFINITION: _____

    MAIN TERM: _____

    ICD-9-CM CODE(S): _____

20. Sick sinus syndrome, exhibiting tachycardia

    DEFINITION: _____

    MAIN TERM: _____

    ICD-9-CM CODE(S): _____

21. Ulcerative phlebitis of the femoral vein

    DEFINITION: _____

    MAIN TERM: _____

    ICD-9-CM CODE(S): _____

22. Unstable angina pectoris

    DEFINITION: _____

    MAIN TERM: _____

    ICD-9-CM CODE(S): _____

ICD-9-CM Volume 3, Chapter 7, Operations on the Cardiovascular System (35–39)

Cardiovascular system operations and some therapeutic treatments are coded to ICD-9-CM volume 3, chapter 7, "Operations on the Cardiovascular System." This chapter includes these major categories:

- **Operations on valves and septa of the heart (35).** Codes in this category range from replacement of heart valve to total repair of certain congenital cardiac anomalies.

- **Operations on vessels of the heart (36).** Codes in this category apply to the coronary arteries.

- **Other operations on the heart and pericardium (37).** Codes in this category range from right heart cardiac catheterization to pacemaker insertion.

- **Incision, excision, and occlusion of vessels (38).** Codes in this category range from endarterectomy to stripping varicose veins. This category has instruction notes for fourth-digit codes, and *code also* directions.

- **Other operations on vessels (39).** Codes in this category exclude coronary vessels.

The instructional note *code also cardiopulmonary bypass [extracorporeal circulation] [heart-lung machine]* is included in several categories and subcategories. The operative or procedure report must confirm whether the patient was placed on a heart-lung machine. There are many instructional notes with all procedure codes. For this reason, **never** assign procedure codes from the *ALPHABETIC INDEX.*

Volume 3, chapter 16, "Miscellaneous Diagnostic and Therapeutic Procedures" (87–99) also contains codes that apply to the cardiovascular system. Chapter 16 includes procedures and tests that are used to diagnose cardiovascular diseases and conditions. Electrocardiography, stress tests, ultrasound examinations, and nuclear medicine imaging are examples of diagnostic tests and procedures.

EXERCISE 6-15

Write a brief definition for each operative, treatment, and diagnostic procedure term. Identify the main term in the statement and assign the correct ICD-9-CM code(s).

1. Mouth-to-mouth cardiopulmonary resuscitation (CPR)

   DEFINITION: _____

   MAIN TERM: _____

   ICD-9-CM CODE(S): _____

2. TEE

   DEFINITION: _____

   MAIN TERM: _____

   ICD-9-CM CODE(S): _____

3. Cardiovascular MUGA scan

   DEFINITION: _____

   MAIN TERM: _____

   ICD-9-CM CODE(S): _____

4. Thallium stress test

   DEFINITION: _____

   MAIN TERM: _____

   ICD-9-CM CODE(S): _____

5. Coronary angiography

   DEFINITION: _____

   MAIN TERM: _____

   ICD-9-CM CODE(S): _____

continued

6. Arteriography of the aortic arch

   DEFINITION: _____

   MAIN TERM: _____

   ICD-9-CM CODE(S): _____

7. 12-lead electrocardiogram

   DEFINITION: _____

   MAIN TERM: _____

   ICD-9-CM CODE(S): _____

8. Left heart catheterization

   DEFINITION: _____

   MAIN TERM: _____

   ICD-9-CM CODE(S): _____

9. Valvoplasty of the aortic valve

   DEFINITION: _____

   MAIN TERM: _____

   ICD-9-CM CODE(S): _____

Current Procedural Terminology (CPT) Cardiovascular System Codes (33010–39599)

CPT cardiovascular system codes are located in the Surgery, Radiology, and Medicine sections. The Surgery guidelines provide important information for all of the Surgery subsections. Review the guidelines in the CPT manual and in chapter 3 of this text. There are additional and extensive instructional notes throughout the Cardiovascular System subsection of the Surgery section. The Cardiovascular System subsection includes the following major categories:

- **Heart and Pericardium (33010–33999).** Codes in this category cover procedures like pacemaker insertion, heart valve procedures, and coronary endarterectomy. There are extensive instruction notes for most of the heart and pericardium subcategories. For example, the instruction notes for pacemaker or pacing cardioverter-defibrillator procedures explain the components of a pacemaker system, the difference between a single-chamber pacemaker system and a dual-chamber pacemaker system, the components of a cardioverter-defibrillator system, and the operative approaches for placing these systems.

  Heart and pericardium subcategories include codes for arterial and venous grafting for coronary artery bypass (33510–33548); septal defect repair, closure, and banding (33641–33697); repair of transposition of the great vessels (33770–33781); and procedures related to aortic artery anomalies and aneurysm (33800–33877).

- **Arteries and Veins (34001–37799).** Codes in this category cover procedures that range from repair of an abdominal aortic aneurysm to insertion of a cannula for hemodialysis. Intravascular ultrasound and surgical vascular endoscopy are also in this category. There are extensive instruction notes for most of the arteries and veins subcategories. For example, endovascular repair of abdominal aortic aneurysm (34800–34834) instruction notes explain the components of endovascular repair of an abdominal aortic aneurysm and describe the procedures that can be reported or coded separately.

  The central venous access procedures subcategory (36555–36598) describes the parameters of a central venous access catheter or device, a description of the five procedure categories, and additional codes that apply to these procedures. The five types of procedures are (1) **insertion**, placement of the catheter through a newly established venous access; (2) **repair**, fixing the device without replacement of either the catheter or port/pump, other than pharmacological or mechanical correction on intracatheter or pericatheter occlusion; (3) **partial replacement**, replacement of only the catheter component associated with a port/pump device, but not the entire device; (4) **complete replacement**, replacement of the entire device via the same venous access site; and (5) **removal**, removal of the entire device.

Cardiovascular diagnostic imaging procedures are coded to the Radiology section. Some of the subsections related to the cardiovascular system include the following:

- **Cardiac Magnetic Resonance Imaging (75557–75564).** Codes in this subsection include magnetic resonance imaging for cardiac function and structure with and without contrast material, with stress imaging, with flow/velocity quantification, and with flow/velocity quantification and stress.

- **Vascular Procedures (75600–75996).** Codes in this subsection apply to imaging procedures of the aorta and arteries; veins and lymphatics; transcatheter radiological supervision associated with contrast injections, road mapping, and fluoroscopic guidance; vessel measurement; and completion angiography/venography. There are extensive instruction notes throughout this subsection.

- **Nuclear Medicine (78414–78499).** Codes in this subsection include cardiac shunt detection, venous thrombosis imaging, and myocardial imaging studies.

Cardiovascular diagnostic procedures are also coded to the Medicine section. Some of the subsections related to the cardiovascular system include the following:

- **Cardiovascular Therapeutic Services (92950–92998).** Codes in this subsection apply to cardiopulmonary resuscitation, percutaneous transluminal coronary and pulmonary vessel procedures, and percutaneous balloon valvuloplasty.

- **Cardiography and Echocardiography (93000–93352).** Codes in this subsection apply to electrocardiogram, electrocardiographic monitoring, transesophageal echocardiography, transthoracic echocardiography, and Doppler echocardiography. The instruction notes for echocardiography include descriptions of a complete transthoracic echocardiography, a follow-up or limited echocardiographic study, and the components of a written report.

- **Cardiac Catheterization (93501–93572).** Codes in this subsection apply to right and left heart catheterization and injection procedures related to the heart and vessels.

EXERCISE 6-16

Write a brief definition for the italicized terms. Assign the correct CPT code(s) for each procedure.

1. *Cardiac catheterization,* right side only, with IV conscious sedation

   DEFINITION: _____

   CPT CODE: _____

2. *Cardiovascular stress test* on a 56-year-old male with recent EKG changes, physician supervision only

   DEFINITION: _____

   CPT CODE: _____

3. 2-D M-Mode *Doppler echocardiography,* color flow imaging

   DEFINITION: _____

   CPT CODE: _____

4. *Atherectomy* and *angioplasty* of the left anterior descending and diagonal coronary artery

   DEFINITION: _____

   CPT CODE: _____

5. 24-hour *Holter electrocardiography* by continuous original ECG waveform recording; scanning analysis with report, physician review, and interpretation

   DEFINITION: _____

   CPT CODE: _____

   Identify the main term in each statement. Assign the correct CPT code(s).

6. Mouth-to-mouth cardiopulmonary resuscitation (CPR)

   MAIN TERM: _____

   CPT CODE(S): _____

7. Transesophageal echocardiography

   MAIN TERM: _____

   CPT CODE(S): _____

8. Cardiovascular MUGA scan

   MAIN TERM: _____

   CPT CODE(S): _____

   continued

9. Thallium stress test

   MAIN TERM: _____

   CPT CODE(S): _____

10. Coronary angiography

    MAIN TERM: _____

    CPT CODE(S): _____

11. 12-lead electrocardiogram, with interpretation and report

    MAIN TERM: _____

    CPT CODE(S): _____

12. Left heart catheterization

    MAIN TERM: _____

    CPT CODE(S): _____

13. Valvuloplasty of the aortic valve; open with cardiopulmonary bypass

    MAIN TERM: _____

    CPT CODE(S): _____

■ SUMMARY

This chapter covered medical terms related to the cardiovascular system, which includes the heart, great vessels, and the peripheral vascular system. Cardiovascular diagnoses and procedures were identified and defined. Cardiovascular diseases and conditions are coded to ICD-9-CM volume 2, chapter 7, "Diseases of the Circulatory System." Cardiovascular procedures are coded to ICD-9-CM volume 3, chapter 7, "Operations on the Cardiovascular System," and chapter 16, "Miscellaneous Diagnostic and Therapeutic Procedures."

Current Procedural Terminology (CPT) cardiovascular procedure codes are found in the CPT Surgery subsection, Cardiovascular System (33010–37799), and in the CPT Radiology and Medicine sections.

■ CHAPTER REVIEW

Read each medical note. Write the diagnosis(es) and identify the main term in the diagnostic statement. Assign the ICD-9-CM diagnostic code(s).

CASE 1

Rosita Chavez has experienced chest pain that in the past has been relieved with nitroglycerine tablets. She presents today with angina that is not relieved, and she is concerned that she may be "a heart attack waiting to happen." After the preliminary workup it is evident that she is experiencing unstable angina. She agreed to be admitted for treatment.

DIAGNOSIS(ES): _____

MAIN TERM(S): _____

ICD-9-CM DIAGNOSIS CODE(S): _____

CASE 2

This 42-year-old male was seen in the emergency department complaining of the sudden onset of substernal chest pain, tightness, and burning. His initial EKG showed some Q-wave and T-wave changes. He was admitted for further evaluation that revealed an acute anterior wall myocardial infarction.

DIAGNOSIS(ES): _____

MAIN TERM(S): _____

ICD-9-CM DIAGNOSIS CODE(S): _____

CASE 3

This 65-year-old female is seen today in the office for her six-month follow-up. She occasionally experiences PAT, which is relieved when she uses the instructions that were reviewed with her previously. She has a copy of the instructions with her today. Other than the PAT, she is doing well.

DIAGNOSIS(ES): _____

MAIN TERM(S): _____

ICD-9-CM DIAGNOSIS CODE(S): _____

CASE 4

After undergoing an abdominal aortic ultrasound, Mr. Brown was informed that he had an abdominal aortic aneurysm that is still intact. He agreed to have surgery and is scheduled for Monday morning. Mr. Brown received information about the procedure and will come to the hospital on Sunday for preoperative preparations.

DIAGNOSIS(ES): _____

MAIN TERM(S): _____

ICD-9-CM DIAGNOSIS CODE(S): _____

CASE 5

Marilyn Shaski is seen today for an annual physical examination. She is 47 years old and smokes about 10 cigarettes per day. Her weight is stable at 125 lb. We discussed smoking cessation options and she agrees that she must "quit al-together." During auscultation, carotid artery sounds on the left side were thready with bruits and at one point nearly absent. She is scheduled for carotid arteriography later this afternoon to confirm carotid artery stenosis.

DIAGNOSIS(ES): _____

MAIN TERM(S): _____

ICD-9-CM DIAGNOSIS CODE(S): _____

CASE 6

David Brindley, a 52-year-old male, is seen today with complaints of severe cramping in his lower leg, "in the calf." He states that the cramping is so severe he would "fall down" if he didn't reach for support. He has been diagnosed with restless leg syndrome, but he says this is "much worse." He will be seen by Dr. Singe to confirm a diagnosis of DVT of the lower extremity.

DIAGNOSIS(ES): _____

MAIN TERM(S): _____

ICD-9-CM DIAGNOSIS CODE(S): _____

CASE 7

Raoul Washington is seen today for a follow-up blood pressure check. He recently started a new medication for hypertension, which was diagnosed six months ago. He presents today with no complaints of dyspnea on exertion, shortness of breath, or tinnitus. BP today is 135/75 mmHg. He has been checking his blood pressure at home with a wrist monitor. BPs at home range between 140/80 mmHg and 130/70 mmHg. At this time, the hypertension is controlled with the current medication. Follow-up will be in three months unless he becomes symptomatic.

DIAGNOSIS(ES): _____

MAIN TERM(S): _____

ICD-9-CM DIAGNOSIS CODE(S): _____

CASE 8

The patient is seen today and states "this vein is really bulging, it hurts, and feels very warm." She is a 56-year-old female, moderately obese, with a superficial varicosity in the groin and upper anterior aspect of the thigh. On palpation the vein is linear, indurated, tender, and warm. Discoloration around the area is indicative of superficial thrombophlebitis. The patient was reassured that at this point, the condition was actually in resolution, and she should be symptom free by the end of the week.

DIAGNOSIS(ES): _____

MAIN TERM(S): _____

ICD-9-CM DIAGNOSIS CODE(S): _____

CASE 9

Ms. Azotes presents with chest pain, dyspnea, fever, pericardial rub, and EKG changes consistent with acute pericarditis, resolving and unknown etiology. CBC reveals leukocytosis and an elevated sed rate. She can take Tylenol #3 for fever and pain, and she should stay off her feet as much as possible. She was advised to stay off work for the rest of the week and was provided with documentation for her employer. She is to call on Monday to report if there is improvement.

DIAGNOSIS(ES): _____

MAIN TERM(S): _____

ICD-9-CM DIAGNOSIS CODE(S): _____

CASE 10

The patient's EKG results are consistent with right bundle branch block.

DIAGNOSIS(ES): _____

MAIN TERM(S): _____

ICD-9-CM DIAGNOSIS CODE(S): _____

Read the procedure note, operative report, and discharge summary excerpts. Write the diagnosis and its ICD-9-CM code. Write the name of the procedure and the main term. Assign the ICD-9-CM procedure code(s).

CASE 11

This 74-year-old female presented with transient ischemic attacks and was investigated with CT scan and carotid angiography that revealed right carotid artery stenosis. In consultation with the cardiologist, she underwent right carotid endarterectomy. Her postoperative course was satisfactory and without incident. She was discharged on 5/12/20xx and was scheduled for an office follow-up in two weeks.

DIAGNOSIS: _____

ICD-9-CM DIAGNOSIS CODE: _____

PROCEDURE(S): _____

MAIN TERM(S): _____

ICD-9-CM DIAGNOSIS CODE(S): _____

CASE 12

PREOPERATIVE DIAGNOSIS: Abdominal aortic aneurysm.

POSTOPERATIVE DIAGNOSIS: Abdominal aortic aneurysm.

PROCEDURE: Aneurysmectomy of abdominal aortic aneurysm with Dacron replacement graft.

DIAGNOSIS: _____

ICD-9-CM DIAGNOSIS CODE: _____

PROCEDURE(S): _____

MAIN TERM(S): _____

ICD-9-CM DIAGNOSIS CODE(S): _____

CASE 13

PREOPERATIVE DIAGNOSIS: End-stage coronary artery disease.

POSTOPERATIVE DIAGNOSIS: End-stage coronary artery disease.

OPERATION: Coronary artery bypass grafting ×2 utilizing:
A. Saphenous vein graft from aorta to left anterior descending coronary artery.
B. Saphenous vein graft from aorta to the obtuse marginal coronary artery.

TECHNIQUE: To begin the operation, a femoral artery line was placed in the left common femoral artery. After this was completed, the saphenous vein was harvested through several small incisions along the left thigh for two lengths. The sternal incision was then made and carried down to the bone. The sternum was divided with a sternal saw and the sternal spreader placed. The pericardium was opened in an inverted T. The patient was placed on cardiopulmonary bypass and cooled. The vein grafts were anastomosed to the aorta and the left anterior descending coronary artery and obtuse marginal coronary artery respectively. While the patient was rewarming, a transmyocardial revascularization was performed, primarily on the inferior, apical, anterior, and anterolateral surfaces.

DIAGNOSIS: _____

ICD-9-CM DIAGNOSIS CODE: _____

PROCEDURE(S): _____

MAIN TERM(S): _____

ICD-9-CM DIAGNOSIS CODE(S): _____

CASE 14

INDICATIONS: 1. Stenosis of the proximal left anterior descending coronary artery, 80%. 2. Stenosis of the diagonal branch of the LADA, 80%.

PROCEDURE: Percutaneous transluminal coronary angioplasty (PTCA) of the left anterior descending and diagonal branch of the left anterior descending coronary artery.

TECHNIQUE: Using sterile preparation a 6 French sheath was inserted percutaneously into the right femoral vein for venous access. Next a 9 French long-sheath introducer was inserted into the right femoral artery, the catheter was advanced through the left coronary artery, and mapping views were taken of several projections. The Thruflex balloon was advanced and dilated ×2, up to nine bars for 60 seconds. The balloon was advanced down the diagonal coronary artery and dilated up to four bars for 60 seconds. Good results were obtained. A review of the cineangiograms following the procedure showed the 80% stenosis in the left proximal anterior descending coronary artery to be virtually eliminated. The diagonal branch 80% stenosis was reduced to 30%–40%.

DIAGNOSIS: _____

ICD-9-CM DIAGNOSIS CODE: _____

PROCEDURE(S): _____

MAIN TERM(S): _____

ICD-9-CM DIAGNOSIS CODE(S): _____

CASE 15

PROCEDURE: Insertion, dual-chamber cardiac pacemaker.

INDICATIONS FOR PROCEDURE: 1. Protracted, high degree, atrial ventricular block. 2. Status post inferior myocardial infarction.

DESCRIPTION: The patient was brought to the heart cath lab. Left infraclavicular area was prepped and draped in the usual sterile fashion. Local anesthesia was achieved with 1% plain Xylocaine. Femoral vein was punctured with an 18-gauge needle. A guide wire was advanced through that needle. Sterile technique was used throughout the entire procedure. Fluoroscopic guidance was employed for all internal manipulations. Afterward, about a 5-cm skin-entry incision was made, and a pocket was made with blunt dissection to the pectoralis major fossa using Metzenbaum scissors and Bovie for proper hemostasis. Afterward, a 10 French introducer was advanced over the wire. Trocar was removed. A permanent ventricular lead was advanced through the sheath, which was peeled away and the lead advanced to the right ventricular apex and affixed in the usual fashion. Afterward, the guide wire, which had been preserved after pulling the first sheath away, was used to implant a second sheath, 10 French, whereupon the Oscor Atrial screw-in wire was advanced through the sheath. The sheath was peeled away and the wire removed. The Oscor was advanced to the region of the right atrium. The stylet was retracted. Then the stay stylet was advanced. Satisfactory pacing numbers were obtained and the lead screwed into the atrial wall with three clockwise screw motions. Prior to this we had obtained satisfactory pacing numbers, threshold numbers, and sensitivity numbers with ventricular wire.

The permanent leads were affixed to the generator, after silica gel applied, screw caps applied, excess wire cooled behind the generator, all housed in the pocket. Wound closed with 2-0 Vicryl, subcutaneous and 3-0 nylon on the skin.

Satisfactory pacing was obtained, and the patient returned to his room with stable vital signs and EKG. No apparent complications.

EQUIPMENT: Bitronic DDD pacer, Gemnose TC04, serial 87006454.

ATRIAL WIRE: Oscor, model XY53, JV. Serial BIK27689. Resistance 670 ohms. P amplitude. 2.4 millivolts. Pacing threshold 0.6 volts.

VENTRICULAR LEAD: Model MP53PB, serial 34340163, manufacturer Biotronic. Pacing threshold 0.7 volts. R wave 10.2 millivolts, resistance 650 ohms. Both the atrial and ventricular leads were bipolar sensing and pacing. AV delay paced was 180 msec. Hysteresis out. Rate 70. Upper tracking rate 130.

DIAGNOSIS: _____

ICD-9-CM DIAGNOSIS CODE: _____

PROCEDURE(S): _____

MAIN TERM(S): _____

ICD-9-CM DIAGNOSIS CODE(S): _____

Using the same excerpts in previous exercises, assign the CPT code(s) to the procedure(s).

CASE 16

This 74-year-old female presented with transient ischemic attacks and was investigated with CT scan and carotid angiography that revealed right carotid artery stenosis. In consultation with the cardiologist, she underwent right carotid endarterectomy. Her postoperative course was satisfactory and without incident. She was discharged on 5/12/20xx and was scheduled for an office follow-up in two weeks.

PROCEDURE(S): _____

MAIN TERM(S): _____

CPT CODE(S): _____

CASE 17

PREOPERATIVE DIAGNOSIS: Abdominal aortic aneurysm.

POSTOPERATIVE DIAGNOSIS: Abdominal aortic aneurysm.

PROCEDURE: Aneurysmectomy of abdominal aortic aneurysm with Dacron replacement graft.

PROCEDURE(S): _____

MAIN TERM(S): _____

CPT CODE(S): _____

CASE 18

PREOPERATIVE DIAGNOSIS: End-stage coronary artery disease.

POSTOPERATIVE DIAGNOSIS: End-stage coronary artery disease.

OPERATION: Coronary artery bypass grafting ×2 utilizing:
A. Saphenous vein graft from aorta to left anterior descending coronary artery.
B. Saphenous vein graft from aorta to the obtuse marginal coronary artery.

TECHNIQUE: To begin the operation, a femoral artery line was placed in the left common femoral artery. After this was completed, the saphenous vein was harvested through several small incisions along the left thigh for two lengths. The sternal incision was then made and carried down to the bone. The sternum was divided with a sternal saw and the sternal spreader placed. The pericardium was opened in an inverted T. The patient was placed on cardiopulmonary bypass and cooled. The vein grafts were anastomosed to the aorta and the left anterior descending coronary artery and obtuse marginal coronary artery respectively. While the patient was rewarming, a transmyocardial revascularization was performed, primarily on the inferior, apical, anterior, and anterolateral surfaces.

PROCEDURE(S): _____

MAIN TERM(S): _____

CPT CODE(S): _____

CASE 19

INDICATIONS: 1. Stenosis of the proximal left anterior descending coronary artery, 80%. 2. Stenosis of the diagonal branch of the LADA, 80%.

PROCEDURE: Percutaneous transluminal coronary angioplasty (PTCA) of the left anterior descending and diagonal branch of the left anterior descending coronary artery.

TECHNIQUE: Using sterile preparation a 6 French sheath was inserted percutaneously into the right femoral vein for venous access. Next a 9 French long-sheath introducer was inserted into the right femoral artery, the catheter was advanced through the left coronary artery, and mapping views were taken of several projections. The Thruflex balloon was advanced and dilated ×2, up to nine bars for 60 seconds. The balloon was advanced down the diagonal coronary artery and dilated up to four bars for 60 seconds. Good results were obtained. A review of the cineangiograms following the procedure showed the 80% stenosis in the left proximal anterior descending coronary artery to be virtually eliminated. The diagonal branch 80% stenosis was reduced to 30%–40%.

PROCEDURE(S): _____

MAIN TERM(S): _____

CPT CODE(S): _____

CASE 20

PROCEDURE: Insertion, dual-chamber cardiac pacemaker.

INDICATIONS FOR PROCEDURE: 1. Protracted, high degree, atrial ventricular block. 2. Status post inferior myocardial infarction.

DESCRIPTION: The patient was brought to the heart cath lab. Left infraclavicular area was prepped and draped in the usual sterile fashion. Local anesthesia was achieved with 1% plain Xylocaine. Femoral vein was punctured with an 18-gauge needle. A guide wire was advanced through that needle. Sterile technique was used throughout the entire procedure. Fluoroscopic guidance was employed for all internal manipulations. Afterward, about a 5-cm skin-entry incision was made, and a pocket was made with blunt dissection to the pectoralis major fossa using Metzenbaum scissors and Bovie for proper hemostasis. Afterward, a 10 French introducer was advanced over the wire. Trocar was removed. A permanent ventricular lead was advanced through the sheath, which was peeled away and the lead advanced to the right ventricular apex and affixed in the usual fashion. Afterward, the guide wire, which had been preserved after pulling the first sheath away, was used to implant a second sheath, 10 French, whereupon the Oscor Atrial screw-in wire was advanced through the sheath. The sheath was peeled away and the wire removed. The Oscor was advanced to the region of the right atrium. The stylet was retracted. Then the stay stylet was advanced. Satisfactory pacing numbers were obtained and the lead screwed into the atrial wall with three clockwise screw motions. Prior to this we had obtained satisfactory pacing numbers, threshold numbers, and sensitivity numbers with ventricular wire.

The permanent leads were affixed to the generator, after silica gel applied, screw caps applied, excess wire cooled behind the generator, all housed in the pocket. Wound closed with 2-0 Vicryl, subcutaneous, and 3-0 nylon on the skin. Satisfactory pacing was obtained, and the patient returned to his room with stable vital signs and EKG. No apparent complications.

EQUIPMENT: Bitronic DDD pacer, Gemnose TC04, serial 87006454.

ATRIAL WIRE: Oscor, model XY53, JV. Serial BIK27689. Resistance 670 ohms. P amplitude. 2.4 millivolts. Pacing threshold 0.6 volts.

VENTRICULAR LEAD: Model MP53PB, serial 34340163, manufacturer Biotronic. Pacing threshold 0.7 volts. R wave 10.2 millivolts, resistance 650 ohms. Both the atrial and ventricular leads were bipolar sensing and pacing. AV delay paced was 180 msec. Hysteresis out. Rate 70. Upper tracking rate 130.

PROCEDURE(S): _____

MAIN TERM(S): _____

CPT CODE(S): _____

MEDICAL TERMINOLOGY CHALLENGE

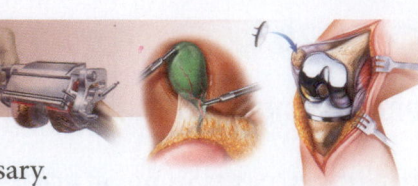

Write a brief definition for each medical term. Use a medical dictionary as necessary.

1. anterolateral _____
2. auscultation _____
3. bruits _____
4. cineangiograms _____
5. dyspnea _____
6. etiology _____
7. femoral _____
8. hemostasis _____
9. infraclavicular _____
10. ischemic _____
11. palpation _____
12. pericardial _____
13. percutaneous _____
14. restless leg syndrome _____
15. stenosis _____
16. subcutaneous _____
17. substernal _____
18. tinnitus _____
19. transmyocardial _____
20. vital signs _____

NOTES:

CHAPTER 7

Blood and Lymph

■ OBJECTIVES

At the completion of this chapter, the student should be able to:

1. Learn the word roots associated with the blood and lymph.
2. Label the structures of the blood and lymph.
3. Discuss the functions of the blood and lymph.
4. Accurately spell and define medical terminology related to the blood and lymph.
5. Accurately assign medical codes to diagnoses and procedures related to the blood and lymph.

■ OVERVIEW

Blood and lymph includes blood plasma, blood cells, lymph fluid, lymph cells, and lymph vessels, nodes, and organs. The main functions of blood are to deliver oxygen, nutrients, and essential chemicals to the cells; to remove carbon dioxide and other waste products from the cells; and to promote wound healing. Blood moves throughout the body by way of arteries and veins. There are three types of blood cells: erythrocytes, leukocytes, and thrombocytes or platelets. Lymph fluid and structures help maintain the fluid balance of body tissues and play an important role in the immune functions of the body. **Hematology** (**hee**-mah-**TALL**-oh-jee) is the study of blood and disorders of blood-forming organs. A physician who specializes in this area is called a **hematologist** (**hee**-mah-**TALL**-oh-jist).

KEY TERMS

ABO blood groups
adenoids
agglutination
agranulocyte
antibody
basophil
blood cell
coagulation
corpuscle
eosinophil
erythrocyte
factors
fibrin
fibrinolysis
granulocyte
hematologist
hematology
hemoglobin
hemolysis
hemolytic disease
 of the newborn
hemostasis
heparin
histamine
interstitial fluid
leukocyte
lingual tonsil
lymph fluid
lymph node
lymph organ
lymph vessel
lymphatic duct
lymphocyte
macrophage
monocyte
neutrophil
palatine tonsils
pathogen
phagocyte
phagocytosis
pharyngeal tonsils
plasma
platelet plug
platelet
right lymphatic duct
spleen
T lymphocyte; T cell
thoracic duct
thrombocyte
thymosin
thymus
tonsils

BLOOD AND LYMPH ROOTS, PREFIXES, AND SUFFIXES

Roots, prefixes, and suffixes associated with blood and lymph are listed in table 7-1. Review the word elements and complete the exercises.

Table 7-1 Roots, Prefixes, and Suffixes for Blood and Lymph

ROOT	MEANING
adenoid/o	adenoid
agglutin/o	to clump
angi/o	vessel
ather/o	fat; fatty plaque
bas/o	base
blast/o	immature cell
coagul/o	clotting
cyt/o	cell
eosin/o	red; rosy
erythr/o	red
granul/o	granules
hem/o; hemat/o	blood
immun/o	protection
is/o	equal
kary/o	nucleus
leuk/o	white
lymph/o	lymph
lymphaden/o	lymph gland
lymphangi/o	lymph vessel
morph/o	form; shape
myel/o	bone marrow; spinal cord
nucle/o	nucleus
phag/o	to eat
poikil/o	varied; irregular
sarc/o	flesh
spher/o	sphere; round
splen/o	spleen
thromb/o	clot; thrombus
thym/o	thymus
tonsill/o	tonsils

PREFIX	MEANING
macro-	large
mono-	one
pan-	all

SUFFIX	MEANING
-cyte	cell
-emia	blood condition
-globin	protein
-lysis; -lytic	destruction; related to destruction
-oma	tumor
-osis	condition

EXERCISE 7-1

Write the root, prefix, suffix, and their meaning. Based on the meanings, write a brief definition for each term.

1. Hematology

   ROOT: _____ MEANING: _____

   PREFIX: _____ MEANING: _____

   SUFFIX: _____ MEANING: _____

   BRIEF DEFINITION: _____

2. Erythremia

   ROOT: _____ MEANING: _____

   PREFIX: _____ MEANING: _____

   SUFFIX: _____ MEANING: _____

   BRIEF DEFINITION: _____

3. Erythrocytopenia

   ROOT: _____ MEANING: _____

   PREFIX: _____ MEANING: _____

   SUFFIX: _____ MEANING: _____

   BRIEF DEFINITION: _____

4. Hemolysis

   ROOT: _____ MEANING: _____

   PREFIX: _____ MEANING: _____

   SUFFIX: _____ MEANING: _____

   BRIEF DEFINITION: _____

5. Leukemia

   ROOT: _____ MEANING: _____

   PREFIX: _____ MEANING: _____

   SUFFIX: _____ MEANING: _____

   BRIEF DEFINITION: _____

6. Splenomegaly

ROOT: _____ MEANING: _____

PREFIX: _____ MEANING: _____

SUFFIX: _____ MEANING: _____

BRIEF DEFINITION: _____

7. Thrombosis

ROOT: _____ MEANING: _____

PREFIX: _____ MEANING: _____

SUFFIX: _____ MEANING: _____

BRIEF DEFINITION: _____

8. Tonsillitis

ROOT: _____ MEANING: _____

PREFIX: _____ MEANING: _____

SUFFIX: _____ MEANING: _____

BRIEF DEFINITION: _____

9. Lymphangiogram

ROOT: _____ MEANING: _____

PREFIX: _____ MEANING: _____

SUFFIX: _____ MEANING: _____

BRIEF DEFINITION: _____

10. Pancytopenia

ROOT: _____ MEANING: _____

PREFIX: _____ MEANING: _____

SUFFIX: _____ MEANING: _____

BRIEF DEFINITION: _____

11. Myeloma

ROOT: _____ MEANING: _____

PREFIX: _____ MEANING: _____

SUFFIX: _____ MEANING: _____

BRIEF DEFINITION: _____

12. Lymphadenopathy

ROOT: _____ MEANING: _____

PREFIX: _____ MEANING: _____

SUFFIX: _____ MEANING: _____

BRIEF DEFINITION: _____

13. Spherocytosis

ROOT: _____ MEANING: _____

PREFIX: _____ MEANING: _____

SUFFIX: _____ MEANING: _____

BRIEF DEFINITION: _____

14. Hemoglobin

ROOT: _____ MEANING: _____

PREFIX: _____ MEANING: _____

SUFFIX: _____ MEANING: _____

BRIEF DEFINITION: _____

15. Anemia

ROOT: _____ MEANING: _____

PREFIX: _____ MEANING: _____

SUFFIX: _____ MEANING: _____

BRIEF DEFINITION: _____

16. Immunology

ROOT: _____ MEANING: _____

PREFIX: _____ MEANING: _____

SUFFIX: _____ MEANING: _____

BRIEF DEFINITION: _____

17. Adenoidectomy

ROOT: _____ MEANING: _____

PREFIX: _____ MEANING: _____

SUFFIX: _____ MEANING: _____

BRIEF DEFINITION: _____

18. Sarcoma

ROOT: _____ MEANING: _____

PREFIX: _____ MEANING: _____

SUFFIX: _____ MEANING: _____

BRIEF DEFINITION: _____

19. Poikilocytosis

ROOT: _____ MEANING: _____

PREFIX: _____ MEANING: _____

SUFFIX: _____ MEANING: _____

BRIEF DEFINITION: _____

20. Lymphangitis

ROOT: _____ MEANING: _____

PREFIX: _____ MEANING: _____

SUFFIX: _____ MEANING: _____

BRIEF DEFINITION: _____

21. Macrocyte

ROOT: _____ MEANING: _____

PREFIX: _____ MEANING: _____

SUFFIX: _____ MEANING: _____

BRIEF DEFINITION: _____

continued

22. Polycythemia

ROOT: _____ MEANING: _____

PREFIX: _____ MEANING: _____

SUFFIX: _____ MEANING: _____

BRIEF DEFINITION: _____

23. Lymphoid

ROOT: _____ MEANING: _____

PREFIX: _____ MEANING: _____

SUFFIX: _____ MEANING: _____

BRIEF DEFINITION: _____

STRUCTURES AND COMPONENTS OF BLOOD

The major components of blood are plasma and cells. **Plasma** is the liquid portion of blood and makes up about 55% of the total blood volume. The plasma is about 90% water and contains dissolved substances such as electrolytes, glucose, gases, protein, and fats. **Blood cells** make up about 45% of the total blood volume. Blood cells are illustrated in figure 7-1. Refer to this figure as you read about these cells.

The blood cells include (1) **erythrocytes** (eh-**RITH**-roh-sights), red blood cells; (2) **leukocytes** (**LOO**-koh-sights), white blood cells; and (3) **platelets** (**PLAYT**-lets) or **thrombocytes** (**THROM**-boh-sights). Leukocytes are further classified as (4) **neutrophils** (**NOO**-troh-fills), (5) **eosinophils** (ee-oh-**SIN**-oh-fills), (6) **basophils** (**BAY**-soh-fills), (7) **monocytes** (**MON**-oh-sights), and (8) **lymphocytes** (**LIM**-foh-sights). Any type of blood cell is also called a **corpuscle** (**KOR**-puss-ehl).

Erythrocytes

Erythrocytes, also called red blood cells (RBCs), are small, biconcave-shaped disks that are thinner in the center than around the edges. Erythrocytes are the most numerous of all blood cells. **Hemoglobin** (**hee**-moh-**GLOH**-bin), which is an iron-protein substance, is the main component of erythrocytes. The primary purpose of erythrocytes is to deliver oxygen to all cells.

Leukocytes

Leukocytes, also called white blood cells (WBCs), are larger than erythrocytes but fewer in number. Leukocytes function as part of our immune system and help fight disease. There are five types of leukocytes, which are grouped into two categories: **granulocytes** (**GRAN**-yoo-loh-sights) and **agranulocytes** (ay-**GRAN**-yoo-loh-sights).

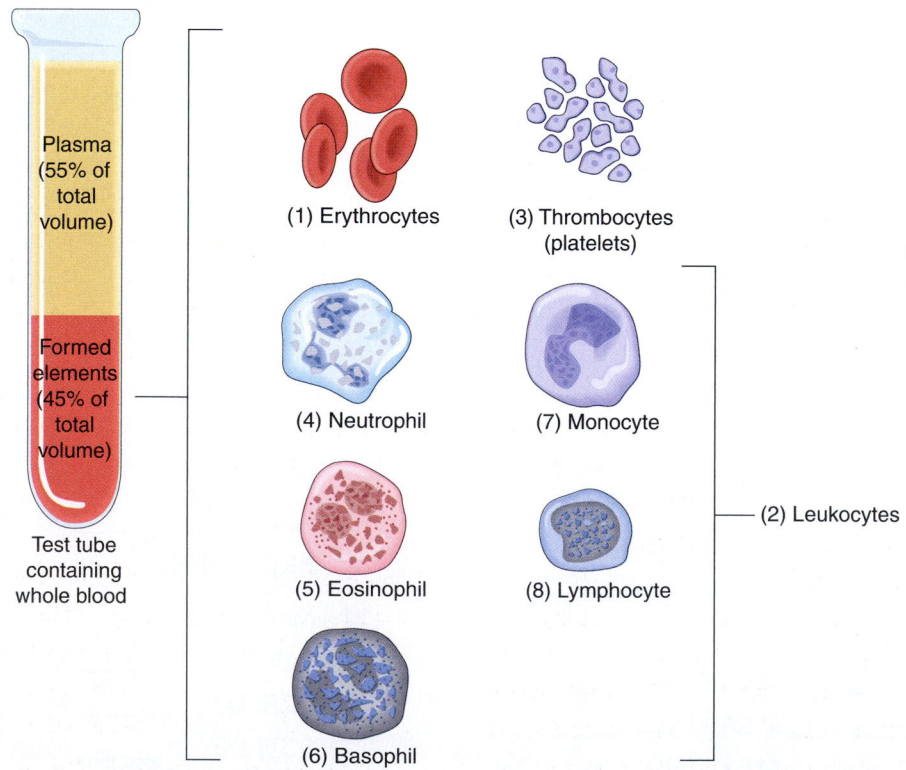

Figure 7-1 Components of blood

Granulocytes have grains or granules in their cytoplasm. These granules absorb different types of stains (also called dyes) that make the cells more visible under a microscope. Figure 7-1 illustrates the three types of granulocytes that include neutrophils, eosinophils, and basophils.

Neutrophils do not absorb any stain and appear neutral in color. Neutrophils are **phagocytes** (**FAG**-oh-sights); they fight disease by engulfing and digesting or destroying bacteria and damaged tissue. **Phagocytosis** (**fag**-oh-sigh-**TOH**-sis) is the process of engulfing and destroying a substance. Eosinophils absorb stain and turn rosy red. The number of eosinophils increases during an allergic reaction and they help defend the body. Basophils absorb stain and turn blue. Basophils release **histamine** (**HISS**-tah-meen) and **heparin** (**HEP**-ah-rin), which help the body respond to an allergic reaction. Histamine increases blood flow, and heparin prevents the blood from clotting.

Agranulocytes do not have granules in their cytoplasm and do not absorb stains. Agranulocytes are categorized by the size of the cell and the shape of the nucleus. Figure 7-1 illustrates the two types of agranulocytes that include monocytes and lymphocytes. Monocytes are the largest leukocytes and have a kidney bean-shaped nucleus. Lymphocytes have a large sphere-shaped nucleus. Monocytes and lymphocytes fight disease by phagocytosis. Some lymphocytes produce **antibodies** (**AN**-tih-**bod**-eez) that destroy bacteria.

Thrombocytes

Thrombocytes, or platelets, are small cells that are essential for normal blood **coagulation** (**koh**-ag-yoo-**LAY**-shun) or clotting. Figure 7-1 illustrates thrombocytes. The coagulation function of platelets is essential to **hemostasis** (**hee**-moh-**STAY**-sis). Hemostasis is defined as stopping or controlling the escape of blood from its vessel by artificial or natural means.

Natural hemostasis is accomplished by a series of reactions that involve the blood vessel wall, platelet activity, and a complex mechanism that involves several plasma coagulation **factors**. Table 7-2 lists 12 coagulation factors.

The hemostatic process is triggered by any injury that damages the lining of a blood vessel. The injury causes platelets to adhere to tissue at the site of the injury. The platelets change shape, aggregate (stick together), and form a **platelet plug** that is able to stop small hemorrhages. Once the platelet plug is formed, the coagulation factors react and **fibrin**, an insoluble, stringy, plasma protein, is deposited on the initial platelet plug to form a fibrin

Table 7-2   Plasma Coagulation Factors

FACTOR NUMBER	FACTOR NAME
Factor I	Fibrinogen
Factor II	Prothrombin
Factor III	Thromboplastin; tissue factor
Factor IV	Calcium
Factor V	Prothrombin accelerator; proaccelerin
Factor VII	Proconvertin
Factor VIII	Antihemophilic factor A; antihemophilic globulin
Factor IX	Christmas factor; antihemophilic B
Factor X	Stuart-Prower factor
Factor XI	Plasma thromboplastin antecedent; antihemophilic C
Factor XII	Hageman factor
Factor XIII	Fibrin-stabilizing factor

clot. This clot stops the escape of blood until the injury heals. Once the clot has served its purpose, **fibrinolysis** (**fih**-brin-**ALL**-ih-sis), destruction of fibrin clots, must be accomplished in a timely manner. If the clot is destroyed too early, hemostasis is compromised.

Blood Groups

Human blood is grouped according to the presence or absence of specific antigens that are present on the surface of red blood cells. Three commonly referenced red blood cell antigens are the *A*, *B*, and *Rh* antigens. The ABO system is commonly used to group or type blood. Group A blood has A antigens, group B blood has B antigens, group AB blood has both A and B antigens, and group O blood has neither antigen.

The presence or absence of the Rh antigen further identifies an individual's blood type. Rh positive (Rh+) means that the red blood cells have the Rh antigen, and Rh negative (Rh−) means that the red blood cells do not contain the Rh antigen. For example, type A positive (A+) means both antigen A and the Rh antigen are present. Blood type A negative (A−) means antigen A is present and the Rh antigen is *not* present. In addition to the blood group antigens associated with red blood cells, blood group antibodies are present in the serum, or plasma, of human blood. Table 7-3 summarizes the **ABO blood groups** and identifies the antigens and antibodies associated with each group.

Identifying an individual's blood group is critical when the individual requires a blood transfusion.

Table 7-3 ABO Blood Groups

BLOOD TYPE	ANTIGEN A/B	RH ANTIGEN	ANTIBODIES
A+ (A positive)	A	Present	Antibody B
A− (A negative)	A	Not present	Antibody B
B+ (B positive)	B	Present	Antibody A
B− (B negative)	B	Not present	Antibody A
AB+ (AB positive)	A and B	Present	None
AB− (AB negative)	A and B	Not present	None
O+ (O positive)	None	Present	Antibody A and B
O− (O negative)	None	Not present	Antibody A and B

An individual should be transfused with blood of the same ABO group and the same Rh designation. If an individual with type A blood receives a transfusion of type B blood, an incompatibility reaction occurs. The B antibodies in the serum of the type A blood react with the B antigens on the red blood cells of the type B blood. There are two types of incompatibility reactions: agglutination and hemolysis. **Agglutination** (ah-**gloo**-tih-**NAY**-shun) means red blood cells clump together and inhibit blood flow. **Hemolysis** (hee-**MALL**-ih-sis) means red blood cells are destroyed.

The Rh antigen does not have naturally occurring antibodies. However, if an individual with Rh− blood is transfused with Rh+ blood, the Rh− individual might produce antibodies to the Rh antigen present in the transfused blood. Once an individual has Rh antibodies, subsequent transfusions with Rh+ blood results in the hemolysis (destruction) of the transfused Rh+ blood cells. Therefore, it is important that transfused blood is the same blood type and Rh designation as the blood of the individual receiving the transfusion.

The production of Rh antibodies might also occur during pregnancy. When an Rh− mother gives birth to an Rh+ infant, the infant's Rh+ blood comes in contact with the mother's Rh− blood. This contact stimulates the production of Rh antibodies in the mother's blood. In subsequent pregnancies, an Rh+ fetus is at risk for a condition called **hemolytic** (**hee**-moh-**LIT**-ik) **disease of the newborn**. In this situation, the Rh antibodies in the mother's blood might enter the fetal bloodstream and react with the fetal Rh+ blood cells. The reaction causes hemolysis of fetal red blood cells, which is a life-threatening condition.

Hemolytic disease of the newborn may be prevented by administering RhoGAM, a commercially prepared immune protein, shortly after the birth of an Rh+ infant by an Rh− mother. RhoGAM helps prevent the formation of Rh antibodies. RhoGAM may also be administered during subsequent pregnancies when an Rh incompatibility exists.

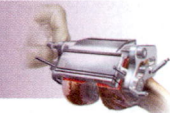

EXERCISE 7-2

Match the component of blood in column 1 with the correct definition in column 2.

COLUMN 1	COLUMN 2
a. agranulocytes	1. absorb different types of stain _____
b. basophils	2. do not absorb stain ____
c. eosinophils	3. iron-protein substance _____
d. granulocytes	4. largest leukocyte _____
e. hemoglobin	5. releases histamine and heparin _____
f. lymphocytes	6. necessary for coagulation _____
g. monocytes	7. engulf, digest, and/or destroy unwanted material _____
h. neutrophils	8. produces antibodies _____
i. phagocytes	9. increases in an allergic reaction _____
j. platelets	10. phagocytic white blood cell _____

EXERCISE 7-3

Write the medical term that best fits the description.

1. clumping together of red blood cells _____
2. destruction of red blood cells _____
3. determine(s) blood type A+ _____
4. determine(s) blood type O– _____
5. determine(s) blood type B _____
6. determine(s) blood type AB– _____
7. plasma antibody(ies) in blood type A _____
8. plasma antibody(ies) in blood type O _____
9. plasma antibody(ies) in blood type B _____
10. plasma antibody(ies) in blood type AB _____

LYMPH AND RELATED STRUCTURES

Lymph and related structures include lymph fluid, (1) **lymph vessels**, (2) **lymph nodes**, and **lymph organs**. These components are an integral part of our immune system and also help maintain our internal fluid balance. Figure 7-2 illustrates lymph vessels, lymph nodes, and lymph organs.

Lymph Fluid

Lymph fluid, usually called lymph, is clear, transparent, and colorless. It consists of proteins, electrolytes, fats, glucose, and lymphocytes. Lymph is derived from the blood and the fluid that collects in body tissue. The smallest lymph vessels, called lymph capillaries, collect **interstitial** (in-ter-**STIH**-shill) **fluid**. Interstitial fluid is located in the spaces between cells, and is the fluid that filters out of the blood capillaries. Once the interstitial fluid enters the lymph capillaries it is called lymph fluid. Figure 7-3 illustrates the relationship between blood capillaries and lymph capillaries.

Lymph Vessels

Lymph capillaries transport lymph fluid to larger lymphatic vessels. The lymphatic vessels allow water and dissolved

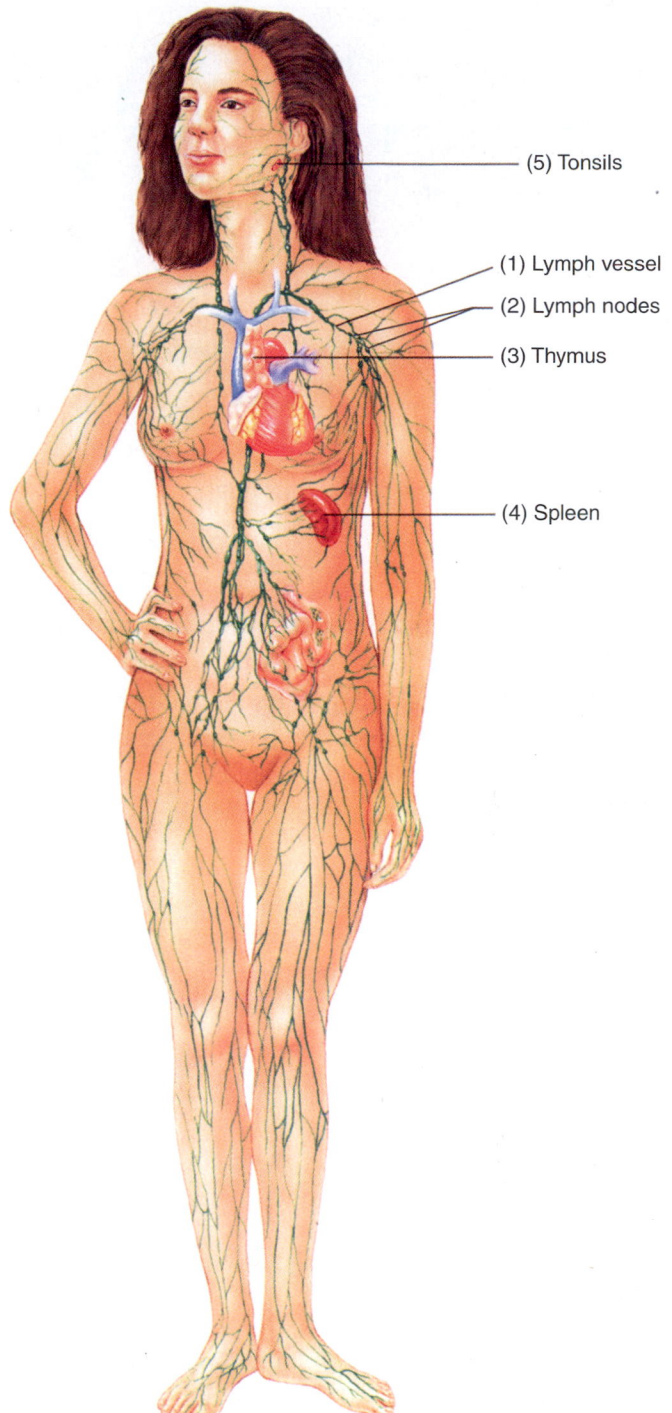

Figure 7-2   Lymph vessels, nodes, and organs

substances to be returned to the blood. Lymph vessels continue to merge and become two **lymphatic ducts**, the **right lymphatic duct** and the **thoracic duct**.

Lymph Nodes

Lymph nodes are collections of lymphatic tissue located at intervals along the course of the lymph vessels. Lymph

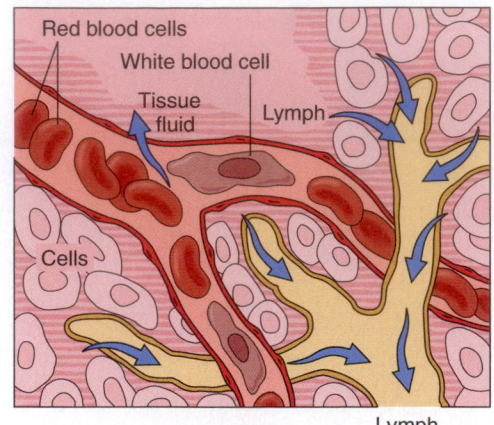

Red blood cells
White blood cell
Blood capillary
Tissue fluid
Lymph
Cells
Lymph capillary

Figure 7-3 Blood and lymph capillaries

nodes function as filters for old, dead cells and bacteria that are present in the lymph fluid. **Macrophages** (**MACK**-roh-fay-jezs), phagocytes located in the lymph nodes, engulf and destroy the bacteria. Lymph nodes also produce antibodies and lymphocytes.

Thymus

The (3) **thymus** is a lymph and endocrine gland. It is located in the mediastinum near the middle of the chest. The thymus secretes a hormone called **thymosin** (thigh-**MOH**-sin), which stimulates the production of **T lymphocytes**, also called **T cells**. T cells are an important part of our immune system because they circulate throughout the body and attack foreign substances and abnormal cells.

Spleen

The (4) **spleen** is the largest lymph organ in the body. It is situated in the upper left quadrant of the abdomen just below the diaphragm and behind the stomach. The spleen filters blood in much the same way the lymph nodes filter lymph fluid. Macrophages in the spleen remove **pathogens** (**PATH**-oh-jens), which are disease-causing substances, from the blood.

Tonsils

The (5) **tonsils**, masses of lymphatic tissue, are located in the mouth at the back of the throat and are divided into three groups. The **pharyngeal tonsils**

(**fair**-in-**JEE**-al **TON**-sills), also called the **adenoids** (**ADD**-eh-noydz), are near the opening of the nasal cavity into the pharynx. The **palatine** (**PAL**-ah-tine) **tonsils** are located on each side of the throat at the back of the oral cavity. The **lingual** (**LING**-gwal) **tonsils** are near the base of the tongue. The tonsils are the first lines of defense against bacteria and other harmful substances that might enter the body through the nose and mouth.

EXERCISE 7-4

Match the lymph terms in column 1 with the definitions in column 2.

COLUMN 1	COLUMN 2
a. interstitial space	1. adenoids _____
b. lingual tonsils	2. attack abnormal cells _____
c. lymph capillaries	3. between the cells of body tissue _____
d. lymph ducts	4. composed of blood and body tissue fluid _____
e. lymph fluid	5. collect interstitial fluid _____
f. macrophages	6. merged lymph vessels _____
g. palatine tonsils	7. filters blood _____
h. pharyngeal tonsils	8. engulf and destroy bacteria _____
i. spleen	9. near the base of the tongue _____
j. T lymphocytes	10. on each side of the throat _____

BLOOD LYMPH MEDICAL TERMINOLOGY

Blood and lymph medical terms are organized by diseases and conditions, and diagnostic procedures, operations, and laboratory tests. There are two categories of medical terminology exercises: (1) those designed to provide opportunities to learn the terms, and (2) those designed to provide opportunities to accurately assign diagnostic or procedure codes. Exercises for learning the terms immediately follow the list of terms and definitions. Medical coding exercises are available after all terms have been presented.

Diseases and Conditions of Blood and Lymph

The medical terms in table 7-4 are signs, symptoms, diseases, and conditions related to blood and lymph. Review the meaning of these terms and complete the exercises.

Table 7-4 Blood and Lymph Signs, Symptoms, Diseases, Disorders, and Conditions

TERM WITH PRONUNCIATION	DEFINITION
acquired immune deficiency syndrome (AIDS)	a syndrome of infections that occur during the final stage of infection by the human immunodeficiency virus (HIV); characterized by the progressive loss of immune system function
acute lymphoblastic leukemia (**lim**-foh-**BLASS**-tik loo-**KEE**-mee-ah) (ALL) lymph/o = lymph cyt/o = cell -ic = pertaining to leuk/o = white -emia = blood condition	a malignant condition characterized by the replacement of normal bone marrow with lymphoblasts, immature lymphocytes; ALL is the most common malignancy in children from 3 to 5 years of age; may spread to the liver, spleen, lymph nodes, central nervous system, kidneys, ovaries, and testes
acute myeloblastic leukemia (AML) (**migh**-eh-loh-**BLASS**-tik loo-**KEE**-mee-ah) myel/o = bone marrow -blast = immature cell -ic = pertaining to leuk/o = white -emia = blood condition	a malignant condition characterized by the replacement of normal bone marrow with myeloblasts, immature agranulocytes; AML occurs at any age; more common in adults than acute lymphocytic leukemia
adenoiditis (**add**-eh-noyd-**EYE**-tis) adenoid/o = adenoid -itis = inflammation	inflammation of the adenoids
anemia (ah-**NEE**-mee-ah) an- = without -emia = blood condition	deficiency in the quantity or quality of blood
anemia, aplastic (ah-**PLAST**-ik ah-**NEE**-mee-ah) a- = without; lack of plast/o = development -ic = pertaining to	deficiency of red blood cell production due to a disorder of the bone marrow
anemia, autoimmune hemolytic (AIHA)	anemia caused by the presence of antibodies that react with red blood cells and cause hemolysis
anemia, hemolytic	anemia due to the premature destruction of red blood cells; hemolytic anemia may be congenital, familial, hereditary, or acquired
anemia, iron deficiency	anemia caused by the lack of an adequate amount of iron in the blood for the production of hemoglobin; the most common cause is blood loss; other causes are diminished iron absorption via the gastrointestinal tract, insufficient iron in the diet, and chronic intravascular hemolysis
anemia, pernicious (PA)	anemia due to a vitamin B_{12} deficiency in the blood; the most common cause of the deficiency is the inability of the gastrointestinal tract to absorb vitamin B_{12}
anemia, sickle cell (**SIK**-ul sell ah-**NEE**-mee-ah) an- = without -emia = blood condition	hereditary form of hemolytic anemia characterized by crescent-shaped erythrocytes (figure 7-4)

continued

Table 7-4 (*continued*)   Blood and Lymph Signs, Symptoms, Diseases, Disorders, and Conditions

TERM WITH PRONUNCIATION	DEFINITION
chronic lymphocytic leukemia (CLL) (**lim**-foh-**SIT**-ik) lymph/o = lymph cyt/o = cell -ic = pertaining to	a condition characterized by a proliferation of mature-appearing lymphocytes in the lymph nodes, spleen, bone marrow, and blood; average age of onset is 60
chronic myelocytic leukemia (CML) (**migh**-eh-loh-**SIT**-ik) myel/o = bone marrow cyt/o = cell -ic = pertaining to	a condition characterized by an excessive production of granulocytes in the bone marrow; occurs at any age, but rarely before age 10
disseminated intravascular coagulation (DIC) intra- = within vascul/o = blood vessel -ar = pertaining to	serious bleeding disorder characterized by overstimulation of clotting and anticlotting body processes; primary DIC involves generalized coagulation within the blood vessels that subsequently leads to a deficiency in clotting factors causing decreased coagulation and hemorrhage
dyscrasia (dis-**KRAY**-zee-ah)	any abnormal condition of blood
embolism (**EM**-boh-lizm)	obstruction of a blood vessel by a foreign substance or a blood clot
embolus (**EM**-boh-lus)	circulating blood clot
erythremia (eh-rih-**THREE**-mee-ah) erythr/o = red -emia = blood condition	an abnormal increase in the number of red blood cells
erythrocytopenia (eh-**rith**-roh-**sigh**-toh-**PEE**-nee-ah) erythr/o = red cyt/o = cell -penia = deficiency; decreased number	decrease in the number of erythrocytes
granulocytosis (**gran**-yoo-loh-sigh-**TOH**-sis) granul/o = granules cyt/o = cell -osis = condition	an increase in the number of granulocytes
hemolysis (hee-**MALL**-ih-sis) hem/o = blood -lysis = destruction; breakdown	destruction or breakdown of red blood cells
hemolytic disease of newborns (**hee**-moh-**LIT**-ik) hem/o = blood -lytic = pertaining to destruction	destruction of newborn or fetal red blood cells caused by a reaction between Rh− maternal blood and Rh+ fetal blood; also called *erythroblastosis fetalis*
hemophilia (**hee**-moh-**FILL**-ee-ah)	hereditary bleeding disorder caused by a deficiency of coagulation factors in the blood in which the blood does not clot
hemophilia A	hereditary bleeding disorder characterized by a deficiency in coagulation factor VIII
hemophilia B	hereditary bleeding disorder characterized by a deficiency in coagulation factor IX

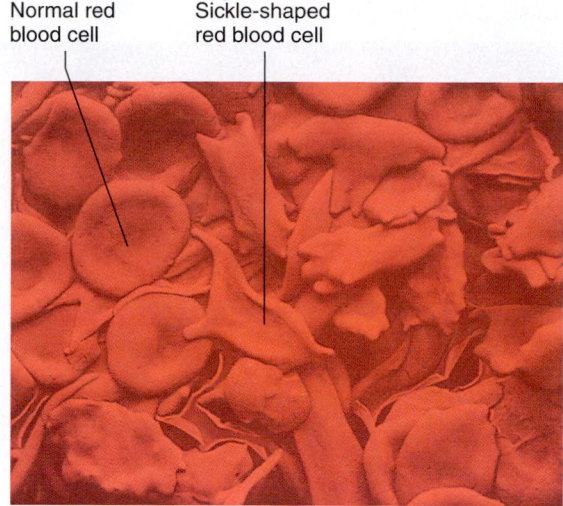

Normal red blood cell

Sickle-shaped red blood cell

Figure 7-4 Sickle-cell anemia

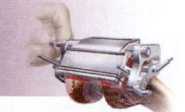

EXERCISE 7-6

Write out each abbreviation and a brief definition of the condition.

1. AIDS _____

   DEFINITION: _____

2. AIHA _____

   DEFINITION: _____

3. ALL _____

   DEFINITION: _____

4. AML _____

   DEFINITION: _____

5. DIC _____

   DEFINITION: _____

EXERCISE 7-5

Circle the medical term that best fits the description.

1. bone marrow disorder; deficient erythrocyte production — *hemolytic anemia or aplastic anemia*

2. proliferation of mature-appearing lymphocytes — *CLL or ALL*

3. excess bone marrow production of granulocytes — *CLL or CML*

4. bleeding disorder — *hemophilia or hemorrhage*

5. deficiency in blood quality or quantity — *dyscrasia or anemia*

6. circulating blood clot — *embolus or embolism*

7. decrease in the number of red blood cells — *erythrocytopenia or hemolysis*

EXERCISE 7-7

Write the medical term for each definition.

1. anemia associated with hemoglobin production _____

2. anemia caused by premature destruction of erythrocytes _____

3. any abnormal blood condition _____

4. destruction or breakdown of red blood cells _____

5. increase in the number of granulocytes _____

6. inflammation of the adenoids _____

7. obstruction of a blood vessel by a foreign substance or blood clot _____

8. anemia characterized by crescent-shaped erythrocytes _____

The medical terms in table 7-5 are signs, symptoms, diseases, and conditions related to blood and lymph. Review the meaning of these terms and complete the exercises.

Table 7-5 Blood and Lymph Signs, Symptoms, Diseases, and Conditions

TERM WITH PRONUNCIATION	DEFINITION
hemorrhage (**HEM**-oh-rij) hem/o = blood -(r)rhage = excessive flow; bursting forth	excessive blood loss, internal or external
Hodgkin disease (**HODJ**-kin)	malignant neoplasm of lymph tissue, also called *Hodgkin lymphoma*
idiopathic thrombocytopenic purpura (ITP)	disorder characterized by decreased thrombocytes and hemorrhages beneath the skin (purpura); in children ITP is usually self-limited and follows a viral infection; in adults ITP is chronic with no apparent cause
leukemia (loo-**KEE**-mee-ah) leuk/o = white -emia = blood condition	abnormal increase in the number of immature white blood cells caused by a malignancy of the blood-forming organs
leukopenia (**loo**-koh-**PEE**-nee-ah) leuk/o = white -penia = deficiency; decreased number	decrease in the number of leukocytes
lymphadenitis (lim-**fad**-en-**EYE**-tis) lymphaden/o = lymph gland -itis = inflammation	inflammation of a lymph gland
lymphadenopathy (lim-**fad**-eh-**NOP**-ah-thee) lymphaden/o = lymph gland -pathy = disease	any disease of a lymph gland
lymphoma (lim-**FOH**-mah) lymph/o = lymph -oma = tumor	a tumor of the lymph tissue, usually malignant
mononucleosis (**mon**-oh-noo-klee-**OH**-sis)	abnormal increase in the number of monocytes accompanied by enlargement of the spleen and lymph nodes; symptoms typically include pharyngitis with exudates, anterior lymphadenopathy, fever, splenomegaly, and posterior cervical or generalized adenopathy; *infectious mononucleosis* is caused by the Epstein-Barr virus (EBV)
neutropenia	decrease in the number of neutrophils in the blood
non-Hodgkin lymphoma (NHL)	a group of malignant lymphomas characterized by a proliferation of lymphoid cells; classification depends on the type of lymph tissue or cells involved: *undifferentiated Burkitt* or *non-Burkitt type, histiocytic, mixed lymphocytic-histiocytic type, lymphocytic type, lymphoblastic type*
polycythemia (**pol**-ee-sigh-**THEE**-mee-ah) poly- = many cyt/o = cells -emia = blood condition	an increase in the number of erythrocytes in the blood
polycythemia vera, primary (PV) (**pol**-ee-sigh-**THEE**-mee-ah **VAIR**-ah) poly- = many cyt/o = cells -emia = blood condition	a chronic myeloproliferative disorder characterized by an increase in hemoglobin concentration, erythrocytosis, hypercellular bone marrow, and an increased production of red blood cells, neutrophils, and platelets
purpura simplex (**PURR**-pyoo-rah)	vascular bleeding disorder characterized by increased bruising and hemorrhages beneath the skin
rouleaux (roo-**LOH**)	abnormal stacking of erythrocytes; also called *rouleaux formation* (figure 7-5)
septicemia (**sep**-tih-**SEE**-mee-ah)	presence of disease-causing bacteria in the blood
spherocytosis (**sfee**-roh-sigh-**TOH**-sis) spher/o = round cyt/o = cell -osis = condition	abnormal condition of round or sphere-shaped erythrocytes
splenomegaly (splee-neh-**MEG**-ah-lee) splen/o = spleen -megaly = enlarged	enlargement of the spleen

continued

Table 7-5 (*continued*) Blood and Lymph Signs, Symptoms, Diseases, and Conditions

TERM WITH PRONUNCIATION	DEFINITION
thalassemia (thal-ah-**SEE**-mee-ah)	hereditary form of hemolytic anemia
thrombocytopenia (**throm-boh-sigh-toh-PEE**-nee-ah) thromb/o = clot cyt/o = cell -penia = deficiency; decreased number	decrease in the number of thrombocytes
thrombosis (throm-**BOH**-sis) thromb/o = clot -osis = condition	presence of a blood clot within a blood vessel
thrombus (**THROM**-bus) thromb/o = clot	a blood clot
tonsillitis (ton-sih-**LIGH**-tis) tonsil/o = tonsils -itis = inflammation	inflammation of the tonsils
von Willebrand disease (VWD)	hereditary disorder characterized by mild to moderate bleeding that includes easy bruising, bleeding from small skin cuts that may stop and start, abnormal postsurgical bleeding, increased menstrual bleeding in women, and a moderate reduction in plasma factor VIII; screening coagulation tests reveal a long bleeding time

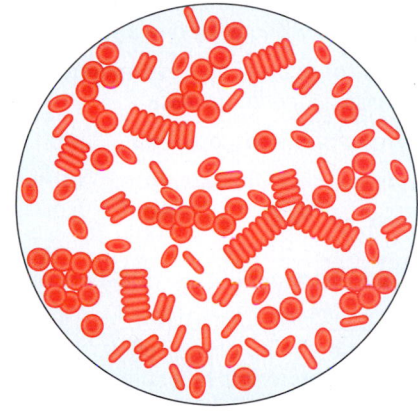

Figure 7-5 Rouleaux

EXERCISE 7-8

Circle the medical term that best fits the description.

1. abnormal stacking of erythrocytes — *polycythemia* or *rouleaux*
2. decrease in the number of leukocytes — *leukocytosis* or *leukopenia*
3. blood clot — *thrombosis* or *thrombus*
4. hemorrhage beneath the skin — *polycythemia* or *purpura simplex*
5. presence of disease-causing bacteria in the blood — *septicemia* or *thalassemia*
6. abnormal increase of all blood cells — *polycythemia vera* or *polycythemia*

EXERCISE 7-9

Write the medical term for each definition.

1. abnormal increase in the number of immature white blood cells _____
2. abnormally round erythrocytes _____
3. any disease of a lymph gland _____
4. hereditary type of hemolytic anemia _____
5. decrease in the number of thrombocytes _____
6. enlarged spleen _____
7. increase in the number of erythrocytes _____
8. inflammation of a lymph gland _____
9. inflammation of the tonsils _____
10. presence of a blood clot in a blood vessel _____
11. tumor of lymph tissue _____

Diagnostic Procedures, Operations, Treatments, and Laboratory Tests of Blood and Lymph

Review the pronunciation and definition of the diagnostic procedures, operations, treatments, and laboratory tests in table 7-6 and complete the exercises.

Table 7-6 Blood and Lymph Diagnostic Procedures, Operations, Treatments, and Laboratory Tests

TERM WITH PRONUNCIATION	DEFINITION
activated partial thromboplastin time (APTT) (**throm**-boh-**PLASS**-tin)	laboratory blood test that is more sensitive than the partial thromboplastin time; measures deficiencies in several coagulation factors
adenoidectomy (**ad**-en-oyd-**EK**-toh-mee) adenoid/o = adenoid -ectomy = surgical removal	surgical removal of the adenoids
bleeding time	laboratory blood test that measures the time required for platelets to interact with a blood vessel wall to form a platelet plug; a platelet plug is an aggregation of platelets that stop or control intravascular bleeding
blood transfusion	administration of blood or components of blood to replace the loss of blood
biopsy, aspiration	withdrawal of tissue for microscopic examination using a needle or trocar; *percutaneous,* through the skin
biopsy, excisional	surgical removal of tissue for microscopic examination; *open biopsy,* tissue is removed via an incision; *closed biopsy,* tissue is removed without making a surgical incision
bone marrow aspiration	withdrawal of a sample of bone marrow for microscopic examination or transplant; usually performed with a biopsy needle or trocar
bone marrow biopsy	removal of a sample of the bone marrow for microscopic examination
bone marrow transplant	infusion of bone marrow from a donor to a recipient; *autologous transplant,* the donor and recipient are the same person; *allogeneic transplant,* the donor and recipient are different individuals
clot retraction time	laboratory blood test that evaluates platelet function, the quality of a fibrin clot, and fibrinolysis
complete blood count (CBC)	a blood test that analyzes the quantity and quality of the cellular components of blood; table 7-7 lists the components of a complete blood count
direct antiglobulin test; Coombs test	blood test that identifies the presence of erythrocyte antibodies in the blood of an Rh− woman, which will cause an incompatibility with an Rh+ fetus
drainage, lymph abscess	removal of fluid and foreign matter from a lymph node or other abscess of lymphatic structures
factor assay test; coagulation factors test	laboratory blood test that measures the plasma concentration of specific coagulation factors
fibrin assay test	laboratory blood test that measures the presence or absence of fibrinogen, coagulation factor I
lymphangiogram (lim-**FAN**-jee-oh-gram) lymphangi/o = lymph vessel -gram = record; picture	a record or picture of an x-ray examination of lymph vessels
lymphangiography	diagnostic imaging (x-ray) of lymph vessels
lymph node biopsy	removal of lymph nodes for microscopic examination
partial thromboplastin time (PTT) (**throm**-boh-**PLASS**-tin)	laboratory blood test that identifies deficiencies in several coagulation factors
platelet aggregation test	laboratory blood test that identifies the ability of platelets to aggregate and form a platelet plug

continued

Table 7-6 (*continued*)   Blood and Lymph Diagnostic Procedures, Operations, Treatments, and Laboratory Tests

TERM WITH PRONUNCIATION	DEFINITION
prothrombin time (PT; pro time) (proh-**THROM**-bin)	laboratory blood test used to identify coagulation problems associated with deficiencies of blood coagulation factors; also used to monitor anti-coagulation therapies or medications
thrombin time; thrombin clotting time	laboratory blood test that measures blood plasma levels of fibrinogen, coagulation factor I
tonsillectomy (**ton**-sill-**EK**-toh-mee) tonsill/o = tonsils -ectomy = surgical removal	surgical removal of the tonsils
tonsillectomy and adenoidectomy (T&A)	surgical removal of the tonsils and adenoids
splenectomy (splen-**EK**-toh-mee) splen/o = spleen -ectomy = surgical removal	removal of all or a portion of the spleen
splenorrhaphy splen/o = spleen -(r)rhaphy = suture; surgical repair	surgical repair of the spleen
transplantation, stem cell	removal and infusion of bone marrow, blood-derived, or umbilical cord stem cells; *autologous transplant,* the donor and recipient are the same person; *allogeneic transplant,* the donor and recipient are different individuals

Table 7-7   Components of a Complete Blood Count

COMPONENT WITH PRONUNCIATION	DESCRIPTION
red blood cell (RBC) count	measures the number of red blood cells, erythrocytes, in a sample of blood
hemoglobin (Hgb) (**hee**-moh-**GLOH**-bin) hem(e) = iron -globin = protein	measures the number of grams of hemoglobin in a sample of blood
hematocrit (Hct) (hee-**MAT**-oh-krit) hemat/o = blood -crit = to separate	measures the percent of red blood cells in a specific sample of blood
red blood cell indices • mean corpuscular volume (MCV) • mean corpuscular hemoglobin (MCH) • mean corpuscular hemoglobin concentration (MCHC)	mathematical calculations that identify erythrocyte size and erythrocyte hemoglobin concentration; MCV is the average size of an erythrocyte; MCH is the average amount of hemoglobin present in an average erythrocyte; and MCHC is the average percentage of hemoglobin in an average erythrocyte
white blood cell (WBC) count	measures the number of white blood cells in a sample of blood
white blood cell differential (diff)	measures the percentage of each type of white blood cell in a sample of blood
platelet count (**PLAYT**-let)	measures the number of platelets in a sample of blood

EXERCISE 7-10

Circle the medical term that best fits the description.

1. measures the percentage of each type of WBC   *diff* or *WBC*

2. identifies antibodies in Rh– woman   *Coombs test* or *CBC*

3. measures platelet plug formation ability   *platelet aggregation* or *clot retraction time*

4. infusion of bone marrow   *bone marrow biopsy* or *bone marrow transplant*

5. grams of hemoglobin in blood   *MCHC* or *Hgb*

6. percent of red blood cells in blood   *Hct* or *MCV*

7. monitors anticoagulation therapies   *thrombin time* or *prothrombin time*

8. identifies coagulation deficiencies   *bleeding time* or *PTT*

EXERCISE 7-11

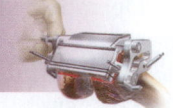

Write a brief definition for each abbreviation or term.

1. RBC _____
2. APTT _____
3. CBC _____
4. WBC _____
5. bleeding time _____
6. platelet count _____
7. clot retraction time _____
8. lymphangiogram _____
9. splenectomy _____

Review the blood and lymph abbreviations in table 7-8. Practice writing out the abbreviations with a brief definition for each phrase or term.

Table 7-8 Blood and Lymph Abbreviations

ABBREVIATION	MEANING
AIDS	acquired immune deficiency syndrome
AIHA	autoimmune hemolytic anemia
ALL	acute lymphoblastic leukemia
AML	acute myeloblastic leukemia
APTT	activated partial thromboplastin time
CBC	complete blood count
CLL	chronic lymphocytic leukemia
CML	chronic myelocytic leukemia
DIC	disseminated intravascular coagulation
diff	white blood cell differential
EBV	Epstein-Barr virus
Hct	hematocrit
Hgb	hemoglobin
HIV	human immunodeficiency virus
ITP	idiopathic thrombocytopenic purpura
MCH	mean corpuscular hemoglobin
MCHC	mean corpuscular hemoglobin concentration
MCV	mean corpuscular volume
NHL	non-Hodgkin lymphoma
PA	pernicious anemia
PT; pro time	prothrombin time
PTT	partial thromboplastin time
PV	polycythemia vera
RBC	red blood cell; red blood cell count
T&A	tonsillectomy and adenoidectomy
VWD	von Willebrand disease
WBC	white blood cell; white blood cell count

BLOOD AND LYMPH MEDICAL CODING

To successfully complete the exercises in this section, the ICD-9-CM volumes 1, 2, and 3, and the CPT (Current Procedural Terminology) coding references must be readily available. The information in this section is presented as follows:

- An introduction to ICD-9-CM volume 1, chapter 4, "Diseases of the Blood and Blood-Forming Organs"
- ICD-9-CM diagnostic coding exercises
- A summary of ICD-9-CM volume 3 coding conventions that apply to the blood and blood-forming organs
- ICD-9-CM procedure coding exercises
- A summary of the CPT Blood and Lymph coding guidelines
- CPT coding exercises

Students are *strongly* encouraged to review the information at the beginning of the ICD-9-CM and CPT coding references. Commercial publishers include instructions on how to use the reference, the ICD-9-CM official coding conventions, additional conventions used by the publisher, and the *ICD-9-CM Official Guidelines for Coding and Reporting*. Some publishers include the three ICD-9-CM volumes in one book and put the *Alphabetic Index* (volume 2) at the beginning of the reference.

The *Introduction* to CPT includes detailed instructions for using this code book, an index to the illustrations throughout the book, and anatomical illustrations of the major structures of the body systems.

ICD-9-CM Volume 1, Chapter 4, Diseases of the Blood and Blood-Forming Organs (280–289)

Blood and lymph diseases are coded to ICD-9-CM volume 1, chapter 4, "Diseases of the Blood and Blood-Forming Organs." This chapter includes the following major categories:

- **Anemia (280–285.9).** Codes in this category cover all types of anemia from aplastic anemia to thalassemia. Both acquired and hereditary forms of anemia are included in this category.

- **Coagulation Defects (286–286.9).** Codes in this category cover congenital, hereditary, and hemorrhagic conditions due to coagulation factor disorders.

- **Purpura and Other Hemorrhagic Conditions (287–287.9).** Codes in this category include a variety of hemorrhagic conditions associated with platelet disorders.

- **Diseases of White Blood Cells (288–288.9).** Codes in this category are related to white blood cell disorders.

- **Other Diseases of Blood and Blood-Forming Organs (289–289.9).** Codes in this category range from lymphadenitis to hypercoagulable disorders.

Conditions related to blood and lymph may also be coded to the following chapters in volume 1: chapter 14, "Congenital Anomalies"; chapter 16, "Symptoms, Signs, and Ill-Defined Conditions"; and chapter 2, "Neoplasms." Because the tonsils and adenoids are also part of the respiratory system, diseases of these lymph structures are coded to ICD-9-CM volume 1, chapter 8, "Diseases of the Respiratory System."

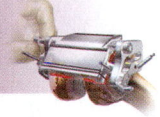

EXERCISE 7-12

Write a brief definition for each diagnosis. Identify the main term in the diagnostic statement and assign the correct ICD-9-CM code(s).

1. Acute viral tonsillitis

   DEFINITION: _____

   MAIN TERM: _____

   ICD-9-CM CODE(S): _____

2. Acute lymphocytic leukemia

   DEFINITION: _____

   MAIN TERM: _____

   ICD-9-CM CODE(S): _____

3. Chronic myelocytic leukemia

   DEFINITION: _____

   MAIN TERM: _____

   ICD-9-CM CODE(S): _____

4. Disseminated intravascular coagulation

   DEFINITION: _____

   MAIN TERM: _____

   ICD-9-CM CODE(S): _____

5. Pernicious anemia

   DEFINITION: _____

   MAIN TERM: _____

   ICD-9-CM CODE(S): _____

6. Thalassemia minima

   DEFINITION: _____

   MAIN TERM: _____

   ICD-9-CM CODE(S): _____

7. Familial polycythemia

   DEFINITION: _____

   MAIN TERM: _____

   ICD-9-CM CODE(S): _____

8. Neutropenia due to infection

   DEFINITION: _____

   MAIN TERM: _____

   ICD-9-CM CODE(S): _____

9. Aplastic anemia, Fanconi

   DEFINITION: _____

   MAIN TERM: _____

   ICD-9-CM CODE(S): _____

10. Chronic lymphocytic leukemia

    DEFINITION: _____

    MAIN TERM: _____

    ICD-9-CM CODE(S): _____

11. Nonfamilial hemophilia

    DEFINITION: _____

    MAIN TERM: _____

    ICD-9-CM CODE(S): _____

continued

12. Hemolytic disease of newborn

    DEFINITION: _____

    MAIN TERM: _____

    ICD-9-CM CODE(S): _____

13. Acute hemolytic anemia, Lederer

    DEFINITION: _____

    MAIN TERM: _____

    ICD-9-CM CODE(S): _____

14. Non-Hodgkin lymphoma, spleen

    DEFINITION: _____

    MAIN TERM: _____

    ICD-9-CM CODE(S): _____

15. Sickle-cell anemia

    DEFINITION: _____

    MAIN TERM: _____

    ICD-9-CM CODE(S): _____

ICD-9-CM Volume 3, Chapter 8, Operations on the Hemic and Lymphatic Systems (40–41)

Blood and lymph operations and some therapeutic treatments are coded to ICD-9-CM volume 3, chapter 8, "Operations on the Hemic and Lymphatic Systems." This chapter includes the following major categories:

■ **Operations on lymphatic system (40–40.9).** Codes in this category include incision, excision, operations, and diagnostic procedures on lymph nodes and ducts. Excisions are identified as simple, regional, or radical. Simple excisions are defined as removal of the lymphatic structure only; regional excisions are defined as removal of a lymph node group from a specific region including skin, subcutaneous tissue, and fat; and radical excisions are defined as removal of a lymph node group down to the muscle and deep fascia.

■ **Operations on bone marrow and spleen (41–41.9).** Codes in this category include bone marrow transplant, operations on the spleen, and diagnostic procedures on the bone marrow and spleen.

The majority of codes in this chapter have four digits. The fourth digit gives additional information about the location and nature of the procedure.

Volume 3, chapter 16, "Miscellaneous Diagnostic and Therapeutic Procedures" (87–99) also contains codes that apply to blood and lymph such as lymphangiography and blood transfusions. Blood tests that screen for disorders of the blood and blood-forming organs, such as iron deficiency anemia, are coded to ICD-9-CM volume 1, V code supplementary classification category V78–V78.9. However, most clinical laboratory tests are coded to the Current Procedural Terminology's Pathology and Laboratory section (80047–89356).

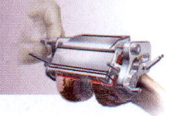

EXERCISE 7-13

Write a brief definition for each operative, treatment, or diagnostic procedure term. Identify the main term in the statement and assign the correct ICD-9-CM code(s).

1. Needle aspiration bone marrow biopsy

   DEFINITION: _____

   MAIN TERM: _____

   ICD-9-CM CODE(S): _____

2. Radical excision of axillary lymph nodes

   DEFINITION: _____

   MAIN TERM: _____

   ICD-9-CM CODE(S): _____

3. Bone marrow transplant, autologous, without purging

   DEFINITION: _____

   MAIN TERM: _____

   ICD-9-CM CODE(S): _____

4. Partial splenectomy

   DEFINITION: _____

   MAIN TERM: _____

   ICD-9-CM CODE(S): _____

5. Lymphadenectomy, simple

   DEFINITION: _____

   MAIN TERM: _____

   ICD-9-CM CODE(S): _____

6. Bone marrow aspiration, from donor for transplant

DEFINITION: _____

MAIN TERM: _____

ICD-9-CM CODE(S): _____

7. Open biopsy of the spleen

DEFINITION: _____

MAIN TERM: _____

ICD-9-CM CODE(S): _____

8. Stem cell transplant, cord blood

DEFINITION: _____

MAIN TERM: _____

ICD-9-CM CODE(S): _____

9. Blood transfusion, platelets

DEFINITION: _____

MAIN TERM: _____

ICD-9-CM CODE(S): _____

10. Autologous whole blood transfusion, previously collected blood

DEFINITION: _____

MAIN TERM: _____

ICD-9-CM CODE(S): _____

Current Procedural Terminology (CPT) Blood and Lymph Codes

CPT blood and lymph codes are included in the Surgery, Radiology, Pathology and Laboratory, and Medicine sections. The range of codes in each section includes, but may not be limited to, the following:

- **Surgery Section, Cardiovascular System, Hemic and Lymphatic System Subsection (38100–38794).** Codes in this subsection cover excision and repair of the spleen, bone marrow or stem cell services and procedures, and procedures of lymph nodes and lymphatic channels.

- **Radiology Section (70010–79999).** Codes in this section cover diagnostic radiology of lymph structures and nuclear medicine procedures of blood and lymph.

- **Pathology and Laboratory Section (80047–89356).** The codes in this section cover diagnostic clinical laboratory tests of blood and lymph, hematology and coagulation tests, blood transfusion procedures and tests, and microscopic evaluation of cells and tissue.

- **Medicine Section (90281–99602).** The codes in this section cover a variety of medical and clinical interventions such as injections, immunizations, chemotherapy, allergy testing, and allergen immunotherapy.

EXERCISE 7-14

Identify the main term in each statement. Assign the correct CPT code(s).

1. Multiple, bilateral iliac crest bone marrow harvesting for transplantation

MAIN TERM: _____

CPT CODE(S): _____

2. Peripheral blood stem cell transplantation, autologous

MAIN TERM: _____

CPT CODE(S): _____

3. Excision of axillary lymph nodes through the subcutaneous tissue, left axilla

MAIN TERM: _____

CPT CODE(S): _____

4. Simple drainage of lymph node abscess

MAIN TERM: _____

CPT CODE(S): _____

5. Bilateral lymphangiography, abdominal, with radiological supervision and interpretation

MAIN TERM: _____

CPT CODE(S): _____

continued

6. CBC with automated differential WBC count

    MAIN TERM: _____

    CPT CODE(S): _____

7. Partial thromboplastin time, whole blood

    MAIN TERM: _____

    CPT CODE(S): _____

8. Peripheral blood smear, interpretation and written report

    MAIN TERM: _____

    CPT CODE(S): _____

9. Splenorrhaphy, with partial splenectomy

    MAIN TERM: _____

    CPT CODE(S): _____

■ SUMMARY

This chapter covered medical terms related to blood, lymph, and lymph structures. Blood and lymph diagnoses and procedures were identified and defined. Blood and lymph diseases and conditions are coded to ICD-9-CM volume 1, chapter 4, "Diseases of the Blood and Blood-Forming Organs." Conditions related to blood and lymph may also be coded to volume 1, chapter 14, "Congenital Anomalies"; chapter 16, "Symptoms, Signs, and Ill-Defined Conditions"; chapter 2, "Neoplasms"; and chapter 8, "Diseases of the Respiratory System." Blood and lymph procedures are coded to ICD-9-CM volume 3, chapter 8, "Operations on the Hemic and Lymphatic Systems."

Current Procedural Terminology (CPT) blood and lymph procedure codes are found in the Surgery, Radiology, Pathology and Laboratory, and Medicine sections.

■ CHAPTER REVIEW

Read each medical note. Write the diagnosis(es) and the main term. Assign the ICD-9-CM diagnosis codes.

CASE 1

Rebecca is a 19-year-old college sophomore who was seen today for a low-grade fever, fatigue, and sore throat off and on for the past three weeks. She states she did not "have time" to come in earlier because she has been "cramming for exams." Examination reveals tenderness in the axilla and neck area consistent with lymphadenopathy. Palpation of the abdomen is positive for marked splenomegaly. Results of the CBC and differential showed an atypical lymphocytosis. Based on these findings, a serum analysis was ordered to confirm infectious mononucleosis. Rebecca was advised to take it easy until we have the serum analysis results. She agreed to seek treatment at the local emergency room should her symptoms worsen.

DIAGNOSIS(ES): _____

MAIN TERM(S): _____

ICD-9-CM DIAGNOSIS CODE(S): _____

CASE 2

Marcel is seen today complaining of tiredness, fatigue, and a general feeling of malaise. He works the midnight shift at the local paint factory and attends college part-time during the day. He states that he hasn't been getting much sleep and his eating habits have gone from "bad to worse." Laboratory tests confirm iron deficiency anemia, which we will try to manage with diet and iron supplements.

DIAGNOSIS(ES): _____

MAIN TERM(S): _____

ICD-9-CM DIAGNOSIS CODE(S): _____

CASE 3

Cho is a 6-year-old boy who is being treated for malignant lymphoma, undifferentiated Burkitt type. He is here today with his parents to discuss the possibility of bone marrow transplantation. They have provided a list of family members who are willing to be tested for potential compatibility. Cho's name has been added to the bone marrow registry.

DIAGNOSIS(ES): _____

MAIN TERM(S): _____

ICD-9-CM DIAGNOSIS CODE(S): _____

CASE 4

Alice, a 65-year-old woman, is seen today to review the results of her recent complete physical examination including lab work. Based on the test results, her problems are related to pernicious anemia. Blood tests also revealed hypogammaglobulinemia, which is fairly common in patients with this diagnosis. She agreed to begin treatment with appropriate medications. A vitamin B_{12} shot was given today.

DIAGNOSIS(ES): _____

MAIN TERM(S): _____

ICD-9-CM DIAGNOSIS CODE(S): _____

CASE 5

Ms. Walenski has been treated for idiopathic thrombocytopenic purpura for approximately two years. She is very unhappy with the side affects of prednisone and is interested in other treatment options. We discussed the risks and benefits of splenectomy. She agreed to give this careful consideration and will decide by the end of the week.

DIAGNOSIS(ES): _____

MAIN TERM(S): _____

ICD-9-CM DIAGNOSIS CODE(S): _____

CASE 6

The patient was admitted with acute myelocytic leukemia, second relapse. On admission, hemoglobin was 8.1 and hematocrit was 23%. The white blood cell count was 23,200 and differential showed 1% segmented neutrophils, 42% lymphocytes, and 57% monocytes. The patient received two units of packed red blood cells. He was started on his usual chemotherapeutic regimen and responded well to this. Due to his nausea and vomiting, he was placed on tube feeding. At discharge he was doing much better. Discharge diagnoses include relapsed acute myelocytic leukemia, severe pancytopenia due to bone marrow hypoplasia, secondary to chemotherapy. We will follow his progress on an outpatient basis.

DIAGNOSIS(ES): _____

MAIN TERM(S): _____

ICD-9-CM DIAGNOSIS CODE(S): _____

CASE 7

Ms. Gervais is a 47-year-old woman who was admitted for complete diagnostic workup related to symptoms that suggest femoral artery thrombosis. She is being treated for ulcerative colitis with high-dose prednisone therapy. Arteriography revealed extensive femoral artery thrombosis with emboli lodging in pedal arterioles. Past medical history reveals several flares of ulcerative colitis with blood loss, over the past six months. Treatment during this hospitalization is consistent with disseminated intravascular coagulation. Aggressive anticoagulation therapy achieved the desired results. The patient was discharged in satisfactory condition. Follow-up will be provided by her internist.

DIAGNOSIS(ES): _____

MAIN TERM(S): _____

ICD-9-CM DIAGNOSIS CODE(S): _____

Read the procedure note, operative report, or discharge summary excerpts. Write the diagnosis(es) and the ICD-9-CM code(s). Write the name of the procedure and the main term. Assign the ICD-9-CM procedure code(s).

CASE 8

PREOPERATIVE DIAGNOSIS: Idiopathic thrombocytopenic purpura.

POSTOPERATIVE DIAGNOSIS: Idiopathic thrombocytopenic purpura.

OPERATIVE PROCEDURE: Splenectomy.

The patient is a 21-year-old woman who noted excessive bruising since last June. She was diagnosed with idiopathic thrombocytopenic purpura. She was treated with prednisone, 20 mg per day. Platelet count has remained low and the patient agreed to undergo elective splenectomy. The patient was taken to the operating room and the splenectomy was performed without incident. She was transfused intraoperatively with 10 units of platelets and postoperatively with an additional 10 units of platelets. She was discharged on the fourth postoperative day in good condition. Platelet count was 77,000. Follow-up will be in the office.

DIAGNOSIS: _____

ICD-9-CM DIAGNOSIS CODE: _____

PROCEDURE(S): _____

MAIN TERM(S): _____

ICD-9-CM PROCEDURE CODE(S): _____

CASE 9

PREOPERATIVE DIAGNOSIS: Hodgkin disease.

POSTOPERATIVE DIAGNOSIS: Hodgkin disease.

PROCEDURE: Bone marrow harvest.

The patient is being treated for Hodgkin disease and has had several relapses. During this admission she underwent an autologous bone marrow harvest. Under general anesthesia, the patient was prepped and draped in the usual sterile manner. She was placed in the prone position. The posterior iliac crests were identified, and multiple bilateral aspirations were taken.

DIAGNOSIS: _____

ICD-9-CM DIAGNOSIS CODE: _____

PROCEDURE(S): _____

MAIN TERM(S): _____

ICD-9-CM PROCEDURE CODE(S): _____

CASE 10

PREOPERATIVE DIAGNOSIS: Lymphadenitis.

POSTOPERATIVE DIAGNOSIS: Abscess, axillary lymph node.

PROCEDURE: Incision and drainage of lymph node abscess.

The patient has been treated for lymphadenitis for several months. Due to the recurrent nature of this problem, she agreed to more aggressive treatment. Under general anesthesia, the patient was prepped and draped in the usual sterile fashion and placed in position for incision and drainage of axillary lymph nodes. The abscess was fully developed and required extensive treatment. The patient tolerated the procedure well and was sent to the recovery room in good condition.

DIAGNOSIS: _____

ICD-9-CM DIAGNOSIS CODE: _____

PROCEDURE(S): _____

MAIN TERM(S): _____

ICD-9-CM PROCEDURE CODE(S): _____

CASE 11

PREOPERATIVE DIAGNOSES: 1. Severe blood loss anemia, due to uncontrolled bleeding. 2. Hemophilia A.

POSTOPERATIVE DIAGNOSES: 1. Severe blood loss anemia, due to uncontrolled bleeding. 2. Hemophilia A.

PROCEDURE: Blood transfusion.

Roger is an 8-year-old boy who has been diagnosed with hemophilia A. He was admitted for severe blood loss anemia due to uncontrolled bleeding. He was given clotting factor and six units of whole blood. Post-transfusion lab results revealed an improved platelet count; hemoglobin and hematocrit are close to normal range. Factor assay results are pending. He was discharged the following day in good spirits.

DIAGNOSIS: _____

ICD-9-CM DIAGNOSIS CODE: _____

PROCEDURE(S): _____

MAIN TERM(S): _____

ICD-9-CM PROCEDURE CODE(S): _____

CASE 12

PREOPERATIVE DIAGNOSIS: Blunt trauma, spleen.

POSTOPERATIVE DIAGNOSIS: Ruptured spleen.

PROCEDURE: 1. Splenorrhaphy. 2. Partial splenectomy.

The patient was seen in the emergency department on Friday evening, after being involved in a motor vehicle accident. Internal injuries included blunt trauma to the spleen. The patient was stabilized and taken to emergency surgery for repair of a ruptured spleen. During the procedure it was necessary to remove a portion of the spleen. The patient was transfused with six units of whole blood. Sponge and needle count was correct ×2. The patient was sent to the recovery room in serious condition and will be transferred to the intensive care unit.

DIAGNOSIS: _____

ICD-9-CM DIAGNOSIS CODE: _____

PROCEDURE(S): _____

MAIN TERM(S): _____

ICD-9-CM PROCEDURE CODE(S): _____

Using the same excerpts in previous cases, write the name of the procedure and the main term. Assign the CPT codes.

CASE 13

PREOPERATIVE DIAGNOSIS: Idiopathic thrombocytopenic purpura.

POSTOPERATIVE DIAGNOSIS: Idiopathic thrombocytopenic purpura.

OPERATIVE PROCEDURE: Splenectomy.

The patient is a 21-year-old woman who noted excessive bruising since last June. She was diagnosed with idiopathic thrombocytopenic purpura. She was treated with prednisone, 20 mg per day. Platelet count has remained low and the patient agreed to undergo elective splenectomy. The patient was taken to the operating room and the splenectomy was performed without incident. She was transfused intraoperatively with 10 units of platelets and postoperatively with an additional 10 units of platelets. She was discharged on the fourth postoperative day in good condition. Platelet count was 77,000. Follow-up will be in the office.

PROCEDURE(S): _____

MAIN TERM(S): _____

CPT CODE(S): _____

CASE 14

PREOPERATIVE DIAGNOSIS: Hodgkin disease.

POSTOPERATIVE DIAGNOSIS: Hodgkin disease.

PROCEDURE: Bone marrow harvest.

The patient is being treated for Hodgkin disease and has had several relapses. During this admission she underwent an autologous bone marrow harvest. Under general anesthesia, the patient was prepped and draped in the usual sterile manner. She was placed in the prone position. The posterior iliac crests were identified, and multiple bilateral aspirations were taken.

PROCEDURE(S): _____

MAIN TERM(S): _____

CPT CODE(S): _____

CASE 15

PREOPERATIVE DIAGNOSIS: Lymphadenitis.

POSTOPERATIVE DIAGNOSIS: Abscess, axillary lymph node.

PROCEDURE: Incision and drainage of lymph node abscess.

The patient has been treated for lymphadenitis for several months. Due to the recurrent nature of this problem, she agreed to more aggressive treatment. Under general anesthesia, the patient was prepped and draped in the usual sterile fashion and placed in position for incision and drainage of axillary lymph nodes. The abscess was fully developed and required extensive treatment. The patient tolerated the procedure well and was sent to the recovery room in good condition.

PROCEDURE(S): _____

MAIN TERM(S): _____

CPT CODE(S): _____

CASE 16

PREOPERATIVE DIAGNOSES: 1. Severe blood loss anemia, due to uncontrolled bleeding. 2. Hemophilia A.

POSTOPERATIVE DIAGNOSES: 1. Severe blood loss anemia, due to uncontrolled bleeding. 2. Hemophilia A.

PROCEDURE: Blood transfusion.

Roger is an 8-year-old boy who has been diagnosed with hemophilia A. He was admitted for severe blood loss anemia due to uncontrolled bleeding. He was given clotting factor and six units of whole blood. Post-transfusion lab results revealed an improved platelet count; hemoglobin and hematocrit are close to normal range. Factor assay results are pending. He was discharged the following day in good spirits.

PROCEDURE(S): _____

MAIN TERM(S): _____

CPT CODE(S): _____

CASE 17

PREOPERATIVE DIAGNOSIS: Blunt trauma, spleen.

POSTOPERATIVE DIAGNOSIS: Ruptured spleen.

PROCEDURE: 1. Splenorrhaphy. 2. Partial splenectomy.

The patient was seen in the emergency department on Friday evening, after being involved in a motor vehicle accident. Internal injuries included blunt trauma to the spleen. The patient was stabilized and taken to emergency surgery for repair of a ruptured spleen. During the procedure it was necessary to remove a portion of the spleen. The patient was transfused with six units of whole blood. Sponge and needle count was correct ×2. The patient was sent to the recovery room in serious condition and will be transferred to the intensive care unit.

PROCEDURE(S): _____

MAIN TERM(S): _____

CPT CODE(S): _____

MEDICAL TERMINOLOGY CHALLENGE

Place an X next to the tests that are directly related to hemophilia and blood clotting.

1. APPT _____
2. bone marrow aspiration _____
3. CBC _____
4. Coombs test _____
5. diff _____
6. factor assay test _____
7. Hct _____
8. MCHC _____
9. PT _____
10. PTT _____

NOTES:

_____   _____

_____   _____

_____   _____

_____   _____

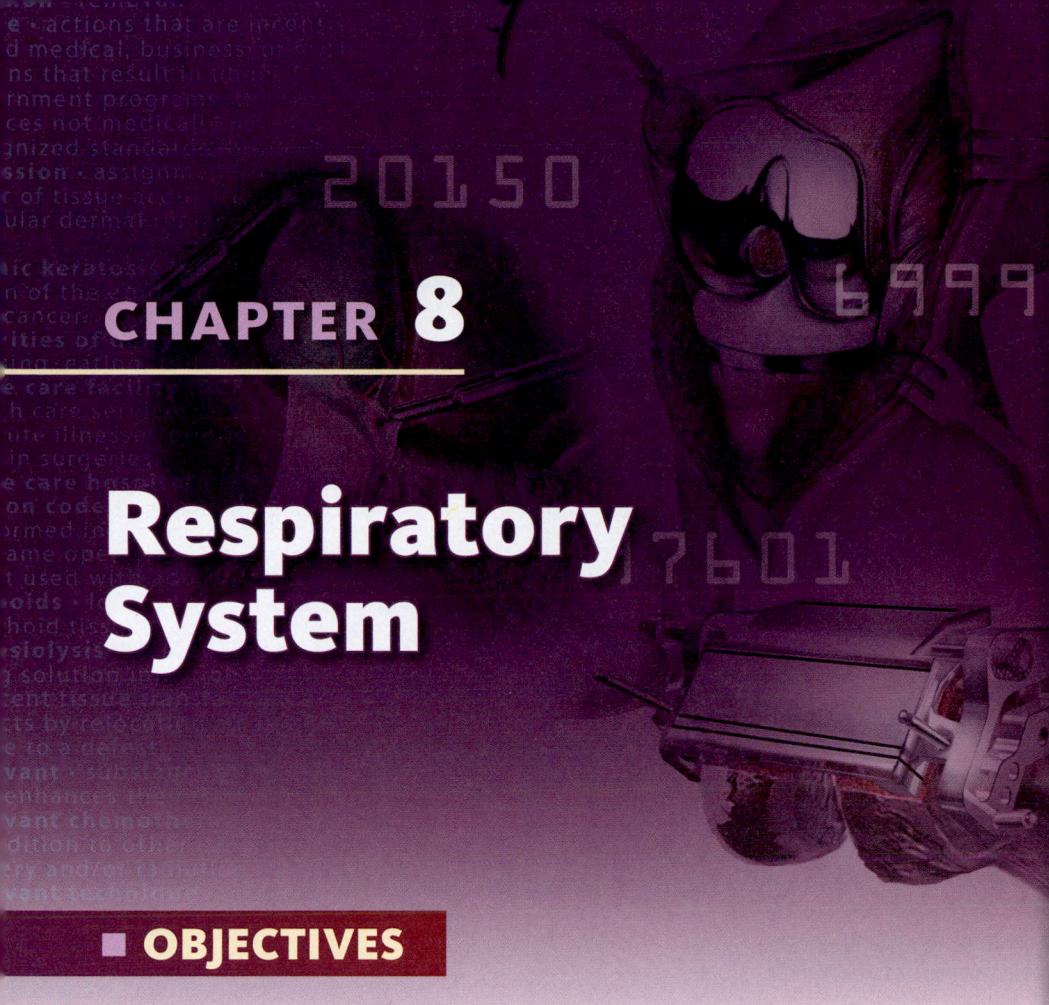

CHAPTER 8

Respiratory System

■ OBJECTIVES

At the completion of this chapter, the student should be able to:

1. Learn the word roots associated with the respiratory system.
2. Label the basic structures of the respiratory system.
3. Discuss the functions of the respiratory system.
4. Accurately spell and define respiratory terminology.
5. Accurately assign medical codes to respiratory system diagnoses and procedures.

■ OVERVIEW

The respiratory system is made up of the nose, pharynx, larynx, trachea, bronchi, and lungs. The structures of the respiratory system function together for the following purposes: (1) to provide oxygen to all body cells, (2) to remove the waste product carbon dioxide from all body cells, (3) to assist the body's defense mechanisms against foreign material, and (4) to produce sound necessary for speech. The medical specialty related to the respiratory system is **pulmonology** (**pull**-mon-**ALL**-oh-jee), and physician specialists are **pulmonologists** (**pull**-mon-**ALL**-oh-jists). A **respiratory therapist** is an allied health professional who conducts various respiratory tests and therapies.

The respiratory system moves oxygen and carbon dioxide by external respiration and internal respiration. **External respiration** is the exchange of air between the lungs and the external environment. When a person inhales, the oxygen in the air is drawn into the lungs and distributed, by way of the blood, to all body cells. During exhalation, carbon dioxide is released into the environment. Normal breathing is called **eupnea** (**YOOP**-nee-ah).

Internal respiration is the exchange of oxygen and carbon dioxide between the cells and the blood. The blood delivers oxygen to every cell and picks up carbon dioxide. The carbon dioxide is then returned to the lungs and, as previously noted, expelled from the body when you exhale.

RESPIRATORY SYSTEM ROOTS, PREFIXES, AND SUFFIXES

Roots, prefixes, and suffixes associated with the respiratory system are listed in table 8-1. Review the word elements and complete the exercises.

Table 8-1   Respiratory System Roots, Prefixes, and Suffixes

ROOT	MEANING
alveol/o	alveolus
anthrac/o	coal
atel/o	incomplete
bronch/o; bronch/i	bronchus
bronchiol/o	bronchus
coni/o	dust
epiglott/o	epiglottis
laryng/o	larynx
muc/o	mucus
nas/o	nose
orth/o	straight
ox/i	oxygen
pector/o	chest
pharyng/o	pharynx
phren/o	diaphragm
pleur/o	pleura
pneum/o	lung; air
pulmon/o	lungs
py/o	pus
rhin/o	nose
sinus/o	sinus
spir/o	breathe; breath
tonsill/o	tonsils
thorac/o	chest
trache/o	trachea

PREFIX	MEANING
eu-	normal

SUFFIX	MEANING
-capnia	carbon dioxide
-ectasis	stretching; dilation
-phonia	sound; voice
-pnea	breathing
-ptysis	coughing; spitting up
-(r)rhea	copious discharge
-thorax	chest

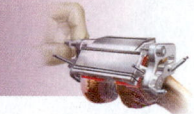

EXERCISE 8-1

Write the root, prefix, suffix, and their meaning. Based on the meanings, write a brief definition for each term.

1. Pharyngitis

   ROOT: _____ MEANING: _____

   PREFIX: _____ MEANING: _____

   SUFFIX: _____ MEANING: _____

   BRIEF DEFINITION: _____

2. Anoxia

   ROOT: _____ MEANING: _____

   PREFIX: _____ MEANING: _____

   SUFFIX: _____ MEANING: _____

   BRIEF DEFINITION: _____

3. Anthracosis

   ROOT: _____ MEANING: _____

   PREFIX: _____ MEANING: _____

   SUFFIX: _____ MEANING: _____

   BRIEF DEFINITION: _____

4. Phrenic

   ROOT: _____ MEANING: _____

   PREFIX: _____ MEANING: _____

   SUFFIX: _____ MEANING: _____

   BRIEF DEFINITION: _____

5. Eupnea

   ROOT: _____ MEANING: _____

   PREFIX: _____ MEANING: _____

   SUFFIX: _____ MEANING: _____

   BRIEF DEFINITION: _____

6. Hypercapnia

ROOT: _____ MEANING: _____

PREFIX: _____ MEANING: _____

SUFFIX: _____ MEANING: _____

BRIEF DEFINITION: _____

7. Rhinorrhagia

ROOT: _____ MEANING: _____

PREFIX: _____ MEANING: _____

SUFFIX: _____ MEANING: _____

BRIEF DEFINITION: _____

8. Rhinorrhea

ROOT: _____ MEANING: _____

PREFIX: _____ MEANING: _____

SUFFIX: _____ MEANING: _____

BRIEF DEFINITION: _____

9. Alveolar

ROOT: _____ MEANING: _____

PREFIX: _____ MEANING: _____

SUFFIX: _____ MEANING: _____

BRIEF DEFINITION: _____

10. Pneumoconiosis

ROOT: _____ MEANING: _____

PREFIX: _____ MEANING: _____

SUFFIX: _____ MEANING: _____

BRIEF DEFINITION: _____

11. Pneumothorax

ROOT: _____ MEANING: _____

PREFIX: _____ MEANING: _____

SUFFIX: _____ MEANING: _____

BRIEF DEFINITION: _____

12. Hypoxemia

ROOT: _____ MEANING: _____

PREFIX: _____ MEANING: _____

SUFFIX: _____ MEANING: _____

BRIEF DEFINITION: _____

13. Hemoptysis

ROOT: _____ MEANING: _____

PREFIX: _____ MEANING: _____

SUFFIX: _____ MEANING: _____

BRIEF DEFINITION: _____

14. Pulmonologist

ROOT: _____ MEANING: _____

PREFIX: _____ MEANING: _____

SUFFIX: _____ MEANING: _____

BRIEF DEFINITION: _____

STRUCTURES OF THE RESPIRATORY SYSTEM

The structures of the respiratory system include the (1) **nose**, (2) **nasal cavity**, (3) **paranasal sinuses**, (4) **pharynx** (**FAIR**-inks), (5) **larynx** (**LAIR**-inks), (6) **trachea** (**TRAY**-kee-ah), (7) **lungs**, (8) **bronchi** (**BRONG**-kigh), (9) **alveoli** (al-**VEE**-oh-ligh), and (10) **diaphragm** (**DIGH**-ah-fram). Figure 8-1 illustrates these structures. Refer to this figure as you read about each structure.

Nose, Pharynx, and Larynx

The nose and mouth direct air into the body. The entrances to the nose are the **nares** (**NAIRZ**), also called *nostrils*. Air enters the nose through the right and left chambers of the nasal cavity. A cartilage wall called the **septum** divides the chambers. Air also passes through the paranasal sinuses, which are cavities in the skull that open into the nasal cavity. The walls of the nasal cavity are lined with scroll-shaped structures called **turbinates** (**TER**-bin-ayts). The turbinates are mucous membranes that warm the air as it passes into the lungs. Hairlike projections called **cilia** (**SEE**-lee-ah) sweep dirt and foreign particles toward the throat and away from the lungs.

The pharynx, or throat, connects the nose and mouth to the larynx, or voice box. The pharynx has three sections: the (11) **nasopharynx** (**nay**-zoh-**FAIR**-inks), the upper section; the (12) **oropharynx** (**or**-oh-**FAIR**-inks), the middle section; and the (13) **laryngopharynx** (lah-**ring**-oh-**FAIR**-inks), the lower portion. The pharynx serves as the passageway for both air and food. As food passes through the pharynx, it must be prevented from entering the lungs. A small flap of cartilage, called the (14) **epiglottis** (ep-ih-**GLOT**-iss), closes over the trachea and prevents food from entering the larynx. The adenoids and tonsils are located in the pharynx.

The larynx, also called the voice box, contains vocal cords that make vocal sounds. As air passes through the spaces between the vocal cords, sound is produced. The space between the vocal cords is called the **glottis** (**GLOT**-iss). The larynx is made up of cartilage.

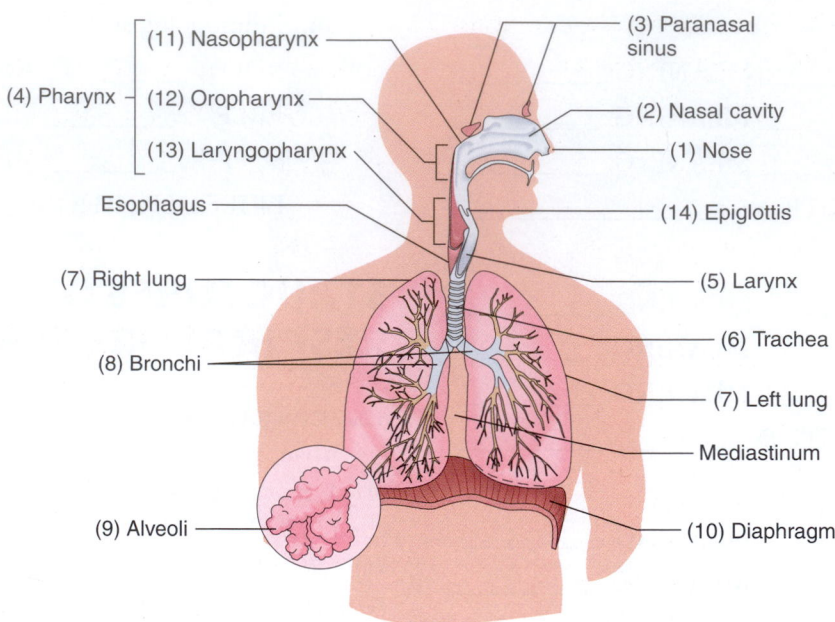

Figure 8-1 Respiratory system structures

The most prominent cartilage, which is actually the thyroid cartilage, is often called the *Adam's apple.*

Trachea, Bronchi, and Lungs

The trachea, bronchi, lungs, and related structures are illustrated in figure 8-2. Refer to this figure as you read about these structures.

The (1) trachea is commonly called the windpipe. It is the passageway for air and consists of muscular tissue that is kept open by a series of C-shaped cartilage rings.

Before entering the lungs, the trachea branches into two tubes, called (2) bronchi. One **bronchus** (**BRONG**-kus) enters the right lung, and the other enters the left lung. Bronchi, nerves, and blood vessels enter the lungs at a specific location called the **hilum** (**HIGH**-lum). In the lungs, the bronchi divide into progressively smaller tubes called (3) **bronchioles** (**BRONG**-kee-ohlz). The bronchioles end in clusters of air sacs called (4) alveoli (al-**VEE**-oh-ligh). The alveoli are surrounded by capillaries. Oxygen and carbon dioxide pass between the alveoli and capillaries. Oxygen passes into the bloodstream and

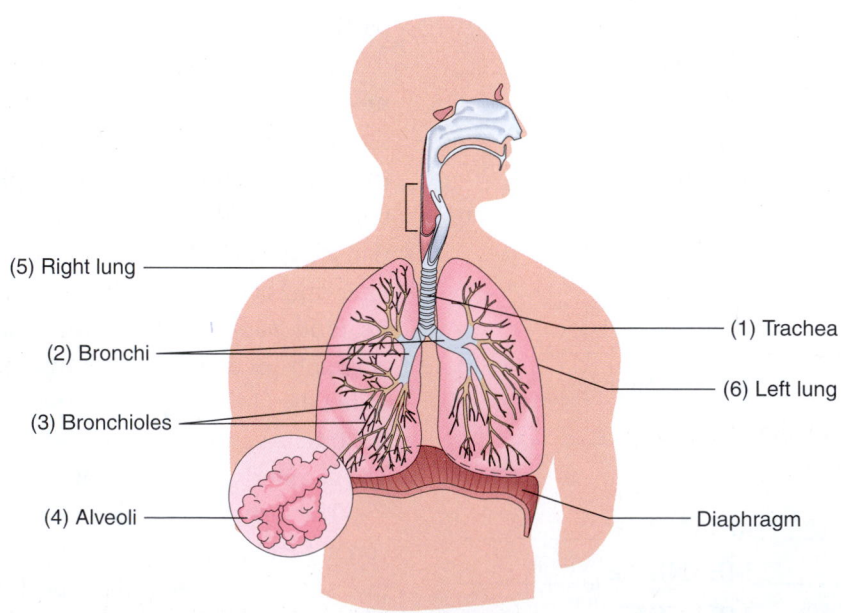

Figure 8-2 Trachea, bronchi, and lungs

is delivered to all parts of the body. Carbon dioxide passes into the alveoli and is expelled during exhalation.

The lungs are cone-shaped, spongy organs that house the bronchi, bronchioles, alveoli, blood vessels, nerves, and elastic tissue. The lungs are divided into lobes. The (5) **right lung** has three lobes and the (6) **left lung** has two lobes. The upper part of the lung is called the apex, and the lower part of the lung is called the base. **Sputum**, material brought or coughed up from the lungs, consists of mucus, cellular debris, or microorganisms. Sputum color, amount, and constituents play an important role in the diagnosis of many diseases.

The **pleura** (**PLOO**-rah) is a double-folded membrane that surrounds the lungs. One layer covers the lungs and the other layer lines the chest cavity. The small space between the layers is the pleural space, which is filled with a fluid that prevents friction between the lungs and ribs during respiration.

The diaphragm is a muscular partition that separates the thoracic and abdominal cavities. During inhalation, the diaphragm drops to enlarge the thoracic cavity and draw air into the lungs. During exhalation, the diaphragm returns to its normal position and helps push air out of the lungs. Drawing air into the lungs is called **inhalation** or **inspiration**. Pushing air out of the lungs is called **exhalation** or **expiration**.

EXERCISE 8-2

Match the term in column 1 with the correct definition in column 2.

TERM	DEFINITION
a. alveoli	1. muscular partition between the thoracic and abdominal cavities _____
b. bronchi	2. entrances to the nose _____
c. bronchioles	3. entrance into the lungs for bronchi, nerves, and blood vessels _____
d. capillaries	4. very small blood vessel in the lungs _____
e. diaphragm	5. membranes surrounding the lungs _____
f. hilum	6. voice box _____
g. larynx	7. throat _____

h. lungs	8. tubes leading to the lungs _____
i. nares	9. airway; windpipe _____
j. pharynx	10. air sacs _____
k. pleura	11. cone-shaped, spongy organs _____
l. trachea	12. "little" bronchi _____

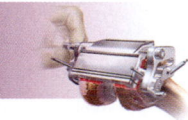

EXERCISE 8-3

Label the structures of the respiratory system identified in figure 8-3. Write your answer on the spaces provided.

1. _____

2. _____

3. _____

4. _____

5. _____

6. _____

7. _____

8. _____

9. _____

10. _____

RESPIRATORY SYSTEM MEDICAL TERMINOLOGY

Respiratory system medical terms are organized by diseases, conditions, diagnostic procedures, and operations. There are two categories of medical terminology exercises: (1) those designed to provide opportunities to learn the terms, and (2) those designed to provide opportunities to accurately assign diagnostic or procedure codes. Exercises for learning the terms immediately follow the lists of terms and definitions. Medical coding exercises are available after all terms have been presented.

Respiratory System Signs, Symptoms, Diseases, and Conditions

The medical terms in table 8-2 are signs or symptoms of diseases or conditions related to the respiratory system. Review the meaning of these terms and complete the exercises.

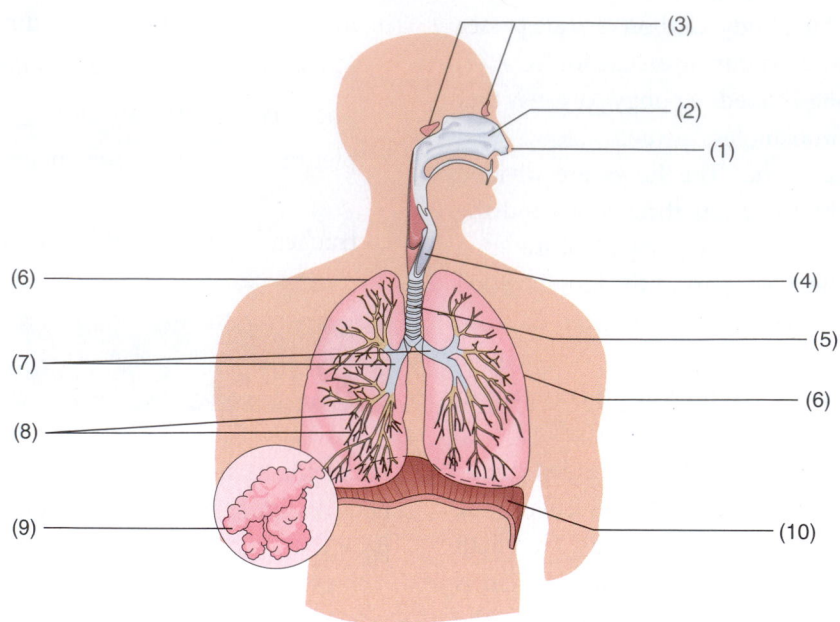

Figure 8-3 Label respiratory system structures

Table 8-2 Respiratory System Signs, Symptoms, Diseases, and Conditions

TERM WITH PRONUNCIATION	DEFINITION
aspirate; aspiration (**ASS**-per-ayt; **ass**-per-**AY**-shun)	to draw foreign material into the lungs (Note: *Aspirate* and *aspiration* also means to withdraw fluid or tissue, as in bone marrow aspiration.)
acapnia (ay-**KAP**-nee-ah) a- = without -capnia = carbon dioxide	absence of carbon dioxide in the blood; less than normal blood levels of carbon dioxide
anoxia (an-**OCKS**-ee-ah) an- = absence; lack of ox/i = oxygen -a = noun ending	absence or lack of the normal level of oxygen in the blood
aphonia (ay-**FOH**-nee-ah) a- = absence; lack of -phonia = sound or voice	inability to produce sound or speech
apnea (ap-**NEE**-ah) a- = absence; lack of -pnea = breathing	absence or lack of breathing; temporary cessation of breathing
dysphonia (diss-**FOH**-nee-ah) dys- = difficult -phonia = voice; sound	difficulty producing speech or vocal sounds
dyspnea (disp-**NEE**-ah) dys- = difficult -pnea = breathing	difficulty breathing
dyspnea on exertion (DOE)	difficulty breathing during any physical activity
hypercapnia (**high**-per-**KAP**-nee-ah) hyper- = excessive; increase -capnia = carbon dioxide	increased or excessive carbon dioxide in the blood
hyperpnea (**high**-perp-**NEE**-ah) hyper- = excessive; increase -pnea = breathing	excessive or increased breathing
hypocapnia (**high**-poh-**KAP**-nee-ah) hypo- = decreased; deficient -capnia = carbon dioxide	deficient carbon dioxide levels in the blood

continued

Table 8-2 (*continued*)   Respiratory System Signs, Symptoms, Diseases, and Conditions

TERM WITH PRONUNCIATION	DEFINITION
hypopnea (**high**-pop-**NEE**-ah) hypo- = decreased; deficient -pnea = breathing	decreased or deficient breathing
hypoxemia (**high**-pocks-**EE**-mee-ah) hypo- = decreased; deficient ox/i = oxygen -emia = blood	deficient or decreased oxygen in the blood
hypoxia (high-**POCKS**-ee-ah) hypo- = decreased; deficient ox/i = oxygen -a = noun ending	deficient or decreased oxygen supply to body tissue
mucopurulent (**myoo**-koh-**PYOOR**-yoo-lent)	containing both mucus and pus
orthopnea (or-**THOP**-nee-ah) orth/o = straight -pnea = breathing	ability to breathe only when upright or in the upright position
rales (**RALZ**)	abnormal chest sound caused by congested or spasmodic bronchi
rhinorrhea (**righ**-noh-**REE**-ah) rhin/o = nose -(r)rhea = copious discharge; drainage	thin, watery discharge from the nose; runny nose
rhonchi (**RONG**-kigh)	rales or rattling in the throat, resembles snoring
stridor (**STRIGH**-dor)	harsh, high-pitched sound during respiration

EXERCISE 8-4

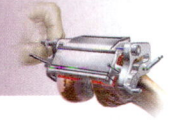

Circle the medical term that best fits the description.

1. difficulty breathing — *eupnea* or *dyspnea*
2. lack of oxygen in the blood — *hypoxemia* or *anoxia*
3. rattling; resembles snoring — *rhonchi* or *rales*
4. high-pitched sound during respiration — *stridor* or *rales*
5. deficient carbon dioxide in the blood — *hypocapnia* or *hypopnea*
6. decreased oxygen supply to body tissue — *acapnia* or *hypoxia*
7. abnormal chest sound related to bronchi — *rales* or *stridor*
8. lack of carbon dioxide in the blood — *acapnia* or *hypopnea*
9. inability to produce speech or sound — *apnea* or *aphonia*

EXERCISE 8-5

Write the medical term for each definition.

1. runny nose _____
2. ability to breathe only when upright _____
3. excessive breathing _____
4. decreased oxygen in the blood _____
5. drawing foreign material into the lungs _____
6. difficulty producing speech or sound _____
7. containing mucus and pus _____
8. temporary cessation of breathing _____

The medical terms in table 8-3 are diseases and conditions of the respiratory system. Review the meaning of these terms and complete the exercises.

Table 8-3   Respiratory Diseases and Conditions

TERM WITH PRONUNCIATION	DEFINITION
acute respiratory distress syndrome; adult respiratory distress syndrome (ARDS)	respiratory failure associated with a variety of acute conditions that directly or indirectly injure the lung, for example, primary bacterial or viral pneumonias, aspiration of gastric contents, and trauma; characterized by hypoxemia and diffuse pulmonary infiltrates
adenoiditis (**ad**-eh-noyd-**EYE**-tis) adenoid/o = adenoids -itis = inflammation	inflammation of the adenoids
anthracosis (an-thrah-**KOH**-sis) anthrac/o = coal -osis = condition	accumulation of carbon deposits in the lungs; black lung disease; also known as *coal worker's pneumoconiosis*
asbestosis (as-bess-**TOH**-sis)	accumulation of asbestos particles in the lungs; a type of nonmalignant pulmonary fibrosis
asphyxia (as-**FICKS**-ee-ah)	oxygen deprivation; suffocation
asthma (**AZ**-mah)	diffuse airway inflammation caused by a variety of stimuli that results in bronchoconstriction, bronchospasm, wheezing, and dyspnea; treatment is based on frequency and severity of asthmatic episodes; often classified as mild, moderate, or severe, persistent or intermittent
atelectasis (**at**-eh-**LEK**-tah-sis) atel/o = incomplete -ectasis = expansion; dilatation	incomplete expansion, usually of the lung; may be caused by disease, trauma, or postoperative complications
bronchiectasis (brong-kee-**EK**-tah-sis) bronch/o = bronchus; bronchi -ectasis = expansion; dilation	abnormal dilation or destruction of the bronchi caused by infection and inflammation; often seen with cystic fibrosis or individuals with immune defects
bronchiolitis (**brong**-kee-oh-**LIGH**-tis) bronchiol/o = bronchiole -itis = inflammation	acute viral infection of the bronchioles; usually occurs in children less than two years old
bronchitis, acute (brong-**KIGH**-tis) bronch/o = bronchus, bronchi -itis = inflammation	acute inflammation of the bronchi that often follows an upper respiratory infection; may be caused by a virus or bacteria; cough is minimally productive or nonproductive
bronchitis, chronic obstructive	chronic bronchitis characterized by airflow obstruction
bronchogenic carcinoma (brong-koh-**JEN**-ic **kar**-sin-**OH**-mah) bronch/o = bronchus -genic = pertaining to development carcin- = cancer; malignant -oma = tumor	malignant lung tumor also called lung carcinoma; primary lung carcinoma is classified as small cell carcinoma, non–small cell carcinoma, or other; small cell carcinomas account for about 15% of lung carcinomas; about 30% of lung cancers are adenocarcinomas; 30% are squamous cell carcinoma; and 10% are large cell carcinoma
bronchopneumonia (**brong**-koh-noo-**MOH**-nee-ah) bronch/o = bronchus pneumon/o = lungs; air -ia = noun ending	inflammation of the bronchi and lungs caused primarily by bacteria
bronchospasm (**BRONG**-koh-spasm) bronch/o = bronchus -spasm = involuntary contraction	involuntary spasms of the bronchi
chronic obstructive pulmonary disease (COPD)	progressive and partially reversible condition characterized by airflow obstruction and diminished lung capacity; chronic obstructive bronchitis and emphysema are often concurrent with COPD
coryza; rhinitis (koh-**RIGH**-zuh) (righ-**NIGH**-tis) rhin/o = nose -itis = inflammation	inflammation of the mucous membranes of the nose; a common cold

continued

Table 8-3 (*continued*)   Respiratory Diseases and Conditions

TERM WITH PRONUNCIATION	DEFINITION
croup (kroop)	acute inflammation of the upper and lower respiratory tracts, usually caused by a virus; affects children between six months and three years of age; characterized by a barking cough, dyspnea, and laryngeal spasms
cystic fibrosis (CF) (**SIS**-tik figh-**BROH**-sis)	a hereditary disorder that affects the gastrointestinal and respiratory system; respiratory features include airway obstructions and infections, excess mucus secretion, mucopurulent substance in the airways, pulmonary atelectasis, and decreased pulmonary function
deviated septum	misalignment of the nasal septum due to malformation or injury
emphysema (em-fih-**SEE**-mah)	distention and destruction of alveolar walls causing decreased elasticity of the lungs; often associated with COPD; cigarette smoking is the primary risk factor
epistaxis, rhinorrhagia (ep-ih-**STAK**-sis) (**righ**-noh-**RAY**-jee-ah) rhin/o = nose -(r)rhagia = hemorrhage	discharge of blood from the nose; nosebleed
hemoptysis (hee-**MOP**-tih-sis) hem/o = blood -ptysis = spitting up	coughing up blood-tinged sputum; spitting up blood
hemothorax (**hee**-moh-**THOR**-aks) hem/o = blood -thorax = chest; chest cavity	blood in the chest cavity or pleural space
influenza (flu) (in-floo-**EN**-zah)	highly contagious infection of the respiratory tract caused by a virus
laryngitis (lair-in-**JIGH**-tis) laryng/o = larynx -itis = inflammation	inflammation of the larynx

EXERCISE 8-6

Write the medical term for each definition.

1. abnormal dilation and destruction of the bronchi _____
2. black lung disease _____
3. blood in the chest cavity _____
4. common cold _____
5. inflammation of the adenoids _____
6. inflammation of the larynx _____
7. spitting up blood _____
8. suffocation _____

EXERCISE 8-7

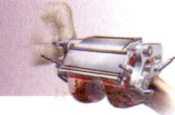

Circle the term that best fits the description.

1. abnormal destruction of alveoli — *atelectasis* or *emphysema*
2. childhood respiratory tract infection — *bronchiolitis* or *croup*
3. contagious respiratory tract infection — *influenza* or *chronic bronchitis*
4. diffuse airway inflammation — *ARDS* or *asthma*
5. hereditary respiratory tract disorder — *cystic fibrosis* or *asbestosis*
6. inflammation of the bronchi — *bronchitis* or *bronchiolitis*
7. progressive airflow obstruction — *COPD* or *ARDS*

EXERCISE 8-8

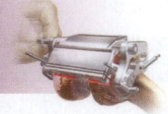

Write a brief definition for each term or abbreviation.

1. ARDS _____
2. asbestosis _____
3. atelectasis _____
4. bronchiolitis _____

5. bronchogenic carcinoma _____
6. bronchopneumonia _____
7. bronchospasm _____
8. deviated septum _____
9. epistaxis _____

The medical terms in table 8-4 are diseases and conditions of the respiratory system. Review the meaning of these terms and complete the exercises.

Table 8-4 Respiratory System Diseases and Conditions

TERM WITH PRONUNCIATION	DEFINITION
laryngospasm (lah-**RING**-oh-spasm) laryng/o = larynx -spasm = involuntary contraction	involuntary or spasmodic contractions of the larynx
Legionnaires disease (**lee**-jeh-**NAIRZ**)	a lobar pneumonia caused by the *Legionella pneumophila* bacteria
lobar pneumonia	a severe infection of one or more of the five lobes of the lung
mesothelioma, pleural	malignant disease of the pleura usually caused by exposure to asbestos; may occur 30 years after exposure; survival time from diagnosis is less than two years
nasopharyngitis (**nay**-zoh-**fair**-in-**JIGH**-tis) nas/o = nose pharyng/o = pharynx -itis = inflammation	inflammation of the nose and pharynx
obstructive sleep apnea (OSA)	temporary absence of breathing during sleep due to repetitive pharyngeal collapse characterized by loud disruptive snoring and recurrent awakening at night
pansinusitis (**pan**-sigh-nus-**EYE**-tis) pan- = all sinus/o = nasal sinus -itis = inflammation	inflammation of all nasal sinuses
pertussis (per-**TUSS**-is)	a highly contagious respiratory disease characterized by coughing and a loud whooping on inspiration; commonly called whooping cough
pleural effusion (**PLOO**-ral eh-**FYOO**-zhun)	escape of fluid into the pleural space
pleuritis, pleurisy (ploo-**RIGH**-tis, **PLOOR**-ih-see) pleur/o = pleura -itis = inflammation	inflammation of the pleural membrane
Pneumocystis jiroveci pneumonia (**noo**-moh-**SISS**-tis jer-oh-**VEE**-see noo-**MOH**-nee-ah)	pneumonia caused by the organism *P. jiroveci*; the organism causes no disease in individuals with healthy immune systems; individuals with compromised immune systems are susceptible to this type of pneumonia (Note: formerly called *Pneumocystis carinii* pneumonia)
pneumonia (noo-**MOH**-nee-ah)	acute inflammation of the lungs; causes may be bacterial, viral, fungal, or parasitic; treatment and prognosis depend on causative organism and whether the pneumonia is acquired in the community or a health care facility, such as a hospital or nursing home
pneumonoconiosis (noo-**mon**-oh-**koh**-nee-**OH**-sis) pneumon/o = lungs con/i = dust -osis = condition	any disease of the lung caused by chronic inhalation of dust, usually mineral dusts of occupational or environmental origin

continued

Table 8-4 (continued) Respiratory System Diseases and Conditions

TERM WITH PRONUNCIATION	DEFINITION
pulmonary edema pulmon/o = lungs -ary = pertaining to	swelling of the lungs caused by an abnormal accumulation of fluid in the lungs
pulmonary embolism	obstruction of one or more of the pulmonary arteries by a thrombus (clot)
pulmonary heart disease; cor pulmonale (cor pull-mon-**ALL**-ee)	heart failure caused by pulmonary disease
pulmonary (arterial) hypertension (PAH), primary PAH	pulmonary hypertension is increased pressure in the arterioles and arteries that supply the lungs; primary pulmonary hypertension is diagnosed when an underlying cause for the hypertension cannot be identified; primary PAH may be familial or acquired
pulmonary (arterial) hypertension (PAH), secondary	increased pressure in the arterioles and arteries that supply the lungs caused by another condition or disease, such as mitral valve stenosis, pulmonary blood clots, COPD, and emphysema
pyothorax, empyema (pigh-oh-**THOR**-raks, em-pigh-**EE**-mah) py/o = pus -thorax = chest	presence of pus in the chest or pleural space
respiratory distress syndrome (RDS) of newborns	disorder associated with premature birth and characterized by diffuse atelectasis and immature development of alveolar membranes, also called *hyaline membrane disease*
severe acute respiratory distress syndrome (SARS)	an acute syndrome of the respiratory system caused by a coronavirus; symptoms resemble influenza; patients with SARS are placed in isolation; mortality rate is 10%
tonsillitis (**ton**-sih-**LIGH**-tis) tonsill/o = tonsils -itis = inflammation	inflammation of the palatine tonsils
tracheostenosis (tray-kee-oh-sten-**OH**-sis) trache/o = trachea -stenosis = narrowing	narrowing of the trachea
tuberculosis, pulmonary (TB) (**too**-ber-kyoo-**LOH**-sis)	a contagious disease that may affect several organs; pulmonary tuberculosis is caused by the organism *Mycobacterium tuberculosis* and accounts for about 75% of all cases; pulmonary TB is characterized by hemoptysis or blood-tinged sputum, chest pain, and a chronic cough; disease is spread by air via droplets expelled when an infected individual sneezes, coughs, or spits; primarily involves the alveoli, but may affect the heart and skeletal muscles
upper respiratory infection (URI)	infection of the pharynx, larynx, trachea, and bronchi

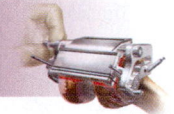

EXERCISE 8-9

Write the medical term for each definition.

1. disease of the lungs caused by mineral dust _____

2. inflammation of all nasal sinuses _____

3. inflammation of the nose and pharynx _____

4. inflammation of the palatine tonsils _____

5. inflammation of the pleural membrane _____

6. involuntary spasms of the larynx _____

7. narrowing of the trachea _____

8. presence of pus in the pleural space or chest cavity _____

EXERCISE 8-10

Write a brief description for each term or abbreviation.

1. OSA _____

2. PAH, primary _____

3. Legionnaires disease _____

4. pleural mesothelioma _____

5. pertussis _____

6. RDS of newborns _____

7. TB _____

8. URI _____

9. cor pulmonale _____

10. pulmonary embolism _____

11. SARS _____

Respiratory System Diagnostic Procedures and Laboratory Tests

Respiratory system diagnostic procedures and laboratory tests are listed in table 8-5. Review the terms and complete the exercises. Pulmonary function tests are used to evaluate air flow, blood flow, and oxygen and carbon dioxide exchange capability. An **oximeter** (ock-**SIM**-eh-ter) is an instrument for measuring oxygen saturation of the blood. A **spirometer** (spigh-**ROM**-eh-ter) is an instrument for measuring breathing activity, air flow, and lung volumes.

Table 8-5   Respiratory System Diagnostic Procedures and Laboratory Tests

TERM WITH PRONUNCIATION	DEFINITION
arterial blood gases (ABG)	examination of arterial blood to determine blood levels of oxygen, carbon dioxide, and other gases
bronchoalveolar lavage (BAL) (**brong**-koh-al-**VEE**-oh-lar lah-**VAHZH**)	endoscopic diagnostic procedure that includes the injection and aspiration of a solution into a specific area of the lung for microscopic evaluation of organisms, malignant cells, or mineral bodies
bronchoscopy (brong-**KOSS**-koh-pee), flexible fiberoptic bronch/o = bronchus -scopy = process of visualization	direct airway visualization using a flexible bronchoscope; samples of secretions and tissue may be taken for analysis; may also be used as a treatment or surgical approach to remove secretions or foreign material from the bronchi (figure 8-4)
chest x-ray	noninvasive process of recording an x-ray film of the lungs, chest wall, diaphragm, and mediastinum; also used to describe the actual film or "picture" of these structures
CT scan	diagnostic imaging study that provides cross-sectional images of the lungs and other thoracic structures
laryngoscopy (lair-in-**GOSS**-koh-pee) laryng/o = larynx -scopy = process of visualization	direct visualization of the larynx with a laryngoscope

continued

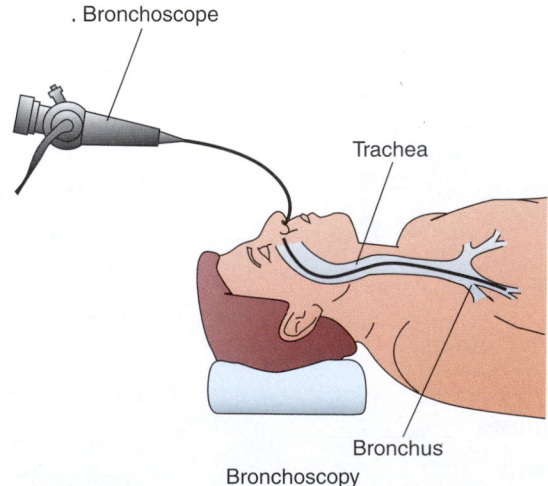

. Bronchoscope

Trachea

Bronchus

Bronchoscopy

Figure 8-4   Bronchoscopy

Table 8-5 (continued)   Respiratory System Diagnostic Procedures and Laboratory Tests

TERM WITH PRONUNCIATION	DEFINITION
lung scan	a nuclear medicine study used to detect abnormalities related to air or blood flow to the lungs
oximetry (ock-**SIM**-ih-tree)	measuring the oxygen saturation of blood
perfusion scan	a nuclear medicine study used to detect inadequate blood flow to the lungs
pulmonary function tests	a group of tests designed to measure respiratory function and to identify abnormalities
spirometry (spigh-**ROM**-eh-tree) spir/o = breathing -metry = to measure	process of measuring breathing or lung volumes
thoracentesis (**thor**-ah-sen-**TEE**-sis), diagnostic thorac/o = thorax; chest -centesis = surgical puncture to withdraw fluid	surgical puncture into the chest wall to remove fluid; diagnostic thoracentesis is used to obtain samples of pleural fluid for analysis; therapeutic thoracentesis is done to alleviate problems associated with pleural effusion
thoracoscopy (**thor**-ah-**KOSS**-koh-pee) thorac/o = chest; thorax -scopy = process of viewing	direct visualization of the pleural space using an endoscope; diagnostic thoracoscopy is used to evaluate pleural space fluid and pulmonary and pleural lesions; thoracoscopy is done when other noninvasive diagnostic tests are inconclusive
thoracotomy (**thor**-ah-**KOT**-ah-mee) thorac/o = chest; thorax -(o)tomy = incision into	surgical incision into the chest wall, accomplished under general anesthesia, to evaluate and treat pulmonary problems; thoracotomy is done when other noninvasive diagnostic tests are inconclusive
ventilation scan	a nuclear medicine study used to detect abnormalities of air flow to the lungs
ventilation/perfusion (lung) (V/Q scan)	a nuclear medicine study used to detect abnormalities of air and blood scan flow to the lungs

EXERCISE 8-11

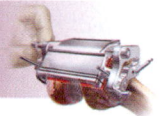

Write a brief definition for the diagnostic tests and describe the difference between each pair.

1. a. CT scan _____

   b. lung scan _____

2. a. perfusion scan _____

   b. ventilation scan _____

3. a. oximetry _____

   b. spirometry _____

2. direct visualization of airways using a flexible scope _____

3. direct visualization of the larynx with a scope _____

4. direct visualization of the pleural space with a scope _____

5. group of tests that measure respiratory function _____

6. nuclear medicine study to evaluate air and blood flow to the lungs _____

7. surgical incision into the chest wall _____

8. surgical puncture into the chest wall to remove fluid _____

EXERCISE 8-12

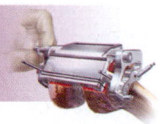

Write the name of the procedure or laboratory test for each definition.

1. diagnostic study that provides cross-sectional images of the lungs _____

Respiratory System Procedures, Operations, and Treatments

Review the procedures, operations, and treatments in table 8-6 and complete the exercises.

Table 8-6 Respiratory System Procedures, Operations, and Treatments

TERM WITH PRONUNCIATION	DEFINITION
adenoidectomy (**add**-eh-noyd-**EK**-toh-mee) adenoid/o = adenoid gland -ectomy = surgical removal	surgical removal of the adenoid glands
bronchoplasty (**BRONG**-koh-**plass**-tee) bronch/o = bronchus; bronchi -plasty = surgical repair	surgical repair of the bronchi
Caldwell-Luc procedure	sinusotomy (antrotomy) of the maxillary sinus with removal of the membrane lining the maxillary cavity
chest physiotherapy	manual or mechanically assisted techniques such as *chest percussion, postural drainage,* and *vibration* for the purpose of mobilizing airway secretions
continuous positive airway pressure (CPAP)	noninvasive treatment for obstructive sleep apnea; a flow of air is delivered at a constant pressure through a ventilator, endotracheal tube, or nasal cannula
decortication	removal of fibrous material from the outer surface of an organ
functional endoscopic sinus surgery (FESS)	sinus surgery performed by using a fiberoptic nasal endoscope
laryngectomy (lair-in-**JEK**-toh-mee) laryng/o = larynx -ectomy = surgical removal	surgical removal of the larynx
laryngoplasty (lah-**RING**-oh-**plass**-tee) laryng/o = larynx -plasty = surgical repair	surgical repair of the larynx
laryngostomy (lair-in-**GOSS**-toh-mee) laryng/o = larynx -(o)stomy = creation of an artificial or new opening	creation of an opening from the neck to the larynx; the opening is usually permanent
laryngotomy (lair-in-**GOT**-oh-mee) laryng/o = larynx -(o)tomy = incision into	incision into the larynx; usually done when a standard tracheotomy cannot be performed
laryngotracheotomy (lair-**ring**-oh-**tray**-kee-**OT**-oh-me) laryng/o = larynx trache/o = trachea -(o)tomy = incision into	incision into the larynx and trachea
lobectomy (loh-**BEK**-toh-mee) lob/o = lobe of the lung -ectomy = surgical removal	surgical removal of a lobe of the lung
lung transplant	placement of a donor lung into a recipient
pneumonectomy (**noo**-mon-**EK**-toh-mee) pneumon/o = lung; air -ectomy = surgical removal	surgical removal of a lung
rhinoplasty (**RIGH**-noh-**plass**-tee) rhin/o = nose -plasty = surgical repair	surgical repair of the nose
septoplasty (**SEP**-toh-**plass**-tee) sept/o = septum; nasal septum -plasty = surgical repair	surgical repair of the nasal septum
sinusotomy (**sign**-nus-**OT**-oh-mee) sinus/o = nasal sinus -(o)tomy = incision into	incision into the nasal sinuses
tonsillectomy (**ton**-sill-**EK**-toh-mee) tonsil/o = tonsils -ectomy = surgical removal	surgical removal of the tonsils

continued

Table 8-6 (*continued*) Respiratory System Procedures, Operations, and Treatments

TERM WITH PRONUNCIATION	DEFINITION
tracheostomy (**tray**-kee-**OSS**-toh-mee) trache/o = trachea -(o)stomy = creation of a new or artificial opening	creation of a new opening through the neck into the trachea; usually performed for insertion of an indwelling tube that allows the individual to breathe; may be temporary or permanent
tracheotomy (**tray**-kee-**OT**-oh-mee) trache/o = trachea -(o)tomy = incision into	incision into the trachea to access a foreign body, tumor, or other blockage
turbinectomy (ter-bin-**EK**-toh-mee)	removal of the nasal turbinate
uvulopalatopharyngoplasty (UPPP; UP$_3$) (**yoo**-vyoo-loh-**pal**-ah-toh-fah-**RING**-oh-plass-tee) video-assisted thoracoscopic surgery (VATS)	surgery of the soft palate, uvula, and other structures of the oropharynx to correct obstructive sleep apnea; when a laser is used, the surgery is called *laser-assisted* uvulopalatopharyngoplasty (LUPPP; LUP$_3$) surgical thoracoscopy

EXERCISE 8-13

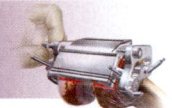

Write a brief definition for the diagnostic tests and describe the difference between each pair.

1. a. tracheostomy
   b. tracheotomy
2. a. laryngostomy
   b. laryngotomy
3. a. lobectomy
   b. pneumonectomy
4. a. Caldwell-Luc procedure
   b. sinusotomy

EXERCISE 8-14

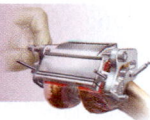

Write the name of the procedure or operation for each definition.

1. incision into the larynx and trachea _____
2. surgical removal of the adenoid glands _____
3. surgical removal of the larynx _____
4. surgical removal of the tonsils _____
5. surgical removal of the nasal turbinate _____
6. surgical repair of the bronchi _____
7. surgical repair of the larynx _____
8. surgical repair of the nose _____
9. surgical repair of the nasal septum _____

ABBREVIATIONS

Respiratory system abbreviations are listed in table 8-7. Practice writing out the abbreviations with a brief definition for each phrase or term.

Table 8-7 Abbreviations

ABBREVIATION	MEANING
ABG	arterial blood gases
ARDS	acute respiratory distress syndrome; adult respiratory distress syndrome
ARF	acute respiratory failure
BAL	bronchoalveolar lavage
CF	cystic fibrosis
CO$_2$	carbon dioxide
COPD	chronic obstructive pulmonary disease
CPAP	continuous positive airway pressure
DOE	dyspnea on exertion
FESS	functional endoscopic sinus surgery
LUPPP; LUP$_3$	laser-assisted uvulopalatopharyngoplasty
OSA	obstructive sleep apnea
PAH	pulmonary arterial hypertension
PFTs	pulmonary function tests
RDS	respiratory distress syndrome
SARS	severe acute respiratory distress syndrome
SOB	shortness of breath
TB	tuberculosis
UPPP; UP$_3$	uvulopalatopharyngoplasty
URI	upper respiratory (tract) infection
VATS	video-assisted thoracoscopic surgery
V/Q scan	ventilation/perfusion scan

RESPIRATORY SYSTEM MEDICAL CODING

To successfully complete the exercises in this section, the ICD-9-CM volumes 1, 2, and 3, and the CPT (Current Procedural Terminology) coding references must be readily available. The information in this section is presented as follows:

- An introduction to ICD-9-CM volume 1, chapter 8, "Diseases of the Respiratory System"
- ICD-9-CM diagnostic coding exercises
- A summary of ICD-9-CM volume 3 coding conventions that apply to respiratory system procedures
- ICD-9-CM procedure coding exercises
- A summary of the CPT Respiratory System coding guidelines
- CPT coding exercises

Students are *strongly* encouraged to review the information at the beginning of the ICD-9-CM and CPT coding references. Commercial publishers include instructions on how to use the ICD-9-CM references, the ICD-9-CM official coding conventions, additional conventions used by the publisher, and the *ICD-9-CM Official Guidelines for Coding and Reporting*. Some publishers include the three ICD-9-CM volumes in one book and put the *Alphabetic Index* (volume 2) at the beginning of the reference.

The *Introduction* to CPT includes detailed instructions for using this code book, an index to the illustrations throughout the book, and anatomical illustrations of the major structures of body systems.

ICD-9-CM Volume 1, Chapter 8, Diseases of the Respiratory System (460–519)

Respiratory system diseases are coded to ICD-9-CM volume 1, chapter 8, "Diseases of the Respiratory System." This chapter includes the following major categories:

- **Acute Respiratory Infections (460–466).** Codes in this section cover acute infections and inflammation of the nose, pharynx, larynx, epiglottis, and bronchi.
- **Other Diseases of the Upper Respiratory Tract (470–478).** Codes in this section include chronic infections and inflammation of the nose, pharynx, and trachea. Other conditions are polyps, cellulitis, paralysis, and allergic reactions that affect the upper respiratory tract.
- **Pneumonia and Influenza (480–488).** Codes in this section cover pneumonia and influenza caused by specific and nonspecific organisms.
- **Chronic Obstructive Pulmonary Disease and Allied Conditions (490–496).** Codes in this section include asthma, emphysema, bronchiectasis, and allergic conditions of the alveoli.
- **Pneumoconioses and Other Lung Diseases Due to External Agents (500–508).** Codes in this section cover diseases of the lungs due to external agents like coal dust, chemical fumes, solids, and liquids.
- **Other Diseases of the Respiratory System (510–519).** Codes in this section include diseases and conditions that cannot be coded to other categories. Examples are empyema, pleurisy, abscess, pneumothorax, and acute respiratory failure.

In order to select a code for pneumonia due to a specific organism, laboratory test results must conclusively identify the organism. Pneumonia category 484, *pneumonia in infectious diseases classified elsewhere,* tells the coder to *code first the underlying disease.*

Conditions related to the respiratory system may also be coded to the following chapters in volume 1: chapter 14, "Congenital Anomalies"; chapter 16, "Symptoms, Signs, and Ill-Defined Conditions"; and chapter 2, "Neoplasms." Obstructive sleep apnea is coded to chapter 6, "Diseases of the Nervous System."

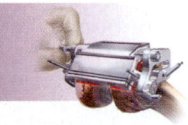

EXERCISE 8-15

Write a brief definition for each diagnosis. Identify the main term in the diagnostic statement and assign the correct ICD-9-CM diagnosis code(s).

1. Acute laryngitis with airway obstruction

   DEFINITION: _____

   MAIN TERM: _____

   ICD-9-CM CODE(S): _____

2. Pneumonia due to streptococcus group A

    DEFINITION: _____

    MAIN TERM: _____

    ICD-9-CM CODE(S): _____

3. Spontaneous pneumothorax

    DEFINITION: _____

    MAIN TERM: _____

    ICD-9-CM CODE(S): _____

4. Acute exacerbation of chronic bronchitis

    DEFINITION: _____

    MAIN TERM: _____

    ICD-9-CM CODE(S): _____

5. Acute sinusitis, frontal and maxillary sinuses

    DEFINITION: _____

    MAIN TERM: _____

    ICD-9-CM CODE(S): _____

6. COPD and emphysema

    DEFINITION: _____

    MAIN TERM: _____

    ICD-9-CM CODE(S): _____

7. Hypertrophy of the tonsils and adenoids

    DEFINITION: _____

    MAIN TERM: _____

    ICD-9-CM CODE(S): _____

8. Acute bronchiolitis due to respiratory syncy-
    tial virus (RSV)

    DEFINITION: _____

    MAIN TERM: _____

    ICD-9-CM CODE(S): _____

9. Late-onset asthma

    DEFINITION: _____

    MAIN TERM: _____

    ICD-9-CM CODE(S): _____

10. Black lung disease

    DEFINITION: _____

    MAIN TERM: _____

    ICD-9-CM CODE(S): _____

11. Adult respiratory distress syndrome

    DEFINITION: _____

    MAIN TERM: _____

    ICD-9-CM CODE(S): _____

12. Obstructive sleep apnea

    DEFINITION: _____

    MAIN TERM: _____

    ICD-9-CM CODE(S): _____

13. Nocturnal dyspnea

    DEFINITION: _____

    MAIN TERM: _____

    ICD-9-CM CODE(S): _____

14. Pulmonary atelectasis

    DEFINITION: _____

    MAIN TERM: _____

    ICD-9-CM CODE(S): _____

15. Primary pulmonary atrial hypertension

    DEFINITION: _____

    MAIN TERM: _____

    ICD-9-CM CODE(S): _____

16. Upper respiratory infection

    DEFINITION: _____

    MAIN TERM: _____

    ICD-9-CM CODE(S): _____

17. Chronic obstructive bronchitis

    DEFINITION: _____

    MAIN TERM: _____

    ICD-9-CM CODE(S): _____

18. Orthopnea

    DEFINITION: _____

    MAIN TERM: _____

    ICD-9-CM CODE(S): _____

19. Giant bullous emphysema

    DEFINITION: _____

    MAIN TERM: _____

    ICD-9-CM CODE(S): _____

20. Lung abscess

    DEFINITION: _____

    MAIN TERM: _____

    ICD-9-CM CODE(S): _____

ICD-9-CM Volume 3, Chapter 6, Operations of the Respiratory System (30–34)

Respiratory system operations and some therapeutic treatments are coded to ICD-9-CM volume 3, chapter 6, "Operations of the Respiratory System." This chapter covers the larynx, trachea, bronchi, and lungs. This chapter includes the following major categories:

- **Excision of Larynx (30–31.5).** Codes in this category include diagnostic treatments and procedures of the larynx and trachea.
- **Repair of Larynx (31.6); Repair and Plastic Operations on Trachea (31.7); Other Operations on Larynx and Trachea (31.9).** Codes in these categories cover repair, revision, reconstruction, and closures of the larynx and trachea.
- **Excision of Lung and Bronchus (32).** Codes in this category include excision of the lungs and bronchi, and excision or destruction of lung tissue or lesions.
- **Other Operations on the Lung and Bronchus (33–33.99).** Codes in this category include incision, resection, biopsy, diagnostic procedures, transplant, and surgical repair of the lungs and bronchi.
- **Operations on Chest Wall, Pleura, Mediastinum, and Diaphragm (34).** Codes in this category cover treatment and diagnostic procedures of the chest wall, pleura, mediastinum, and diaphragm. Types of procedures include incision, excision, destruction, repair, and biopsy of these structures.

Operations and procedures of the nose, mouth, and pharynx are coded to ICD-9-CM volume 3, chapter 5, "Operations on the Nose, Mouth, and Pharynx" (21–29). This chapter includes the following categories that apply to these structures as part of the respiratory system:

- **Operations on Nose (21).** Codes in this category cover diagnostic and treatment procedures of the nose, nasal septum, and nasal turbinates.

- **Operations on Nasal Sinuses (22).** Codes in this category include diagnostic and treatment procedures of the nasal sinuses such as aspiration, lavage, and repair.
- **Operations on Tonsils and Adenoids (28).** Codes in this category cover diagnostic and treatment procedures of the tonsils and adenoids.
- **Operations on Pharynx (29).** Codes in this category cover diagnostic and treatment procedures of the pharynx.

EXERCISE 8-16

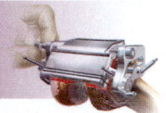

Write a brief definition for each operative, treatment, or diagnostic procedure term. Identify the main term in the statement and assign the correct ICD-9-CM code(s).

1. Fiberoptic bronchoscopy, diagnostic

   DEFINITION: _____

   MAIN TERM: _____

   ICD-9-CM CODE(S): _____

2. Thoracentesis to remove fluid from the chest cavity

   DEFINITION: _____

   MAIN TERM: _____

   ICD-9-CM CODE(S): _____

3. Caldwell-Luc procedure

   DEFINITION: _____

   MAIN TERM: _____

   ICD-9-CM CODE(S): _____

4. Permanent, open tracheostomy

   DEFINITION: _____

   MAIN TERM: _____

   ICD-9-CM CODE(S): _____

5. Septoplasty with submucosal resection of the nasal septum

   DEFINITION: _____

   MAIN TERM: _____

   ICD-9-CM CODE(S): _____

6. Limited rhinoplasty to restore the tip of the nose

   DEFINITION: _____

   MAIN TERM: _____

   ICD-9-CM CODE(S): _____

7. Hemilaryngectomy due to necrotizing infection

   DEFINITION: _____

   MAIN TERM: _____

   ICD-9-CM CODE(S): _____

8. Thoracoscopic lobectomy, left lung

   DEFINITION: _____

   MAIN TERM: _____

   ICD-9-CM CODE(S): _____

9. Tonsillectomy and adenoidectomy, recurrent strep infections

   DEFINITION: _____

   MAIN TERM: _____

   ICD-9-CM CODE(S): _____

10. Bilateral lung transplantation, with extracorporeal circulation

    DEFINITION: _____

    MAIN TERM: _____

    ICD-9-CM CODE(S): _____

11. Decortication of the lung

    DEFINITION: _____

    MAIN TERM: _____

    ICD-9-CM CODE(S): _____

12. Lysis of laryngeal adhesions

    DEFINITION: _____

    MAIN TERM: _____

    ICD-9-CM CODE(S): _____

13. Control of epistaxis with cauterization and packing

    DEFINITION: _____

    MAIN TERM: _____

    ICD-9-CM CODE(S): _____

14. Aspiration and lavage of nasal sinus

    DEFINITION: _____

    MAIN TERM: _____

    ICD-9-CM CODE(S): _____

15. Radical laryngectomy due to malignancy

    DEFINITION: _____

    MAIN TERM: _____

    ICD-9-CM CODE(S): _____

Current Procedural Terminology (CPT) Respiratory System Codes (30000–32999)

CPT respiratory system codes are located in the Surgery, Radiology, and Medicine sections. The Surgery guidelines provide important information for all of the Surgery subsections. Review the guidelines in the CPT manual and in chapter 3 of this text. There are additional instruction notes for the Respiratory System subsection of the Surgery section. The Respiratory System subsection includes the following categories:

- **Nose (30000–30999).** Codes in this category cover incisions, excisions, repair, destruction, and other procedures of the nose, nasal septum, and nasal turbinates.
- **Accessory Sinuses (31000–31299).** Codes in this category include lavage, sinusotomy, surgical removal, and endoscopic procedures of the nasal sinuses.
- **Larynx (31300–31599).** Codes in this category cover excisions, intubation, repair, destruction, and endoscopic procedures of the larynx.
- **Trachea and Bronchi (31600–31899).** Codes in this category include incisions, excisions, endoscopic procedures, and repair of the trachea and bronchi.
- **Lungs and Pleura (32035–32820).** Codes in this category cover incisions, excisions, removal, destruction, repair, and endoscopic procedures of the lungs and pleura.

continued

■ **Lung Transplantation (32850–32856).**
Codes in this category cover all aspects of
lung transplantation. There are three distinct
components associated with lung transplantation: (1) removing the donor lungs from a
cadaver and preserving the donor lungs;
(2) preparation of a cadaver donor for a
single or double lung transplantation, also
called *backbench work;* and (3) transplantation of the donor lungs into the recipient.
Lung transplantation is categorized as an
allotransplantation because the lungs are
provided via a cadaver.

Respiratory system diagnostic imaging procedures are
coded to the Radiology section. Some of the subsections related to the respiratory system include the
following:

■ **Diagnostic Radiology (Diagnostic Imaging)
(71010–71555).** Codes in this subsection
include radiography of the chest. Magnetic
resonance imaging (MRI) and computerized
tomography (CT) scans are covered in this
subsection.

■ **Nuclear Medicine: Respiratory System
(78580–78599).** Codes in this subsection
cover pulmonary ventilation and perfusion
scans.

Ventilator management, spirometry, continuous
positive airway pressure ventilation (CPAP), some pulmonary function tests, and miscellaneous respiratory
treatments are coded to the Medicine section, codes
94002–94799.

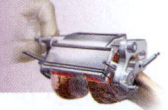

EXERCISE 8-17

Identify the main term in each statement. Assign the
correct CPT code(s).

1. Thoracentesis to remove fluid from the chest
cavity

   MAIN TERM: _____

   CPT CODE(S): _____

2. Caldwell-Luc procedure, removal of polyps

   MAIN TERM: _____

   CPT CODE(S): _____

3. Permanent, open tracheostomy, 36-year-old
male

   MAIN TERM: _____

   CPT CODE(S): _____

4. Septoplasty with submucosal resection of the
nasal septum

   MAIN TERM: _____

   CPT CODE(S): _____

5. Total laryngectomy without radical neck
dissection

   MAIN TERM: _____

   CPT CODE(S): _____

6. Thorascopic lobectomy, left lung

   MAIN TERM: _____

   CPT CODE(S): _____

7. Bilateral lung transplantation, with extracorporeal circulation

   MAIN TERM: _____

   CPT CODE(S): _____

8. Thoracoscopic partial decortication of
the lung

   MAIN TERM: _____

   CPT CODE(S): _____

9. Extensive excision of nasal polyps

   MAIN TERM: _____

   CPT CODE(S): _____

10. Bilateral control of nasal hemorrhage, anterior,
with limited cautery and packing

    MAIN TERM: _____

    CPT CODE(S): _____

11. Pulmonary perfusion scan with ventilation
imaging

    MAIN TERM: _____

    CPT CODE(S): _____

12. Primary rhinoplasty

    MAIN TERM: _____

    CPT CODE(S): _____

13. Chest x-ray, A/P and lateral view

    MAIN TERM: _____

    CPT CODE(S): _____

14. Continuous positive airway pressure ventilation (CPAP), initiation and management

    MAIN TERM: _____

    CPT CODE(S): _____

15. Pulse oximetry, single determination

    MAIN TERM: _____

    CPT CODE(S): _____

■ SUMMARY

This chapter covered medical terms related to the respiratory system. Respiratory diagnoses and procedures were identified and defined. Respiratory diseases and conditions are coded to ICD-9-CM volume 1, chapter 8, "Diseases of the Respiratory System"; chapter 2, "Neoplasms"; chapter 14, "Congenital Anomalies"; and chapter 16, "Signs, Symptoms, and Ill-Defined Conditions." Respiratory system procedures are coded to ICD-9-CM volume 3, chapter 6, "Operations of the Respiratory System"; chapter 5, "Operations on the Nose, Mouth, and Pharynx"; and chapter 16, "Miscellaneous Diagnostic and Therapeutic Procedures."

Current Procedural Terminology (CPT) respiratory procedure codes are found in the CPT Surgery subsection, Respiratory System, and in the Radiology and Medicine sections.

■ CHAPTER REVIEW

Read each medical note or medical report excerpt. Write the diagnosis(es) and the main term. Assign the ICD-9-CM diagnosis code.

CASE 1

Ms. Romsberg has had a sore throat for the past several days with a temperature to 101 degrees F. She complains of abundant postnasal drip and a pleuritic cough. Examination today reveals tender sinuses in the maxillary and frontal areas. Tympanic membranes are gray, bilaterally. The pharynx is reddened and there is obvious purulent material in the left posterior pharynx. The neck is supple and no nodes are palpable. The chest is clear. Heart has a regular rate and rhythm and is without murmur. Sinus films are normal. Diagnosis is clinical chronic sinusitis. A strep test was done to rule out strep throat. She is to use Beconase nasal spray, one whiff to each nostril, q.i.d. for one week, then one whiff to each nostril. If she has not improved in three weeks, referral to ear, nose, and throat specialist is needed.

DIAGNOSIS(ES): _____

MAIN TERM(S): _____

ICD-9-CM DIAGNOSIS CODE(S): _____

CASE 2

Mr. Hsu is seen today for evaluation of an abnormal chest x-ray. He was seen at the walk-in clinic complaining of right pleuritic chest pain. Cardiac events were ruled out. Mr. Hsu is generally healthy. Weight today is 190 lb. Blood pressure is 130/84. AP and lateral chest x-ray today is consistent for acute lower respiratory infection with pleurisy, responding well to erythromycin. He was instructed to complete the full course of antibiotics. Barring any emergency situations, he will return to the office in 10 days.

DIAGNOSIS(ES): _____

MAIN TERM(S): _____

ICD-9-CM DIAGNOSIS CODE(S): _____

CASE 3

ADMITTING DIAGNOSIS: Stridor.

DISCHARGE DIAGNOSIS: Laryngeal airway obstruction secondary to bilateral true vocal cord paralysis.

HOSPITAL COURSE: Mr. Whales was admitted for increasing stridor and respiratory distress. He has multiple medical problems that include severe coronary artery disease, mitral valve regurgitation, congestive heart failure, and diabetes mellitus type 2, well-controlled. Flexible fiberoptic nasopharyngoscopy and laryngoscopy were performed and revealed laryngeal airway obstruction secondary to bilateral true vocal cord paralysis. He was discharged in fair condition.

DIAGNOSIS(ES): _____

MAIN TERM(S): _____

ICD-9-CM DIAGNOSIS CODE(S): _____

CASE 4

ADMITTING DIAGNOSIS: Shortness of breath.

DISCHARGE DIAGNOSES: 1. Severe bronchospasm. 2. Status asthmaticus.

BRIEF HISTORY: The patient is a 22-year-old male who presented at the walk-in clinic with a three-day history of a runny nose, headaches, and worsening dyspnea. He was using his inhaler more frequently than usual. He received nebulizer therapy. Despite repeated treatments, he did not improve. He was admitted to the ICU with status asthmaticus. He was started on oxygen, 40% by face mask, appropriate IV medications, and nebulizers every hour ×4 and then every two hours. He responded well and was discharged to home.

DIAGNOSIS(ES): _____

MAIN TERM(S): _____

ICD-9-CM DIAGNOSIS CODE(S): _____

CASE 5

Marqueesha is an 18-year-old female who presented to the walk-in clinic with the sudden onset of shortness of breath. She stated that she "never had anything like this before." She also complained of pleuritic chest pain. Initial evaluation revealed a right spontaneous pneumothorax. She was observed for 48 hours. Repeat x-ray showed improvement of the pneumothorax. She was discharged in stable condition with restricted activity and a regular diet. She will be followed in the office and understands that she should return to the clinic immediately if her symptoms worsen.

DIAGNOSIS(ES): _____

MAIN TERM(S): _____

ICD-9-CM DIAGNOSIS CODE(S): _____

CASE 6

ADMITTING DIAGNOSIS: Severe shortness of breath.

DISCHARGE DIAGNOSES: 1. Left lower pneumonia due to *Actinomycosis.* 2. Acute bronchitis. 3. Chronic obstructive pulmonary diseases. 4. Cor pulmonale.

HOSPITAL COURSE: This 67-year-old woman was admitted for severe shortness of breath. She was treated with intravenous antibiotics. Sputum culture grew *Actinobacillus.* She underwent bronchoscopy which was unremarkable. Bronchial washings were negative for malignant cells. At discharge, she was able to ambulate with limitations and was sent home on appropriate medications.

DIAGNOSIS(ES): _____

MAIN TERM(S): _____

ICD-9-CM DIAGNOSIS CODE(S): _____

CASE 7

Mr. Smith is seen today for a persistent cough over the past six weeks. He was unconcerned until this past week when he began experiencing shortness of breath "even when I wasn't doing anything." He has been retired from the construction industry for two years. During the last 15 years he has worked as a foreman. However, early in his career he worked primarily in demolition and reconstruction of "historical buildings." He states he spent about 20 years working in that type of environment. Chest x-ray today shows some suspicious lesions that could be scar tissue or plaque. Given his work history and very probable exposure to asbestos, a CT scan is recommended to confirm the nature of the pulmonary lesions seen on chest x-ray. It was explained to Mr. Smith that we are most likely looking at a diagnosis of pulmonary fibrosis due to asbestos exposure. A differential diagnosis of mesothelioma was also discussed, but this is quite unlikely. CT scan will be scheduled for early next week. Probable diagnosis is asbestosis, unless CT findings demonstrate otherwise.

DIAGNOSIS(ES): _____

MAIN TERM(S): _____

ICD-9-CM DIAGNOSIS CODE(S): _____

Read the procedure note, operative report, or discharge summary excerpt. Write the diagnosis and its ICD-9-CM code. Write the name of the procedure and the main term. Assign the ICD-9-CM procedure code(s).

CASE 8

PREPROCEDURE DIAGNOSIS: Nodule, left lung lower lobe.

POSTPROCEDURE DIAGNOSIS: Nodule, left lung lower lobe.

PROCEDURES: 1. Video-assisted thoracoscopy, left side. 2. Wedge resection biopsy, left lower lobe ×2. 3. Bronchoscopy, right upper lobe with transbronchial biopsy ×2.

INDICATIONS: The patient has a long history of smoking. CT scan of the chest revealed a nodule in the left lung, lower lobe and some consolidation in the right lung, upper lobe.

PROCEDURE: The patient was brought into the procedure room and placed on the table in the supine position. General endotracheal anesthesia was accomplished and a Foley catheter was placed. The patient was then turned into the left lateral decubitus position and the area was prepped and draped in the usual sterile manner. A small incision was made and dissected down into the chest cavity. Two ports were placed to provide access to the site.

Visualization was accomplished. Gross inspection of the chest showed no adhesions, and no pleural fluid was present. The nodule was removed via wedge resection biopsy and sent to pathology for evaluation. Bronchoscopy was then performed with the patient in the supine position. The trachea and intermediate bronchus appeared normal. With biopsy forceps, several specimens were obtained from the right segment of the right upper lobe.

All instruments were removed and the patient was sent to the recovery room in good condition having tolerated the procedure well.

DIAGNOSIS(ES): _____

ICD-9-CM DIAGNOSIS(ES) CODES: _____

PROCEDURE(S): _____

MAIN TERM(S): _____

ICD-9-CM PROCEDURE CODE(S): _____

CASE 9

PREOPERATIVE DIAGNOSIS: Recurrent maxillary and ethmoid sinusitis.

POSTOPERATIVE DIAGNOSES: 1. Maxillary sinusitis. 2. Obstruction of the natural ostia. 3. Ethmoiditis.

PROCEDURES: 1. Bilateral functional endoscopic sinus surgery (FESS). 2. Bilateral enlargement of the natural ostia and anterior ethmoidectomy.

ANESTHESIA: General endotracheal.

PROCEDURE: The patient was taken to the operating room and placed in the supine position. After successful endotracheal anesthesia, saturated pledgets were placed intranasally. The nose was prepped and draped in the usual sterile fashion. Using an endoscope, the right middle meatus was examined as was the left. There was some thickening noted.

The natural ostia was identified and was edematous, but not completely obstructed. It was enlarged using rongeurs and forceps. The anterior ethmoid was opened and layer cells removed. The left middle meatus was completely obstructed and thusly enlarged. The left maxillary sinus was irrigated with saline until clear. The patient tolerated the procedure well and was taken to the recovery room in good condition. All counts were correct ×2.

DIAGNOSIS(ES): _____

ICD-9-CM DIAGNOSIS(ES) CODES: _____

PROCEDURE(S): _____

MAIN TERM(S): _____

ICD-9-CM PROCEDURE CODE(S): _____

CASE 10

PREOPERATIVE DIAGNOSES: 1. Deviated nasal septum. 2. Chronic maxillary sinusitis. 3. Turbinate hypertrophy with nasal obstruction.

POSTOPERATIVE DIAGNOSES: 1. Deviated nasal septum. 2. Chronic maxillary sinusitis. 3. Turbinate hypertrophy with nasal obstruction.

PROCEDURE: 1. Septoplasty. 2. Nasal endoscopy with bilateral maxillary antroscopy. 3. Bilateral submucous resection of the inferior turbinates.

The patient was brought to the operating room. Under general anesthesia, she was prepped and draped. An incision was made along the left caudal columnar region of the septum to the mucoperichondrium. The portion of the deviation was carefully exposed. The deviation was removed and a large septal spur was also removed.

A much improved septum was noted. A piece of cartilage was morselized and inserted between the nasal mucosa layers and the submucosa was closed with 4-0 plain suture, interrupted. The middle turbinates were then medialized.

The left nasal chamber was examined endoscopically and the natural os was located and enlarged. The right os was also located and the natural os was widely enlarged. The inferior turbinates were infractured, clamped, and submucosal resection was performed, bilaterally. Splints were sewn in place along the septum with 3-0 Ethilon. Both nasal chambers were packed with Bactroban-coated packing. The patient tolerated the procedure well and was taken to the recovery room in good condition. All counts were correct ×2.

DIAGNOSIS(ES): _____

ICD-9-CM DIAGNOSIS(ES) CODES: _____

PROCEDURE(S): _____

MAIN TERM(S): _____

ICD-9-CM PROCEDURE CODE(S): _____

CASE 11

PREOPERATIVE DIAGNOSIS: Loculated left thoracic empyema with hemothorax.

POSTOPERATIVE DIAGNOSIS: Left thoracic fibrinous hemothorax.

PROCEDURE: Posterolateral thoracotomy with evacuation of loculated hemothorax, decortication of fibrothorax, and insertion of two 36 French chest tubes.

The patient was taken to the operating room in the supine position. Endotracheal anesthesia was administered and the patient was placed in the chest-up position. The chest and back were prepped and draped in the usual sterile fashion. A posterolateral thoracotomy incision was made over the fifth interspace. It was carried from the nipple to left posterior axillary line. Dissection was made down to the intercostal musculature. A fibrinous exudate accounted for severe adhesions of the left lower lobe to the parietal pleura. This was separated manually and sharp dissection was used to decorticate a fixed fibrinous line from the surface of the left lower lobe, anteriorly and laterally. The left thoracic cavity was copiously irrigated. Two 36 French chest tubes were inserted through separate stab incisions and secured to the skin. The chest wall musculature was closed, the subcutaneous tissue was reapproximated, and staples were used to close the skin. The patient was transferred to the intensive care unit in stable condition. Blood loss was minimal. All counts were correct ×2.

DIAGNOSIS(ES): _____

ICD-9-CM DIAGNOSIS(ES) CODES: _____

PROCEDURE(S): _____

MAIN TERM(S): _____

ICD-9-CM PROCEDURE CODE(S): _____

CASE 12

PREOPERATIVE DIAGNOSIS: Bronchogenic carcinoma, right upper lobe.

POSTOPERATIVE DIAGNOSIS: Occluded right upper lobe posterior and superior segments.

PROCEDURE: 1. Flexible fiberoptic bronchoscopy with radiation catheter placement, right upper lobe. 2. Placement of radiation beads.

ANESTHESIA: One percent topical lidocaine, 4% nebulized lidocaine, 25 mg of Demerol, and IV incremental doses of Versed.

PROCEDURE: With the patient in the supine position under supplemental oxygen, the flexible fiberoptic bronchoscope was passed through the left nostril without difficulty. The upper airway vocal cords were within normal limits. The trachea was within normal limits. The carina was sharp and within normal limits. The bilateral endobronchial tree was observed in detail and all airways were patent, other than the superior and posterior segments of the right upper lobe, which were occluded by tumor. Using fluoroscopic guidance, a radiation catheter was placed in the superior segment of the right upper lobe. The patient tolerated the procedure well. Only mild oozing of blood occurred with less than 5 cc estimated blood loss. Vital signs remained stable. Oxygen saturation remained stable.

After observation in the endoscopy suite recovery area, the patient was transferred to the radiation department in stable condition and radiation beads were loaded into the catheter.

DIAGNOSIS(ES): _____

ICD-9-CM DIAGNOSIS(ES) CODES: _____

PROCEDURE(S): _____

MAIN TERM(S): _____

ICD-9-CM PROCEDURE CODE(S): _____

Using the excerpts in previous cases, write the name of the procedure and the main term. Assign the CPT code(s) to the procedures.

CASE 13

PREPROCEDURE DIAGNOSIS: Nodule, left lung lower lobe.

POSTPROCEDURE DIAGNOSIS: Nodule, left lung lower lobe.

PROCEDURES: 1. Video-assisted thoracoscopy, left side. 2. Wedge resection biopsy, left lower lobe ×2. 3. Bronchoscopy, right upper lobe with transbronchial biopsy ×2.

INDICATIONS: The patient has a long history of smoking. CT scan of the chest revealed a nodule in the left lung, lower lobe and some consolidation in the right lung, upper lobe.

PROCEDURE: The patient was brought into the procedure room and placed on the table in the supine position. General endotracheal anesthesia was accomplished and a Foley catheter was placed. The patient was then turned into the left lateral decubitus position and the area was prepped and draped in the usual sterile manner. A small incision was made and dissected down into the chest cavity. Two ports were placed to provide access to the site.

Visualization was accomplished. Gross inspection of the chest showed no adhesions and no pleural fluid was present. The nodule was removed via wedge resection biopsy and sent to pathology for evaluation. Bronchoscopy was then performed with the patient in the supine position. The trachea and intermediate bronchus appeared normal. With biopsy forceps, several specimens were obtained from the right segment of the right upper lobe.

All instruments were removed and the patient was sent to the recovery room in good condition having tolerated the procedure well.

PROCEDURE(S): _____

MAIN TERM(S): _____

CPT PROCEDURE CODE(S): _____

CASE 14

PREOPERATIVE DIAGNOSIS: Recurrent maxillary and ethmoid sinusitis.

POSTOPERATIVE DIAGNOSES: 1. Maxillary sinusitis. 2. Obstruction of the natural ostia. 3. Ethmoiditis.

PROCEDURES: 1. Bilateral functional endoscopic sinus surgery (FESS). 2. Bilateral enlargement of the natural ostia and anterior ethmoidectomy.

ANESTHESIA: General endotracheal.

PROCEDURE: The patient was taken to the operating room and placed in the supine position. After successful endotracheal anesthesia, saturated pledgets were placed intranasally. The nose was prepped and draped in the usual sterile fashion. Using an endoscope, the right middle meatus was examined as was the left. There was some thickening noted and the natural ostia was identified and was edematous, but not completely obstructed. It was enlarged using rongeurs and forceps. The anterior ethmoid was opened and layer cells removed. The left middle meatus was completely obstructed and thusly enlarged. The left maxillary sinus was irrigated with saline until clear. The patient tolerated the procedure well and was taken to the recovery room in good condition. All counts were correct ×2.

PROCEDURE(S): _____

MAIN TERM(S): _____

CPT PROCEDURE CODE(S): _____

CASE 15

PREOPERATIVE DIAGNOSES: 1. Deviated nasal septum. 2. Chronic maxillary sinusitis. 3. Turbinate hypertrophy with nasal obstruction.

POSTOPERATIVE DIAGNOSES: 1. Deviated nasal septum. 2. Chronic maxillary sinusitis. 3. Turbinate hypertrophy with nasal obstruction.

PROCEDURES: 1. Septoplasty. 2. Nasal endoscopy with bilateral maxillary antroscopy. 3. Bilateral submucous resection of the inferior turbinates.

The patient was brought to the operating room. Under general anesthesia, she was prepped and draped. An incision was made along the left caudal columnar region of the septum to the mucoperichondrium. The portion of the deviation was carefully exposed. The deviation was removed and a large septal spur was also removed.

A much improved septum was noted. A piece of cartilage was morselized and inserted between the nasal mucosa layers and the submucosa was closed with 4-0 plain suture, interrupted. The middle turbinates were then medialized.

The left nasal chamber was examined endoscopically and the natural os was located and enlarged. The right os was also located and the natural os was widely enlarged. The inferior turbinates were infractured, clamped, and submucosal resection was performed, bilaterally. Splints were sewn in place along the septum with 3-0 Ethilon. Both nasal chambers were packed with Bactroban-coated packing. The patient tolerated the procedure well and was taken to the recovery room in good condition. All counts were correct ×2.

PROCEDURE(S): _____

MAIN TERM(S): _____

CPT PROCEDURE CODE(S): _____

CASE 16

PREOPERATIVE DIAGNOSIS: Loculated left thoracic empyema with hemothorax.

POSTOPERATIVE DIAGNOSIS: Left thoracic fibrinous hemothorax.

PROCEDURE: Posterolateral thoracotomy with evacuation of loculated hemothorax, decortication of fibrothorax, and insertion of two 36 French chest tubes.

The patient was taken to the operating room in the supine position. Endotracheal anesthesia was administered and the patient was placed in the chest-up position. The chest and back were prepped and draped in the usual sterile fashion. A posterolateral thoracotomy incision was made over the fifth interspace. It was carried from the nipple to the left posterior axillary line. Dissection was made down to the intercostal musculature. A fibrinous exudate accounted for severe adhesions of the left lower lobe to the parietal pleura. This was separated manually and sharp dissection was used to decorticate a fixed fibrinous line from the surface of the left lower lobe, anteriorly and laterally. The left thoracic cavity was copiously irrigated. Two 36 French chest tubes were inserted through separate stab incisions and secured to the skin. The chest wall musculature was closed, the subcutaneous tissue was reapproximated, and staples were used to close the skin. The patient was transferred to the intensive care unit in stable condition. Blood loss was minimal. All counts were correct ×2.

PROCEDURE(S): _____

MAIN TERM(S): _____

CPT PROCEDURE CODE(S): _____

CASE 17

PREOPERATIVE DIAGNOSIS: Bronchogenic carcinoma, right upper lobe.

POSTOPERATIVE DIAGNOSIS: Occluded right upper lobe posterior and superior segments.

PROCEDURES: 1. Flexible fiberoptic bronchoscopy with radiation catheter placement, right upper lobe. 2. Placement of radiation beads.

ANESTHESIA: One percent topical lidocaine, 4% nebulized lidocaine, 25 mg of Demerol, and IV incremental doses of Versed.

PROCEDURE: With the patient in the supine position under supplemental oxygen, the flexible fiberoptic bronchoscope was passed through the left nostril without difficulty. The upper airway vocal cords were within normal limits. The trachea was within normal limits. The carina was sharp and within normal limits. The bilateral endobronchial tree was observed in detail and all airways were patent, other than the superior and posterior segments of the right upper lobe, which were occluded by tumor. Using fluoroscopic guidance, a radiation catheter was placed in the superior segment of the right upper lobe. The patient tolerated the procedure well. Only mild oozing of blood occurred with less than 5 cc estimated blood loss. Vital signs remained stable. Oxygen saturation remained stable. After observation in the endoscopy suite recovery area, the patient was transferred to the radiation department in stable condition and radiation beads were loaded into the catheter.

PROCEDURE(S): _____

MAIN TERM(S): _____

CPT PROCEDURE CODE(S): _____

MEDICAL TERMINOLOGY CHALLENGE

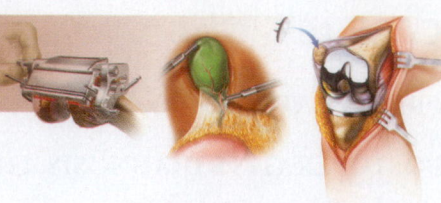

Read the operative report and write a brief definition for each medical term.
Use a dictionary as necessary.

PREOPERATIVE DIAGNOSIS: Bilateral nasal (1) *polyposis.*

POSTOPERATIVE DIAGNOSIS: Bilateral nasal polyposis.

PROCEDURE: Bilateral endoscopic nasal (2) *polypectomy,* and total (3) *ethmoidectomy,* and middle (4) *meatal antrostomies.*

ANESTHESIA: General (5) *endotracheal.*

DETAILS: The patient was prepped and draped in the usual fashion under general endotracheal anesthesia. The nose was packed with pledgets followed by injection of the nose with 2% Xylocaine, 1:100,000 epinephrine. The polyps in the right middle meatus were removed. The polyps had completely filled and eroded the (6) *ethmoid sinuses.* All this was removed. The left side was then attended to in the same manner. It was noted that there appeared to be some bulging on the (7) *medial wall* of the *maxillary sinus.* At this time there was noted some bleeding in the (8) *middle meatus* on the left side and the meatus was packed with gauze packing. The packing on the right side was removed. The patient was (9) *extubated* and returned to the recovery room in satisfactory condition.

1. _____
2. _____
3. _____
4. _____
5. _____
6. _____
7. _____
8. _____
9. _____

NOTES:

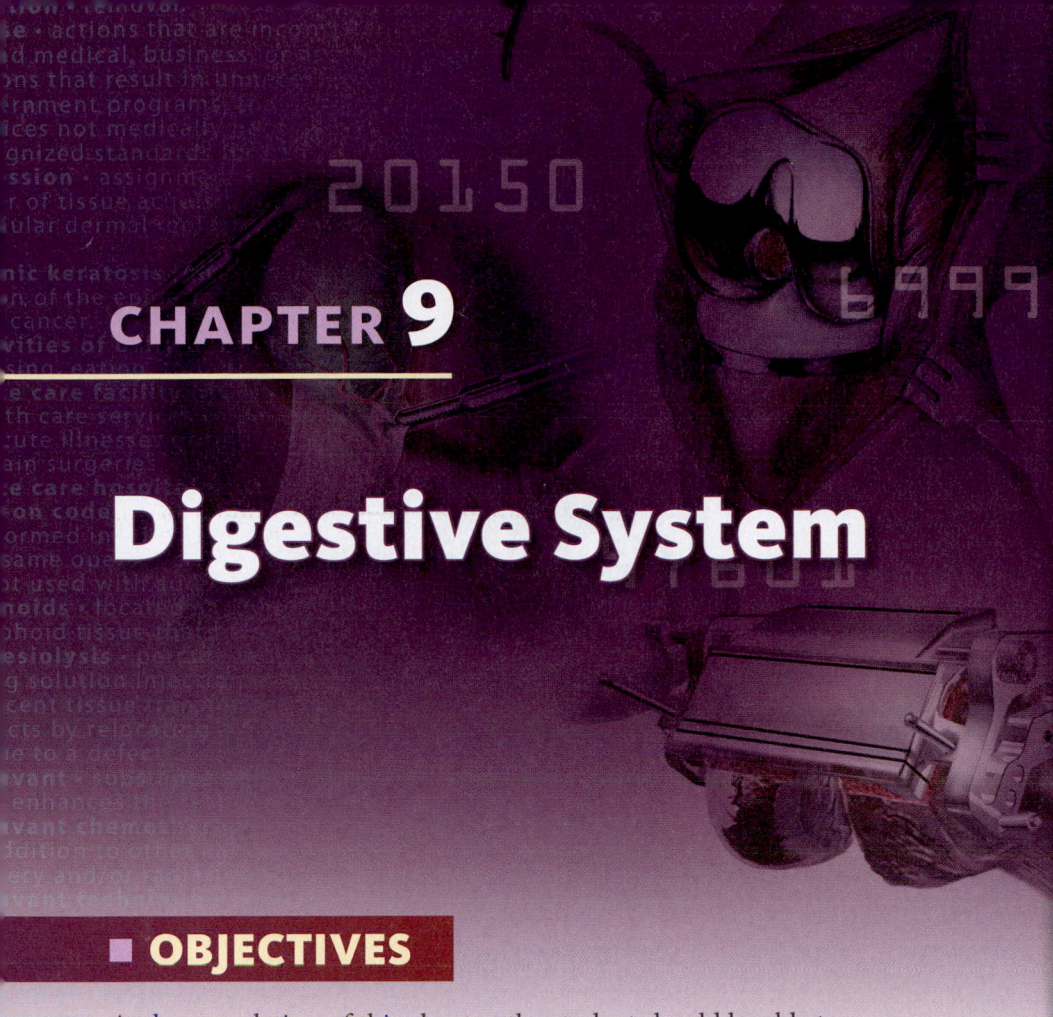

CHAPTER 9

Digestive System

■ OBJECTIVES

At the completion of this chapter, the student should be able to:

1. Learn the word roots associated with the digestive system.
2. Label the basic structures of the digestive system.
3. Discuss the functions of the digestive system.
4. Accurately spell and define digestive system terminology.
5. Accurately assign medical codes to digestive system diagnoses and procedures.

■ OVERVIEW

The digestive system, also called the **gastrointestinal (GI) tract**, **alimentary canal**, or **digestive tract**, is made up of the mouth, pharynx, esophagus, stomach, small intestine, large intestine, and accessory organs, including the salivary glands, liver, gallbladder, and pancreas. The structures of the digestive system function together for the following purposes: (1) to digest food, (2) to absorb nutrients into the bloodstream, and (3) to eliminate solid waste products. The medical specialty related to the digestive system is **gastroenterology** (**gass**-troh-en-ter-**ALL**-oh-jee) and the physician specialist is a **gastroenterologist** (**gass**-troh-en-ter-**ALL**-oh-jist). **Proctology** (prok-**TALL**-oh-jee) is a subspecialty of gastroenterology and the physician specialist is a **proctologist** (prok-**TALL**-oh-jist).

DIGESTIVE SYSTEM ROOTS, PREFIXES, AND SUFFIXES

Roots, prefixes, and suffixes associated with the digestive system are listed in table 9-1. Review the word elements and complete the exercises.

Table 9-1 Digestive System Roots, Prefixes, and Suffixes

ROOT	MEANING
abdomin/o; celi/o	abdomen
an/o	anus
append/o; appendic/o	appendix
bil/i	bile
bucc/o	cheek
cec/o	cecum
cheil/o	lips
chol/e	bile; gall
cholangi/o	bile duct
cholecyst/o	gallbladder
choledoch/o	common bile duct
col/o; colon/o	colon
duoden/o	duodenum
enter/o	intestines
esophag/o	esophagus
gastr/o	stomach
gingiv/o	gums
gloss/o; lingu/o	tongue
hepat/o	liver
ile/o	ileum
jejun/o	jejunum
lapar/o	abdominal wall
leuk/o	white
lip/o	fat
lith/o	stone
or/o; stomat/o	mouth
pancreat/o	pancreas
peritone/o	peritoneum
pharyng/o	pharynx
polyp/o	polyp
proct/o; rect/o	rectum
sial/o	salivary gland; saliva
sigmoid/o	sigmoid colon

PREFIX	MEANING
endo-	within
retro-	backward

SUFFIX	MEANING
-cele	hernia; herniation
-iasis	condition
-pepsia	digestion
-phagia	swallowing; to swallow
-tripsy	crushing

EXERCISE 9-1

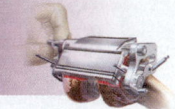

Write the root, prefix, suffix, and their meaning. Based on the meanings, write a brief definition for each term.

1. Abdominal
   ROOT: _abdomin/o_ MEANING: _abdomen_
   PREFIX: _____ MEANING: _____
   SUFFIX: _____ MEANING: _al_
   BRIEF DEFINITION: _pertaining to abdomen_

2. Anal
   ROOT: _an/o_ MEANING: _anus_
   PREFIX: _____ MEANING: _____
   SUFFIX: _al_ MEANING: _pertaing to_
   BRIEF DEFINITION: _pertaining to the anus_

3. Buccal
   ROOT: _bucc/o_ MEANING: _cheek_
   PREFIX: _____ MEANING: _____
   SUFFIX: _al_ MEANING: _pertaining to_
   BRIEF DEFINITION: _pertaining to the cheek_

4. Gastric
   ROOT: _gastr/o_ MEANING: _stomach_
   PREFIX: _____ MEANING: _____
   SUFFIX: _ic_ MEANING: _pertaining to_
   BRIEF DEFINITION: _pertaining to stomach_

5. Ileocecal
   ROOT: _ile/o cec/o_ MEANING: _ileum cecum_
   PREFIX: _____ MEANING: _____
   SUFFIX: _al_ MEANING: _pertaining to_
   BRIEF DEFINITION: _pertaining to ileum & cecum_

6. Nasogastric
ROOT: _nas/o_ (gastr/o)   MEANING: _nose & stomach_
PREFIX: _____   MEANING: _____
SUFFIX: _ic_   MEANING: _pertaining to_
BRIEF DEFINITION: _pertaining to nose and stomach_

7. Peritoneal
ROOT: _peritone/o_   MEANING: _peritoneum_
PREFIX: _____   MEANING: _____
SUFFIX: _al_   MEANING: _pertaining to_
BRIEF DEFINITION: _pertaining to peritoneum_

8. Proctologist
ROOT: _proct/o_   MEANING: _rectum_
PREFIX: _____   MEANING: _____
SUFFIX: _(o)logist_   MEANING: _specialist_
BRIEF DEFINITION: _specialist studying rectum_

9. Proctology
ROOT: _proct/o_   MEANING: _rectum_
PREFIX: _____   MEANING: _____
SUFFIX: _ology_   MEANING: _study of_
BRIEF DEFINITION: _study of rectum_

10. Sublingual
ROOT: _lingu/o_   MEANING: _tongue_
PREFIX: _sub_   MEANING: _____
SUFFIX: _____   MEANING: _al_
BRIEF DEFINITION: _pertaining to below tongue_

11. Hepatobiliary
ROOT: _Hepat/o_ _bil/i_   MEANING: _liver; bile_
PREFIX: _____   MEANING: _____
SUFFIX: _ary_   MEANING: _pertaining to_
BRIEF DEFINITION: _pertaining to liver & bile_

12. Lithotripsy
ROOT: _lith/o_   MEANING: _stone_
PREFIX: _____   MEANING: _____
SUFFIX: _tripsy_   MEANING: _crushing_
BRIEF DEFINITION: _crushing stones_

13. Dyspepsia
ROOT: _____   MEANING: _____
PREFIX: _dys_   MEANING: _difficult_
SUFFIX: _pepsia_   MEANING: _digestion_
BRIEF DEFINITION: _difficult digestion_

14. Dysphagia
ROOT: _____   MEANING: _____
PREFIX: _dys_   MEANING: _difficult_
SUFFIX: _phagia_   MEANING: _swallowing_
BRIEF DEFINITION: _difficult swallowing_

15. Sialolithiasis
ROOT: _sial/o_ _lith/o_   MEANING: _saliva / stone_
PREFIX: _____   MEANING: _____
SUFFIX: _iasis_   MEANING: _condition_
BRIEF DEFINITION: _condition of salivary glands and stone_

16. Colonoscopy
ROOT: _colon/o_   MEANING: _colon_
PREFIX: _____   MEANING: _____
SUFFIX: _(o)scopy_   MEANING: _process of viewing_
BRIEF DEFINITION: _process of viewing the colon_

17. Colorectal
ROOT: _col/o_ _rect/o_   MEANING: _colon & rectum_
PREFIX: _____   MEANING: _____
SUFFIX: _al_   MEANING: _pertaining to_
BRIEF DEFINITION: _pertaining to colon and rectum_

18. Rectocele
ROOT: _rect/o_   MEANING: _rectum_
PREFIX: _____   MEANING: _____
SUFFIX: _cele_   MEANING: _hernia_
BRIEF DEFINITION: _herniation of rectum_

19. Hemicolectomy
ROOT: _col/o_   MEANING: _colon_
PREFIX: _hemi_   MEANING: _half_
SUFFIX: _ectomy_   MEANING: _surgical removal_
BRIEF DEFINITION: _removal of half the colon_

20. Laparoscopy
ROOT: _lapar/o_   MEANING: _abdominal wall_
PREFIX: _____   MEANING: _____
SUFFIX: _(o)scopy_   MEANING: _process of viewing_
BRIEF DEFINITION: _process of viewing the abdominal wall w/ scope_

21. Choledocholithiasis
ROOT: _choledoch/o_ _lith/o_   MEANING: _common bile duct_ _stone_
PREFIX: _____   MEANING: _____
SUFFIX: _iasis_   MEANING: _condition_
BRIEF DEFINITION: _condition of stones in the common bile duct_

continued

22. Sigmoidoscopy

ROOT: _Sigmoid/o_ MEANING: _Sigmoid colon_

PREFIX: _____ MEANING: _____

SUFFIX: _____ MEANING: _Process of viewing_

BRIEF DEFINITION: _Process of Viewing the sigmoid colon_

STRUCTURES OF THE DIGESTIVE SYSTEM

Structures of the digestive system include the (1) **mouth**, also called the oral cavity, and all that is in it; (2) **salivary glands**; (3) **pharynx** (**FAIR**-inks), commonly called the throat; (4) **esophagus** (eh-**SOFF**-ah-gus), a 10-inch tube that extends from the pharynx to the stomach; (5) **stomach**; (6) **small intestine**; (7) **large intestine**; (8) **anus**; (9) **liver**; (10) **gallbladder**; and (11) **pancreas** (**PAN**-kree-ass). Figure 9-1 illustrates these structures.

Mouth/Oral Cavity, Pharynx, Esophagus, and Salivary Glands

The mouth, also called the oral cavity, includes the lips, gingiva (gums), teeth, tongue, hard and soft palate, and uvula. The lips form the opening to the oral cavity, and the teeth are used to mechanically break down food. The tongue moves the food around the mouth, provides the sense of taste, and helps push the food into the throat. The hard palate forms the roof of the mouth, and the soft palate prevents food from entering the nasal cavity. The uvula can trigger the gag reflex and also helps produce sounds and speech.

The salivary glands produce saliva, a watery substance that contains digestive enzymes. The digestive process begins when food mixes with saliva. There are three pairs of salivary glands: **parotid** (pah-**ROT**-id) **glands**, located in front of and slightly below the ear; **sublingual** (sub-**LING**-gwall) **glands**, located underneath the tongue; and **submandibular** (sub-man-**DIB**-yoo-lar) **glands**, located on the posterior floor of the mouth. Figure 9-2 illustrates the salivary glands.

The **bolus** (**BOH**-lus), which is foodstuffs mixed with salivary secretions, passes through the pharynx into the esophagus. The esophagus is a muscular tube that leads to the stomach. The bolus is pushed to the stomach by wavelike muscular contractions called **peristalsis** (pair-ih-**STALL**-sis).

Stomach and Small Intestine

Refer to figure 9-3 as you learn about the stomach and small intestine.

The bolus of food enters the (1) stomach through the (2) **cardiac sphincter** (**KAR**-dee-ak **SFINGK**-ter), a muscular ring at the upper end of the stomach that prevents food from moving back into the esophagus. In the stomach, the bolus mixes with digestive juices and hydrochloric acid. The digestive process continues in the stomach. The bulge at the lower end of the stomach is called the (3) **antrum** (**AN**-trum) or **pylorus** (pigh-**LOR**-us). The (4) **pyloric sphincter** (pigh-**LOR**-ik **SFINGK**-ter), a muscular ring at the end of the antrum, allows the partially digested food, called **chyme** (**KIGHM**), to move into the small intestine.

The first 10 to 12 inches of the small intestine is the (5) **duodenum** (doo-oh-**DEE**-num, doo-**ODD**-eh-num); it is here that most digestion occurs. The small intestine is approximately 20 feet in length and extends from the pyloric sphincter to the large intestine. The (6) **jejunum** (jeh-**JOO**-num), the second segment of the small intestine, is approximately 8 feet long; and the (7) **ileum** (**ILL**-ee-um), the third segment of the small intestine, is approximately 11 feet long. As the digested food passes through the small intestine, nutrients are passed into the bloodstream. The remaining waste is liquid and is passed into the large intestine.

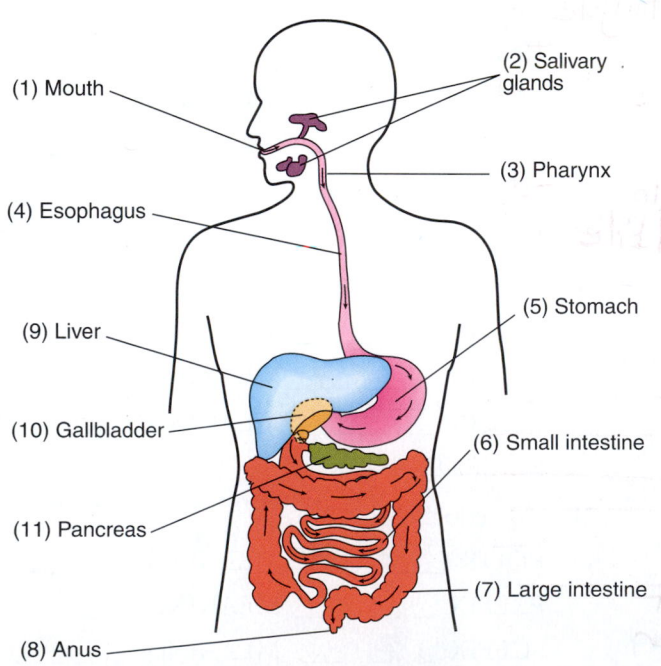

(1) Mouth

(2) Salivary glands

(3) Pharynx

(4) Esophagus

(9) Liver

(10) Gallbladder

(11) Pancreas

(8) Anus

(5) Stomach

(6) Small intestine

(7) Large intestine

Figure 9-1 Digestive system structures

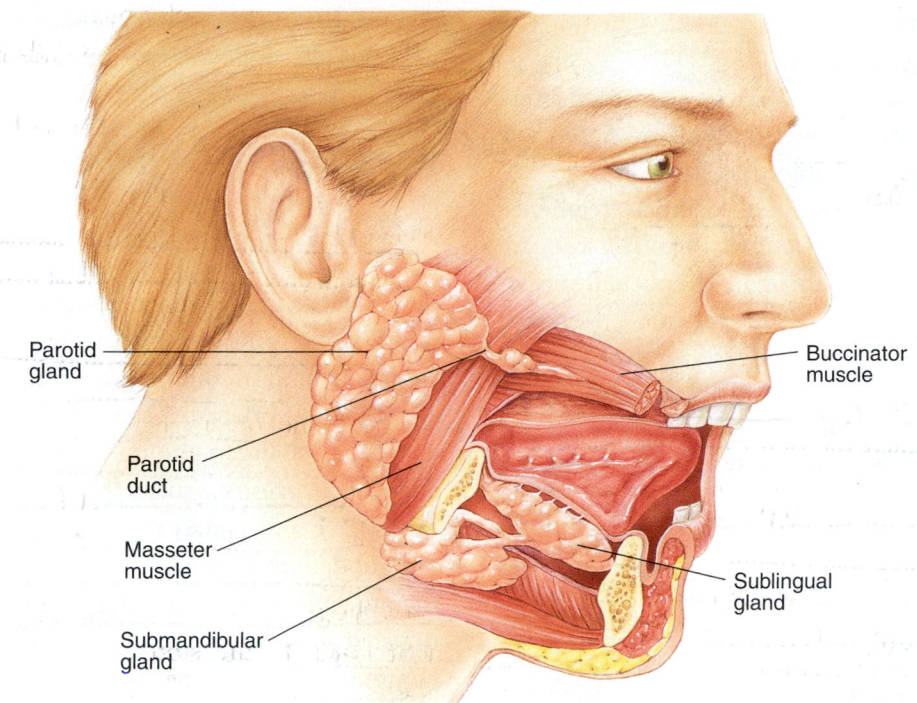

Figure 9-2   Salivary glands

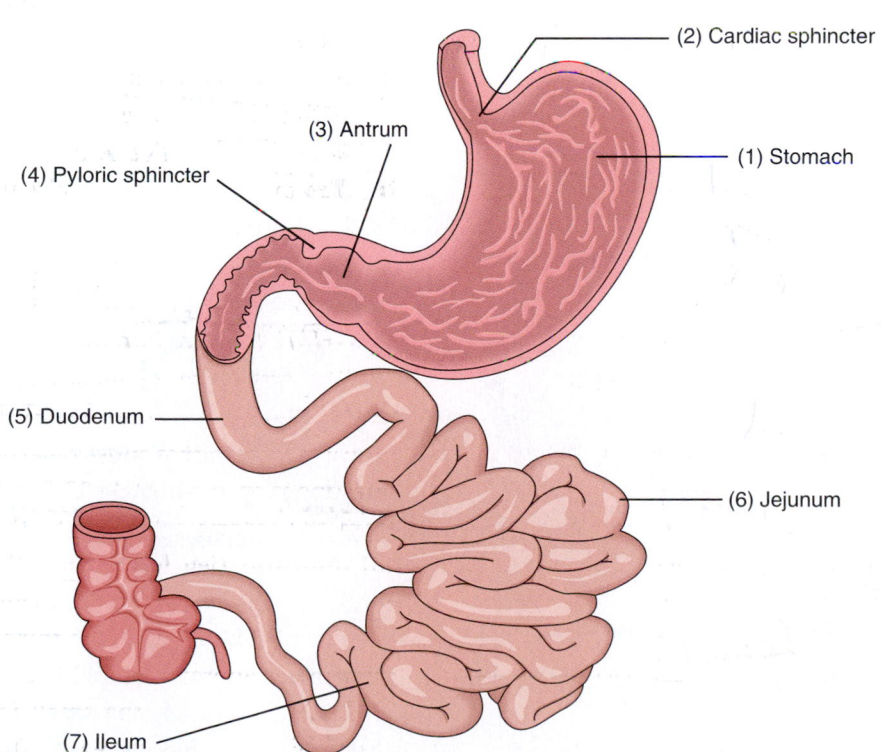

Figure 9-3   Stomach and small intestine

Large Intestine

The large intestine is approximately 5 to 6 feet long and extends from the cecum to the anus. Refer to figure 9-4 as you learn about the large intestine.

The large intestine has six distinct segments and two major corners or curves: the (1) **cecum** (**SEE**-kum), (2) **ascending colon**, (3) **hepatic flexure**, (4) **transverse colon**, (5) **splenic flexure**, (6) **descending colon**, (7) **sigmoid colon**, and (8) **rectum**. The cecum, the pouchlike beginning of the large intestine, is connected to the ileum by the (10) **ileocecal** (**ill**-ee-oh-**SEE**-kal) **valve**. The valve is a muscular ring that prevents the liquid waste from flowing back into the small intestine. The **vermiform appendix**, commonly called the appendix, is a narrow, wormlike tube connected to the cecum. Inflammation of this tube is called appendicitis.

As the waste product moves through the large intestine, water and minerals are absorbed into the bloodstream. The solid to semisolid waste is stored in the rectum. The (9) anus, another sphincter muscle, holds the waste in the rectum until we voluntarily release the waste.

Liver, Gallbladder, and Pancreas

The (1) liver, (2) gallbladder, and (3) pancreas are commonly called the accessory organs of the digestive system. Refer to figure 9-5 as you learn about these organs.

The liver produces bile, which is necessary for the digestion of fats. Bile is stored in the gallbladder, a small saclike structure. The pancreas, which functions as a digestive organ and an endocrine gland, produces additional digestive juices that help digest all types of foods. Bile and pancreatic digestive juices empty into the duodenum by a series of ducts. Note in figure 9-5 that the (4) right and (5) left **hepatic ducts** come together to form the (6) **common hepatic duct**. The common hepatic duct joins with the (7) **cystic duct** to form the (8) **common bile duct**. The common bile duct joins with the (9) **pancreatic ducts** and enters the duodenum.

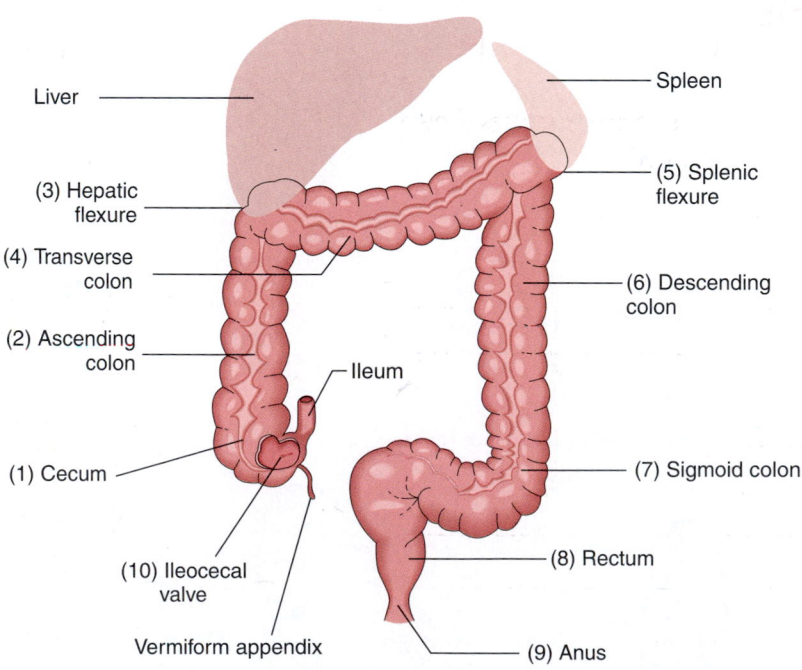

Figure 9-4 Large intestine

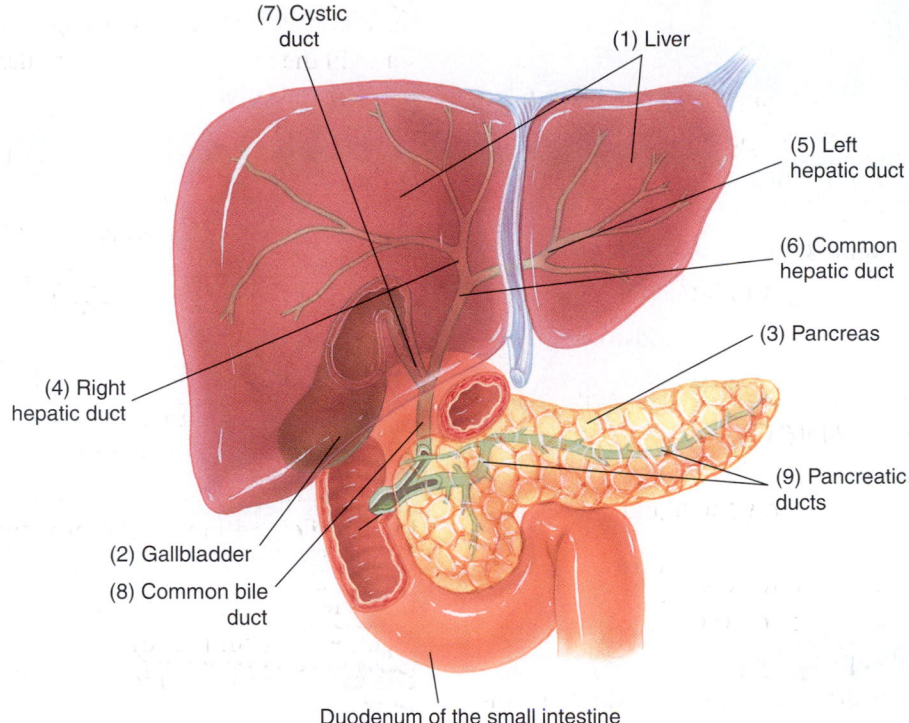

Figure 9-5 Liver, gallbladder, pancreas

EXERCISE 9-2

Write the names of the digestive system structures shown in figure 9-6 on the spaces provided.

1. _____
2. _____
3. _____
4. _____
5. _____
6. _____
7. _____
8. _____
9. _____
10. _____

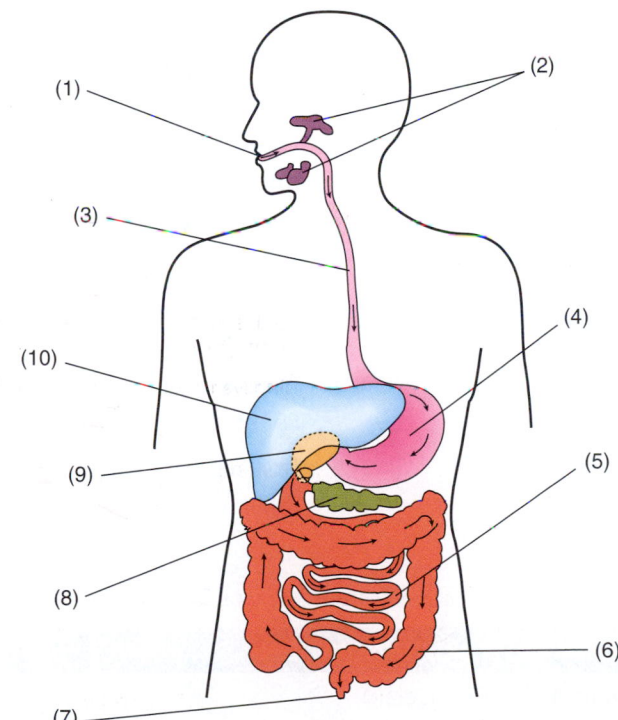

Figure 9-6 Label digestive system structures

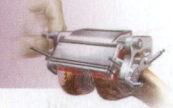

EXERCISE 9-3

Write the name of the digestive system organ or structure that fits each description.

1. adds digestive juices to the duodenum
2. adds hydrochloric acid to foodstuffs
3. nutrients absorbed into the bloodstream
4. pouch for storing solid waste
5. produces bile _liver_
6. produce saliva
7. stores bile
8. water absorbed into the bloodstream

EXERCISE 9-4

Match the sections and structures associated with the small and large intestine in column 1 with the correct definition in column 2.

COLUMN 1

a. anus

b. ascending colon

c. cecum

d. descending colon

e. duodenum

COLUMN 2

1. beginning section, large intestine _____ c
2. connects small and large intestine _____ g
3. curve between the ascending and transverse colon _____ f
4. curve between the transverse and descending colon _____ l
5. first segment, small intestine _____ e

f. hepatic flexure

g. ileocecal valve

h. ileum

i. jejunum

j. rectum

k. sigmoid colon

l. splenic flexure

m. transverse colon

6. last segment, large intestine _____
7. located across the abdomen ___ m ___
8. located on the left side ___ d ___
9. located on the right side ___ b ___
10. second segment, small intestine __ jejunum __
11. sphincter muscle, holds waste ___ a ___
12. stores solid waste ___ j ___
13. third segment, small intestine __ ileum __

DIGESTIVE SYSTEM MEDICAL TERMINOLOGY

Digestive system medical terms are organized by diseases, conditions, diagnostic procedures, and operations. There are two categories of medical terminology exercises: (1) those designed to provide opportunities to learn the terms, and (2) those designed to provide opportunities to accurately assign diagnostic or procedure codes. Exercises for learning the terms immediately follow the lists of terms and definitions. Medical coding exercises are available after all terms have been presented.

Digestive System Signs, Symptoms, Diseases, and Conditions

The medical terms in table 9-2 are digestive system signs or symptoms. Review the meanings of these terms and complete the exercise.

Table 9-2 Digestive System Signs or Symptoms

TERM WITH PRONUNCIATION	MEANING
aphagia (ah-**FAY**-jee-ah) a- = lack of; without -phagia = to swallow	loss of the ability to swallow
ascites (ah-**SIGH**-teez)	abnormal accumulation of fluid in the peritoneal cavity
dyspepsia (diss-**PEP**-see-ah) dys- = abnormal; painful; difficult -pepsia = digestion	painful or abnormal digestion; indigestion

continued

Table 9-2 (*continued*) Digestive System Signs or Symptoms

TERM WITH PRONUNCIATION	MEANING
dysphagia (diss-**FAY**-jee-ah) dys- = abnormal; painful; difficult -phagia = swallowing	difficulty swallowing
eructation (eh-ruk-**TAY**-shun)	expelling gas from the stomach through the mouth; belch, burp
flatus	gas in the digestive tract; expelling gas from the anus
gastrodynia, gastralgia (gass-troh-**DIN**-ee-ah; gass-**TRAL**-jee-ah) gastr/o = stomach -dynia = pain -algia = pain	pain in the stomach; stomachache
hematemesis (hem-at-**EM**-eh-sis) hemat/o = blood -emesis = vomiting	vomiting blood
hematochezia (**hem**-at-oh-**KEE**-zha) hemat/o = blood -chezia = feces	passage of gross (visible) red blood from the rectum
melena (**MELL**-eh-nah)	abnormal, black, tarry stool
nausea (**NAW**-zee-ah)	unpleasant sensation usually preceding vomiting
occult blood; occult bleeding	passage of occult (hidden) blood from the GI tract; blood is identified via chemical testing of feces

EXERCISE 9-5

Write the medical term for each definition.

1. abnormal accumulation of fluid in the peritoneal cavity _ascites_
2. abnormal, black, tarry stool _melena_
3. belch, burp _eructation_
4. difficulty swallowing _dysphagia_
5. indigestion _dyspepsia_
6. loss of the ability to swallow _aphagia_
7. passing visible blood from the rectum _hematochezia_
8. stomachache _gastrodynia_
9. vomiting blood _hematemesis_
10. unpleasant sensation, usually precedes vomiting _nausea_

The medical terms in table 9-3 are diseases and conditions of the digestive system. Review the meanings of these terms and complete the exercises.

Table 9-3 Digestive System Diseases and Conditions

TERM WITH PRONUNCIATION	DEFINITION
achalasia (ak-ah-**LAY**-zee-ah)	decreased mobility of the lower two-thirds of the esophagus with lower esophageal sphincter constriction
anorexia nervosa (an-oh-**REK**-see-ah ner-**VOH**-sah)	loss of appetite and emaciation accompanied by an extreme and unfounded fear of obesity
aphthous stomatitis (**AFF**-thuss stoh-mah-**TIGH**-tis) stomat/o = mouth -itis = inflammation	inflammatory, noninfectious ulcerated lesion of the lips, tongue, and mouth; canker sore
appendicitis (ah-**pen**-dih-**SIGH**-tis) appendic/o = appendix -itis = inflammation	inflammation of the vermiform appendix

continued

Table 9-3 (*continued*) Digestive System Diseases and Conditions

TERM WITH PRONUNCIATION	DEFINITION
bulimia (buh-**LIM**-ee-ah)	condition characterized by alternately overeating and inducing vomiting
celiac sprue (**SEE**-lee-ak sproo)	hereditary disorder characterized by sensitivity to gluten, a protein found in wheat, rye, and barley
cholecystitis (**koh**-lee-sist-**EYE**-tis) cholecyst/o = gallbladder -itis = inflammation	inflammation of the gallbladder
choledocholithiasis (koh-lee-**doh**-koh-lih-**THIGH**-ah-sis) choledoch/o = bile duct lith/o = stones; calculi -iasis = abnormal condition	presence of calculi (stones) in the common bile duct (figure 9-7)
cholelithiasis (**koh**-lee-lih-**THIGH**-ah-sis) chole/o = bile lith/o = stones -iasis = abnormal condition	formation or presence of bile stones in the gallbladder; gallstones (figure 9-7)
cirrhosis (sih-**ROH**-sis)	chronic disease of the liver characterized by the destruction of liver cells
colorectal carcinoma (koh-loh-**REK**-tal kar-sin-**OH**-mah) col/o = colon rect/o = rectum -al = pertaining to carcin- = cancer; malignant -oma = tumor	malignant neoplasm of the colon and rectum
Crohn disease (**KROHN**)	chronic inflammation of the ileum characterized by ulcerations along the intestinal wall and the formation of scar tissue; also called regional ileitis or regional enteritis
diarrhea (digh-ah-**REE**-ah)	frequent passage of loose, watery stools
diverticulitis (**digh**-ver-**tik**-yoo-**LIGH**-tis) diverticul/o = diverticulum -itis = inflammation	inflammation of a diverticulum or several diverticula
diverticulosis (**digh**-ver-**tik**-yoo-**LOH**-sis) diverticul/o = diverticulum -osis = condition	presence of diverticula in the colon
diverticulum (**digh**-ver-**TIK**-yoo-lum)	a sac or pouch in the walls of an organ; often exhibited in the large intestine
duodenal ulcer (doo-oh-**DEE**-nal, doo-**OD**-eh-nal **ULL**-sir) duoden/o = duodenum -al = pertaining to	ulceration of the mucous membrane of the duodenum; peptic ulcer; caused by *Helicobacter pylori* (*H. pylori*) or nonsteroidal anti-inflammatory drug (NSAID) use
dysentery (**DISS**-en-ter-ee)	infection of the intestinal tract by bacteria, virus, or microbes that cause an inflammation of the intestinal mucosa characterized by loose, bloody, mucuslike stools
emaciation (ee-**may**-she-**AY**-shun)	state of being abnormally and extremely lean
epigastric hernia	protrusion of an organ in an area above the stomach
femoral hernia	protrusion of the intestine into the femoral canal and groin
gastric ulcer (**GASS**-trik **ULL**-sir) gastr/o = stomach -ic = pertaining to	ulcer of the mucosa of the stomach; peptic ulcer; caused by *H. pylori* or NSAID use
gastroenteritis (**gass**-troh-**en**-ter-**EYE**-tis) gastr/o = stomach enter/o = intestines -itis = inflammation	inflammation of the stomach and intestinal tract

continued

Table 9-3 (continued) Digestive System Diseases and Conditions

TERM WITH PRONUNCIATION	DEFINITION
gastroesophageal reflux disease (GERD) (**gass**-troh-eh-**soff**-oh-**JEE**-al **REE**-flux) gastr/o = stomach esophag/o = esophagus -eal = pertaining to	reflux or moving backward of gastric contents into the esophagus

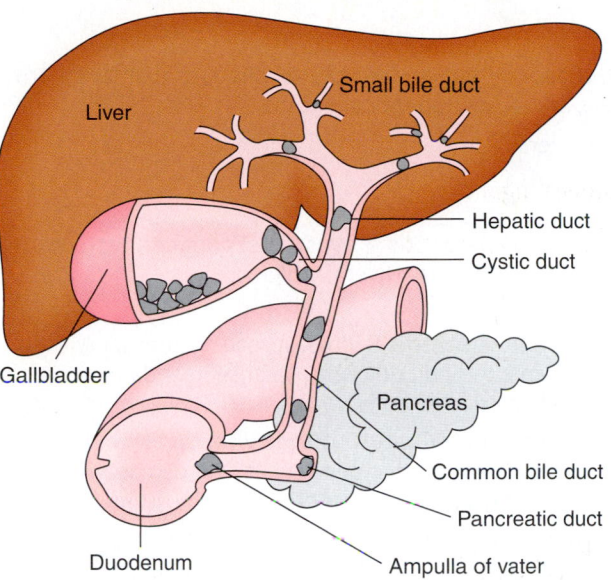

Figure 9-7 Choledocholithiasis and cholelithiasis

Labels: Liver; Small bile duct; Hepatic duct; Cystic duct; Gallbladder; Pancreas; Common bile duct; Pancreatic duct; Duodenum; Ampulla of vater

EXERCISE 9-6

Replace the italicized phrase with the correct medical term.

1. Carlos's lower GI series identified the presence of *sacs or pouches in his large intestine.* diverticulum

2. As a result of Marjorie's *overeating and induced vomiting,* her parents requested a mental health consultation. bulimia

3. *Canker sores* may be caused by poor dietary habits. aphthous stomatitis

4. Because of a family history of *malignancy of the colon and rectum,* Jerald made an appointment with his family physician. colorectal carcinoma

5. Regina's *regional ileitis* was treated with prednisone. Crohn disease

6. *Decreased esophageal mobility and sphincter constriction* made it difficult for Luke to swallow. achalasia

7. Repeated episodes of *loose, watery stools* caused baby Rosita's dehydration. diarrhea

8. *Inflammation of the appendix* usually requires surgical intervention. appendicitis

9. Young women are more likely to be diagnosed with *loss of appetite, emaciation, and an extreme fear of obesity* than young men. anorexia

10. Marcus was diagnosed with *sensitivity to gluten* and was placed on a wheat-free diet. celiac sprue

11. George was scheduled for surgery to remove *gallstones.* cholelithiasis

EXERCISE 9-7

Write the name of the digestive system organ or structure identified in each term. Write a brief definition for the term.

1. Cholecystitis
   ORGAN/STRUCTURE: gall bladder
   DEFINITION: inflammation of gallbladder

2. Choledocholithiasis
   ORGAN/STRUCTURE: bile duct
   DEFINITION: presence of calculi (stones) in common bile duct

3. Gastroenteritis
   ORGAN/STRUCTURE: Stomach
   DEFINITION: inflammation within the stomach

4. Gastroesophageal reflux disease
   ORGAN/STRUCTURE: Stomach
   DEFINITION: reflux or moving backward of gastric contents into the esophagus

continued

5. Duodenal ulcer

ORGAN/STRUCTURE: _duodenum_

DEFINITION: _Ulceration of mucous membrane of the doudenun_

The medical terms in table 9-4 are diseases and conditions of the digestive system. Review the meanings of these terms and complete the exercises.

Table 9-4   Digestive System Diseases and Conditions

TERM WITH PRONUNCIATION	DEFINITION
gingivitis (jin-jih-**VIGH**-tis) gingiv/o = gingiva; gums -itis = inflammation	inflammation of the gums or gingiva
Helicobacter pylori (H. pylori) infection	_H. pylori_ is a spiral-shaped organism that causes diseases such as gastritis, peptic ulcer disease, and gastric adenocarcinoma
hepatitis (hep-ah-**TIGH**-tis) hepat/o = liver -itis = inflammation	inflammation of the liver
hepatitis A (hep-ah-**TIGH**-tis A) hepat/o = liver -itis = inflammation	liver infection caused by the hepatitis A virus; most common type of hepatitis; does not lead to long-term liver problems
hepatitis B (hep-ah-**TIGH**-tis B) hepat/o = liver -itis = inflammation	liver infection caused by the hepatitis B virus; spread by contact with blood or body fluids of an infected person; may cause liver damage; passes from mother to baby during delivery
hepatitis C (hep-ah-**TIGH**-tis C) hepat/o = liver -itis = inflammation	liver infection caused by hepatitis C virus; spread by contact with the blood of an infected person; may lead to permanent liver damage, liver cancer, and liver failure; rarely passes from mother to baby during delivery
hernia (**HER**-nee-ah)	protrusion of an organ or part of an organ through the wall of a cavity; usually refers to some part of the intestinal tract protruding through the abdominal wall
herpetic stomatitis (her-**PEH**-tik **stoh**-mah-**TIGH**-tis) stomat/o = mouth -itis = inflammation	inflammatory infectious lesions of the oral cavity caused by the herpes simplex virus; cold sores, fever blisters
hiatal hernia (high-**AY**-tal **HER**-nee-ah)	herniation of a portion of the stomach through the esophageal opening in the diaphragm (figure 9-8)
Hirschsprung disease (**HIRSH**-sproong)	congenital condition characterized by a lack of enervation to the colon that results in absent or inefficient peristalsis of the lower intestine; also known as _congenital megacolon_
ileus (**ILL**-ee-us)	temporary stoppage of intestinal peristalsis; may result in an obstruction of the intestine
incisional hernia	protrusion of the intestine through a surgical scar in the abdominal wall
inguinal hernia, direct	protrusion of the intestine into the groin
inguinal hernia, indirect	protrusion of the intestine into the inguinal canal
intestinal obstruction (in-**TESS**-tin-al ob-**STRUK**-shun)	complete or partial interruption of the movement of the contents of the small or large intestine
intussusception (in-**tuh**-suh-**SEP**-shun)	telescoping of one portion of the large intestine into another portion of the large intestine
irritable bowel syndrome (IBS)	increased motility of the small or large intestines resulting in abdominal pain, flatulence, nausea, anorexia, and trapped gas throughout the intestines; spastic colon
lower esophageal ring	mucosal stricture of the esophagus that causes a ringlike narrowing of the lower end of the esophagus; also called _Schatzki ring_ and _B ring;_ may be a congenital condition
oral leukoplakia (**OR**-al **loo**-koh-**PLAY**-kee-ah)	presence of white spots or patches on the mucous membrane of the tongue or cheek; lesions may become malignant

continued

Table 9-4 (*continued*)   Digestive System Diseases and Conditions

TERM WITH PRONUNCIATION	DEFINITION
pancreatitis (**pan**-kree-ah-**TIGH**-tis) pancreat/o = pancreas -itis = inflammation	inflammation of the pancreas
peritonitis (**pair**-ih-toh-**NIGH**-tis) peritone/o = peritoneum -itis = inflammation	inflammation of the peritoneum
polyp (**PALL**-ip)	a small growth projecting from the mucous membrane of organs such as the colon, nose, or uterus
polyposis, chronic (pall-ee-**POH**-sis) polyp/o = polyp -osis = condition	presence of a large number of polyps in the large intestine
pruritus ani (proo-**RIGH**-tus **AN**-eye)	severe itching around the anus
sialolithiasis (**sigh**-ah-loh-lih-**THIGH**-ah-sis) sial/o = saliva; salivary glands lith/o = stones; calculi -iasis = abnormal condition	presence of salivary stones or calculi in the salivary gland or duct
toxic megacolon	a life-threatening condition associated with complications related to ulcerative colitis; peristalsis absent or abnormal, the colon becomes dilated; perforation, septicemia, or death may result
thrush	a fungal infection of the mouth and throat that produces creamy white patches on the tongue and other oral surfaces
ulcerative colitis (**ULL**-ser-ah-tiv koh-**LIGH**-tis) col/o = colon; large intestine -itis = inflammation	a chronic inflammatory condition characterized by the formation of ulcerated lesions in the mucous membrane lining of the colon; inflammatory bowel disease (IBD)
umbilical hernia	protrusion of the intestine through a weakness in the abdominal wall around the umbilicus
volvulus (**VOL**-vyoo-lus)	twisting of loops of the bowel or colon that results in an intestinal obstruction

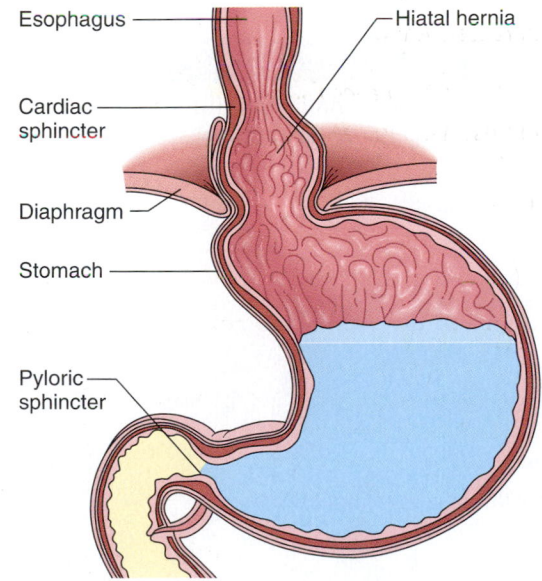

Figure 9-8   Hiatal hernia

EXERCISE 9-8

Circle the term that best fits the definition.

1. temporary stoppage of intestinal peristalsis — *ileus* or *intussusception*

2. twisting of loops of the bowels or large intestine — *intussusception* or *volvulus*

3. increased motility of the small or large intestines — *IBS* or *ulcerative colitis*

4. fungal infection of the mouth and throat — *thrush* or *oral leukoplakia*

5. mucosal stricture of the esophagus — *hiatal hernia* or *Schatzki ring*

continued

6. white patches on the oral mucous membrane — *oral leukoplakia* or *thrush*

7. telescoping of the large intestine into itself — *volvulus* or *intussusception*

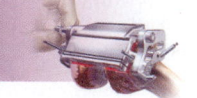

EXERCISE 9-9

Replace the italicized phrase with the correct medical term.

1. Surgery was scheduled to repair a/an *protrusion of the small intestine through the abdominal wall* that was incarcerated. — *umbilical hernia*

2. Many hospitals require immunization for *inflammation of the liver* for all employees. — *hepatitis*

3. *Fever blisters* often occur around the lips. — *herpetic stomatitis*

4. "Heartburn" might be caused by a/an *herniation of the stomach into the esophagus*. — *hiatal hernia*

5. *Inflammation of the gums* is often characterized by swelling and bleeding. — *gingivitis*

6. *Inflammation of the peritoneum* is associated with a ruptured appendix. — *peritonitis*

7. Pinworms often cause *severe itching around the anus*. — *pruritis*

8. During a recent colonoscopy, Dr. Mosheed removed several *small growths projecting from the lining of the colon*. — *polyp*

9. Martina's lack of salivary secretions was attributed to *salivary stones in the salivary ducts*. — *sialolithiasis*

Digestive System Diagnostic Procedures and Laboratory Tests

Digestive system diagnostic procedures and laboratory tests are listed in table 9-5. Review the terms and complete the exercises. Note that many of the diagnostic tests are accomplished with an endoscope, which is an instrument used to visualize internal structures and tissues. Diagnostic procedures such as colonoscopy also function as a surgical or treatment approach. For example, during a diagnostic colonoscopy, the gastroenterologist discovers several suspicious-looking polyps. With the patient's consent, the gastroenterologist removes the polyps. In this example, the diagnostic colonoscopy has become the surgical approach for a polypectomy.

Table 9-5 Digestive System Diagnostic Procedures and Laboratory Tests

TERM WITH PRONUNCIATION	DEFINITION
abdominocentesis (ab-**dom**-ih-noh-sen-**TEE**-sis) abdomin/o = abdomen -centesis = surgical puncture to remove fluid	surgical puncture into the abdominal/peritoneal cavity to remove excess fluid; also known as paracentesis
cholangiogram (kohl-**AN**-jee-oh-gram) cholangi/o = bile ducts -gram = picture; x-ray	x-ray of the bile ducts
cholangiography (**kohl**-an-jee-**OG**-rah-fee) cholangi/o = bile ducts -graphy = process of recording; x-ray examination	x-ray examination of the bile ducts
cholecystogram (**koh**-lee-**SISS**-toh-gram) cholecyst/o = gallbladder -gram = picture; x-ray	x-ray of the gallbladder
cholecystography (**koh**-lee-sist-**OG**-rah-fee) cholecyst/o = gallbladder -graphy = process of recording; x-ray examination	x-ray examination of the gallbladder
colonoscopy (koh-lon-**OSS**-koh-pee) colon/o = colon; large intestine -scopy = process of visualization with a scope	endoscopic visualization and examination of the large intestine from the anus to the ileocecal junction

continued

Table 9-5 (continued)   Digestive System Diagnostic Procedures and Laboratory Tests

TERM WITH PRONUNCIATION	DEFINITION
endoscopic retrograde cholangiopancreatogram (en-doh-**SKOP**-ic **REH**-troh-grayd kohl-**an**-jee-oh-**PAN**-kree-**ah**-toh-gram) endo- = within -scopic = pertaining to visualization with a scope cholangi/o = bile duct pancreat/o = pancreas -gram = picture; x-ray	x-ray of the pancreatic ducts and bile ducts
endoscopic retrograde cholangiopancreatography (ERCP) (en-doh-**SKOP**-ic **REH**-troh-grayd kohl-**an**-jee-oh-**pan**-kree-ah-**TOG**-rah-fee) cholangi/o = bile duct pancreat/o = pancreas -graphy = process of recording; x-ray examination	x-ray examination of the pancreatic ducts and bile ducts
esophagogastroduodenoscopy (EGD) (eh-**soff**-ah-goh-**gass**-troh-doo-**wah**-den-**OSS**-koh-pee) esophag/o = esophagus gastr/o = stomach duoden/o = duodenum -scopy = process of visualization with a scope	endoscopic visualization and examination of the esophagus, stomach, and duodenum
esophagoscopy (eh-**soff**-ah-**GOSS**-koh-pee) esophag/o = esophagus -scopy = process of visualization with a scope	endoscopic visualization and examination of the esophagus
gastroscopy (gass-**TROSS**-koh-pee) gastr/o = stomach -scopy = process of visualization with a scope	endoscopic visualization and examination of the stomach
Helicobacter pylori (*H. pylori*) (hee-lih-koh-**BAK**-ter pigh-**LOR**-eye) test	a blood test to determine the presence of *H. pylori* antibodies, which indicate infection with the bacteria; *H. pylori* is also found in the lining of the stomach and causes duodenal ulcers
laparoscopy (lap-ah-**ROSS**-koh-pee) lapar/o = abdominal wall -scopy = process of visualization with a scope	endoscopic visualization and examination of the abdominal and pelvic cavities
lower gastrointestinal series; barium enema (**gass**-troh-in-**TESS**-tin-al) gastr/o = stomach intestin/o = intestines -al = pertaining to	x-ray examination of the rectum and large intestine aided by a contrast medium
occult blood test (uh-**KULT**)	microscopic examination of feces to detect the presence of blood that is not otherwise visible; screen for colorectal cancer
proctoscopy (prok-**TOSS**-koh-pee) proct/o = rectum, anus -scopy = process of visualization with a scope	endoscopic visualization and examination of the anus and rectum
sigmoidoscopy (sig-moyd-**OSS**-koh-pee) sigmoid/o = sigmoid colon -scopy = process of visualization with a scope	endoscopic visualization and examination of the sigmoid colon
small bowel follow-through (SBF)	x-ray examination of the small intestine aided by a contrast medium; often done with an upper gastrointestinal series
upper gastrointestinal series (**gass**-troh-in-**TESS**-tin-al) gastr/o = stomach intestin/o = intestines -al = pertaining to	x-ray examination of the esophagus, stomach, and small intestine aided by a contrast medium

EXERCISE 9-10

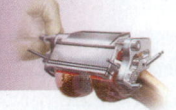

Replace the italicized phrase or abbreviation with the correct medical term.

1. The *microscopic screen for colorectal cancer* is usually ordered for all patients age 50 and older. *occult blood test*

2. A patient is sedated but conscious during the *endoscopic examination of the entire large intestine.* *colonoscopy*

3. The *x-ray of the bile ducts* showed several large gallstones in the common bile duct. *cholangiogram*

4. Kwan was told not to eat or drink the night before his scheduled *ERCP.* *endoscopic retrograde cholangiopancreatography*

5. An upper GI series often includes a/an *SBF.* *small bowel follow-through*

EXERCISE 9-11

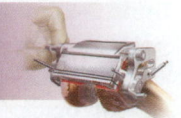

Write the name of the digestive system organs or structures associated with each diagnostic procedure.

1. cholangiography — *bile ducts*
2. cholecystography — *gall bladder*
3. ERCP — *bile ducts & pancreastic duct*
4. EGD — *esophagus, stomach, duodenum*
5. proctoscopy — *rectum, anus*
6. sigmoidoscopy — *sigmoid colon*
7. SBF — *small intestine*
8. lower gastrointestinal series — *rectum, large intestine*
9. upper gastrointestinal series — *esophagus, stomach, small, intestine*

Digestive System Procedures, Operations, and Treatments

Review the procedures, operations, and treatments in table 9-6 and complete the exercises.

Table 9-6 Digestive System Procedures, Operations, and Treatments

TERM WITH PRONUNCIATION	DEFINITION
abdominoplasty (ab-**dom**-in-oh-**PLASS**-tee) abdomin/o = abdomen -plasty = surgical repair	plastic surgery of the abdomen
anoplasty (**AY**-noh-**plass**-tee) an/o = anus -plasty = surgical repair	surgical repair of the anus
appendectomy (ap-en-**DEK**-toh-mee) append/o = appendix -ectomy = surgical removal	surgical removal of the appendix
bariatric surgery (bair-ee-**AT**-rik)	weight-loss surgical procedure accomplished by gastric bypass or adjustable gastric banding
Billroth I	surgical removal of the pylorus of the stomach with the proximal end of the duodenum anastomosed to the stomach
Billroth II	surgical removal of the pylorus of the stomach and the duodenum with the stomach anastomosed to the jejunum
celiotomy (see-lee-**OT**-oh-mee) celi/o = abdomen -(o)tomy = incision into	surgical incision into the abdominal cavity

continued

Table 9-6 (*continued*)   Digestive System Procedures, Operations, and Treatments

TERM WITH PRONUNCIATION	DEFINITION
cheiloplasty (**KIGH**-loh-**plass**-tee) cheil/o = lip -plasty = surgical, plastic repair	surgical or plastic repair of the lip
cheilorrhaphy (kigh-**LOR**-ah-fee) cheil/o = lip -(r)rhaphy = to suture	suturing the lip
cholecystectomy (**koh**-lee-sist-**EK**-toh-mee) cholecyst/o = gallbladder -ectomy = surgical removal	surgical removal of the gallbladder
choledocholithotomy (koh-leh-**doh**-koh-lith-**OT**-oh-mee) choledoch/o = bile duct lith/o = stones; calculi -(o)tomy = incision into	removal of gallstones through an incision into the common bile duct
choledocholithotripsy (koh-leh-**doh**-koh-**LITH**-oh-trip-see) choledoch/o = bile duct lith/o = stones; calculi -tripsy = crushing	crushing of gallstones in the common bile duct
colectomy (koh-**LEK**-toh-mee) col/o = colon; large intestine -ectomy = surgical removal	surgical removal of all or part of the colon or large intestine
colostomy (koh-**LOSS**-toh-mee) col/o = colon; large intestine -(o)stomy = creating a new or artificial opening	creation of a new or artificial opening for the colon through the abdominal wall to its outside surface
diverticulectomy (**digh**-ver-**tik**-yoo-**LEK**-toh-mee) diverticul/o = diverticulum -ectomy = surgical removal	surgical removal of diverticulum or diverticula
esophagogastroplasty (eh-**soff**-ah-goh-**GASS**-troh-plass-tee) esophag/o = esophagus gastr/o = stomach -plasty = surgical repair	surgical repair of the esophagus and stomach
extracorporeal shock wave lithotripsy (ESWL) (**eks**-trah-kor-**POR**-ee-al shock wave **LITH**-oh-trip-see) lith/o = stones; calculi -tripsy = crushing	crushing of gallstones using ultrasound and shock waves; nonsurgical treatment for gallstone
gastrectomy (gass-**TREK**-toh-mee) gastr/o = stomach -ectomy = surgical removal	surgical removal of all or a portion of the stomach; also known as gastric resection
gastric lavage (**GASS**-trik lah-**VAHZH**) gastr/o = stomach -ic = pertaining to	washing out the contents of the stomach; commonly called "pumping the stomach"

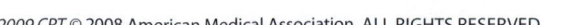

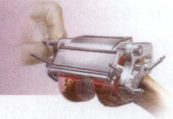

EXERCISE 9-12

Write the name of the digestive system organ or structure associated with each procedure. Write a brief definition of the procedure.

1. Celiotomy
   ORGAN/STRUCTURE: *abdomen cavi?*
   DEFINITION: *Surgical incision into abdominal cavity*

2. Cheilorrhaphy
   ORGAN/STRUCTURE: *lip*
   DEFINITION: *suturing the lip*

3. Cholecystectomy
   ORGAN/STRUCTURE: *gall bladder*
   DEFINITION: *Surgical removal of the gallbladder*

4. Cheiloplasty
   ORGAN/STRUCTURE: *lip*
   DEFINITION: *Surgical repair of lip*

5. Choledocholithotomy
   ORGAN/STRUCTURE: *bile duct*
   DEFINITION: *removal of gallstones through incision into common bile duct*

6. Choledocholithotripsy
   ORGAN/STRUCTURE: *bile duct*
   DEFINITION: *Crushing of gallstones in the common bile ducts*

7. Esophagogastroplasty
   ORGAN/STRUCTURE: *esophagus & stomach*
   DEFINITION: *Surgical repair of esophagus & stomach*

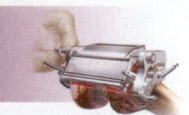

EXERCISE 9-13

Write the name of the procedure, operation, or treatment for each definition or abbreviation.

1. creation of a new opening for the colon *Colostom*
2. ESWL *extra corporal shock wave lithotripsy*
3. plastic surgery of the abdomen *abdominoplasty*
4. "pumping the stomach" *gastric lavage*
5. surgical procedure for weight loss *bariatric surgery*
6. surgical removal of all or part of the large intestine *Colectomy*
7. surgical removal of the appendix *appendectomy*
8. surgical removal of diverticula *diverticulectomy*
9. surgical removal of all or part of the stomach *gastrectomy*
10. surgical repair of the anus *anoplasty*

Review the procedures, operations, and treatments in table 9-7 and complete the exercises.

Table 9-7 Digestive System Procedures, Operations, and Treatments

TERM WITH PRONUNCIATION	DEFINITION
gastric banding, bariatric	restrictive bariatric surgical procedure during which a silicone band is placed around a portion of the stomach to limit the volume of the contents of the stomach
gastric bypass, bariatric	weight-loss surgical procedure characterized by reducing the size of the stomach and connecting it to a portion of the small intestine; part of the stomach and the first segment of the small intestine are bypassed
gastroduodenostomy (**gass**-troh-doo-**wah**-den-**OSS**-toh-mee) gastr/o = stomach duoden/o = duodenum -(o)stomy = creation of a new or artificial opening	creation of a new or artificial opening between the stomach and the duodenum, usually after a portion of the stomach is removed
gavage (gah-**VAHZH**)	procedure in which an individual receives nutrition through a tube passed through the nose or mouth or both (nasogastric); commonly known as *tube feeding*
gingivectomy (jin-jih-**VEK**-toh-mee) gingiv/o = gingival -ectomy = surgical removal	surgical removal of the gingiva (gums)

continued

Table 9-7 (*continued*)   Digestive System Procedures, Operations, and Treatments

TERM WITH PRONUNCIATION	DEFINITION
glossorrhaphy (gloss-**OR**-ah-fee) gloss/o = tongue -(r)rhaphy = to suture	suture of a wound of the tongue
herniorrhaphy (her-nee-**OR**-ah-fee)	suture repair of a hernia
ileostomy (ill-ee-**OSS**-toh-mee) ile/o = ileum -(o)stomy = creation of a new or artificial opening	surgical creation of a new or artificial opening for the ileum through the abdominal wall to its outside surface
laparoscopic adjustable gastric banding (LAGB) lapar/o = abdominal wall -scopy = process of viewing -ic = pertaining to gastr/o = stomach	bariatric surgical procedure in which a silicone band is placed around a portion of the stomach; the band, which is inserted via laparoscope, can be tightened or loosened
laparotomy (lap-ah-**ROT**-oh-mee) lapar/o = abdomen; abdominal wall -(o)tomy = incision into	surgical incision into the abdominal wall
nasogastric intubation (nay-zoh-**GASS**-trik in-too-**BAY**-shun) nas/o = nose gastr/o = stomach -ic = pertaining to	insertion of a tube through the nose into the stomach
palatoplasty (**PAL**-at-oh-plass-tee) palat/o = palate -plasty = surgical repair	surgical repair of the palate, usually to repair a cleft palate
percutaneous endoscopic gastrostomy (PEG) per- = through cutan/e = skin -ous = pertaining to endo- = within -scopy = process of visualization -ic = pertaining to gastr/o = stomach -(o)stomy = creating an opening	endoscopic placement of a feeding tube into the stomach through an incision made in the skin
polypectomy (pall-ih-**PEK**-toh-mee) polyp/o = polyp -ectomy = surgical removal	surgical removal of a polyp
proctocolectomy (**prock**-toh-koh-**LEK**-toh-mee) proct/o = rectum; anus col/o = colon; large intestine -ectomy = surgical removal	surgical removal of the large intestine and rectum
pyloroplasty (pigh-**LOR**-oh-plass-tee) pylor/o = pylorus -plasty = surgical repair	surgical procedure for enlarging the opening between the stomach and duodenum
Roux-en-Y gastric bypass (**ROO**-en-wigh) (RYGBP) gastr/o = stomach -ic = pertaining to	bariatric surgical procedure during which the size of the stomach is reduced and subsequently connected to a portion of the small intestine; also called proximal gastric bypass
total parenteral nutrition (TPN)	provision of nutritional and caloric needs by an intravenous route in order to bypass the digestive tract
uvulopalatopharyngoplasty (UPPP; UP$_3$) (**yoo**-vyoo-loh-**pal**-ah-toh-fah-**RING**-oh-plass-tee) uvul/o = uvula palat/o = palate pharyng/o = pharynx -plasty = surgical repair	surgical repair of the uvula, soft palate, and pharynx

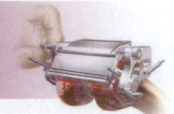

EXERCISE 9-14

Replace the italicized phrase or abbreviation with the correct medical term or phrase.

1. After the anesthesia took effect, the surgical nurse proceeded with *the insertion of a tube through the nose into the stomach.* nasogastric intubation

2. *Surgical incision into the abdominal wall* might serve as a diagnostic or treatment procedure. laparotomy

3. Due to injuries sustained in a motor vehicle accident, Jennifer underwent *surgical repair of the palate.* palatoplasty

4. Caleb's physician recommended *the surgical removal of polyps* to correct rectal bleeding. polypectomy

5. Removal of the small intestine might result in the need for *TPN.* total parenteral nutrition

6. As a result of ulcerative colitis, Milton underwent a/an *removal of the colon and rectum.* total proctocolectomy

7. Ms. Hsu discussed the risks and benefits of *LAGB* with her family physician. Laparoscopic adjustable gastic bending

8. Premature infants may require *tube feeding.* gavage

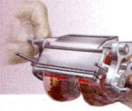

EXERCISE 9-15

Write the name of the digestive system organ or structure associated with each procedure. Write a brief definition of the procedure.

1. Gastroduodenostomy

   ORGAN/STRUCTURE: Stomach & duodenum

   DEFINITION: Creation of new opening between stomach & duodenum

2. Gingivectomy

   ORGAN/STRUCTURE: gums

   DEFINITION: Surgical removal of gums

3. Glossorrhaphy

   ORGAN/STRUCTURE: tongue

   DEFINITION: Suture of the wound on the tongue

4. Herniorrhaphy

   ORGAN/STRUCTURE: hernia (small intestine)

   DEFINITION: sututure of the hernia

5. Ileostomy

   ORGAN/STRUCTURE: ileum

   DEFINITION: Surgical creation of new opening for ileum through abdominal wall

6. Pyloroplasty

   ORGAN/STRUCTURE: Pylorus

   DEFINITION: Sugical procedure enlarging the opening between stomach & dueodun

7. UPPP

   ORGAN/STRUCTURE: uvula, soft palate, pharnx

   DEFINITION: Surgigal repair of uvula, soft palate & pharnx

ABBREVIATIONS

Review the digestive system abbreviations in table 9-8. Practice writing out the meaning of each abbreviation.

Table 9-8   Abbreviations

ABBREVIATION	MEANING
BE	barium enema
EGD	esophagogastroduodenoscopy
ERCP	endoscopic retrograde cholangiopancreatography
GERD	gastroesophageal reflux disease
GI	gastrointestinal
LAGBP	laparoscopic adjustable gastric bypass
NG	nasogastric
PEG	percutaneous endoscopic gastrostomy
RYGBP	Roux-en-Y gastric bypass
SBF	small bowel follow-through
TPN	total parenteral nutrition
UGI	upper gastrointestinal
UPPP	uvulopalatopharyngoplasty

DIGESTIVE SYSTEM MEDICAL CODING

To successfully complete the exercises in this section, the ICD-9-CM volumes 1, 2, and 3, and the CPT (Current Procedural Terminology) coding references must be readily available. The information in this section is presented as follows:

- An introduction to ICD-9-CM, chapter 9, "Diseases of the Digestive System"
- ICD-9-CM diagnostic coding exercises
- A summary of ICD-9-CM volume 3 coding conventions that apply to digestive system procedures
- ICD-9-CM procedure coding exercises
- A summary of the CPT Digestive System coding guidelines
- CPT coding exercises

Students are *strongly* encouraged to review the information at the beginning of the ICD-9-CM and CPT coding references. Commercial publishers include instructions on how to use the ICD-9-CM references, the ICD-9-CM official coding conventions, additional conventions used by the publisher, and the *ICD-9-CM Official Guidelines for Coding and Reporting*. Some publishers include the three ICD-9-CM volumes in one book and put the *Alphabetic Index* (volume 2) at the beginning of the reference.

The *Introduction* to CPT includes detailed instructions for using this code book, an index to the illustrations throughout the book, and anatomical illustrations of the major structures of body systems.

ICD-9-CM Volume 1, Chapter 9, Diseases of the Digestive System (520–579)

Digestive system diseases are coded to ICD-9-CM volume 1, chapter 9, "Diseases of the Digestive System." This chapter includes the following major categories:

- **Diseases of Oral Cavity, Salivary Glands, and Jaws (520–529).** Codes in this section cover conditions of the teeth, gingiva, jaws, salivary glands, lips, and tongue. Many categories require fifth digits, especially codes related to the teeth.
- **Diseases of Esophagus, Stomach, and Duodenum (530–538).** Codes in this section cover conditions of the esophagus, stomach, and duodenum, which is the first segment of the small intestine. Fifth digits are needed to

identify obstruction, perforation, or hemorrhage associated with ulcers and inflammatory diseases such as gastric ulcer and gastritis.

- **Hernia of Abdominal Cavity (550–553).** Codes in this section cover epigastric hernias, hiatal hernias, incisional hernias, inguinal hernias, umbilical hernias, and ventral hernias. This section has extensive fourth- and fifth-digit codes that identify whether the hernia is bilateral or unilateral, and whether gangrene, obstruction, or both are present. Other terms for an obstructed hernia include *incarcerated, irreducible,* and *strangulated.* Hernias due to adhesions with obstruction are coded to 560.81.

  Inguinal hernias may be further identified as *indirect* (*external or oblique*) or *direct* (*internal*) depending on whether the hernia passes through the inguinal canal. An indirect (external or oblique) inguinal hernia passes through the inguinal canal.
- **Noninfectious Enteritis and Colitis (555–558).** Codes in this section cover inflammatory conditions of the small and large intestine such as Crohn disease and ulcerative colitis. Infectious diseases, which can be transmitted from one individual to another, are excluded from these categories.
- **Other Diseases of Intestines and Peritoneum (560–569).** Codes in this section cover a variety of digestive system conditions that range from obstruction without mention of herniation to rectal prolapse. Diverticulosis, with or without hemorrhage, constipation, irritable bowel syndrome, and postgastric surgery are coded to this section. Fourth- and fifth-digit codes are used to identify hemorrhage, fistulas, ulceration, and complications.
- **Other Diseases of Digestive System (570–579).** Codes in this section cover the accessory organs of the digestive system. Liver diseases are coded to categories 570–573, gallbladder and bile duct conditions are

continued

coded to categories 574–576, diseases of the pancreas are coded to category 577, gastrointestinal bleeding and hemorrhage not associated with other conditions such as ulcers and diverticulitis are coded to category 578, and intestinal malabsorption conditions are coded to category 579.

In order to select the correct code for cholelithiasis, the location of the stones, obstruction, concurrent cholecystitis, and acute or chronic conditions are identified with fourth and fifth digits. As with all codes, documentation in the medical record must support the selected code.

Conditions related to the digestive system may also be coded to the following chapters in volume 1: chapter 14, "Congenital Anomalies"; chapter 16, "Symptoms, Signs, and Ill-Defined Conditions"; and chapter 2, "Neoplasms."

EXERCISE 9-16

Write a brief definition for each diagnosis. Identify the main term in the diagnostic statement and assign the correct ICD-9-CM diagnosis code(s).

1. Atrophic gastritis

   DEFINITION: _____

   MAIN TERM: _____

   ICD-9-CM CODE(S): _535.10_

2. Abdominal pain secondary to constipation

   DEFINITION: _____

   MAIN TERM: _____

   ICD-9-CM CODE(S): _789.00_

3. Bilateral inguinal hernias, left greater than right

   DEFINITION: _____

   MAIN TERM: _____

   ICD-9-CM CODE(S): _550.92_

4. Incarcerated incisional hernia with obstruction

   DEFINITION: _____

   MAIN TERM: _____

   ICD-9-CM CODE(S): _552.21_

5. Chronic duodenal ulcer, perforated with hemorrhage

   DEFINITION: _____

   MAIN TERM: _____

   ICD-9-CM CODE(S): _532.60_

6. Hepatitis due to infectious mononucleosis

   DEFINITION: _____

   MAIN TERM: _____

   ICD-9-CM CODE(S): _075 [573.1]_

7. Aphthous stomatitis

   DEFINITION: _____

   MAIN TERM: _____

   ICD-9-CM CODE(S): _528.2_

8. Toxic megacolon due to severe ulcerative colitis

   DEFINITION: _____

   MAIN TERM: _____

   ICD-9-CM CODE(S): _556.9_

9. Acute appendicitis with perforation and peritonitis

   DEFINITION: _____

   MAIN TERM: _____

   ICD-9-CM CODE(S): _540.0_

10. Small bowel obstruction due to peritoneal adhesions

    DEFINITION: _____

    MAIN TERM: _____

    ICD-9-CM CODE(S): _560.81_

11. Cholelithiasis with acute cholecystitis

    DEFINITION: _____

    MAIN TERM: _____

    ICD-9-CM CODE(S): _574.00_

12. Choledocholithiasis with chronic cholecystitis

    DEFINITION: _____

    MAIN TERM: _____

    ICD-9-CM CODE(S): _574.40_

13. Gastritis with hemorrhage due to alcoholism

    DEFINITION: _____

    MAIN TERM: _____

    ICD-9-CM CODE(S): _535.31_
    _303.90_

14. Gastroenteritis due to *Salmonella*

    DEFINITION: _____

    MAIN TERM: _____

    ICD-9-CM CODE(S): _003.0_____

15. Reflux esophagitis with hiatal hernia

    DEFINITION: _____

    MAIN TERM: _____

    ICD-9-CM CODE(S): _530.11___553.3__

16. Obstructed hiatal hernia

    DEFINITION: _____

    MAIN TERM: _____

    ICD-9-CM CODE(S): _552.3_____

17. Intestinal obstruction due to volvulus

    DEFINITION: _____

    MAIN TERM: _____

    ICD-9-CM CODE(S): _560.2_____

18. Herpetic stomatitis

    DEFINITION: _____

    MAIN TERM: _____

    ICD-9-CM CODE(S): _054.2_____

19. Oral leukoplakia

    DEFINITION: _____

    MAIN TERM: _____

    ICD-9-CM CODE(S): _528.6_____

20. Esophageal achalasia

    DEFINITION: _____

    MAIN TERM: _____

    ICD-9-CM CODE(S): _530.0_____

21. Chronic polyposis of the colon

    DEFINITION: _____

    MAIN TERM: _____

    ICD-9-CM CODE(S): _211.3_____

22. Sialolithiasis, etiology unknown

    DEFINITION: _____

    MAIN TERM: _____

    ICD-9-CM CODE(S): _527.5_____

23. Acute, generalized peritonitis

    DEFINITION: _____

    MAIN TERM: _____

    ICD-9-CM CODE(S): _567.21_____

ICD-9-CM Volume 3, Chapter 6, Operations on the Digestive System (42–54)

Digestive system operations and some therapeutic treatments are coded to ICD-9-CM volume 3, chapter 6, "Operations on the Digestive System." This chapter covers the esophagus, stomach, small and large intestine, appendix, rectum, anus, and accessory structures of the digestive system. This chapter includes the following major categories:

- **Operations on Esophagus (42).** Codes in this category include diagnostic and operative procedures of the esophagus.
- **Incision and Excision of Stomach (43); Other Operations on Stomach (44).** Codes in these categories cover incision, excision, destruction, resection, repair, and gastric restrictive procedures of the stomach.
- **Incision, Excision, Anastomosis, and Diagnostic Procedures on Small and Large Intestine (45).** Codes in this category cover diagnostic and operative procedures ranging from biopsies to total intra-abdominal colectomy.
- **Other Operations on Intestine (46).** Codes in this category include colostomy, ileostomy, closure of fistulas, and dilation and manipulation of the small and large intestine.
- **Operations on Appendix (47).** Codes in this category cover surgical interventions related to the appendix.
- **Operations on Rectum, Rectosigmoid, and Perirectal Tissue (48).** Codes in this category cover incision, excision, repair, and resection of the rectum and surrounding tissue.
- **Operations on Anus (49).** Codes in this category cover procedures related to the anus.
- **Operations on Liver (50).** Codes in these categories cover biopsy, incision, excision, repair, and transplantation of the liver.
- **Operations on Gallbladder and Biliary Tract (51).** Codes in this category cover biopsy, incision, excision, and repair of the gallbladder, cystic duct, hepatic duct, and common bile duct.

continued

- **Operations on Pancreas (52).** Codes in this category cover biopsy, incision, excision, repair, and transplant of the pancreas and pancreatic duct.
- **Repair of Hernia (53).** As the name implies, this category covers hernia repairs.
- **Other Operations on Abdominal Region (54).** Codes in this category cover biopsy, incision, excision or destruction, drainage, and repair of the abdominal region, abdominal wall, and peritoneum.

The majority of the codes related to operations and procedures on the digestive system require four digits. Many of the diagnostic procedures are accomplished with an endoscope. When a diagnostic endoscopy becomes a surgical approach, the code for the diagnostic endoscopy is omitted. For example, during a diagnostic sigmoidoscopy the physician removes several polyps. The medical coder assigns the appropriate ICD-9-CM procedure code for endoscopic polypectomy.

Digestive system diagnostic and therapeutic procedures are also coded to ICD-9-CM volume 3, chapter 16, "Miscellaneous Diagnostic and Therapeutic Procedures." These procedures include diagnostic radiology, nuclear medicine scans, nonoperative removal of therapeutic devices and foreign bodies, and nonoperative intubation and irrigation.

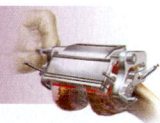

EXERCISE 9-17

Write a brief definition for each operative, treatment, or diagnostic procedure. Identify the main term in the statement and assign the correct ICD-9-CM procedure code(s).

1. Bilateral herniorrhaphy, indirect inguinal hernias

   DEFINITION: _____

   MAIN TERM: _____

   ICD-9-CM CODE(S): 53.12

2. Endoscopic polypectomy, sigmoid colon *large colon*

   DEFINITION: _____

   MAIN TERM: _____

   ICD-9-CM CODE(S): 454.2

3. Laparoscopic cholecystectomy with exploration of the common bile duct

   DEFINITION: _____

   MAIN TERM: _____

   ICD-9-CM CODE(S): 51.23   51.51

4. Percutaneous endoscopic gastrostomy tube placement

   DEFINITION: _____

   MAIN TERM: _____

   ICD-9-CM CODE(S): 43.11

5. Open cholecystectomy and choledocholithotomy

   DEFINITION: _____

   MAIN TERM: _____

   ICD-9-CM CODE(S): 51.22 , 51.41

6. Partial gastrectomy with gastrojejunostomy (Billroth II procedure)

   DEFINITION: _____

   MAIN TERM: _____

   ICD-9-CM CODE(S): 43.7

7. Repair of esophageal stricture

   DEFINITION: _____

   MAIN TERM: _____

   ICD-9-CM CODE(S): 42.85

8. Gastric banding, insertion of adjustable gastric band and port

   DEFINITION: _____

   MAIN TERM: _____

   ICD-9-CM CODE(S): 44.68 44.95

9. EGD with gastric biopsy

   DEFINITION: _____

   MAIN TERM: _____

   ICD-9-CM CODE(S): 45.16

10. Endoscopic ligation of esophageal varices

    DEFINITION: _____

    MAIN TERM: _____

    ICD-9-CM CODE(S): 42.33

11. Partial gastrectomy with gastroduodenostomy (Billroth I procedure)

    DEFINITION: _____

    MAIN TERM: _____

    ICD-9-CM CODE(S): 43.6

12. Total colectomy and proctectomy with permanent ileostomy

    DEFINITION: _____

    MAIN TERM: _____

    ICD-9-CM CODE(S): 45.8 48.69, 46.23

13. Percutaneous liver biopsy

    DEFINITION: _____

    MAIN TERM: _____

    ICD-9-CM CODE(S): _____50.11_____

14. Endoscopic retrograde cholangiopancreatography

    DEFINITION: _____

    MAIN TERM: _____

    ICD-9-CM CODE(S): _____51.10_____

15. Repair of umbilical hernia with mesh graft

    DEFINITION: _____

    MAIN TERM: _____

    ICD-9-CM CODE(S): _____

16. Fiberoptic flexible sigmoidoscopy

    DEFINITION: _____

    MAIN TERM: _____

    ICD-9-CM CODE(S): _____

17. Extracorporeal shock wave lithotripsy

    DEFINITION: _____

    MAIN TERM: _____

    ICD-9-CM CODE(S): _____

18. Roux-en-Y gastric bypass

    DEFINITION: _____

    MAIN TERM: _____

    ICD-9-CM CODE(S): _____

19. Laparoscopic lysis of peritoneal adhesions

    DEFINITION: _____

    MAIN TERM: _____

    ICD-9-CM CODE(S): _____

20. Exploratory laparotomy

    DEFINITION: _____

    MAIN TERM: _____

    ICD-9-CM CODE(S): _____

Current Procedural Terminology (CPT) Digestive System Codes (40490–49999)

CPT digestive system codes are located in the Surgery, Radiology, and Medicine sections. The Surgery guidelines provide important information for all of the Surgery subsections. Review the guidelines in the CPT manual and in chapter 3 of this text. There are additional instruction notes for the Digestive System subsection of the Surgery section. The Digestive System subsection includes these major categories:

- **Lips (40490–40799).** Codes in this category cover excision and repair of the lips.

- **Vestibule of Mouth (40800–40899).** Codes in this category cover incision, excision, and repair of the vestibule of the mouth. The vestibule includes the mucosal and submucosal tissue of the lips and cheeks and excludes the teeth and gums.

- **Tongue and Floor of Mouth (41000–41599).** Codes in this category include incision, excision, repair, and other procedures of the tongue and floor of the mouth.

- **Dentoalveolar Structures (41800–41899).** Codes in this category include incision, excision, destruction, and other procedures related to the tooth socket and gums.

- **Palate and Uvula (42000–42299).** Codes in this category include incision, excision, destruction, repair, and other procedures of the hard and soft palate and the uvula.

- **Salivary Gland and Ducts (42300–42699).** Codes in this category include incision, excision, destruction, repair, and other procedures related to the salivary glands and ducts.

- **Pharynx, Adenoids, and Tonsils (42700–42999).** Codes in this category include incision, excision, repair, and other procedures related to the throat, adenoids, and tonsils.

- **Esophagus (43020–43499).** Codes in this category include incision, excision, endoscopic and laparoscopic procedures, repair, manipulation, and other procedures of the esophagus. The procedures in the endoscopy

continued

subcategory are flagged to denote that moderate (conscious) sedation is used. CPT codes for moderate sedation are in the Medicine section (99143–99150). Surgical laparoscopy always includes the diagnostic laparoscopy.

- **Stomach (43500–43999).** Codes in this category include incision, excision, laparoscopy, introduction of tubes, bariatric surgery, and other procedures related to the stomach.

- **Intestines (Except Rectum) (44005–44799).** Codes in this category include incision, excision, laparoscopy, enterostomy, endoscopy, repair, and other procedures related to the small and large intestine. Enterostomies include colostomy, ileostomy, and jejunostomy.

- **Rectum (45000–45999).** Codes in this category include incision, excision, destruction, endoscopy, laparoscopy, manipulation, and other procedures related to the rectum. Endoscopies include proctosigmoidoscopy, sigmoidoscopy, and colonoscopy.

- **Anus (46020–46999).** Codes in this category include incision, excision, endoscopy, repair, destruction, suture, and other procedures related to the anus. Hemorrhoid procedures are part of this category.

- **Liver (47000–47399).** Codes in this category include incision, excision, transplantation, repair, laparoscopy, and other procedures related to the liver. Instruction notes for liver transplantation direct the medical coder to additional codes that apply to this procedure.

- **Biliary Tract (47400–47999).** Codes in this category include incision, endoscopy, injections and introductions, laparoscopy, excision, repair, and other procedures related to the biliary tract. The biliary tract includes the cystic, hepatic, and common bile ducts.

- **Pancreas (48000–48999).** Codes in this category include incision, excision, repair, and pancreas transplantation. Instruction notes for pancreas transplantation direct the medical coder to additional codes that apply to this procedure.

- **Abdomen, Peritoneum, and Omentum (49000–49999).** Codes in this category include incision, excision, laparoscopy, revision, removal, and hernia repair. Hernia repair codes are categorized primarily by type of hernia. The instruction notes in the hernia subcategory direct the medical coder to additional codes that apply to hernia procedures. Hernia repair includes hernioplasty, herniorrhaphy, and herniotomy.

Transplantation procedures involve three distinct components of the physician's work: (1) **cadaver donor** or **living donor** organ or graft removal and preservation; (2) **backbench work**, which includes preparing the organ or graft for transplantation; and (3) **recipient allotransplantation** of the harvested organ or graft.

Digestive system diagnostic imaging procedures are coded to the Radiology section. Some of the subsections related to the digestive system include the following:

- **Diagnostic Radiology (Diagnostic Imaging) (74000–74363).** Codes in this subsection include radiology of the abdomen and gastrointestinal tract. Magnetic resonance imaging (MRI) and computerized tomography (CT) scans are covered in this subsection.

- **Nuclear Medicine: Gastrointestinal System (78201–78299).** Codes in this subsection include procedures of the liver, salivary glands, esophagus, stomach, and intestines.

The Medicine section also has codes that apply to the digestive system. The Gastroenterology subsection (91000–91299) covers procedures like intubation, reflux tests, gastric lavage and aspiration, and irrigation of fecal impaction.

EXERCISE 9-18

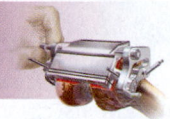

Identify the main term in each statement. Assign the correct CPT code(s).

1. Proximal gastrectomy for chronic gastric ulcer

   MAIN TERM: _____

   CPT CODE(S): _____

2. Colonoscopy with polypectomy by snare technique and biopsy

   MAIN TERM: _____

   CPT CODE(S): _____

3. Repair of incarcerated incisional hernia with obstruction

   MAIN TERM: _____

   CPT CODE(S): _____

4. Percutaneous endoscopic gastrostomy tube placement

   MAIN TERM: _____

   CPT CODE(S): _____

5. Esophagogastroduodenoscopy with Maloney dilation

   MAIN TERM: _____

   CPT CODE(S): _____

6. Repair of femoral hernia with graft, unilateral

   MAIN TERM: _____

   CPT CODE(S): _____

7. Endoscopic retrograde cholangiopancreatography

   MAIN TERM: _____

   CPT CODE(S): _____

8. Hemiglossectomy

   MAIN TERM: _____

   CPT CODE(S): _____

9. Revision of ileostomy stoma, simple

   MAIN TERM: _____

   CPT CODE(S): _____

10. Intraoral sialolithotomy of the sublingual salivary gland, uncomplicated

    MAIN TERM: _____

    CPT CODE(S): _____

11. Incision and drainage of peritonsillar abscess

    MAIN TERM: _____

    CPT CODE(S): _____

12. Hemorrhoidectomy, internal and external, simple

    MAIN TERM: _____

    CPT CODE(S): _____

13. Percutaneous liver biopsy

    MAIN TERM: _____

    CPT CODE(S): _____

14. Exploratory laparotomy

    MAIN TERM: _____

    CPT CODE(S): _____

15. Diagnostic laparoscopy with collection of specimens by brushing

    MAIN TERM: _____

    CPT CODE(S): _____

■ SUMMARY

This chapter covered medical terms related to the digestive system. Digestive system diagnoses and procedures were identified and defined. Digestive diseases are coded to ICD-9-CM volume 1, chapter 9, "Diseases of the Digestive System"; chapter 2, "Neoplasms"; chapter 14, "Congenital Anomalies"; and chapter 16, "Signs, Symptoms, and Ill-Defined Conditions." Digestive system procedures are coded to ICD-9-CM volume 3, chapter 6, "Operations on the Digestive System" and chapter 16, "Miscellaneous Diagnostic and Therapeutic Procedures."

Current Procedural Terminology (CPT) digestive procedure codes are found in the CPT Surgery section, Digestive System subsection, and the Radiology and Medicine sections.

■ CHAPTER REVIEW

Read each medical note or medical report excerpt. Write the diagnosis(es) and the main term. Assign the ICD-9-CM diagnosis code.

CASE 1

Ms. Burr is seen today for follow-up of endoscopic gastrostomy tube placement for intestinal Hirschsprung disease. She states that she is feeling "much better." She is somewhat confined due to her illness, but this does not seem to be problematic. The gastrostomy site is negative for edema, redness, or tenderness. Pupils are equal and reactive. The pharynx is benign and the neck is supple without adenopathy. The extremities are negative for cyanosis, clubbing, or edema. She is to continue with her current medications. She was advised to increase her activities as tolerated and to call if she experiences any problems.

DIAGNOSIS(ES): _____

MAIN TERM: _____

ICD-9-CM DIAGNOSIS CODE(S): _____

CASE 2

Mr. Kwan is seen for the first time today. He noted a change in the quality of bowel movements in that they became segmented. Two weeks ago occult blood was found in the stool on Hemoccult testing ×3. Bowel movements occur every 2 to 3 hours, and stool is flat and hemispheric. He has no weight loss and his appetite is good. Other health problems include hypertension for over 20 years, well controlled with medication. He also had a recent episode of parotitis. He admits no allergies. Rectal exam revealed normal tone, an external hemorrhoid anteriorly, and a normal prostate. No masses were palpable in the rectum. Verbal report of pathology report from barium enema reveals a 2-cm apple core type lesion in lower sigmoid colon, findings compatible with carcinoma. Assessment: Constricting lesion, lower sigmoid colon. Plan: Colonoscopy with biopsies to confirm or rule out colon cancer.

DIAGNOSIS(ES): _____

MAIN TERM: _____

ICD-9-CM DIAGNOSIS CODE(S): _____

CASE 3

Three years ago today this patient was noted to have a bulge in his left side. He reports that his bowel movements have been normal. No bloody or black, tarry stools. In the standing position, there is a left inguinal hernia that exits the external ring and a right inguinal hernia that is beginning to do this. Rectal examination is normal. Prostate is normal. The stool Hemoccult is negative. Assessment: Bilateral inguinal hernias, left greater than right.

DIAGNOSIS(ES): _____

MAIN TERM: _____

ICD-9-CM DIAGNOSIS CODE(S): _____

CASE 4

PREOPERATIVE DIAGNOSIS: Cholelithiasis.

POSTOPERATIVE DIAGNOSIS: Cholelithiasis.

SPECIMEN SUBMITTED: Gallbladder and stone.

GROSS DESCRIPTION: Specimen received in one container labeled "gallbladder." Specimen consists of a 9-cm gallbladder measuring 2 cm in average diameter. The serosal surface demonstrates diffuse fibrous adhesion. The wall is thickened and hemorrhagic. The mucosa is eroded and there is a single large stone measuring 2 cm in diameter within the lumen. Representative sections are submitted in one cassette.

MICROSCOPIC DIAGNOSIS: Gallbladder, hemorrhagic chronic cholecystitis with cholelithiasis.

DIAGNOSIS(ES): _____

MAIN TERM: _____

ICD-9-CM DIAGNOSIS CODE(S): _____

CASE 5

Mr. Schatzki is seen today for follow-up of a recent endoscopy. The biopsies of the esophagus showed chronic inflammation. No malignancy was identified. He complains of abdominal pain that is "worse than usual." He denies melena, hematochezia, or hematemesis. Physical examination was unremarkable except for mild epigastric discomfort with no guarding or rebound. Assessment: Reflux esophagitis, duodenitis, and hiatal hernia, confirmed by endoscopy.

DIAGNOSIS(ES): _____

MAIN TERM: _____

ICD-9-CM DIAGNOSIS CODE(S): _____

CASE 6

Ms. Withers is seen today with complaints of abdominal pain, nausea, and flatulence. She states that the "gas" is bad enough, but the cramps are nearly unbearable. In addition, her bowel movements are loose and watery, nearly explosive, and very urgent. A recent colonoscopy was negative for inflammation, diverticulitis, and ulcerations. The mucosa was unremarkable. We discussed various dietary factors and she was advised to avoid dairy products for two weeks. At this time we are probably looking at irritable bowel syndrome. She was advised to seek immediate treatment if there is blood in the stool.

DIAGNOSIS(ES): _____

MAIN TERM: _____

ICD-9-CM DIAGNOSIS CODE(S): _____

CASE 7

CLINICAL HISTORY: Polyps.

MACROSCOPIC EXAMINATION: Specimen A: Labeled "splenic flexure." The specimen consists of two 1- to 2-mm soft tissue fragments wrapped and submitted in formalin.

Specimen B: Labeled "cecal biopsy." The specimen is a 2-mm soft tissue fragment wrapped and submitted in formalin.

Specimen C: Labeled "sigmoid polyp." The specimen is a 2- to 3-mm soft tissue fragment wrapped and submitted in formalin.

MICROSCOPIC EXAMINATION: Specimen A: The splenic flexure biopsy consists of portions of adenomatous colonic mucosa. The surface epithelium is intact. Many of the underlying glands exhibit tall columnar epithelium with stratification of elongated hyperchromatic nuclei. No malignant cells are identified.

Specimen B: The cecal biopsy consists of colonic mucosa.

Specimen C: The sigmoid biopsy consists of colonic mucosa with focal hyperplastic changes. No dysplastic cells are identified.

DIAGNOSES: 1. Specimens A and B: Adenomatous polyps. 2. Specimen C: Hyperplastic polyp.

DIAGNOSIS(ES): _____

MAIN TERM: _____

ICD-9-CM DIAGNOSIS CODE(S): _____

Read the procedure note, operative report, or discharge summary excerpt. Write the diagnosis and its ICD-9-CM code. Write the name of the procedure and the main term. Assign the ICD-9-CM procedure code(s).

CASE 8

PREOPERATIVE DIAGNOSIS: Chronic cholecystitis and cholelithiasis.

POSTOPERATIVE DIAGNOSIS: Cholecystitis, cholelithiasis, and common duct stone.

OPERATION PERFORMED: Cholecystectomy and common bile duct exploration.

INDICATIONS: The patient is a 48-year-old female who was admitted to the hospital with a chronic history of right upper quadrant pain and with associated dyspepsia.

FINDINGS: Surgical intervention revealed numerous cholesterol stones. The initial cystic duct cholangiogram failed to reveal clear passage of dye into the duodenum. There was a concentric defect in the terminal common bile duct. After 1 mg of glucagon was given, cholangiograms were repeated and the common duct was open.

DIAGNOSIS(ES): _____ ICD-9-CM DIAGNOSIS(ES) CODE(S): _____

PROCEDURE(S): _____ MAIN TERM(S): _____

ICD-9-CM PROCEDURE CODE(S): _____

CASE 9

PREOPERATIVE DIAGNOSIS: Foreign body in the upper esophagus.

POSTOPERATIVE DIAGNOSIS: Foreign body in the upper esophagus, a penny.

PROCEDURE: Upper esophagoscopy and removal of foreign body.

DESCRIPTION: With the patient in the supine position, general anesthesia was then administered. A laryngoscope was introduced and passed posteriorly into the hypopharynx and beyond the level of the cricopharynx. The foreign body was visualized in the upper esophagus. The penny was grasped with alligator-type forceps. The instrument and the penny were removed at the same time. The mucosa of the esophagus was intact and there was no laceration. The patient tolerated the procedure well and without complications.

DIAGNOSIS(ES): _____   ICD-9-CM DIAGNOSIS(ES) CODE(S): _____

PROCEDURE(S): _____   MAIN TERM(S): _____

ICD-9-CM PROCEDURE CODE(S): _____

CASE 10

ADMITTING DIAGNOSIS: Morbid obesity.

DISCHARGE DIAGNOSIS: Morbid obesity.

PROCEDURES: 1. Open Roux-en-Y gastric bypass. 2. Removal of gastroplasty ring. 3. Liver biopsy. 4. G tube placement.

HOSPITAL COURSE: The patient was admitted for open Roux-en-Y gastric bypass, removal of gastroplasty ring, and liver biopsy. The patient did very well postoperatively. By the fourth postoperative day, she was tolerating bypass soft diet. She was discharged home with pain medications and discharge instructions. Activities of daily living as tolerated.

DIAGNOSIS(ES): _____   ICD-9-CM DIAGNOSIS(ES) CODE(S): _____

PROCEDURE(S): _____   MAIN TERM(S): _____

ICD-9-CM PROCEDURE CODE(S): _____

CASE 11

PREOPERATIVE DIAGNOSIS: Hernia through the hiatus, a diaphragmatic hernia with incarceration of the transverse colon.

POSTOPERATIVE DIAGNOSIS: Hernia through the hiatus, a diaphragmatic hernia with incarceration of the transverse colon.

PROCEDURES: 1. Abdominal exploration with repair of hiatus paraesophageal-type hernia. 2. Partial colectomy, transverse colon.

DESCRIPTION: Under general anesthesia, the patient was prepped and draped in the usual sterile manner. An upper midline incision was made through the fascia. The patient had a very large hernia through the hiatus with the stomach going into the hernia sac. The transverse colon had been reduced with induction of anesthesia. The diaphragmatic defect was repaired and the stomach was tacked laterally and medially to the crus of the diaphragm. The transverse colon was then removed and reanastomosed using a side-to-side functional end-to-end anastomosis. The abdomen was irrigated with saline solution. The fascia was closed in the usual manner. The skin was closed using staples. The patient tolerated the procedure well and was transferred to the recovery room in satisfactory condition. Sponge, needle, and instrument counts were correct ×2.

DIAGNOSIS(ES): _____   ICD-9-CM DIAGNOSIS(ES) CODE(S): _____

PROCEDURE(S): _____   MAIN TERM(S): _____

ICD-9-CM PROCEDURE CODE(S): _____

CASE 12

PREOPERATIVE DIAGNOSES: 1. Rectosigmoid colon cancer. 2. Umbilical hernia.

POSTOPERATIVE DIAGNOSES: 1. Rectosigmoid colon cancer. 2. Umbilical hernia.

PROCEDURES: 1. Exploratory laparotomy with low anterior resection with primary anastomosis of the colon. 2. Umbilical hernia repair.

DESCRIPTION: With the patient in the supine position, general anesthesia was obtained. A Foley catheter and NG tube were placed. The anterior abdomen was prepped and draped in the usual sterile manner. A midline incision was taken to the fascia which was divided. The colon cancer was palpated at the pelvic inlet at the rectosigmoid junction. We divided the sigmoid colon at approximately the midsigmoid level. The distal portion of the sigmoid was then grasped and held up. The rectum was divided in the usual manner. A primary end-to-end anastomosis was accomplished. On insufflation there were no leaks at the anastomosis. The abdomen was thoroughly irrigated with warm saline. We then closed the abdominal wall incision. A small umbilical hernia sac was removed. The fascia at the umbilicus was reapproximated. The skin was reapproximated with staples. The patient tolerated the procedure well and was taken to the recovery room in stable condition. Sponge, needle, and instrument counts were correct ×2.

DIAGNOSIS(ES): _____   ICD-9-CM DIAGNOSIS(ES) CODE(S): _____

PROCEDURE(S): _____   MAIN TERM(S): _____

ICD-9-CM PROCEDURE CODE(S): _____

Using the same excerpts in previous cases, write the name of the procedure and identify the main term. Assign the CPT codes to the procedures.

CASE 13

PREOPERATIVE DIAGNOSIS: Chronic cholecystitis and cholelithiasis.

POSTOPERATIVE DIAGNOSIS: Cholecystitis, cholelithiasis, and common duct stone.

OPERATION PERFORMED: Cholecystectomy and common bile duct exploration.

INDICATIONS: The patient is a 48-year-old female who was admitted to the hospital with a chronic history of right upper quadrant pain and with associated dyspepsia.

FINDINGS: Surgical intervention revealed numerous cholesterol stones. The initial cystic duct cholangiogram failed to reveal clear passage of dye into the duodenum. There was a concentric defect in the terminal common bile duct. After 1 mg of glucagon was given, cholangiograms were repeated and the common duct was open.

PROCEDURE(S): _____ MAIN TERM(S): _____

CPT PROCEDURE CODE(S): _____

CASE 14

PREOPERATIVE DIAGNOSIS: Foreign body in the upper esophagus.

POSTOPERATIVE DIAGNOSIS: Foreign body in the upper esophagus, a penny.

PROCEDURE: Upper esophagoscopy and removal of foreign body.

DESCRIPTION: With the patient in the supine position, general anesthesia was then administered. A laryngoscope was introduced and passed posteriorly into the hypopharynx and beyond the level of the cricopharynx. The foreign body was visualized in the upper esophagus. The penny was grasped with alligator-type forceps. The instrument and the penny were removed at the same time. The mucosa of the esophagus was intact and there was no laceration. The patient tolerated the procedure well and without complications.

PROCEDURE(S): _____ MAIN TERM(S): _____

CPT PROCEDURE CODE(S): _____

CASE 15

ADMITTING DIAGNOSIS: Morbid obesity.

DISCHARGE DIAGNOSIS: Morbid obesity.

PROCEDURES: 1. Open Roux-en-Y gastric bypass. 2. Removal of gastroplasty ring. 3. Liver biopsy. 4. G tube placement.

HOSPITAL COURSE: The patient was admitted for open Roux-en-Y gastric bypass, removal of gastroplasty ring, and liver biopsy. The patient did very well postoperatively. By the fourth postoperative day, she was tolerating bypass soft diet. She was discharged home with pain medications and discharge instructions. Activities of daily living as tolerated.

PROCEDURE(S): _____ MAIN TERM(S): _____

CPT PROCEDURE CODE(S): _____

CASE 16

PREOPERATIVE DIAGNOSIS: Hernia through the hiatus, a diaphragmatic hernia with incarceration of the transverse colon.

POSTOPERATIVE DIAGNOSIS: Hernia through the hiatus, a diaphragmatic hernia with incarceration of the transverse colon.

PROCEDURES: 1. Abdominal exploration with repair of hiatus paraesophageal-type hernia. 2. Partial colectomy, transverse colon.

DESCRIPTION: Under general anesthesia, the patient was prepped and draped in the usual sterile manner. An upper midline incision was made through the fascia. The patient had a very large hernia through the hiatus with the stomach going into the hernia sac. The transverse colon had been reduced with induction of anesthesia. The diaphragmatic defect was repaired and the stomach was tacked laterally and medially to the crus of the diaphragm. The transverse colon was then removed and reanastomosed using a side-to-side functional end-to-end anastomosis. The abdomen was irrigated with saline solution. The fascia was closed in the usual manner. The skin was closed using staples. The patient tolerated the procedure well and was transferred to the recovery room in satisfactory condition. Sponge, needle, and instrument counts were correct ×2.

PROCEDURE(S): _____ MAIN TERM(S): _____

CPT PROCEDURE CODE(S): _____

CASE 17

PREOPERATIVE DIAGNOSES: 1. Rectosigmoid colon cancer. 2. Umbilical hernia.

POSTOPERATIVE DIAGNOSES: 1. Rectosigmoid colon cancer. 2. Umbilical hernia.

PROCEDURES: 1. Exploratory laparotomy with low anterior resection with primary anastomosis of the colon. 2. Umbilical hernia repair.

DESCRIPTION: With the patient in the supine position, general anesthesia was obtained. A Foley catheter and NG tube were placed. The anterior abdomen was prepped and draped in the usual sterile manner. A midline incision was taken to the fascia which was divided. The colon cancer was palpated at the pelvic inlet at the rectosigmoid junction. We divided the sigmoid colon at approximately the midsigmoid level. The distal portion of the sigmoid was then grasped and held up. The rectum was divided in the usual manner. A primary end-to-end anastomosis was accomplished. On insufflation there were no leaks at the anastomosis. The abdomen was thoroughly irrigated with warm saline. We then closed the abdominal wall incision. A small umbilical hernia sac was removed. The fascia at the umbilicus was reapproximated. The skin was reapproximated with staples. The patient tolerated the procedure well and was taken to the recovery room in stable condition. Sponge, needle, and instrument counts were correct ×2.
Note: The patient is 60 years old.

PROCEDURE(S): _____ MAIN TERM(S): _____

CPT PROCEDURE CODE(S): _____

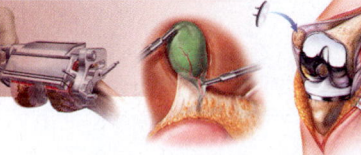

MEDICAL TERMINOLOGY CHALLENGE

Write a brief definition for each medical term. Use a medical dictionary as necessary.

1. anastomosis _____

2. clubbing _____

3. cricopharynx _____

4. cyanosis _____

5. Foley catheter _____

6. formalin _____

7. glucagon _____

8. hypopharynx _____

9. incarceration _____

10. insufflation _____

11. intraoral _____

12. lumen _____

13. mucosa _____

14. palpated _____

15. parotitis _____

16. percutaneous _____

17. serosal _____

18. splenic flexure _____

19. supine _____

NOTES:

_____   _____

_____   _____

_____   _____

_____   _____

_____   _____

_____   _____

_____   _____

_____   _____

NOTES:

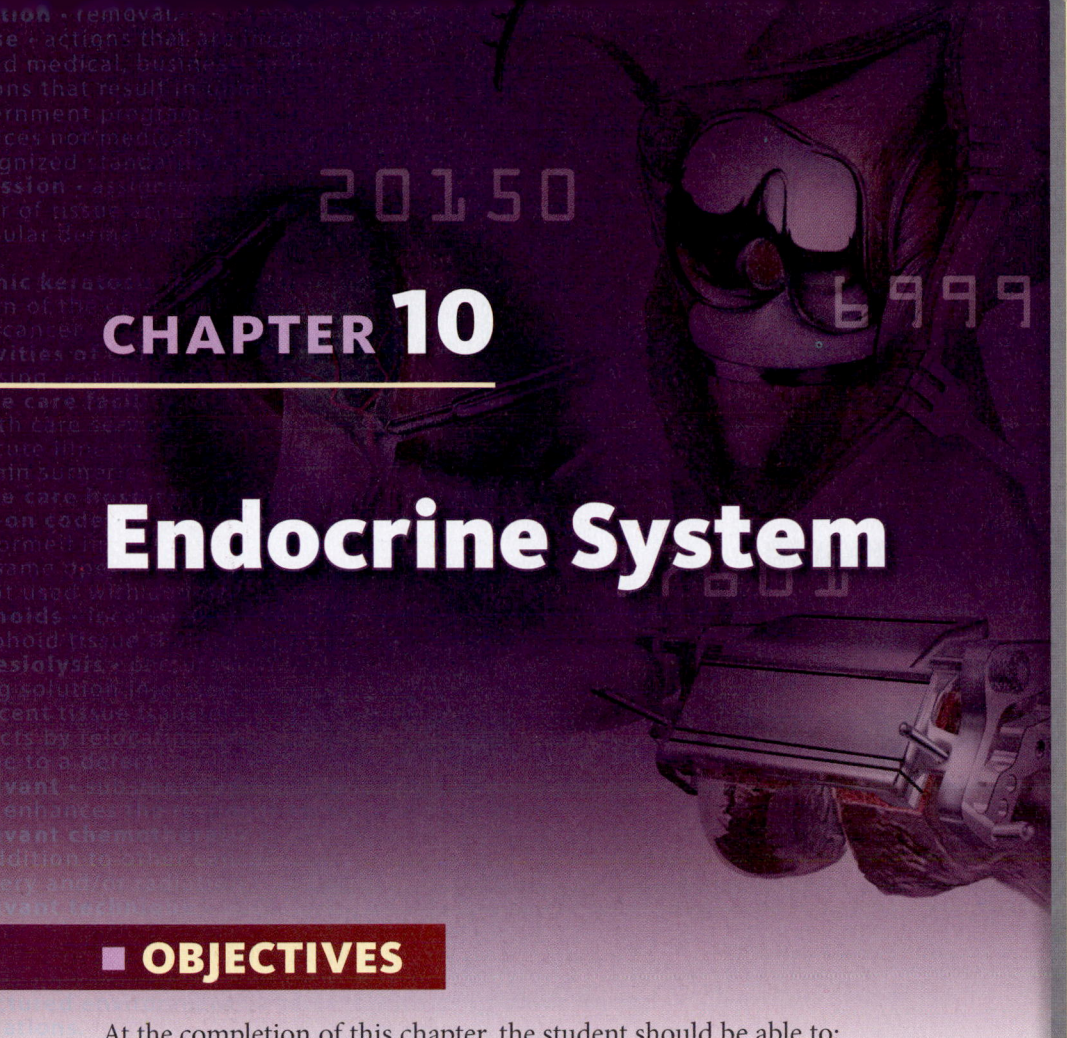

CHAPTER 10

Endocrine System

■ OBJECTIVES

At the completion of this chapter, the student should be able to:

1. Learn the word roots associated with the endocrine system.
2. Label the basic structures of the endocrine system.
3. Discuss the functions of the endocrine system.
4. Accurately spell and define endocrine system terminology.
5. Accurately assign medical codes to endocrine system diagnoses and procedures.

■ OVERVIEW

The endocrine system is made up of the pituitary gland, pineal gland, thyroid gland, parathyroid glands, thymus, adrenal gland, pancreas, ovaries, and testes. Endocrine glands are ductless and release their hormones directly into the bloodstream. **Hormones** are chemicals that maintain and regulate the growth and activity of specific organs and the body as a whole. For example, hormones from the thyroid gland regulate metabolism, adrenal gland hormones help maintain the body's fluid balance, and the hormones from the testes and ovaries are important to the development of secondary sex characteristics. In fact, every single aspect of human growth and development is affected by the hormones of the endocrine system. The medical specialty related to the endocrine system is **endocrinology** (en-doh-krin-**ALL**-oh-jee), and physician specialists are **endocrinologists** (en-doh-krin-**ALL**-oh-jists).

KEY TERMS

adrenal cortex
adrenal gland
adrenal medulla
adrenaline
adrenocorticotropic hormone (ACTH)
aldosterone
androgen
antidiuretic hormone (ADH)
calcitonin
cortisol
endocrinologist
endocrinology
epinephrine
estrogen
follicle-stimulating hormone (FSH)
glucagon
glucocorticoid
gonadocorticoid
growth hormone (GH)
hormone
hydrocortisone
insulin
islets of Langerhans
lactogenic hormone
luteinizing hormone (LH)
melanocyte-stimulating hormone (MSH)
melatonin
metabolism
mineralocorticoid
noradrenaline
norepinephrine
ovary
oxytocin
pancreas
parathyroid glands
parathyroid hormone (PTH)
pineal gland
pituitary gland
progesterone
prolactin
somatotropic hormone (STH)
testes
testosterone
thymopoietin
thymosin
thymus
thyroid gland
thyroid-stimulating hormone (TSH)
thyroxine (T_4)
triiodothyronine (T_3)
vasopressin

ENDOCRINE SYSTEM ROOTS, PREFIXES, AND SUFFIXES

Roots, prefixes, and suffixes associated with the endocrine system are listed in table 10-1. Review the word elements and complete the exercises.

Table 10-1 Endocrine System Roots, Prefixes, and Suffixes

ROOT	MEANING
acid/o	sour; bitter
acr/o	extremities
aden/o	gland
adren/o; adrenal/o	adrenal glands
andr/o	male; man
calc/i	calcium
cortic/o	cortex
dips/o	thirst
endocrin/o	endocrine
gonad/o	sex glands
gluc/o; glyc/o	glucose; sugar; sweet
kal/i	potassium
ket/o	ketone bodies
lact/o	milk
natr/o	sodium
pancreat/o	pancreas
parathyroid/o	parathyroid glands
somat/o	body
toxic/o	poison
thym/o	thymus gland
thyr/o; thyroid/o	thyroid gland

PREFIX	MEANING
eu-	same; normal
oxy-	sharp; quick
poly-	excessive

SUFFIX	MEANING
-crine	secrete
-emia	blood condition
-tropin	stimulating effect of a hormone

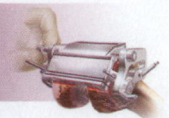

EXERCISE 10-1

Write the root, prefix, suffix, and their meaning. Based on the meanings, write a brief definition for each term.

1. Cortical
   ROOT: _cortic/o_ MEANING: _cortex_
   PREFIX: _____ MEANING: _____
   SUFFIX: _-al_ MEANING: _pertaining to_
   DEFINITION: _pertaining to the cortex_

2. Corticoid
   ROOT: _cortic/o_ MEANING: _cortex_
   PREFIX: _____ MEANING: _____
   SUFFIX: _-oid_ MEANING: _resembling_
   DEFINITION: _resembling the cortex_

3. Endocrinologist
   ROOT: _endocrin/o_ MEANING: _endocrine_
   PREFIX: _____ MEANING: _____
   SUFFIX: _ologist_ MEANING: _specialist_
   DEFINITION: _endocrine specialist_

4. Endocrinology
   ROOT: _endocrin/o_ MEANING: _endocrine_
   PREFIX: _endo-_ MEANING: _____
   SUFFIX: _-ology_ MEANING: _study of_
   DEFINITION: _study of within the endocrine_

5. Euthyroid
   ROOT: _thyroid/o_ MEANING: _thyroid gland_
   PREFIX: _eu_ MEANING: _normal_
   SUFFIX: _____ MEANING: _____
   DEFINITION: _normal thyroid_

6. Hypercalcemia
   ROOT: _calc/i_ MEANING: _calcium_
   PREFIX: _hyper-_ MEANING: _excessive_
   SUFFIX: _-emia_ MEANING: _blood condition_
   DEFINITION: _excessive calcium in the blood_

7. Hyperglycemia
   ROOT: _glyc/o_ MEANING: _glucose_
   PREFIX: _hyper-_ MEANING: _excessive_
   SUFFIX: _-emia_ MEANING: _blood condition_
   DEFINITION: _increased glucose in the blood_

8. Hyperkalemia
   ROOT: _Kal/i_ MEANING: _potassium_
   PREFIX: _hyper-_ MEANING: _excessive_
   SUFFIX: _-emia_ MEANING: _blood condition_
   DEFINITION: _excessive potassium in the blood_

9. Hypocalcemia
   ROOT: _calc/i_ MEANING: _calcium_
   PREFIX: _hypo-_ MEANING: _decreased_
   SUFFIX: _-emia_ MEANING: _blood condition_
   DEFINITION: _decreased calcium in the blood_

10. Hypoglycemia
    ROOT: _gly/o_ MEANING: _glucose_
    PREFIX: _hypo-_ MEANING: _deficient-decreased_
    SUFFIX: _-emia_ MEANING: _blood condition_
    DEFINITION: _decreased glucose in the blood._

11. Hypokalemia
    ROOT: _kal/i_ MEANING: _potassium_
    PREFIX: _hypo-_ MEANING: _decreased_
    SUFFIX: _-emia_ MEANING: _blood condition_
    DEFINITION: _decreased potassium in the blood._

12. Hyponatremia
    ROOT: _natr/o_ MEANING: _sodium_
    PREFIX: _hypo-_ MEANING: _deficient, decreased_
    SUFFIX: _-emia_ MEANING: _blood condition_
    DEFINITION: _decreased sodium in the blood_

13. Polydipsia
    ROOT: _dips/o_ MEANING: _thirst_
    PREFIX: _poly_ MEANING: _many, excessive_
    SUFFIX: _a_ MEANING: _noun ending_
    DEFINITION: _excessive thirst_

14. Somatotropin
    ROOT: _somat/o_ MEANING: _body_
    PREFIX: _____ MEANING: _____
    SUFFIX: _-tropin_ MEANING: _stimulating effect of a_
    DEFINITION: _stimulating effect of a hormone in the body — stimulating body growth_

15. Adrenalectomy
    ROOT: _adrenal/o_ MEANING: _adrenal gland_
    PREFIX: _____ MEANING: _____
    SUFFIX: _ectomy_ MEANING: _surgical removal_
    DEFINITION: _surgical excision of of the adrenal gland_

STRUCTURES OF THE ENDOCRINE SYSTEM

The major structures of the endocrine system include the (1) **pituitary gland**, (2) **pineal gland**, (3) **thyroid gland**, (4) **parathyroid glands**, (5) **thymus**, (6) **adrenal glands**, (7) **pancreas**, (8) **ovaries**, and (9) **testes**. The endocrine system structures are located throughout the body. Figure 10-1 illustrates the location of these structures.

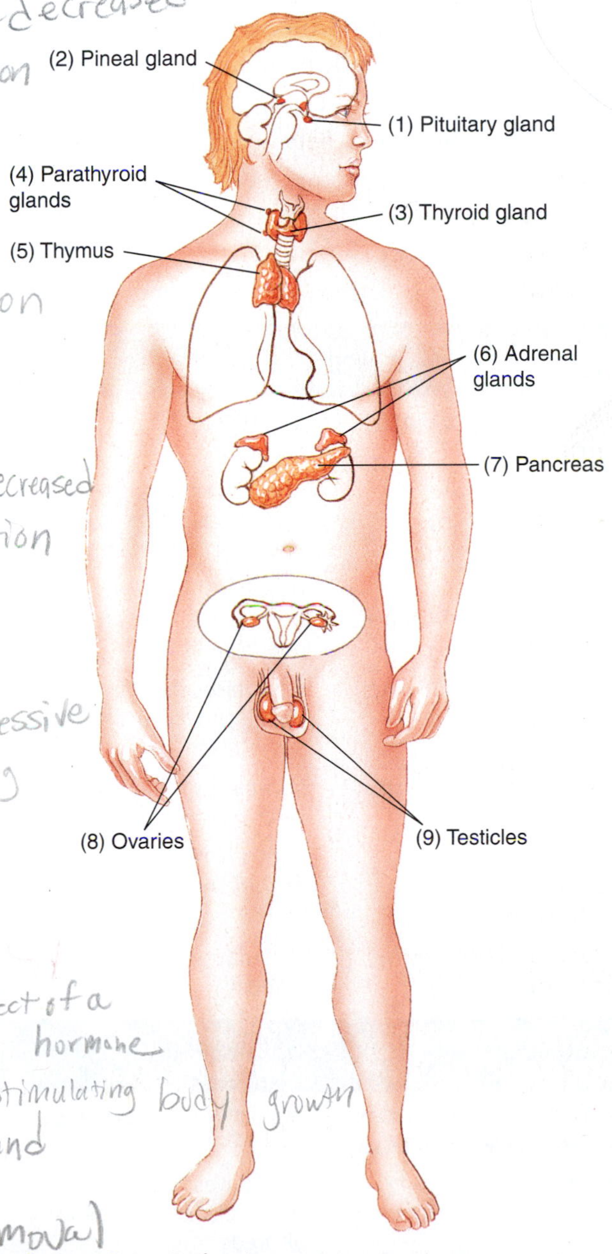

Figure 10-1 Endocrine system structures

Pituitary Gland

The pituitary gland, often called the *master gland,* is a pea-sized structure located at the base of the brain. The pituitary gland has two lobes, anterior and posterior, that secrete specific hormones. Table 10-2 describes the hormones of the anterior and posterior lobes of the pituitary gland. Pituitary gland hormones affect nearly all body functions.

Pineal Gland

The pineal gland is a pinecone-shaped gland located in the midbrain. The pineal gland secretes **melatonin** (mell-ah-**TOH**-nin), a hormone that seems to have a role in promoting sleep. Although the precise function of the pineal gland is not clearly understood, evidence suggests that this gland helps regulate our biological clock.

Table 10-2 Pituitary Gland Hormones

ANTERIOR LOBE HORMONES	FUNCTION
adrenocorticotropic hormone (ACTH)	stimulates the adrenal cortex
follicle-stimulating hormone (FSH)	stimulates estrogen secretion, ovum production, and sperm production
growth hormone (GH), or **somatotropic hormone (STH)**	regulates the growth of body tissues (i.e., muscles and bones)
lactogenic hormone, or **prolactin**	stimulates breast development and milk production
luteinizing hormone (LH)	stimulates ovulation and testosterone production
melanocyte-stimulating hormone (MSH)	controls the pigmentation of skin cells
thyroid-stimulating hormone (TSH)	stimulates the thyroid gland
POSTERIOR LOBE HORMONES	FUNCTION
antidiuretic hormone (ADH), or **vasopressin**	regulates urine secretion
oxytocin	stimulates uterine contractions and release of breast milk

Thyroid Gland and Parathyroid Glands

The thyroid gland is located in the neck and is attached to the trachea. The thyroid gland has two lobes, one on either side of the trachea, that are connected by a strip of tissue called the *isthmus.* The parathyroid glands are four round bodies of tissue on the back of the thyroid gland, two on each thyroid lobe. Figure 10-2 illustrates the (1) thyroid gland and the (2) parathyroid glands.

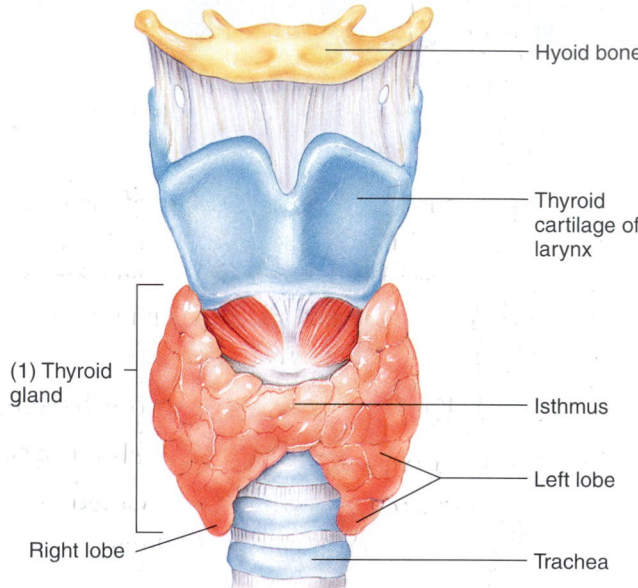

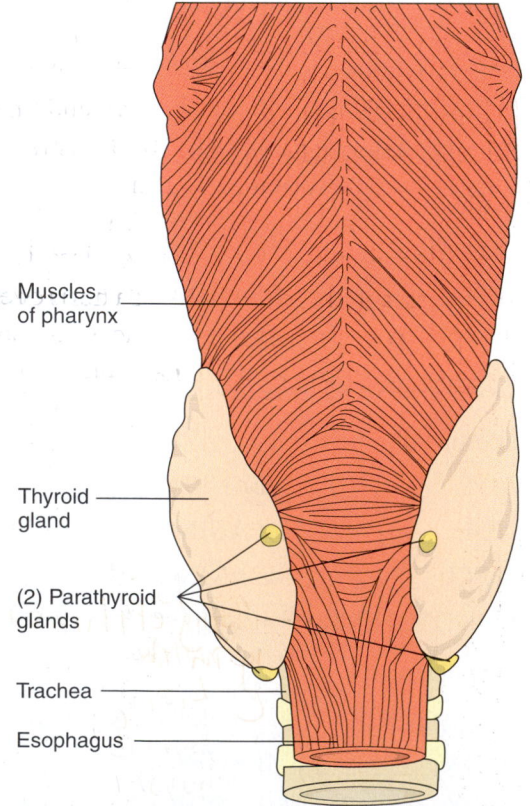

Figure 10-2 Thyroid and parathyroid glands

Thyroid gland hormones include **triiodothyronine** (try-**eye**-oh-doh-**THIGH**-roh-neen) (**T₃**), **thyroxine** (thigh-**ROCKS**-in) (**T₄**), and **calcitonin** (**kal**-sih-**TOH**-nin). T_3 and T_4 regulate growth and control body temperature and metabolism. **Metabolism** (meh-**TAB**-eh-lizm) is the total of all chemical processes that take place in a living organism. Calcitonin helps regulate the amount of calcium in the blood. The parathyroid glands secrete **parathyroid hormone (PTH)**. This hormone, in partnership with calcitonin, regulates the amount of calcium in the blood.

Thymus Gland

The thymus gland is located in the middle of the pleural cavity. It is large in infants and shrinks as the body ages. The thymus gland is primarily responsible for the development of the immune system. Figure 10-1 illustrates the location of this important gland. Thymus gland hormones include **thymosin** (thigh-**MOH**-sin) and **thymopoietin** (**thigh**-moh-**POY**-eh-tin), which stimulate the production of T cells. T cells are specialized lymphocytes and are part of the immune system.

Adrenal Glands

The (1) adrenal glands are two small glands that sit on top of each kidney. The adrenal gland consists of two parts: the (2) **adrenal cortex** (outer part) and the (3) **adrenal medulla** (inner part). Figure 10-3 illustrates the location and sections of the adrenal glands.

Each part of the adrenal gland secretes different hormones. The adrenal cortex hormones are classified as steroid hormones, and the adrenal medulla hormones are classified as nonsteroid hormones. Table 10-3 lists and describes the adrenal gland hormones.

Table 10-3 Adrenal Gland Hormones

STEROID HORMONES OF THE ADRENAL CORTEX	
Mineralocorticoids: regulate the fluid and electrolyte balance in the body	**Aldosterone** is the primary mineralocorticoid of the adrenal cortex
Glucocorticoids: influence the metabolism of carbohydrates, fats, and proteins; maintain normal blood pressure; have an anti-inflammatory effect during times of stress	**Cortisol**, also called **hydrocortisone**, is the primary glucocorticoid of the adrenal cortex and electrolyte balance in the body
Gonadocorticoids: sex hormones that contribute to the secondary sex characteristics in males and females	**Androgen** is one of the gonadocorticoid hormones secreted by the adrenal cortex
NONSTEROID HORMONES OF THE ADRENAL MEDULLA	
Epinephrine or **adrenaline:** increases heart rate, dilates the bronchioles, raises blood glucose levels	This hormone plays an important role in the body's response to stress by increasing the availability of oxygen and glucose in the blood
Norepinephrine or **noradrenaline:** causes the blood vessels to constrict and thereby raises the blood pressure	This hormone also plays an important role in the body's response to stress by raising the individual's blood pressure

Pancreas

The pancreas is a gland that is located in the upper left quadrant of the abdomen, under the stomach. Specialized pancreatic cells called the **islets** (**EYE**-lets) **of Langerhans** (**LONG**-er-honz) produce **insulin** and **glucagon** (**GLOO**-kah-gon), the pancreatic hormones.

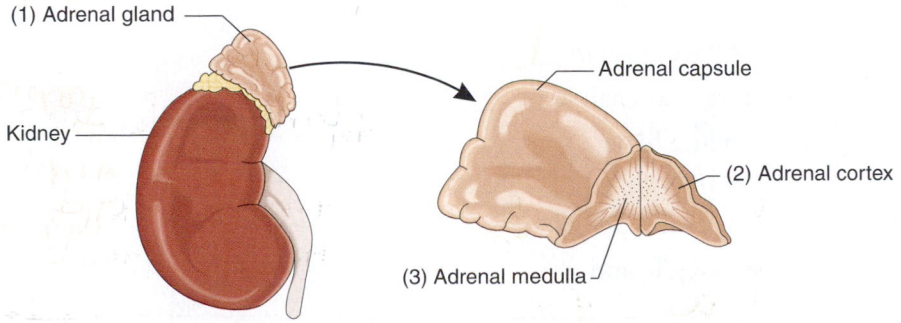

Figure 10-3 Adrenal glands

Insulin is responsible for decreasing the amount of glucose in the blood. Glucagon is responsible for increasing the amount of glucose in the blood. Figure 10-1 illustrates the pancreas.

Ovaries and Testes

The ovaries are female sex glands or gonads. There are two ovaries, one on each side of the pelvic cavity. The ovaries produce the hormones **estrogen** (**ESS**-troh-jen) and **progesterone** (proh-**JESS**-ter-ohn). Estrogen promotes the maturation of the ovum (egg) and prepares the uterus for implantation of a fertilized ovum. Estrogen is necessary for the development of female secondary sex characteristics. Progesterone also helps prepare the uterus for implantation and is responsible for the growth and development of the placenta.

Testes are the male sex organs, or gonads, and are contained in the scrotum. The testes produce **testosterone** (tess-**TOSS**-ter-ohn), the hormone responsible for the maturation of sperm and the development of male secondary sex characteristics. A complete discussion of the functions of the ovaries and testes is presented in chapters 11 and 12.

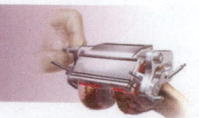

EXERCISE 10-3

Label the structures of the endocrine system identified in figure 10-4. Write your answer on the spaces provided.

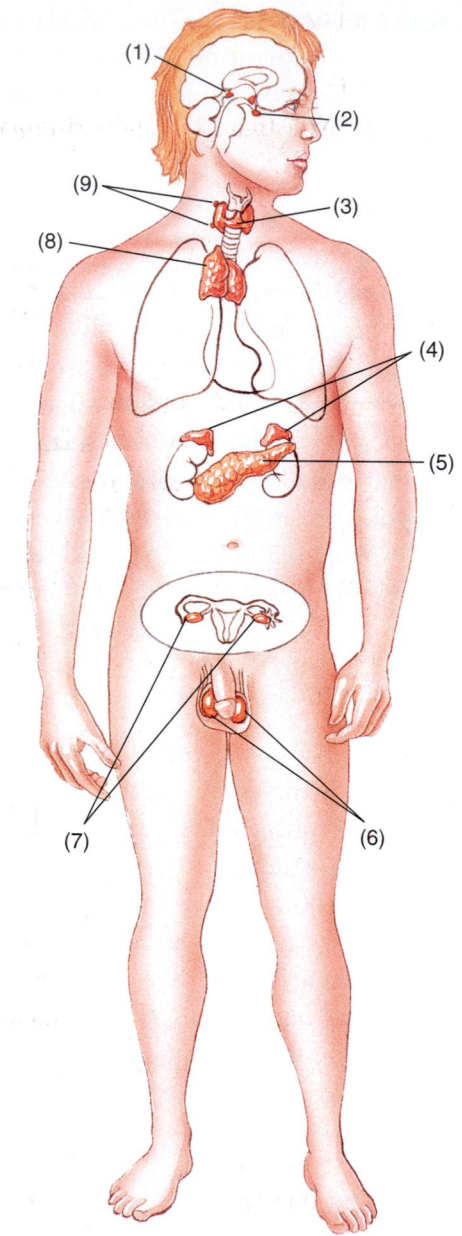

Figure 10-4 Label endocrine system structures

1. _Pineal gland_
2. _Pituitary gland_
3. _Thyroid glands_
4. _Adrenal glands_
5. _Pancreas_
6. _Testicles_

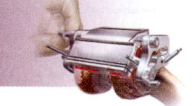

EXERCISE 10-2

Match the endocrine gland in column 1 with the correct definition in column 2.

COLUMN 1

a. thyroid gland

b. pancreas

c. testes

d. parathyroid glands

e. pituitary gland

f. adrenal glands

g. thymus

h. ovaries

COLUMN 2

1. produce male hormones _c_

2. primarily functions during childhood _g_

3. produces insulin _b_

4. secrete adrenaline _f_

5. produce female hormones _h_

6. four round bodies _d_

7. secretes T_3 and T_4 _a_

8. the master gland _e_

7. _Ovaries_
8. _thymus_
9. _parathyroid glands_

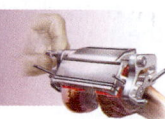

EXERCISE 10-4

Match the endocrine gland in column 1 with the hormone in column 2. Note that some endocrine glands will be used more than once.

COLUMN 1

a. adrenal cortex

b. adrenal medulla

c. anterior lobe of the pituitary gland

d. ovaries

e. pancreas

f. parathyroid glands

g. posterior lobe of the pituitary gland

h. testes

i. thymus gland

j. thyroid gland

COLUMN 2

1. adrenocorticotropic hormone _c_

2. androgen _a_

3. antidiuretic hormone _g_

4. calcitonin _j_

5. cortisol _a_

6. epinephrine _b_

7. estrogen _d_

8. glucagon _e_

9. growth hormone _c_

10. insulin _e_

11. testosterone _h_

12. PTH _f_

13. T_3, T_4 _j_

14. thymopoietin _i_

15. thyroid-stimulating hormone _c_

ENDOCRINE SYSTEM MEDICAL TERMINOLOGY

Endocrine system medical terms are organized by diseases, conditions, diagnostic procedures, and operations. There are two categories of medical terminology exercises: (1) those designed to provide opportunities to learn the terms, and (2) those designed to provide opportunities to accurately assign diagnosis and procedure codes. Medical coding exercises are available after all terms have been presented.

Endocrine System Signs, Symptoms, Diseases, and Conditions

Endocrine system medical terms include conditions related to endocrine system glands and hormones, nutritional deficiency conditions, and metabolic conditions. Nutritional conditions range from vitamin deficiencies to malnutrition. Metabolic conditions occur as a result of the inability of the body to process carbohydrates, fats, and proteins. The medical terms in table 10-4 are signs, symptoms, diseases, and conditions related to the endocrine system, nutritional conditions, and metabolic conditions. Review the meaning of these terms and complete the exercises.

Table 10-4 Endocrine System Signs, Symptoms, Diseases, and Conditions

TERM WITH PRONUNCIATION	DEFINITION
acidosis (ass-ih-**DOH**-sis) acid/o = sour; bitter -osis = condition	excessive acidity of body fluids
acromegaly (ak-roh-**MEG**-ah-lee) acr/o = extremities -megaly = enlargement	enlargement of the bones of the extremities and face due to excessive secretion of growth hormone
Addison disease	deficiency in the secretion of adrenal cortex hormones characterized by decreased functioning of the adrenal cortex; also called *primary or chronic adrenocortical insufficiency*

continued

Table 10-4 (*continued*) Endocrine System Signs, Symptoms, Diseases, and Conditions

TERM WITH PRONUNCIATION	DEFINITION
adrenalitis (ah-**dree**-nah-**LIGH**-tis) adren/o = adrenal gland -itis = inflammation	inflammation of the adrenal gland
adrenomegaly (ah-**dree**-noh-**MEG**-ah-lee) adren/o = adrenal gland -megaly = enlargement	enlargement of the adrenal gland
cretinism (**KREE**-tin-izm)	congenital condition related to severe hypothyroidism and a lack of thyroid hormone secretion; characterized by dwarfism and mental retardation
Cushing syndrome	metabolic condition characterized by chronic and excessive production of cortisol, an adrenal cortex hormone
diabetes insipidus (**digh**-ah-**BEE**-teez in-**SIP**-ih-dus)	a metabolic condition caused by a disorder of the pituitary gland characterized by copious secretion of urine and excessive thirst
diabetes mellitus (**digh**-ah-**BEE**-teez **MELL**-ih-tus)	condition characterized by the inability to metabolize carbohydrates, proteins, and fats due to insufficient insulin production, secretion, or the inability of insulin to perform its function; diabetes mellitus can be insulin-dependent (IDDM), which means the individual must inject insulin to control blood glucose levels, or non-insulin-dependent (NIDDM), which means blood glucose levels are controlled by diet alone or by diet and oral medication
diabetes mellitus, secondary	secondary diabetes mellitus can be caused by other health problems such as pancreatitis and cystic fibrosis that have a significant effect on the pancreas
diabetes mellitus, type 1	absence of insulin production due to pancreatic beta-cell dysfunction or destruction; formerly called juvenile-onset diabetes; also known as *insulin-dependent diabetes mellitus*
diabetes mellitus, type 2	insufficient secretion, production, or functional ability of insulin; formerly called adult-onset or late-onset diabetes mellitus; may be insulin-dependent or non-insulin-dependent
diabetic ketoacidosis (**kee**-toh-**ass**-ih-**DOH**-sis) (DKA) ket/o = ketone bodies acid/o = sour; bitter -osis = condition	accumulation of ketone bodies in the blood and excessive acidity of body fluid as a complication of diabetes mellitus
dwarfism	congenital condition characterized by abnormal underdevelopment due to a deficiency of human growth hormone
exophthalmia (**eks**-off-**THAL**-mee-ah) ex- = outward ophthalm/o = eye -ia = condition	abnormal outward protrusion of the eyeball; one of the signs of hyperthyroidism, specifically Graves disease; also called *exophthalmos*
gigantism	excessive size and height caused by excessive secretion of human growth hormone
goiter (**GOY**-ter)	hyperplasia of the thyroid gland due to a lack of dietary iodine; iodine is necessary for the production of thyroid hormones T_3 and T_4; classified as nontoxic and toxic, nodular or diffuse
Graves disease	hyperthyroidism characterized by excessive secretion or introduction of thyroid hormone and exophthalmia; also called *toxic diffuse goiter*
Hashimoto thyroiditis (**HASH**-ee-moh-to **thigh**-royd-**EYE**-tis) thyr/o = thyroid gland -itis = inflammation	an autoimmune disease in which the immune system produces antibodies that target thyroid cells; also called *Hashimoto disease* or *chronic lymphocytic thyroiditis*
hirsutism	excessive body hair, especially on a female in a male distribution pattern

continued

Table 10-4 (*continued*)   Endocrine System Signs, Symptoms, Diseases, and Conditions

TERM WITH PRONUNCIATION	DEFINITION
hypercalcemia (**high**-per-kal-SEE-mee-ah) hyper- = excessive calc/o = calcium -emia = blood condition	abnormal increase of calcium in the blood
hypercholesterolemia (**high**-per-koh-**less**-ter-oh-**LEE**-mee-ah) hyper- = increase cholesterol/o = cholesterol -emia = blood condition	abnormal increase of cholesterol in the blood; a disorder of lipid metabolism; other names include *familial hypercholesterolemia* and *hyperlipidemia group A*

EXERCISE 10-5

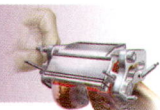

Circle the term that best fits the description.

1. primary adrenocortical insufficiency _____
   (Addison disease) or *Cushing syndrome*
2. disorder of the pituitary gland _____
   (diabetes insipidus) or *diabetes mellitus*
3. insulin-dependent diabetes mellitus _____
   DM type 2 or (*DM type 1*)
4. excessive body hair, male pattern _____
   (hirsutism) or *virilism*
5. autoimmune thyroiditis _____
   Graves disease or (Hashimoto disease)
6. chronic, excessive production of cortisol ____
   Addison disease or (Cushing syndrome)

EXERCISE 10-6

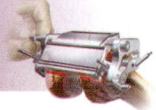

Write the medical term for each definition.

1. abnormal increase of calcium in the blood
   hypercalcemia

2. abnormal increase of cholesterol in the blood *hypercholesterolemia*
3. abnormal protrusion of the eyeball *exophthalmos; exophthalmia*
4. enlargement of facial and extremity bones *acromegaly*
5. enlargement of the adrenal gland *andrenomegaly*
6. excessive acidity of body fluids *diabetic Ketoacidosis*
7. hyperplasia of the thyroid gland *goiter*
8. inability to metabolize carbohydrates, proteins, and fats *diabetes mellitus*
9. inflammation of the adrenal gland *adrenalitis*
10. toxic diffuse goiter *graves disease*

The medical terms in table 10-5 are signs, symptoms, diseases, and conditions of the endocrine system. Review the meaning of these terms and complete the exercises.

Table 10-5   Endocrine System Signs, Symptoms, Diseases, and Conditions

TERM WITH PRONUNCIATION	DEFINITION
hyperglycemia (**high**-per-gligh-**SEE**-mee-ah) hyper- = increase glyc/o = glucose; sugar; sweet -emia = blood condition	abnormal increase of glucose in the blood
hyperkalemia (**high**-per-kal-**EE**-mee-ah) hyper- = increase kal/i = potassium -emia = blood condition	abnormal increase of potassium in the blood

continued

Table 10-5 (continued) Endocrine System Signs, Symptoms, Diseases, and Conditions

TERM WITH PRONUNCIATION	DEFINITION
hyperlipidemia (**high**-per-lip-ih-**DEE**-mee-ah) hyper- = excessive lipid/o = fat; lipids -emia = blood condition	abnormal increase of lipids, lipoproteins, and phospholipids in the blood
hyperthyroidism (**high**-per-**THIGH**-royd-izm) hyper- = excessive thyroid/o = thyroid gland -ism = condition	overactivity of the thyroid gland
hypocalcemia (**high**-poh-kal-**SEE**-mee-ah) hypo- = decreased calc/o = calcium -emia = blood condition	abnormal decrease of calcium in the blood
hypoglycemia (**high**-poh-gligh-**SEE**-mee-ah) hypo- = decreased glyc/o = glucose; sugar; sweet -emia = blood condition	abnormal decrease of glucose in the blood
hypokalemia (**high**-poh-kal-**EE**-mee-ah) hypo- = decrease kal/i = potassium -emia = blood condition	abnormal decrease of potassium in the blood
hyponatremia (**high**-poh-nah-**TREE**-mee-ah) hypo- = decrease natr/o = sodium -emia = blood condition	abnormal decrease of sodium in the blood
hypothyroidism (**high**-poh-**THIGH**-royd-izm) hypo- = decrease thyroid/o = thyroid gland -ism = condition	decreased activity of the thyroid gland
ketoacidosis (**kee**-toh-**ass**-ih-**DOH**-sis) ket/o = ketone bodies acid/o = sour; bitter -osis = condition	accumulation of ketone bodies in the blood and excessive acidity of body fluids; usually caused by extensive breakdown of fats due to inadequate carbohydrate metabolism; primarily occurs as a complication of diabetes mellitus
multiple endocrine neoplasia (MEN)	a hereditary hormonal disorder characterized by neoplasms occurring in several endocrine glands; types of neoplasms include hyperplasia, adenoma, or carcinoma
multiple endocrine neoplasia, type I (MEN-I)	hereditary disorder that affects the parathyroid glands, pancreatic islet cells, and pituitary gland; also called *multiple endocrine adenomatosis type I* and *Wermer syndrome*
multiple endocrine neoplasia, type IIA (MEN-IIA)	hereditary disorder that affects the adrenal glands, thyroid gland, and parathyroid glands; also called *multiple endocrine adenomatosis type II* and *Sipple syndrome*
multiple endocrine neoplasia, type IIB (MEN-IIB)	a syndrome characterized by multiple mucosal neuromas, carcinoma of the thyroid, and a vascular tumor of the adrenal medulla; also called *MEN-III, multiple endocrine adenomatosis type IIB,* and *mucosal neuroma syndrome*
myxedema (miks-eh-**DEE**-mah)	the most severe form of adult hypothyroidism, may lead to coma and death
pancreatitis (**pan**-kree-ah-**TIGH**-tis) pancreat/o = pancreas -itis = inflammation	inflammation of the pancreas
polydipsia (**pall**-ee-**DIP**-see-ah) poly- = many; excessive dips/o = thirst -ia = condition	excessive thirst

continued

Table 10-5 (*continued*) Endocrine System Signs, Symptoms, Diseases, and Conditions

TERM WITH PRONUNCIATION	DEFINITION
thyroiditis (**thigh**-royd-**EYE**-tis) thyroid/o = thyroid -itis = inflammation	inflammation of the thyroid gland; *acute thyroiditis* is caused by an infection; *subacute thyroiditis* is characterized by fever and painful enlargement of the thyroid gland; *chronic lymphocytic thyroiditis* is an autoimmune disease of the thyroid
thyrotoxicosis (**thigh**-roh-toks-ih-**KOH**-sis) thyr/o = thyroid gland toxic/o = poison -osis = condition	hyperthyroidism characterized by excess quantities of thyroid hormones in tissues; also called *Graves disease*
thyroid storm; thyroid crisis	a condition seen in poorly controlled or uncontrolled hyperthyroidism characterized by a high fever (may reach 106°F), acute respiratory distress, apprehension, and irritability; left untreated, coma and heart failure can occur
virilism (**VEER**-il-izm)	development of masculine physical traits in a female

EXERCISE 10-7

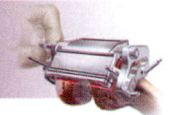

Replace the italicized phrase with the correct medical term.

1. Uncontrolled diabetes mellitus might result in *an accumulation of ketone bodies and increased acidity in the blood.* Ketoacidosis

2. *The most severe form of adult hypothyroidism is a life-threatening endocrine disease.* myx edema

3. Lack of female hormones might contribute to *the development of masculine traits in a female.* Viralism

4. *Excessive thirst* is a symptom of diabetes mellitus. polydipsia

5. *A decreased amount of potassium in the blood* has serious implications for heart function. hypoKalemia

6. Insufficient insulin secretion leads to *an abnormal increase of glucose in the blood.* hyperglycemia

7. *Inflammation of the pancreas* might interfere with adequate hormone secretion. pancreatitis

8. Weight control is an issue for individuals who have *decreased activity of the thyroid gland.* hypothyroidism

9. *Overactivity of the thyroid gland* may result in a goiter. hyperthyroidism

10. *An abnormal increase of lipids in the blood* may contribute to cardiovascular disease. hyperlipidemia

EXERCISE 10-8

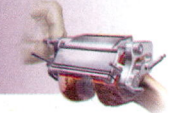

Match the condition in column 1 with the description in column 2.

COLUMN 1

a. acute thyroiditis

b. chronic lymphocytic thyroiditis

c. hyperkalemia

d. hyponatremia

e. MEN

f. MEN-I

g. MEN-IIA

h. MEN-IIB

i. subacute thyroiditis

j. thyroid storm

k. Thyrotoxicosis

COLUMN 2

1. abnormal increase of potassium in the blood __c__

2. autoimmune disease __b__

3. decrease of sodium in the blood __d__

4. Graves disease __K__

5. mucosal neuroma syndrome __h__

6. multiple endocrine neoplasia __e__

7. painful enlargement of the thyroid gland __i__

8. Sipple syndrome __g__

9. thyroid condition caused by an infection __a__

10. uncontrolled hyperthyroidism __j__

11. Wermer syndrome __f__

Endocrine System Diagnostic, Laboratory, and Treatment Terms

Endocrine system diseases and conditions, nutritional deficiencies, and metabolic disorders are treated with medication, dietary adjustments, and surgery. Review the pronunciation and definition of the diagnostic, laboratory, and treatment terms in table 10-6 and complete the exercise.

Table 10-6 Endocrine System Diagnostic, Laboratory, and Treatment Terms

LABORATORY/DIAGNOSTIC TEST	DEFINITION
diagnostic imaging	any diagnostic test that produces an image of the gland or organ under study; includes radiography, nuclear medicine (MRI, CT) scans, and ultrasonography
fasting plasma glucose (FPG)	blood test that measures the amount of glucose in the blood, the individual must fast 8–12 hours before the test; also called *fasting blood sugar* (FBS)
glucose tolerance test (GTT)	blood test that measures blood glucose levels 2–3 hours after the individual drinks a concentrated glucose solution
hemoglobin A_{1c} (HbA_{1c})	blood test that evaluates and measures blood glucose levels for the preceding two or three months; used to monitor blood glucose control in individuals with diabetes
radioactive iodine uptake (RAIU)	thyroid function test that measures thyroid activity by determining the amount of radioactive iodine that is taken up by the thyroid; a trace amount of radioactive iodine is administered orally or intravenously
thyroid scan	nuclear medicine imaging scan to determine the size, shape, and function of the thyroid gland
thyroid-stimulating hormone test	blood test that measures the concentration of thyroid-stimulating hormone in the blood
TREATMENT TERMS WITH PRONUNCIATION	**DEFINITION**
adrenalectomy (ah-**dreen**-al-**EK**-toh-mee) adrenal/o = adrenal gland -ectomy = surgical removal	surgical removal of one or both of the adrenal glands
hormone replacement	replacement of endocrine gland hormones
parathyroidectomy (**pair**-ah-**thigh**-royd-**EK**-toh-mee) parathyroid/o = parathyroid gland -ectomy = surgical removal	surgical removal of one or all of the parathyroid glands
thyroidectomy (**thigh**-royd-**EK**-toh-mee) thyroid/o = thyroid -ectomy = surgical removal	surgical removal of all or part of the thyroid gland

EXERCISE 10-9

Place an X next to the endocrine system blood test.

1. diagnostic imaging _____

2. fasting plasma glucose _____

3. glucose tolerance test _____

4. hemoglobin A_{1c} _____

5. radioactive iodine uptake _____

6. thyroid-stimulating hormone test _____

ABBREVIATIONS

Endocrine system abbreviations are listed in table 10-7. Practice writing out the abbreviations with a brief definition for each phrase or term.

Table 10-7 Abbreviations

ABBREVIATION	MEANING
ACTH	adrenocorticotropic hormone
ADH	antidiuretic hormone
DM-I	diabetes mellitus, type 1
DM-II	diabetes mellitus, type 2
DKA	diabetic ketoacidosis
FBS	fasting blood sugar
FPG	fasting plasma glucose
FSH	follicle-stimulating hormone
GH	growth hormone
GTT	glucose tolerance test
HbA_{1c}	hemoglobin A_{1c}
IDDM	insulin-dependent diabetes mellitus
LH	luteinizing hormone
MEN	multiple endocrine neoplasia
MEN-I	multiple endocrine neoplasia, type I
MEN-IIA	multiple endocrine neoplasia, type IIA
MEN-IIB	multiple endocrine neoplasia, type IIB
MSH	melanocyte-stimulating hormone
NIDDM	non-insulin-dependent diabetes mellitus
PTH	parathyroid hormone
RAIU	radioactive iodine uptake test
STH	somatotropin hormone
T_3	triiodothyronine
T_4	thyroxine
TSH	thyroid-stimulating hormone

ENDOCRINE SYSTEM MEDICAL CODING

To successfully complete the exercises in this section, the ICD-9-CM volumes 1, 2, and 3, and the CPT (Current Procedural Terminology) coding references must be readily available. The information in this section is presented as follows:

- An introduction to ICD-9-CM, chapter 3, "Endocrine, Nutritional, and Metabolic Diseases and Immunity Disorders"
- ICD-9-CM diagnosis coding exercises

- A summary of ICD-9-CM volume 3 coding conventions that apply to endocrine system procedures
- ICD-9-CM procedure coding exercises
- A summary of the CPT Endocrine System coding guidelines
- CPT coding exercises

Students are *strongly* encouraged to review the information at the beginning of the ICD-9-CM and CPT coding references. Commercial publishers include instructions on how to use the ICD-9-CM references, the ICD-9-CM official coding conventions, additional conventions used by the publisher, and the *ICD-9-CM Official Guidelines for Coding and Reporting*. Some publishers include the three ICD-9-CM volumes in one book and put the *Alphabetic Index* (volume 2) at the beginning of the reference.

The *Introduction* to CPT includes detailed instructions for using this code book, an index to the illustrations throughout the book, and anatomical illustrations of the major structures of body systems.

ICD-9-CM Volume 1, Chapter 3, Endocrine, Nutritional, and Metabolic Diseases and Immunity Disorders (240–279)

Endocrine system disorders or diseases are coded to ICD-9-CM volume 1, chapter 3, "Endocrine, Nutritional, and Metabolic Diseases and Immunity Disorders." The coding categories related to the endocrine system include the following:

- **Disorders of Thyroid Gland (240–246).** Codes in this section cover goiters, hyperthyroidism, hypothyroidism, thyrotoxicosis, thyroiditis, and other disorders of the thyroid gland.
- **Diseases of Other Endocrine Glands (249–259).** Codes in this section include diabetes mellitus, secondary diabetes, and disorders or diseases of the parathyroid glands, pituitary gland, thymus, adrenal glands, ovaries, testes, polyglandular dysfunction, and other endocrine disorders.

continued

- **Nutritional Deficiencies (260–269).** Codes in this section cover malnutrition, vitamin deficiencies, and other conditions related to poor nutrition.

- **Other Metabolic and Immunity Disorders (270–279).** Codes in this section cover various metabolic conditions, disorders of lipid metabolism, gout, cystic fibrosis, obesity, and immunodeficiencies related to a lack of various immunoglobulins.

240.0   253.0   250.01   272.0   244.9

In order to accurately code diabetes mellitus, the medical coder must pay close attention to *includes* and *excludes* notes, fifth-digit notes, and *use additional code* instructions. For example, diabetic retinopathy requires two codes. The first-listed code reflects the status of the diabetes mellitus (insulin-dependent or non-insulin-dependent; not stated as uncontrolled or uncontrolled), and the additional code identifies the type of retinopathy. Retinopathy is a disease of the retina of the eye and is coded to chapter 6, "Diseases of the Nervous System and Sense Organs." Documentation in the health record must clearly support the selected codes.

Conditions related to the endocrine system may also be coded to the following chapters in volume 1: chapter 14, "Congenital Anomalies"; chapter 16, "Symptoms, Signs, and Ill-Defined Conditions"; and chapter 2, "Neoplasms."

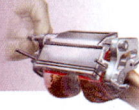

EXERCISE 10-10

245.2

Write a brief definition for each diagnosis. Identify the main term in the diagnostic statement and assign the correct ICD-9-CM diagnosis code(s).

1. Goiter, simple

   DEFINITION: _____

   MAIN TERM: _____

   ICD-9-CM CODE(S): *240.0*

2. Multinodular goiter of the thyroid, toxic

   DEFINITION: _____

   MAIN TERM: _____

   ICD-9-CM CODE(S): _____

3. Acromegaly

   DEFINITION: _____

   MAIN TERM: _____

   ICD-9-CM CODE(S): *253.0*

4. Cushing syndrome

   DEFINITION: _____

   MAIN TERM: _____

   ICD-9-CM CODE(S): _____

5. Diabetes mellitus, type 1, insulin-dependent

   DEFINITION: _____

   MAIN TERM: _____

   ICD-9-CM CODE(S): *250.01*

6. Toxic diffuse goiter

   DEFINITION: _____

   MAIN TERM: _____

   ICD-9-CM CODE(S): _____

7. Familial hypercholesterolemia

   DEFINITION: _____

   MAIN TERM: _____

   ICD-9-CM CODE(S): *272.0*

8. Diabetic ketoacidosis

   DEFINITION: _____

   MAIN TERM: _____

   ICD-9-CM CODE(S): _____

9. Myxedema

   DEFINITION: _____

   MAIN TERM: _____

   ICD-9-CM CODE(S): *244.9*

10. Postsurgical hypothyroidism

    DEFINITION: _____

    MAIN TERM: _____

    ICD-9-CM CODE(S): _____

11. Hashimoto disease

    DEFINITION: _____

    MAIN TERM: _____

    ICD-9-CM CODE(S): *245.2*

12. Diabetes mellitus, type 2

DEFINITION: _____

MAIN TERM: _____

ICD-9-CM CODE(S): _____

13. Addison disease

DEFINITION: _____

MAIN TERM: _____

ICD-9-CM CODE(S): _255.41_

14. Vitamin B$_{12}$ deficiency

DEFINITION: _____

MAIN TERM: _____

ICD-9-CM CODE(S): _____

15. Gouty arthritis

DEFINITION: _____

MAIN TERM: _____

ICD-9-CM CODE(S): _274.0_

16. Morbid obesity

DEFINITION: _____

MAIN TERM: _____

ICD-9-CM CODE(S): _____

17. Hypocalcemia

DEFINITION: _____

MAIN TERM: _____

ICD-9-CM CODE(S): _275.41_

18. Hypokalemia

DEFINITION: _____

MAIN TERM: _____

ICD-9-CM CODE(S): _____

19. Cystic fibrosis

DEFINITION: _____

MAIN TERM: _____

ICD-9-CM CODE(S): _277.00_

20. Diabetes insipidus

DEFINITION: _____

MAIN TERM: _____

ICD-9-CM CODE(S): _____

ICD-9-CM Volume 3, Chapter 2, Operations on the Endocrine System (06–07)

Endocrine system operations and diagnostic procedures are coded to ICD-9-CM volume 3, chapter 2, "Operations on the Endocrine System." This chapter includes the following major categories:

- **Operations on the Thyroid and Parathyroid Glands (06).** Codes in this category cover incision, aspiration, excision, and biopsies of the thyroid and parathyroid glands.

- **Operations on Other Endocrine Glands (07).** Codes in this category cover explorations, incisions, excisions, and biopsies of the adrenal glands, pituitary gland, pineal gland, and thymus.

Two categories in ICD-9-CM volume 3, chapter 16, Miscellaneous Diagnostic and Therapeutic Procedures, include codes that specifically mention endocrine glands or endocrine hormones. The categories are *Nuclear medicine* (92) and *Injection or infusion of therapeutic or prophylactic substance* (99.1).

EXERCISE 10-11

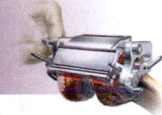

Write a brief definition for each operative, treatment, or diagnostic procedure term. Identify the main term in the statement and assign the correct ICD-9-CM code(s).

1. Complete parathyroidectomy

DEFINITION: _____

MAIN TERM: _____

ICD-9-CM CODE(S): _06.81_

2. Iodine uptake scan of the thyroid gland

DEFINITION: _____

MAIN TERM: _____

ICD-9-CM CODE(S): _____

continued

3. Percutaneous aspiration biopsy of the thyroid gland

DEFINITION: _____

MAIN TERM: _____

ICD-9-CM CODE(S): _____O6.11_____

4. Radioisotope scan of the parathyroid glands

DEFINITION: _____

MAIN TERM: _____

ICD-9-CM CODE(S): _____

5. Thoracoscopic total excision of the thymus

DEFINITION: _____

MAIN TERM: _____

ICD-9-CM CODE(S): _____07.84_____

6. Total excision of the pituitary gland, frontal approach

DEFINITION: _____

MAIN TERM: _____

ICD-9-CM CODE(S): _____

Current Procedural Terminology (CPT) Endocrine System Codes (60000–60699)

60100   60220   60254   82951

CPT endocrine system codes are located in the Surgery section, the Radiology section, and the Chemistry subsection of the Pathology and Laboratory section.

- **Endocrine System (60000–60699).** Codes in this subsection include incision, excision, and removal of the endocrine glands.

- **Radiology/Nuclear Medicine (78000–78099).** Endocrine system codes in this subsection cover nuclear imaging of the thyroid, parathyroid, and adrenal glands; thyroid uptake studies; and thyroid cancer metastases imaging.

- **Pathology and Laboratory, Chemistry Subsection (82000–84999).** Codes in this subsection include blood tests for hormone levels in the blood, glucose tolerance tests, and laboratory test panels that include glucose blood levels.

Identify the main term in each statement. Assign the correct CPT code(s).

1. Percutaneous core needle biopsy of the thyroid gland

MAIN TERM: _____

CPT CODE(S): _____60100_____

2. Total thyroidectomy

MAIN TERM: _____

CPT CODE(S): _____

3. Unilateral total thyroid lobectomy

MAIN TERM: _____

CPT CODE(S): _____60220_____

4. Re-exploration of the parathyroid glands

MAIN TERM: _____

CPT CODE(S): _____

5. Total thyroidectomy for thyroid carcinoma with radical neck dissection

MAIN TERM: _____

CPT CODE(S): _____60254_____

6. Thyroid-stimulating hormone blood test

MAIN TERM: _____

CPT CODE(S): _____

7. Glucose tolerance test, three specimens taken

MAIN TERM: _____

CPT CODE(S): _____82951_____

■ SUMMARY

This chapter covered medical terms related to the endocrine system. Endocrine system diagnoses and procedures were identified and defined. Endocrine diseases are coded to ICD-9-CM volume 1, chapter 3, "Endocrine, Nutritional, and Metabolic Diseases and Immunity Disorders"; chapter 2, "Neoplasms"; chapter 14, "Congenital Anomalies"; and chapter 16, "Symptoms, Signs, and Ill-Defined Conditions."

Current Procedural Terminology (CPT) endocrine procedure codes are found in the CPT Surgery subsection, Endocrine System (60000–60699), and the Radiology, Medicine, and Pathology and Laboratory sections.

■ CHAPTER REVIEW

790.29

Read the medical report excerpts. Write the diagnosis(es) and the main term. Assign the correct ICD-9-CM diagnosis(es) code(s).

CASE 1

Viola was seen today for a glucose tolerance test. Her fasting blood sugar, which was done two days ago, revealed hyperglycemia, which is indicative of diabetes mellitus. The results of the GTT will confirm or rule out that diagnosis.

DIAGNOSIS(ES): _____

MAIN TERM(S): _____

ICD-9-CM DIAGNOSIS(ES) CODE(S): ___790.21_____

CASE 2

Gerald has recent complaints of fatigue, lack of energy, and weight gain. His initial thyroid function test showed a decreased level of T_3 and T_4. A follow-up thyroid-stimulating hormone test ruled out pituitary malfunction. Thyroid scan reveals several cold thyroid nodules. Biopsy is scheduled for tomorrow. 241.0

DIAGNOSIS(ES): _____

MAIN TERM(S): _____

ICD-9-CM DIAGNOSIS(ES) CODE(S): _____

CASE 3

Ms. Shim was seen today to discuss the results of her recent thyroid lab and diagnostic imaging workup. Based on the results, Ms. Shim was informed that she definitely has hyperthyroidism with a nodular goiter. She asked if there was an appropriate medical course of treatment. We discussed the pros and cons of thyroid hormone replacement therapy and that definitive treatment is partial thyroidectomy. She will call tomorrow with her final decision. If she opts for surgery, our office will make the appropriate referral. 242.30

DIAGNOSIS(ES): _____

MAIN TERM(S): _____

ICD-9-CM DIAGNOSIS(ES) CODE(S): ___242.30_____

CASE 4

Mrs. Morris is here today with her son Jerome who is five years old. We have been following Jerome for the past two years because his growth pattern has remained in the 2nd percentile since infancy. His growth has been abnormally slow, with normal proportions. After a thorough review of his nutritional status, we continued with a complete endocrinological workup. Based on bone maturation, as revealed via a left hand x-ray last week, we suspected some type of pituitary problem. MRI of the head was within normal limits. There were no pituitary growths, tumors, or pituitary

253.2

atrophy. Laboratory test results confirm idiopathic hypopituitarism. Jerome will begin a course of recombinant growth hormone, titrated to his current weight. We will monitor his progress on a monthly basis.

DIAGNOSIS(ES): _____

MAIN TERM(S): _____

ICD-9-CM DIAGNOSIS(ES) CODE(S): _____

CASE 5

Ms. Fisher has been a patient for six months, with an initial complaint of having a "hairy body, almost like a man." Initial laboratory and imaging tests effectively ruled out hypomenorrhea and elevated testosterone associated with polycystic ovary syndrome. MRI of the adrenals was normal, with no tumors, growths, or adrenal hypertrophy. Ms. Fisher continued to experience hirsutism, selective alopecia, acne, and most recently deepening of her voice. Laboratory tests demonstrated elevated blood levels of adrenal androgens. This is consistent with adrenal virilism syndrome with hirsutism. We will begin treatment with appropriate medications. Ms. Fisher understands that most symptoms will disappear, with hirsutism and virilism taking more time. She is aware that her voice may remain a little deeper than before. Fertility issues were discussed. Further workup to determine long-range fertility problems will be deferred until androgen levels are normal for six months.

DIAGNOSIS(ES): _____

MAIN TERM(S): _____

ICD-9-CM DIAGNOSIS(ES) CODE(S): _255.2_____704.1_____

Note: Due to the limited availability of endocrinology operative and procedure reports, only one full report is available for the next set of medical coding exercises.

    Read the operative report. Write the diagnosis and the ICD-9-CM diagnosis code. Write the name of the procedure and main terms. Assign the correct ICD-9-CM procedure code.

CASE 6

INDICATIONS: This 65-year-old male was recently worked up for suspected thyroid cancer. A thyroid scan revealed an enlargement of the thyroid, both lobes, with hot nodules in each lobe. Fine-needle aspiration biopsy confirmed the malignancy, either papillary or follicular carcinoma of the thyroid. Due to the possibility of follicular carcinoma, surgery was scheduled this week.

PREOPERATIVE DIAGNOSIS: Thyroid nodules, both lobes, rule out follicular carcinoma.

POSTOPERATIVE DIAGNOSIS: Follicular carcinoma, both lobes of the thyroid.

PROCEDURE: Total thyroidectomy with isthmusectomy, frozen section, and lymph node resection and frozen section.

DETAILS: The patient was given adequate general anesthesia, prepped, and draped in the usual sterile manner. A sand bag was placed under the shoulder blades, and the neck was extended and stabilized. A transverse skin incision was made in the anterior part of the neck, and deepened through the subcutaneous tissue and platysma. Hemostasis was obtained with cautery. The midline fascia was incised and strap muscles were separated from the thyroid gland. Retractors were placed and the entire thyroid was exposed. The left lobe of the thyroid was excised and sent for frozen section. The pathology report confirmed follicular carcinoma of the thyroid. Since the nodules in both lobes were histologically similar, the decision was made to proceed with total thyroidectomy, isthmusectomy, and resection of local lymph nodes. Frozen sections of lymph nodes were free of any abnormal cells. At the end of the procedure the vocal cords were inspected and were moving equally well. Sponge, instruments, and needle counts were correct ×2. The patient tolerated the procedure well and was sent to the recovery room in stable condition. Blood loss was minimal.

DIAGNOSIS: _____ ICD-9-CM DIAGNOSIS CODE: _____

PROCEDURE(S): _____ MAIN TERM(S): _____

ICD-9-CM PROCEDURE CODE(S): _____

Using the procedure statements from previous cases, write the main term(s) for each procedure. Assign the correct CPT codes.

CASE 7

PROCEDURE: Complete parathyroidectomy.

MAIN TERM: _____

CPT CODE(S): _____60500_____

CASE 8

PROCEDURE: Iodine uptake scan of the thyroid gland.

MAIN TERM: _____

CPT CODE(S): _____

CASE 9

PROCEDURE: Percutaneous aspiration biopsy of the thyroid gland.

MAIN TERM: _____

CPT CODE(S): _____60100_____

CASE 10

PROCEDURE: Radioisotope scan of the parathyroid glands.

MAIN TERM: _____

CPT CODE(S): _____

CASE 11

PROCEDURE: Thoracoscopic total excision of the thymus.

MAIN TERM: _____

CPT CODE(S): _____60521_____

CASE 12

PROCEDURE: Total excision of the pituitary gland, intracranial approach.

MAIN TERM: _____

CPT CODE(S): _____

CASE 13

INDICATIONS: This 65-year-old male was recently worked up for suspected thyroid cancer. A thyroid scan revealed an enlargement of the thyroid, both lobes, with hot nodules in each lobe. Fine-needle aspiration biopsy confirmed the malignancy, either papillary or follicular carcinoma of the thyroid. Due to the possibility of follicular carcinoma, surgery was scheduled this week.

PREOPERATIVE DIAGNOSIS: Thyroid nodules, both lobes, rule out follicular carcinoma.

POSTOPERATIVE DIAGNOSIS: Follicular carcinoma, both lobes of the thyroid.

PROCEDURE: Total thyroidectomy with isthmusectomy, frozen section, and lymph node resection and frozen section.

DETAILS: The patient was given adequate general anesthesia, prepped, and draped in the usual sterile manner. A sand bag was placed under the shoulder blades, and the neck was extended and stabilized. A transverse skin incision was made in the anterior part of the neck, and deepened through the subcutaneous tissue and platysma. Hemostasis was obtained with cautery. The midline fascia was incised and strap muscles were separated from the thyroid gland. Retractors were placed and the entire thyroid was exposed. The left lobe of the thyroid was excised and sent for frozen section. The pathology report confirmed follicular carcinoma of the thyroid. Since the nodules in both lobes were histologically similar, the decision was made to proceed with total thyroidectomy, isthmusectomy, and resection of local lymph nodes. Frozen sections of lymph nodes were free of any abnormal cells. At the end of the procedure the vocal cords were inspected and were moving equally well. Sponge, instruments, and needle counts were correct ×2. The patient tolerated the procedure well and was sent to the recovery room in stable condition. Blood loss was minimal.

PROCEDURE(S): _____

MAIN TERM(S): _____

CPT CODE(S): _____

MEDICAL TERMINOLOGY CHALLENGE

Write a brief description of the disease, condition, or abbreviation. Identify the endocrine gland that is associated with the listed diseases and conditions.

1. Acromegaly

   DESCRIPTION: _____

   ENDOCRINE GLAND: _____

2. Addison disease

   DESCRIPTION: _____

   ENDOCRINE GLAND: _____

3. IDDM

   DESCRIPTION: _____

   ENDOCRINE GLAND: _____

4. Diabetes insipidus

   DESCRIPTION: _____

   ENDOCRINE GLAND: _____

5. Cushing syndrome

   DESCRIPTION: _____

   ENDOCRINE GLAND: _____

6. Graves disease

   DESCRIPTION: _____

   ENDOCRINE GLAND: _____

7. Hashimoto disease

   DESCRIPTION: _____

   ENDOCRINE GLAND: _____

8. Virilism

   DESCRIPTION: _____

   ENDOCRINE GLAND: _____

NOTES:

_____ _____

_____ _____

_____ _____

_____ _____

_____ _____

_____ _____

NOTES:

CHAPTER 11

Genitourinary System

■ OBJECTIVES

At the completion of this chapter, the student should be able to:

1. Learn the word roots associated with the genitourinary system.
2. Label the basic structures of the genitourinary system.
3. Discuss the functions of the genitourinary system.
4. Accurately spell and define genitourinary system terminology.
5. Accurately assign medical codes to genitourinary system diagnoses and procedures.

■ OVERVIEW

The genitourinary system includes the structures of the urinary system and the male reproductive system. Urinary system structures are the kidneys, ureters, urinary bladder, and urethra. These structures function together for the following purposes: (1) to filter the blood; (2) to maintain the proper balance of water, salts, and other substances found in our body fluids; and (3) to remove waste and excess fluids from the body.

The structures of the male reproductive system include the testes, epididymis, vas deferens, seminal vesicle, ejaculatory duct, prostate gland, Cowper gland, urethra, and penis. These structures function to produce male hormones and to produce, sustain, and transport **spermatozoa** (sper-**mat**-oh-**ZOH**-ah), usually called **sperm**. The reproductive structures are collectively known as the male **genitalia** (jen-ih-**TAY**-lee-ah). **Urology** is the medical specialty for this system and the physician specialist is a **urologist**.

KEY TERMS

ammonia
bulbourethral gland
circumcision
cortex
Cowper gland
creatinine
ejaculatory duct
epididymis
genitalia
glans penis
glomerulus
kidneys
medulla
micturition
nephron
penis
prepuce
prostate gland
renal pelvis
renal tubule
scrotum
semen
seminal vesicle
seminiferous tubule
sperm
spermatic cord
spermatozoa
testes
urea
ureters
urethra
urethral meatus
urinary bladder
urinary meatus
urologist
urology
vas deferens

GENITOURINARY SYSTEM ROOTS, PREFIXES, AND SUFFIXES

Roots, prefixes, and suffixes associated with the genito-urinary system are listed in table 11-1. Review the word elements and complete the exercises.

Table 11-1   Genitourinary System Roots, Prefixes, and Suffixes

ROOT	MEANING
andr/o	male
balan/o	glans penis
crypt/o	hidden
cyst/o	bladder; sac; urinary bladder
glomerul/o	glomerulus
hydr/o	water
lith/o	stone
meat/o	meatus (opening)
nephr/o	kidney
noct/o	night
olig/o	few; diminished
orch/o; orchi/o; orchid/o	testis; testes
prostat/o	prostate
pyel/o	renal pelvis
ren/o	kidney
semin/i	semen
sperm/o; spermat/o	sperm; spermatic cord
test/o; testicul/o	testes; testis; testicle
ur/o	urine; urinary system
ureter/o	ureter
varic/o	twisted veins or vessels
vas/o	vessel
vesic/o	urinary bladder

PREFIX	MEANING
a-; an-	without; lack of
carcin-	cancer
epi-	upon; on

SUFFIX	MEANING
-cele	hernia; protrusion
-genesis	producing
-pexy	surgical fixation
-ptosis	drooping; sagging
-(r)rhea	flow; discharge
-trophy	growth; development
-uria	urine

EXERCISE 11-1

Write the root, prefix, suffix, and their meaning. Based on the meanings, write a brief definition for each term.

1. Spermatogenesis
   ROOT: _spermat/o_ MEANING: _sperm_
   PREFIX: _____ MEANING: _____
   SUFFIX: _genesis_ MEANING: _producing_
   DEFINITION: _producing sperm_

2. Anuria
   ROOT: _____ MEANING: _____
   PREFIX: _an-_ MEANING: _____
   SUFFIX: _-uria_ MEANING: _urine_
   DEFINITION: _without urine_

3. Dysuria
   ROOT: _____ MEANING: _____
   PREFIX: _dys-_ MEANING: _difficult_
   SUFFIX: _-uria_ MEANING: _urine_
   DEFINITION: _difficult urination_

4. Nocturia
   ROOT: _noct/o_ MEANING: _night_
   PREFIX: _____ MEANING: _____
   SUFFIX: _-uria_ MEANING: _urine_
   DEFINITION: _night urination_

5. Hematuria
   ROOT: _hemat/o_ MEANING: _blood_
   PREFIX: _____ MEANING: _____
   SUFFIX: _-uria_ MEANING: _urine_
   DEFINITION: _blood in the urine_

6. Nephropexy
   ROOT: _nephr/o_ MEANING: _kidney_
   PREFIX: _____ MEANING: _____
   SUFFIX: _-pexy_ MEANING: _surgical fixation_
   DEFINITION: _surgical fixation of the kidney_

7. Nephroptosis
   ROOT: _nephr/o_ MEANING: _kidney_
   PREFIX: _____ MEANING: _____
   SUFFIX: _-ptosis_ MEANING: _sagging_
   DEFINITION: _sagging kidney_

8. Spermatocele

   ROOT: _____ MEANING: _____

   PREFIX: _____ MEANING: _____

   SUFFIX: _____ MEANING: _____

   DEFINITION: _____

9. Orchiditis

   ROOT: _Orchid/o_ MEANING: _testes_

   PREFIX: _____ MEANING: _____

   SUFFIX: _itis_ MEANING: _inflammation_

   DEFINITION: _inflammation of the testes_

10. Cystitis

    ROOT: _Cyst/o_ MEANING: _bladder_

    PREFIX: _____ MEANING: _____

    SUFFIX: _itis_ MEANING: _inflammation_

    DEFINITION: _inflammation of bladder_

STRUCTURES OF THE URINARY SYSTEM

The major structures of the urinary system include the kidneys, ureters, urinary bladder, and urethra. The (1) **kidneys** are responsible for filtering the blood and producing urine. The (2) **ureters** transport the urine from the kidney to the (3) **urinary bladder**, which is the storage sac for the urine. Urine leaves the body through the (4) **urethra** (yoo-**REE**-thrah). Figure 11-1 illustrates the major structures of the urinary system.

Kidneys

The kidneys are bean-shaped organs located on the posterior wall of the abdominal cavity. There is one kidney on each side of the spinal column. The kidneys are superfilters for the blood. They remove waste products from the bloodstream and help maintain the proper balance of water, salts, and other necessary substances found in body fluids.

The outer layer of the kidney is called the (1) **cortex** (**KOR**-tecks) and contains the **nephrons** (**NEFF**-ronz), or kidney cells. The inner layer of the kidney is called the (2) **medulla** (meh-**DULL**-ah). The (3) **renal pelvis** is the upper, expanded section of the ureters. Urine collects in the renal pelvis and then travels to the urinary bladder by way of the ureters. Figure 11-2 illustrates the areas of the kidney.

Nephrons are microscopic structures and are responsible for filtering blood and forming urine. Figure 11-3 illustrates two major parts of a nephron: the (1) **glomerulus** (glom-**AIR**-yoo-lus) and (2) **renal**

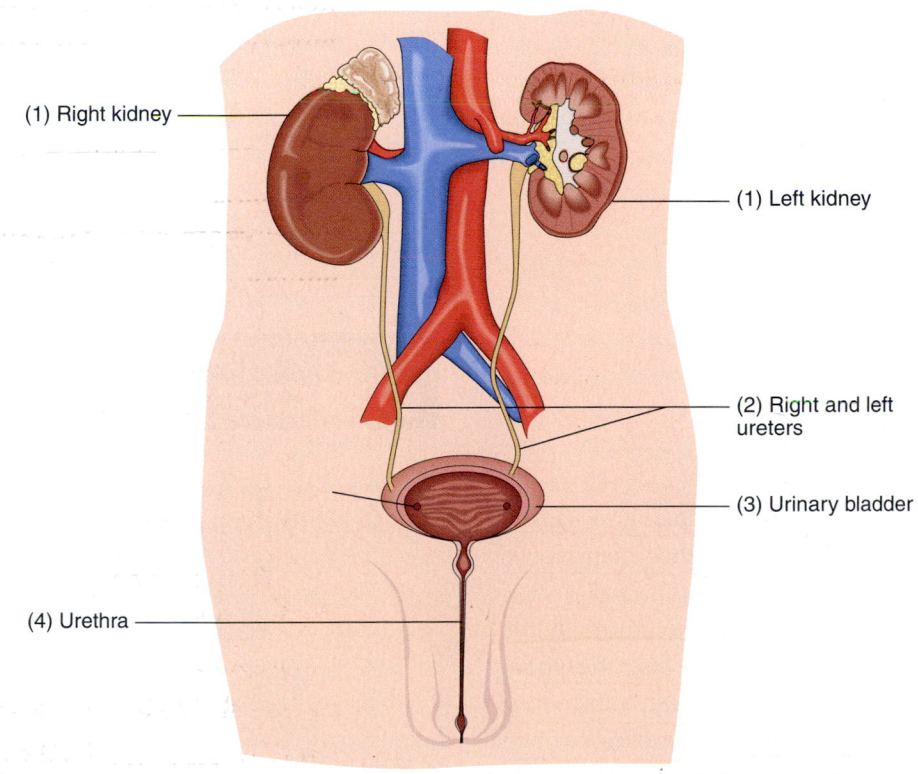

(1) Right kidney

(1) Left kidney

(2) Right and left ureters

(3) Urinary bladder

(4) Urethra

Figure 11-1 Urinary system structures

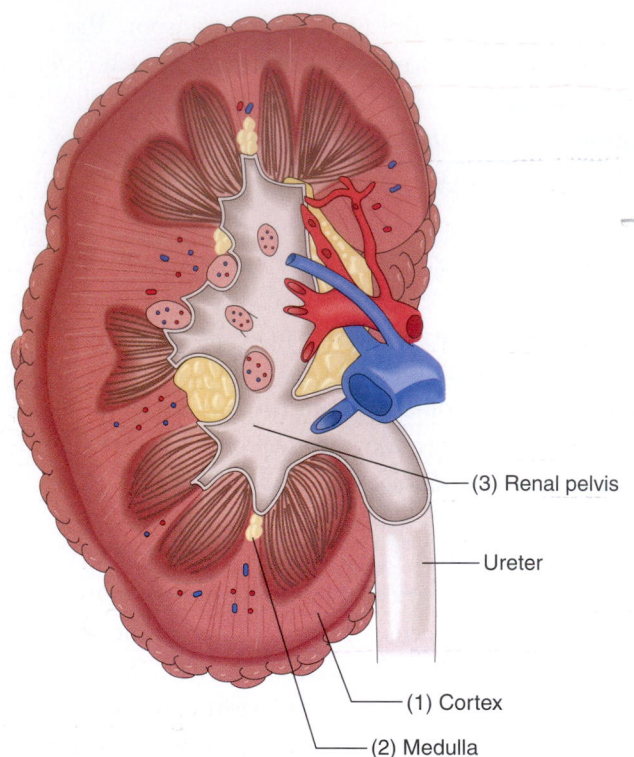

Figure 11-2   Kidney

(3) Renal pelvis

Ureter

(1) Cortex

(2) Medulla

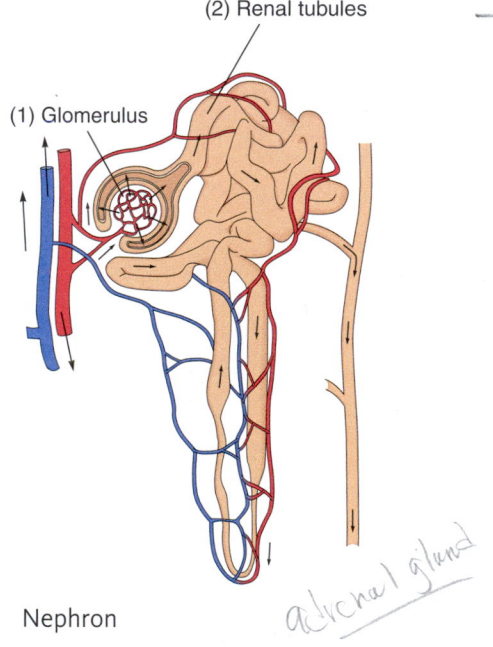

(2) Renal tubules

(1) Glomerulus

adrenal gland

Figure 11-3   Nephron

tubules (**TOOB**-yoolz). The glomerulus is a cluster or ball of capillaries. The renal tubule has many loops and coils.

As blood enters the kidney it passes through the glomeruli of the nephrons. The glomeruli filter the blood, removing water, waste products, and other substances. When the blood leaves the glomeruli, it moves through a network of capillaries that surround the renal tubules. The renal tubules capture water and waste products to

form urine. The renal tubules deposit the urine into the renal pelvis. The filtered blood continues to flow through the blood vessels that surround the renal tubules and eventually leaves the kidney.

Urine is the liquid waste of the body. It is made up of 95% water and 5% of other substances. These substances, known as *waste products,* include **urea** (yoo-**REE**-ah), **creatinine** (kree-**AT**-in-in), **ammonia**, and mineral salts.

Ureters, Urinary Bladder, and Urethra

The ureters, urinary bladder, and urethra are responsible for moving urine out of the body. Figure 11-1 illustrates these structures. The ureters are narrow tubes about 10 to 12 inches in length. The upper ends of the ureters are located in the kidney and called the renal pelvis. From the kidney, the ureters narrow and connect to the urinary bladder. The urinary bladder is a hollow, muscular organ or sac that temporarily stores urine. When the body is ready to release urine, the bladder contracts and expels the urine. *Urination, voiding,* and **micturition** (mick-too-**RIH**-shun) are terms that mean the normal process of expelling urine.

The urethra is the tube leading from the urinary bladder to the outside of the body. The male urethra is about 8 inches long, and the female urethra is about 1.5 inches long. The male urethra transports both urine and semen through the penis, but not at the same time. Only urine passes through the female urethra. The **urinary meatus** (mee-**AY**-tus), also called the **urethral meatus**, is the external opening of the urethra. In the male, the urinary meatus is at the tip of the penis; in the female, it is located between the clitoris and the vaginal opening.

EXERCISE 11-2

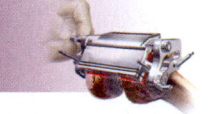

Label the structures of the urinary system identified in figure 11-4. Write your answers on the spaces provided.

1. *right kidney*
2. *Urethra*
3. *urinary bladder*
4. *right & left ureters*
5. *adrenal medulla*
6. *left Kidney*

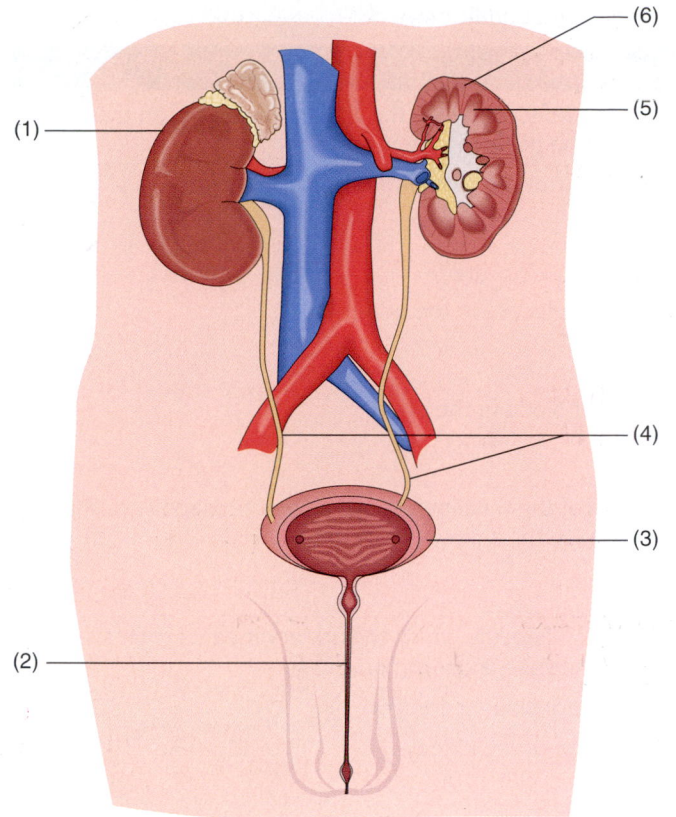

Figure 11-4   Label urinary system structures

URINARY STRUCTURE MEDICAL TERMINOLOGY

Urinary medical terms are organized by diseases, conditions, diagnostic procedures, and operations. There are two categories of medical terminology exercises for the genitourinary system: (1) those designed to provide opportunities to learn the terms, and (2) those designed to provide opportunities to accurately assign diagnostic or procedure codes. Medical terminology exercises follow the list of terms for the urinary and male reproductive structures. Medical coding exercises are available after all terms have been presented.

Urinary Structure Signs, Symptoms, Diseases, and Conditions

The medical terms in table 11-2 are signs, symptoms, diseases, and conditions related to urinary structures. Review the meaning of these terms and complete the exercises.

Table 11-2   Urinary Structure Signs, Symptoms, Diseases, and Conditions

TERM WITH PRONUNCIATION	DEFINITION
anuria (an-**YOO**-ree-ah) an- = lack of; without -uria = urine	absence of urine
azoturia (azz-oh-**TOO**-ree-ah)	an increase of urea in urine
cystitis (siss-**TIGH**-tis) cyst/o = urinary bladder -itis = inflammation	inflammation of the urinary bladder
cystocele (**SISS**-toh-seel) cyst/o = urinary bladder -cele = hernia; protrusion	hernia of the urinary bladder through the vaginal wall
diuresis (**digh**-yoo-**REE**-siss)	secretion of large amounts of urine
diuretic (**digh**-yoo-**RET**-ik)	increasing the secretion of urine; a substance that increases the secretion of urine
dysuria (diss-**YOO**-ree-ah) dys- = abnormal; painful; difficult -uria = urine	painful or difficult urination
enuresis (en-yoo-**REE**-siss)	involuntary release of urine; bedwetting

continued

Table 11-2 (*continued*) Urinary Structure Signs, Symptoms, Diseases, and Conditions

TERM WITH PRONUNCIATION	DEFINITION
epispadias (ep-ih-**SPAY**-dee-as)	congenital defect in which the urinary meatus is on the upper surface of the penis (figure 11-5)
glomerulonephritis (glom-**air**-yoo-loh-neh-**FRIGH**-tis) glomerul/o = glomerulus nephr/o = kidney -itis = inflammation	inflammation of the glomerulus of the kidneys
glycosuria (**gligh**-kohs-**YOO**-ree-ah) glycos/o = glucose -uria = urine	presence of glucose in the urine
hematuria (**hee**-mah-**TOO**-ree-ah) hemat/o = blood -uria = urine	presence of blood in the urine
hydronephrosis (**high**-droh-neh-**FROH**-sis) hydro- = water nephr/o = kidney -osis = condition	distention of the renal pelvis caused by the inability of the urine to leave the kidney (figure 11-6)
hypospadias (**high**-poh-**SPAY**-dee-as)	a congenital defect in which the urinary meatus is on the under surface of the penis (figure 11-5)
incontinence (in-**KON**-tin-ents)	loss of urinary bladder control
nephritis (neh-**FRIGH**-tis) nephr/o = kidney -itis = inflammation	inflammation of the kidney
nephrolithiasis (**neh**-froh-lih-**THIGH**-ah-sis) nephr/o = kidney lith/o = stone -iasis = condition	presence of stones in the kidneys; kidney stones; also called renal calculi
nephroma (neh-**FROH**-mah) nephr/o = kidney -oma = tumor	kidney tumor

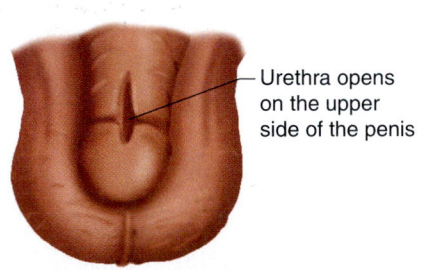 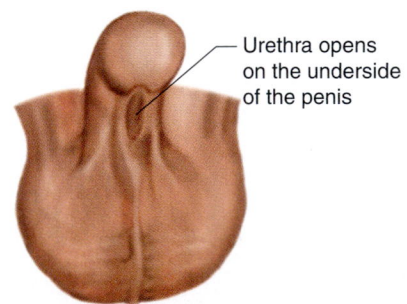

Figure 11-5 Epispadias and Hypospadias

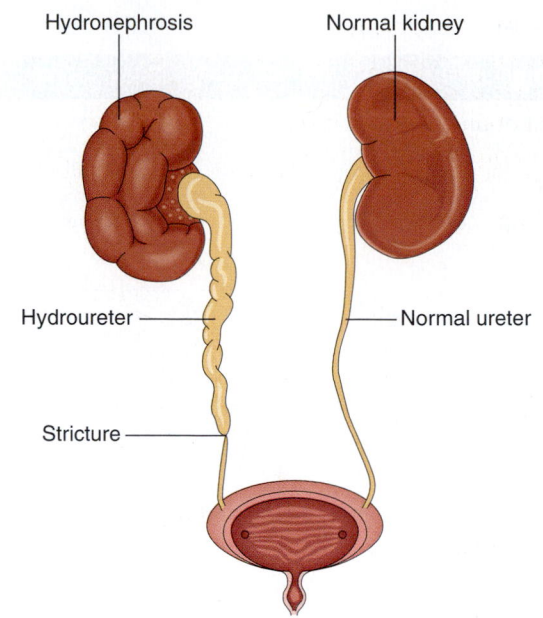

Figure 11-6 Hydronephrosis

h. hematuria

i. hydronephrosis

j. hypospadias

k. incontinence

8. inflammation of the glomerulus of the kidney _f_

9. urinary meatus on the under surface of the penis _j_

10. involuntary release of urine _e_

11. hernia of the bladder through the vaginal wall _c_

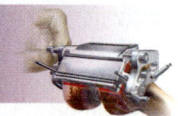

EXERCISE 11-3

Match the medical term in column 1 with the correct definition in column 2.

COLUMN 1

a. anuria

b. azoturia

c. cystocele

d. diuresis

e. enuresis

f. glomerulonephritis

g. glycosuria

COLUMN 2

1. absence of urine _a_

2. secretion of large amounts of urine _d_

3. glucose in the urine _g_

4. blood in the urine _h_

5. distention of the renal pelvis _i_

6. loss of urinary bladder control _k_

7. increased urea in the urine _b_

EXERCISE 11-4

Replace the italicized word or phrase with the correct medical term.

1. To relieve fluid overload, the physician might prescribe a/an *medication that increases the secretion of urine.* diuretic

2. Surgical intervention might correct *a urinary meatus on the upper surface of the penis.* epispadias

3. *Painful urination* may be a symptom of a urinary tract infection. dysuria

4. Rhonda was taking an antibiotic for *an inflammation of the urinary bladder.* cystitis

5. A/an *kidney tumor* may be malignant or benign. nephroma

6. *Kidney stones* may be removed via lithotripsy. nephrolithiasis

7. A systemic infection may lead to *inflammation of the kidney.* nephritis

The medical terms in table 11-3 are signs, symptoms, diseases, and conditions of urinary structures. Review the meaning of these terms and complete the exercises.

Table 11-3 Urinary Structure Signs, Symptoms, Diseases, and Conditions

TERM WITH PRONUNCIATION	DEFINITION
nephromegaly (**neh**-froh-**MEG**-ah-lee) nephr/o = kidney -megaly = enlarged; enlargement	enlargement of one or both kidneys
nephroptosis (**neh**-frop-**TOH**-sis) nephr/o = kidney -ptosis = drooping; sagging	downward displacement of drooping kidney; also known as a *floating kidney*
nocturia (nok-**TOO**-ree-ah) noct/o = night -uria = urine	excessive urination at night
oliguria (all-ig-**YOO**-ree-ah) olig/o = few; diminished -uria = urine	diminished urine secretion
polycystic kidney (pall-ee-**SISS**-tik) poly- = many cyst/o = fluid-filled sac -ic = pertaining to	a hereditary kidney disorder in which fluid-filled cysts or sacs replace normal kidney tissue
polyuria (pall-ee-**YOO**-ree-ah) poly- = many -uria = urine	excessive urination
pyelitis (**pigh**-eh-**LIGH**-tis) pyel/o = renal pelvis -itis = inflammation	inflammation of the renal pelvis
pyelonephritis (**pigh**-eh-loh-neh-**FRIGH**-tis) pyel/o = renal pelvis nephr/o = kidney -itis = inflammation	inflammation of the renal pelvis and kidney
pyuria (pigh-**YOO**-ree-ah) py/o = pus -uria = urine	presence of pus in the urine
renal hypertension (**REE**-nal)	increased blood pressure caused by kidney disease
uremia (yoo-**REE**-mee-ah)	presence of urea and other waste products in the blood
ureteritis (yoo-**ree**-ter-**EYE**-tis) ureter/o = ureter -itis = inflammation	inflammation of the ureters
ureterocele (yoo-**REE**-ter-oh-seel) ureter/o = ureter -cele = hernia; protrusion	herniation or protrusion of the ureter into the urinary bladder
ureterolithiasis (yoo-**ree**-ter-oh-lih-**THIGH**-ah-sis) ureter/o = ureter lith/o = stone -iasis = condition	presence of stones in the ureter
ureterostenosis (yoo-**ree**-ter-oh-sten-**OH**-sis) ureter/o = ureter -stenosis = narrowing	narrowing or stricture of the ureter
urethrocystitis (yoo-**ree**-throh-siss-**TIGH**-tis) urethr/o = urethra cyst/o = urinary bladder -itis = inflammation	inflammation of the urethra and urinary bladder
urinary retention (**YOOR**-in-air-ee ree-**TEN**-shun) ur/o = urine -ary = pertaining to	inability to empty the urinary bladder
urinary tract infection (UTI)	infection of the urinary tract that can include the urethra, urinary bladder, and ureters

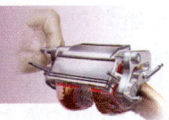

EXERCISE 11-5

Circle the medical term that best fits the description.

1. enlarged kidney — polycystic kidney or *nephromegaly*

2. pus in the urine — pyelitis or *pyuria*

3. excessive urination at night — polyuria or *nocturia*

4. stricture of the ureter — *ureterostenosis* or urinary retention

5. diminished urine secretion — uremia or *oliguria*

3. herniation of the ureter into the urinary bladder *ureterocele*

4. inflammation of the renal pelvis *pyelitis*

5. inflammation of the renal pelvis and kidney *pyelonephritis*

6. inflammation of the ureters *ureteritis*

7. inflammation of the urethra and urinary bladder *urethrocystitis*

8. stones in the ureter *ureterolithiasis*

9. urea in the blood *uremia*

10. UTI *urinary tract infection*

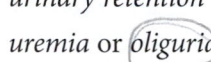

EXERCISE 11-6

Write the medical term for each definition or abbreviation.

1. excessive urination *polyuria*

2. floating kidney *nephroptosis*

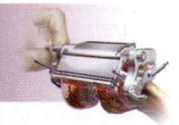

Urinary Structure Diagnostic Procedure and Laboratory Terms

Urinary structure diagnostic procedure and laboratory terms are listed in table 11-4. Review the terms and complete the exercises.

Table 11-4 Urinary Structure Diagnostic Procedure and Laboratory Terms

TERM WITH PRONUNCIATION	DEFINITION
blood urea nitrogen (BUN) (yoo-**REE**-ah **NIGH**-tro-jen)	blood test that measures the urea and nitrogen in the blood; urea and nitrogen are normally excreted by the kidneys
creatinine clearance test (kree-**AT**-in-in)	blood test that measures the amount of creatinine in the blood; creatinine is normally excreted by the kidneys
cystography (siss-**TOG**-rah-fee) cyst/o = urinary bladder -graphy = process of recording	process of recording an x-ray of the urinary bladder
cystometrography (**siss**-toh-meh-**TROG**-rah-fee) cyst/o = urinary bladder metr/o = to measure -graphy = process of recording	process of measuring and recording bladder pressure during filling and voiding
cystoscopy (sist-**OSS**-koh-pee) cyst/o = urinary bladder -scopy = visual examination	visual examination of the interior of the urinary bladder using a cystoscope
intravenous pyelography (IVP) (in-trah-**VEE**-nus **pigh**-eh-**LOG**-rah-fee) intra- = within ven/o = vein -ous = pertaining to pyel/o = renal pelvis -graphy = process of recording	process of recording the internal structures of the kidneys, ureters, urinary bladder, and urethra after a contrast medium is injected into a vein; also called *intravenous urography*
kidneys, ureters, and bladder (KUB)	an x-ray of the lower abdomen that displays the size, shape, and location of the kidneys, ureters, and bladder; also called a *scout film*

continued

Table 11-4 (continued) Urinary Structure Diagnostic Procedure and Laboratory Terms

TERM WITH PRONUNCIATION	DEFINITION
retrograde pyelography (RP) (**REH**-troh-grayd **pigh**-eh-**LOG**-rah-fee)	process of recording the internal structure of the ureters and renal pelvis; contrast medium is injected into the ureters and travels up the ureters into the renal pelvis
urinalysis (UA) (**yoo**-rin-**AL**-ih-sis)	a physical, microscopic, or chemical examination of urine; physical examination includes color, turbidity, specific gravity, and pH; microscopic examination identifies the presence or absence of blood cells, crystals, pus, and bacteria; chemical analysis identifies the presence or absence of ketones, glucose (sugar), protein, or microscopic blood
urinary catheterization (**YOOR**-in-air-ee **kath**-eh-ter-ih-**ZAY**-shun)	insertion of a catheter (i.e., a small tube) into the urinary bladder for the purpose of collecting urine
voiding cystourethrography (VCUG) (**siss**-toh-yoo-ree-**THROG**-rah-fee) cyst/o = urinary bladder urethr/o = urethra -graphy = process of recording	recording the activity and internal condition of the urinary bladder and urethra during the voiding process

EXERCISE 11-7

Replace the italicized phrase or abbreviation with the correct medical term.

1. Unrelenting lower back pain, radiating both left and right, was justification for a/an *IVP*. _intravenous pyelography_

2. The *test to measure the amount of creatinine in the blood* provides information about the kidneys' ability to filter blood. _creatine clearance test_

3. A/an *VCUG* requires the patient to drink substantial amounts of water. _voiding cystourethrography_

4. A/an *microscopic examination of urine* is a screening test for urinary system diseases and disorders. _urinalysis_

5. *Collecting urine with a catheter* is a common postoperative physician's order. _urinary catheterization_

6. A/an *BUN* is often ordered to assess kidney function. _blood urea nitrogen_

EXERCISE 11-8

Write a brief description for the diagnostic tests and describe the difference between each pair.

1. a. voiding cystourethrography _recording the activity of urinary bladder and urethra during voiding_
   b. cystometrography _measuring bladder pressure during filling & voiding_

2. a. intravenous pyelography _Process of recording kidney, ureters, urinary bladder & urethra Contrast medium inve'_
   b. retrograde pyelography _Process of recording ureters and renal pelvis contrast medium inject into ureters_

3. a. physical examination of urine _includes color, turbidity, specific gravity & pH_
   b. chemical analysis of urine _identifies the presence or absense of ketones, glucose, protein_

4. a. cystography _Process of recording x-ray of urinary bladder_
   b. cystoscopy _visual examination of the urinary bladder using cystoscope_

Urinary Structure Procedures, Operations, and Treatments

Review the procedures, operations, and treatments in table 11-5 and complete the exercises.

Table 11-5 Urinary Structure Procedures, Operations, and Treatments

TERM WITH PRONUNCIATION	DEFINITION
cystectomy (siss-**TEK**-toh-mee) cyst/o = urinary bladder -ectomy = surgical removal	surgical removal of the bladder; excision of the bladder
cystolithotomy (**siss**-toh-lith-**OT**-oh-mee) cyst/o = urinary bladder lith/o = stone -(o)tomy = incision into	incision into the bladder to remove a stone

continued

Table 11-5 (continued) Urinary Structure Procedures, Operations, and Treatments

TERM WITH PRONUNCIATION	DEFINITION
cystopexy (**SISS**-toh-**pek**-see) cyst/o = urinary bladder -pexy = surgical fixation	surgical fixation of the urinary bladder
cystoplasty (**SISS**-toh-**plass**-tee) cyst/o = urinary bladder -plasty = surgical repair	surgical repair of the urinary bladder
cystorrhaphy (sist-**OR**-ah-fee) cyst/o = urinary bladder -(r)rhaphy = suturing	suturing of the urinary bladder
cystostomy (sist-**OSS**-toh-mee) cyst/o = urinary bladder -(o)stomy = surgical creation of a new or artificial opening	surgical creation of a new or artificial opening between the urinary bladder and the surface of the bladder
hemodialysis	a treatment procedure to filter blood when the kidneys are unable to function; blood is circulated through a dialysis machine, filtered, and returned to the body (figure 11-7)
kidney transplant	replacing a failed kidney with a donated kidney; also called a *renal transplant*
lithotripsy (**LITH**-oh-trip-see) lith/o = stone -tripsy = crushing	intentional crushing of stones for the purpose of removal
meatotomy (mee-ah-**TOT**-oh-mee) meat/o = urinary meatus -(o)tomy = incision into	incision into the urinary meatus to enlarge the opening
nephrectomy (neh-**FREK**-toh-mee) nephr/o = kidney -ectomy = surgical removal	surgical removal of a kidney; excision of a kidney
nephrolithotomy (**neh**-froh-lith-**OT**-oh-mee) nephr/o = kidney lith/o = stone -(o)tomy = incision into	surgical incision into a kidney to remove stones
nephropexy (**NEFF**-roh-pek-see) nephr/o = kidney -pexy = surgical fixation	surgical fixation of a fallen or prolapsed kidney
peritoneal dialysis	a treatment to filter blood when the kidneys are unable to function; the peritoneum, the membrane that lines the abdominal cavity, is the filter and blood does not leave the body; *continuous ambulatory peritoneal dialysis* (CAPD), gravity-assisted dialysis that requires three to five exchanges of solution during the waking hours; *continuous cycler-assisted peritoneal dialysis* (CCPD), and *nocturnal intermittent peritoneal dialysis* (NIPD), machine-assisted dialysis that uses an automated cycler to perform three to five exchanges of solution during sleeping hours (figure 11-8)
pyelolithotomy (**pigh**-eh-loh-lith-**OT**-oh-mee) pyel/o = renal pelvis lith/o = stone -(o)tomy = incision into	incision into the renal pelvis to remove stones
ureterectomy (yoo-**ree**-ter-**ECK**-toh-mee) ureter/o = ureter -ectomy = surgical removal	surgical removal of a ureter; excision of a ureter
ureteroplasty (yoo-**ree**-ter-oh-**PLASS**-tee) ureter/o = ureter -plasty = surgical repair	surgical repair of the ureter

continued

Table 11-5 (*continued*)   Urinary Structure Procedures, Operations, and Treatments

TERM WITH PRONUNCIATION	DEFINITION
urethrectomy (yoo-ree-**THREK**-toh-mee) urethr/o = urethra -ectomy = surgical excision	surgical excision of the urethra
urethropexy (yoo-**REE**-throh-pek-see) urethr/o = urethra -pexy = surgical fixation	surgical fixation of the urethra
urethrostomy (yoo-ree-**THROSS**-toh-mee) urethr/o = urethra -(o)stomy = creation of a new or artificial opening	creation of a new or artificial opening for the urethra
urethroplasty (yoo-**REE**-throh-plass-tee) urethr/o = urethra -plasty =surgical repair	surgical repair of the urethra
vesicourethral suspension (**vess**-ih-koh-yoo-**REETH**-ral)	surgical suspension of a drooping or prolapsed urinary bladder and urethra

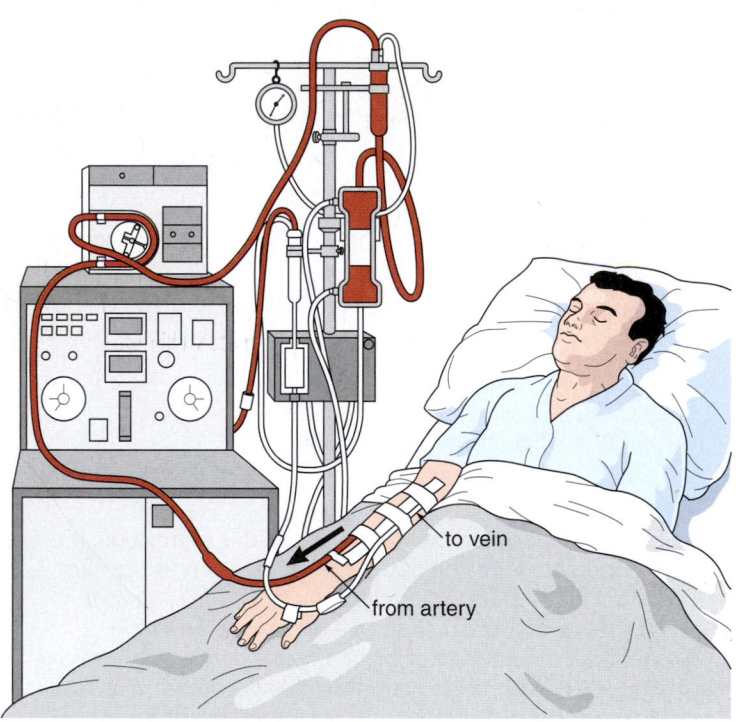

Figure 11-7   Hemodialysis

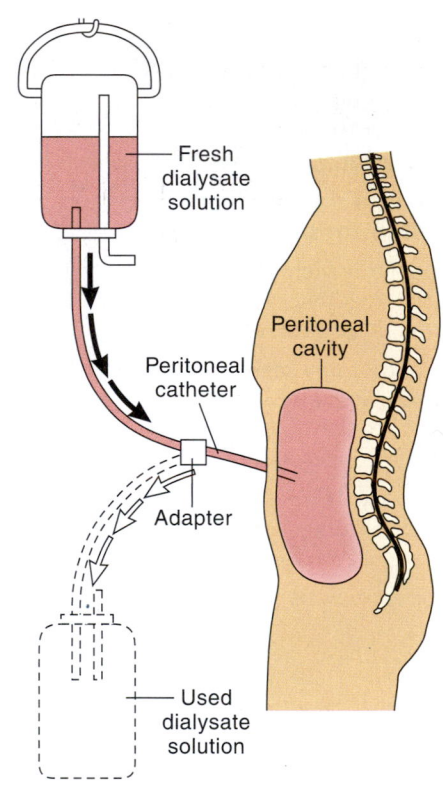

Figure 11-8   Peritoneal dialysis

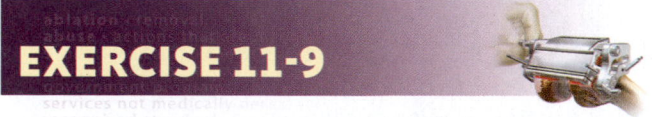

EXERCISE 11-9

Circle the medical term that best fits the definition.

1. urinary bladder incision to remove a stone — *cystotomy* or *cystolithotomy*

2. surgical repair of the urinary bladder — *cystoplasty* or *cystorrhaphy*

3. surgical fixation of the kidney — *nephroplasty* or *nephropexy*

4. surgical excision of the urethra — *urethrectomy* or *ureterectomy*

5. surgical fixation of the urinary bladder — *cystoplasty* or *cystopexy*

6. surgical repair of the ureter — *ureteroplasty* or *ureteropexy*
7. creating a new opening for the urethra — *urethrotomy* or *urethrostomy*

EXERCISE 11-10

Write the medical term for each definition or abbreviation.

1. creation of a new opening for the urinary bladder ___Cystostomy___
2. CAPD ___Continuous ambulatory peritoneal dialysis___
3. suturing the urinary bladder ___cystorrhaphy___
4. excision of the urinary bladder ___cystectomy___
5. incision into the meatus ___meatotomy___
6. CCPD ___Continuous cycler-assisted peritoneal dialysis___
7. incision into the kidney to remove stones ___nephrolithotomy___
8. NIPD ___nocturnal intermittent peritoneal dialysis___
9. incision into the renal pelvis to remove stones ___pyelolithotomy___
10. excision of the kidney ___nephrectomy___

ABBREVIATIONS

Urinary structure abbreviations are listed in table 11-6. Practice writing out the abbreviations with a brief definition for each phrase or term.

Table 11-6 Urinary Structure Abbreviations

ABBREVIATION	MEANING
BUN	blood urea nitrogen
CAPD	continuous ambulatory peritoneal dialysis
CCPD	continuous cycler-assisted peritoneal dialysis
IVP	intravenous pyelography
IVU	intravenous urography
KUB	kidneys, ureters, and bladder
NIPD	nocturnal intermittent peritoneal dialysis
UA	urinalysis
UTI	urinary tract infection
VCUG	voiding cystourethrography

STRUCTURES OF THE MALE REPRODUCTIVE SYSTEM

The male reproductive system is made up of the (1) **testes** (**TESS**-teez) (pl.), (2) **scrotum** (**SKROH**-tum), (3) **epididymis** (**ep**-ih-**DID**-ih-miss), (4) **vas deferens** (**VAZ DEFF**-er-enz), (5) **seminal vesicle** (**SEM**-ih-nall **VESS**-ih-kal), (6) **ejaculatory** (ee-**JACK**-yoo-lah-**tor**-ee) **duct**, (7) **prostate** (**PROSS**-tayt) **gland**, (8) **Cowper** (**COW**-per) **glands**, (9) urethra, and (10) **penis**. Figure 11-9 illustrates the structures of the male reproductive system.

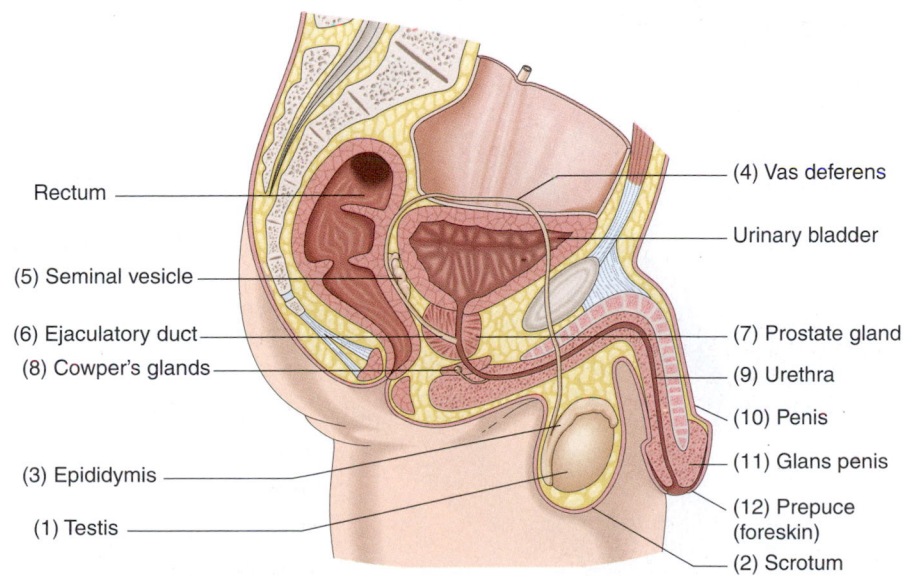

Figure 11-9 Male reproductive system structures

Testes, Epididymis, and Vas Deferens

The testes, also called *testicles,* are the male gonads, or sex organs. They develop in the abdominal cavity and eventually descend into the scrotum, the sac that houses the testes. Figure 11-10 illustrates a testis and related structures.

The (1) testes are composed of tiny, coiled tubules called (2) **seminiferous tubules** (sem-ih-**NIFF**-er-us **TOO**-byools) that are responsible for sperm production. The tissue between the tubules secretes the male sex hormone testosterone.

The (3) epididymis, a continuation of the seminiferous tubules, is a tightly coiled tube on the testes. Sperm mature and become motile in the epididymis. The (4) vas deferens, a continuation of the epididymis, leaves the scrotum, passes around the urinary bladder, and eventually connects with the urethra. Each testicle is suspended by a (5) **spermatic cord** that contains blood and lymph vessels, nerves, and the vas deferens.

Seminal Vesicles, Ejaculatory Duct, and Cowper Glands

Refer to figure 11-9 for an illustration of the seminal vesicles, ejaculatory duct, and Cowper glands. The (5) seminal vesicles, two glands located behind the urinary bladder, open into the vas deferens and secrete a thick fluid called seminal fluid. Seminal fluid is part of the **semen**, which is the substance discharged from the penis. The seminal vesicles narrow into a straight duct that joins with the vas deferens to form the (6) ejaculatory duct. The ejaculatory duct passes through the (7) prostate gland and joins with the urethra.

The (8) Cowper glands, also called the **bulbourethral** (**bull**-boh-yoo-**REE**-thrall) **glands**, are a pair of glands that lie just below the prostate gland. The Cowper glands secrete a mucus-like fluid into the urethra. The fluid, which is a component of semen, provides lubrication during intercourse.

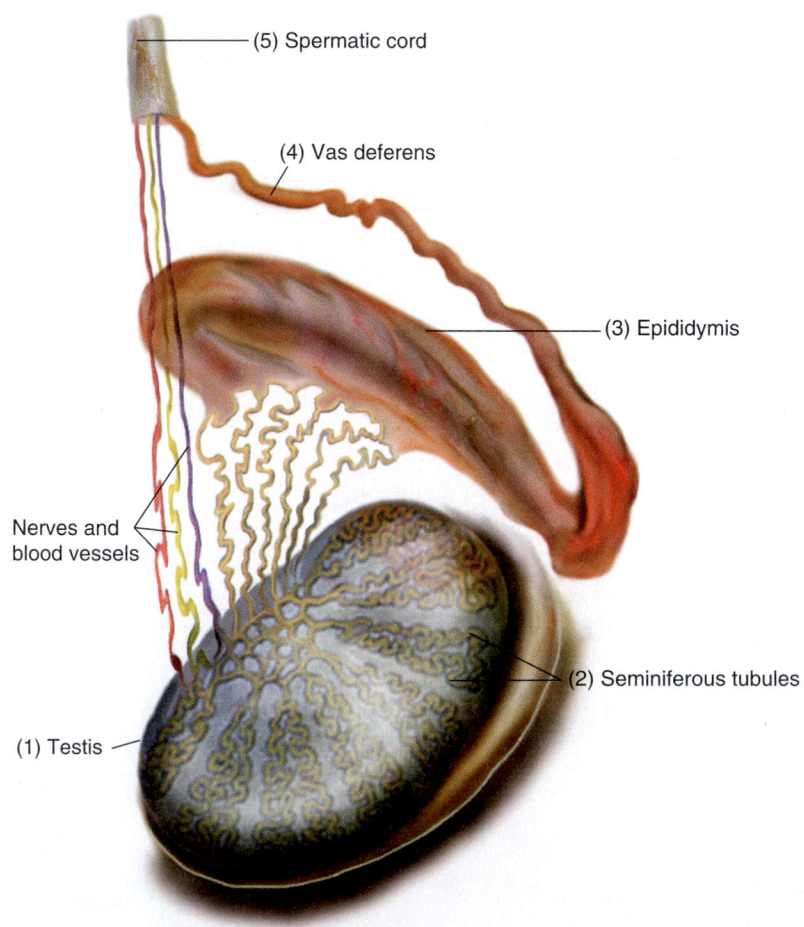

Figure 11-10 Testis

Prostate Gland

The (7) prostate gland lies at the base of the bladder and surrounds the urethra. Refer to figure 11-9 for an illustration of the prostate gland. The prostate gland secretes a milky-colored fluid that enhances sperm motility and helps neutralize vaginal secretions. Prostate fluid is added to the semen via ducts that open into the urethra. During ejaculation, the muscular action of the prostate gland helps propel semen through the urethra into the vagina.

Penis

The (10) penis consists of a base that attaches the penis to the pubic region, a shaft or body that becomes engorged with blood during arousal, and a tip or head called the (11) **glans penis**. Refer to figure 11-9 for an illustration of the penis. A retractable fold of skin called the (12) **prepuce** (**PREE**-pus), or foreskin, covers the glans penis. The prepuce is often removed by a procedure known as **circumcision**.

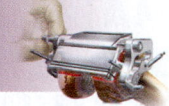

EXERCISE 11-11

Label the structures of the male reproductive system as shown in figure 11-11. Write your answer in the spaces provided.

1. Vas deferens
2. Prostate glands
3. Urethra
4. Penis
5. glans penis
6. Prepuce (foreskin)
7. Scrotum
8. testes
9. epididymis
10. seminal vesicle

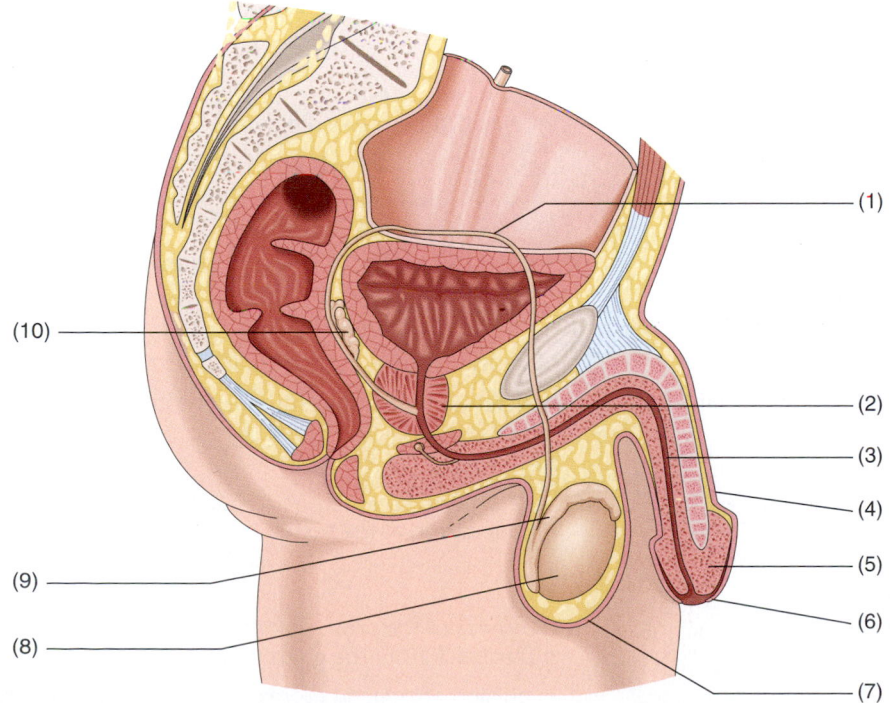

Figure 11-11   Label male reproductive system structures

MALE REPRODUCTIVE STRUCTURE MEDICAL TERMINOLOGY

Male reproductive structure medical terms are organized by diseases, conditions, diagnostic procedures, and operations. Table 11-7 lists diseases and conditions related to male reproductive structures. Review the terms and complete the exercises.

EXERCISE 11-12

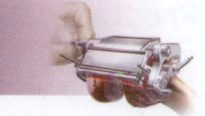

Replace the italicized phrase or abbreviation with the correct medical term.

1. Calhoun's diagnosis was *BPH*.
   benign prostatic hypertrophy
2. The *inability to achieve or maintain an erection* may be caused by a physical or psychological condition. *erectile dysfunction or impotence*

Table 11-7 Male Reproductive Structure, Diseases, and Conditions

TERM WITH PRONUNCIATION	DEFINITION
anorchism (an-**ORK**-izm) an- = without orch/i = testes -ism = condition	absence of one or both testes
aspermia (ah-**SPERM**-ee-ah) a- = lack of; without sperm/o = sperm -ia = condition	lack or absence of sperm
balanitis (bal-ah-**NIGH**-tis) balan/o = glans penis -itis = inflammation	inflammation of the glans penis
benign prostatic hypertrophy (BPH) (bee-**NIGHN** pross-**TAT**-ik high-**PER**-troh-fee) prostat/o = prostate -ic = pertaining to hyper- = excessive -trophy = growth; development	noncancerous enlargement of the prostate gland
cryptorchidism (kript-**OR**-kid-izm) crypt/o = hidden orchid/o = testes -ism = condition	undescended testicle; failure of one or both testes to descend into the scrotum
epididymitis (**ep**-ih-**did**-ih-**MIGH**-tis) epididym/o = epididymis -itis = inflammation	inflammation of the epididymis
erectile dysfunction	inability to achieve or maintain an erection; impotence
hydrocele (**HIGH**-droh-seel) hydr/o = water -cele = hernia; protrusion	accumulation of fluid in the scrotum or along the spermatic cord
impotence (**IM**-poh-tens)	inability to achieve or maintain an erection; erectile dysfunction
oligospermia (**all**-ih-goh-**SPER**-mee-ah) olig/o = few; deficient sperm/o = sperm -ia = condition	deficient number of sperm present in semen
orchitis (or-**KIGH**-tis) orch/i = testes -itis = inflammation	inflammation of the testes
phimosis (fih-**MOH**-sis)	tightness of the prepuce, or foreskin, that prevents it from being pulled back from the glans penis
premature ejaculation	expulsion of semen before complete erection or immediately after vaginal penetration

continued

Table 11-7 (continued)   Male Reproductive Structure Diseases and Conditions

TERM WITH PRONUNCIATION	DEFINITION
priapism	abnormal, painful, and prolonged erection of the penis not related to sexual arousal
prostate cancer	malignant tumor or neoplasm of the prostate gland
prostatitis (**pross**-tah-**TIGH**-tis) prostat/o = prostate gland -itis = inflammation	inflammation of the prostate gland
spermatolysis (sper-mah-**TALL**-ih-sis) spermat/o = sperm -lysis = destruction; breakdown	destruction, dissolution, or breakdown of sperm
testicular carcinoma (tess-**TICK**-yoo-lar **kar**-sin-**OH**-ma) testicul/o = testes; testicles -ar = pertaining to -carcin = cancer; malignant -oma = tumor	malignant tumor of one or both testes
varicocele (**VAIR**-ih-koh-seel) varic/o = enlarged; twisted veins -cele = hernia; protrusion	enlarged, twisted, and swollen veins of the spermatic cord

3. *Tightness of the foreskin* prevents proper cleansing of the penis. _phimosis_

4. Ziad sought treatment for *abnormal, painful, and prolonged erection of the penis.* _priapism_

5. Surgical intervention or radiation may be used to treat *a malignant tumor of one or both testes.* _testicular carcinoma_

6. *Enlargement of the veins of the spermatic cord* may lead to male infertility. _varicocele_

7. Johnson had surgery to correct *undescended testicles.* _Cryptorchidism_

8. Semen analysis can identify *a deficiency of sperm.* _oligospermia_

tight foreskin

3. a. hydrocele _accumulation of fluid in the scrotum or along the spermatic cord_

   b. varicocele _enlarge, twisted and swollen veins of the spermatic cord_

4. a. phimosis _tightness of the prepuce, or foreskin, prevents it from being pulled back from the glans penis._

   b. priapism _Abnormal, painful, and prolonged erection of the penis not related to sexual arousal_

Male Reproductive Structure Procedures, Operations, and Treatments

prolonged painful erection

Male reproductive structure procedures, operations, and treatments are listed in table 11-8. Review the terms and complete the exercises.

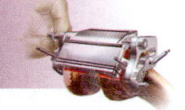

EXERCISE 11-13

Write a brief definition for each medical term and describe the difference between each pair.

1. a. anorchism _absence of one or both testes_

   b. aspermia _absence or lack of sperm_

2. a. balanitis _inflammation of the glans penis_

   b. epididymitis _inflammation of the epididymis_

EXERCISE 11-14

Replace the italicized phrase or abbreviation with the correct medical term.

1. Due to recurrent balanitis, Malcolm underwent *the removal of the foreskin.* _Circumcision_

2. The *PAP test* is used to rule out prostate cancer. _Phosphatase_

3. The *PSA* laboratory blood test is a screening test for prostate cancer. _Prostate specific antigen_

continued

Table 11-8 Male Reproductive Structure Procedures, Operations, and Treatments

TERM WITH PRONUNCIATION	DEFINITION
circumcision (sir-kum-**SIH**-shun)	surgical removal of the foreskin (prepuce) of the penis (figure 11-12)
epididymectomy (**ep**-ih-**did**-ih-**MEK**-toh-mee) epididym/o = epididymis -ectomy = surgical removal	surgical removal of the epididymis
orchidectomy (or-kid-**ECK**-toh-mee) orchid/o = testes -ectomy = surgical removal	surgical removal of one or both testes
orchidopexy; orchiopexy (**OR**-kid-oh-**pek**-see; **or**-kee-oh-**PEK**-see) orchid/o; orchi/o = testes -pexy = surgical fixation	surgical fixation of one or both testes
orchidoplasty; orchioplasty (**OR**-kid-oh-**plass**-tee; **OR**-kee-oh-**plass**-tee) orchid/o; orchi/o = testes -plasty = surgical repair	surgical repair of one or both testes; placement of undescended testes into the scrotum
prostatectomy (**pross**-tah-**TEK**-toh-mee) prostat/o = prostate gland -ectomy = surgical removal	surgical removal of all or part of the prostate
prostatic acid phosphatase (PAP) (pross-**STAT**-ic acid **FOSS**-fah-tays) prostat/o = prostate gland -ic = pertaining to	laboratory test that measures the level of acid phosphatase, an enzyme present in prostate cells and in the blood; elevated levels indicate prostate cancer
prostate-specific antigen (PSA) (**PROSS**-tayt specific **AN**-tih-jen) prostate/o = prostate gland -ic = pertaining to	laboratory test that measures the blood levels of PSA, a protein produced by the prostate gland; elevated PSA levels indicate benign prostatic hypertrophy or prostate cancer; a screening test for prostate cancer
semen analysis	laboratory analysis of the physical and chemical components of semen
sterilization	any procedure that renders a male incapable of producing sperm or impregnating a woman
suprapubic prostatectomy (**soo**-prah-**PYOO**-bic **pross**-tah-**TEK**-toh-mee) supra- = above pub/o = pubis, pubic bone -ic = pertaining to prostat/o = prostate gland -ectomy = surgical removal	surgical removal of all or part of the prostate gland through an incision just above the pubic bone
transurethral resection of the prostate (TURP) (**tranz**-yoo-**REE**-thral) trans- = through urethr/o = urethra -al = pertaining to	surgical removal of all or part of the prostate gland by passing an instrument into and through the urethra (figure 11-13)
varicocelectomy (**vair**-ih-koh-see-**LEK**-toh-mee) varic/o = twisted veins -cele = hernia; protrusion -ectomy = surgical removal	surgical removal of a varicocele by excision of a portion of the scrotum and tying off (ligation) of the enlarged, twisted veins
vasectomy (vas-**EK**-toh-mee) vas/o = vas deferens -ectomy = surgical removal	surgical removal of all or a portion of the vas deferens; *male sterilization*

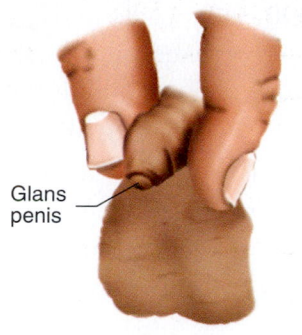
Glans
penis

(A) Before Circumcision

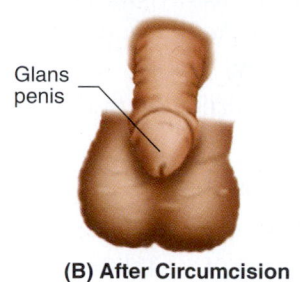
Glans
penis

(B) After Circumcision

Figure 11-12   Circumcision

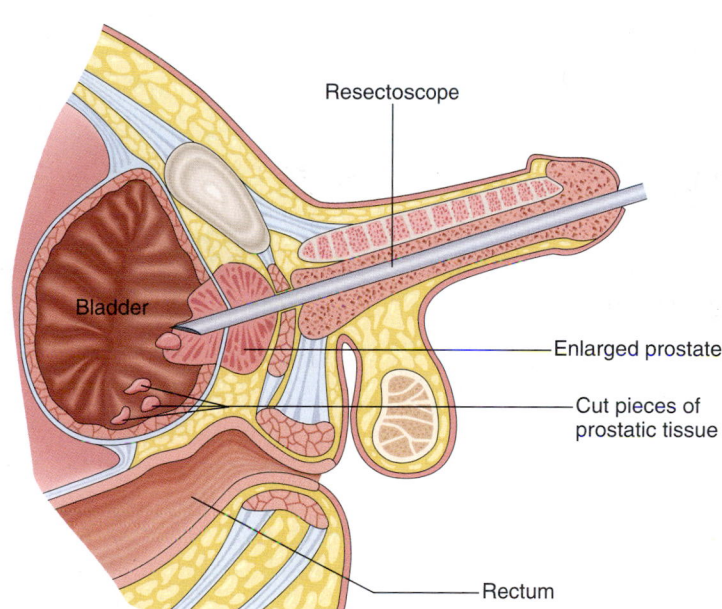

Resectoscope

Bladder

Enlarged prostate

Cut pieces of
prostatic tissue

Rectum

Figure 11-13   Transurethral resection of the prostate

4. A/an *TURP* may result in an inability to
   achieve or sustain an erection.
   transurethral resection of the prostate

5. *Surgical removal of all or part of the vas
   deferens* is a procedure for male
   sterilization. *vasectomy*

6. Cryptorchidism can be corrected with *surgical
   repair of the testes.* *orchidoplasty*

7. Testicular cancer may require *the surgical
   removal of one or both testes.*
   orchidectomy

8. *Surgical fixation of the testes* is a treatment for
   retractile testicles.

   orchiodopexy

MALE REPRODUCTIVE STRUCTURE ABBREVIATIONS

Male reproductive structure abbreviations are listed in table 11-9. Practice writing out the abbreviations with a brief definition for each phrase or term.

Table 11-9   Male Reproductive Structure Abbreviations

ABBREVIATION	MEANING
BPH	benign prostatic hypertrophy
PAP	prostatic acid phosphatase
PSA	prostate specific antigen
TURP	transurethral resection of the prostate

Know

GENITOURINARY SYSTEM MEDICAL CODING

To successfully complete the exercises in this section, the ICD-9-CM volumes 1, 2, and 3, and the CPT (Current Procedural Terminology) coding references must be readily available. The information in this section is presented as follows:

- An introduction to ICD-9-CM, chapter 10, "Diseases of the Genitourinary System"
- ICD-9-CM diagnostic coding exercises
- A summary of ICD-9-CM volume 3 coding conventions that apply to genitourinary system procedures
- ICD-9-CM procedure coding exercises
- A summary of the CPT Genitourinary System coding guidelines
- CPT coding exercises

Students are *strongly* encouraged to review the information at the beginning of the ICD-9-CM and CPT coding references. Commercial publishers include instructions on how to use the ICD-9-CM references, the ICD-9-CM official coding conventions, additional conventions used by the publisher, and the *ICD-9-CM Official Guidelines for Coding and Reporting*. Some publishers include the three ICD-9-CM volumes in one book and put the *Alphabetic Index* (volume 2) at the beginning of the reference.

The *Introduction* to CPT includes detailed instructions for using this code book, an index to the illustrations throughout the book, and anatomical illustrations of the major structures of body systems.

ICD-9-CM Volume 1, Chapter 10, Diseases of the Genitourinary System (580–629)

Genitourinary system diseases are coded to ICD-9-CM volume 1, chapter 10, "Diseases of the Genitourinary System." This chapter includes the following major sections:

- **Nephritis, Nephrotic Syndrome, and Nephrosis (580–589).** Codes in this section include glomerulonephritis, acute renal failure, chronic kidney disease, renal failure, and disorders resulting from impaired renal function. Several categories instruct the medical coder to *code first the underlying condition.*

- **Other Diseases of Urinary System (590–599).** Codes in this section include diseases of the kidney, ureters, urethra, acute and chronic cystitis, disorders of the bladder, and urinary obstruction.

- **Diseases of Male Genital Organs (600–608).** Codes in this section cover diseases and disorders of the prostate, penis, seminal vesicles, male infertility, and spermatic cord.

This chapter also includes medical codes related to the female reproductive organs and breasts. These codes are covered in chapter 12 of this text, "Female Reproductive System." Conditions related to the genitourinary system may also be coded to the following chapters in volume 1: chapter 14, "Congenital Anomalies"; chapter 16, "Symptoms, Signs, and Ill-Defined Conditions"; and chapter 2, "Neoplasms."

583.9   584.9   604.90   592.0   593.70

EXERCISE 11-15

Write a brief definition for each diagnosis. Identify the main term in the diagnostic statement and assign the correct ICD-9-CM diagnosis code(s).

1. Hemorrhagic glomerulonephritis
   DEFINITION: *inflammation and bleeding of the glomerus of the kidney*
   MAIN TERM: *glomerulonephritis*
   ICD-9-CM CODE(S): *583.9*

2. Chronic glomerulonephritis
   DEFINITION: *long lasting inflammation of the glomerus of the kidney*
   MAIN TERM: *glomerulonephritis*
   ICD-9-CM CODE(S): *582.9*

3. Acute renal failure
   DEFINITION: *intense rapid failure pertaining to the kidney*
   MAIN TERM: *renal*
   ICD-9-CM CODE(S): *584.9*

4. End-stage renal disease
   DEFINITION: *end stage of disease pertaining to the kidney*
   MAIN TERM: *renal*
   ICD-9-CM CODE(S): *585.6*

5. Chronic epididymitis

DEFINITION: *Chronic inflammation of the epididymis*

MAIN TERM: *epididymitis*

ICD-9-CM CODE(S): *604.90*

6. Distal hypospadias

DEFINITION: *Distal congenital defect in which the urinary meatus is on the undersurface of penis*

MAIN TERM: *hypospadias*

ICD-9-CM CODE(S): *752.61*

7. Staghorn calculus of the kidney

DEFINITION: *Calculus in the renal pelvis shape like antlers*

MAIN TERM: *Calculus*

ICD-9-CM CODE(S): *592.0*

8. Polycystic kidney disease

DEFINITION: *Pertaining to many cysts in the kidney*

MAIN TERM: *Kidney*

ICD-9-CM CODE(S): *753.12*

9. Vesicoureteral reflux, without reflux nephropathy

DEFINITION: *Passage of urine from bladder back into the ureter; reflux*

MAIN TERM: *reflux*

ICD-9-CM CODE(S): *593.70*

10. Chronic interstitial cystitis

DEFINITION: *Chronic inflammation of the urinary bladder*

MAIN TERM: *Cystitis*

ICD-9-CM CODE(S): *595.89*

11. Urinary tract infection due to *E. coli*

DEFINITION: *infection of urinary tract due to E. coli*

MAIN TERM: *infection*

ICD-9-CM CODE(S): *599.0 041.4*

12. BPH with urinary retention

DEFINITION: _____

MAIN TERM: *Urinary*

ICD-9-CM CODE(S): *788.20*

13. Spermatic cord hydrocele

DEFINITION: _____

MAIN TERM: _____

ICD-9-CM CODE(S): *603.9*

14. Acute prostatitis

DEFINITION: _____

MAIN TERM: *Prostatitis*

ICD-9-CM CODE(S): *601.1*

15. Cryptorchidism, bilateral

DEFINITION: _____

MAIN TERM: *Cryptorchidism*

ICD-9-CM CODE(S): *752.51*

ICD-9-CM Volume 3, Operations on the Genitourinary System

601.1

Genitourinary system operations and some therapeutic treatments are coded to ICD-9-CM volume 3, chapter 10, "Operations on the Urinary System" (55–59) and chapter 11, "Operations on the Male Genital Organs" (60–64). Chapter 10 includes the following major categories:

599.0, 014.4   603.9   752.51

- **Operations on Kidney (55).** Codes in this category include diagnostic and operative procedures of the kidney.

- **Operations on Ureter (56).** Codes in this category include diagnostic and operative procedures of the ureter.

- **Operations on Urinary Bladder (57).** Codes in this category include diagnostic and operative procedures of the urinary bladder.

- **Operations on Urethra (58).** Codes in this category include diagnostic and operative procedures of the urethra.

- **Other Operations on Urinary Tract (59).** Codes in this category include diagnostic and operative procedures of the urinary tract such as repair of urinary incontinence and ureteral catheterization.

Nearly all of the procedure codes require a fourth digit. Diagnostic procedures include biopsy and endoscopy. Hemodialysis is coded to category V56 and peritoneal dialysis is coded to V56.8. Diagnostic imaging procedures of the genitourinary system are coded to chapter 16, "Miscellaneous Diagnostic and Therapeutic Procedures."

Chapter 11, "Operations on the Male Genital Organs (60–64)," includes these major categories:

62.5, 62.5   63.01   63.1   58.45

- **Operations on Prostate and Seminal Vesicles (60).** Codes in this category include diagnostic and operative procedures of the prostate and seminal vesicles.

- **Operations on Scrotum and Tunica Vaginalis (61).** Codes in this category include diagnostic and operative procedures of the scrotum and tunica vaginalis. The tunica vaginalis is a serous membrane that surrounds the testes and epididymis.

- **Operations on Testes (62).** Codes in this category include diagnostic and operative procedures of the testes.

- **Operations on Spermatic Cord, Epididymis, and Vas Deferens (63).** Codes in this category include diagnostic and operative procedures of the spermatic cord, epididymis, and vas deferens.

- **Operations on Penis (64).** Codes in this category include diagnostic and operative procedures of the penis.

64.0   55.23

Nearly all of the procedure codes require a fourth digit. Diagnostic procedures include open and closed biopsies.

EXERCISE 11-16

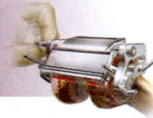

Write a brief definition for each operative, treatment, or diagnostic procedure term. Identify the main term in the statement and assign the correct ICD-9-CM code(s).

1. Bilateral orchiopexy

   DEFINITION: _____

   MAIN TERM: _Orchiopexy_

   ICD-9-CM CODE(S): _62.5   62.5_

2. Laparoscopic retropubic radical prostatectomy

   DEFINITION: _____

   MAIN TERM: _____

   ICD-9-CM CODE(S): _60.5_

3. Biopsy and exploration of epididymis

   DEFINITION: _____

   MAIN TERM: _biopsy_

   ICD-9-CM CODE(S): _63.01_

4. Right radical nephrectomy

   DEFINITION: _55.51_

   MAIN TERM: _nephrectomy_

   ICD-9-CM CODE(S): _55.51_   _40.50_

5. Hydrocelectomy, spermatic cord

   DEFINITION: _____

   MAIN TERM: _hydro celetomy_

   ICD-9-CM CODE(S): _63.1_

6. Laparoscopic ureteral stone extraction

   DEFINITION: _____

   MAIN TERM: _extration_

   ICD-9-CM CODE(S): _56.2_

7. Hypospadias repair, distal

   DEFINITION: _____

   MAIN TERM: _repair_

   ICD-9-CM CODE(S): _58.45_

8. Extracorporeal shock wave lithotripsy of right kidney stone

   DEFINITION: _____

   MAIN TERM: _lithotripsy_

   ICD-9-CM CODE(S): _56.0_

9. Circumcision

   DEFINITION: _____

   MAIN TERM: _circumcision_

   ICD-9-CM CODE(S): _64.0_

10. Vasectomy

    DEFINITION: _____

    MAIN TERM: _vesectomy_

    ICD-9-CM CODE(S): _63.73_

11. Percutaneous biopsy of the kidney

    DEFINITION: _____

    MAIN TERM: _biosy_

    ICD-9-CM CODE(S): _55.23_

12. Transurethral cystoscopy

DEFINITION: _____

MAIN TERM: _Cystoscopy_

ICD-9-CM CODE(S): _57.32_

13. Bladder suspension

DEFINITION: _____

MAIN TERM: _suspension_

ICD-9-CM CODE(S): _57.89_

14. Aspiration of the testes

DEFINITION: _____

MAIN TERM: _aspiration_

ICD-9-CM CODE(S): _62.91_

15. Voiding cystourethrography

DEFINITION: _____

MAIN TERM: _cystourethrography_

ICD-9-CM CODE(S): _87.76_

Current Procedural Terminology (CPT) Genitourinary System Codes

CPT genitourinary system codes are located in the Surgery, Radiology, and Medicine sections. The Surgery guidelines provide important information for all sections of the chapter. Review the guidelines in the CPT manual and in chapter 3 of this text. Procedures related to genitourinary structures are in the Urinary System (50010–53899) and Male Genital System (54000–55980) subsections of the Surgery section. The Urinary System subsection includes the following major categories:

_57.89   87.76_

- **Kidney (50010–50593).** Codes in this category cover incision, excision, transplantation, introduction, repair, laparoscopy, and endoscopy procedures of the kidneys.
- **Ureter (50600–50980).** Codes in this category cover incision, excision, transplantation, introduction, repair, laparoscopy, and endoscopy procedures of the ureters.
- **Bladder (51020–51999).** Codes in this category cover incision, excision, transplantation,

introduction, urodynamic studies, repair, laparoscopy, and endoscopy procedures of the urinary bladder.

- **Endoscopy (52000–52010).** Codes in this category include cystoscopy, urethroscopy, and cystourethroscopy.
- **Transurethral Surgery (52204–52355).** Codes in this category include procedures of the urethra, bladder, ureters, and pelvis that are accomplished via cystoscopy.
- **Vesical Neck and Prostate (52400–52700).** Codes in this category apply to the prostate, ejaculatory ducts, and bladder neck.
- **Urethra (53000–53665).** Codes in this category cover incision, excision, repair, and manipulation of the urethra.

The Male Genital System subsection includes these major categories:

- **Penis (54000–54450).** Codes in this category cover incision, excision, introduction, repair, and manipulation of the penis and foreskin.
- **Testis and Epididymis (54500–54901).** Codes in these categories cover excision, exploration, repair, and laparoscopy of the testes and epididymis.
- **Tunica Vaginalis, Scrotum, Vas Deferens, Spermatic Cord, and Seminal Vesicles (55000–55680).** Codes in these categories cover incision, excision, repair, suture, and laparoscopy of the tunica vaginalis, scrotum, vas deferens, spermatic cord, and seminal vesicles.

Genitourinary system diagnostic imaging procedures are coded to the Radiology section. Some of the categories related to the genitourinary system include the following:

- **Diagnostic Radiology (Diagnostic Imaging): Urinary Tract (74400–74485).** Codes in this category include radiography of the kidneys, ureters, and urinary bladder.
- **Nuclear Medicine: Genitourinary System (78700–78799).** Codes in this category cover kidney function, ureteral reflux, and urinary bladder residual studies.

Other procedures related to the genitourinary system are coded to the Medicine section. Categories related to this system include the following:

54300 52601 54865 54150 51565 (handwritten)

- **Hemodialysis (90935–90947).** Codes in this category include hemodialysis, hemodialysis with evaluation, hemodialysis flow study, and miscellaneous dialysis procedures.
- **End-Stage Renal Disease Services (90951–90970).** Codes in this category include end-stage renal disease services based on the patient's age and the number of face-to-face physician services. Extensive instructional notes precede this category.

EXERCISE 11-17

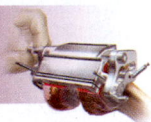

Identify the main term in each statement. Assign the correct CPT code(s).

1. Distal hypospadias repair
   MAIN TERM: _hypospadias_
   CPT CODE(S): _54300_

2. Radical nephrectomy, right kidney
   MAIN TERM: _nephrectomy_
   CPT CODE(S): _50230_

3. Transurethral resection of the prostate
   MAIN TERM: _prostate_
   CPT CODE(S): _52601_

4. Laparoscopic orchidectomy
   MAIN TERM: _____
   CPT CODE(S): _54690_

5. Biopsy and exploration of the epididymis
   MAIN TERM: _biopsy_
   CPT CODE(S): _54865_

6. Extracorporeal shock wave lithotripsy, kidney stone, right kidney
   MAIN TERM: _lithotripsy_
   CPT CODE(S): _50590_

7. Clamp circumcision, neonate
   MAIN TERM: _circumcision_
   CPT CODE(S): _54150_

8. Ureteral stent insertion
   MAIN TERM: _Ureteral_
   CPT CODE(S): _50393_

9. Partial cystectomy with reimplantation of ureters into the bladder
   MAIN TERM: _cystectomy_
   CPT CODE(S): _51565_

10. Voiding cystourethrography (VCUG)
    MAIN TERM: _cystourethrography_
    CPT CODE(S): _51600_

11. Intravenous urography
    MAIN TERM: _urography_
    CPT CODE(S): _74400_

12. Unilateral excision of left hydrocele, tunica vaginalis
    MAIN TERM: _hydrocele_
    CPT CODE(S): _55040_

13. Total urethrectomy with cystostomy, 52-year-old male
    MAIN TERM: _urethrectomy_
    CPT CODE(S): _53215_

14. Laparoscopic urethral suspension for stress incontinence
    MAIN TERM: _laparoscopic_
    CPT CODE(S): _51990_

15. Cystometrography, simple
    MAIN TERM: _cytometrography_
    CPT CODE(S): _51725_

■ SUMMARY

74400 53215 51725 (handwritten)

This chapter covered medical terms related to the genitourinary system. The genitourinary system includes urinary and male reproductive structures. Genitourinary system diagnoses and procedures were identified and defined. Genitourinary system diseases and conditions are coded to ICD-9-CM volume 1, chapter 10, "Diseases of the Genitourinary System"; chapter 2, "Neoplasms"; chapter 14, "Congenital Anomalies"; and chapter 16, "Symptoms, Signs, and Ill-Defined Conditions." Genitourinary system procedures are coded to ICD-9-CM volume 3, chapter 10, "Operations of the Urinary System"; chapter 11, "Operations of the Male Reproductive System"; and chapter 16, "Miscellaneous Diagnostic and Therapeutic Procedures."

Current Procedural Terminology (CPT) genitourinary system procedure codes are found in the Surgery subsections Urinary System (50010–53899) and Male Genital System (54000–55980), and the Radiology and Medicine sections.

■ CHAPTER REVIEW

Read each medical note or medical report excerpt. Write the diagnosis(es) and the main term. Assign the ICD-9-CM diagnosis code(s).

CASE 1

Jeneesha is a six-year-old female who came to the walk-in clinic with her mother. Mom states that her daughter has been treated for cystitis three times in the past year and she was again complaining about dysuria. Urinalysis confirmed a urinary tract infection and pyuria.

DIAGNOSIS(ES): _____

MAIN TERM: _____

ICD-9-CM CODE(S): _____599.0____791.9_____

CASE 2

Mr. Lopez was seen today with complaints of nocturnal frequency of urination, about every two hours. He noticed a slowing of the urinary stream and a feeling of incomplete bladder emptying. There was no dysuria or blood in the urine. Rectal exam today revealed a normal sphincter tone and a 1+ to 2+ enlarged prostate. Diagnosis at this time is enlarged prostate with bladder neck obstruction. A cystoscopy is scheduled for Tuesday morning.

DIAGNOSIS(ES): _____

MAIN TERM: _____

ICD-9-CM CODE(S): _____600.01____596.0_____

CASE 3

Malcolm is a 12-year-old male who is seen today for enuresis occurring approximately three times a week. His mother states that he is becoming withdrawn and refuses to participate in any overnight activities away from home. Malcolm denies any pain with urination and he doesn't drink any fluid between dinner and bedtime. Physical examination is unremarkable. We discussed the social implications of enuresis. A trial of imipramine 10 mg once a day was prescribed. Follow-up will be in two weeks.

DIAGNOSIS(ES): _____

MAIN TERM: _____

ICD-9-CM CODE(S): _____788.30_____

CASE 4

Mr. Yoha is seen today for routine follow-up for polycystic kidney disease. He has no new complaints and states that he "feels pretty good for an old guy." Blood pressure is 110/80. Metabolic panel is normal. Urinalysis was negative for protein. He has been free from urinary tract infections for the past three months. Creatinine clearance and BUN are negative. We discussed the long-term effects of his condition. He will continue on his current medications and return in one month. 753.12

DIAGNOSIS(ES): _____

MAIN TERM: _____

ICD-9-CM CODE(S): _____ 753.12 _____

CASE 5

This patient is seen today with complaints of nocturia, dysuria, low back pain, and a burning sensation during urination. On examination blood pressure is 120/80. Temperature is 100.9°F. There is tenderness in the suprapubic region. Clean-catch urine sample is turbid with microscopic hematuria. Microscopic analysis and urine dipstick test results are consistent for cystitis. The patient left with a prescription for antibiotics and will return in two weeks unless symptoms worsen.

595.9

DIAGNOSIS(ES): _____

MAIN TERM: _____

ICD-9-CM CODE(S): _____ 5 95.9 _____

CASE 6

The patient is a nine-month-old uncircumcised male who presents with balanitis. His mother states that she has a hard time cleaning the glans penis because she can't fully retract the foreskin. On examination the glans penis is moderately swollen with redness. The foreskin is tight and retraction revealed a significant amount of secretions and detritus, which is the likely cause of the balanitis. The area was irrigated and the mother was instructed to retract the foreskin with each diaper change. If this continues to be problematic, circumcision may be needed. 607.1

DIAGNOSIS(ES): _____

MAIN TERM: _____

ICD-9-CM CODE(S): _____ 607.1 _____

Read the procedure note, operative report, or discharge summary excerpt. Write the diagnosis and its ICD-9-CM code. Write the name of the procedure and the main term. Assign the ICD-9-CM procedure code(s).

CASE 7

PREOPERATIVE DIAGNOSIS: Right kidney stone. 592.0

592.0 98.51

POSTOPERATIVE DIAGNOSIS: Right kidney stone.

PROCEDURE: Extracorporeal shock wave lithotripsy of right kidney stone. 98.51

98.51

DESCRIPTION: Under intravenous sedation, the patient was placed in the supine position and prepped and draped in the usual sterile manner. Lithotripsy was started at 21 kilovolts and increased to a maximum of 30 kilovolts. The stone was revisualized and appeared to be in the same place. Additional shocks were delivered. The stone was ad-equately fragmented after a total of 2,500 shocks. Sedation was discontinued. The patient tolerated the procedure well and was released to his spouse.

DIAGNOSIS(ES): _____

ICD-9-CM DIAGNOSIS(ES) CODE(S): _____ 592.0 _____

PROCEDURE(S): _____

MAIN TERM(S): _____

ICD-9-CM PROCEDURE CODE(S): _____ 98.51 _____

CASE 8

ADMITTING DIAGNOSIS: Nephroptosis and hydronephrosis.

DISCHARGE DIAGNOSIS: Nephroptosis and hydronephrosis.

HOSPITAL COURSE: The patient was admitted on 11/15/xx for a scheduled nephropexy. The indications for surgery are based on the results of the intravenous pyelography that was done last week. The IVP demonstrated nephroptosis and hydronephrosis. The patient's preoperative course was uneventful. He tolerated the procedure and was returned to his unit in good condition. On the fifth postoperative day, he developed urinary retention, which necessitated urinary catheterization. Urinary output continued to be diminished. The KUB was negative for ureterostenosis and uretero-lithiasis. The patient was encouraged to increase fluids, and by the ninth postoperative day, urinary output was normal. The patient was discharged home on restricted activity for six weeks.

DISCHARGE PLAN: He is scheduled for a follow-up office visit next week.

DIAGNOSIS(ES): _____

ICD-9-CM DIAGNOSIS(ES) CODE(S): _____

PROCEDURE(S): _____

MAIN TERM(S): _____

ICD-9-CM PROCEDURE CODE(S): _____

CASE 9

PREOPERATIVE DIAGNOSIS: Left ureterolithiasis.

POSTOPERATIVE DIAGNOSIS: Left ureterolithiasis.

PROCEDURE: Cystoscopy and left retrograde pyelogram. Left ureteroscopic stone extraction with placement of a left double-J ureteral stent.

DESCRIPTION: The patient was premedicated and brought to the operating room in the supine position. Intravenous sedation was administered and the patient was repositioned to the dorsolithotomy position, prepped, and draped in the usual sterile fashion. Cystoscopy was performed and the bladder mucosa was smooth and without evidence of tu-mors or stones. The left ureteral orifice was seen and entered with an open-tip ureteral stent. Left retrograde pyelogram confirmed calculus in the distal ureter. The stone was quite large and grasped with grasping forceps. It was broken into a couple of pieces and the largest piece was removed and sent to pathology. Multiple small fragments were irrigated into the bladder. The ureteroscope was removed and a 7 French 26-cm double-J stent was passed into the ureter with the proximal end lying within the renal pelvis and the distal end lying within the bladder. The bladder was drained. There were no complications and the patient was sent to the recovery room in good condition.

DIAGNOSIS(ES): _____

ICD-9-CM DIAGNOSIS(ES) CODE(S): _____

PROCEDURE(S): _____

MAIN TERM(S): _____

ICD-9-CM PROCEDURE CODE(S): _____

CASE 10

PREOPERATIVE DIAGNOSIS: Stress urinary incontinence.

POSTOPERATIVE DIAGNOSIS: Stress urinary incontinence.

ANESTHESIA: General endotracheal.

PROCEDURE: Cystoscopy and raised bladder neck suspension.

DESCRIPTION: The patient was brought to the operating room in the supine position. She was placed under general endotracheal anesthesia and placed in the dorsolithotomy position. She was prepped and draped in the usual sterile fashion. A Foley catheter was inserted and the bladder was drained. A midline vaginal incision was made. Using a combination of sharp and blunt dissection, the vaginal mucosa was dissected free from the bladder. Two stitches were placed for elevation of the bladder neck. There was excellent elevation of the bladder neck. Cystourethroscopy was then performed. There was no evidence of bladder injuries and the urine was clear. The ureteral orifices were visualized and found to be patent with clear efflux from each orifice. The incision was closed and a vaginal pack was placed. Sponge, instrument, and needle counts were correct ×2. There were no complications and the patient was sent to the recovery room in good condition.

DIAGNOSIS(ES): _____

ICD-9-CM DIAGNOSIS(ES) CODE(S): _____

PROCEDURE(S): _____

MAIN TERM(S): _____

ICD-9-CM PROCEDURE CODE(S): _____

CASE 11

PREOPERATIVE DIAGNOSIS: Cryptorchidism.

POSTOPERATIVE DIAGNOSIS: Cryptorchidism.

OPERATION: Bilateral orchiopexy.

INDICATIONS: This four-year-old Native American male presented with undescended testes, nonresponsive to hormone treatment. His parents have consented to surgical intervention and were advised of the risks and benefits of the procedure.

PROCEDURE: After adequate general anesthesia, the patient was prepped and draped in the usual manner. He was placed in the supine position, and an incision was made in the inguinal canal. The testes were freed with sharp dissection. The spermatic cord was stripped, and the vas deferens and spermatic vessels were left intact. The testes were placed away from the operative site. A channel for each testis was created from the inguinal incision to the bottom of the scrotum. Each testis was delivered through the respective channels, and the scrotal wound was closed. Sponge, needle, and instrument counts were correct ×2. The patient was returned to the recovery room in good condition.

DIAGNOSIS(ES): _____

ICD-9-CM DIAGNOSIS(ES) CODE(S): _____

PROCEDURE(S): _____

MAIN TERM(S): _____

ICD-9-CM PROCEDURE CODE(S): _____

CASE 12

PREOPERATIVE DIAGNOSIS: Benign prostatic hypertrophy with bladder neck obstruction.

POSTOPERATIVE DIAGNOSIS: Benign prostatic hypertrophy with bladder neck obstruction.

PROCEDURE: Cystourethroscopy and transurethral resection of the prostate.

ANESTHESIA: Spinal block.

DESCRIPTION: Under spinal anesthesia, the patient was placed in the lithotomy position and prepped and draped in the usual sterile manner. Cystourethroscopy was done with a #17 French cystourethroscope. The anterior urethra was normal. Prostatic urethra revealed predominantly lateral lobar type of enlargement with obstruction to the bladder neck. The bladder showed fine to moderate trabeculation and no evidence of bladder tumor, diverticulum, or calculus. Ureteral orifices were normal in location. The efflux was clear bilaterally and the cystoscope was removed. The urethra was dilated to a #28 French with van Buren sounds. A #27 French continuous-flow resectoscope was introduced and the prostatic tissue was resected out, first by dissection of the median lobe, then the left lateral lobe, and finally the right lateral lobe. All the bleeding points were controlled. Prostatic chips were evacuated. A #24 French three-way Foley catheter was left indwelling. Approximate blood loss, 200 cc. Blood replacement, none. The patient left the operating room in satisfactory condition.

DIAGNOSIS(ES): _____

ICD-9-CM DIAGNOSIS(ES) CODE(S): _____

PROCEDURE(S): _____

MAIN TERM(S): _____

ICD-9-CM PROCEDURE CODE(S): _____

Using the same excerpts from previous cases, write the name of the procedure and main term. Assign the correct CPT procedure codes.

CASE 13

PREOPERATIVE DIAGNOSIS: Right kidney stone.

POSTOPERATIVE DIAGNOSIS: Right kidney stone.

PROCEDURE: Extracorporeal shock wave lithotripsy of right kidney stone.

DESCRIPTION: Under intravenous sedation, the patient was placed in the supine position and prepped and draped in the usual sterile manner. Lithotripsy was started at 21 kilovolts and increased to a maximum of 30 kilovolts. The stone was revisualized and appeared to be in the same place. Additional shocks were delivered. The stone was adequately fragmented after a total of 2,500 shocks. Sedation was discontinued. The patient tolerated the procedure well and was released to his spouse.

PROCEDURE(S): _____

MAIN TERM(S): _____

CPT PROCEDURE CODE(S): _____

CASE 14

ADMITTING DIAGNOSIS: Nephroptosis and hydronephrosis.

DISCHARGE DIAGNOSIS: Nephroptosis and hydronephrosis.

HOSPITAL COURSE: The patient was admitted on 11/15/xx for a scheduled nephropexy. The indications for surgery are based on the results of the intravenous pyelography that was done last week. The IVP demonstrated nephroptosis and hydronephrosis. The patient's preoperative course was uneventful. He tolerated the procedure and was returned to his unit in good condition. On the fifth postoperative day, he developed urinary retention, which necessitated urinary catheterization. Urinary output continued to be diminished. The KUB was negative for ureterostenosis and ureterolithiasis. The patient was encouraged to increase fluids, and by the ninth postoperative day, urinary output was normal. The patient was discharged home on restricted activity for six weeks.

DISCHARGE PLAN: He is scheduled for a follow-up office visit next week.

PROCEDURE(S): _____

MAIN TERM(S): _____

CPT PROCEDURE CODE(S): _____

CASE 15

PREOPERATIVE DIAGNOSIS: Left ureterolithiasis.

POSTOPERATIVE DIAGNOSIS: Left ureterolithiasis.

PROCEDURE: Cystoscopy and left retrograde pyelogram. Left ureteroscopic stone extraction with placement of a left double-J ureteral stent.

DESCRIPTION: The patient was premedicated and brought to the operating room in the supine position. Intravenous sedation was administered and the patient was repositioned to the dorsolithotomy position, prepped, and draped in the usual sterile fashion. Cystoscopy was performed and the bladder mucosa was smooth and without evidence of tumors or stones. The left ureteral orifice was seen and entered with an open-tip ureteral stent. Left retrograde pyelogram confirmed calculus in the distal ureter. The stone was quite large and grasped with grasping forceps. It was broken into a couple of pieces and the largest piece was removed and sent to pathology. Multiple small fragments were irrigated into the bladder. The ureteroscope was removed, and a 7 French 26-cm double-J stent was passed into the ureter with the proximal end lying within the renal pelvis and the distal end lying within the bladder. The bladder was drained. There were no complications and the patient was sent to the recovery room in good condition.

PROCEDURE(S): _____

MAIN TERM(S): _____

CPT PROCEDURE CODE(S): _____

CASE 16

PREOPERATIVE DIAGNOSIS: Stress urinary incontinence.

POSTOPERATIVE DIAGNOSIS: Stress urinary incontinence.

ANESTHESIA: General endotracheal.

PROCEDURE: Cystoscopy and raised bladder neck suspension.

DESCRIPTION: The patient was brought to the operating room in the supine position. She was placed under general endotracheal anesthesia and placed in the dorsolithotomy position. She was prepped and draped in the usual sterile fashion. A Foley catheter was inserted and the bladder was drained. A midline vaginal incision was made. Using a combination of sharp and blunt dissection, the vaginal mucosa was dissected free from the bladder. Two stitches were placed for elevation of the bladder neck. There was excellent elevation of the bladder neck. Cystourethroscopy was then performed. There was no evidence of bladder injuries and the urine was clear. The ureteral orifices were visualized and found to be patent with clear efflux from each orifice. The incision was closed and a vaginal pack was placed. Sponge, instrument, and needle counts were correct ×2. There were no complications and the patient was sent to the recovery room in good condition.

PROCEDURE(S): _____

MAIN TERM(S): _____

CPT PROCEDURE CODE(S): _____

CASE 17

PREOPERATIVE DIAGNOSIS: Cryptorchidism.

POSTOPERATIVE DIAGNOSIS: Cryptorchidism.

OPERATION: Bilateral orchiopexy.

INDICATIONS: This four-year-old Native American male presented with undescended testes, nonresponsive to hormone treatment. His parents have consented to surgical intervention and were advised of the risks and benefits of the procedure.

PROCEDURE: After adequate general anesthesia, the patient was prepped and draped in the usual manner. He was placed in the supine position, and an incision was made in the inguinal canal. The testes were freed with sharp dissection. The spermatic cord was stripped, and the vas deferens and spermatic vessels were left intact. The testes were placed away from the operative site. A channel for each testis was created from the inguinal incision to the bottom of the scrotum. Each testis was delivered through the respective channels, and the scrotal wound was closed. Sponge, needle, and instrument counts were correct ×2. The patient was returned to the recovery room in good condition.

PROCEDURE(S): _____

MAIN TERM(S): _____

CPT PROCEDURE CODE(S): _____

CASE 18

PREOPERATIVE DIAGNOSIS: Benign prostatic hypertrophy with bladder neck obstruction.

POSTOPERATIVE DIAGNOSIS: Benign prostatic hypertrophy with bladder neck obstruction.

PROCEDURE: Cystourethroscopy and transurethral resection of the prostate.

ANESTHESIA: Spinal block.

DESCRIPTION: Under spinal anesthesia, the patient was placed in the lithotomy position and prepped and draped in the usual sterile manner. Cystourethroscopy was done with a #17 French cystourethroscope. The anterior urethra was normal. Prostatic urethra revealed predominantly lateral lobar type of enlargement with obstruction to the bladder neck. The bladder showed fine to moderate trabeculation and no evidence of bladder tumor, diverticulum, or calculus. Ureteral orifices were normal in location. The efflux was clear bilaterally and the cystoscope was removed. The urethra was dilated to a #28 French with van Buren sounds. A #27 French continuous-flow resectoscope was introduced and the prostatic tissue was resected out, first by dissection of the median lobe, then the left lateral lobe, and finally the right lateral lobe. All the bleeding points were controlled. Prostatic chips were evacuated. A #24 French three-way Foley catheter was left indwelling. Approximate blood loss, 200 cc. Blood replacement, none. The patient left the operating room in satisfactory condition.

PROCEDURE(S): _____

MAIN TERM(S): _____

CPT PROCEDURE CODE(S): _____

MEDICAL TERMINOLOGY CHALLENGE

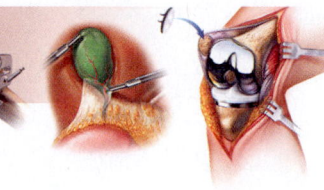

Read the operative report excerpts and write a brief description for each italicized medical term. Use a medical dictionary as necessary.

A. PREOPERATIVE DIAGNOSIS: Possible intermittent left (1) *testicular torsion.*

POSTOPERATIVE DIAGNOSIS: Torsion and (2) *necrosis* of left testicular appendix.

OPERATIONS: Left (3) *testicular appendectomy*, hydrocelectomy, and (4) *bilateral* orchiopexy.

DESCRIPTION: The patient was placed in the (5) *supine* position and prepped and draped in the usual sterile manner. A midline scrotal incision was made on the left side. There was considerable reaction around the (6) *tunica vaginalis.* The tunica vaginalis was (7) *imbricated* to the visceral margin. The left testicle was then fixed to prevent subsequent torsion.

A1. _____

A2. _____

A3. _____

A4. _____

A5. _____

A6. _____

A7. _____

B. PREOPERATIVE DIAGNOSIS: (1) *Adenocarcinoma* of the prostate.

POSTOPERATIVE DIAGNOSIS: Adenocarcinoma of the prostate.

PROCEDURE: (2) *Radioactive seed implantation* to the prostate using (3) *fluoroscopic* and ultrasound guidance.

DESCRIPTION: The patient was given satisfactory anesthesia. He was placed in the (4) *lithotomy* position and prepped and draped in the usual fashion. A (5) *Foley catheter* was inserted and the bladder was filled with 200 cc of fluid. A (6) *transrectal* probe was inserted using the stepper device. A #1 French cystoscope was introduced through the urethra. The (7) *anterior urethra* was normal. The (8) *prostatic urethra* had one small, slightly traumatized area.

B1. _____

B2. _____

B3. _____

B4. _____

B5. _____

B6. _____

B7. _____

B8. _____

NOTES:

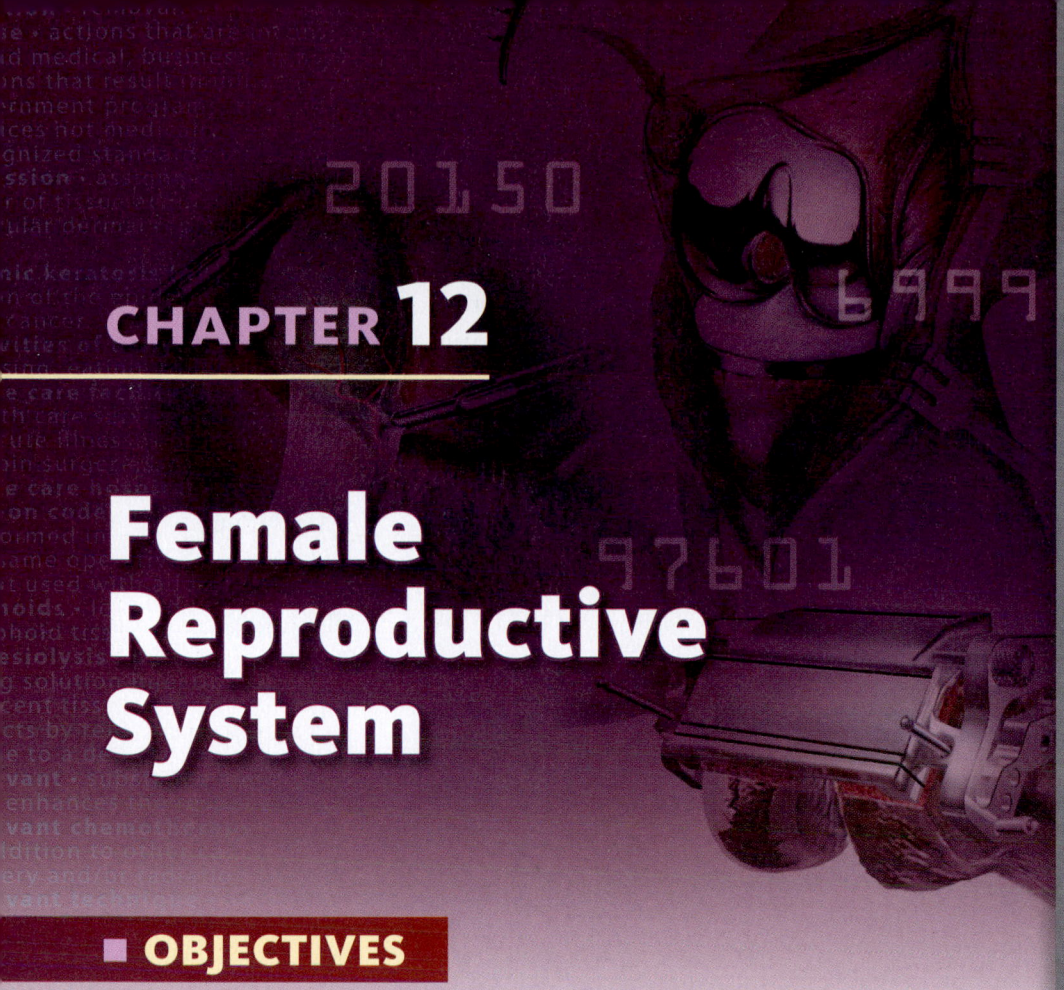

CHAPTER 12

Female Reproductive System

■ OBJECTIVES

At the completion of this chapter, the student should be able to:

1. Learn the word roots associated with the female reproductive system.
2. Label the basic structures of the female reproductive system.
3. Discuss the functions of the female reproductive system.
4. Accurately spell and define female reproductive system terminology.
5. Accurately assign medical codes to female reproductive system diagnoses and procedures.

■ OVERVIEW

The female reproductive system consists of external and internal **genitalia** (jen-ih-**TAY**-lee-ah). The **internal genitalia**—the vagina, uterus, fallopian tubes, and ovaries—function together to produce female hormones and provide an environment for the development and birth of a baby. The **external genitalia**—the mons pubis, labia majora and minora, clitoris, vaginal orifice, Bartholin glands, and perineum—function as a protective covering for internal female reproductive organs. **Gynecology** (**gigh**-neh-**KALL**-oh-jee; **jin**-eh-**KALL**-oh-jee) is the medical specialty related to the female reproductive system, and the physician specialist is a **gynecologist** (**gigh**-neh-**KALL**-oh-jist; **jin**-eh-**KALL**-oh-jist). **Obstetrics** is the medical specialty related to pregnancy, and the physician specialist is an **obstetrician**. These two specialties are often practiced together.

Medical terms and exercises related to female reproductive system structures are presented in the first section of this chapter. Medical terms

KEY TERMS

adnexa
amnion
amniotic fluid
amniotic sac
areola
Bartholin glands
breech presentation
cervix
cesarean delivery
chorion
clitoris
embryo
embryologist
embryology
endometrium
external genitalia
fallopian tube
fetal membrane
fetus
fimbriae
fundus
gamete
genitalia
gestation
glandular tissue
graafian follicle
gynecologist
gynecology
hymen
internal genitalia
labia majora
labia minora
lactation
lactiferous duct
menarche
menopause
menorrhea
menses
mons pubis
myometrium
nipple
obstetrician
obstetrics
occiput anterior
occiput posterior
ovary
ovulation
ovum
perimetrium
perineum
placenta
transverse presentation
umbilicus
uterus
vagina
vaginal orifice
zygote

Hysterosalpinguoophoruectomy

and exercises related to the female reproductive system during pregnancy are presented in the second section of this chapter. Medical coding exercises are available after all terms are presented.

FEMALE REPRODUCTIVE SYSTEM ROOTS, PREFIXES, AND SUFFIXES

Roots, prefixes, and suffixes associated with the female reproductive system are listed in table 12-1. Review the word elements and complete the exercise.

Table 12-1 Female Reproductive System Roots, Prefixes, and Suffixes

ROOT	MEANING
cervic/o	cervix
colp/o	vagina
cry/o	cold
cyst/o	sac
epis/o	vulva
fibr/o	fibrous tissue
gyn/o; gynec/o	woman
hyster/o	uterus
lapar/o	abdominal wall
mamm/o; mast/o	breast
men/o	menses; menstruation
metr/o; metr/i	uterus
oophor/o	ovary
ov/o	ovum; egg
ovari/o	ovary
salping/o	fallopian tubes; oviducts
uter/o	uterus
vagin/o	vagina
vulv/o	vulva

PREFIX	MEANING
ante-	before; forward
endo-	within
retro-	behind; backward; upward

SUFFIX	MEANING
-arche	beginning; onset
-cele	herniation; protrusion
-version	to turn

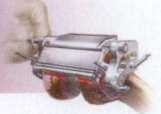

EXERCISE 12-1

Write the root, prefix, suffix, and their meanings. Based on the meanings, write a brief definition for each term.

1. Menarche
   ROOT: _men/o_ MEANING: _menstruation_
   PREFIX: _____ MEANING: _____
   SUFFIX: _arche_ MEANING: _beginning_
   DEFINITION: _beginning of Menses_

2. Endometrium
   ROOT: _Metr/o_ MEANING: _uterus_
   PREFIX: _endo_ MEANING: _within_
   SUFFIX: _ium_ MEANING: _____
   DEFINITION: _pertaining to within the uterus_

3. Laparoscopy
   ROOT: _Lapar/o_ MEANING: _abdominal wall_
   PREFIX: _____ MEANING: _____
   SUFFIX: _scopy_ MEANING: _process of visualization_
   DEFINITION: _visualization through the abdominal wall with a scope_

4. Episiotomy
   ROOT: _epis/o_ MEANING: _vulva_
   PREFIX: _____ MEANING: _____
   SUFFIX: _otomy_ MEANING: _incision into_
   DEFINITION: _incision into the vulva_

5. Fibroid
   ROOT: _fibr/o_ MEANING: _fibrous tissue_
   PREFIX: _____ MEANING: _____
   SUFFIX: _oid_ MEANING: _resembling_
   DEFINITION: _resembling fibrous tissue_

6. Hysterocele
   ROOT: _hyster/o_ MEANING: _uterus_
   PREFIX: _____ MEANING: _____
   SUFFIX: _cele_ MEANING: _protrusion_
   DEFINITION: _hernia or protrusion of uterus_

7. Salpingitis
   ROOT: <u>Salping/o</u> MEANING: <u>fallopian tubes</u>
   PREFIX: _____ MEANING: _____
   SUFFIX: <u>itis</u> MEANING: <u>inflammation</u>
   DEFINITION: <u>inflammation of the fallopian tubes</u>

8. Endometriosis
   ROOT: <u>metr/o</u> MEANING: <u>uterus</u>
   PREFIX: <u>endo</u> MEANING: <u>within</u>
   SUFFIX: <u>osis</u> MEANING: <u>condition</u>
   DEFINITION: <u>a condition within the uterus</u>

9. Cervical
   ROOT: <u>Cervic/o</u> MEANING: <u>cervix</u>
   PREFIX: _____ MEANING: _____
   SUFFIX: <u>al</u> MEANING: <u>pertaining to</u>
   DEFINITION: <u>pertaining to the cervix</u>

10. Dysmenorrhea
    ROOT: <u>men/o</u> MEANING: <u>menses</u>
    PREFIX: <u>dys</u> MEANING: _____
    SUFFIX: <u>orrhea</u> MEANING: <u>discharge</u>
    DEFINITION: <u>painful discharge (flow) of menses</u>

STRUCTURES OF THE FEMALE REPRODUCTIVE SYSTEM

The external genitalia includes the (1) **mons pubis** (**MONS PYOO**-bis), (2) **labia majora** (**LAY**-bee-ah mah-**JOR**-ah), (3) **clitoris** (**KLIT**-oh-ris), (4) **labia minora** (min-**OR**-ah), (5) **vaginal orifice**, (6) **hymen**, and **Bartholin glands**. These structures, collectively called the *vulva,* are illustrated in figure 12-1, with the exception of the Bartholin glands. The (7) **perineum** (pair-ih-**NEE**-um) is the area between the vaginal orifice and the anus.

The mons pubis, which is covered with hair in adult women, is a pad of fatty tissue that covers the symphysis pubis. The labia majora are two folds of fatty tissue, one on each side of the vaginal opening. The labia minora are two thinner folds of tissue that are located within the labia majora. The clitoris, located above the urinary orifice, is made of highly sensitive, erectile tissue. The vaginal orifice, which is surrounded by a thin layer of elastic connective tissue called the hymen, is the opening to the vagina. Bartholin glands, located on each side of the vaginal opening, secrete a mucous substance that lubricates the vagina.

The internal genitalia of the female reproductive system include the (1) **vagina**, (2) **uterus**, (3) **fallopian tubes**, and (4) **ovaries**. These structures are illustrated in figure 12-2.

Vagina and Uterus

The vagina, commonly called the *birth canal,* is a muscular, elastic tube, about three inches long, that expands during childbirth. The vagina receives the penis during intercourse and is the outlet for the menstrual flow.

The uterus is a hollow, pear-shaped, muscular organ commonly called the *womb.* It holds the fertilized ovum as it develops during pregnancy. The uterus has three distinct areas that are called the (5) **fundus**, the rounded upper section; the (6) **body**, the central section; and the

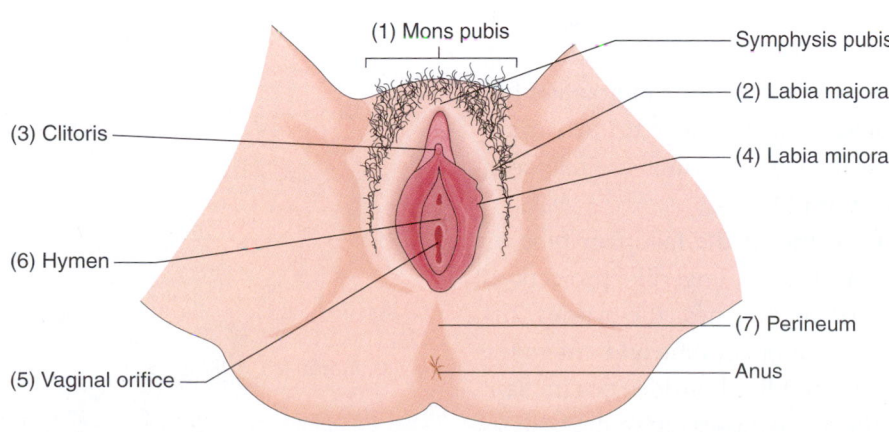

Figure 12-1 External genitalia

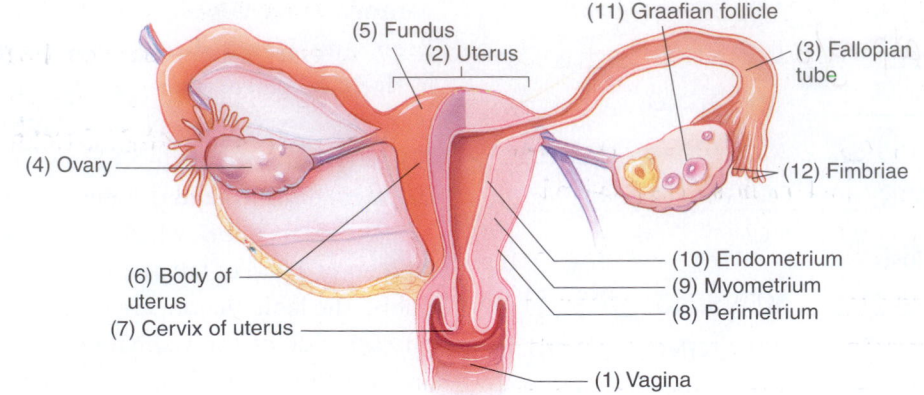

Figure 12-2 Internal genitalia

(7) **cervix**, the lower end of the uterus. The walls of the uterus consist of the (8) **perimetrium** (pair-ih-**MEE**-tree-um), the outer layer; the (9) **myometrium** (my-oh-**MEE**-tree-um), the thick muscular layer; and the (10) **endometrium** (en-doh-**MEE**-tree-um), the inner layer or lining. The endometrium thickens each month in preparation for implantation of a fertilized egg. When implantation does not occur, the endometrium is shed in a bloody discharge called **menses** (**MEN**-seez) or menstrual flow.

Ovaries and Fallopian Tubes

The ovaries are two small, almond-shaped organs located in the pelvic cavity on either side of the uterus. The fallopian tubes, also called *uterine tubes* and *oviducts,* are attached to the uterus and lie close to the ovaries. The ovaries and fallopian tubes are collectively known as the **adnexa** (add-**NECKS**-ah).

The ovaries are the female gonads and are responsible for producing the mature **ovum**. Ova, commonly called *eggs,* are the female sex cells. Immature ova are stored in the microscopic sacs of the ovaries, called (11) **graafian follicles** (**GRAFF**-ee-an **FALL**-ih-kals). During the menstrual cycle, the ovum and graafian follicles mature. The graafian follicles move to the surface of the ovary and release the mature ovum. The release of a mature ovum is called **ovulation**.

The ovum is coaxed toward the fallopian tube by the (12) **fimbriae** (**FIM**-bree-ay), fingerlike projections of the fallopian tubes that are very near the ovaries. The ovum travels through the fallopian tube and enters the uterus. If the ovum is not fertilized or does not implant in the endometrium, the ovum passes out of the body as part of the menstrual flow.

The onset of menstruation is called **menarche** (men-**AR**-kee). **Menorrhea** (men-oh-**REE**-ah) is normal menstrual flow. **Menopause** is the normal and gradual cessation of menstrual cycles and menstruation.

Mammary Glands

The mammary glands, or breasts, are responsible for the production of milk. This process is called **lactation** (lak-**TAY**-shun). Figure 12-3 illustrates the basic parts of the breast.

Each breast consists of a (1) **nipple** that is surrounded by a pigmented area called the (2) **areola** (air-ee-**OH**-lah). Areolar pigmentation can range from pink-flesh tones to a dark brown. The main internal structures of the breasts include (3) **glandular tissue** and (4) **lactiferous** (lak-**TIFF**-er-us) **ducts**. The glandular tissue produces milk that moves through the lactiferous ducts to the nipple.

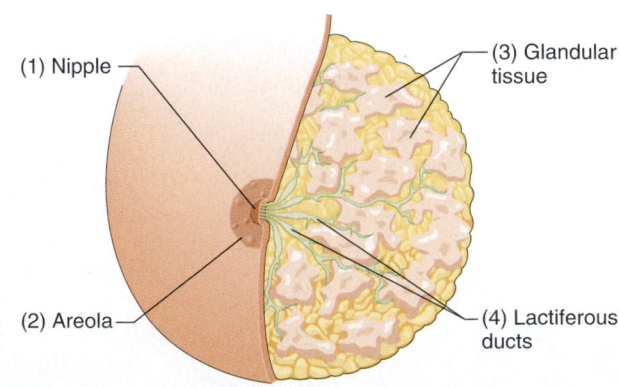

Figure 12-3 Mammary glands

EXERCISE 12-2

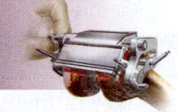

Write the names of the female reproductive system structures illustrated in figure 12-4 on the spaces provided.

1. _Uterus_
2. _Cervix of uterus_
3. _Vagina_
4. _Fallopian tube_
5. _Fimbriae_
6. _endometrium_
7. _myometrium_
8. _perimetrium_
9. _graafian_

EXERCISE 12-3

Write the medical term for each definition.

1. area between the vaginal orifice and anus _Perinum_
2. folds of fatty tissue surrounding the vaginal opening _Labia majora_
3. highly sensitive erectile tissue _clitoris_
4. menstrual flow _menstruation_
5. milk production _lactation_

6. normal cessation of menstruation _Menopause_
7. onset of menstruation _menometrorrhagia_
8. pad of fatty tissue; covers the symphysis pubis _Mons pubis_
9. secretes a lubricating substance _premenstrual syndrome_
10. thinner folds of tissue around the vaginal opening

FEMALE REPRODUCTIVE SYSTEM MEDICAL TERMINOLOGY

Female reproductive system medical terms are organized by diseases, conditions, diagnostic procedures, and operations. There are two categories of medical terminology exercises: (1) those designed to provide opportunities to learn the terms, and (2) those designed to provide opportunities to accurately assign diagnostic or procedure codes. Exercises for learning the medical terms immediately follow the list of terms and definitions. Medical coding exercises are available after all terms have been presented.

Female Reproductive System Signs, Symptoms, Diseases, and Conditions

The medical terms in table 12-2 are signs, symptoms, diseases, or conditions related to female reproductive system structures. Review the meaning of these terms and complete the exercises.

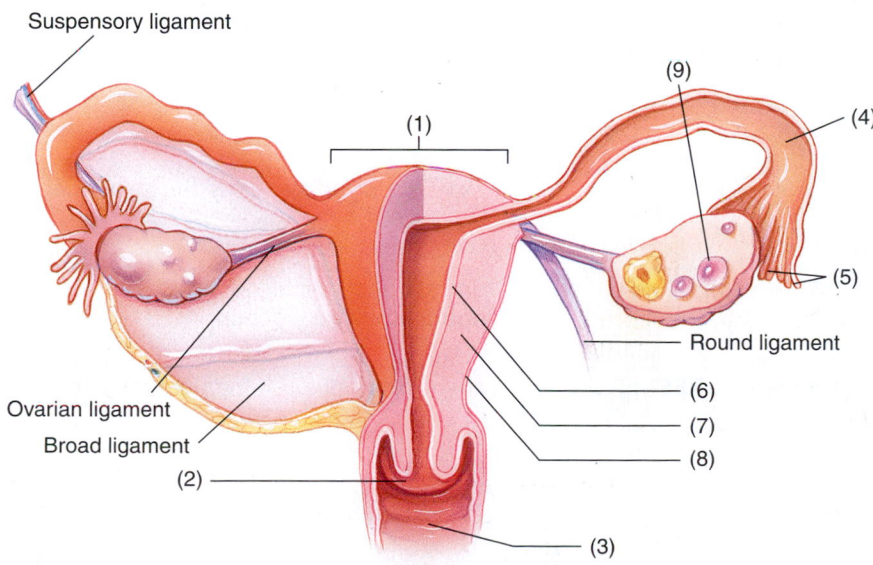

Figure 12-4 Label female reproductive system structures

Table 12-2 Female Reproductive System Signs, Symptoms, Diseases, and Conditions

TERM WITH PRONUNCIATION	DEFINITION
amenorrhea (**ah**-men-oh-**REE**-ah) a- = lack of; without men/o = menses; menstrual flow -(r)rhea = discharge; flow	absence or lack of menstruation
anteflexion of the uterus (**an**-tee-**FLEX**-shun) ante- = before	forward displacement of the uterus
carcinoma of the breast (kar-sin-**OH**-mah) carcin/o = cancer; malignant -oma = tumor	malignant tumor of the breast tissue; also called *breast cancer;* usually involves glandular breast cells in the ducts or lobules; DCIS is ductal carcinoma in situ (noninvasive); LCIS is lobular carcinoma in situ; invasive breast carcinoma is usually an adenocarcinoma
cervical carcinoma cervic/o = cervix; neck -al = pertaining to carcin/o = cancer; malignant -oma = tumor	squamous cell carcinoma of the cervix caused by the human papillomavirus (HPV) infection or by an adenocarcinoma; also called *cervical cancer*
cervicitis (**ser**-vih-**SIGH**-tis) cervic/o = cervix; neck -itis = inflammation	inflammation of the cervix
dysmenorrhea (**diss**-men-oh-**REE**-ah) dys- = painful; difficult; abnormal men/o = menses; menstruation -(r)rhea = flow; discharge	painful or abnormal menstrual flow
endometriosis (**en**-doh-**mee**-tree-**OH**-sis) endo- = within metr/i = uterus -osis = condition	presence and growth of endometrial tissue in areas outside of the uterus
fibroadenoma of the breast (**figh**-broh-**add**-eh-**NOH**-mah) fibr/o = fibrous tissue aden/o = gland -oma = tumor	small painless lumps that are benign, circumscribed, and mobile; may be felt during breast self-examination
fibrocystic breast changes (figh-broh-**SISS**-tik) fibr/o = fibrous tissue cyst/o = sac; cyst -ic = pertaining to	general term that includes mastalgia (painful breasts), breast cysts, and nondescript lumpiness of the breast; usually not associated with an increased risk of breast cancer; also called *fibrocystic breast disease* (FBD)
menometrorrhagia (**men**-oh-**met**-roh-**RAY**-jee-ah) men/o = menses; menstruation metr/i = uterus -(r)rhagia = hemorrhage	excessive bleeding during and between the normal menstrual period
menorrhagia (men-oh-**RAY**-jee-ah) men/o = menses; menstruation -(r)rhagia = hemorrhage	excessive bleeding during the menstrual period
metrorrhagia (meh-tro-**RAY**-jee-ah) metr/i = uterus -(r)rhagia = hemorrhage	excessive uterine bleeding at times other than during the normal menstrual period
oligomenorrhea (**oh**-lig-oh-**men**-oh-**REE**-ah) olig/o = few; diminished men/o = menses; menstruation -(r)rhagia = hemorrhage	abnormally light or infrequent menstruation
oophoritis (**oh**-off-or-**EYE**-tis) oophor/o = ovary -itis = inflammation	inflammation of the ovaries

continued

Table 12-2 (*continued*) Female Reproductive System Signs, Symptoms, Diseases, and Conditions

TERM WITH PRONUNCIATION	DEFINITION
ovarian carcinoma	malignant or cancerous tumor of the ovary
ovarian cyst	fluid-filled, multichambered sac in the ovary; also called *polycystic ovary syndrome*
pelvic inflammatory disease (PID)	inflammation of the vagina, cervix, fallopian tubes, and broad ligament; often a result of untreated sexually transmitted infections; also caused by bacteria associated with bacterial vaginitis
premature ovarian failure	early onset of the signs and symptoms of menopause characterized by decreased estrogen production of the ovaries; may be caused by enzyme or genetic defects, immune disturbances, or physical and environmental factors; also called *premature menopause*
premenstrual syndrome (PMS) (pre-**MEN**-stroo-al) pre- = before men/o = menses; menstruation -al = pertaining to	a group of symptoms such as irritability, anxiety, mood changes, headaches, breast swelling, and water retention that begin several days before the onset of menstruation and end a short time after the onset of menstruation
prolapse of the uterus	protrusion of the uterus into the vaginal opening
retroversion of the uterus retro- = backward; toward the back -version = to turn	backward displacement of the uterus
salpingitis (sal-pin-**JIGH**-tis) salping/o = fallopian tube -itis = inflammation	inflammation of the fallopian tube
toxic shock syndrome (TSS)	a rare and sometimes fatal disease caused by an infection of the female reproductive organs associated with certain strains of *Staphylococcus aureus*
uterine fibroids	benign uterine tumors originating in the smooth muscle of the uterus; may cause abnormal vaginal bleeding, pelvic pain and pressure, and pregnancy complications; also known as *leiomyomas, myomas,* and *fibromyomas* of the uterus
vaginitis (vaj-in-**EYE**-tis) vagin/o = vagina -itis = inflammation	inflammation of the vagina caused by bacteria, virus, or autoimmune disorders
vulvovaginitis (**vull**-voh-**vaj**-in-**EYE**-tis) vulv/o = vulva vagin/o = vagina -itis = inflammation	inflammation of the vulva (external genitalia) and vagina

EXERCISE 12-4

Replace the italicized phrase or abbreviation with the correct medical term.

1. After three abnormal evaluations, the final diagnosis was *a malignant tumor of the cervix.*
   cervical carcinoma
2. *Forward displacement* of the uterus might affect a woman's ability to become pregnant.
   anteflexion of the uterus
3. Female athletes sometimes exhibit *abnormally light or infrequent menstruation.*
   oligomenorrhea

4. *Painful menstrual flow* might be alleviated with pain relievers. *dysmenorrhea*
5. *Excessive bleeding during the menstrual period* might be a symptom of uterine polyps. *menorrhea*
6. Marlena informed her family physician that both her mother and sister had *malignant tumors of the breast* before they were 45 years of age.
   carcinoma of the breast
7. *Excessive bleeding during and between the normal menstrual period* may result in anemia.
   menometrorrhagia
8. Recurrent and severe vaginitis may lead to *PID.*
   pelvic inflammatory disease

continued

9. *PMS* can limit an individual's activities of daily living. *premenstral syndrome*

10. Bacteria cause *TSS*, a rare and sometimes fatal infection. *toxic shock syndrome*

EXERCISE 12-5

Match the medical term or abbreviation in column 1 with the definition in column 2.

MEDICAL TERM

a. amenorrhea

b. cervicitis

c. DCIS

d. endometriosis

e. fibroadenoma

DEFINITION

1. breast cancer *c*

2. excessive uterine bleeding *f*

3. growth of endometrial tissue outside of the uterus *d*

4. inflammation of the cervix *b*

5. inflammation of the external genitalia and vagina *k*

f. metrorrhagia

g. oophoritis

h. uterine prolapse

i. salpingitis

j. fibromyoma

k. vulvovaginitis

6. inflammation of the fallopian tube *i*

7. inflammation of the ovaries *g*

8. lack or absence of menstruation *a*

9. protrusion of the uterus into the vaginal opening *h*

10. small, benign lump in the breast *e*

11. uterine fibroid *j*

Female Reproductive System Operations and Diagnostic Procedures

Female reproductive system operations and diagnostic procedures are listed in table 12-3. Review the terms and complete the exercises.

Table 12-3 Female Reproductive System Operations and Diagnostic Procedures

TERM WITH PRONUNCIATION	DEFINITION
breast augmentation	implanting a prosthesis to enlarge the size of the breast for cosmetic reasons or breast reconstruction
breast reduction	mammoplasty to reduce the size of the breast for cosmetic or clinical reasons
colposcopy (kol-**POSS**-koh-pee) colp/o = vagina -scopy = examination with a scope	examination of vaginal and cervical tissue using a scope
conization (kon-ih-**ZAY**-shun)	surgical removal of a cone-shaped segment of the cervix for diagnosis or treatment; also called *cone biopsy*
cryosurgery (**krigh**-oh-**SER**-jer-ee) cry/o = cold	destruction and removal of tissue by rapid freezing
dilation and curettage (D & C) (**DIGH**-lay-shun and koo-reh-**TAHZH**)	widening of the cervical canal followed by scraping of the uterine lining (figure 12-5)
hysterectomy (**hiss**-ter-**EK**-toh-mee) hyster/o = uterus -ectomy = surgical removal; excision	surgical removal of the uterus; *total abdominal hysterectomy* (TAH) includes the uterus and cervix; *radical hysterectomy* includes the uterus, cervix, ovaries, fallopian tubes, lymph nodes, and lymph channels
hysterosalpingography (**hiss**-ter-oh-**sal**-ping-**OG**-rah-fee) hyster/o = uterus salping/o = fallopian tubes -graphy = process of recording	x-ray of the uterus and fallopian tubes using a contrast medium

continued

Table 12-3 (*continued*)   Female Reproductive System Operations and Diagnostic Procedures

TERM WITH PRONUNCIATION	DEFINITION
laparoscopy (lap-ar-**OSS**-koh-pee) lapar/o = abdominal wall -scopy = examination with a scope	examination of the contents of the abdominal and pelvic cavity using a scope
loop electrosurgical excision procedure (LEEP)	excision of abnormal cervical tissue using a thin, low-voltage electrified wire loop
mammography (mam-**OG**-rah-fee) mamm/o = breast -graphy = process of recording	x-ray examination of the soft tissue of the breast (figure 12-6)
mastectomy (mass-**TEK**-toh-mee) mast/o = breast -ectomy = surgical removal	surgical removal of the breast and surrounding tissue; *simple mastectomy* includes only the breast; *radical mastectomy* includes the removal of chest muscles and axillary lymph nodes; *modified radical mastectomy* allows the chest muscles that move the arm to be preserved
oophorectomy (oh-**off**-or-**EK**-toh-mee) oophor/o = ovary -ectomy = surgical removal	surgical removal of the ovary or ovaries
oophoropexy (oh-**off**-or-oh-**PEK**-see) oophor/o = ovary -pexy = surgical fixation	surgical fixation of the ovary or ovaries; also called *ovariopexy*
Papanicolaou smear (pap-ah-**NIK**-oh-low)	microscopic examination of cervical cells; diagnostic test for cervical cancer; Pap smear, Pap test (figure 12-7)
salpingo-oophorectomy (sal-**ping**-oh-oh-**off**-or-**EK**-toh-mee) salping/o = fallopian tubes oophor/o = ovary -ectomy = surgical removal	surgical removal of the fallopian tubes and ovaries
tubal ligation	surgical cutting and tying of the fallopian tubes to prevent passage of the sperm and ova through the tube; female sterilization (figure 12-8)
uteropexy (**YOO**-ter-oh-pek-see) uter/o = uterus -pexy = surgical fixation	surgical fixation of the uterus to the abdominal wall

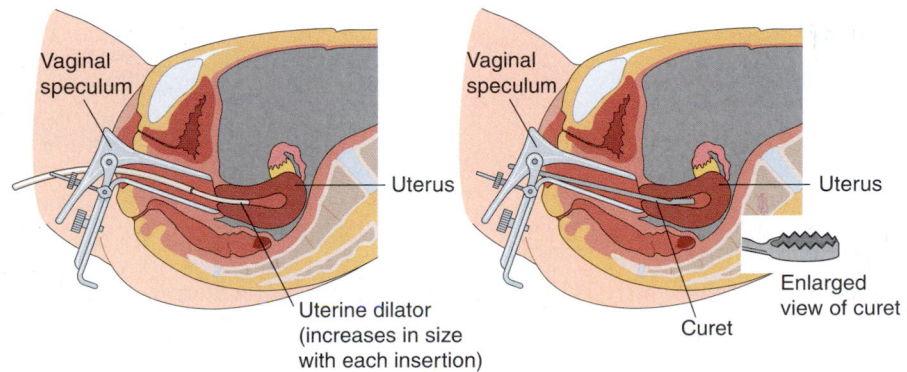

Figure 12-5   Dilation and curettage

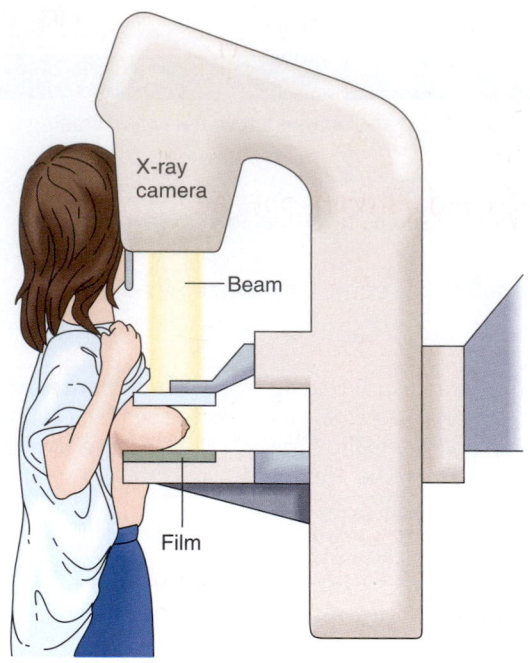

Figure 12-6   Mammography

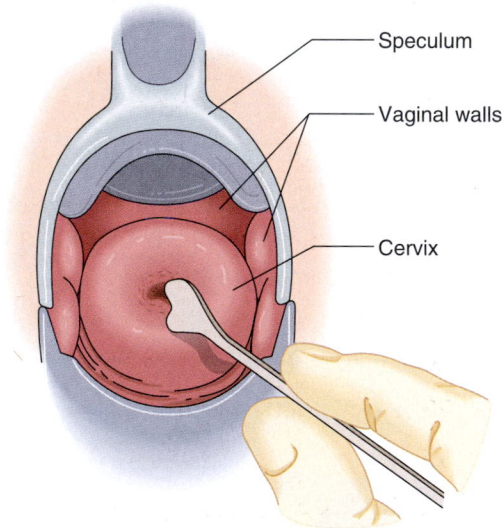

Figure 12-7   Pap smear

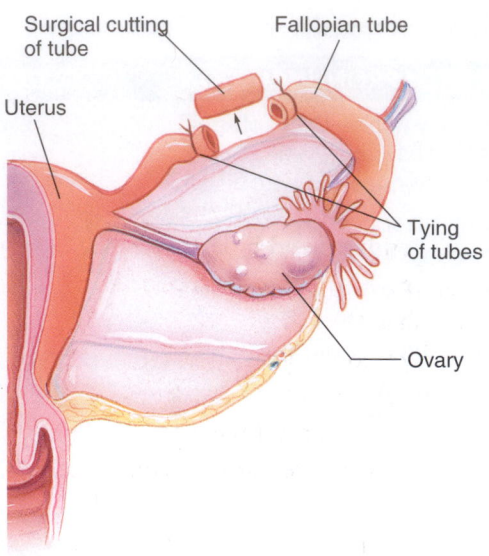

Figure 12-8   Tubal ligation

4. Irregular menstrual periods sometimes necessitate a *D & C*. _dilation and curettage_

5. After two abnormal cervical smears, the physician recommended a/an *surgical removal of cone-shaped segment of the cervix.* _conization, cone biopsy_

6. *Rapid freezing, destruction, and removal of tissue* is a procedure for treating abnormal cervical tissue growth. _cryosurgery_

7. Structural problems of the uterus and oviducts can be identified via *x-ray of the uterus and fallopian tubes using a contrast medium.* _hysterosalpingography_

8. *Endoscopic examination of the vagina and cervical tissue* is often done as a result of abnormal Pap smear test results. _colposcopy_

9. A prolapsed uterus may be repaired via *surgical fixation of the uterus to the abdominal wall.* _uteropexy_

10. *Surgical fixation of the ovaries* may be done to bring the ovaries closer to the fallopian tubes. _uteropexy_

EXERCISE 12-6

Replace the italicized phrase or abbreviation with the correct medical term.

1. Carmen made every effort to have an annual *x-ray examination of her breasts.* _mammography_

2. Melinda's initial *microscopic examination of cervical cells* was abnormal. _papanicolaou smear_

3. Helen chose *female sterilization* to prevent future pregnancies. _tubal ligation_

EXERCISE 12-7

Write the name of the female reproductive organ or structure associated with the listed terms.

1. hysterectomy   _uterus_
2. mastectomy   _breast_
3. oophorectomy   _ovary_
4. salpingo-oophorectomy   _fallopian tubes & ovaries_

PREGNANCY

This section of the chapter covers medical terms related to pregnancy, labor, and delivery. The generic medical term for male and female sex cells (ovum and sperm) is **gamete** (**GAM**-eet). Pregnancy occurs when an ovum has been fertilized by a sperm and is implanted into the endometrium. Fertilization usually takes place in the fallopian tube. The fertilized ovum is called a **zygote** (**ZIGH**-goht). From the second week through the eighth week of pregnancy, the fertilized ovum is called an **embryo** (**EM**-bree-oh). For the remainder of the pregnancy, the fertilized ovum is called a **fetus** (**FEE**-tus).

Pregnancy lasts 40 weeks or 280 days, which is about 9 calendar months or 10 lunar months. A lunar month is 4 weeks or 28 days. Pregnancy is divided into trimesters; each trimester is about 3 months long. The time between fertilization, also known as conception, and labor is called **gestation** (JESS-**TAY**-shun), or the gestational period. **Embryology** (em-bree-**ALL**-oh-jee) is the medical specialty related to the study of the embryo, and the physician specialist is called an **embryologist** (em-bree-**ALL**-oh-jist). Roots, prefixes, and suffixes associated with pregnancy are listed in table 12-4. Review the word elements and complete the exercises.

Table 12-4 Pregnancy Roots, Prefixes, and Suffixes

ROOT	MEANING
amni/o; amnion/o	amnion
chori/o	chorion
embry/o	embryo
episi/o; vulv/o	vulva
fet/o; fet/i	fetus
gravid/o	pregnancy
lact/o	milk
nat/o	birth
par/o; part/o	bear; give birth to; labor; childbirth
pelv/i	pelvis
perine/o	perineum
puerper/o	childbirth; puerperium
PREFIX	**MEANING**
micro-	small
multi-	many

PREFIX	MEANING
nulli-	none
post-	after
primi-	first; one
SUFFIX	**MEANING**
-centesis	surgical puncture
-metry	to measure
-(o)tomy	incision into
-(r)rhexis	rupture
-tocia	labor; birth

EXERCISE 12-8

Write the root, prefix, suffix, and their meaning. Based on the meanings, write a brief definition for each term.

1. Antepartum
   ROOT: _part/o_ MEANING: _give birth_
   PREFIX: _ante_ MEANING: _before_
   SUFFIX: _um_ MEANING: _pertaining to_
   DEFINITION: _pertainting to giving birth_

2. Embryology
   ROOT: _____ MEANING: _____
   PREFIX: _____ MEANING: _____
   SUFFIX: _____ MEANING: _____
   DEFINITION: _____

3. Multigravida
   ROOT: _gravid/o_ MEANING: _pregnancy_
   PREFIX: _multi_ MEANING: _many_
   SUFFIX: _a_ MEANING: _noun ending_
   DEFINITION: _many pregnancy_

4. Multipara
   ROOT: _____ MEANING: _____
   PREFIX: _____ MEANING: _____
   SUFFIX: _____ MEANING: _____
   DEFINITION: _____

continued

5. Nulligravida

ROOT: gravid/o MEANING: pregnancy

PREFIX: nulli MEANING: none

SUFFIX: a MEANING: noun ending

DEFINITION: never having been pregnant

6. Nullipara

ROOT: _____ MEANING: _____

PREFIX: _____ MEANING: _____

SUFFIX: _____ MEANING: _____

DEFINITION: _____

7. Postpartum

ROOT: part/o MEANING: give birth

PREFIX: post MEANING: after

SUFFIX: um MEANING: pertaining to

DEFINITION: pertaining to after giving birth

8. Primigravida

ROOT: par/o MEANING: give birth

PREFIX: _____ MEANING: _____

SUFFIX: _____ MEANING: _____

DEFINITION: _____

9. Primipara

ROOT: par/o MEANING: give birth

PREFIX: primi MEANING: first, one

SUFFIX: a MEANING: noun ending

DEFINITION: first time giving birth

10. Amniocentesis

ROOT: _____ MEANING: _____

PREFIX: _____ MEANING: _____

SUFFIX: _____ MEANING: _____

DEFINITION: _____

11. Perinatal

ROOT: nat/o MEANING: birth

PREFIX: peri MEANING: around

SUFFIX: al MEANING: pertaining to

DEFINITION: pertaining to the time around birth

12. Episiotomy

ROOT: _____ MEANING: _____

PREFIX: _____ MEANING: _____

SUFFIX: _____ MEANING: _____

DEFINITION: _____

STRUCTURES RELATED TO PREGNANCY

In addition to the female reproductive organs already presented, the specific structures related to pregnancy include the **amniotic sac** (**am**-nee-**OT**-ik sac), (1) **placenta** (plah-**SEN**-tah), (2) **umbilicus** (um-**BILL**-ih-kus), and (3) **amniotic fluid** (**am**-nee-**OT**-ik fluid). Figure 12-9 illustrates these structures.

The amniotic sac, also called the **fetal membrane**, houses the developing fetus. The sac is filled with amniotic fluid, which cushions and protects the fetus. The outer layer of the amniotic sac is the (4) **chorion** (**KOR**-ee-on), and the inner layer is the (5) **amnion** (**AM**-nee-on). Note that the umbilicus, also called the umbilical cord, connects the fetus to the placenta. The placenta, a temporary organ embedded in the wall of the uterus, allows blood, nutrients, oxygen, and waste to be exchanged between the mother and fetus. The placenta also produces several hormones necessary for a normal pregnancy.

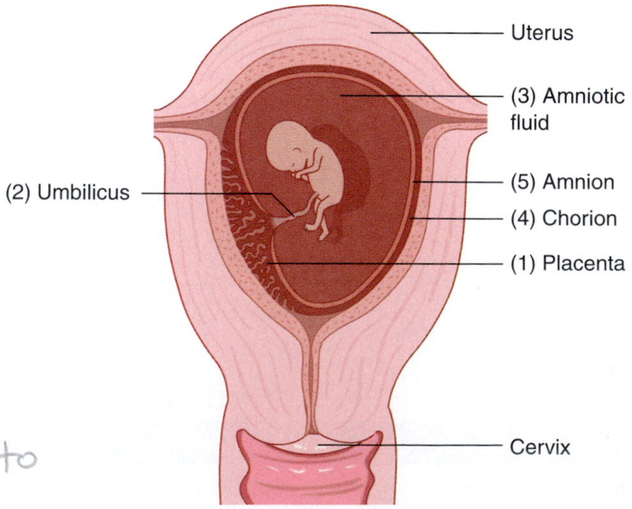

Figure 12-9 Amniotic sac, placenta, umbilicus

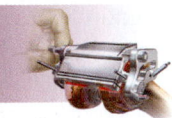

EXERCISE 12-9

Write the medical term for each definition.

1. connects the fetus to the placenta *umbilical cord*
2. fertilized ovum
3. fertilized ovum, ninth to fortieth week of pregnancy *fetus*
4. fertilized ovum, second to eighth week of pregnancy
5. inner layer of the structure that houses the developing fetus *amnion*
6. male and female sex cell
7. outer layer of the structure that houses the developing fetus *chorion*
8. period between fertilization and labor
9. structure that houses the developing fetus
10. temporary organ embedded in the uterine wall *amniotic sac*

Labor and Delivery

Labor and delivery are the time periods it takes to give birth. Normal, uncomplicated labor is divided into three stages:

- Stage one begins with productive uterine contractions and continues until the cervix is fully dilated at 10 centimeters.
- Stage two begins the actual process of delivery. Contractions push the infant downward toward the vaginal opening, and the mother assists the process by pushing with each contraction.
- Stage three begins when the placenta, membranes of the amniotic sac, and umbilical cord are expelled from the uterus.

A spontaneous vaginal delivery (SVD) is characterized by the infant in the (A) **occiput** (**OK**-sih-put) **anterior** position, which is head down and face toward the mother's back. Other positions include (B) **breech presentation**, or buttocks first; (C) **transverse presentation**, the infant is lying across the birth canal; and (D) **occiput posterior**, which is head down and face toward the mother's front. Delivery presentations are illustrated in figure 12-10.

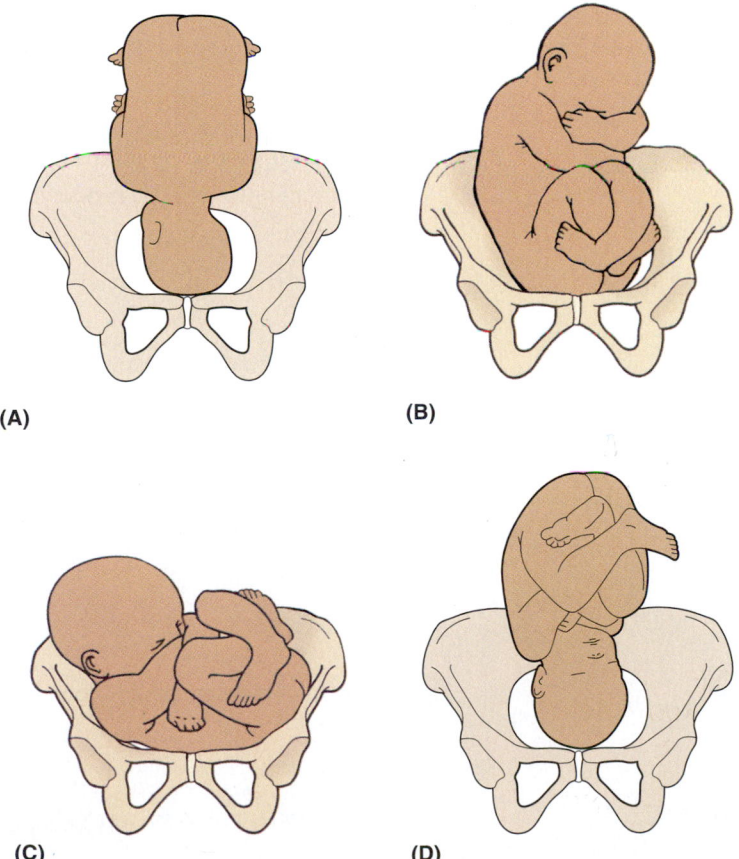

(A) (B) (C) (D)

Figure 12-10 Delivery presentations

These delivery presentations may require repositioning of the infant, forceps-assisted delivery, or **cesarean** (sih-ZAYR-ee-an) **delivery**, also called a C-section. A C-section is an operative procedure and the infant is delivered via an incision into the abdominal wall and uterus.

MEDICAL TERMS RELATED TO PREGNANCY

Pregnancy medical terms are organized as (1) general medical terms; (2) complications and disorders of pregnancy; and (3) diagnostic, surgical, and laboratory test terms.

Pregnancy General Medical Terms

The medical terms in table 12-5 are unique to pregnancy and childbearing. Review the pronunciation and meaning for each term and complete the exercises.

Table 12-5   General Medical Terms of Pregnancy

TERM WITH PRONUNCIATION	DEFINITION
Braxton-Hicks contractions	irregular and nonproductive contractions of the uterus that may occur throughout pregnancy
Chadwick sign	bluish-violet hue of the cervix and vagina; usually seen after the sixth week of pregnancy
effacement (ee-**FACE**-ment)	normal thinning and shortening of the cervix; occurs during labor
lochia (**LOH**-kee-ah)	vaginal discharge from the uterus that occurs for the first week or two after childbirth
meconium (meh-**KOH**-nee-um)	first feces of a newborn
multigravida (**mull**-tee-**GRAV**-ih-dah) multi- = many gravid/o = pregnancy	having been pregnant more than two times
multipara (mull-**TIP**-ah-rah) multi- = many par/o = giving birth to -a = a noun ending	having given birth two or more times to a viable fetus
neonatal intensive care unit (NICU) (**NIK**-yoo)	a hospital unit equipped and staffed to provide care to infants with special needs immediately following birth
neonate (**NEE**-oh-nayt)	an infant from birth to 28 days of age
nulligravida (**null**-ee-**GRAV**-ih-dah) nulli- = none gravid/o = pregnancy -a = a noun ending	never having been pregnant
nullipara (null-**IP**-ah-rah) nulli- = none par/o = giving birth to -a = a noun ending	never having given birth to a viable fetus
parturition (par-too-**RISH**-un)	act of giving birth; childbirth; delivery
prenatal	pertaining to the time period before giving birth
primigravida (**prigh**-mih-**GRAV**-ih-dah) primi- = first gravid/o = pregnancy -a = noun ending	first pregnancy
primipara (prigh-**MIP**-pah-rah) primi- = first par/o = giving birth to -a = noun ending	giving birth for the first time following 20 or more weeks of gestation
puerperium (pyoo-er-**PEER**-ee-um) puerper/o = childbirth -um = noun ending	the time period three to six weeks following childbirth

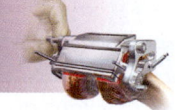

EXERCISE 12-10

Describe the difference between the paired terms.

1. a. multigravida _Many pregnancies_
   b. nulligravida _never pregnant_
2. a. multipara _____
   b. nulligravida _____
3. a. primigravida _first pregnancy_
   b. primipara _first child birth_
4. a. parturition _____
   b. puerperium _____

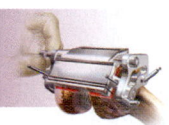

EXERCISE 12-11

Write the medical term for each definition.

1. bluish-violet hue of the cervix and vagina _Chadwick sign_
2. first feces of a newborn _____

3. hospital unit for newborns with special medical needs _neonatal intensive care unit_
4. infant from birth to 28 days of age _____
5. irregular, nonproductive contractions _Braxton-hicks contraction_
6. pertaining to the time period before giving birth _____
7. vaginal discharge during the first week or two after childbirth _lochia_

Pregnancy Complication and Disorder Terms

The medical terms in table 12-6 are complications and disorders associated with pregnancy and delivery. Review the meaning of the terms and complete the exercises.

Table 12-6   Complications and Disorders of Pregnancy

TERM WITH PRONUNCIATION	DEFINITION
abortion (ah-**BOR**-shun)	spontaneous or induced termination of pregnancy; a spontaneous abortion is commonly called a *miscarriage*
abruptio placentae (ah-**BRUP**-shee-oh plah-**SEN**-tee)	premature separation of the placenta from the uterine wall
amnionitis (**am**-nee-oh-**NIGH**-tis) amni/o = amnion -itis = inflammation	inflammation of the amnion
amniorrhea (**am**-nee-oh-**REE**-ah) amni/o = amnion -(r)rhea = flow; discharge	discharge of amniotic fluid from the amniotic sac; leaking of amniotic fluid
breech birth	delivery presentation with the buttocks appearing first
dystocia (diss-**TOH**-see-ah) dys- = abnormal; painful; difficult -tocia = labor; birth	difficult or painful labor
eclampsia (ee-**KLAMP**-see-ah) ectopic pregnancy	most severe form of gestation hypertension characterized by seizures abnormal implantation of a fertilized ovum outside the uterus; also called a *tubal pregnancy*

continued

Table 12-6 (*continued*) Complications and Disorders of Pregnancy

TERM WITH PRONUNCIATION	DEFINITION
gestational diabetes (jess-**TAY**-shun-al digh-ah-**BEE**-teez)	diabetes that develops during pregnancy and that usually resolves after pregnancy
gestational hypertension (jess-**TAY**-shun-al high-per-**TEN**-shun)	hypertension that develops during pregnancy and usually resolves after pregnancy; also called *pregnancy-induced hypertension* (PIH)
hydatidiform mole (**high**-day-**TID**-ih form)	a cystic mass resembling a cluster of grapes that develops in place of a placenta and fetus; also called a *molar pregnancy*
hyperemesis gravidarum (**high**-per-**EM**-eh-sis **grav**-ih-**DAR**-um) hyper- = excessive -emesis = vomiting gravid/o = pregnancy -um = noun ending	condition characterized by excessive and severe vomiting that results in maternal dehydration and weight loss
hysterorrhexis (**hiss**-ter-oh-**REKS**-iss) hyster/o = uterus -(r)rhexis = rupture	rupture of the uterus
incompetent cervix	inability of the cervix to retain the contents of the pregnant uterus that results in a spontaneous abortion
occiput posterior position	delivery presentation with the infant's head downward and facing the mother's back
placenta previa (plah-**SEN**-tah **PREE**-vee-ah)	condition in which the placenta is implanted in a lower part of the uterus and precedes the fetus during delivery (figure 12-11)
pre-eclampsia (**pre**-ee-**KLAMP**-see-ah)	gestational hypertension characterized by edema and proteinuria; the presence of protein in the urine
Rh incompatibility	reaction between Rh negative (Rh−) maternal blood and the Rh positive (Rh+) fetal blood of a first pregnancy that causes the immune system of the mother to develop antibodies against Rh+ blood cells; in subsequent pregnancies the antibodies will attack Rh+ fetal blood cells
transverse presentation	delivery presentation with the infant lying across the birth canal
tubal pregnancy	implantation of a fertilized ovum in the wall of a fallopian tube; also called ectopic pregnancy

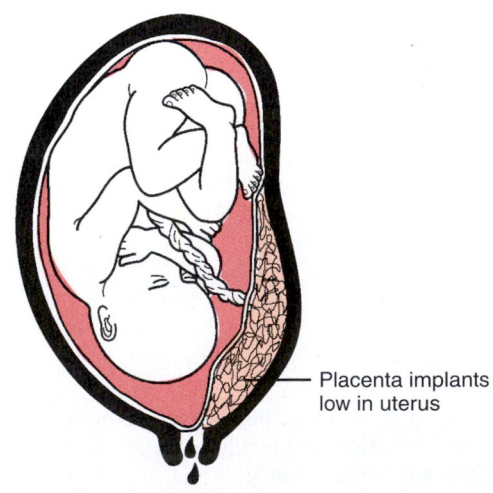

Placenta implants low in uterus

Figure 12-11 Placenta previa

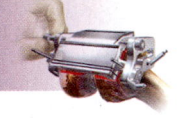

EXERCISE 12-12

Replace the italicized phrase or abbreviation with the correct medical term.

1. At 12 weeks of gestation, Marcia had a spontaneous *termination of pregnancy*. abortion
2. *Premature separation of the placenta* is a life-threatening condition for both mother and child.
3. Cheryl experienced *diabetes during pregnancy* for each of her pregnancies.
4. Due to a/an *implantation of a fertilized ovum outside the uterus,* Sara underwent removal of a fallopian tube.

5. Melinda's labor was prolonged due to a/an *delivery presentation with buttocks appearing first.*

6. Irina's first ultrasound revealed *placental implantation in the lower part of the uterus.*

7. *Excessive vomiting* may result in maternal dehydration and weight loss.

8. The obstetrician reassured Bonita that the medication for *PIH* would not affect fetal development.

EXERCISE 12-13

Match the condition in column 1 with the correct definition in column 2.

COLUMN 1	COLUMN 2
a. amnionitis	1. cystic mass resembling a cluster of grapes ___*e*___
b. amniorrhea	2. difficult labor _____
c. dystocia	3. gestational hypertension with edema and proteinuria ___*i*___

d. eclampsia

e. hydatidiform mole

f. hysterorrhexis

g. incompetent cervix

h. occiput posterior position

i. pre-eclampsia

j. transverse presentation

4. head downward and facing toward the back _____

5. inability of the cervix to retain uterine contents ___*g*___

6. infant lying across the birth canal _____

7. inflammation of the amnion ___*a*___

8. leaking of amniotic fluid _____

9. most severe form of gestational hypertension ___*d*___

10. rupture of the uterus _____

Pregnancy Diagnostic Procedure, Operative, and Laboratory Tests

Diagnostic procedure, operative, and laboratory tests related to pregnancy are listed in table 12-7. Review the meaning of the terms and complete the exercises.

Table 12-7   Pregnancy Diagnostic Procedure, Operative, and Laboratory Tests

TERM WITH PRONUNCIATION	DEFINITION
amniocentesis (**am**-nee-oh-sen-**TEE**-sis) amni/o = amnion -centesis = surgical puncture to remove fluid	surgical puncture into the amniotic sac to remove fluid for analysis; identifies genetic disorders; usually performed during the 15th week of pregnancy or later (figure 12-12)
amniography (**am**-nee-**OG**-rah-fee) amni/o = amnion -graphy = process of recording	process of taking an x-ray of the amniotic sac using a contrast medium
amnioscopy (**am**-nee-**OSS**-koh-pee) amni/o = amnion -scopy = visualization with a scope	visualization of the fetus with a scope that enters the amniotic cavity through the abdominal wall
amniotomy (**am**-nee-**OT**-oh-mee) amni/o = amnion -(o)tomy = incision into	incision into or rupture of the amniotic membranes to induce labor; also called "breaking the water"
cerclage (ser-**KLOZH**)	suturing the cervical opening to prevent spontaneous abortion; treatment for a history of incompetent cervix
cesarean section (see-**SAYR**-ee-an) (C-section)	incision into the abdominal wall and uterus to deliver a baby

continued

Table 12-7 (*continued*) Pregnancy Diagnostic Procedure, Operative, and Laboratory Tests

TERM WITH PRONUNCIATION	DEFINITION
chorionic villus sampling (**kor**-ee-**ON**-ik **VILL**-us) (CVS) chori/o = chorion -ic = pertaining to	removal of a small sample of the placenta by inserting a catheter or needle through the cervix and withdrawing placental tissue for analysis to identify genetic disorders of the fetus; usually performed between the 10th and 12th weeks of pregnancy
contraction stress test (CST)	introduction of an intravenous solution containing the hormone oxytocin to stimulate uterine contractions to evaluate whether the fetus can tolerate the stress of labor and delivery; also called the *oxytocin challenge test*
electronic fetal monitoring	application and use of an internal or external electronic device to monitor fetal heart rate and maternal uterine contractions; assesses the quality of the uterine contractions and the effects of labor on the fetus
episiotomy (eh-**pihz**-ee-**OT**-oh-mee) episi/o = vulva -(o)tomy = incision into	incision into the perineum to facilitate delivery and prevent perineal laceration or tearing
fetal ultrasonography (**ull**-trah-soh-**NOG**-rah-fee)	noninvasive examination of the fetus in utero using high-frequency sound waves
fetometry (fee-**TOM**-eh-tree) fet/o = fetus -metry = process of measuring	measuring or estimating the size of the fetus or the fetal head before delivery
pelvimetry (pell-**VIM**-eh-tree) pelv/i = pelvis -metry = process of measuring	measuring the pelvic outlet to determine if its size is adequate for childbirth
pregnancy test	laboratory blood and urine tests to determine pregnancy

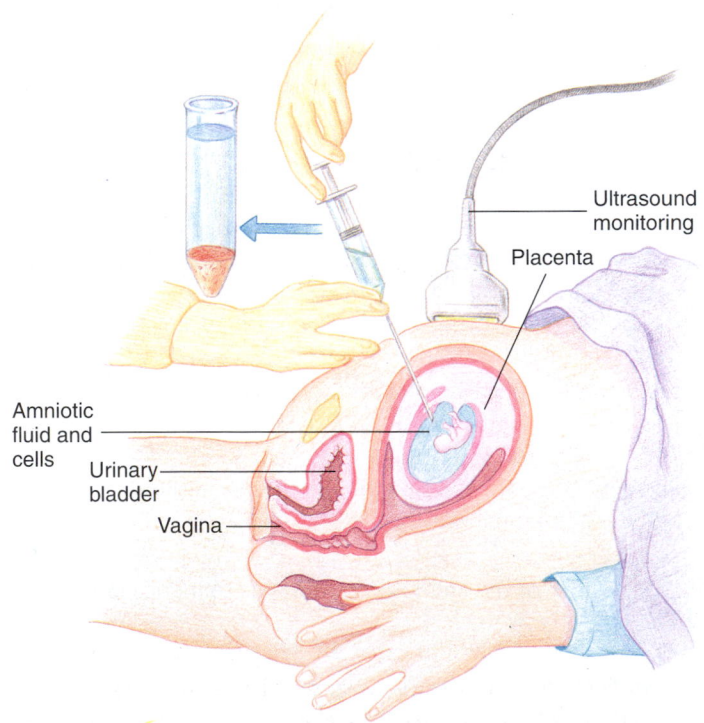

Figure 12-12 Amniocentesis

EXERCISE 12-14

Circle the medical term or abbreviation that best fits the description.

1. surgical puncture to remove fluid — *amniotomy* or *amniocentesis*

2. estimating fetal size before delivery — *fetometry* or *fetography*

3. incision into the perineum — *cerclage* or *episiotomy*

4. endoscopic visualization of the fetus — *fetal ultrasound* or *amnioscopy*

5. measuring the pelvic outlet — *pelvimetry* or *CST*

6. rupture of the amniotic membranes — *amniotomy* or *C-section*

7. suturing the cervical opening — *CVS or cerclage*
8. labor and delivery fetal stress test — *electronic fetal monitoring or CST*
9. incision to deliver a baby — *cesarean section or amniotomy*
10. removal of a sample of the placenta — *CST or CVS*

ABBREVIATIONS

Female reproductive system and pregnancy abbreviations are listed in table 12-8. Practice writing out the abbreviations with a brief definition for each phrase or term.

Table 12-8   Abbreviations

ABBREVIATION	MEANING
C-section	cesarean section
CST	contraction stress test
CVS	chorionic villus sampling
D & C	dilation and curettage
EDB	estimated date of birth
EDC	expected or estimated date of confinement
EDD	expected date of delivery
FHR	fetal heart rate
GYN	gynecology
L & D	labor and delivery
LEEP	loop electrosurgical excision procedure
LMP	last menstrual period
NSD	normal spontaneous delivery
OB	obstetrics
Pap smear	*Papanicolaou* smear
PID	pelvic inflammatory disease
PIH	pregnancy-induced hypertension
PMS	premenstrual syndrome
SVD	spontaneous vaginal delivery
TAH	total abdominal hysterectomy
TSS	toxic shock syndrome
TVH	total vaginal hysterectomy

FEMALE REPRODUCTIVE SYSTEM AND PREGNANCY MEDICAL CODING

To successfully complete the exercises in this section, the ICD-9-CM volumes 1, 2, and 3, and the CPT (Current Procedural Terminology) coding references must be readily available. The information in this section is presented as follows:

- An introduction to ICD-9-CM, chapter 10, "Diseases of the Genitourinary System," categories 610–629; and chapter 11, "Complications of Pregnancy, Childbirth, and the Puerperium"
- ICD-9-CM diagnostic coding exercises
- A summary of ICD-9-CM volume 3, chapter 12, "Operations on the Female Genital Organs"; and chapter 13, "Obstetrical Procedures"
- ICD-9-CM procedure coding exercises
- A summary of CPT Female Reproduction System and Pregnancy coding guidelines
- CPT coding exercises

Students are *strongly* encouraged to review the information at the beginning of the ICD-9-CM and CPT coding references. Commercial publishers include instructions on how to use the ICD-9-CM references, the ICD-9-CM official coding conventions, additional conventions used by the publisher, and the *ICD-9-CM Official Guidelines for Coding and Reporting*. Some publishers include the three ICD-9-CM volumes in one book and put the *Alphabetic Index* (volume 2) at the beginning of the reference.

The *Introduction* to CPT includes detailed instructions for using this code book, an index to the illustrations throughout the book, and anatomical illustrations of the major structures of body systems.

ICD-9-CM Volume 1, Chapter 10, Diseases of the Genitourinary System (610–629)

Female reproductive system diseases are coded to ICD-9-CM volume 1, chapter 10, "Diseases of the Genitourinary System," sections 610–629. These sections include the following:

- **Disorders of Breast (610–612).** Codes in this section include dysplasia, inflammatory diseases, hypertrophy and atrophy, and unspecified disorders of the breast.

- **Inflammatory Disease of Female Pelvic Organs (614–616).** Codes in this section include inflammatory diseases of the ovaries, fallopian tubes, peritoneum, uterus, cervix, vagina, and vulva.

- **Other Disorders of Female Genital Tract (617–629).** Codes in this section include endometriosis, prolapse of female organs, and noninflammatory diseases of the ovaries, fallopian tubes, uterus, cervix, vagina, and vulva. Disorders of menstruation, menopause, and infertility are also covered in this section.

Pregnancy disorders and conditions are coded to ICD-9-CM volume 1, chapter 11, "Complications of Pregnancy, Childbirth, and the Puerperium" (630–679). The codes in this chapter apply to the mother. The major sections in this chapter include the following:

- **Ectopic and Molar Pregnancy (630–633).** Codes in this section include hydatidiform and ectopic pregnancies involving the fallopian tubes and ovaries.

- **Other Pregnancy with Abortive Outcome (634–639).** Codes in this section cover all disorders and conditions related to spontaneous abortion, legally induced abortion, illegally induced abortion, complications following abortion, and ectopic and molar pregnancies. There are extensive fourth- and fifth-digit instructions for this section.

- **Complications Mainly Related to Pregnancy (640–649).** Codes in this section cover complications such as placenta previa, abruptio placentae, hypertension, pre-eclampsia, and diseases and conditions in the mother that complicate pregnancy.

- **Normal Delivery, and Other Indications for Care in Pregnancy, Labor, and Delivery (650–659).** Codes in this section apply to multiple gestations, fetal position, congenital abnormalities of the uterus and vulva, and

any fetal conditions that affect the management of the care of the mother.

- **Complications Occurring Mainly in the Course of Labor and Delivery (660–669).** Codes in this section cover conditions related to labor and delivery such as obstructed labor, uterine inertia, prolonged labor, postpartum hemorrhage, retained placenta, and complications related to anesthesia or sedation during labor and delivery.

- **Complications of the Puerperium (670–677).** The puerperium is the time period three to six weeks following delivery. Codes in this section include conditions such as infection, thrombophlebitis, pulmonary embolism, and disorders of lactation. Fifth-digit subclassifications are used throughout the section.

- **Other Maternal and Fetal Complications (678–679).** Codes in this section include conditions such as conjoined twins and complications in utero.

Conditions related to the female reproductive system may also be coded to the following chapters in volume 1: chapter 14, "Congenital Anomalies"; chapter 16, "Symptoms, Signs, and Ill-Defined Conditions"; and chapter 2, "Neoplasms."

EXERCISE 12-15

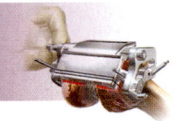

Write a brief definition for each diagnosis. Identify the main term in the diagnostic statement and assign the correct ICD-9-CM diagnosis code(s).

1. Fibrocystic breast disease
   DEFINITION: _lump of the breast_
   MAIN TERM: _breast cyst_
   ICD-9-CM CODE(S): _610.1_

2. Acute salpingitis and oophoritis
   DEFINITION: _____
   MAIN TERM: _____
   ICD-9-CM CODE(S): _____

3. Vulvovaginitis due to *E. coli*

   DEFINITION: *inflammation of the vulva*

   MAIN TERM: _____

   ICD-9-CM CODE(S): 616.10 , 041.4

4. Parametrial endometriosis

   DEFINITION: _____

   MAIN TERM: _____

   ICD-9-CM CODE(S): _____

5. Anteflexion of the uterus

   DEFINITION: _____

   MAIN TERM: _____

   ICD-9-CM CODE(S): 621.6

6. Lateral cystocele and rectocele

   DEFINITION: _____

   MAIN TERM: _____

   ICD-9-CM CODE(S): _____

7. Squamous cell carcinoma of the cervix, in situ

   DEFINITION: _____

   MAIN TERM: _____

   ICD-9-CM CODE(S): 233.1

8. Multiple uterine fibroids

   DEFINITION: _____

   MAIN TERM: _____

   ICD-9-CM CODE(S): _____

9. Follicular cyst of the ovary

   DEFINITION: _____

   MAIN TERM: _____

   ICD-9-CM CODE(S): 620.0

10. Ectopic tubal pregnancy without uterine pregnancy

    DEFINITION: _____

    MAIN TERM: _____

    ICD-9-CM CODE(S): _____

11. Incomplete spontaneous abortion

    DEFINITION: _____

    MAIN TERM: _____

    ICD-9-CM CODE(S): 634.91

12. Frank breech presentation, successfully delivered

    DEFINITION: _____

    MAIN TERM: _____

    ICD-9-CM CODE(S): _____

13. Antepartum threatened abortion

    DEFINITION: _____

    MAIN TERM: _____

    ICD-9-CM CODE(S): 640.03

14. Hyperemesis gravidarum with dehydration

    DEFINITION: _____

    MAIN TERM: _____

    ICD-9-CM CODE(S): _____

15. Hydatidiform mole

    DEFINITION: _____

    MAIN TERM: _____

    ICD-9-CM CODE(S): 630

16. Mild pre-eclampsia, antepartum condition

    DEFINITION: _____

    MAIN TERM: _____

    ICD-9-CM CODE(S): _____

17. Cesarean delivery due to transverse presentation

    DEFINITION: _____

    MAIN TERM: _____

    ICD-9-CM CODE(S): 652.31

18. Pregnancy-induced hypertension, delivered

    DEFINITION: _____

    MAIN TERM: _____

    ICD-9-CM CODE(S): _____

19. Abruptio placentae

    DEFINITION: _____

    MAIN TERM: _____

    ICD-9-CM CODE(S): 641.20

ICD-9-CM Volume 3, Chapter 12, Operations on the Female Genital Organs (65–71); and Chapter 13, Obstetrical Procedures (72–75)

Female reproductive system and pregnancy procedures are coded to ICD-9-CM volume 3, chapter 12, "Operations on the Female Genital Organs"; and chapter 13, "Obstetrical Procedures." Chapter 12 includes the following categories:

- ■ **Operations on Ovary (65).** Codes in this category cover excision, biopsy, and repair of the ovaries. There are separate codes for bilateral and unilateral procedures.

- ■ **Operations on Fallopian Tubes (66).** Codes in this category cover excision, biopsy, repair, and insufflation of the fallopian tubes. There are separate codes for bilateral and unilateral procedures.

- ■ **Operations on Cervix (67).** Codes in this category cover excision, biopsy, and repair of the cervix.

- ■ **Other Incision and Excision of Uterus (68); Other Operations on Uterus and Supporting Structures (69).** Codes in these categories cover procedures related to the uterus and uterine ligaments. Procedures include hysterectomy, dilation and curettage, biopsy, and repair. Hysterectomy is classified as cervical or abdominal, total, subtotal, and radical.

- ■ **Operations on Vagina and Cul-de-sac (70).** Codes in this category cover excision, biopsy, and repair of the vagina.

- ■ **Operations on Vulva and Perineum (71).** Codes in this category cover incision, excision, biopsy, and repair of the external genitalia and perineum.

Obstetrical procedures related to delivery are coded to ICD-9-CM volume 3, chapter 13. This chapter includes the following main categories:

- ■ **Forceps, Vacuum, and Breech Delivery (72).** Codes in this category cover delivery assisted by forceps, rotation of the fetal head, breech extraction, and vacuum extraction.

- ■ **Other Procedures Inducing or Assisting Delivery (73).** Codes in this category cover artificial rupture of amniotic membranes, manually assisted delivery, and episiotomy.

- ■ **Cesarean Section and Removal of Fetus (74).** Codes in this category cover delivery by cesarean section.

- ■ **Other Obstetric Operations (75).** Codes in this category cover diagnostic amniocentesis, intrauterine transfusion, intrauterine operations on the fetus, repair of lacerations occurring during delivery, and manual exploration of the uterus.

Some diagnostic and therapeutic procedures related to the female reproductive system and pregnancy are also coded to volume 3, chapter 16, "Miscellaneous Diagnostic and Therapeutic Procedures."

EXERCISE 12-16

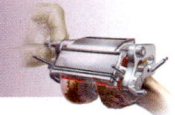

Write a brief definition for each operative, treatment, or diagnostic procedure term. Identify the main term in the statement and assign the correct ICD-9-CM code(s).

1. Bilateral mammogram

   DEFINITION: _____

   MAIN TERM: _____

   ICD-9-CM CODE(S): *87.37, 87.37*

2. Laparoscopic aspiration of ovarian cyst

   DEFINITION: _____

   MAIN TERM: _____

   ICD-9-CM CODE(S): _____

3. Vaginal hysterectomy with bilateral salpingo-oophorectomy

   DEFINITION: _____

   MAIN TERM: _____

   ICD-9-CM CODE(S): *68.59   65.61*

4. LEEP cone biopsy of the cervix

   DEFINITION: _____

   MAIN TERM: _____

   ICD-9-CM CODE(S): _____

5. D & C performed for dysfunctional bleeding

   DEFINITION: _____

   MAIN TERM: _____

   ICD-9-CM CODE(S): _____69.09_____

6. Total abdominal hysterectomy with bilateral salpingo-oophorectomy

   DEFINITION: _____

   MAIN TERM: _____

   ICD-9-CM CODE(S): _____

7. Primary low transverse cesarean section

   DEFINITION: _____

   MAIN TERM: _____

   ICD-9-CM CODE(S): _____74.1_____

8. Low forceps delivery with episiotomy

   DEFINITION: _____

   MAIN TERM: _____

   ICD-9-CM CODE(S): _____

9. Modified radical mastectomy

   DEFINITION: _____

   MAIN TERM: _____

   ICD-9-CM CODE(S): _____85.43_____

10. Repair of rectocele and cystocele

    DEFINITION: _____

    MAIN TERM: _____

    ICD-9-CM CODE(S): _____

11. Diagnostic amniocentesis

    DEFINITION: _____

    MAIN TERM: _____

    ICD-9-CM CODE(S): _____75.1_____

Current Procedural Terminology (CPT) Female Genital System Codes (56405–59899)

CPT female genital system codes are located in the Surgery, Radiology, and Medicine sections. The Surgery guidelines provide important information for all of the Surgery subsections. Review the guidelines in the CPT manual and in chapter 3 of this text. There are additional instruction notes for the Female Genital System subsection of the Surgery section. The Female Genital System subsection includes the following major categories:

- **Vulva, Perineum, and Introitus (56405–56821).** Codes in this category include incision, destruction, excision, repair, and endoscopy of the vulva, perineum, and introitus. Vulvectomies are classified as *simple,* removal of skin and superficial subcutaneous tissues; *radical,* removal of skin and deep subcutaneous tissue; *partial,* removal of less than 80% of the vulvar area; and *complete,* removal of greater than 80% of the vulvar area.

- **Vagina (57000–57425).** Codes in this category include incision, destruction, excision, introduction, repair, manipulation, and endoscopy of the vagina.

- **Cervix Uteri (57452–57800).** Codes in this category cover endoscopy, excision, repair, and manipulation of the cervix of the uterus.

- **Corpus Uteri (58100–58579).** Codes in this category cover excision, hysterectomy, introduction, repair, and laparoscopy or hysteroscopy of the uterus.

- **Oviduct/Ovary (58600–58999).** Codes in this category cover incision, excision, repair, and laparoscopy of the ovaries and fallopian tubes. In vitro fertilization procedures are also included.

- **Maternity Care and Delivery (59000–59899).** Codes in this category cover procedures related to antepartum care, vaginal delivery and postpartum care, cesarean delivery, delivery after previous cesarean delivery, and abortion. Instruction notes at the beginning of this category describe the services provided in uncomplicated maternity cases.

Female reproductive system and pregnancy diagnostic imaging procedures are coded to the Radiology section. Some of the subsections related to the female reproductive system include the following:

- **Diagnostic Radiology (Diagnostic Imaging) (72170–72910; 74000–74190; 74710–74775).** Codes in these subsections

continued

include radiography of the abdomen and pelvis, and gynecological and obstetrical radiography.

■ **Diagnostic Ultrasound (76801–76828).** Codes in this subsection include ultrasonography of the pregnant uterus and Doppler studies of fetal arteries and the cardiovascular system. There are extensive instruction notes at the beginning of this subsection.

EXERCISE 12-17

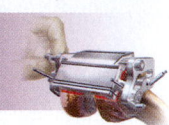

Identify the main term in each statement. Assign the correct CPT code(s).

1. Laparoscopic fulguration of fallopian tubes, bilateral

   MAIN TERM: _____

   CPT CODE(S): _58670_

2. D & C for incomplete spontaneous abortion, 8 weeks pregnant

   MAIN TERM: _____

   CPT CODE(S): _____

3. Chorionic villus sampling by needle

   MAIN TERM: _____

   CPT CODE(S): _59015_

4. Laparoscopic aspiration of an ovarian cyst, left ovary

   MAIN TERM: _____

   CPT CODE(S): _____

5. Total abdominal hysterectomy with bilateral salpingo-oophorectomy

   MAIN TERM: _____

   CPT CODE(S): _58150_

6. Incision and drainage of Bartholin gland abscess

   MAIN TERM: _____

   CPT CODE(S): _____

7. Insertion of intrauterine device (IUD)

   MAIN TERM: _____

   CPT CODE(S): _58300_

8. Cesarean delivery only

   MAIN TERM: _____

   CPT CODE(S): _____

9. Abdominal cerclage of cervix, pregnant uterus

   MAIN TERM: _____

   CPT CODE(S): _59325_

■ SUMMARY

This chapter covered medical terms related to the female reproductive system and pregnancy. Diagnoses and procedures were identified and defined. Female reproductive system and pregnancy diseases and conditions are coded to ICD-9-CM volume 1, chapter 10, "Diseases of the Genitourinary System," categories 610–629; and chapter 11, "Complications of Pregnancy, Childbirth, and the Puerperium." Female reproductive system and pregnancy-related procedures are coded to ICD-9-CM volume 3, chapter 12, "Operations on the Female Genital Organs"; and chapter 13, "Obstetrical Procedures."

Current Procedural Terminology (CPT) female reproductive system and pregnancy-related procedure codes are found in the CPT Surgery subsection, Female Genital System (56405–59899), and the Radiology and Medicine sections.

■ CHAPTER REVIEW

Read each medical note or medical report excerpt. Write the diagnosis(es) and the main term. Assign the ICD-9-CM diagnosis code.

CASE 1

Ms. Bohiden is seen today for menometrorrhagia, present for the past six months. She is very frustrated with this situation and it definitely interferes with her quality of life. We discussed several options, the first being oral contraceptives to regulate her menstrual cycles. She is somewhat hesitant and stated she must discuss this with her husband. We also discussed dilation and curettage as an alternative. She left the office with several pamphlets and will schedule another office visit next month.

DIAGNOSIS(ES): _____

MAIN TERM: _____

ICD-9-CM DIAGNOSIS CODE(S): _626.2_____

CASE 2

CLINICAL HISTORY: Pelvic pain with pelvic mass.

MICROSCOPIC EXAMINATION: Histological sections of right ovarian cyst wall reveal portions of ovarian tissue with definite follicles present. Within the wall there is focal hemorrhage and hemosiderin deposits, along with chronic inflammatory cells. No malignant cells are present.

DIAGNOSIS: Hemorrhagic follicular cyst with chronic oophoritis.

DIAGNOSIS(ES): _____

MAIN TERM: _____

ICD-9-CM DIAGNOSIS CODE(S): _____

CASE 3

ADMITTING DIAGNOSES: 1. Menorrhagia. 2. Dysmenorrhea with probable adenomyosis and persistent pelvic endometriosis.

DISCHARGE DIAGNOSES: 1. Endometriosis of the posterior uterine serosa and left fallopian tube. 2. Fibrous adhesions. 3. Adenomyosis of the uterus.

BRIEF HISTORY: This 40-year-old nulligravida female has a three-year history of menorrhagia, pelvic pain, and pelvic endometriosis. Given the severity of her symptoms, she was admitted for exploratory laparotomy and possible hysterectomy with salpingo-oophorectomy.

DIAGNOSIS(ES): _____

MAIN TERM: _____

ICD-9-CM DIAGNOSIS CODE(S): _617.0 417.2 614.6 417.0_____

CASE 4

Ms. Smith is seen today to review the lab and radiology results of her recent annual physical examination. Lab tests are within normal limits. Pap smear is negative for dysplastic cells or inflammation. Bilateral mammography revealed atrophic breasts with moderate fibrocystic breast changes and moderate ductal hyperplasia. There is no evidence of malignant mass lesion at this time. We discussed breast self-exam and dietary changes that are helpful in relieving some of the tenderness of fibrocystic breast changes.

DIAGNOSIS(ES): _____

MAIN TERM: _____

ICD-9-CM DIAGNOSIS CODE(S): _____

CASE 5

The patient has a lifelong history of markedly enlarged breasts. In the past year she has experienced increasing neck, back, and shoulder discomfort. She states she has been subjected to cruel "teasing" since the fourth grade. As an adult, she believes that most people cannot see "past my breasts." On physical exam, the breasts are symmetrical and markedly enlarged with grade III ptosis. There is marked cutaneous grooving on both shoulders, obviously a result of the weight the breasts exert on her bra straps. She is a good candidate for breast reduction. We discussed the risks and benefits. She is scheduled for bilateral breast reduction next week.

IMPRESSION: Bilateral hypertrophy of the breasts with grade III ptosis.

DIAGNOSIS(ES): _____

MAIN TERM: _____

ICD-9-CM DIAGNOSIS CODE(S): _611.1_____611.81_____

CASE 6

Ms. Smith is a 28-year-old female who has a six-year history of spontaneous abortion ✕3 at 14 weeks of gestation. Current status is intrauterine pregnancy at 12 weeks. She was admitted today for McDonald cerclage placement due to cervical incompetence. The procedure was without complication and the patient was taken to the recovery room in good condition.

DIAGNOSIS(ES): _____

MAIN TERM: _____

ICD-9-CM DIAGNOSIS CODE(S): _____

Read the procedure note, operative report, or discharge summary excerpt. Write the diagnosis and its ICD-9-CM code. Write the name of the procedure and main term. Assign the ICD-9-CM procedure code(s).

CASE 7

PREOPERATIVE DIAGNOSES: 1. Cyclic pelvic pain. 2. Menorrhagia. 3. Endometriosis, uterine serosa.

POSTOPERATIVE DIAGNOSES: 1. Cyclic pelvic pain. 2. Menorrhagia. 3. Endometriosis, uterine serosa.

OPERATION: Diagnostic laparoscopy with biopsy; hysteroscopy with endometrial sampling.

FINDINGS: There was a prior appendectomy and some adhesions to the cecum down to the right lower quadrant. The liver edge was normal. Gallbladder was not visualized. Both tubes and ovaries were normal. Anterior bladder flap was normal other than prior cesarean scarring. No endometriosis. The uterine serosa had a mosaic pattern and vesicular pattern consistent with serosal endometriosis. Down in the cul-de-sac was a blue powder-burn cluster of endometriosis along the right uterosacral ligament consistent with the patient's pain and a few vesicular peritoneal changes also consistent with endometriosis scattered about.

DIAGNOSES: _____ ICD-9-CM DIAGNOSES CODE(S): _____

PROCEDURE(S): _____ MAIN TERM(S): _____

ICD-9-CM PROCEDURE CODE(S): _____

CASE 8

ADMITTING DIAGNOSIS: Ruptured left isthmic ectopic pregnancy.

DISCHARGE DIAGNOSIS: 1. Ruptured left isthmic ectopic pregnancy. 2. Status post partial left salpingectomy without complications.

BRIEF HISTORY: This 29-year-old gravida II, para II female presented with acute abdominal pain. A serum pregnancy test was positive. Pelvic ultrasound was negative for an intrauterine pregnancy. No pelvic mass was palpated.

HOSPITAL COURSE: The patient was taken to the operating room and culdocentesis was positive. Laparoscopy revealed a ruptured left isthmic ectopic pregnancy, and a left partial salpingectomy was completed without complication.

DISCHARGE INSTRUCTIONS: The patient was discharged on a regular diet, ambulating without difficulty, with normal bowel movements. She was given postoperative instructions regarding this episode of care and information about ectopic pregnancies in general.

DIAGNOSES: _____ ICD-9-CM DIAGNOSES CODE(S): _____

PROCEDURE(S): _____ MAIN TERM(S): _____

ICD-9-CM PROCEDURE CODE(S): _____

CASE 9

PREOPERATIVE DIAGNOSIS: Menometrorrhagia and cervical stenosis.

POSTOPERATIVE DIAGNOSIS: Menometrorrhagia and cervical stenosis.

OPERATION: Diagnostic hysteroscopy and dilation and curettage of the uterus.

DESCRIPTION OF PROCEDURE: Under adequate general anesthesia, the patient was prepped and draped in the low lithotomy position. Bimanual examination revealed the uterus to be 6-weeks' size and midline. A speculum was placed in the vagina, and the cervix was grasped with a single-toothed tenaculum. It was very stenotic, and we started with the smallest dilator available and dilated up to a No. 9 Pratt. An Olympus fiberoptic hysteroscope was then inserted, and inspection was carried out. There was extensive glandular- and abnormal-appearing tissue along the entire posterior wall of the uterus that appeared to be hyperplastic. The hysteroscope was removed from the uterus, and the cervix was then dilated. Endometrial curettage was performed, with removal of a very large amount of glandular-appearing tissue. The patient tolerated the procedure well and left the operating room in good condition.

DIAGNOSES: _____ ICD-9-CM DIAGNOSES CODE(S): _____

PROCEDURE(S): _____ MAIN TERM(S): _____

ICD-9-CM PROCEDURE CODE(S): _____

CASE 10

PROCEDURE: Colposcopy with cervical biopsy.

DESCRIPTION: The patient was taken to the procedure suite and placed in the lithotomy position. Her vagina and cervix were examined and a speculum was inserted. Cervical biopsies were performed at the indicated areas. There were no complications and the patient went to recovery in good condition.

IMPRESSION: 1. Class II cervical dysplasia, per Pap smear results. 2. Cervicitis.

DIAGNOSES: _____ ICD-9-CM DIAGNOSES CODE(S): _____

PROCEDURE(S): _____ MAIN TERM(S): _____

ICD-9-CM PROCEDURE CODE(S): _____

CASE 11

DISCHARGE DIAGNOSIS: Uterine papillary serous carcinoma involving the corpus and cervix with no invasion.

PROCEDURES: Total abdominal hysterectomy, bilateral salpingo-oophorectomy, pelvic lymphadenectomy with partial omentectomy.

HOSPITAL COURSE: The patient was brought to the operating room and given general anesthesia. The surgery noted above was carried out without incident. The next day we attempted to remove the Foley catheter, but she had 300 cc retention. She also experienced mild febrile morbidity and a modest ileus. Nasogastric intubation was not needed. By the fourth postoperative day she was voiding well and ready for discharge.

PATHOLOGY RESULTS: Peritoneal washings were negative. Omental biopsy was negative. Tubes and ovaries were negative. High-grade papillary serous cancer of the endometrium was confirmed.

DIAGNOSES: _____ ICD-9-CM DIAGNOSES CODE(S): _____

PROCEDURE(S): _____ MAIN TERM(S): _____

ICD-9-CM PROCEDURE CODE(S): _____

CASE 12

PREOPERATIVE DIAGNOSIS: Intrauterine pregnancy at 40 weeks' estimated gestational age, cephalopelvic disproportion, prolonged second-stage labor, and fetal stress.

POSTOPERATIVE DIAGNOSIS: Intrauterine pregnancy at 40 weeks' estimated gestational age, cephalopelvic disproportion, prolonged second-stage labor, and fetal stress.

PROCEDURE: Primary low transverse cesarean section under epidural anesthesia.

DESCRIPTION: The patient was taken to the operating room and placed in the supine position. The abdomen was prepped and draped in the usual sterile fashion. The neonatologist was in attendance. A Pfannenstiel skin incision was made approximately two fingerbreadths above the symphysis pubis and carried down through the subcutaneous layer and fascia. Upon entering the uterine cavity, clear amniotic fluid was noted. The uterine incision was extended horizontally in a curvilinear fashion. A viable 8-pound 2-ounce female infant was delivered in the left occiput and anterior position. The placenta was removed and the uterus was then exteriorized out of the abdominal cavity.

The interior of the uterine cavity was then cleaned with a moist lap sponge. The uterine incision was then closed and the uterus placed back into the abdominopelvic cavity. Estimated blood loss was 1000 cc. Sponge, lap, needle, and instrument counts were correct ×3. The patient was awakened in the operating room and taken to the recovery room in stable condition.

DIAGNOSES: _____ ICD-9-CM DIAGNOSES CODE(S): _____

PROCEDURE(S): _____ MAIN TERM(S): _____

ICD-9-CM PROCEDURE CODE(S): _____

Using the excerpts from previous cases, write the name of the procedure and main term. Assign the CPT codes to the procedures.

CASE 13

PREOPERATIVE DIAGNOSES: 1. Cyclic pelvic pain. 2. Menorrhagia. 3. Endometriosis, uterine serosa.

POSTOPERATIVE DIAGNOSES: 1. Cyclic pelvic pain. 2. Menorrhagia. 3. Endometriosis, uterine serosa.

OPERATION: Diagnostic laparoscopy with biopsy; hysteroscopy with endometrial sampling.

FINDINGS: There was a prior appendectomy and some adhesions to the cecum down to the right lower quadrant. The liver edge was normal. Gallbladder was not visualized. Both tubes and ovaries were normal. Anterior bladder flap was normal other than prior cesarean scarring. No endometriosis. The uterine serosa had a mosaic pattern and vesicular pattern consistent with serosal endometriosis. Down in the cul-de-sac was a blue powder-burn cluster of endometriosis along the right uterosacral ligament consistent with the patient's pain and a few vesicular peritoneal changes also consistent with endometriosis scattered about.

PROCEDURE(S): _____ MAIN TERM(S): _____

CPT PROCEDURE CODE(S): _____

CASE 14

ADMITTING DIAGNOSIS: Ruptured left isthmic ectopic pregnancy.

DISCHARGE DIAGNOSIS: 1. Ruptured left isthmic ectopic pregnancy. 2. Status post partial left salpingectomy without complications.

BRIEF HISTORY: This 29-year-old gravida II, para II female presented with acute abdominal pain. A serum pregnancy test was positive. Pelvic ultrasound was negative for an intrauterine pregnancy. No pelvic mass was palpated.

HOSPITAL COURSE: The patient was taken to the operating room and culdocentesis was positive. Laparoscopy revealed a ruptured left isthmic ectopic pregnancy, and a left partial salpingectomy was completed without complication.

DISCHARGE INSTRUCTIONS: The patient was discharged on a regular diet, ambulating without difficulty, with normal bowel movements. She was given postoperative instructions regarding this episode of care and information about ectopic pregnancies in general.

PROCEDURE(S): _____ MAIN TERM(S): _____

CPT PROCEDURE CODE(S): _____

CASE 15

PREOPERATIVE DIAGNOSIS: Menometrorrhagia and cervical stenosis.

POSTOPERATIVE DIAGNOSIS: Menometrorrhagia and cervical stenosis.

OPERATION: Diagnostic hysteroscopy and dilation and curettage of the uterus.

DESCRIPTION OF PROCEDURE: Under adequate general anesthesia, the patient was prepped and draped in the low lithotomy position. Bimanual examination revealed the uterus to be 6-weeks' size and midline. A speculum was placed in the vagina, and the cervix was grasped with a single-toothed tenaculum. It was very stenotic, and we started with the smallest dilator available and dilated up to a No. 9 Pratt. An Olympus fiberoptic hysteroscope was then inserted, and inspection was carried out. There was extensive glandular- and abnormal-appearing tissue along the entire posterior wall of the uterus that appeared to be hyperplastic. The hysteroscope was removed from the uterus, and the cervix was then dilated. Endometrial curettage was performed, with removal of a very large amount of glandular-appearing tissue. The patient tolerated the procedure well and left the operating room in good condition.

PROCEDURE(S): _____ MAIN TERM(S): _____

CPT PROCEDURE CODE(S): _____

CASE 16

PROCEDURE: Colposcopy with cervical biopsy.

DESCRIPTION: The patient was taken to the procedure suite and placed in the lithotomy position. Her vagina and cervix were examined and a speculum was inserted. Cervical biopsies were performed at the indicated areas. There were no complications and the patient went to recovery in good condition.

IMPRESSION: 1. Class II cervical dysplasia, per Pap smear results. 2. Cervicitis.

PROCEDURE(S): _____ MAIN TERM(S): _____

CPT PROCEDURE CODE(S): _____

CASE 17

DISCHARGE DIAGNOSIS: Uterine papillary serous carcinoma involving the corpus and cervix with no invasion.

PROCEDURES: Total abdominal hysterectomy, bilateral salpingo-oophorectomy, pelvic lymphadenectomy with partial omentectomy.

HOSPITAL COURSE: The patient was brought to the operating room and given general anesthesia. The surgery noted above was carried out without incident. The next day we attempted to remove the Foley catheter, but she had 300 cc retention. She also experienced mild febrile morbidity and a modest ileus. Nasogastric intubation was not needed. By the fourth postoperative day she was voiding well and ready for discharge.

PATHOLOGY RESULTS: Peritoneal washings were negative. Omental biopsy was negative. Tubes and ovaries were negative. High-grade papillary serous cancer of the endometrium was confirmed.

PROCEDURE(S): _____ MAIN TERM(S): _____

CPT PROCEDURE CODE(S): _____

CASE 18

PREOPERATIVE DIAGNOSIS: Intrauterine pregnancy at 40 weeks' estimated gestational age, cephalopelvic disproportion, prolonged second-stage labor, and fetal stress.

POSTOPERATIVE DIAGNOSIS: Intrauterine pregnancy at 40 weeks' estimated gestational age, cephalopelvic disproportion, prolonged second-stage labor, and fetal stress.

PROCEDURE: Primary low transverse cesarean section under epidural anesthesia.

DESCRIPTION: The patient was taken to the operating room and placed in the supine position. The abdomen was prepped and draped in the usual sterile fashion. The neonatologist was in attendance. A Pfannenstiel skin incision was made approximately two fingerbreadths above the symphysis pubis and carried down through the subcutaneous layer and fascia. Upon entering the uterine cavity, clear amniotic fluid was noted. The uterine incision was extended horizontally in a curvilinear fashion. A viable 8-pound 2-ounce female infant was delivered in the left occiput and anterior position. The placenta was removed and the uterus was then exteriorized out of the abdominal cavity. The interior of the uterine cavity was then cleaned with a moist lap sponge. The uterine incision was then closed and the uterus placed back into the abdominopelvic cavity. Estimated blood loss was 1000 cc. Sponge, lap, needle, and instrument counts were correct ×3. The patient was awakened in the operating room and taken to the recovery room in stable condition.

PROCEDURE(S): _____ MAIN TERM(S): _____

CPT PROCEDURE CODE(S): _____

MEDICAL TERMINOLOGY CHALLENGE

Read the operative description and write a brief definition for the italicized medical terms. Use a dictionary as necessary.

PROCEDURE: Laparoscopic-assisted vaginal hysterectomy with (1) *bilateral* salpingo-oophorectomy.

DESCRIPTION: The patient was taken to the operating room and placed in the supine position. After adequate general anesthesia had been obtained, the patient was prepped and draped in the usual fashion. The bladder was drained with a red rubber catheter. A small (2) *infraumbilical* skin incision was made with the scalpel, and 10-mm laparoscopic sleeve and (3) *trocar* were introduced without difficulty. The trocar was removed. The laparoscope was placed, and 2 L of CO_2 gas was (4) *insufflated* into the abdomen. A small incision was made (5) *suprapubically* and a 12-mm laparoscope sleeve was introduced under direct visualization. A 5-mm laparoscope sleeve and trocar were placed in the left lower quadrant under direct visualization. A manipulator was used to examine the patient's pelvic organs.

There was a small cyst on the right ovary. Both ovaries were free from adhesions. The ureters were free from the operative field. After measuring the ovarian distal pedicles, the endo-GIA staple was placed across each round ligament.

Attention was turned to the vaginal part of the procedure. A weighted (6) *speculum* was placed in the vagina. The anterior lip of the cervix was grasped with a Lahey (7) *tenaculum*. Posterior (8) *colpotomy* incision was made and the posterior (9) *peritoneum* was entered. The (10) *uterosacral ligaments* were bilaterally clamped, cut, and (11) *ligated*. After the uterus was free of a vascular supply, it was removed (12) *en bloc* with tubes and ovaries attached. All surgical wounds were closed appropriately with (13) *purse-string suture* to the peritoneum and (14) *figure-of-eight suture* to the vaginal cuff. (15) *Hemostasis* was excellent.

1. _____
2. _____
3. _____
4. _____
5. _____
6. _____
7. _____
8. _____
9. _____
10. _____
11. _____
12. _____
13. _____
14. _____
15. _____

NOTES:

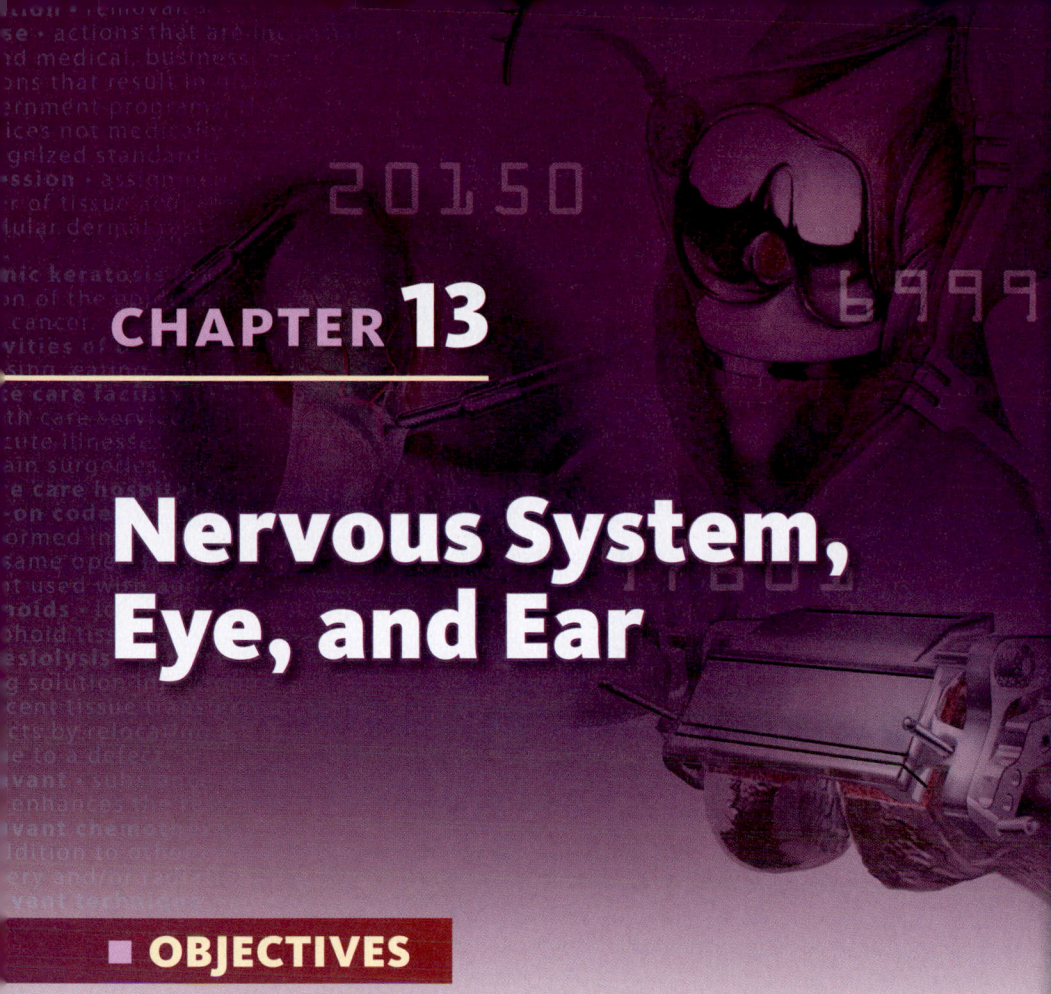

CHAPTER 13

Nervous System, Eye, and Ear

■ OBJECTIVES

At the completion of this chapter, the student should be able to:

1. Learn the word roots, prefixes, and suffixes associated with the nervous system, eye, and ear.
2. Label the basic structures of the nervous system, eye, and ear.
3. Discuss the functions of the nervous system, eye, and ear.
4. Accurately spell and define nervous system, eye, and ear terminology.
5. Accurately assign medical codes to nervous system, eye, and ear diagnoses and procedures.

■ OVERVIEW

This chapter includes medical terms, diagnoses, and procedures of the nervous system, the eyes, and the ears. Information is presented as follows: (1) nervous system medical terms, diagnoses, and procedures; (2) medical terms, diagnoses, and procedures related to the eyes; and (3) medical terms, diagnoses, and procedures related to the ears.

KEY TERMS

acoustic nerve
afferent nerve
anterior chamber
aqueous humor
arachnoid membrane
astrocyte
audiologist
audiology
auricle
autonomic nervous
    system (ANS)
axon
brain
brain stem
cauda equina
cell body
central nervous system (CNS)
cerebellum
cerebral cortex
cerebrospinal fluid (CSF)
cerebrum
cerumen
ceruminous glands
choroid
cilia
ciliary body
cochlea
cones
conjunctiva
cornea
corpus callosum
cranial nerves
crystalline lens
dendrite
dura mater
efferent nerves
eustachian tube
external auditory canal
external ear
eye socket
eyebrow
eyelash
eyelid
frontal lobe
gyri
gyrus
hypothalamus
incus
inner ear
internal ear
iris
labyrinth
lacrimal duct
lacrimal fluid

continued

KEY TERMS *continued*

lacrimal glands
lacrimal sac
lens
malleus
medulla oblongata
meibomian gland
meninges
microglia
midbrain
middle ear
motor nerves
myelin
nasolacrimal duct
neuroglia
neurologist
neurology
neuron
neurosurgeon
nucleus
occipital lobe
oligodendroglia
ophthalmologist
ophthalmology
optic disk
optic nerve
optician
optometrist
optometry
orbit
organ of Corti
ossicles
otologist

otology
otorhinolaryngologist
otorhinolaryngology
oval window
parietal lobe
peripheral nervous system (PNS)
pia mater
pinna
pons
posterior chamber
pupil
retina
rods
sclera
semicircular canals
sensory nerve
somatic nervous system (SNS)
spinal cord
spinal nerve
stapes
sulci
sulcus
suspensatory ligament
synapse
temporal lobe
terminal end fibers
thalamus
tunic
tympanic membrane
uvea
vestibule
vitreous humor

NERVOUS SYSTEM

The nervous system includes nerve cells, the brain, the spinal cord, 12 pairs of cranial nerves, and 31 pairs of spinal nerves. The **central nervous system (CNS)** is the brain and spinal cord, and the **peripheral nervous system (PNS)** includes the cranial and spinal nerves. The structures of the nervous system function together to (1) regulate all activities of the body, (2) control consciousness, (3) detect environmental stimuli, (4) respond to environmental stimuli, (5) process and store sensory and motor information, and (6) transmit sensory and motor impulses between the brain and all parts of the body. **Neurology** (noo-**RALL**-oh-jee) is the medical specialty for the nervous system, and the physician specialist is a **neurologist** (noo-**RALL**-oh-jist). A physician who specializes in surgery of the nervous system is called a **neurosurgeon**.

NERVOUS SYSTEM WORD ROOTS, PREFIXES, AND SUFFIXES

Roots, prefixes, and suffixes related to the nervous system are listed in table 13-1. Review the word elements and complete the exercises.

Table 13-1 Nervous System Roots, Prefixes, and Suffixes

ROOT	MEANING
arachn/o	spider
cerebr/o	cerebrum; brain
crani/o	cranium; skull
dendr/o	branching; dendrite
electr/o	electricity
encephal/o	brain
gli/o	neuroglia; nerve cell
hydr/o	water; fluid
mening/o	meninges
myel/o	spinal cord (also bone marrow)
neur/o	nerve
olig/o	few; diminished
quadr/i	four
thec/o	sheath
thromb/o	clot
vascul/o	blood vessels
ventricul/o	ventricle

PREFIX	MEANING
dura-	hard
echo-	sound

SUFFIX	MEANING
-algia	pain
-malacia	softening
-paresis	partial paralysis
-pathy	disease
-plegia	paralysis

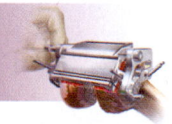

EXERCISE 13-1

Write the root, prefix, suffix, and their meaning. Based on the meanings, write a brief definition for each term.

1. Cerebral

   ROOT: _____ MEANING: _____

   PREFIX: _____ MEANING: _____

   SUFFIX: _____ MEANING: _____

   DEFINITION: _____

2. Craniocerebral

   ROOT: _____ MEANING: _____

   PREFIX: _____ MEANING: _____

   SUFFIX: _____ MEANING: _____

   DEFINITION: _____

3. Neurologist

   ROOT: _____ MEANING: _____

   PREFIX: _____ MEANING: _____

   SUFFIX: _____ MEANING: _____

   DEFINITION: _____

4. Neurology

   ROOT: _____ MEANING: _____

   PREFIX: _____ MEANING: _____

   SUFFIX: _____ MEANING: _____

   DEFINITION: _____

5. Neurosurgeon

   ROOT: _____ MEANING: _____

   PREFIX: _____ MEANING: _____

   SUFFIX: _____ MEANING: _____

   DEFINITION: _____

6. Quadriplegia

   ROOT: _____ MEANING: _____

   PREFIX: _____ MEANING: _____

   SUFFIX: _____ MEANING: _____

   DEFINITION: _____

7. Hemiplegia

   ROOT: _____ MEANING: _____

   PREFIX: _____ MEANING: _____

   SUFFIX: _____ MEANING: _____

   DEFINITION: _____

8. Cerebrovascular

   ROOT: _____ MEANING: _____

   PREFIX: _____ MEANING: _____

   SUFFIX: _____ MEANING: _____

   DEFINITION: _____

9. Intrathecal

   ROOT: _____ MEANING: _____

   PREFIX: _____ MEANING: _____

   SUFFIX: _____ MEANING: _____

   DEFINITION: _____

STRUCTURES OF THE NERVOUS SYSTEM

The structures of the nervous system include the nerve cells, brain, cranial nerves, spinal cord, and spinal nerves. There are two general categories of nerve cells: **neurons** (**NOO**-ronz), which transmit nerve impulses from the body to the brain and back to the body, and **neuroglia** (noo-**ROG**-lee-ah), the nerve cells that support the nervous system. Neurons consist of a (1) **cell body** that contains the cell **nucleus**; (2) **dendrites** (**DEN**-drights), which are branchlike structures that receive impulses and send them to the cell body; an (3) **axon** (**ACKS**-on), which sends impulses away from the cell body; (4) **myelin** (**MIGH**-eh-lin), a white fatty tissue that covers the axon; and (5) **terminal end fibers**, branching fibers that lead the impulse away from the axon. The space between neurons or a neuron and an organ is called a (6) **synapse** (**SIN**-apps). Figure 13-1 illustrates the structures of a neuron.

Neuroglia are the supportive and connective cells of the nervous system and do not conduct impulses. There are three types of neuroglial cells: (1) **astrocytes** (**ASS**-troh-sights), (2) **microglia** (my-**KROG**-lee-ah), and (3) **oligodendroglia** (**all**-ih-goh-den-**DROG**-lee-ah). Figure 13-2 illustrates the neuroglia.

Brain and Spinal Cord

The **brain** and **spinal cord** are called the *central nervous system*. The brain weighs about three pounds and

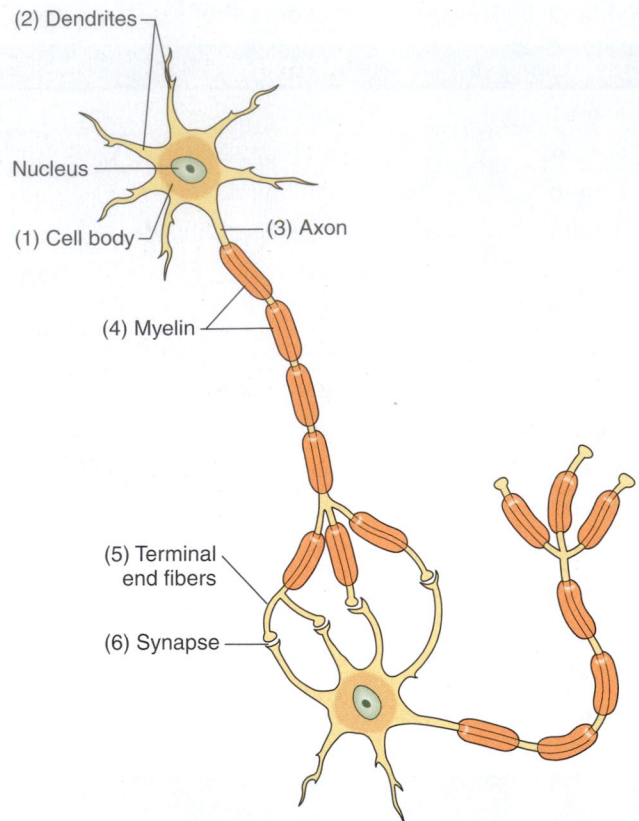

Figure 13-1   Neuron

controls physical and mental activities of the body. The spinal cord transmits nerve impulses to and from the brain to all parts of the body. Figure 13-3 illustrates the structures of the brain and brain stem.

Major structures of the brain include the (1) **cerebrum** (seh-**REE**-brum), (2) **cerebellum** (ser-eh-**BELL**-um),

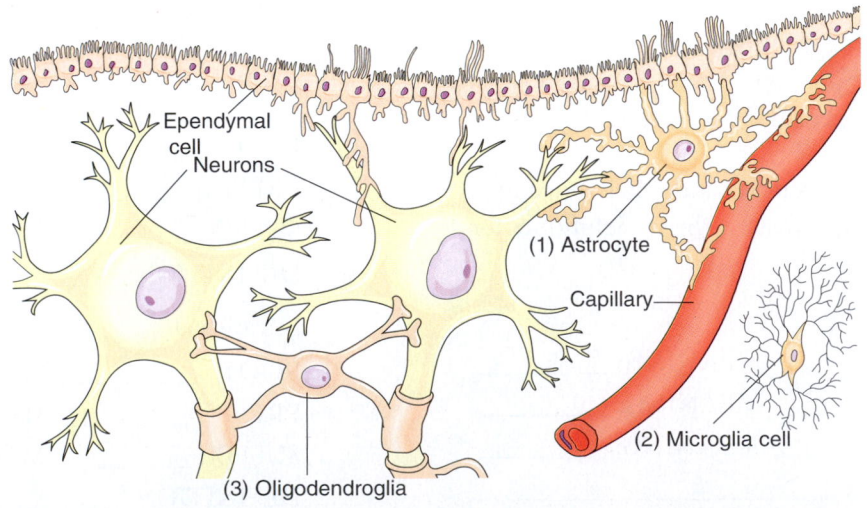

Figure 13-2   Neuroglial cells

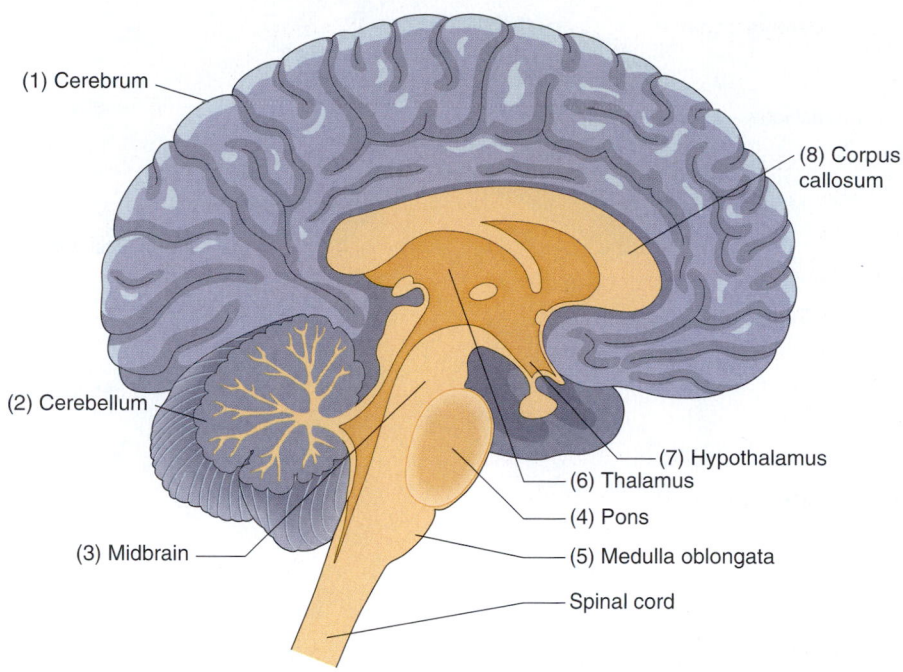

(1) Cerebrum

(8) Corpus callosum

(2) Cerebellum

(7) Hypothalamus

(6) Thalamus

(4) Pons

(3) Midbrain

(5) Medulla oblongata

Spinal cord

Figure 13-3   Brain and brain stem

(3) **midbrain**, (4) **pons** (PONZ), (5) **medulla oblongata** (meh-**DULL**-ah ob-long-**AH**-tah), (6) **thalamus** (**THAL**-ah-mus), (7) **hypothalamus** (**high**-poh-**THAL**-ah-mus), and (8) **corpus callosum** (**KOR**-pus kal-**OH**-sum). The midbrain, pons, and medulla oblongata are collectively known as the **brain stem**. Table 13-2 lists the parts of the brain and describes their functions.

The cerebrum is divided into right and left hemispheres. The **cerebral cortex** (seh-**REE**-bral **KOR**-teks)

is the outer layer of the cerebrum and is characterized by folds and grooves. The cerebral cortex folds are called **gyri** (**JIGH**-righ), and the grooves are called **sulci** (**SULL**-kigh), or fissures. A single fold is a **gyrus**, and a single groove is a **sulcus**. Each hemisphere of the cerebrum has four distinct lobes, which are illustrated in figure 13-4.

The (1) **frontal lobe** is responsible for motor function. The (2) **temporal** (**TEM**-por-al) **lobe** is responsible

Table 13-2   Parts of the Brain

PART OF THE BRAIN	DESCRIPTION
cerebrum	largest section of the brain; controls consciousness, memory, sensations, emotions, and voluntary movement
cerebellum	attaches the brain to the brain stem; maintains muscle tone, movement, and balance
midbrain	area of the brain that provides nerve conduction pathways to and from the brain
pons	literally means "bridge"; nerve cells cross from one side of the brain to control the opposite side of the body
medulla oblongata	lowest section of the brain stem; controls the muscles of respiration, heart rate, and blood pressure
thalamus	relays nerve impulses to and from the cerebral cortex and the sense organs of the body
hypothalamus	regulates heart rate, blood pressure, respiratory rate, digestive activities, emotional responses, behavior, body temperature, water balance and thirst, sleep-wake cycles, hunger sensations, and endocrine system activities; often called the "thermostat" of the body
corpus callosum	structure that connects the two hemispheres of the brain

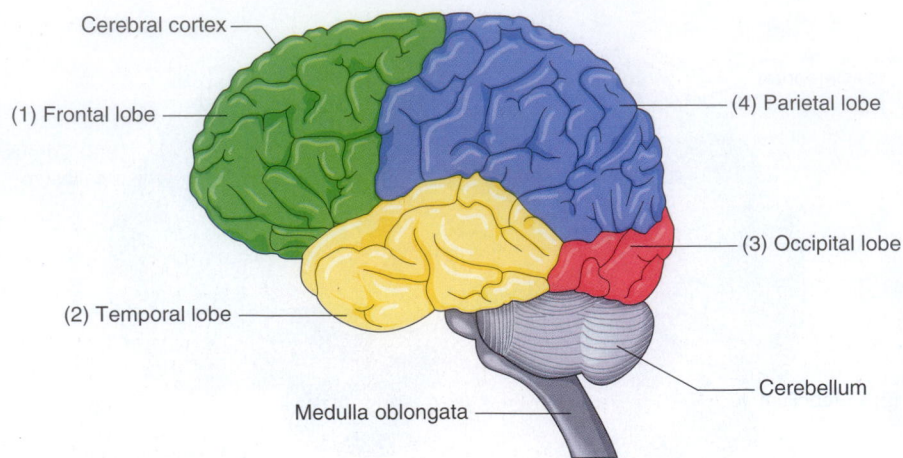

Figure 13-4 Lobes of the cerebrum

for hearing and smell. The (3) **occipital** (ok-**SIP**-ih-tal) **lobe** is responsible for sight. The (4) **parietal** (pah-**RIGH**-eh-tal) **lobe** receives and interprets nerve impulses from the sensory receptors located throughout the body.

The spinal cord is the pathway for impulses traveling to and from the brain. It houses 31 pairs of spinal nerves that affect the limbs and lower part of the body. The spinal cord is protected by cerebrospinal fluid, the three layers of the meninges, and the vertebrae. The lower end of the spinal cord and spinal nerve roots are called the **cauda equina** (**KAW**-dah ee-**KWIGH**-nah) and resemble a horse's tail.

EXERCISE 13-2

Label the parts of a neuron and the structures of the brain and brain stem shown in figure 13-5a and 13-5b. Write your answers on the spaces provided.

A. Neuron

1. _____

2. _____

3. _____

4. _____

5. _____

6. _____

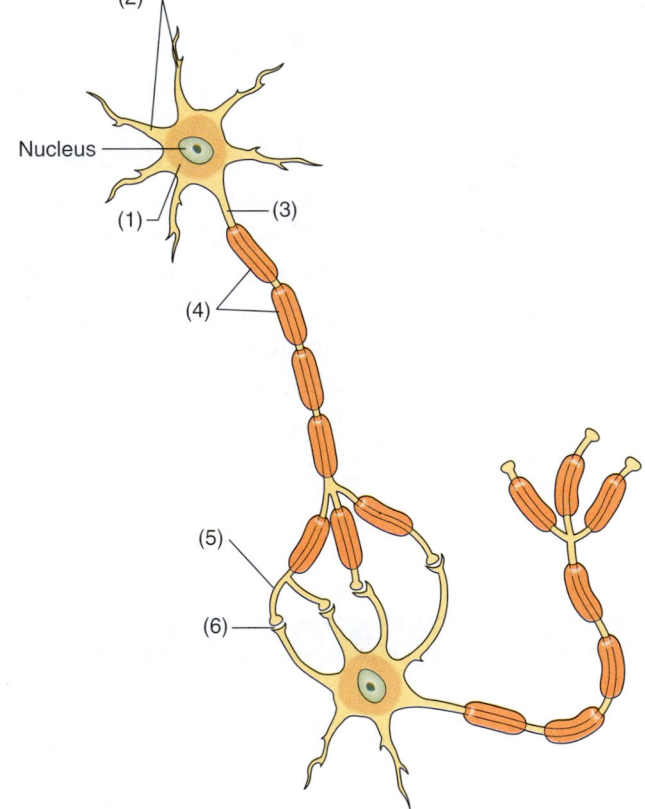

Figure 13-5(a) Label neuron

B. Brain and brain stem

1. _____

2. _____

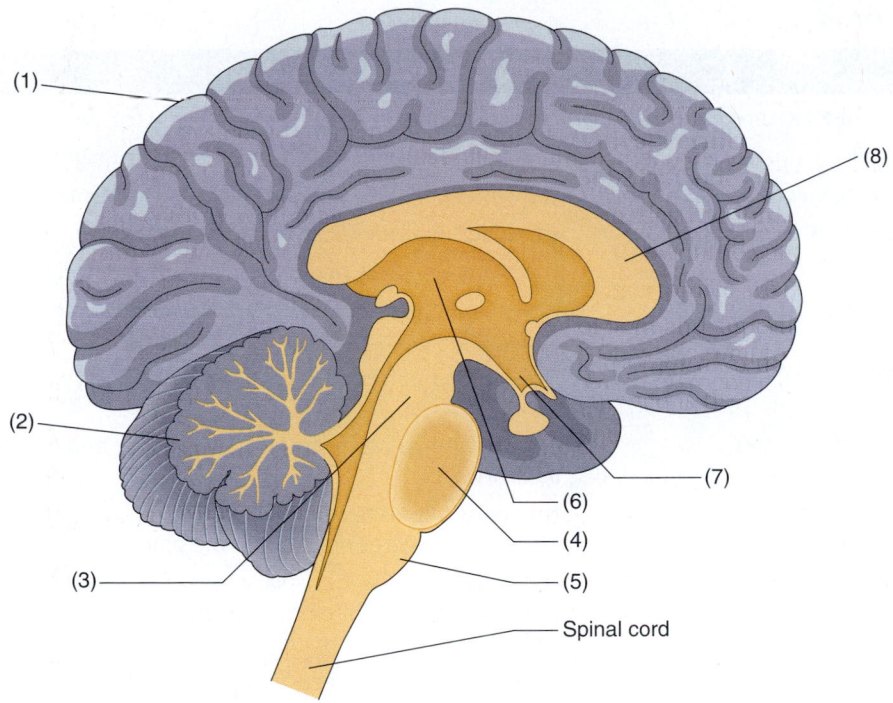

Figure 13-5(b) Label brain and brain stem

3. _____

4. _____

5. _____

6. _____

7. _____

8. _____

Meninges and Cerebrospinal Fluid

The **meninges** (men-**IN**-jeez) are three layers of membranes that surround and protect the brain and spinal cord. The outer membrane layer is the **dura mater** (**DOO**-rah **MAY**-ter), which is a tough, white connective tissue just beneath the skull. The middle layer is the **arachnoid** (ah-**RAK**-noyd) **membrane**, a web-like tissue with several strands that attach to the inner membrane layer. The inner membrane layer is the **pia mater** (**PEE**-ah **MAY**-ter), which is attached directly to the surface of the brain and spinal cord.

Cerebrospinal (seh-**ree**-broh-**SPIGH**-nal) **fluid (CSF)** flows in and around the brain and spinal cord. CSF cushions the brain and spinal cord and also provides some nutrients to those structures.

Cranial and Spinal Nerves

The 12 pairs of **cranial nerves** and 31 pairs of **spinal nerves** are known as the peripheral nervous system (PNS). The peripheral nervous system transmits information from all parts of the body to the brain and back to the body. **Afferent nerves**, or **sensory nerves**, carry impulses from the body to the brain, and **efferent nerves**, or **motor nerves**, carry impulses from the brain to the appropriate body structure. The peripheral nervous system is further classified as the **somatic** (soh-**MAT**-ik) **nervous system (SNS)** and the **autonomic** (**ot**-oh-**NOM**-ik) **nervous system (ANS)**. The somatic nervous system is responsible for voluntary movements and responses such as walking, talking, and swimming. The autonomic nervous system is responsible for involuntary movement and responses such as hormone secretion, heart rate, blood flow, and digestive system functions.

The cranial nerves are numbered from 1 to 12, using Roman numerals. Table 13-3 lists the cranial nerves and provides a brief description of their functions. The 31 pairs of spinal or peripheral nerves transmit impulses to all parts of the body. The spinal nerves are attached to the spinal cord and exit the vertebral column through openings in the vertebrae. These nerves have many branches that eventually reach every part of the body.

Figure 13-6 illustrates the body areas affected by the cranial nerves.

Table 13-3   Cranial Nerves

CRANIAL NERVE	DESCRIPTION
I olfactory nerve (ohl-**FAK**-tor-ee)	transmits sensory impulses necessary for the sense of smell
II optic nerve (**OP**-tik)	transmits sensory impulses necessary for sight
III oculomotor nerve (**ok**-yoo-loh-**MOH**-tor)	transmits impulses necessary for eye movement
IV trochlear nerve (**TROK**-lee-ar)	transmits impulses necessary for eye movement and eye muscle sensations
V trigeminal nerve (trigh-**JEM**-ih-nal)	transmits impulses necessary for chewing and facial sensations
VI abducens nerve (ab-**DOO**-senz)	transmits impulses necessary to turn the eyeball outward or away from the midline
VII facial nerve (**FAY**-shee-al)	transmits impulses to the scalp, forehead, eyelids, cheek, jaw, and other facial muscles
VIII acoustic nerve (ah-**KOO**-stik)	transmits impulses necessary for hearing and balance; also called the *auditory nerve*
IX glossopharyngeal nerve (**gloss**-oh-fair-in-**JEE**-al)	transmits impulses necessary for taste, some sensations from the viscera, and secretions from some glands
X vagus nerve (**VAY**-gus)	transmits impulses necessary for speech, swallowing, as well as the activity of cardiac muscle, smooth muscle, and glands and ducts of the respiratory system
XI accessory nerve	transmits impulses necessary for speech, swallowing, and some head and shoulder movements
XII hypoglossal nerve (**high**-poh-**GLOSS**-al)	transmits impulses necessary for swallowing and moving the tongue

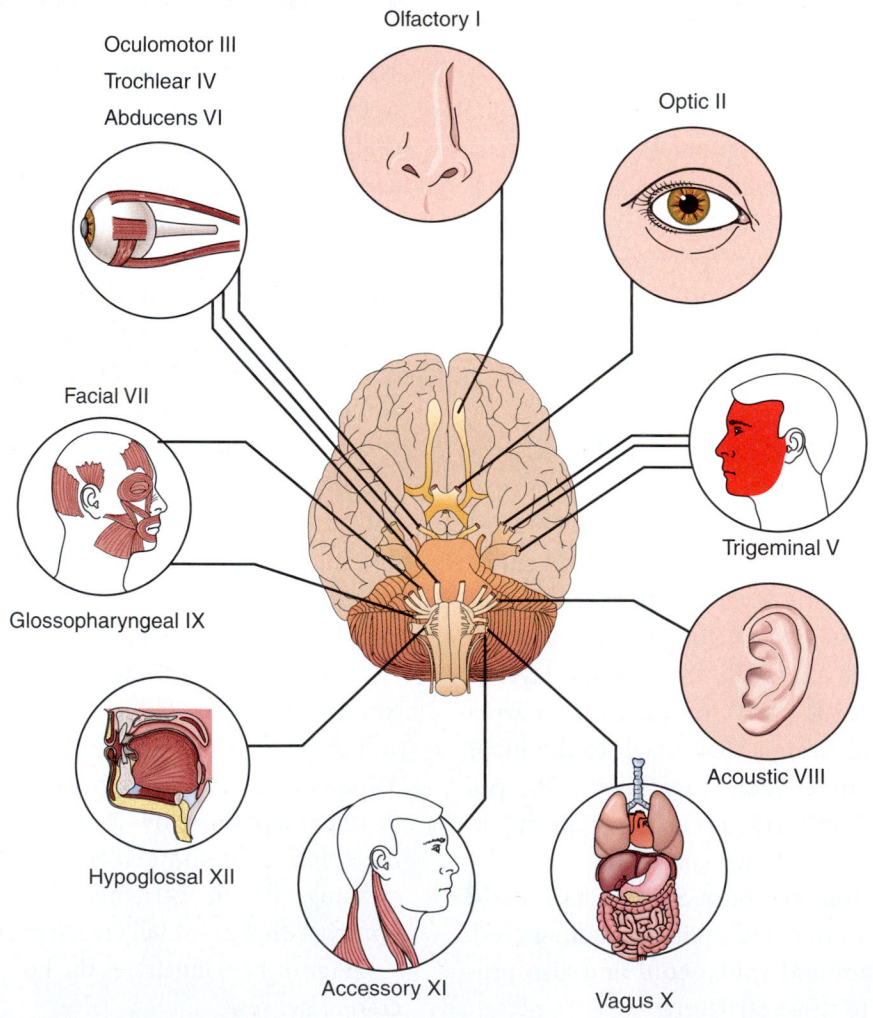

Figure 13-6   Body areas affected by cranial nerves

NERVOUS SYSTEM MEDICAL TERMINOLOGY

Nervous system medical terms are organized by diseases, conditions, diagnostic procedures, and operations. There are two categories of medical terminology exercises: (1) those designed to provide opportunities to learn the terms, and (2) those designed to provide opportunities to accurately assign diagnostic or procedure codes. Exercises for learning the terms immediately follow the lists of terms and definitions. Medical coding exercises are available after all terms have been presented.

Nervous System Signs, Symptoms, Diseases, and Conditions

The medical terms in table 13-4 are signs, symptoms, diseases, and conditions related to the nervous system. Review the meaning of these terms and complete the exercises.

Table 13-4 Nervous System Signs, Symptoms, Diseases, and Conditions

TERM WITH PRONUNCIATION	DEFINITION
Alzheimer disease (**ALTS**-high-mer)	progressive, extremely debilitating deterioration of an individual's intellectual functioning
amyotrophic lateral sclerosis (ALS) (ah-**migh**-oh-**TROFF**-ik **LAT**-er-al skleh-**ROH**-sis)	severe weakening and wasting of various muscle groups due to loss of motor neuron function in the brain stem and spinal cord
anencephaly (**an**-en-**SEFF**-ah-lee) an- = lack of; absence encephal/o = brain -y = noun ending	congenital absence of the brain and, in some cases, the spinal cord
ataxia (ah-**TAK**-see-ah)	lacking muscular coordination, especially voluntary muscle movement
Bell palsy (Bell **PALL**-zee)	weakness or paralysis of the muscles of one side of the face
cephalalgia (seff-al-**AL**-jee-ah) cephal/o = head -algia = pain	pain in the head; headache
cerebral aneurysm (seh-**REE**-bral **AN**-yoo-rizm)	dilation of a cerebral artery that might put pressure on cerebral tissue and interfere with cerebral function
cerebral hemorrhage (seh-**REE**-bral **HEM**-oh-rij)	bursting forth of blood into cerebral tissue due to rupture of a cerebral vessel
cerebral palsy (CP) (seh-**REE**-bral **PALL**-zee)	lack of voluntary muscle control and/or coordination caused by a lack of oxygen to the brain at or near the time of birth
cerebral thrombosis (seh-**REE**-bral throm-**BOH**-sis) thromb/o = clot -osis = condition	presence of an atherosclerotic clot in a cerebral blood vessel that causes death of a specific portion of brain tissue
cerebrovascular accident (CVA) (seh-**REE**-broh-**VASS**-kyoo-lar) cerebr/o = cerebrum vascul/o = vessel -al = pertaining to	occlusion or rupture of a cerebral blood vessel resulting in decreased blood flow to the affected area and death of a specific portion of brain tissue; a *stroke*
Chiari malformation (kee-**AR**-ee)	a structural defect characterized by portions of the cerebellum extending downward through the foramen magnum; *type I*, the cerebellar tonsils extend into the foramen magnum; *type II*, cerebellar and brain stem tissue extends into the foramen magnum; *type III*, the cerebellum and brain stem protrude through the foramen magnum into the spinal cord; *type IV*, an incomplete or underdeveloped cerebellum, also called cerebellar hypoplasia
concussion (kon-**KUSH**-on)	violent jarring, shaking, or other blunt nonpenetrating injury to the brain; may or may not involve loss of consciousness
contusion (kon-**TOO**-zhun)	small venous hemorrhages in the brain caused by the brain striking the cranium; also called a bruise

continued

Table 13-4 (*continued*)   Nervous System Signs, Symptoms, Diseases, and Conditions

TERM WITH PRONUNCIATION	DEFINITION
dementia (deh-**MEN**-shee-ah)	progressive, irreversible deterioration of memory, judgment, and other thought processes
encephalitis (**en**-seff-ah-**LIGH**-tis) encephal/o = brain -itis = inflammation	inflammation of the brain
encephalomalacia (**en**-seff-ah-loh-mah-**LAY**-shee-ah) encephal/o = brain -malacia = softening	softening of brain tissue
encephalopathy (**en**-seff-ah-**LOP**-ah-thee) encephal/o = brain -pathy = disease	any disease of the brain
epidural hematoma (ep-ih-**DOO**-ral **hee**-mah-**TOH**-mah) epi- = above dura- = dura mater -al = pertaining to	a swelling or mass of blood between the cranium and dura mater that applies pressure on the brain tissue in the affected area
epilepsy (**EP**-ih-lep-see)	recurring episodes of excessive or irregular electrical activity of the central nervous system; *intractable epilepsy* is resistant to treatment with medication; epilepsy is also called *seizure disorder*
glioma (gligh-**OH**-mah) gli/o = neuroglia; nerve cell -oma = tumor	malignant tumor of neuroglial cells
Guillain-Barré syndrome (**GEE**-yon bah-**RAY SIN**-drohm)	acute inflammation of several nerves of the peripheral nervous system characterized by symmetrical pain and weakness of the extremities; paralysis may also develop
hemiparesis (**hem**-ee-pah-**REE**-sis) hemi- = half -paresis = partial paralysis	partial paralysis of one side of the body
hemiplegia (**hem**-ee-**PLEE**-jee-ah) hemi- = half -plegia = paralysis	paralysis of one side of the body
Huntington disease (HD)	genetic disorder characterized by progressive, irreversible degeneration of cerebral neurons that results in uncontrolled movements, loss of intellectual capabilities, and emotional disturbances; also called *Huntington chorea*
hydrocephalus (**high**-droh-**SEFF**-ah-lus) hydr/o = water; fluid cephal/o = head -us = noun ending	abnormal accumulation of cerebrospinal fluid around the brain, often causing swelling of the head; commonly called *water on the brain*

EXERCISE 13-3

Replace the italicized phrase or abbreviation with the correct medical term.

1. The computerized tomography (CT) scan revealed a/an *dilation of a cerebral artery.*

2. Shayna's diagnosis of *facial muscle paralysis* was established by her family physician.

3. After a/an *CVA,* Victoria was paralyzed on her left side.

4. A/an *atherosclerotic clot* resulted in temporal lobe brain tissue death.

5. *ALS* is also called Lou Gehrig's disease, after the famous baseball player who had this condition.

6. Bridget was diagnosed with *CP* as a result of a lack of oxygen during delivery.

7. Lillian's diagnosis was a/an *malignant tumor of neuroglial cells.*

8. Armando's *seizure disorder* was successfully treated with medication.

9. *Paralysis of one side of the body* can be the result of a stroke.

10. Belinda's *abnormal accumulation of cerebrospinal fluid around the brain* was relieved by the placement of a shunt.

EXERCISE 13-4

Write a brief definition for each term and describe the difference between each pair.

1. a. anencephaly _____

   b. encephalitis _____

2. a. encephalopathy _____

   b. encephalomalacia _____

3. a. Guillain-Barré syndrome _____

   b. Huntington disease _____

4. a. concussion _____

   b. contusion _____

5. a. hemiparesis _____

   b. hemiplegia _____

The medical terms in table 13-5 are signs, symptoms, diseases, and conditions related to the nervous system. Review the meaning of these terms and complete the exercises.

Table 13-5   Nervous System Signs, Symptoms, Diseases, and Conditions

TERM WITH PRONUNCIATION	DEFINITION
meningioma (men-**in**-jee-**OH**-mah) mening/o = meninges -oma = tumor	slow-growth tumor of the meninges of the brain, primarily from the arachnoid membrane
meningitis (**men**-in-**JIGH**-tis) mening/o = meninges -itis = inflammation	infection or inflammation of the membranes covering the brain or spinal cord (meninges); may be bacterial or viral and is by severe headache, vomiting, and pain and stiffness in the neck
meningocele (men-**IN**-goh-seel) mening/o = meninges -cele = hernia; protrusion	herniation of the meninges through a hole in the skull or vertebral column
meningomyelocele (men-**in**-goh-my-**ELL**-oh-seel) mening/o = meninges myel/o = spinal cord -cele = hernia; protrusion	herniation of the spinal cord and meninges through a defect in the vertebral column
multiple sclerosis (MS) (sklair-**OH**-sis)	degenerative inflammatory disease of the central nervous system that attacks the myelin sheath of the spinal cord and brain, resulting in hardening and scarring
myelomalacia (**migh**-eh-loh-mah-**LAY**-shee-ah) myel/o = spinal cord -malacia = softening	abnormal softening of the spinal cord
neuralgia (noo-**RAL**-jee-ah) neur/o = nerve -algia = pain	severe sharp pain of a nerve or along the course of a nerve
neuritis (noo-**RIGH**-tis) neur/o = nerve -itis = inflammation	inflammation of nerve or nerves
neuroblastoma (**noo**-roh-blast-**OH**-mah) neur/o = nerve blast/o = embryonic stage of development -oma = tumor	highly malignant tumor composed of cells derived from embryonic neural tissue; usually occurs in young children
neuropathy (noo-**ROP**-ah-thee) neur/o = nerve -pathy = disease	any disease of the nerves

continued

Table 13-5 (continued) Nervous System Signs, Symptoms, Diseases, and Conditions

TERM WITH PRONUNCIATION	DEFINITION
paraplegia (pair-ah-**PLEE**-jee-ah) para- = around -plegia = paralysis	paralysis of the lower half of the body, including the legs
Parkinson disease	chronic, progressive nervous disease characterized by tremor, muscular weakness, and rigidity
poliomyelitis (**poh**-lee-oh-**migh**-eh-**LIGH**-tis)	infectious viral disease that affects the motor (efferent) neurons of the brain and spinal cord, resulting in muscle paralysis and wasting
polyneuritis (**pall**-ee-noo-**RIGH**-tis) poly- = many neur/o = nerve -itis = inflammation	inflammation of many nerves or nerve fibers
postpolio syndrome	slow, progressive weakening of muscles that occurs in approximately 25% of poliomyelitis survivors 20–30 years after the initial illness
quadriplegia (**kwad**-rih-**PLEE**-jee-ah) quadr/i = four -plegia = paralysis	paralysis of all four limbs, usually resulting from spinal cord injury
Reye syndrome (**RIGH SIN**-drohm)	acute encephalopathy following an acute viral infection
sciatica (sigh-**AT**-ih-kah)	severe pain along the course of the sciatic nerve, from the back of the thigh and down the inside of the leg
seizure (**SEE**-zhoor)	excessive irregular electrical activity of the central nervous system associated with epilepsy
shingles; herpes zoster (**HER**-peez **ZOSS**-ter)	acute viral infection characterized by an inflammation of a spinal or cranial nerve pathway that produces painful vesicular eruptions on the skin
subdural hematoma (sub-**DOO**-ral **hee**-mah-**TOH**-mah) sub- = beneath; below dura- = hard -al = pertaining to	collection of blood below the dura mater and above the arachnoid membrane, usually the result of a closed head injury (figure 13-7)
syncope (**SIN**-koh-pee)	loss of consciousness due to a lack of blood supply to the brain; fainting
transient ischemic (iss-**KEE**-mik) attack (TIA)	temporary interference or interruption of the blood supply to a portion of the brain
trigeminal neuralgia; tic douloureaux (trigh-**JEM**-ih-nal noo-**RAL**-jee-ah; **TIK DOO**-loh-roo)	severe pain that radiates along the fifth cranial nerve and usually affects one side of the head and face

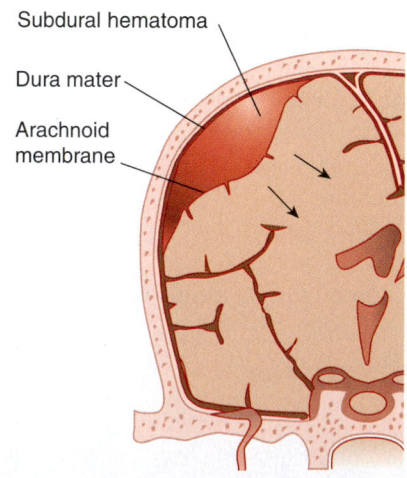

Figure 13-7 Subdural hematoma

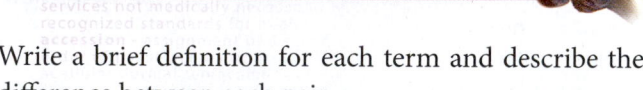

EXERCISE 13-5

Write a brief definition for each term and describe the difference between each pair.

1. a. meningioma _____
    b. neuroblastoma _____

2. a. meningocele _____
    b. meningomyelocele _____

3. a. neuralgia _____
    b. neuropathy _____

4. a. Parkinson disease _____

   b. Multiple sclerosis _____

5. a. syncope _____

   b. transient ischemic attack _____

6. a. poliomyelitis _____

   b. polyneuritis _____

7. a. paraplegia _____

   b. quadriplegia _____

EXERCISE 13-6

Match the medical term in column 1 with the definition in column 2.

COLUMN 1

a. meningitis

b. myelomalacia

c. neuritis

d. Reye syndrome

e. sciatica

f. seizure

g. shingles

h. subdural hematoma

i. trigeminal neuralgia

COLUMN 2

1. abnormal softening of the spinal cord _____

2. acute encephalopathy following an acute viral infection _____

3. acute viral infection; inflammation along a nerve pathway _____

4. collection of blood below the dura mater and above the arachnoid membrane _____

5. inflammation of the membranes covering the brain _____

6. inflammation of the nerves _____

7. irregular electrical activity of the CNS associated with epilepsy _____

8. severe pain along the fifth cranial nerve _____

9. severe pain from the back of the thigh down the inside of the leg _____

Nervous System Diagnostic Procedures, Operations, and Laboratory Tests

Nervous system diagnostic procedures, operations, and laboratory tests are listed in table 13-6. Review the terms and complete the exercises.

Table 13-6 Nervous System Diagnostic Procedures, Operations, and Laboratory Tests

TERM WITH PRONUNCIATION	DEFINITION
cerebrospinal fluid analysis (seh-**ree**-broh-**SPIGH**-nal) cerebr/o = cerebrum spin/o = spine -al = pertaining to	laboratory analysis of cerebrospinal fluid (CSF) to detect the presence of bacteria, blood, and malignant cells, and to measure glucose and protein content
craniotomy (**kray**-nee-**OT**-oh-me) crani/o = skull -(o)tomy = incision into	incision into the skull to provide access to the brain or to relieve intracranial pressure
echoencephalography (**ek**-oh-en-**seff**-ah-**LOG**-rah-fee) echo- = sound encephal/o = brain -graphy = process of recording	process of recording a picture of the structures of the brain using sound waves
electroencephalogram (ee-**lek**-troh-en-**SEFF**-ah-loh-gram) electr/o = electricity encephal/o = brain -gram = record of	graphic record of the electrical activity of the brain
electroencephalography (EEG) (ee-**lek**-troh-en-**seff**-ah-**LOG**-rah-fee) electr/o = electricity encephal/o = brain -graphy = process of recording	process of recording the electrical activity of the brain

continued

Table 13-6 (*continued*) Nervous System Diagnostic Procedures, Operations, and Laboratory Tests

TERM WITH PRONUNCIATION	DEFINITION
evoked potential studies	electroencephalographic test that measures the brain activity in response to various types of electrical stimulation
lumbar puncture (LP)	insertion of a needle into the subarachnoid space, usually between the third and fourth lumbar vertebrae, to withdraw cerebrospinal fluid; also called *spinal tap* (figure 13-8)
myelography (**migh**-eh-**LOG**-rah-fee) myel/o = spinal cord -graphy = process of recording	process of recording an x-ray picture of the spinal cord and spinal cavity
myelogram (**MIGH**-eh-loh-gram) myel/o = spinal cord -gram = record of	x-ray record of the spinal cord and spinal cavity
neurectomy (noo-**REK**-toh-me) neur/o = nerve -ectomy = surgical removal	surgical excision of a nerve or nerve fibers
pneumoencephalography (PEG) (**noo**-moh-en-**seff**-ah-**LOG**-rah-fee) pneum/o = air encephal/o = brain -graphy = process of recording	process of recording an x-ray picture of the ventricles and other fluid-filled cavities of the central nervous system; air or another type of gas is used as the contrast medium
Romberg test (**ROM**-berg)	technique used to assess and evaluate cerebellar function and balance
transcutaneous electrical nerve stimulation (TENS) (**tranz**-kyoo-**TAY**-nee-us) trans- = across, through cutane/o = skin -ous = pertaining to	pain-relief treatment during which electrical impulses are delivered through the skin to nerve endings near the pain site; the impulses prevent the transmission of pain signals to the brain

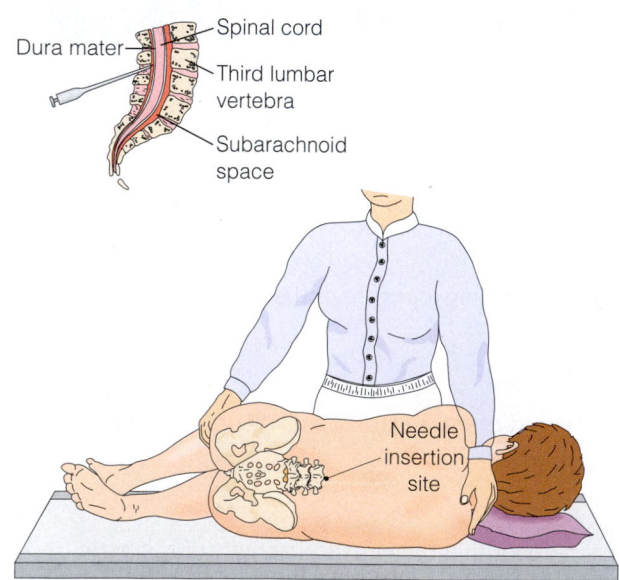

Figure 13-8 Lumbar puncture

EXERCISE 13-7

Place an X next to the medical term or abbreviation that identifies an x-ray of the nervous system and an E next to the electrical activity tests.

1. CSF analysis _____

2. EEG _____

3. LP _____

4. myelography _____

5. PEG _____

6. evoked potential studies _____

7. Romberg test _____

EXERCISE 13-8

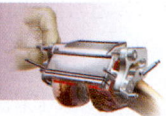

Write out each abbreviation with a brief definition of the phrase.

1. TENS _____

   DEFINITION: _____

2. EEG _____

   DEFINITION: _____

3. PEG _____

   DEFINITION: _____

4. LP _____

   DEFINITION: _____

5. CSF analysis _____

   DEFINITION: _____

ABBREVIATIONS

Nervous system abbreviations are listed in table 13-7. Practice writing out the abbreviations with a brief definition for each phrase or term.

Table 13-7   Abbreviations

ABBREVIATION	MEANING
ALS	amyotrophic lateral sclerosis
ANS	autonomic nervous system
CNS	central nervous system
CP	cerebral palsy
CSF	cerebrospinal fluid
CVA	cerebrovascular accident
EEG	electroencephalography
HD	Huntington disease
ICP	intracranial pressure
LP	lumbar puncture
MS	multiple sclerosis
PEG	pneumoencephalography
PNS	peripheral nervous system
PPS	postpolio syndrome
SNS	somatic nervous system
TENS	transcutaneous electrical nerve stimulation
TIA	transient ischemic attack

THE EYE AND VISION

The eyes are located in the bony orbits at the front of the skull. The structures of the eyes are arranged in three layers called **tunics**. The eyes receive light rays; bend, or refract, the rays; and transmit the nerve impulses generated by the light rays to the occipital lobe of the brain. After the impulses reach the occipital lobe, they are interpreted as images and we are able to "see." Vision is dependent on the health of the eyes, the sight-related nerves, and the brain.

Ophthalmology (**off**-thall-**MALL**-oh-jee) is the medical specialty related to the eye, and the physician specialist is called an **ophthalmologist** (**off**-thall-**MALL**-oh-jist). An **optometrist** is a nonphysician eye specialist who has a degree in **optometry**. Both groups use *doctor* as their professional title. An **optician** is an allied-health technician who is trained to fit prescription eyeglasses and contact lenses, and also grinds lenses for eyeglasses.

ROOTS, PREFIXES, AND SUFFIXES OF THE EYE

Roots, prefixes, and suffixes associated with the eye are listed in table 13-8. Review these word elements and complete the exercises.

Table 13-8   Roots, Prefixes, and Suffixes of the Eye

ROOT	MEANING
aque/o	watery
blast/o	immature
blephar/o	eyelid
conjunctiv/o	conjunctiva
corne/o	cornea
dacry/o	tears
dacryocyst/o	tear sac
dipl/o	double
fund/o	fundus; base
glauc/o	silver; gray
ir/o; irid/o	iris
kerat/o	cornea
lacrim/o	tears
ocul/o	eye
ophthalm/o	eye
opt/o	eye; vision

continued

Table 13-8 (*continued*) Roots, Prefixes, and Suffixes of the Eye

ROOT	MEANING
palpebr/o	eyelid
phac/o; phak/o	lens
phot/o	light
pupill/o	pupil
retin/o	retina
scler/o	sclera; hard
uve/o	uvea
vitre/o	glassy; jelly-like

PREFIX	MEANING
ect-	outside; out
en-; eso-	in; inward
ex-	out; outward
presby-	aging; old

SUFFIX	MEANING
-metry	to measure
-opia	vision
-tropia; -tropion	to turn; turning

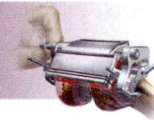

EXERCISE 13-9

Write the root, prefix, suffix, and their meaning. Based on the meanings, write a brief definition for each term.

1. Intraocular

    ROOT: _____ MEANING: _____

    PREFIX: _____ MEANING: _____

    SUFFIX: _____ MEANING: _____

    DEFINITION: _____

2. Lacrimal

    ROOT: _____ MEANING: _____

    PREFIX: _____ MEANING: _____

    SUFFIX: _____ MEANING: _____

    DEFINITION: _____

3. Nasolacrimal

    ROOT: _____ MEANING: _____

    PREFIX: _____ MEANING: _____

    SUFFIX: _____ MEANING: _____

    DEFINITION: _____

4. Ophthalmologist

    ROOT: _____ MEANING: _____

    PREFIX: _____ MEANING: _____

    SUFFIX: _____ MEANING: _____

    DEFINITION: _____

5. Ophthalmology

    ROOT: _____ MEANING: _____

    PREFIX: _____ MEANING: _____

    SUFFIX: _____ MEANING: _____

    DEFINITION: _____

6. Optometry

    ROOT: _____ MEANING: _____

    PREFIX: _____ MEANING: _____

    SUFFIX: _____ MEANING: _____

    DEFINITION: _____

7. Corneal

    ROOT: _____ MEANING: _____

    PREFIX: _____ MEANING: _____

    SUFFIX: _____ MEANING: _____

    DEFINITION: _____

8. Vitreous

    ROOT: _____ MEANING: _____

    PREFIX: _____ MEANING: _____

    SUFFIX: _____ MEANING: _____

    DEFINITION: _____

9. Hyperopia

    ROOT: _____ MEANING: _____

    PREFIX: _____ MEANING: _____

    SUFFIX: _____ MEANING: _____

    DEFINITION: _____

10. Presbyopia

    ROOT: _____ MEANING: _____

    PREFIX: _____ MEANING: _____

    SUFFIX: _____ MEANING: _____

    DEFINITION: _____

STRUCTURES OF THE EYE

The structures of the eye are arranged in three layers, or tunics. The outer layer is the **sclera** (**SKLAIR**-ah), the middle layer is the **choroid** (**KOH**-royd), and the inner

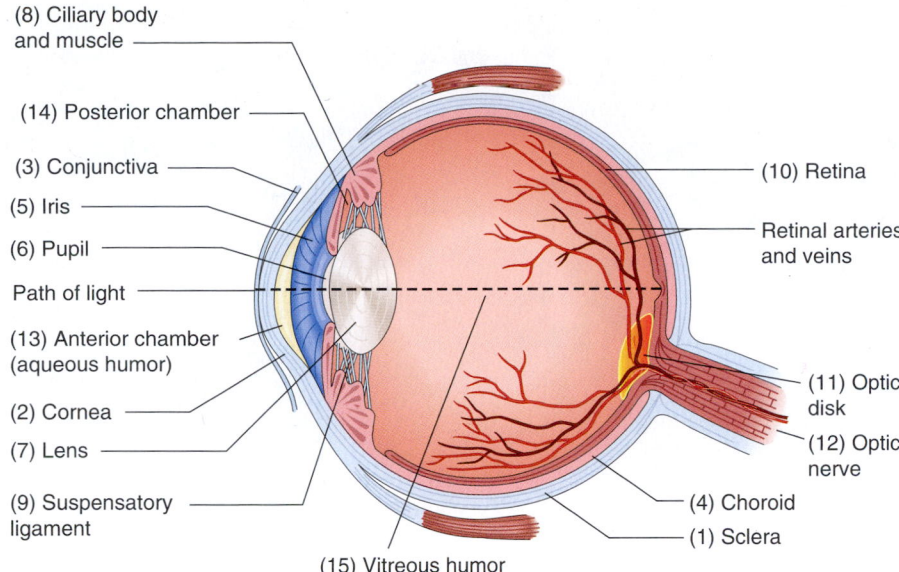

(8) Ciliary body and muscle

(14) Posterior chamber

(3) Conjunctiva

(5) Iris

(6) Pupil

Path of light

(13) Anterior chamber (aqueous humor)

(2) Cornea

(7) Lens

(9) Suspensatory ligament

(10) Retina

Retinal arteries and veins

(11) Optic disk

(12) Optic nerve

(4) Choroid

(1) Sclera

(15) Vitreous humor

Figure 13-9   Structures of the eye

layer is the **retina** (**RET**-ih-nah). The structures of each layer have specific functions related to vision. Figure 13-9 illustrates the structures of the eye. Refer to this figure as you learn about each layer and its structures.

The outer layer of the eye consists of the sclera, cornea, and conjunctiva. The (1) sclera, the white of the eye, is a fibrous tissue that maintains the shape of the eyeball and serves as its protective covering. The (2) **cornea** (**KOR**-nee-ah) is the transparent anterior portion of the sclera that covers the iris. The (3) **conjunctiva** (**kon**-junk-**TIGH**-vah) is a mucous membrane that lines the outer surface of the eye and the inside of the eyelid.

The middle layer of the eye includes the choroid, iris, pupil, lens, and ciliary body. The (4) choroid is a layer of tissue beneath the sclera. The choroid contains blood vessels that supply oxygen and nutrients to the eye. The (5) **iris**, which gives the eyes color, is a muscular ring that surrounds the (6) **pupil**. The iris adjusts the opening of the pupil to control the amount of light that enters the eye. The (7) **lens**, also called the **crystalline** (**KRIS**-tah-lin) **lens**, is connected to the choroid by the (8) **ciliary** (**SILL**-ee-air-ee) **body** and the (9) **suspensatory** (suh-**SPEN**-sah-tor-ee) **ligaments**. The choroid, iris, and ciliary body are collectively known as the **uvea** (**YOO**-vee-ah). The ciliary body and suspensatory ligaments adjust the shape of the lens to help focus light rays on the retina. When an object is near, the lens is shortened and becomes thicker; when an object is distant, the lens is lengthened and becomes thinner.

The inner layer of the eye includes the retina, nerve cells, and optic disk. The (10) retina is sensory nerve tissue that coats the inside of the eye. It contains nerve cells called **rods** and **cones**, which convert light rays into nerve impulses. Rods are responsible for vision in dim light and peripheral vision. Cones are responsible for the vision in bright light, central vision, and color vision. The (11) **optic disk**, located at the back of the eye, is the area where the nerve endings of the retina come together to form the (12) **optic nerve**. The optic nerve transmits impulses to the occipital lobe of the brain.

Cavities of the Eye

The interior of the eye has two cavities: the anterior cavity and the posterior cavity. The anterior cavity consists of the (13) **anterior chamber**, the area in the front of the lens; and the (14) **posterior chamber**, the area behind the lens. These chambers are filled with a watery fluid called **aqueous** (**AY**-kwee-us) **humor**; this fluid maintains the proper pressure within the eye.

The posterior cavity is filled with a clear, jelly-like substance called (15) **vitreous** (**VIH**-tree-us) **humor**; this fluid gives the eyeball its shape. Vitreous humor is necessary for sight. If the eyeball is injured and vitreous humor escapes, blindness can result. Both aqueous and vitreous humor help bend light rays as they pass through the eye and focus on the retina.

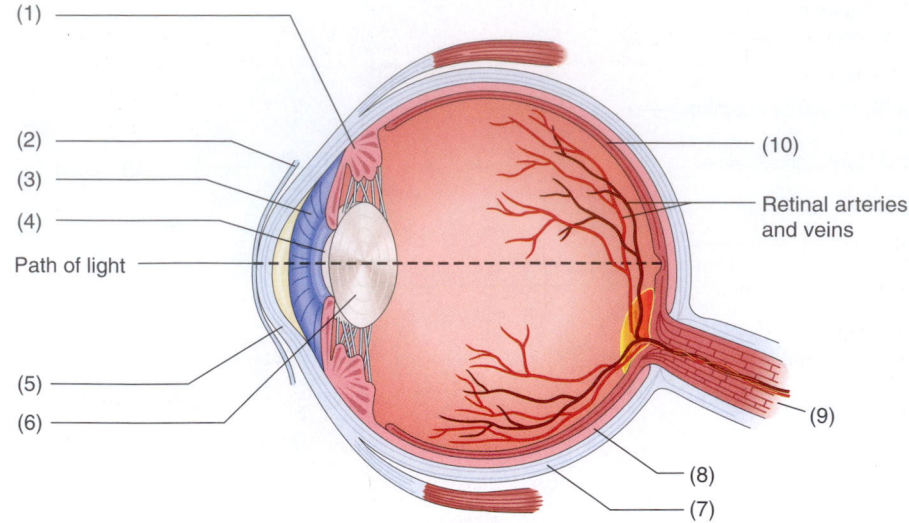

(1)

(2)
(3)
(4)
Path of light

(5)
(6)

(10)

Retinal arteries
and veins

(9)

(8)
(7)

Figure 13-10   Label the eye

EXERCISE 13-10

Write the names of the labeled structures in figure 13-10 on the spaces provided.

1. _____

2. _____

3. _____

4. _____

5. _____

6. _____

7. _____

8. _____

9. _____

10. _____

Accessory Structures of the Eye

Accessory structures of the eye include the orbit; eyebrows; eyelashes; oil glands; and lacrimal glands, fluid, sacs, and ducts. The purpose of the accessory structures is to protect the eye from disease and injury. The **orbit**, also called the **eye socket**, is the bony cavity of the skull that houses and protects the eyeball. The **eyelids**, **eyelashes**, and **eyebrows** prevent foreign matter from reaching the eyes.

The **meibomian** (migh-**BOH**-mee-an) **glands**, located between the conjunctiva and the tissue of the upper and lower eyelids, are small oil glands that lubricate the eyes. These glands are not visible unless they become obstructed. The **lacrimal** (**LAK**-rih-mal) **glands**, located above the outer corner of each eye, produce **lacrimal fluid** (tears) that moistens the anterior surface of the eyeball. The **lacrimal ducts** drain lacrimal fluid away from the eye and into the nose via the **nasolacrimal duct**. The upper expanded portion of the lacrimal duct is called the **lacrimal sac**.

MEDICAL TERMS RELATED TO THE EYE

Medical terms related to the eye are organized by diseases, conditions, diagnostic procedures, and operations. There are two categories of medical terminology exercises: (1) those designed to provide opportunities to learn the terms, and (2) those designed to provide opportunities to accurately assign diagnostic or procedure codes. Exercises for learning the terms immediately follow the lists of terms and definitions. Medical coding exercises are available after all terms have been presented.

Signs, Symptoms, Diseases, and Conditions of the Eye

The medical terms in table 13-9 are signs, symptoms, diseases, and conditions of the eye. Review the pronunciation and meaning of these terms and complete the exercises.

Table 13-9   Signs, Symptoms, Diseases, and Conditions of the Eye

TERM WITH PRONUNCIATION	DEFINITION
astigmatism (ah-**STIG**-mah-tizm)	a refractive error causing light rays to be focused irregularly on the retina due to an abnormally shaped cornea
blepharitis (**bleh**-fah-**RIGH**-tis) blephar/o = eyelids -itis = inflammation	inflammation of the eyelids
blepharoptosis (**bleh**-fah-rop-**TOH**-sis) blephar/o = eyelid -ptosis = drooping	drooping of an eyelid
cataract (**KAT**-ah-rakt)	progressive cloudiness of the crystalline lens
chalazion (kah-**LAY**-zee-on)	cyst or nodule on the eyelid as a result of an obstructed meibomian gland
color blindness	inability to recognize or "see" certain colors
conjunctivitis (kon-**junk**-tih-**VIGH**-tis) conjunctiv/o = conjunctiva -itis = inflammation	inflammation of the conjunctiva; commonly called *pinkeye*
dacryocystitis (**dak**-ree-oh-sis-**TIGH**-tis) dacryocyst/o = tear sac -itis = inflammation	inflammation of the tear sac or lacrimal sac
detached retina	separation of the retina from the choroid layer of the eye
diabetic retinopathy (**digh**-ah-**BEH**-tik **reh**-tin-**OP**-ah-thee) retin/o = retina -pathy = disease	disease of the retina and its capillaries caused by long-standing and usually poorly controlled diabetes mellitus
diplopia (dih-**PLOH**-pee-ah) dipl/o = two; double -opia = vision	double vision; may be in one or both eyes
ectropion (ek-**TROH**-pee-on) ect- = outside; out -tropion = turning	turning outward of the eyelash margins, usually affects the lower eyelid
entropion (en-**TROH**-pee-on) en- = in; inward -tropion = turning	turning inward of the eyelash margins, usually affects the lower eyelid
esotropia (ess-oh-**TROH**-pee-ah) eso- = in; inward -tropia = turning	inward turning of the eyes; also known as *convergent strabismus;* commonly called *cross-eyed*
exophthalmia (**ecks**-off-**THAL**-mee-ah) ex- = out; outward ophthalm/o = eye -ia = noun ending	abnormal protrusion of the eyeball(s)
exotropia (**ecks**-oh-**TROH**-pee-ah) ex- = out; outward -tropia = turning	outward turning of the eyes; also known as *divergent strabismus;* commonly called *walleyed*
glaucoma (glaw-**KOH**-mah)	increased intraocular pressure

EXERCISE 13-11

Replace the italicized phrase with the correct medical term.

1. *Cloudiness of the crystalline lens* is a common problem associated with aging.

2. *A refractive error of irregularly focused light rays* can be corrected with glasses.

3. Trauma to the eye can result in *double vision*.

4. Surgical intervention might be needed to correct *convergent strabismus*.

5. A thorough eye examination includes an assessment for *increased intraocular pressure*.

6. *Walleye* is often caused by a problem with the muscles of the eye.

7. An obstructed meibomian gland is a common cause of a/an *cyst on the eyelid*.

8. *Abnormal protrusion of the eyeballs* is often seen in severe hyperthyroidism.

9. *Turning outward of the eyelash margin* usually affects the lower eyelid.

10. *Turning inward of the eyelash margin* might cause irritation of the eye.

EXERCISE 13-12

Write a brief definition for each term and describe the difference between each pair.

1. a. blepharitis _____
   b. blepharoptosis _____

2. a. conjunctivitis _____
   b. dacryocystitis _____

3. a. detached retina_____
   b. diabetic retinopathy _____

The medical terms in table 13-10 are signs, symptoms, diseases, and conditions of the eye. Review the pronunciation and meaning of these terms and complete the exercises.

Table 13-10 Signs, Symptoms, Diseases, and Conditions of the Eye

TERM WITH PRONUNCIATION	DEFINITION
hordeolum (hor-**DEE**-oh-lum)	bacterial infection of an eyelash follicle or sebaceous gland; commonly called a *sty*
hyperopia (**high**-per-**OH**-pee-ah) hyper- = increased; excessive -opia = vision	impaired vision of close objects; light rays focus beyond the retina; commonly called *farsightedness*
iritis (ir-**RIGH**-tis) ir/o = iris -itis = inflammation	inflammation of the iris
keratitis (**kair**-ah-**TIGH**-tis) kerat/o = cornea -itis = inflammation	inflammation of the cornea
myopia (my-**OH**-pee-ah)	impaired vision of distant objects; light rays focus in front of the retina; commonly called *nearsightedness*
nyctalopia (**nik**-tah-**LOH**-pee-ah)	impaired or inadequate vision at night; commonly called *night blindness*
nystagmus (niss-**TAG**-mus)	involuntary movements of the eye(s), which may or may not be apparent to the individual

continued

Table 13-10 (*continued*) Signs, Symptoms, Diseases, and Conditions of the Eye

TERM WITH PRONUNCIATION	DEFINITION
ophthalmia neonatorum (off-**THAL**-mee-ah nee-oh-nay-**TOR**-um) ophthalm/o = eye -ia = condition neo- = new nat/o = birth	inflammation of the conjunctiva of a newborn caused by irritation, a blocked tear duct, or a bacterial or viral infection contracted as the infant passes through the birth canal; bacterial infections include *Chlamydia,* and viral infections include genital herpes; also called *newborn* or *neonatal conjunctivitis*
photophobia (foh-toh-**FOH**-bee-ah) phot/o = light -phobia = fear	abnormal sensitivity to light
photoretinitis (**foh**-toh-reh-tih-**NIGH**-tis) phot/o = light retin/o = retina -itis = inflammation	damage or inflammation of the retina due to excessive exposure to light
presbyopia (prez-bee-**OH**-pee-ah) presby- = old -opia = vision	impaired vision due to aging
pterygium (ter-**IJ**-ee-um)	irregular growth and thickening of the conjunctiva on the nasal side of the cornea
retinitis pigmentosa (**reh**-tih-**NIGH**-tis **pig**-men-**TOH**-sah) retin/o = retina -itis = inflammation	degenerative disease of the retina without inflammation that results in defective night vision and a decreased field of vision
retinoblastoma (**reh**-tih-noh-blass-**TOH**-mah) retin/o = retina blast/o = immature cell -oma = tumor	malignant tumor of the retina
retinopathy (**reh**-tih-**NOP**-ah-thee) retin/o = retina -pathy = disease	any disease or disorder of the retina
sclerokeratitis (**sklair**-oh-**kair**-ah-**TIGH**-tis) scler/o = sclera kerat/o = cornea -itis = inflammation	inflammation of the sclera and cornea
strabismus (strah-**BIZ**-mus)	inability of the eyes to gaze in the same direction because of weakness of the eye muscles
trachoma (tray-**KOH**-mah)	chronic, contagious form of conjunctivitis characterized by hypertrophy of the conjunctiva
uveitis (yoo-vee-**EYE**-tis) uve/o = uvea -itis = inflammation	inflammation of the iris, ciliary body, and choroid

EXERCISE 13-13

Circle the medical term that best fits the description.

1. farsightedness — *myopia* or *hyperopia*

2. sty — *hordeolum* or *pterygium*

3. involuntary eye movements — *strabismus* or *nystagmus*

4. night blindness — *photophobia* or *nyctalopia*

5. nearsightedness — *myopia* or *hyperopia*

6. pinkeye — *trachoma* or *conjunctivitis*

EXERCISE 13-14

Replace the italicized phrase with the correct medical term.

1. Excessive ultraviolet light exposure can cause *irregular growth of the conjunctiva.*

2. During Shawna's well-baby visit, the pediatrician noted *an inability of the eyes to gaze in the same direction.*

3. *Conjunctivitis with hypertrophy of the conjunctiva* is prevalent in third-world countries.

4. A decreased field of vision is often the result of *a degenerative disease of the retina.*

5. Chlamydia in the mother may lead to *neonatal conjunctivitis.*

6. Mr. Johnson needed reading glasses due to *impaired vision due to aging.*

EXERCISE 13-15

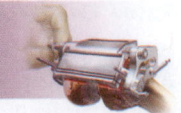

Write a brief definition for each term and describe the difference between each pair.

1. a. photophobia _____
   b. photoretinitis _____

2. a. iritis _____
   b. uveitis _____

3. a. keratitis _____
   b. sclerokeratitis _____

4. a. retinoblastoma _____
   b. retinopathy _____

Diagnostic Procedures, Operations, and Laboratory Tests of the Eye

Procedures and tests related to the eye are listed in table 13-11. Review the terms and complete the exercises.

Table 13-11 Diagnostic Procedures, Operations, and Laboratory Tests of the Eye

TERM WITH PRONUNCIATION	DEFINITION
blepharoplasty (**BLEFF**-ah-roh-**plass**-tee) blephar/o = eyelid -plasty = surgical repair	surgical repair or plastic surgery of the eyelid
corneal transplant (**KOR**-nee-al) corne/o = cornea -al = pertaining to	surgical transplantation of a donor cornea into the eye of a recipient
cryoextraction of the lens (**krigh**-oh-ecks-**TRAK**-shun)	removal of the crystalline lens with a cooling probe
enucleation of the eye (ee-**noo**-klee-**AY**-shun)	removal of the eye from the orbit
extracapsular cataract extraction (ECCE) (**eks**-trah-**KAP**-syoo-lar KAT-ah-rakt)	removal of the crystalline lens and the anterior segment of the lens capsule
funduscopy (fun-**DOSS**-koh-pee) fund/o = fundus; base -scopy = examination with a scope	examination of the posterior inner part of the eye, known as the fundus, using an ophthalmoscope
intraocular lens implant (in-trah-**OK**-yoo-lar) intra- = within ocul/o = eye -ar = pertaining to	surgical implantation of a crystalline lens; usually done at the same time as cataract extraction
iridectomy (**ir**-id-**EK**-toh-mee) irid/o = iris -ectomy = surgical removal	excision of a section of the iris
keratoplasty (**KAIR**-ah-toh-plass-tee) kerat/o = cornea -plasty = surgical repair	surgical repair of the cornea characterized by the excision of an opaque section of the cornea

continued

Table 13-11 (continued)   Diagnostic Procedures, Operations, and Laboratory Tests of the Eye

TERM WITH PRONUNCIATION	DEFINITION
laser in situ keratomileusis (LASIK) (**kair**-ah-toh-mill-**YOO**-sis)	procedure to correct vision problems, especially myopia, by removing tissue and permanently changing the shape of the cornea
ophthalmoscopy (**off**-thal-**MOSS**-koh-pee) ophthalm/o = eye -scopy = visualization with a scope	examination of the interior of the eye
phacoemulsification (**fak**-oh-ee-**MULL**-sih-fih-kay-shun)	breaking the crystalline lens or its cataract into tiny particles that can be removed by suction or aspiration
photorefractive keratectomy (PRK) (**FOH**-toh ree-**FRAK**-tiv **kair**-ah-**TEK**-toh-mee) kerat/o = cornea -ectomy = surgical removal	surgical removal of corneal surface cells to correct or reduce myopia
radial keratotomy (RK) (**RAY**-dee-al **kair**-ah-**TOT**-oh-mee) kerat/o = cornea -(o)tomy = incision into	spoke-like incisions into the cornea to correct nearsightedness
retinal photocoagulation (**REH**-tin-al **foh**-toh-koh-**ag**-yoo-**LAY**-shun) retin/o = retina -al = pertaining to	laser surgery of the retina to correct retinal detachment and prevent hemorrhage of retinal blood vessels
scleral buckling (**SKLAIR**-al **BUK**-ling) scler/o = sclera -al = pertaining to	repair of retinal detachment by resecting or folding in the sclera
trabeculectomy (trah-**bek**-yoo-**LEK**-toh-mee)	surgical excision of a portion of corneal and scleral tissue to decrease intraocular pressure
trabeculoplasty (trah-**BEK**-yoo-loh-**plass**-tee)	surgical creation of a permanent fistula to drain excess aqueous humor from the anterior chamber of the eye in order to relieve the intraocular pressure associated with glaucoma
vitrectomy (vih-**TREK**-toh-mee) vitre/o = glassy; jelly-like -ectomy = surgical removal	surgical removal of all or part of the vitreous humor

EXERCISE 13-16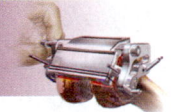

Place an X next to the procedures that are related to lens replacement or cataract surgery and an R next to retinal procedures.

1. corneal transplant _____
2. ECCE _____
3. funduscopy _____
4. iridectomy _____
5. LASIK _____
6. phacoemulsification _____
7. PRK _____
8. RK _____
9. scleral buckling _____
10. cryoextraction _____

EXERCISE 13-17

Identify the specific part of the eye affected by each procedure.

1. blepharoplasty _____
2. funduscopy _____
3. iridectomy _____
4. keratoplasty _____
5. ophthalmoscopy _____
6. trabeculectomy _____
7. vitrectomy _____

ABBREVIATIONS

Abbreviations related to the eye are listed in table 13-12. Practice writing out the abbreviations with a brief definition for each phrase or term.

Table 13-12 Eye Abbreviations

ABBREVIATION	MEANING
ECCE	extracapsular cataract extraction
EOM	extraocular movement
ICCE	intracapsular cataract extraction
IOL	intraocular lens
IOP	intraocular pressure
LASIK	laser in situ keratomileusis
OD	right eye (oculus dexter)
OS	left eye (oculus sinister)
OU	each eye (oculus uterque)
PERRLA	pupils equal, round, reactive to light and accommodation
PRK	photorefractive keratectomy
REM	rapid eye movement
RK	radial keratotomy
VA	visual acuity
VF	visual field

THE EAR

The visible parts of our ears, located on either side of the head, are called the **external ear**. The **internal ear** structures, called the **middle ear** and **inner ear**, are buried in the bony framework of the cranium. The structures of the ear function to provide our sense of hearing, balance, and equilibrium. Sound waves enter the ear, travel through the structures of the middle and inner ear, and are converted to electrical impulses that are transmitted to the cerebral cortex. In the cerebral cortex, the impulses are interpreted into the sounds that we hear.

Otorhinolaryngology (**oh**-toh-**right**-noh-**lair**-in-**GALL**-oh-jee) is the medical specialty of the ears, nose, and throat, and the physician specialist is an **otorhinolaryngologist** (**oh**-toh-**right**-noh-**lair**-in-**GALL**-oh-jist).

Otology (oh-TALL-oh-jee) is the medical specialty related to the study of the diseases and treatments of the ear, and the physician specialist is an **otologist** (oh-TALL-oh-jist). **Audiology** (aw-dee-ALL-oh-jee) is the health profession related to the study, evaluation, and measurement of hearing potential and loss. An **audiologist** (aw-dee-ALL-oh-jist) is an individual who specializes in evaluating hearing potential and hearing loss.

EAR AND HEARING ROOTS, PREFIXES, AND SUFFIXES

Roots, prefixes, and suffixes associated with the ear and hearing are listed in table 13-13. Review the word elements and complete the exercise.

Table 13-13 Ear and Hearing Roots, Prefixes, and Suffixes

ROOT	MEANING
acoust/o	hearing
audi/o	hearing; sound
cochle/o	cochlea
labyrinth/o	inner ear; labyrinth
laryng/o	larynx
myc/o	fungus
myring/o	eardrum; tympanic membrane
ot/o	ear
rhin/o	nose
staped/o	stapes; middle ear bones
tympan/o	eardrum; tympanic membrane
PREFIX	**MEANING**
presby-	old; aging
SUFFIX	**MEANING**
-algia	pain
-cusis; -cusia	hearing
-metry	to measure
-plasty	surgical repair
-(r)rhea	flow; discharge

EXERCISE 13-18

Write the root, suffix, and their meaning. Based on the meanings, write a brief definition for each term.

1. Acoustic

   ROOT: _____ MEANING: _____

   SUFFIX: _____ MEANING: _____

   DEFINITION: _____

2. Audiologist

   ROOT: _____ MEANING: _____

   SUFFIX: _____ MEANING: _____

   DEFINITION: _____

3. Audiology

   ROOT: _____ MEANING: _____

   SUFFIX: _____ MEANING: _____

   DEFINITION: _____

4. Auditory

   ROOT: _____ MEANING: _____

   SUFFIX: _____ MEANING: _____

   DEFINITION: _____

5. Cochlear

   ROOT: _____ MEANING: _____

   SUFFIX: _____ MEANING: _____

   DEFINITION: _____

6. Otologist

   ROOT: _____ MEANING: _____

   SUFFIX: _____ MEANING: _____

   DEFINITION: _____

7. Otology

   ROOT: _____ MEANING: _____

   SUFFIX: _____ MEANING: _____

   DEFINITION: _____

8. Otoscope

   ROOT: _____ MEANING: _____

   SUFFIX: _____ MEANING: _____

   DEFINITION: _____

9. Tympanoplasty

   ROOT: _____ MEANING: _____

   SUFFIX: _____ MEANING: _____

   DEFINITION: _____

10. Otorrhea

    ROOT: _____ MEANING: _____

    SUFFIX: _____ MEANING: _____

    DEFINITION: _____

11. Audiometry

    ROOT: _____ MEANING: _____

    SUFFIX: _____ MEANING: _____

    DEFINITION: _____

STRUCTURES OF THE EAR

The major structures of the ear are illustrated in figure 13-11. Refer to the figure as you learn about these structures.

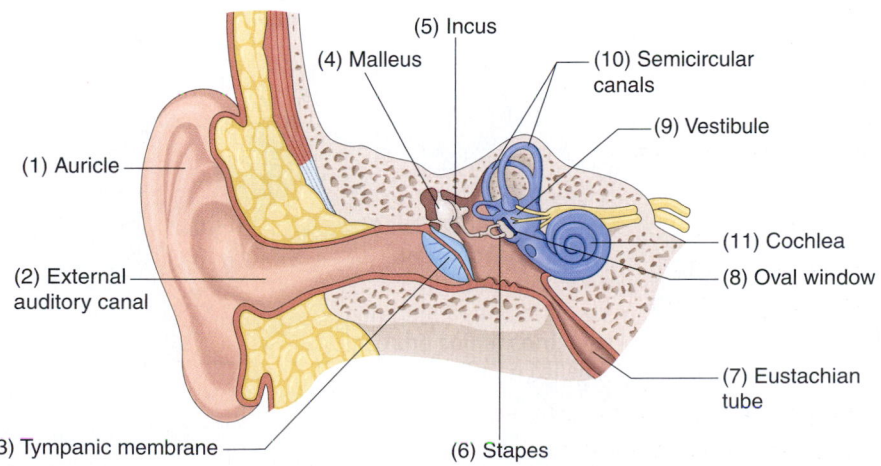

Figure 13-11   Structures of the ear

The external ear includes the (1) **auricle** (**OR**-ih-kal), or **pinna** (**PIN**-ah), which is a cartilaginous flap that directs sound waves into the (2) **external auditory canal**. The auditory canal is lined with hairs called **cilia** (**SILL**-ee-ah) and **ceruminous** (seh-**ROOM**-ih-nus) **glands**. Cilia help direct sound waves through the canal, and the ceruminous glands produce **cerumen** (seh-**ROO**-men), a substance commonly called *earwax* that protects and lubricates the ear. The external ear is separated from the middle ear by the (3) **tympanic** (tim-**PAN**-ik) **membrane**, or eardrum. The tympanic membrane transmits sound waves to the middle ear.

The middle ear includes three small bones called the **ossicles** (**OSS**-ih-kuhlz). The bone closest to the tympanic membrane is the (4) **malleus** (**MAL**-ee-us), commonly known as the *hammer;* the next bone is the (5) **incus** (**INK**-us), commonly known as the *anvil;* and the third bone is the (6) **stapes** (**STAY**-peez), commonly known as the *stirrup.* The middle ear also includes the (7) **eustachian** (yoo-**STAY**-shun) **tube** that connects the middle ear to the pharynx. Yawning and swallowing cause the eustachian tube to open and equalize the pressure between the middle ear and the outside atmosphere.

Sound waves cause the tympanic membrane to vibrate and the ossicles are set in motion. The malleus transmits sound waves to the incus, which in turn transmits sound waves to the stapes. The stapes vibrate against the (8) **oval window**, which separates the middle ear from the inner ear.

The inner ear, called the **labyrinth** (**LAB**-ih-rinth), includes the (9) **vestibule** (**VESS**-tih-byool), the (10) **semicircular canals**, and the (11) **cochlea** (**KOK**-lee-ah). The cochlea is a spiral or snail-shaped structure that contains auditory fluids and the **organ of Corti**. The organ of Corti receives sound wave vibrations and converts them into nerve impulses. The impulses are carried to the brain by the **acoustic** (ah-**KOO**-stik) **nerve** and are then recognized as specific sounds. The semicircular canals are continuous with the vestibule and are filled with fluid necessary for balance and equilibrium.

EXERCISE 13-19

Identify the names of the structures shown in figure 13-12. Write your answers on the spaces provided.

1. _____

2. _____

3. _____

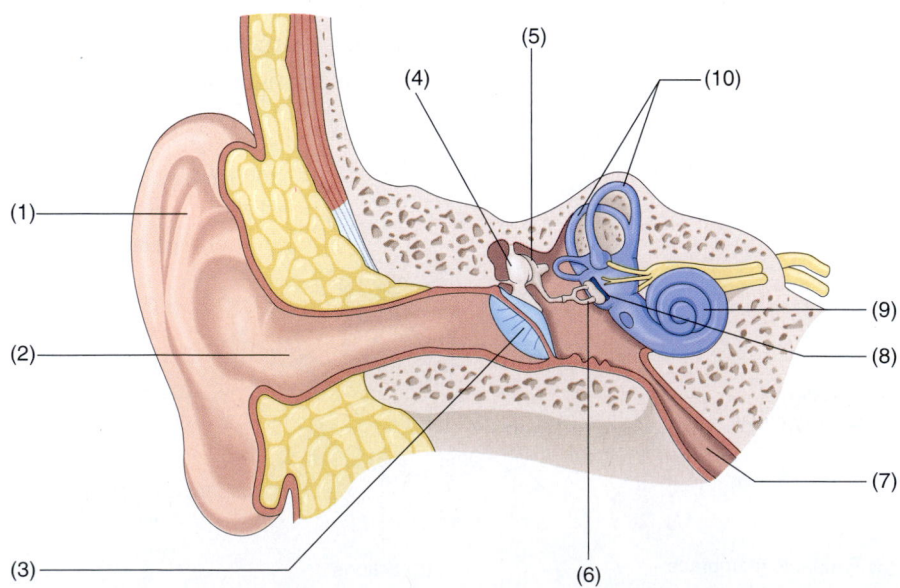

Figure 13-12 Label the ear

4. _____

5. _____

6. _____

7. _____

8. _____

9. _____

10. _____

MEDICAL TERMS RELATED TO THE EAR

Medical terms related to the ear are organized by diseases, conditions, diagnostic procedures, and operations. There are two categories of medical terminology exercises: (1) those designed to provide opportunities to learn the terms, and (2) those designed to provide opportunities to accurately assign diagnostic or procedure codes. Exercises for learning the terms immediately follow the lists of terms and definitions. Medical coding exercises are available after all terms have been presented.

Signs, Symptoms, Diseases, and Conditions of the Ear

The medical terms in table 13-14 are signs, symptoms, diseases, and conditions of the ear. Review the pronunciation and meaning of these terms and complete the exercises.

Table 13-14 Signs, Symptoms, Diseases, and Conditions of the Ear

TERM WITH PRONUNCIATION	DEFINITION
acoustic neuroma (ah-**KOO**-stik noo-**ROH**-mah) acoust/o = hearing -ic = pertaining to neur/o = nerve -oma = tumor; mass	benign tumor of the acoustic nerve
cholesteatoma (**koh**-lee-**stee**-ah-**TOH**-mah)	slow-growth cystic mass or tumor made up of epithelial cell debris and cholesterol; commonly occurs in the middle ear
conductive deafness	hearing loss caused by impaired transmission of sound waves through the middle or external ear
impacted cerumen (seh-**ROO**-men)	excessive accumulation of cerumen (earwax)
labyrinthitis (**lab**-ih-rin-**THIGH**-tis) labyrinth/o = labyrinth -itis = inflammation	inflammation or infection of the labyrinth or inner ear
Meniere disease (man-ee-**AYR**)	chronic inner ear disease characterized by vertigo, sensorial hearing loss, and tinnitus; nausea, vomiting, and sweating may also be present
myringitis (mir-in-**JIGH**-tis) myring/o = tympanic membrane; eardrum -itis = inflammation	inflammation of the tympanic membrane (eardrum)
otalgia (oh-**TAL**-jee-ah) ot/o = ear -algia = pain	pain in the ear; earache
otitis externa (oh-**TIGH**-tis eks-**TER**-nah) ot/o = ear -itis = inflammation	inflammation of the external ear canal; commonly called *swimmer's ear*
otitis media (oh-**TIGH**-tis **MEE**-dee-ah) ot/o = ear -itis = inflammation	infection and inflammation of the middle ear; commonly called a *middle ear infection*

continued

Table 13-14 (continued)   Signs, Symptoms, Diseases, and Conditions of the Ear

TERM WITH PRONUNCIATION	DEFINITION
otomycosis (**oh**-toh-my-**KOH**-sis) ot/o = ear myc/o = fungus -osis = condition	fungal infection of the external auditory meatus (opening)
otorrhea (oh-toh-**REE**-ah) ot/o = ear -(r)rhea = flow; discharge	discharge or drainage from the ear
otosclerosis (**oh**-toh-sklair-**OH**-sis) ot/o = ear -sclerosis = hardening	hereditary condition characterized by irregular ossification of the bones of the middle ear, especially the stapes, causing tinnitus and deafness
perforation of the tympanic membrane	rupture or development of holes in the eardrum
presbycusis (prez-bee-**KOO**-sis) presby- = old -cusis = hearing	impaired hearing related to the aging process
sensorineural deafness (**sen**-soh-ree-**NOO**-ral)	loss of hearing resulting from impaired or damaged auditory nerve cells or tissue
serous otitis media (**SEER**-us oh-**TIGH**-tis) ot/o = ear -itis = inflammation	middle ear infection characterized by an accumulation of serous fluid and air bubbles behind the tympanic membrane
suppurative otitis media (**SOO**-per-ah-tiv oh-**TIGH**-tis) ot/o = ear -itis = inflammation	middle ear infection characterized by an accumulation of purulent (pus-filled) fluid behind the tympanic membrane; symptoms might include dizziness and tinnitus
tinnitus (tin-**NIGH**-tus)	ringing or tinkling sensation in the ears
tympanitis (**tim**-pah-**NIGH**-tis) tympan/o = eardrum -itis = inflammation	inflammation of the tympanic membrane; often associated with otitis media
vertigo (**VER**-tih-goh)	sensation of spinning or dizziness, usually a result of a disturbance of equilibrium

EXERCISE 13-20

Replace the italicized phrase with the correct medical term.

1. Felipe's hearing loss was caused by a/an *benign tumor of the acoustic nerve.*

2. Reggie was fitted for a hearing aid due to *loss of hearing due to aging.*

3. Chronic otitis media might lead to a/an *cystic mass of cell debris and cholesterol.*

4. Many individuals experience *dizziness* in high places.

5. *Ringing in the ears* might be a symptom of inner ear problems.

6. Marta's *inner ear infection* did not respond to antibiotic therapy.

7. Bart had *an excessive accumulation of earwax* removed by his family physician.

EXERCISE 13-21

Write a brief definition for each term and describe the difference between each pair.

1. a. conductive deafness _____

   b. sensorineural deafness _____

2. a. otitis externa _____

   b. otitis media _____

3. a. otomycosis _____

   b. otosclerosis _____

4. a. serous otitis media _____

   b. suppurative otitis media _____

5. a. Meniere disease _____

   b. labyrinthitis _____

6. a. otalgia _____

   b. otorrhea _____

Diagnostic Procedures, Operations, and Laboratory Tests of the Ear

Procedures and tests related to the ear are listed in table 13-15. Review the terms and complete the exercises.

Table 13-15 Diagnostic Procedures, Operations, and Laboratory Tests of the Ear

TERM WITH PRONUNCIATION	DEFINITION
audiogram (**AW**-dee-oh-gram) audi/o = hearing -gram = record	graphic record of hearing
audiometry (**aw**-dee-**OM**-eh-tree) audi/o = hearing -metry = to measure	measuring the sense of hearing
myringoplasty (mir-**IN**-goh-**plass**-tee) myring/o = tympanic membrane; eardrum -plasty = surgical repair	surgical repair of the tympanic membrane
myringotomy (mir-in-**GOT**-oh-mee) myring/o = tympanic membrane; eardrum -(o)tomy = incision into	incision into the tympanic membrane
myringotomy and tubes (mir-in-**GOT**-oh-mee) myring/o = tympanic membrane; eardrum -(o)tomy = incision into	incision into the tympanic membrane and insertion of tubes to allow drainage of fluid that might accumulate behind the eardrum
otoplasty (**OH**-toh-**plass**-tee) ot/o = ear -plasty = surgical repair	surgical repair of one or both of the ears; usually refers to repair of the outer ear
otoscopy (oh-**TOSS**-koh-pee) ot/o = ear -scopy = examination with a scope	visualization and examination of the tympanic membrane using an otoscope
Rinne test (**RIN**-nee)	hearing examination that compares bone and air conduction of sound waves using a vibrating tuning fork
stapedectomy (**stay**-pee-**DEK**-toh-mee) staped/o = stapes -ectomy = surgical removal	excision of the stapes
tympanoplasty (**tim**-pan-oh-**PLASS**-tee) tympan/o = tympanic membrane; eardrum -plasty = surgical repair	surgical repair of the tympanic membrane
tympanotomy (**tim**-pan-**OT**-oh-mee) tympan/o = tympanic membrane; eardrum -(o)tomy = incision into	incision into the tympanic membrane
Weber test	examination of auditory acuity to determine whether a hearing deficit is conductive or sensorineural

EXERCISE 13-22

Circle the term that best fits the definition.

1. surgical repair of the tympanic membrane — *myringotomy* or *myringoplasty*

2. incision into the tympanic membrane — *myringotomy* or *myringoplasty*

3. surgical repair of the ear(s) — *otoplasty* or *ototomy*

4. measurement of hearing — *otometry* or *audiometry*

5. graphic record of hearing — *audiogram* or *audiometry*

6. conductive, sensorial hearing loss test — *Weber test* or *Rinne test*

7. visualization of the inner ear — *otography* or *otoscopy*

8. tests bone and air sound wave conduction — *Weber test* or *Rinne test*

ABBREVIATIONS

Abbreviations related to the ear are listed in table 13-16. Practice writing out the abbreviations with a brief definition for each phrase or term.

Table 13-16 Ear Abbreviations

ABBREVIATION	MEANING
AC	air conduction
AD	right ear (auris dextra)
AS	left ear (auris sinistra)
AU	each ear (auris unitas)
BC	bone conduction
BOM	bilateral otitis media
EENT	eyes, ears, nose, throat
ENT	ears, nose, throat
TM	tympanic membrane

NERVOUS SYSTEM, EYE, AND EAR MEDICAL CODING

To successfully complete the exercises in this section, the ICD-9-CM volumes 1, 2, and 3 and the CPT (Current Procedural Terminology) coding references must be readily available. The information in this section is presented as follows:

- An introduction to ICD-9-CM volume 1, chapter 6, "Diseases of the Nervous System and Sense Organs"
- ICD-9-CM diagnostic coding exercises
- A summary of ICD-9-CM volume 3 coding conventions that apply to nervous system, eye, and ear procedures
- ICD-9-CM procedure coding exercises
- A summary of the CPT Nervous System, Eye, and Ear coding guidelines
- CPT coding exercises

Students are *strongly* encouraged to review the information at the beginning of the ICD-9-CM and CPT coding references. Commercial publishers include instructions on how to use the ICD-9-CM references, the ICD-9-CM official coding conventions, additional conventions used by the publisher, and the *ICD-9-CM Official Guidelines for Coding and Reporting*. Some publishers include the three ICD-9-CM volumes in one book and put the *Alphabetic Index* (volume 2) at the beginning of the reference.

The *Introduction* to CPT includes detailed instructions for using this code book, an index to the illustrations throughout the book, and anatomical illustrations of the major structures of body systems.

ICD-9-CM Volume 1, Chapter 6, Diseases of the Nervous System and Sense Organs (320–389)

Nervous system, eye, and ear diseases are coded to ICD-9-CM volume 1, chapter 6, "Diseases of the Nervous System and Sense Organs." This chapter includes the following major sections:

- **Inflammatory Diseases of the Central Nervous System (320–326).** Codes in this section cover bacterial, viral, acute, and chronic meningitis, and encephalitis. The *code* *first underlying disease* convention is used extensively in the encephalitis categories. Intracranial and intraspinal abscesses are also included in this section.

- **Organic Sleep Disorders (327).** Codes in this section cover organic sleep disorders such as insomnia and hypersomnia (excessive sleeping). Fifth digits are common in this section, as is the convention *code first the underlying disease* or *mental disorder.*

- **Hereditary and Degenerative Diseases of the Central Nervous System (330–337).** Codes in this section cover cerebral degeneration, hydrocephalus, Parkinson disease, abnormal movement diseases, diseases of the spinal cord, and various disorders of the brain and spinal cord.

- **Pain (338).** Codes in this section cover acute and chronic pain disorders and syndromes. Fifth digits are commonly used in this section.

- **Other Headache Syndromes (339).** Codes in this section cover tension, cluster, and post-traumatic headaches.

- **Other Disorders of the Central Nervous System (340–349).** Codes in this section cover demyelinating diseases, multiple sclerosis, paralysis, epilepsy, migraine, and other disorders of the brain, spinal cord, and cerebrospinal fluid. Fifth digits are used to identify specific information related to right- and left-side paralysis, tractable and intractable migraine, and tractable or intractable epilepsy.

- **Disorders of the Peripheral Nervous System (350–359).** Codes in this section cover conditions specific to facial nerves, cranial nerves, and peripheral nerves. Muscular dystrophy codes are also included in this section. The convention *code first the underlying condition* appears in categories 357–359.

- **Disorders of the Eye and Adnexa (360–379).** Codes in this section cover disorders of the eyeball, called the globe; retinal detachments and retinal disorders; and diseases, disorders, and conditions of the structures of the eye. Glaucoma is coded to category 365, cataract to category 366, disorders of refraction and accommodation to category 367, and vision defects and blindness to categories 368–369. Conditions related to the cornea are coded to categories 370–371, disorders of the conjunctiva are coded to 372, and diseases and conditions of the eyelids are coded to categories 373–374. Disorders of the lacrimal system are coded to category 375, and disorders of the orbit of the eye are coded to category 376. Optic nerve and visual pathway conditions are coded to category 377. Strabismus and other disorders of binocular eye movements are coded to category 378. Category 379, other disorders of the eye, includes conditions like scleritis, nystagmus, and anomalies of papillary function. Nearly every category in this section includes fifth-digit codes.

- **Diseases of the Ear and Mastoid Process (380–389).** Codes in this section cover conditions related to the external ear, categories 380–384; the middle ear and mastoid, category 385; and the inner ear, category 386. Category 387 includes otosclerosis of the oval window and cochlea. Degenerative, vascular disorders of the ear, tinnitus, otorrhea, and otalgia are coded to category 388. Hearing loss is coded to category 389. Nearly every category in this section includes fifth-digit codes.

Conditions related to the nervous system, eye, and ear may also be coded to the following chapters in volume 1: chapter 14, "Congenital Anomalies"; chapter 16, "Symptoms, Signs, and Ill-Defined Conditions"; and chapter 2, "Neoplasms."

EXERCISE 13-23

Write a brief definition for each diagnosis. Identify the main term in the diagnostic statement and assign the correct ICD-9-CM diagnosis code(s).

1. Acute follicular conjunctivitis

    DEFINITION: _____

    MAIN TERM: _____

    ICD-9-CM CODE(S): _____

continued

2. Classical migraine

   DEFINITION: _____

   MAIN TERM: _____

   ICD-9-CM CODE(S): _____

3. Bacterial meningitis

   DEFINITION: _____

   MAIN TERM: _____

   ICD-9-CM CODE(S): _____

4. Trigeminal neuralgia

   DEFINITION: _____

   MAIN TERM: _____

   ICD-9-CM CODE(S): _____

5. Senile macular degeneration

   DEFINITION: _____

   MAIN TERM: _____

   ICD-9-CM CODE(S): _____

6. Acute suppurative otitis media, right ear, tympanic membranes intact

   DEFINITION: _____

   MAIN TERM: _____

   ICD-9-CM CODE(S): _____

7. Partial retinal detachment, single defect noted

   DEFINITION: _____

   MAIN TERM: _____

   ICD-9-CM CODE(S): _____

8. Severe dementia due to Alzheimer disease

   DEFINITION: _____

   MAIN TERM: _____

   ICD-9-CM CODE(S): _____

9. Mild, nonproliferative diabetic retinopathy

   DEFINITION: _____

   MAIN TERM: _____

   ICD-9-CM CODE(S): _____

10. Progressive peripheral pterygium

    DEFINITION: _____

    MAIN TERM: _____

    ICD-9-CM CODE(S): _____

11. Concomitant convergent strabismus, congenital

    DEFINITION: _____

    MAIN TERM: _____

    ICD-9-CM CODE(S): _____

12. Retinitis pigmentosa

    DEFINITION: _____

    MAIN TERM: _____

    ICD-9-CM CODE(S): _____

13. Senile cataract

    DEFINITION: _____

    MAIN TERM: _____

    ICD-9-CM CODE(S): _____

14. Bell palsy, right side

    DEFINITION: _____

    MAIN TERM: _____

    ICD-9-CM CODE(S): _____

15. Streptococcal meningitis

    DEFINITION: _____

    MAIN TERM: _____

    ICD-9-CM CODE(S): _____

16. Obstructive hydrocephalus, acquired

    DEFINITION: _____

    MAIN TERM: _____

    ICD-9-CM CODE(S): _____

17. Amyotrophic lateral sclerosis

    DEFINITION: _____

    MAIN TERM: _____

    ICD-9-CM CODE(S): _____

18. Diplegic infantile cerebral palsy

    DEFINITION: _____

    MAIN TERM: _____

    ICD-9-CM CODE(S): _____

19. Generalized convulsive epilepsy, intractable

    DEFINITION: _____

    MAIN TERM: _____

    ICD-9-CM CODE(S): _____

20. Quadriplegia, C1–C4, complete

    DEFINITION: _____

    MAIN TERM: _____

    ICD-9-CM CODE(S): _____

ICD-9-CM Volume 3, Nervous System, Eye, and Ear Procedures

Nervous system operations and some therapeutic treatments are coded to ICD-9-CM volume 3, chapter 1, "Operations on the Nervous System" (01–05); eye operations and some therapeutic treatments are coded to chapter 3, "Operations on the Eye" (08–16); and ear operations and some therapeutic procedures are coded to chapter 4, "Operations on the Ear" (18–20). Chapter 1 includes the following major sections:

- **Incision and Excision of Skull, Brain, and Cerebral Meninges (01–02).** Codes in this section include diagnostic procedures and operations such as biopsy, incision, excision, destruction, and repair of structures associated with the skull, brain, and cerebral meninges. Insertion, revision, removal, and irrigation of ventricular shunts are included in category 02. Fourth digits are required for all but two of the categories in this section.

- **Operations on Spinal Cord and Spinal Canal Structures (03).** Codes in this section include exploration, decompression, diagnostic procedures, repair, lysis of lesions, and injections related to the spinal cord. Repair of meningocele and myelomeningocele are coded to category 03.5. Fourth digits are used extensively in this section.

- **Operations on Cranial and Peripheral Nerves (04).** Codes in this section include incision, division, excision, diagnostic procedures, repair, and other operations on the cranial and peripheral nerves. Carpal tunnel release is coded to category 04.4. Fourth digits are used extensively in this section.

- **Operations on Sympathetic Nerves or Ganglia (05).** Codes in this section include diagnostic and operative procedures.

Chapter 3, "Operations on the Eye" (08–16), includes the following major sections:

- **Operations on Eyelids (08).** Codes in this section include incision, excision, diagnostic procedures, repair, reconstruction, and adjustments of the eyelid. Codes in this section require fourth digits.

- **Operations on Lacrimal System (09).** Codes in this section include incision, excision, diagnostic procedures, repair, and reconstruction of the lacrimal sac, glands, and nasolacrimal ducts. Codes in this section require fourth digits.

- **Operations on Conjunctiva (10).** Codes in this section include incision, excision, diagnostic procedures, repair, and reconstruction of the conjunctiva. Most codes in this section require fourth digits.

- **Operations on Cornea (11).** Codes in this section include incision, excision, diagnostic procedures, repair, transplantation, and reconstruction and refractive surgery of the cornea. Most codes in this section require fourth digits.

- **Operations on Iris, Ciliary Body, Sclera, and Anterior Chamber (12).** Codes in this section include incision, excision, diagnostic procedures, and repair of the iris, ciliary body, sclera, and anterior chamber of the eye. Procedures to relieve elevated intraocular pressure are coded to category 12.7. Additional procedures of the sclera are coded to category 12.8. Most codes in this section require fourth digits.

- **Operations on Lens (13).** Codes in this section include incision, excision, diagnostic procedures, repair, reconstruction, and adjustments of the lens. Removal of the lens and insertion of a prosthetic lens are covered in this section. Most codes in this section require fourth digits.

- **Operations on Retina, Choroid, Vitreous, and Posterior Chamber (14).** Codes in this section include incision, excision, diagnostic procedures, repair, and removal of foreign body and surgically implanted

continued

material. Most codes in this section require fourth digits.

- **Operations on Extraocular Muscles (15).** Codes in this section include lengthening, detachment, repair, and diagnostic procedures of the extraocular muscles.

- **Operations on Orbit and Eyeball (16).** Codes in this section include diagnostic procedures, incision, and repair of the orbit of the eye. Categories 16.3–16.8 cover evisceration, enucleation, removal, and repair of the eyeball.

Chapter 4, "Operations on the Ear" (18–20), includes the following major sections:

- **Operations on External Ear (18).** Codes in this section include incision, excision, diagnostic procedures, repair, and reconstruction of the external ear. Many codes in this section require fourth digits.

- **Reconstructive Operations on Middle Ear (19).** Codes in this section include incision, excision, and repair of the middle ear and tympanic membrane. Many codes in this section require fourth digits.

- **Other Operations on Middle and Inner Ear (20).** Codes in this section include incision, excision, diagnostic procedures, repair, and reconstruction of the middle and inner ear, the mastoid process, and the eustachian tube. Category 20.9 covers cochlear implants and replacement. Many codes in this section require fourth digits.

EXERCISE 13-24

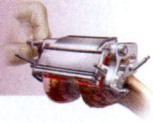

Write a brief definition for each operative, treatment, or diagnostic procedure term. Identify the main term and assign the correct ICD-9-CM code(s).

1. Drainage of subdural hematoma via cranial burr holes

   DEFINITION: _____

   MAIN TERM: _____

   ICD-9-CM CODE(S): _____

2. Diagnostic lumbar puncture (spinal tap); rule out meningitis

   DEFINITION: _____

   MAIN TERM: _____

   ICD-9-CM CODE(S): _____

3. Pterional craniotomy, right side with clipping of aneurysm

   DEFINITION: _____

   MAIN TERM: _____

   ICD-9-CM CODE(S): _____

4. Suboccipital craniectomy, C-1 laminectomy with duraplasty for Chiari type I malformation

   DEFINITION: _____

   MAIN TERM: _____

   ICD-9-CM CODE(S): _____

5. Image-guided left craniotomy for resection of dural arteriovenous fistula

   DEFINITION: _____

   MAIN TERM: _____

   ICD-9-CM CODE(S): _____

6. Phacoemulsification of cataract, left eye, with lens implantation

   DEFINITION: _____

   MAIN TERM: _____

   ICD-9-CM CODE(S): _____

7. Labyrinthectomy with mastoidectomy

   DEFINITION: _____

   MAIN TERM: _____

   ICD-9-CM CODE(S): _____

8. Penetrating keratoplasty, phakic, left eye

   DEFINITION: _____

   MAIN TERM: _____

   ICD-9-CM CODE(S): _____

9. Blepharoplasty and levator repair

   DEFINITION: _____

   MAIN TERM: _____

   ICD-9-CM CODE(S): _____

10. Scleral buckling, retina, left eye

    DEFINITION: _____

    MAIN TERM: _____

    ICD-9-CM CODE(S): _____

11. Extracapsular cataract extraction with implantation of posterior chamber intraocular lens, right eye

    DEFINITION: _____

    MAIN TERM: _____

    ICD-9-CM CODE(S): _____

12. Bilateral myringotomy with tube insertion

    DEFINITION: _____

    MAIN TERM: _____

    ICD-9-CM CODE(S): _____

13. Removal of posterior foreign body with magnet, right eye

    DEFINITION: _____

    MAIN TERM: _____

    ICD-9-CM CODE(S): _____

14. Stapedotomy and repair of ossicular chain

    DEFINITION: _____

    MAIN TERM: _____

    ICD-9-CM CODE(S): _____

15. Cochlear implant, right ear

    DEFINITION: _____

    MAIN TERM: _____

    ICD-9-CM CODE(S): _____

Current Procedural Terminology (CPT) Nervous System, Eye, and Ear Codes (61000–69990)

CPT nervous system, eye, and ear codes are located in the Surgery, Radiology, and Medicine sections. The Surgery guidelines provide important information for all of the Surgery subsections. Review the guidelines in the CPT manual and in chapter 3 of this text. There are three Surgery subsections related to the nervous system, eye, and ear. The Nervous System subsection includes the following categories:

- ■ **Skull, Meninges, and Brain (61000–62258).** Codes in this category cover subdural and cisternal or lateral cervical puncture for drainage, aspiration, or injection; craniectomy or craniotomy; surgery of the skull base; surgery for aneurysm, arteriovenous malformation, or vascular disease; stereotaxis; implantation of neurostimulators; repair; neuroendoscopy; and cerebrospinal fluid shunt procedures. There are extensive instruction notes and definitions in this category. The medical coder must review and follow the notes before assigning CPT codes.

- ■ **Spine and Spinal Cord (62263–63746).** Codes in this category cover injection, drainage, or aspiration; catheter implantation; reservoir/pump implantation; laminotomy or laminectomy; removal or repair of herniated disks; resection of all or parts of the vertebra; stereotaxis; implantation of neurostimulators; repair of meningocele; and creation of a shunt for cerebrospinal fluid. There are extensive instruction notes and definitions in this category. The medical coder must review and follow the notes before assigning CPT codes.

- ■ **Extracranial Nerves, Peripheral Nerves, and Autonomic Nervous System (64400–64999).** Codes in this category cover introduction or injection of anesthetic agents, application of neurostimulators, destruction of nerves, and repair and excision of nerves.

Procedure codes for the eye are coded to the Eye and Ocular Adnexa subsection of the Surgery section. The Eye and Ocular Adnexa subsection includes the following categories:

- ■ **Eyeball (65091–65290).** Codes in this category include removal of the eye and foreign bodies, implants, and laceration repair of the eyeball.

- ■ **Anterior Segment (65400–66999).** Codes in this category include excision, removal, incision, repair, and destruction of the anterior chamber of the eye, the sclera, the iris, the ciliary body, and the lens; and intraocular lens procedures.

continued

- **Posterior Segment (67005–67299).** Codes in this category include removal, repair, or destruction of the vitreous, retina or choroid, and sclera.

- **Ocular Adnexa (67311–67999).** Codes in this category include surgery on the extraocular muscles; exploration, excision, and decompression of the orbit of the eye; and incision, destruction, repair, and reconstruction of the eyelids.

- **Conjunctiva (68020–68399).** Codes in this category include incision and drainage; excision, destruction, and repair of the conjunctiva.

- **Lacrimal System (68400–68899).** Codes in this category include incision, drainage, repair, removal of stones, and probing lacrimal structures.

The Ophthalmology subsection of the Medicine section (92002–92499) covers services such as medical evaluation, contact lens services, and prescription lens services.

Procedure codes for the ear are coded to the Auditory System subsection of the Surgery section. The Auditory System subsection includes these categories:

- **External Ear (69000–69399).** Codes in this category include incision, excision, removal, and repair of the external ear and auditory canal.

- **Middle Ear (69400–69799).** Codes in this category include incision, excision, removal, and repair of the tympanic membrane and ossicles (malleus, incus, and stapes); implantation, replacement, removal, or repair of conduction hearing devices; and decompression of the facial nerve.

- **Inner Ear (69801–69949).** Codes in this category include procedures related to the labyrinth, vestibule, and cochlea.

- **Temporal Bone, Middle Fossa Approach (69950–69979).** Codes in this category cover vestibular nerve section, facial nerve decompression, decompression of the internal auditory canal, and removal of a tumor of the temporal bone.

The Special Otorhinolaryngologic subsection of the Medicine section (92502–92700) covers services such as examination under general anesthesia; vestibular function tests; audiologic function tests; and evaluation and therapeutic services related to cochlear implants, speech-generating devices, swallowing function, and auditory rehabilitation status.

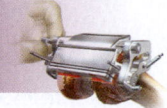

EXERCISE 13-25

Identify the main term in each procedure statement. Assign the correct CPT code(s).

1. Removal and replacement of cerebrospinal fluid shunt system

   MAIN TERM: _____

   CPT CODE(S): _____

2. Total removal of implanted spinal neurostimulator

   MAIN TERM: _____

   CPT CODE(S): _____

3. Brain stem biopsy, mandibular approach

   MAIN TERM: _____

   CPT CODE(S): _____

4. Craniectomy for posterior fossa tumor

   MAIN TERM: _____

   CPT CODE(S): _____

5. Right frontoparietal craniotomy with evacuation of subdural hematoma

   MAIN TERM: _____

   CPT CODE(S): _____

6. Craniotomy for repair of encephalocele, skull base

   MAIN TERM: _____

   CPT CODE(S): _____

7. Corneal laceration repair with tissue glue, right eye

   MAIN TERM: _____

   CPT CODE(S): _____

8. Total reconstruction of the right upper eyelid

   MAIN TERM: _____

   CPT CODE(S): _____

9. Radial keratotomy

   MAIN TERM: _____

   CPT CODE(S): _____

10. Incision and drainage of the lacrimal gland, right eye

    MAIN TERM: _____

    CPT CODE(S): _____

11. Bilateral otoplasty

    MAIN TERM: _____

    CPT CODE(S): _____

12. Stapedotomy for repair of ossicular chain, left ear

    MAIN TERM: _____

    CPT CODE(S): _____

13. Cochlear implant, right ear

    MAIN TERM: _____

    CPT CODE(S): _____

14. Removal of a foreign body, left external auditory canal, general anesthesia

    MAIN TERM: _____

    CPT CODE(S): _____

15. Labyrinthectomy with mastoidectomy, right ear

    MAIN TERM: _____

    CPT CODE(S): _____

■ SUMMARY

This chapter covered medical terms related to the nervous system, the eye, and the ear. Diagnoses and procedures were identified and defined. Nervous system, eye, and ear diseases are coded to ICD-9-CM volume 1, chapter 6, "Diseases of the Nervous System and Sense Organs"; chapter 2, "Neoplasms"; chapter 14, "Congenital Anomalies"; and chapter 16, "Symptoms, Signs, and Ill-Defined Conditions." Nervous system operations and some therapeutic treatments are coded to ICD-9-CM volume 3, chapter 1, "Operations on the Nervous System"; eye operations and some therapeutic treatments are coded to chapter 3, "Operations on the Eye"; and ear operations and some therapeutic procedures are coded to chapter 4, "Operations on the Ear."

Current Procedural Terminology (CPT) nervous system, eye, and ear codes are found in three of the CPT Surgery subsections: Nervous System, Eye and Ocular Adnexa, and Auditory System. Additional codes for the nervous system, eye, and ear are also found in the Radiology and Medicine sections.

■ CHAPTER REVIEW

Read each medical note or medical report excerpt. Write the diagnosis(es) and the main term. Assign the ICD-9-CM diagnosis code(s).

CASE 1

Ms. Theilen is a 40-year-old female who is seen today for follow-up of strep throat. She states her throat feels better, but now her ears are bothering her. On examination, this is an alert female in no acute distress. Vital signs are within normal limits. Review of systems is negative except for the right ear. The tympanic membrane is very distended, with a cloudy yellowish fluid behind it. The ear canal is very red, inflamed, tender, and swollen. The left tympanic membrane and canal are clear. Her throat is clear. Assessment: Acute right otitis media and externa. She will take erythromycin 500 mg four times per day, by mouth, for two weeks. Another follow-up visit is scheduled in two weeks.

DIAGNOSIS(ES): _____

MAIN TERM(S): _____

ICD-9-CM DIAGNOSIS CODE(S): _____

CASE 2

Mr. Rolando is seen today for irritation of the right eye, about one week's duration. He states that the eye feels itchy and he rubs it a great deal. Examination today reveals a healthy appearing male in no acute distress. Vital signs are normal. Review of systems is normal, except for the right eye. Under slit-lamp examination the anterior chamber of the right eye is normal, but there is a 3-mm pterygium, temporally. The left eye, disk, macula, and vessels are within normal limits. Assessment: Pterygium, right eye with limited inflammation. He will apply a topical antihistamine, four times per day as needed for the symptoms. Follow-up is scheduled in two weeks.

DIAGNOSIS(ES): _____

MAIN TERM(S): _____

ICD-9-CM DIAGNOSIS CODE(S): _____

CASE 3

This one-month-old infant is accompanied by her mother. There is a thick discharge from both eyes, which has been present almost since birth. Review of systems is normal except for the discharge from both eyes. Assessment: We will treat this as a chronic relapsing conjunctivitis and treat with erythromycin ointment, both eyes, at bedtime. Cultures of conjunctival scrapings are sent for bacteria and *Chlamydia*. Recheck in three weeks, unless the cultures are positive for bacteria or *Chlamydia*.

DIAGNOSIS(ES): _____

MAIN TERM(S): _____

ICD-9-CM DIAGNOSIS CODE(S): _____

CASE 4

This 62-year-old man is a new patient and is here for an annual physical examination. He states that he sustained a head injury at age 4 that resulted in post-traumatic epilepsy. He has been on antiseizure medication for the past 40 years. He has had approximately two or three cortical petit mal seizures over that period of time. Assessment: We discussed the fact that he has had only three seizures in 40 years. His medication dosage is subtherapeutic. He will taper off the medication. If there is no further seizure activity the medication will not be renewed.

DIAGNOSIS(ES): _____

MAIN TERM(S): _____

ICD-9-CM DIAGNOSIS CODE(S): _____

CASE 5

This 75-year-old patient is visiting her daughter, who found her mother on the floor of the guest room this morning. Upon arriving at the emergency department, a small occipital laceration was found and sutured. The patient was quadriplegic at the time of her evaluation. A CT of the head was essentially normal. X-rays of the cervical spine were inconclusive. CT scan of the cervical spine revealed a fracture at the upper end on C-7, but did not include the vertebral body. Impression: Quadriplegia, incomplete. Fracture of the upper end of C-7. Probable spinal cord compression or injury.

DIAGNOSIS(ES): _____

MAIN TERM(S): _____

ICD-9-CM DIAGNOSIS CODE(S): _____

CASE 6

Mr. Nigele has been experiencing increasing disorientation and confusion over this past month. He states that the left side of his body "feels funny" and he doesn't feel he has complete control of left side movement. He is seen today to discuss the results of the MRI brain scan, which was done on Monday. The scan revealed a large arachnoid cyst in the anterior temporal fossa, extending up into the front parietal area. Compression of the gyri adjacent to the lesion is noted. There is mild compression of the right lateral ventricle from the arachnoid cyst. There is no evidence of ventricular obstruction. The brain stem and upper cervical spinal cord are normal. Mr. Nigele was upset about the findings and he said he cannot discuss treatment options until his wife returns from visiting their son. A meeting will be held with both of them next Wednesday.

DIAGNOSIS(ES): _____

MAIN TERM(S): _____

ICD-9-CM DIAGNOSIS CODE(S): _____

CASE 7

Mrs. Wentworth is a 68-year-old female with long-standing insulin-dependent diabetes mellitus, type 2, somewhat poorly controlled in the past. Today she reports decreased visual acuity in the right eye, heavy floaters, and red vision for the past six weeks. On examination, the fundus of the right eye is not visualized. There is a red reflex present. The left eye is within normal limits, but preproliferative diabetic retinopathy changes are seen. The remainder of the exam is unremarkable. Assessment: Acute vitreous hemorrhage, right eye.

DIAGNOSIS(ES): _____

MAIN TERM(S): _____

ICD-9-CM DIAGNOSIS CODE(S): _____

Read the procedure note, operative report, or discharge summary excerpt. Write the diagnosis and its ICD-9-CM code. Write the name of the procedure and the main term. Assign the ICD-9-CM procedure code(s).

CASE 8

PREOPERATIVE DIAGNOSIS: Aphakia, left eye.

POSTOPERATIVE DIAGNOSIS: Aphakia, left eye.

OPERATION: Anterior vitrectomy with implantation of anterior chamber intraocular lens.

DESCRIPTION: After receiving appropriate anesthesia, the eye was prepped and draped in the usual manner. A lid speculum was inserted. Fornices were cleaned and a fixation suture was placed through the superior rectus muscle.

A clear 6-mm corneal incision was made and reflected into a wide flap. The automated vitrector was introduced into the anterior chamber and a core vitrectomy was completed. The incision was enlarged to allow introduction of an intraocular lens. This was inserted and rotated into proper position. The wound was closed per standard procedures with 10-0 nylon suture. All counts were correct ×2 and the patient was returned to the recovery room in good condition.

DIAGNOSIS(ES): _____

ICD-9-CM DIAGNOSIS(ES) CODES: _____

PROCEDURE(S): _____

MAIN TERM(S): _____

ICD-9-CM PROCEDURE CODE(S): _____

CASE 9

PREOPERATIVE DIAGNOSIS: Recurrent bilateral otitis media with persistent middle ear effusion.

POSTOPERATIVE DIAGNOSIS: Recurrent bilateral otitis media with persistent middle ear effusion.

PROCEDURE: Bilateral myringotomy with tube insertion.

DESCRIPTION: Under general anesthesia the patient was prepped and draped in the usual fashion. The right ear was examined and cleaned of cerumen. Myringotomy was performed in the anterior-inferior quadrant and thick fluid suctioned from the middle ear space. A Type 1 Paparella tube was then inserted. The left ear was examined and cleaned of cerumen. Myringotomy was performed in the anterior-inferior quadrant and again thick fluid was suctioned from the middle ear space. A Type 1 Paparella tube was then inserted. Cortisporin Otic Suspension drops were then placed in both ear canals and cotton in the ears. The patient was awakened and returned to the recovery room in satisfactory condition.

DIAGNOSIS(ES): _____

ICD-9-CM DIAGNOSIS(ES) CODES: _____

PROCEDURE(S): _____

MAIN TERM(S): _____

ICD-9-CM PROCEDURE CODE(S): _____

CASE 10

PREOPERATIVE DIAGNOSIS: Essential tremor.

POSTOPERATIVE DIAGNOSIS: Essential tremor.

OPERATION: Placement of right internal pulse generator (Medtronic Soletra No. 7426).

HISTORY: This 70-year-old male has a history of essential tremor and underwent implantation of a right deep-brain-stimulating electrode in the thalamus for control of his left-upper-extremity tremor. He has done well following electrode implantation and is here for placement of the generator.

DIAGNOSIS(ES): _____

ICD-9-CM DIAGNOSIS(ES) CODES: _____

PROCEDURE(S): _____

MAIN TERM(S): _____

ICD-9-CM PROCEDURE CODE(S): _____

CASE 11

PREOPERATIVE DIAGNOSIS: Rhegmatogenous retinal detachment, left eye.

POSTOPERATIVE DIAGNOSIS: Rhegmatogenous retinal detachment, left eye.

PROCEDURES: 1. Scleral buckle, left eye. 2. Cryotherapy. 3. External drainage.

COMPLICATIONS: 1. Small subretinal hemorrhage superiorly. 2. Retinal incarceration at the drainage site.

DESCRIPTION: The patient was taken to the operating room after receiving the retrobulbar block in the holding area. The usual prep and drape was performed and appropriate incision made. The retina was fairly bullous in the supertemporal quadrant, and a small scleral incision was made. Diathermy was applied to the bed of the incision. Using a sharp blade, the subretinal fluid was drained. The buckle was then tied with a Mersilene mattress stitch in the supertemporal quadrant. Visualization through the pupil revealed incarceration of the retina at the location of the drainage site. The operation was completed and the eye was covered with a pressure patch and a Fox shield was applied. Sponge, needle, and instrument counts were correct ×3. The patient was taken to the recovery room in excellent condition.

DIAGNOSIS(ES): _____

ICD-9-CM DIAGNOSIS(ES) CODES: _____

PROCEDURE(S): _____

MAIN TERM(S): _____

ICD-9-CM PROCEDURE CODE(S): _____

CASE 12

PREOPERATIVE DIAGNOSES: 1. Corneal perforation, left eye. 2. Possible corneal ulcer, left eye.

POSTOPERATIVE DIAGNOSES: 1. Corneal perforation, left eye. 2. Intraocular foreign body (wood), left eye. 3. Possible corneal ulcer, left eye.

OPERATION: 1. Pseudophakic penetrating keratoplasty, left eye (patch graft). 2. Removal of intraocular foreign body, left eye. 3. Injection of intravitreal antibiotics, left eye.

HISTORY: The patient is a 43-year-old man who sustained trauma to the left eye while operating a chainsaw. He underwent closure of a corneal laceration, and subsequently cataract extraction with intraocular lens implantation and revision of the corneal wound. He now has persistent corneal perforation with a shallow anterior chamber and a soft eye. He also appears to have a soupy-appearing inferior cornea and will require a patch graft to repair the eye. Risks and benefits of surgery have been discussed with the patient and he wishes to proceed.

DIAGNOSIS(ES): _____

ICD-9-CM DIAGNOSIS(ES) CODES: _____

PROCEDURE(S): _____

MAIN TERM(S): _____

ICD-9-CM PROCEDURE CODE(S): _____

Using the excerpts from previous cases, identify the procedure and main term. Assign the correct CPT code(s).

CASE 13

PREOPERATIVE DIAGNOSIS: Aphakia, left eye.

POSTOPERATIVE DIAGNOSIS: Aphakia, left eye.

OPERATION: Anterior vitrectomy with implantation of anterior chamber intraocular lens.

DESCRIPTION: After receiving appropriate anesthesia, the eye was prepped and draped in the usual manner. A lid speculum was inserted. Fornices were cleaned and a fixation suture was placed through the superior rectus muscle. A clear 6-mm corneal incision was made and reflected into a wide flap. The automated vitrector was introduced into the anterior chamber and a core vitrectomy was completed. The incision was enlarged to allow introduction of an intraocular lens. This was inserted and rotated into proper position. The wound was closed per standard procedures with 10-0 nylon suture. All counts were correct ×2 and the patient was returned to the recovery room in good condition.

PROCEDURE(S): _____

MAIN TERM(S): _____

CPT PROCEDURE CODE(S): _____

CASE 14

PREOPERATIVE DIAGNOSIS: Recurrent bilateral otitis media with persistent middle ear effusion.

POSTOPERATIVE DIAGNOSIS: Recurrent bilateral otitis media with persistent middle ear effusion.

PROCEDURE: Bilateral myringotomy with tube insertion.

DESCRIPTION: Under general anesthesia the patient was prepped and draped in the usual fashion. The right ear was examined and cleaned of cerumen. Myringotomy was performed in the anterior-inferior quadrant and thick fluid suctioned from the middle ear space. A Type 1 Paparella tube was then inserted. The left ear was examined and cleaned of cerumen. Myringotomy was performed in the anterior-inferior quadrant and again thick fluid was suctioned from the middle ear space. A Type 1 Paparella tube was then inserted. Cortisporin Otic Suspension drops were then placed in both ear canals and cotton in the ears. The patient was awakened and returned to the recovery room in satisfactory condition.

PROCEDURE(S): _____

MAIN TERM(S): _____

CPT PROCEDURE CODE(S): _____

CASE 15

PREOPERATIVE DIAGNOSIS: Essential tremor.

POSTOPERATIVE DIAGNOSIS: Essential tremor.

OPERATION: Placement of right internal pulse generator (Medtronic Soletra No. 7426).

HISTORY: This 70-year-old male has a history of essential tremor and underwent implantation of a right deep-brain-stimulating electrode in the thalamus for control of his left-upper-extremity tremor. He has done well following electrode implantation and is here for placement of the generator.

PROCEDURE(S): _____

MAIN TERM(S): _____

CPT PROCEDURE CODE(S): _____

CASE 16

PREOPERATIVE DIAGNOSIS: Rhegmatogenous retinal detachment, left eye.

POSTOPERATIVE DIAGNOSIS: Rhegmatogenous retinal detachment, left eye.

PROCEDURES: 1. Scleral buckle, left eye. 2. Cryotherapy. 3. External drainage.

COMPLICATIONS: 1. Small subretinal hemorrhage superiorly. 2. Retinal incarceration at the drainage site.

DESCRIPTION: The patient was taken to the operating room after receiving the retrobulbar block in the holding area. The usual prep and drape was performed and appropriate incision made. The retina was fairly bullous in the supertemporal quadrant, and a small scleral incision was made. Diathermy was applied to the bed of the incision. Using a sharp blade, the subretinal fluid was drained. The buckle was then tied with a Mersilene mattress stitch in the supertemporal quadrant. Visualization through the pupil revealed incarceration of the retina at the location of the drainage site. The operation was completed and the eye was covered with a pressure patch and a Fox shield was applied. Sponge, needle, and instrument counts were correct ×3. The patient was taken to the recovery room in excellent condition.

PROCEDURE(S): _____

MAIN TERM(S): _____

CPT PROCEDURE CODE(S): _____

CASE 17

PREOPERATIVE DIAGNOSES: 1. Corneal perforation, left eye. 2. Possible corneal ulcer, left eye.

POSTOPERATIVE DIAGNOSES: 1. Corneal perforation, left eye. 2. Intraocular foreign body (wood), left eye. 3. Possible corneal ulcer, left eye.

OPERATION: 1. Pseudophakic penetrating keratoplasty, left eye (patch graft). 2. Removal of intraocular foreign body, left eye. 3. Injection of intravitreal antibiotics, left eye.

HISTORY: The patient is a 43-year-old man who sustained trauma to the left eye while operating a chainsaw. He underwent closure of a corneal laceration, and subsequently cataract extraction with intraocular lens implantation and revision of the corneal wound. He now has persistent corneal perforation with a shallow anterior chamber and a soft eye. He also appears to have a soupy-appearing inferior cornea and will require a patch graft to repair the eye. Risks and benefits of surgery have been discussed with the patient and he wishes to proceed.

PROCEDURE(S): _____

MAIN TERM(S): _____

CPT PROCEDURE CODE(S): _____

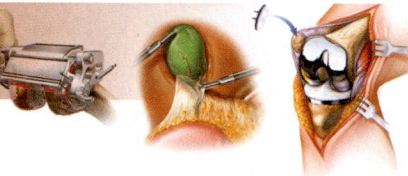

MEDICAL TERMINOLOGY CHALLENGE

The listed medical terms were used in the medical coding exercises.
Use a dictionary as necessary and write a brief definition for each term.

1. bilateral _____

2. bullous _____

3. burr holes _____

4. diathermy _____

5. diplegia _____

6. duraplasty _____

7. effusion _____

8. incarceration (of the retina) _____

9. intravitreal _____

10. neurostimulator _____

11. pseudophakic _____

12. pterional _____

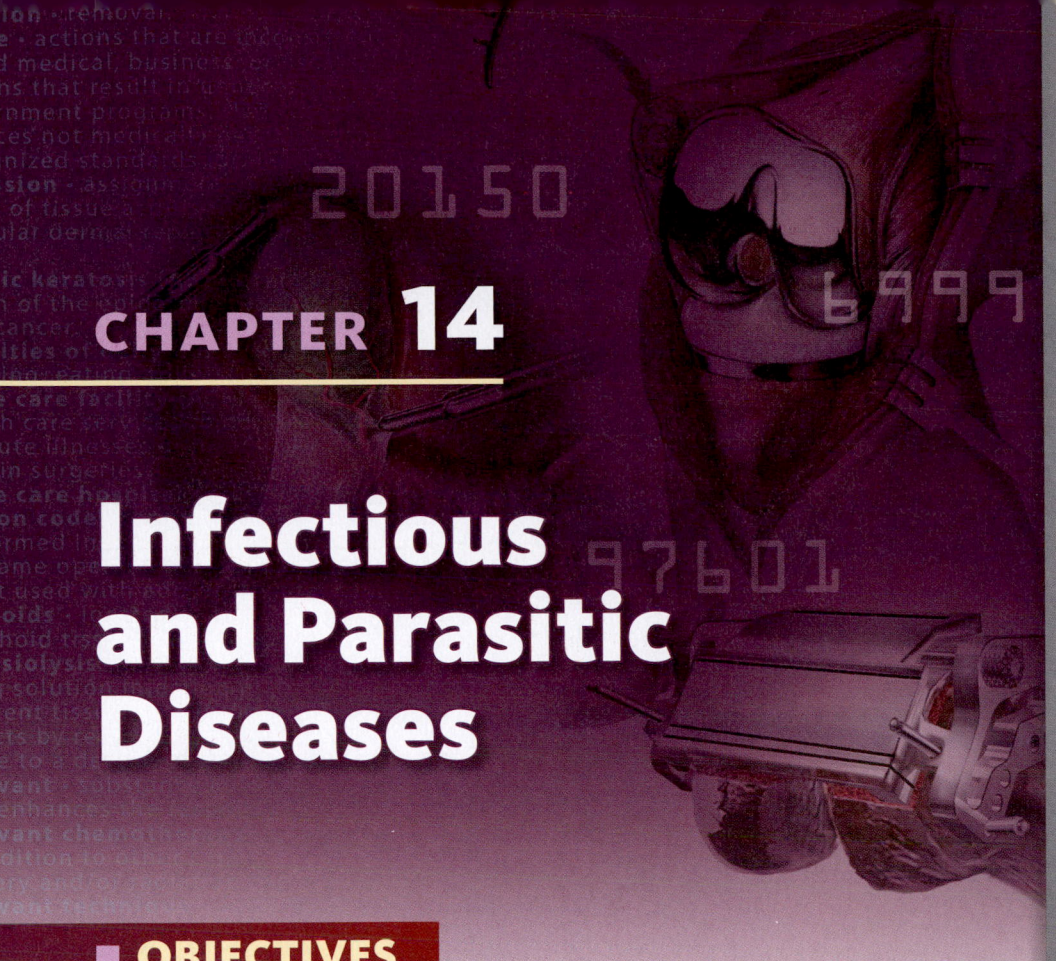

CHAPTER 14

Infectious and Parasitic Diseases

■ OBJECTIVES

At the completion of this chapter, the student should be able to:

1. Learn the word roots associated with infectious and parasitic diseases.
2. Explain the difference between bacteria, viruses, and parasites.
3. Accurately spell and define terminology related to infectious and parasitic diseases.
4. Accurately assign medical codes to infectious and parasitic diseases.

■ OVERVIEW

Infectious and parasitic diseases are caused by bacteria, viruses, fungi (**fungus**, singular), and parasites. There are literally hundreds of thousands of bacteria, viruses, and fungi, most of which do not cause diseases in humans. **Microorganisms** (**migh**-kroh-**OR**-gan-izms) that cause disease are called **pathogens** (**PATH**-oh-jens). **Microbiology** (**migh**-kroh-bigh-**AH**-loh-jee) is the study of microorganisms such as bacteria and viruses. This chapter is an introduction to the medical terminology and diseases associated with infectious and parasitic diseases. Some of the diseases caused by microorganisms and parasites are included in the body system chapters. Sexually transmitted infections (STIs) are covered in this chapter.

Infectious and parasitic diseases can be **transmitted** (passed) from person to person; from animals or insects to people; and from contaminated water, soil, and air to people. Infectious diseases are passed between people through body fluids or by close contact with an individual who has a disease. Animal or insect bites can transmit diseases to people.

ROOTS AND SUFFIXES

Many of the roots, prefixes, and suffixes associated with infectious and parasitic diseases were presented in previous chapters. Table 14-1 lists the word elements commonly associated with the diseases and conditions presented in this chapter.

Table 14-1   Roots and Suffixes

ROOT	MEANING
arthr/o	joint
dipl/o	two
enter/o	within; intestine
hist/o	tissue
myc/o	fungus
spir/o	coil; spiral
staphyl/o	cluster-like
strept/o	curved

SUFFIX	MEANING
-coccus	round
-emia	blood
-itis	inflammation
-osis	condition
-pod	foot

EXERCISE 14-1

Write a brief definition for each medical term.

1. arthropod _____
2. mycosis _____
3. enteritis _____
4. diplococcus _____
5. staphylococcus _____
6. streptococcus _____

BACTERIA

Bacteria (bak-**TEE**-ree-ah) are defined as small unicellular microorganisms that exhibit metabolic activity and are therefore classified as living organisms. A single organism is a bacterium, and the multiplication or growth of bacterium results in a **colony**. Bacteria are identified by their **morphology** (mor-**FALL**-oh-jee), which is their shape, as **coccus** (**KOCK**-us) or round, **bacillus** (bah-**SILL**-us) or rod, **spirochete** (**SPEER**-oh-keet) or spiral, and **vibrio** (**VIB**-ree-oh) or comma shaped. Cocci can occur in pairs called **diplococci** (dip-loh-**KOH**-sigh) or in clusters. Figure 14-1 illustrates the morphological types of bacteria.

Most bacteria do not cause disease and exist as independent cells in soil, in water, and as part of the normal **flora** in the human body. Flora are defined as microorganisms that live within the body, compete with disease-producing organisms, and provide a natural immunity against certain infections. An example of flora is the bacteria *Escherichia coli* (eh-shih-**RIGH**-kee-ah **KOH**-ligh) (*E. coli*) that lives in the lower intestine. Most strains

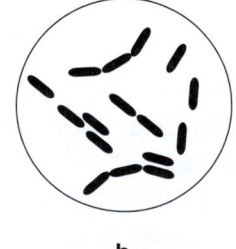
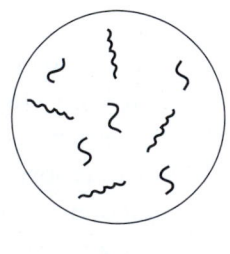
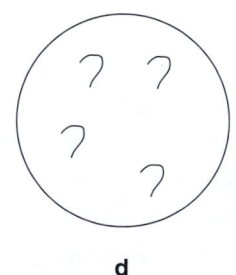

a   b   c   d

Figure 14-1   Morphological types of bacteria: (a) cocci and diplococci, (b) bacilli, (c) spirochete, (d) vibrios

(types) of *E. coli* are harmless and cause no disease. In fact, some strains of *E. coli* are actually helpful to the human body. Bacteria that are capable of causing disease are called pathogens.

VIRUSES

Viruses are defined as microorganisms that can only replicate by invading a living cell. Viruses are much smaller than bacteria. Figure 14-2 illustrates the relative size of an animal cell, bacterial cell, and different viruses.

Viruses have a nucleus that allows the virus to multiply within a living cell. As the virus multiplies, it will eventually cause the cell membrane to rupture and release the virus into the bloodstream. Each virus then has the opportunity to invade another cell and promote the disease process. As with bacteria, viruses that cause

disease are called pathogens. Viral diseases range from herpes simplex (cold sore) to human immunodeficiency virus (HIV) infections.

FUNGI

Fungi are defined as thallus-forming organisms with a defined nucleus. Most fungi are found in the soil and on decaying plant matter. Mushrooms are actually the "budding" evidence of fungi. There are more than 250,000 species of fungi, and less than 250 are considered capable of causing disease.

Fungal diseases range from diaper rash, which is confined to the superficial layers of the skin, to histoplasmosis, which is caused by inhaling *Histoplasma capsulatum* mold spores that grow in the soil or dust contaminated with bird or bat droppings.

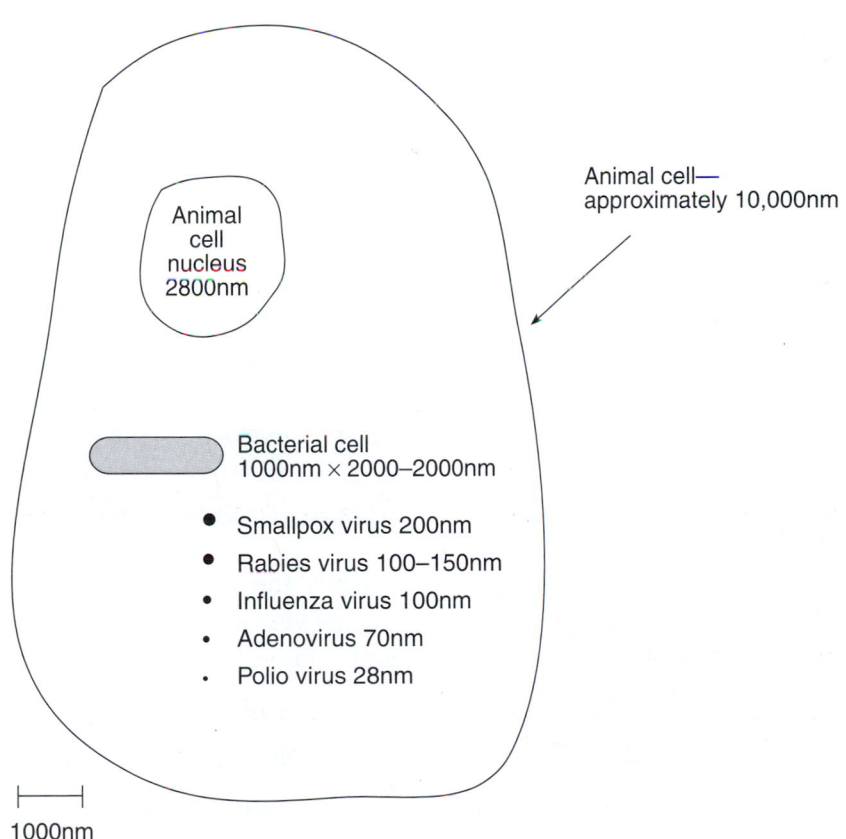

Figure 14-2 Relative size of different viruses

PARASITES

Parasites are organisms that live in a host and receive nutrients from the host and often at the expense of the host. There are three main classes of parasites that can cause diseases in humans:

- **Protozoa** (**proh**-toh-**ZOH**-ah) are microscopic, one-celled organisms that can live within or outside of a host. Protozoa are transmitted to humans via contaminated food or water, person-to-person contact, or insect bites. For example, protozoa that live in human blood are transmitted through a mosquito bite.

- **Helminthes** (**HELL**-minth-eez) are large, multicellular organisms that may be visible to the naked eye, especially in their adult stages. Parasitic helminthes in humans are types of worms such as flatworms (flukes and tapeworms), thorny-headed worms, and roundworms (pinworms).

- **Ectoparasites** are usually defined as organisms such as ticks, fleas, lice, and mites that bite, attach to, or burrow into the skin and may remain there for a long period of time. These arthropods can cause disease themselves, but they are more important as transmitters of different pathogens.

Parasitic infections are very common in tropical and subtropical climates. Of all the parasitic diseases, malaria causes the most deaths worldwide, especially in certain areas of Africa. Parasitic diseases in the United States and other developed countries are caused by *Trichomonas* (trik-oh-**MOH**-ness), *Giardia* (jee-**AR**-dee-ah), *Cryptosporidium* (**krip**-toh-spor-**IH**-dee-um), and *Toxoplasma* (**tok**-soh-**PLAZ**-mah).

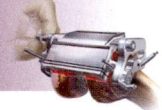

EXERCISE 14-2

Write a brief definition for each medical term.

1. bacteria _____
2. bacillus _____
3. coccus _____
4. ectoparasite _____
5. flora _____
6. helminth _____
7. parasite _____

8. protozoa _____
9. spirochete _____
10. vibrio _____

INFECTIOUS AND PARASITIC DISEASE MEDICAL TERMS

Medical terms related to infectious, parasitic, and sexually transmitted diseases are organized by diseases, conditions, and diagnostic procedures. There are two categories of medical terminology exercises: (1) those designed to provide opportunities to learn the terms, and (2) those designed to provide opportunities to accurately assign diagnostic or procedure codes. Exercises for learning the terms immediately follow the lists of terms and definitions. Medical coding exercises are available after all terms have been presented.

Bacterial, Viral, Fungal, and Parasitic Diseases

Many of the diseases caused by bacteria, viruses, fungi, and parasites are included in the body system chapter associated with the specific disease and may not be included in this chapter. For example, meningitis, which is caused by bacteria or viruses, is in chapter 13, "Nervous System." Therefore, most of the diseases and conditions listed in table 14-2 are named for the organism that causes the disease and affect more than one body system. Review the terms and complete the exercise.

EXERCISE 14-3

Identify the type of microorganism that causes each disease with a B for bacteria, F for fungal, P for parasite, and V for virus.

1. actinomycosis _____
2. amebiasis _____
3. ascariasis _____
4. aspergillosis _____
5. babesiosis _____
6. blastomycosis _____
7. botulism _____

continued

Table 14-2   Bacterial, Viral, Fungal, and Parasitic Diseases and Conditions

DISEASE AND CONDITION	DEFINITION
actinomycosis (**ak**-tin-oh-migh-**KOH**-sis)	a chronic bacterial infection caused by *Actinomyces israelii,* characterized by localized abscesses of the face, thorax, and abdomen that produce a purulent discharge
amebiasis (**ah**-mee-**BIGH**-ah-sis)	an intestinal infection with the protozoa *Entamoeba histolytica* transmitted by ingesting food or water that is contaminated by human feces; symptoms, which may not be present, include intermittent diarrhea and constipation, flatulence, and cramping abdominal pain
ascariasis (**as**-kah-**RIGH**-ah-sis)	a parasitic infection caused by the roundworm *Ascaris lumbricoides,* when the eggs are transmitted to humans via water, hands, or food that has been contaminated by human feces; ingested eggs hatch in the duodenum and larvae migrate to the lungs, and eventually return to the small intestine and develop into mature worms
aspergillosis (**ah**-sper-jill-**OH**-sis)	a fungal infection caused by inhaling the spores of *Aspergillus,* the most common environmental mold, characterized by hemorrhagic necrosis, hemoptysis, skin lesions, and sinusitis; may involve the liver, kidneys, and brain; neutropenia, high-dose steroid therapy, and organ transplantation increase the risk of acquiring aspergillosis
babesiosis (bah-**bee**-see-**OH**-sis)	an infection with the protozoa *Babesia microti* transmitted via a tick bite; *Babesia* enter red blood cells, mature, replicate, and cause the cell membrane to rupture, releasing organisms that infect other red blood cells; symptoms may be absent for years; when present, symptoms include malaise, fatigue, chills, fever, headache, myalgia, and arthralgia; jaundice, hemolytic anemia, and mild neutropenia may also occur
blastomycosis (**blass**-toh-migh-**KOH**-sis)	a fungal infection caused by inhaling the spores of *Blastomyces dermatitidis,* a mold that grows at room temperature in soil containing animal feces, and in moist, decaying, organic material; infection may stay in the lungs or involve the skin, prostate, epididymis, testes, kidneys, brain, and other organs or tissue
botulism (**BAH**-chuh-**liz**-ism)	a neuromuscular poisoning from the toxins associated with the bacteria *Clostridium botulinum;* four *C. botulinum* toxins, type A, B, E, and F (rarely), affect humans; foodborne botulism is caused by type A, B, and E toxins; home-canned foods are the most common source, although commercially prepared foods may account for 10% of the outbreaks; neurologic symptoms begin with the cranial nerves and descend along the spinal column
candidiasis (**kan**-dih-**DIGH**-eh-sis)	a fungal infection usually caused by *Candida albicans,* usually associated with immune suppression and prolonged hospitalizations; involves the skin and mucous membranes, and may involve the bones, joints, liver, spleen, kidneys, eyes, and other tissues; also called *invasive candidiasis, candidosis,* or *moniliasis*
cholera (**KALL**-eh-rah)	an acute bacterial infection of the small bowel by *Vibrio cholerae;* signs or symptoms include copious, watery diarrhea leading to dehydration, oliguria, and possible circulatory collapse; spread by ingestion of contaminated water, seafood, and other foods
coccidioidomycosis (kok-**sid**-ee-**OY**-doh-migh-**koh**-sis)	a fungal infection caused by inhaling the spores of *Coccidioides immitis;* symptoms are not always present, but may include respiratory symptoms resembling influenza or bronchitis; disseminated disease may lead to extensive pulmonary involvement, hemoptysis, and cyanosis; coccidioidomycosis is endemic in the southwestern United States
cryptosporidiosis (**krip**-toh-spor-**ih**-dee-**OH**-sis)	an intestinal infection caused by the protozoa *Cryptosporidium* transmitted to humans via focally contaminated food or water, or direct person-to-person contact; symptoms include profuse watery diarrhea, abdominal cramping, and at times nausea, anorexia, fever, and malaise
cytomegalic inclusion disease (CID)	an infection caused by *Cytomegalovirus* (CMV), human herpes virus type 5, that exhibits a wide range of severity from retinitis in HIV-infected individuals to severe systemic disease in newborns; CMV is transmitted through blood, body fluids, or transplanted organs; CMV crosses the placenta from mother to infant (congenital cytomegalic inclusion disease)

continued

Table 14-2 (*continued*) Bacterial, Viral, Fungal, and Parasitic Diseases and Conditions

DISEASE AND CONDITION	DEFINITION
diphtheria (diff-**THIR**-ee-ah; dip-**THIR**-ee-ah)	an acute bacterial infection caused by *Corynebacterium diphtheriae* that involves the throat, skin, heart, and nervous system
ehrlichiosis (er-**lik**-ee-**OH**-sis)	an infection caused by the bacteria *Ehrlichia* that is transmitted to humans by tick bites; characterized by fever, chills, headache, nausea, vomiting, a rash, diarrhea, and in some cases disseminated intravascular coagulation
enterobiasis (**en**-ter-oh-**BIGH**-ah-sis)	an intestinal infestation by the roundworm *Enterobius vermicularis* that usually occurs in children; also called pinworm infestation; the most common helminthic infection in the U.S.; infestation is almost always limited to the lower gastrointestinal tract; perianal itching is the most common symptom

8. candidiasis _____

9. cholera _____

10. coccidioidomycosis _____

11. cryptosporidiosis _____

12. cytomegalic inclusion disease _____

13. diphtheria _____

14. ehrlichiosis _____

15 enterobiasis _____

Review the medical terms in table 14-3 and complete the exercises.

Table 14-3 Bacterial, Viral, Fungal, and Parasitic Diseases and Conditions

DISEASE OR CONDITION	DEFINITION
giardiasis (jee-**ar**-**DEE**-ah-sis)	an intestinal infection with the protozoa *Giardia lamblia,* usually by waterborne transmission; symptoms, when present, include watery, foul-smelling diarrhea, abdominal cramps and distention, flatulence and eructation, intermittent nausea, and epigastric discomfort
histoplasmosis (**hiss**-toh-plaz-**MOH**-sis)	a fungal infection caused by inhaling the spores of *Histoplasma capsulatum* in soil or dust contaminated with bird or bat droppings; initial infection is in the lungs; *acute primary histoplasmosis* is characterized by fever, cough, myalgia, chest pain, and pneumonia; *progressive disseminated histoplasmosis* is characterized by hepatomegaly, splenomegaly, lymphadenopathy, and bone marrow involvement; *chronic cavitary histoplasmosis* is characterized by pulmonary lesions, cough, dyspnea, and respiratory dysfunction
influenza (in-floo-**EN**-zah)	a viral respiratory infection caused by influenza viruses characterized by fever, coryza, cough, headache, and malaise
Lyme disease	a bacterial infection caused by *Borrelia burgdorferi* that is transmitted to humans via a deer tick bite; there are three stages characterized by progressive myalgia, arthralgia, and polyneuropathy; the first sign of the disease is a red macule or papule called erythema migrans (EM)
measles	a highly contagious viral infection caused by a paramyxovirus; characterized by fever, cough, conjunctivitis, and a rash; also called rubeola or nine-day measles
rickettsialpox (rih-**KET**-see-al-**pocks**)	an infection caused by *Rickettsia akari,* a microorganism with bacterial and viral characteristics; the infection is transmitted to humans via a mite or chigger bite
rickettsiosis	generic term for an infection caused by various *Rickettsia,* transmitted to humans via a tick bite; symptoms include fever, malaise, headache, and rash

continued

Table 14-3 (*continued*) Bacterial, Viral, Fungal, and Parasitic Diseases and Conditions

DISEASE OR CONDITION	DEFINITION
Rocky Mountain spotted fever (RMSF)	an infection caused by *Rickettsia rickettsii* and transmitted to humans via a tick bite: in the western U.S. by wood ticks, in the eastern and southern U.S. by dog ticks; characteristics of the infection include severe headache, chills, muscle pain, high fever, rash, and lesions on the skin; neurologic symptoms range from severe headache to coma
rubella	a contagious viral infection caused by the *rubella* virus, which is spread by respiratory droplets through close contact or through the air; characteristic symptoms include fever, malaise, lymphadenopathy, and a rash similar to measles; infection during early pregnancy can cause spontaneous abortion, stillbirth, or congenital defects; also called German measles or three-day measles
toxoplasmosis (**tocks**-oh-plaz-**MOH**-sis)	a protozoan infection caused by *Toxoplasma gondii;* exposure to toxoplasmosis is common wherever cats are found; *T. gondii* can pass through the placenta to the fetus, which can cause severe problems such as bilateral retinochoroiditis, cerebral calcifications, hydrocephalus or microcephaly, and psychomotor retardation
trichinosis (**trik**-ih-**NOH**-sis)	an infection with the roundworm *Trichinella spiralis* or related species; infection occurs by eating raw, undercooked, or processed meat from infected animals such as pigs, wild boars, or bear; symptoms, when present, include nausea, abdominal cramps, diarrhea, myalgia, eye pain, and photophobia; also called trichiniasis
typhus, epidemic	an infection caused by *Rickettsia prowazekii* transmitted via body lice; symptoms include prolonged high fever, intractable headache, and a maculopapular rash; also called jail fever and louseborne typhus
typhus, murine	an infection caused by *Rickettsia typhi* transmitted by rat fleas and probably cat fleas; symptoms include chills, headache, fever, and rash; also called endemic typhus and rat-flea typhus

EXERCISE 14-4

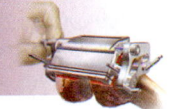

Place an X next to the disease or condition associated with flea, chigger, or tick bites.

1. giardiasis _____
2. histoplasmosis _____
3. Lyme disease _____
4. rickettsiosis _____
5. Rocky Mountain spotted fever _____
6. toxoplasmosis _____
7. trichinosis _____
8. murine typhus _____

EXERCISE 14-5

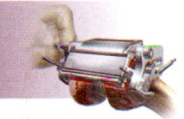

Write the names of the diseases next to the correct category: giardiasis, histoplasmosis, influenza, Lyme disease, measles, rickettsialpox, rickettsiosis, Rocky Mountain spotted fever, rubella, toxoplasmosis, trichinosis, typhus

1. bacterial disease _____
2. viral disease_____
3. fungal disease _____
4. parasitic disease _____

Sexually Transmitted Infections

As the name implies, **sexually transmitted infections (STIs)** are passed from person to person via sexual activity that includes contact with the skin and mucous membranes of the genitals, mouth, and rectum. STIs are usually named for the bacteria or viruses that cause the infection. Review the pronunciation and description for each term in table 14-4 and complete the exercises. Note that symptoms might not be present, especially during the early stages of the infection.

Table 14-4 Sexually Transmitted Infections

TERM WITH PRONUNCIATION	DEFINITION
chancre (**SHANG**-ker)	highly contagious pustule or lesion located on the penis, characteristic of primary syphilis (figure 14-3)
chancroid (**SHANG**-kroyd)	a bacterial infection of the genital skin or mucous membranes caused by *Haemophilus ducreyi;* symptoms include painful ulcers, suppurative inguinal lymph nodes, phimosis, and urethral stricture
Chlamydia (klah-**MID**-ee-ah)	a bacterial infection caused by *Chlamydia trachomatis;* symptoms are usually mild or absent and might include abnormal discharge from the penis or cervix and burning sensation during urination; epididymitis and cervicitis may develop (figure 14-4)
genital herpes (**JEN**-ih-tal **HER**-peez)	a viral infection caused by herpes simplex virus (HSV), type 2; symptoms are called outbreaks, which appear two weeks after infection; outbreaks are characterized by small blisters in the genital area, penis, cervix, vagina, or urethra; blisters rupture, leaving an ulceration that heals without leaving a scar; genital herpes can recur spontaneously once the virus has been acquired; also called venereal herpes
genital warts	a viral disease caused by the human papillomavirus (HPV), characterized by small, cauliflower-like fleshy growth along the penis and in or near the vagina or anus; also called venereal warts (figure 14-5)
gonorrhea (gon-oh-**REE**-ah)	a bacterial infection caused by *Neisseria gonorrhoeae,* characterized by yellow or bloody vaginal discharge; white, yellow, or green and painful discharge from the penis; painful or burning sensations during urination; swollen testicles; untreated, gonorrhea can lead to infection of the entire male and female reproductive tracts
syphilis (**SIF**-ih-lis)	a bacterial infection caused by *Treponema pallidum* that has three distinct stages, each more serious than the previous stage; lesions may involve any organ or tissue; syphilis can be passed from mother to fetus via the placenta
trichomoniasis (**trik**-oh-moh-**NIGH**-ah-sis)	an infection caused by the protozoa *Trichomonas vaginalis;* men are usually asymptomatic but may experience dysuria, urinary frequency, or urethritis; symptoms in women include itching, burning, and a strong-smelling, frothy, greenish yellow vaginal discharge; on examination, the cervix has a strawberry-like appearance

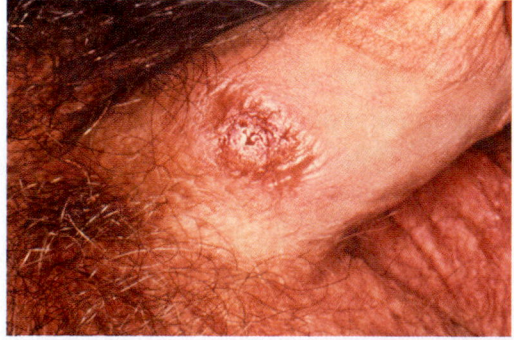

Figure 14-3 Chancre in primary syphilis/Centers for Disease Control (Dr. Gavin Hart, Dr. N.J. Flumara)

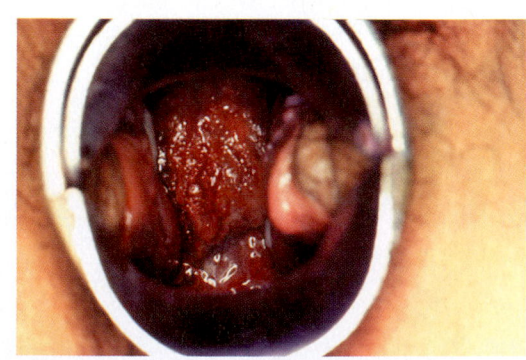

Figure 14-4 Chlamydia, cervix/Centers for Disease Control (Dr. Lourdes Fraw, Jim Pledger)

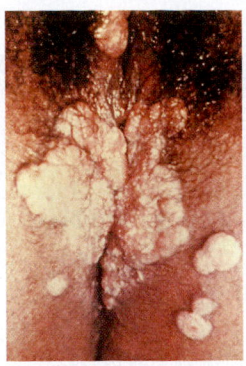

Figure 14-5 Genital warts/Centers for Disease Control

EXERCISE 14-6

Write the name of the sexually transmitted infection for each description.

1. cauliflower-like, fleshy growths
2. bacterial infection of genital mucous membranes
3. caused by herpes simplex virus type 2
4. parasitic infection of the genitourinary tract
5. disease with three distinct stages

EXERCISE 14-7

Rewrite the misspelled terms.

1. shancre
2. chlamydia
3. gonnorrhea
4. syphillis
5. trichomoniasis
6. venerial herpes

Infectious, Parasitic, and Sexually Transmitted Disease Diagnostic Tests

Infectious, parasitic, and sexually transmitted diseases are identified by blood or other body fluid tests. The most common specimen used for testing is serum derived from a clotted blood sample. Some urine and fecal tests are also used for diagnostic purposes. General types of tests include microscopy, culture, and immunodiagnostic blood tests. Review the terms in table 14-5 and complete the exercise.

Table 14-5 Infectious, Parasitic, and Sexually Transmitted Disease Diagnostic Tests

DIAGNOSTIC TEST	DEFINITION
cellophane tape test	method of identifying pinworm infestation by patting the perianal skinfolds with a strip of cellophane tape, which is placed on a slide and examined under a microscope for pinworm ova (eggs)
complement fixation test	serology (blood serum) or other body fluid test; used to diagnose some viral and fungal infections
culture and sensitivity test (C & S)	clinical laboratory test that identifies a pathogenic microorganism (**culture**), and the antimicrobial medications that inhibit the growth of the microorganism (sensitivity); *culture:* specimens such as blood, urine, stool, sputum, wound exudates, and secretions or scrapings from the skin, nose, throat, genitalia, and anus are placed on a growth medium; *sensitivity:* after the specimen is placed on the growth medium, antimicrobial discs are placed on the surface, the microorganism will not grow in the area around an effective antimicrobial (figure 14-6)
enzyme immunoassay (EIA); enzyme-linked immunosorbent assay (ELISA)	a serology test used to identify viral or parasitic diseases
fluorescent stain	microscopic examination of serum or other body fluids that is used to classify bacteria, mycobacteria, and fungi
fluorescent treponemal antibody absorption (FTA-ABS) test	serology test for confirming a diagnosis of primary syphilis
Gram stain test	a microscopic examination of serum or other body fluids that is used to classify bacteria and highlight morphology (bacilli or cocci)

continued

Table 14-5 (*continued*)   Infectious, Parasitic, and Sexually Transmitted Disease Diagnostic Tests

DIAGNOSTIC TEST	DEFINITION
microhemagglutination treponemal pallidum antibody (MHA-TP) test	serology test used to confirm a positive RPR or VDRL test result
polymerase chain reaction (PCR) test	a molecular clinical laboratory test that utilizes blood or other specimens to diagnose viral, fungal, and other microbial diseases that are not readily identified by culture or other methods
rapid plasma reagin test (RPR)	screening serology test for syphilis
TORCH test; toxoplasmosis, rubella, cytomegalovirus, herpes virus	blood test that is used as a screening test panel to identify the mother's exposure to viruses that are harmful to the fetus
trichrome stain; iron hematoxylin stain	microscopic examination of serum that is used to detect parasites in the blood
Venereal Disease Research Laboratory (VDRL) test	screening serology test for syphilis
Western blot assay test	serology or other body fluid test; used to diagnose viral diseases and Lyme disease
Wright stain; Giemsa stain	microscopic examination of blood and other specimens that detects parasites, *Histoplasma capsulatum,* and intracellular inclusions formed by viruses and *Chlamydia*

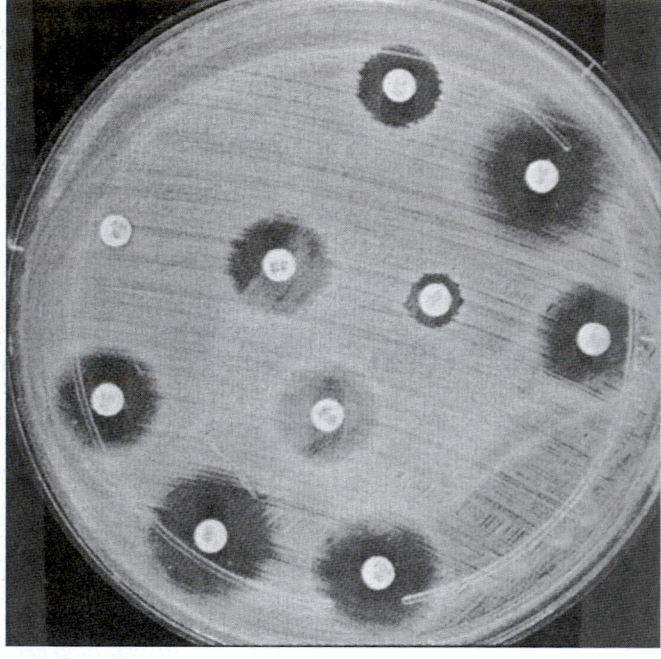

Figure 14-6   Culture and sensitivity plate

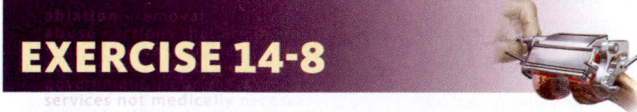

EXERCISE 14-8

Match the test in column 1 with the description in column 2.

COLUMN 1

a. cellophane tape test

b. culture and sensitivity test

c. Gra m stain test

COLUMN 2

1. confirmatory test for syphilis _____

2. detects parasites in the blood _____

3. diagnostic test for viral and fungal infections _____

d. RPR

e. trichrome stain test

f. Western blot assay test

g. complement fixation test

h. FTA-ABS

i. TORCH

j. EIA; ELISA

4. highlights morphology of bacteria _____

5. identifies microorganism and medications _____

6. pinworm test _____

7. screening test for syphilis _____

8. serology test for Lyme disease _____

9. serology test for viral or parasitic diseases _____

10. test panel for maternal exposure to viruses _____

ABBREVIATIONS

Review the abbreviations in table 14-6. Practice writing out the abbreviations with a brief definition for each phrase or term.

Table 14-6 Abbreviations

ABBREVIATION	MEANING
C & S	culture and sensitivity
CMV	cytomegalovirus
DNA	deoxyribonucleic acid
EIA	enzyme immunoassay
ELISA	enzyme-linked immunosorbent assay
EM	erythema migrans
FTA-ABS	fluorescent treponemal antibody absorption
HIV	human immunodeficiency virus
HPV	human papillomavirus
HSV	herpes simplex virus
MHA-TP	microhemagglutination treponemal pallidum
MMR	measles, mumps, rubella
PCR	polymerase chain reaction
RPR	rapid plasma reagin
STI	sexually transmitted infection
TORCH	toxoplasmosis, rubella, cytomegalovirus, herpes virus
VDRL	Venereal Disease Research Laboratory test

INFECTIOUS AND PARASITIC DISEASES MEDICAL CODING

To successfully complete the exercises in this section, the ICD-9-CM volumes 1, 2, and 3 and the CPT (Current Procedural Terminology) coding references must be readily available. The information in this section is presented as follows:

- An introduction to ICD-9-CM volume 1, chapter 1, "Infectious and Parasitic Diseases"
- ICD-9-CM diagnostic coding exercises
- A summary of ICD-9-CM volume 3 coding conventions that apply to infectious and parasitic disease procedures
- ICD-9-CM procedure coding exercises
- A summary of the CPT infectious and parasitic diseases coding guidelines
- CPT coding exercises

Students are *strongly* encouraged to review the information at the beginning of the ICD-9-CM and CPT coding references. Commercial publishers include instructions on how to use the ICD-9-CM references, the ICD-9-CM official coding conventions, additional conventions used by the publisher, and the *ICD-9-CM Official Guidelines for Coding and Reporting*. Some publishers include the three ICD-9-CM volumes in one book and put the *Alphabetic Index* (volume 2) at the beginning of the references.

The *Introduction* to CPT includes detailed instructions for using this code book, an index to the illustrations throughout the book, and anatomical illustrations of the major structures of body systems.

ICD-9-CM Volume 1, Chapter 1, Infectious and Parasitic Diseases (001–139)

Infectious and parasitic diseases are coded to ICD-9-CM volume 1, chapter 1, "Infectious and Parasitic Diseases." This chapter includes the following major sections:

- **Intestinal Infectious Diseases (001–009).** Codes in this section cover bacterial, viral, and protozoan infections of the intestinal tract. Fourth and fifth digits are used to identify specific organisms and other clinical information such as abscess or ulceration.

- **Tuberculosis (010–018).** Codes in this section cover tuberculosis of respiratory, digestive, nervous, and genitourinary systems and other body structures. Fifth digits that represent the type of examination used to identify the disease are required for all categories.

- **Zoonotic Bacterial Diseases (020–027).** Codes in this section cover plague, tularemia, anthrax, brucellosis, and other zoonotic bacterial diseases. Zoonotic diseases are caused by infectious agents that are transmitted between or shared by humans and animals.

- **Other Bacterial Diseases (030–041).** Codes in this section cover specific diseases such as leprosy, diphtheria, whooping cough, septicemia, and other specified bacterial infections.

- **Human Immunodeficiency Virus (HIV) Infection (042).** This code covers HIV infection, acquired immune deficiency syndrome (AIDS), and AIDS-like syndrome.

- **Poliomyelitis and Other Non-Arthropod-Borne Viral Diseases of and Prion Diseases of Central Nervous System (045–049).** Codes in this section cover viral diseases that affect the brain, meninges, and spinal cord.

- **Viral Diseases Accompanied by Exanthem (050–059).** Codes in this section cover viral diseases that present with characteristic skin eruptions (exanthema). Arthropod-borne viral diseases are excluded from this section.

- **Arthropod-Borne Viral Diseases (060–066).** Codes in this section cover viral diseases that are associated with insect bites. The instruction note in this section directs the medical coder to *use additional code* to identify any associated meningitis.

- **Other Diseases Due to Viruses and Chlamydiae (070–079).** Codes in this section cover hepatitis, rabies, mumps, and other diseases associated with specific viruses and chlamydiae. Fourth or fifth digits are required for many categories in this section.

- **Rickettsioses and Other Arthropod-Borne Diseases (080–088).** Codes in this section cover diseases transmitted via lice, ticks, and mosquitoes. Arthropod-borne viral diseases are excluded from this section. Fourth or fifth digits are required for many categories in this section.

- **Syphilis and Other Venereal Diseases (090–099).** Codes in this section cover sexually transmitted infections. Note the extensive use of fourth and fifth digits.

- **Other Spirochetal Diseases (100–104).** Codes in this section cover diseases caused by specific bacteria classified as spirochetes.

- **Mycoses (110–118).** Codes in this section cover fungal diseases. The instruction note in this section directs the medical coder to *use additional code* to identify manifestation as arthropathy, meningitis, and otitis externa. Codes are organized by specific fungi such as *Candida, Coccidioides*, and *Histoplasma capsulatum*.

- **Helminthiases (120–129).** Codes in this section cover conditions related to pinworms, flukes, tapeworms, and the larvae or ova of these parasites.

- **Other Infectious and Parasitic Diseases (130–136).** Codes in this section cover diseases such as toxoplasmosis, trichomoniasis, and unspecified infectious and parasitic conditions. Fourth and fifth digits are required in nearly all categories.

- **Late Effects of Infectious and Parasitic Diseases (137–139).** Codes in this section are used to indicate conditions specified as late effects, as sequclae, or as due to old or inactive tuberculosis, poliomyelitis, viral encephalitis, trachoma, and other and unspecified infectious and parasitic diseases.

Chapter 16, "Symptoms, Signs, and Ill-Defined Conditions," category 795, *Other and nonspecific abnormal cytological, histological, immunological, and DNA test findings,* has a few codes associated with infectious and parasitic diseases.

EXERCISE 14-9

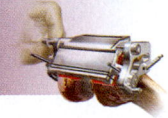

Write a brief definition for each diagnosis. Identify the main term in the diagnostic statement and assign the correct ICD-9-CM diagnosis code(s).

1. Cervicofacial actinomycosis

   DEFINITION: _____

   MAIN TERM: _____

   ICD-9-CM CODE(S): _____

2. Pulmonary tuberculosis, bacilli identified via microscopy

   DEFINITION: _____

   MAIN TERM: _____

   ICD-9-CM CODE(S): _____

3. Pulmonary blastomycosis

   DEFINITION: _____

   MAIN TERM: _____

   ICD-9-CM CODE(S): _____

4. Foodborne botulism

   DEFINITION: _____

   MAIN TERM: _____

   ICD-9-CM CODE(S): _____

5. Chlamydial vaginitis

   DEFINITION: _____

   MAIN TERM: _____

   ICD-9-CM CODE(S): _____

6. Shigella dysenteriae

   DEFINITION: _____

   MAIN TERM: _____

   ICD-9-CM CODE(S): _____

7. Progressive disseminated histoplasmosis

   DEFINITION: _____

   MAIN TERM: _____

   ICD-9-CM CODE(S): _____

8. Multisystem toxoplasmosis

   DEFINITION: _____

   MAIN TERM: _____

   ICD-9-CM CODE(S): _____

9. Genital warts

   DEFINITION: _____

   MAIN TERM: _____

   ICD-9-CM CODE(S): _____

10. Epididymitis due to *Chlamydia trachomatis*

    DEFINITION: _____

    MAIN TERM: _____

    ICD-9-CM CODE(S): _____

11. Herpetic ulceration of the vulva

    DEFINITION: _____

    MAIN TERM: _____

    ICD-9-CM CODE(S): _____

12. Acute gonococcal cervicitis

    DEFINITION: _____

    MAIN TERM: _____

    ICD-9-CM CODE(S): _____

ICD-9-CM Infectious and Parasitic Disease Prevention and Diagnostic Test Codes

Preventing infectious and parasitic diseases is accomplished by vaccination and inoculation. Medical codes related to prevention are included in the following V code categories:

- **V03**—vaccination and inoculation against bacterial diseases
- **V04**—vaccination and inoculation against viral diseases
- **V05**—vaccination and inoculation against a single disease
- **V06**—vaccination and inoculation against a combination of diseases

Vaccination is the main term, and **prophylactic**, which means prevention, is the subterm in the *Alphabetic Index to Diseases* for categories V03–V06.

Prevention codes are also included in ICD-9-CM volume 3, chapter 16, "Miscellaneous Diagnostic and Therapeutic Procedures," categories 99.3, 99.4, and 99.5.

- **Prophylactic Vaccination and Inoculation Against Certain Bacterial Diseases (99.3).** Codes in this category require a fourth digit that identifies the bacteria or bacterial disease associated with the vaccination or inoculation.
- **Prophylactic Vaccination and Inoculation Against Certain Viral Diseases (99.4).** Codes in this category require a fourth digit that identifies the virus or viral disease associated with the vaccination or inoculation.
- **Other Vaccination and Inoculation (99.5).** Codes in this category require a fourth digit that identifies the disease or type of antitoxin associated with the vaccination or inoculation.

Diagnostic test codes for infectious and parasitic disease are covered in the following V code categories:

- **V73**—special screening examination for viral and chlamydial diseases
- **V74**—special screening examination for bacterial and spirochetal diseases
- **V75**—special screening examination for other infectious diseases

ICD-9-CM *Alphabetic Index* main terms for these V codes include *carrier (suspected) of, examination, exposure, history (personal) of, screening, test(s),* and *vaccination.*

Diagnostic test codes for infectious and parasitic diseases are also covered in ICD-9-CM volume 3, chapter 16, "Miscellaneous Diagnostic and Therapeutic Procedures," categories 90 and 91. Both of these categories require fourth digits to identify the type of examination as bacterial smear, culture, culture and sensitivity, parasitology, toxicology, cell block and Pap smear, or

other microscopic examination. The Index to Procedures in ICD-9-CM volume 3 lists *examination (for)* as the main term for chapter 16 categories 90 and 91.

- **Microscopic Examination I (90).** Codes in this category cover microscopic examinations of blood, lymph, sputum, and specimens taken from the nervous system, spinal fluid, endocrine gland, eye, ear, nose, throat, trachea, lungs, lymph nodes, and upper and lower digestive tracts.
- **Microscopic Examination II (91).** Codes in this category cover microscopic examinations of joint fluid, semen, stool, urine, and specimens taken from the liver, pancreas, urinary tract, male and female genital tract, skin, musculoskeletal system, an operative wound, and other or unspecified sites.

EXERCISE 14-10

Write a brief definition for each prevention or diagnostic term. Identify the main term and assign both the ICD-9-CM V code and chapter 16 code.

1. Stool culture for *Salmonella*

   MAIN TERM: _____

   V CODE: _____

   CHAPTER 16 CODE: _____

2. Skin test for histoplasmosis

   MAIN TERM: _____

   V CODE: _____

   CHAPTER 16 CODE: _____

3. Rubella antibody screening blood test

   MAIN TERM: _____

   V CODE: _____

   CHAPTER 16 CODE: _____

4. Urine culture, suspected gonococcal infection

   MAIN TERM: _____

   V CODE: _____

   CHAPTER 16 CODE: _____

5. Measles, mumps, and rubella vaccination (MMR), combined

MAIN TERM: _____

V CODE: _____

CHAPTER 16 CODE: _____

Current Procedural Terminology (CPT) Codes

CPT codes related to infectious and parasitic diseases are covered in the Pathology and Laboratory section and in the Medicine section. Review the guidelines for these sections in the CPT manual and in chapter 3 of this text. Subsections of the Pathology and Laboratory section related to infectious and parasitic diseases include the following:

- **Immunology (86000–86593).** Codes in this subsection cover blood tests for bacterial, viral, and fungal infections. For example, the CPT code for the RPR test for syphilis is 86592.

- **Immunology, Antibody Detection Tests (86602–86804).** Codes in this subsection cover blood tests for the detection of antibodies to bacterial, viral, and fungal infections. For example, the CPT test for *Borrelia burgdorferi,* the infectious agent for Lyme disease, antibodies is 86617 *Borrelia burgdorferi* (Lyme disease) confirmatory test.

- **Microbiology (87001–87999).** The Microbiology subsection includes bacteriology, mycology, parasitology, and virology. Codes in this subsection cover tests that identify infectious agents via culture, culture and sensitivity, complement fixation, immunoassays (EIA, ELIA), stains, agglutination tests, and nucleic acid tests. The codes identify the infectious agent and in some cases the specimen. For example, culture for fungi using skin, hair, or nail is coded to 87101; when blood is the specimen the code is 87103.

The Organ or Disease-Oriented Panels subsection has two codes that relate to infectious disease: (1) 80055, *Obstetric panel,* includes hepatitis B, rubella, and syphilis; and (2) 80074, *Acute hepatitis panel,* includes hepatitis A antibody, hepatitis B core antibody, hepatitis B surface antigen, and hepatitis C antibody.

Subsections of the Medicine section related to infectious and parasitic diseases include the following:

- **Immunization Administration for Vaccines/Toxoids (90465–90474).** Codes in this subsection are used to identify the administration of vaccinations for infectious diseases. Codes 90465–90468 indicate that the physician was present during the administration of a vaccine. Codes 90471–90474 are used when the physician is not present. An additional code that identifies the vaccine that is administered must be reported with the administration code.

- **Vaccines, Toxoids (90476–90749).** Codes in this subsection identify the vaccine product only. For example, code 90707 covers the vaccine for measles, mumps, and rubella virus (MMR) that is administered subcutaneously. The code for administering the vaccine is selected from 90465–90474.

Laboratory tests for infectious and parasitic diseases are listed in the CPT alphabetic index under the name of the test such as culture and immunoassay, the name type of specimen such as blood or urine, or the name of the organism.

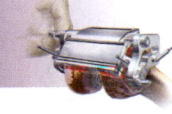

EXERCISE 14-11

Write the main term for each test. Assign the CPT codes, including administration codes as applicable.

1. Stool culture for *Salmonella*

   MAIN TERM: _____

   CPT CODE(S): _____

2. Skin test for histoplasmosis

   MAIN TERM: _____

   CPT CODE(S): _____

3. Rubella antibody screening blood test

   MAIN TERM: _____

   CPT CODE(S): _____

continued

4. Measles, mumps, and rubella vaccination (MMR), combined

MAIN TERM: _____

CPT CODE(S): _____

5. Cellophane tape test, pinworm exam

MAIN TERM: _____

CPT CODE(S): _____

6. Tuberculosis skin test

MAIN TERM: _____

CPT CODE(S): _____

7. Subcutaneous injection, measles, mumps, rubella, and varicella vaccine, live

MAIN TERM: _____

CPT CODE(S): _____

8. Intranasal influenza virus vaccine

MAIN TERM: _____

CPT CODE(S): _____

9. TB skin test, PPD

MAIN TERM: _____

CPT CODE(S): _____

10. Rapid strep test (streptococcus, group A, direct optical observation)

MAIN TERM: _____

CPT CODE(S): _____

■ SUMMARY

This chapter covered medical terms related to infectious and parasitic diseases. Diagnoses and prevention and test procedures were identified and defined. Infectious and parasitic diseases are coded to ICD-9-CM volume 1, chapter 1, "Infectious and Parasitic Diseases." Diagnostic and prevention tests for infectious and parasitic diseases are coded to the supplementary classification V codes and ICD-9-CM volume 3, chapter 16, "Miscellaneous Diagnostic and Therapeutic Procedures." Current Procedural Terminology (CPT) infectious and parasitic disease codes are found in the Pathology and Laboratory section and the Medicine section.

■ CHAPTER REVIEW

Read the progress notes and write the main term. Assign the ICD-9-CM V code; volume 3, chapter 16 code; and CPT codes for the laboratory tests.

CASE 1

Mr. Wallace is seen today to discuss the results of his recent blood tests, which included immunoassay evaluation for *Actinomyces israelii,* the bacteria most likely responsible for his diagnosis of cervicofacial actinomycosis. We discussed his current antibiotic treatment and based on the positive test results, he will complete this course of medications. Follow-up is scheduled in two weeks.

MAIN TERM: _____

ICD-9-CM CODE(S): _____

CPT CODE(S): _____

CASE 2

Ms. Rowland is seen today complaining of dysuria and an unusual vaginal discharge. On examination the presumptive diagnosis is chlamydial vaginitis. Blood was drawn for EIA to identify *Chlamydia trachomatis*. Culture of the vaginal discharge was taken to identify the suspected organism.

MAIN TERM: _____

ICD-9-CM CODE(S): _____

CPT CODE(S): _____

CASE 3

Mr. Gervais has recently experienced gripping abdominal pain, episodes of diarrhea, and urgency to defecate. He states that these episodes "get worse every time" and his stool "looks almost slimy." Diagnostic workup to rule out irritable bowel syndrome, gastroenteritis, and colitis was completed. Stool culture to identify group-A shigella bacteria was taken, since it is quite possibly *Shigella dysenteriae*. Mr. Gervais was advised to increase his fluid intake and pay close attention to hand washing.

MAIN TERM: _____

ICD-9-CM CODE(S): _____

CPT CODE(S): _____

CASE 4

Ms. Rowland is seen today for ulcerations in the vulvar area. She states that these are "painful, especially when urinating." On visual examination the ulcers appear to be due to herpes simplex, type 2. A sample of the exudates was taken for smear and stain analysis to confirm the diagnosis herpetic ulceration of the vulva. Ms. Rowland was advised to abstain from all sexual activity.

MAIN TERM: _____

ICD-9-CM CODE(S): _____

CPT CODE(S): _____

CASE 5

The patient is seen today for cervical examination. The cervix is inflamed and friable, and considerable exudates are present. Samples of the exudates were taken for agar culture and sensitivity testing. Presumptive diagnosis, acute gonococcal cervicitis; presumptive bacteria, *Neisseria gonorrhoeae*. She will begin an antibiotic course of treatment, until the C & S results are available.

MAIN TERM: _____

ICD-9-CM CODE(S): _____

CPT CODE(S): _____

MEDICAL TERMINOLOGY CHALLENGE

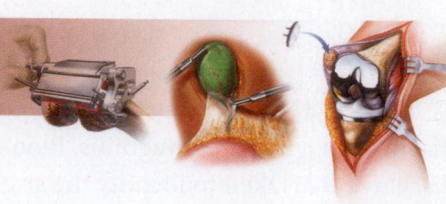

Write a brief definition for each term. Use a medical dictionary as necessary.

1. antibody _____

2. arthropod _____

3. cytological _____

4. exanthema _____

5. histological _____

6. immunological _____

7. inoculation _____

8. larva _____

9. ova _____

10. parasitology _____

11. sequelae _____

12. specimen _____

13. toxicology _____

14. vaccination _____

15. vaccine _____

NOTES:

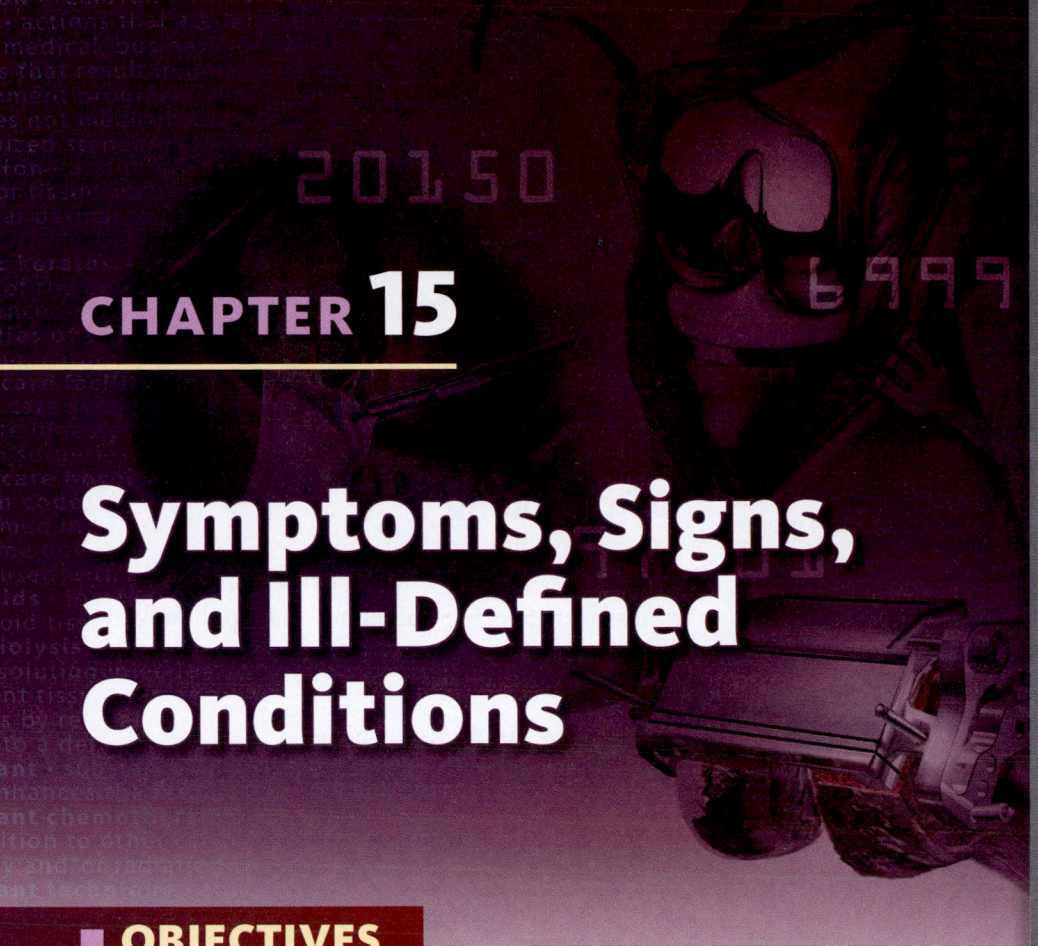

CHAPTER **15**

Symptoms, Signs, and Ill-Defined Conditions

■ OBJECTIVES

At the completion of this chapter, the student should be able to:

1. Define symptoms, signs, and ill-defined conditions.
2. Discuss the encounter form as a source document.
3. Describe the Evaluation and Management section of the Current Procedural Terminology coding reference.
4. Describe the significance of the first-listed diagnosis.
5. Accurately assign medical codes to signs, symptoms, ill-defined conditions, and physician office services.

■ OVERVIEW

This chapter covers medical terminology and coding principles related to the physician office or clinic setting. The medical terminology presented in the system chapters of this text is used in all health care settings. The coding principles presented in chapters 2 and 3 also apply to the physician office and clinic setting. Therefore, the information in this chapter is presented in the following format:

- Encounter form
- ICD-9-CM diagnosis coding principles
- CPT coding principles
- Coding exercises

ENCOUNTER FORM

The **encounter form**, also called a **charge slip**, **routing form,** or **superbill**, is generated when an individual comes to the physician office for an appointment. The encounter form is one of the **source documents** for financial, diagnostic, and treatment information related to a specific appointment or episode of care. Figure 15-1 is a sample of an encounter form developed for an internal medicine office.

The encounter form is usually attached to the patient record and routed to the examination room and other areas of the office or clinic. The physician, or other health care practitioner, completes the following sections of this form:

- Checks encounter category and level: **new patient**, **established patient**, office consultation, or other type service
- Checks the lab tests, procedures, or treatments ordered or performed during the current episode of care
- Circles the diagnosis(es) or writes in the diagnosis(es), as necessary
- Enters any comments or referral information in the section marked Referral/Comments

Most preprinted encounter forms include ICD-9-CM diagnosis and CPT codes. Since the codes are updated annually, the encounter forms must be reviewed to be sure that the preprinted codes are accurate.

The information at the bottom of the encounter form may be printed when the form is generated before the appointment or written when the appointment is finished. The patient usually takes the encounter form to the billing clerk who enters the fees (charges) for the services rendered during the current appointment. The patient signs and dates the original and keeps a copy of the encounter form. The encounter form and the patient's medical record are used as source documents for medical coding and insurance billing procedures.

ICD-9-CM DIAGNOSIS CODES

In the physician office setting, diagnoses are reported using ICD-9-CM diagnosis codes. ICD-9-CM coding conventions as described in chapter 2 apply to physician office coding. Additional ICD-9-CM guidelines are covered in Section IV of the *ICD-9-CM Official Guidelines for Coding and Reporting*. Under the *Guidelines*, the terms **encounter** and **visit** are used interchangeably to describe outpatient service contacts. In all cases, the reason for the encounter or visit is referred to as the **first-listed diagnosis**, although some practitioners may also use the term *primary diagnosis*.

Guidelines for Physician Office Coding

The entire Section IV Guidelines are included in chapter 2 of this text. Specific guidelines that apply to physician office coding are summarized in this chapter.

Guideline IV.A. Selection of first-listed condition

In the physician office setting the term *first-listed diagnosis* is used in lieu of principal diagnosis. In determining the first-listed diagnosis, ICD-9-CM coding conventions as well as the general and disease-specific guidelines take precedence over the outpatient guidelines. Diagnoses often are not established at the time of the initial encounter/visit. It may take two or more visits before the diagnosis is confirmed.

Guideline IV.B. Codes from 001.0 through V86.1

Appropriate ICD-9-CM codes, from 001.0 through V86.1, must be used to identify diagnoses, symptoms, problems, complaints, or other reason(s) for the encounter/visit.

Guideline IV.C. Accurate reporting of ICD-9-CM diagnosis codes

For accurate reporting of ICD-9-CM diagnosis codes, the documentation should describe the patient's condition, using terminology that includes specific diagnoses as well as symptoms, problems, or reasons for the encounter. There are ICD-9-CM codes to describe all of these.

Guideline IV.D. Selection of codes 001.0 through 999.9

These ICD-9-CM codes will frequently be used to describe the reason for the encounter.

Elizabeth Foy, MD
Charles French, MD
Robert Howard, MD
Denzel Hamilton, MD
Roberta Pharyngeal, MD
Henry Romero, MD

Superiorland Clinic
714 Hennepin Avenue
Blueberry, ME 49855
Phone: (906) 336-4600 Fax: (906) 336-4020 Tax ID #: 49-4134726

NEW PATIENT	X	CODE	FEE	LAB TESTS	X	CODE	FEE	LAB TESTS	X	CODE	FEE
Level I		99201		AST		84450		LDH		83615	
Level II		99202		Albumin		82040		Lipid Panel		80061	
Level III		99203		Alk Phos		84075		Metabolic Panel		80053	
Level IV		99204		BUN		84520		Obstetric Panel		80055	
Level V	X	99205		CBC		85027		Occult blood		82270	
ESTABLISHED PATIENT				CBC/diff		85025		PAP smear		88150	
Level I		99211		CK/CPK		82550		PPD Skin Test		86585	
Level II		99212		Drug Screen		80100		Prothrombin Time		85610	
Level III		99213		Electrolyte Panel		80051		PSA		84152	
Level IV		99214		Estrogen		82671		Rapid Strep Screen		87880	
Level V		99215		Glucose		82947		Sed Rate		85651	
OFFICE CONSULTATION				HgbA1C		83020		TSH		84443	
Level I		99241		Hepatitis Panel		80074		Urinalysis		81000	
Level II		99242		HIV Screen		86703					
Level III		99243									
Level IV		99244									
Level V		99245		OTHER TESTS				OTHER TESTS			
HOSPITAL INPATIENT				A/P Chest X-ray				Holter 24 hr			
Initial/Complex		99223		DXA Scan		76075		Sigmoidoscopy		45330	
Subsequent		99231		EKG Int & Report		93000		Stress Test		93015	
EMERGENCY DEPARTMENT SERV.				EKG Single Lead		93040					
Level I		99281									
Level II		99282									
Level III		99283		TREATMENTS	X	CODE	FEE	TREATMENTS	X	CODE	FEE
Level IV		99284		Flu Shot		90658					
Level V		99285									

DIAGNOSIS						
Abdominal Pain	789.00	Gastritis	535.50	OTHER DIAGNOSIS		CODE
Angina Pectoris, Unspec.	413.9	Hemorrhoids, NOS	455.6			
Asthma, Unspecified	493.90	Hiatal hernia	553.3			
Bronchitis, Acute	466.0	Hyperlipidemia, Unspec.	272.4			
Bursitis	727.3	Hypertension, Unspec.	401.9			
CHF	428.0	Hyperthyroidism	242.90	REFERRAL/COMMENTS		
Colon polyp	211.3	Hypothyroidism	244.9			
Conjunctivitis, Unspec.	372.00	Osteoarthritis, Unspec.	715.99			
Diabetes Mellitus, Type I	250.01	Osteoporosis, postmen.	733.01			
Diabetes Mellitus, Type II	250.00	Pleurisy	511.0			
Diverticulosis	562.10	Serous Otitis Media, Acute	381.01			
Emphysema	492.8	UTI	599.0			

DATE:	PATIENT NAME	DOB	CHARGES	PAYMENT	BALANCE

I authorize my insurance benefits to be paid directly to the above named physician. I understand that I am obligated to pay deductibles, copayments, and non-covered services. I authorize release of my medical information for billing purposes.

PATIENT SIGNATURE: DATE:

Figure 15-1 Encounter form

Guideline IV.E. Codes that describe symptoms and signs

Codes that describe symptoms and signs, as opposed to diagnoses, are acceptable for reporting purposes when a diagnosis has not been established (confirmed) by the provider. Chapter 16, "Symptoms, Signs, and Ill-Defined Conditions," contains many but not all codes for symptoms.

Guideline IV.F. Encounters for circumstances other than disease or injury

ICD-9-CM V codes are used to report encounters for reasons other than disease or injury.

Guideline IV.G. Level of detail in coding

All ICD-9-CM codes must be assigned to the highest level of specificity based on the documentation in the patient's record. This means that a three-digit code must not be assigned when a four-digit code is available, and a four-digit code must not be assigned when a five-digit code is available.

Guideline IV.H. ICD-9-CM code for the diagnosis, condition, problem, or other reason for encounter/visit

List first the ICD-9-CM code for the diagnosis, condition, problem, or other reason for the encounter/visit shown in the medical record to be chiefly responsible for the services provided. List additional codes that describe any coexisting conditions. In some cases the first-listed diagnosis may be a symptom when a diagnosis has not been established (confirmed) by the physician.

Guideline IV.I. Uncertain diagnosis

Do not code diagnoses documented as *probable, suspected, questionable, rule out, working diagnosis, provisional,* or other similar terms indicating uncertainty. Rather, code the condition(s) to the highest degree of certainty for that encounter/visit, such as symptoms, signs, abnormal test results, or other reasons for the visit.

Guideline IV.J. Chronic diseases

Chronic diseases treated on an ongoing basis may be coded and reported as many times as the patient receives treatment and care for the condition(s).

Guideline IV.K. Code all documented conditions that coexist

Code all problems that are documented, coexist at the time of the encounter/visit, and require treatment or affect the care of the patient. However, history codes (V10–V19) may be used as secondary codes if the historical condition or family history has an impact on current care or influences treatment.

Guideline IV.L. Patients receiving diagnostic services only

When a patient is seen for diagnostic services only, sequence first the diagnosis, condition, problem, or other reason for encounter/visit shown in the medical record to be chiefly responsible for the outpatient services provided during the encounter/visit. Codes for other diagnoses (e.g., chronic conditions) may be sequenced as additional codes.

For encounters for routine laboratory/radiology testing in the absence of any signs, symptoms, or associated diagnoses, assign V72.5 and V72.6. If routine testing is performed during the same encounter as a test to evaluate a sign, symptom, or diagnosis, it is appropriate to assign both the V code and the code describing the reason for the nonroutine test.

For outpatient encounters for diagnostic tests that have been interpreted by a physician, and the final report is available at the time of coding, code any confirmed or definitive diagnosis(es) documented in the interpretation. Do not code related signs and symptoms as additional diagnoses.

Guideline IV.M. Patients receiving therapeutic services only

For patients receiving therapeutic services only during the encounter/visit, sequence first the diagnosis, condition, problem, or other reason for the encounter/visit shown in the medical record to be chiefly responsible for the outpatient services provided during the encounter/visit. Codes for other diagnoses (e.g., chronic conditions) may be sequenced as additional diagnoses.

The only exception to this rule is that when the primary reason for the admission/encounter is chemotherapy, radiation therapy, or rehabilitation, the appropriate V code for the service is listed first, and the diagnosis or problem for which the service is being performed is listed second.

Guideline IV.N. Patients receiving preoperative evaluation only

For patients receiving preoperative evaluation only, sequence first a code from category V72.8, *Other specified examinations,* to describe the preoperative consultations. Assign a code for the condition to describe the reason for the surgery as an additional diagnosis. Code also any findings related to the preoperative evaluation.

Guideline IV.P. Routine outpatient prenatal visits

For routine outpatient prenatal visits when no complications are present, codes V22.0, *Supervision of normal first pregnancy,* or V22.1, *Supervision of other normal pregnancy,* should be used as the principal diagnosis. These codes should not be used in conjunction with chapter 11, "Complications of Pregnancy, Childbirth, and the Puerperium," codes.

The coding conventions and coding guidelines are intended to ensure accurate and consistent assignment of medical codes. Although all of the conventions and guidelines are equally important, one coding rule actually supersedes all others: code **only** the conditions, diagnoses, problems, and procedures that are **clearly** documented in the patient's medical record.

ICD-9-CM Volume 1, Chapter 16, Symptoms, Signs, and Ill-Defined Conditions (780–799)

The *ICD-9-CM Official Guidelines for Coding and Reporting* allows codes from chapter 16, "Symptoms, Signs, and Ill-Defined Conditions," to be used as the first-listed diagnosis. The instruction note at the beginning of this chapter states that these codes should be used when a more specific diagnosis is not available. The major sections in this chapter include the following:

■ **Symptoms (780–789).** Codes in this section cover general symptoms such as coma, persistent vegetative state, fainting, dizziness, malaise, and fatigue. Symptoms involving specific body systems such as rash, edema, anorexia, headache, and hyperventilation are also included. The exclusion notes in each subsection direct the medical coder to other more specific codes. For example, code 780.4, *Dizziness and giddiness,* includes vertigo NOS, but excludes using this code when the symptom is associated with *Meniere disease.*

■ **Non-Specific Abnormal Findings (790–796).** Codes in this section cover abnormal test results of blood, urine, cerebrospinal fluid, stool, and semen. Abnormal diagnostic imaging results related to the structure or function of body organs or systems are also included. Exclusion notes direct the medical coder to more specific codes. For example, code 790.6, *Other abnormal blood chemistry,* includes abnormal blood levels of cobalt, copper, iron, lead, and other trace minerals, but excludes abnormal findings such as hypoglycemia, lead poisoning, or lipid metabolism.

■ **Ill-Defined and Unknown Causes of Morbidity and Mortality (797–799).** Codes in this section cover sudden death of unknown causes, asphyxia, hypoxemia, or cachexia.

EXERCISE 15-1

Write the main term for each diagnostic statement. Assign the correct ICD-9-CM code(s).

1. Umbilical mass, rectal bleeding; possible umbilical cyst or hernia

   MAIN TERM(S): _____

   ICD-9-CM CODE(S): _____

2. Chronic sinusitis; IDDM, well controlled

   MAIN TERM(S): _____

   ICD-9-CM CODE(S): _____

3. Chronic hypertension, follow-up visit to renew hypertensive medication

   MAIN TERM(S): _____

   ICD-9-CM CODE(S): _____

4. Hypercholesterolemia, recently diagnosed

   MAIN TERM(S): _____

   ICD-9-CM CODE(S): _____

continued

5. Fever of unknown origin, possibly viral; anemia; HIV-AIDS

   MAIN TERM(S): _____

   ICD-9-CM CODE(S): _____

6. Swelling and rash, right forearm, possibly due to an insect bite

   MAIN TERM(S): _____

   ICD-9-CM CODE(S): _____

7. Febrile convulsions, simple

   MAIN TERM(S): _____

   ICD-9-CM CODE(S): _____

8. Insomnia, three nights per week

   MAIN TERM(S): _____

   ICD-9-CM CODE(S): _____

CURRENT PROCEDURAL TERMINOLOGY (CPT) CODES

CPT codes are assigned to all services provided by the physician and other health care professionals. Codes that apply to the physician office setting are located in the Evaluation and Management, Medicine, Laboratory and Pathology, Radiology, and other sections depending on the medical specialty. For example, a gastroenterology office would use codes from the Digestive subsection of the Surgery section.

Evaluation and Management Codes (99201–99499)

Evaluation and Management codes, which are described in chapter 3 of this text, are used to report physician or provider activities associated with evaluating an individual's health status and managing or implementing a plan of care related to that status. Evaluation and management services range from a routine sports physical to planning and implementing care for critically ill or injured individuals. Refer to chapter 3 and the CPT manual for the complete guidelines associated with Evaluation and Management codes.

In the physician office setting, the Evaluation and Management codes are often preprinted on the encounter form (Figure 15-1). The physician selects the E/M code at the time the service is rendered. In some offices, the E/M codes are assigned by the medical coders who

carefully compare the documentation in the medical record with the requirements for the E/M code. The medical coder selects the code that is supported by the documentation. Evaluation and Management modifiers are listed and described in table 3-7. Refer to this table, if necessary, to complete the coding exercises in this chapter.

References that help guide the coder to the correct E/M code include (1) the section and subsection guidelines for E/M codes; (2) appendix C of the CPT manual, which lists clinical examples of E/M codes; and (3) *CPT Assistant,* a monthly publication of the American Medical Association that provides practical advice from coding specialists.

Medicine Section Codes (90281–99607)

Medicine section codes include a range of medical services and procedures, from routine childhood vaccinations to renal dialysis. Refer to table 3-18 for a brief description of the categories and medical services and procedures. Medicine codes are listed in the CPT alphabetic index by type of service and anatomical site. For example, heart catheterization is indexed under *Catheterization, cardiac, left heart, right heart,* and *Heart, catheterization.*

The physician or provider circles the tests and procedures on a preprinted encounter form and may write in additional services as needed. The medical coder reviews the patient's record to be certain that tests and procedures were completed, and to determine if other tests, procedures, or treatments were performed. The medical coder must also be sure that there is an appropriate ICD-9-CM diagnosis code for each CPT code.

Pathology and Laboratory Section Codes (80047–89356)

The Pathology and Laboratory section codes include services provided by the physician or by technicians under the supervision of a physician. This section includes codes for services and procedures that range from a straightforward urinalysis to the more complex cytogenetic studies. Refer to table 3-17 for a list of pathology and laboratory services. A physician office may have its own laboratory that is capable of completing most lab tests. When a lab test is performed by a different lab, CPT **modifier-90**, *reference (outside) laboratory,* is used to indicate that the test was performed elsewhere.

Radiology Section Codes (70010–79999)

Radiology section codes are organized by type of imaging, such as radiography, ultrasonography, and nuclear medicine, and by anatomical site. Radiology subsections include instructional notes that contribute to coding accuracy. Refer to table 3-16 for a list of radiology subsections and codes. Some physician offices may have radiography equipment and staff that allows the physician or provider to have some diagnostic imaging procedures done in the office. Types of equipment associated with specific physician offices include the following:

- Bone density equipment—internal medicine or primary care physician offices
- Ultrasound equipment—obstetrics and gynecology offices
- Radiography equipment—orthopedic, internal medicine, and primary care physician offices

When the physician completes the interpretation and report of a diagnostic imaging study, the CPT code for *interpretation* and *report* is assigned.

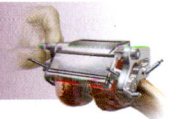

EXERCISE 15-2

Write the main term for each procedure or treatment. Assign the correct CPT codes.

1. Comprehensive preventive medicine, new patient age 65

   MAIN TERM(S): _____

   CPT CODE(S): _____

2. Office consultation, management of systolic hypertension, 70-year-old male, expanded problem-focused history and physical examination, straightforward medical decision making

   MAIN TERM(S): _____

   CPT CODE(S): _____

3. Established patient office visit, syncopal attacks, comprehensive history and physical examination and high-complexity medical decision making

   MAIN TERM(S): _____

   CPT CODE(S): _____

4. Lipid panel, blood test

   MAIN TERM(S): _____

   CPT CODE(S): _____

5. CBC, with differential, automated

   MAIN TERM(S): _____

   CPT CODE(S): _____

■ SUMMARY

This chapter covered ICD-9-CM volume 1, chapter 16, "Symptoms, Signs, and Ill-Defined Conditions"; CPT Evaluation and Management, Medicine, Laboratory, and Radiology sections and subsections; and ICD-9-CM *Official Guidelines for Coding and Reporting* related to physician office and clinic settings. Medical terms in this chapter describe signs or symptoms that are unspecified or describe abnormal test results.

■ CHAPTER REVIEW

Read the office notes and write the reason for the office visit and the services provided. Write the main term for each reason and service. Assign the ICD-9-CM diagnosis code(s), V code(s), and CPT code(s).

1. OFFICE NOTE

Ms. Walleye is a 45-year-old established patient who is seen today for her annual physical examination and Pap test. She also complains of dysuria, urgency, and frothy urine. Urinalysis with microscopy, today, confirms a bladder infection. CBC, automated with differential, showed a mild elevation in WBCs consistent with the bladder infection. Diagnoses: Comprehensive preventative physical examination. Bladder infection, confirmed.

REASON(S): _____

DIAGNOSIS(ES): _____

ICD-9-CM CODE(S): _____

SERVICE(S): _____

CPT CODE(S): _____

2. OFFICE NOTE

Mr. Jones is a new patient who is seen today for initial history and physical examination, comprehensive, and concerns about frequent nosebleeds. He describes the nosebleeds as "starting for no reason, although when I blow my nose really hard that can get everything going." He states this can happen as many as three times per week. He also describes "heart palpitations" every so often. Nasal cautery was done for episodes of epistaxis. A 12 lead EKG with interpretation revealed cardiac arrhythmia. CBC and metabolic panel were ordered. Overall, a relatively healthy 50-year-old with few systemic complaints.

REASON(S): _____

DIAGNOSIS(ES): _____

ICD-9-CM CODE(S): _____

SERVICE(S): _____

CPT CODE(S): _____

3. COMPREHENSIVE HISTORY AND PHYSICAL EXAMINATION/NEW PATIENT

NEW PATIENT: Peter Fraun
DATE: August 2, 20xx

CHIEF COMPLAINT

Fever, chills for the past four days.

HISTORY OF PRESENT ILLNESS

Mr. Fraun is a new patient and is seen today with complaints of fever and chills over the past four days. He has had a fever of 103 degrees, one day, and dysuria for two days. He has not traveled or consumed any unusual foods. He denies nausea, vomiting, diarrhea, chest pain, cough, sore throat, or abdominal pain.

PAST MEDICAL HISTORY

Mr. Fraun has a history of hypertension, controlled with medication, hypercholesterolemia, and urinary retention.

PAST SURGICAL HISTORY

He has had a transurethral resection of the prostate and repair of a right leg fracture. Both procedures were done within the past five years.

FAMILY HISTORY

Both parents lived well into their 80s with few health problems. He has a sister with Type II diabetes, a brother with hypertension and BPH, and a maternal uncle who was an alcoholic.

SOCIAL HISTORY

Mr. Fraun is a research chemist. He and his wife recently moved to Blueberry. She is a housewife and volunteers with several organizations. They have two children, a son aged 22 and a daughter aged 24. According to Mr. Fraun, both children enjoy good health and are pursuing their careers. He denies tobacco use, drinks about 4 cups of coffee per day, and has an occasional drink.

REVIEW OF SYSTEMS

Head and Neck: No change in vision, but frequent watering of the eyes. He does have an ophthalmologist in the area. No complaints of headaches or hearing problems.
Pulmonary: No complaint of cough or dyspnea. No history of TB or pneumonia.
Cardiovascular: No complaint of chest pain, palpitations, or history of heart murmur or rheumatic fever. EKG done today revealed normal sinus rhythm with no apparent abnormalities.
Gastrointestinal: No history of ulcers or hepatitis. His appetite has diminished in the last two days because of his recent illness. Denies diarrhea.
Genitourinary: Mr. Fraun reports dysuria for the last two days.
Endocrine: No history of diabetes, thyroid disease or anemia. He has a long standing history of hypertension and hypercholesterolemia.

PHYSICAL EXAMINATION

Examination today reveals a well-developed, well-nourished male patient who is in some distress due to fever and chills X four days. Blood pressure 170/90. Pulse 90 and regular. Respirations 20 and unlabored. Temperature today is 101.8 degrees. Height 5'11". Weight 220 lb. **Patient denies any allergies.**

continued

HEENT

Pupils are equal, round, and reactive to light and accommodation. There are small bilateral cataracts with mild arteriolar narrowing. The tympanic membranes and nares are clear. The pharynx is clear, and the mucous membranes are dry.

NECK

Supple. No adenopathy or thyromegaly.

CHEST

Clear, without rales or rhonchi.

HEART

Regular rate and rhythm. No clicks, murmur, or gallop. Pulses are 2+ and equal. There are no carotid bruits and there is no edema.

ABDOMEN

The abdomen is obese. There are active bowel sounds. The abdomen is soft, without masses, tenderness, or organomegaly.

GENITALIA

The testes are descended bilaterally and soft. The patient is an uncircumcised male with some phimosis. No discharge is noted.

RECTAL

Sphincter tone is normal. Prostate is minimally enlarged, but smooth and symmetric. The stool is brown and guiac negative.

EXTREMITIES

No lesions are noted. He does have decreased range of motion and some stiffness in the right knee.

IMPRESSION

Possible sepsis. Hypercholesterolemia. Hypertension, controlled.

PLAN

Obtain following labs today: CBC with differential, lipid panel, blood glucose, and urinalysis. In addition, blood and urine cultures are needed. Antibiotic therapy to be determined based on lab results. The patient was advised to take analgesics to relieve symptoms until results confirm or rule out sepsis and causative agent. He is to call tomorrow to let me know how he feels, and seek immediate treatment if his fever reaches 103.5 degrees.

SIGNED

Elizabeth Foy, MD

REASON(S): _____

DIAGNOSIS(ES): _____

ICD-9-CM CODE(S): _____

SERVICE(S): _____

CPT CODE(S): _____

MEDICAL TERMINOLOGY CHALLENGE

Write a brief definition for each medical term or abbreviation.
Use a medical dictionary as needed.

1. arrhythmia _____

2. bruits _____

3. cachexia _____

4. CBC _____

5. EKG _____

6. febrile _____

7. hypercholesterolemia _____

8. hypoxia _____

9. nares _____

10. organomegaly _____

11. palpitations _____

12. sepsis _____

13. syncopal _____

14. TB _____

15. WBC _____

NOTES:

_____   _____

_____   _____

_____   _____

_____   _____

_____   _____

NOTES:

Appendix A

■ PART 1:   WORD ELEMENT TO MEANING

WORD ROOTS

ROOT	MEANING
abdomin/o	abdomen
acid/o	sour; bitter
acoust/o	hearing
acr/o	extremities
aden/o	gland
adenoid/o	adenoid
adip/o	fat
adren/o	adrenal glands
adrenal/o	adrenal glands
agglutin/o	to clump
alveol/o	alveolus
amni/o	amnion
amnion/o	amnion
an/o	anus
andr/o	male; man
aneurysm/o	aneurysm
angi/o	vessel
ankyl/o	stiff
anthrac/o	coal
append/o	appendix
appendic/o	appendix
aque/o	watery
arachn/o	spider
arter/o	artery
arteri/o	artery
arteriol/o	arteriole
arthr/o	joint
articul/o	joint

ROOT	MEANING
atel/o	incomplete
ather/o	fat; fatty plaque; fatty, yellowish plaque
audi/o	hearing; sound
balan/o	glans penis
bas/o	base
bil/i	bile; gall
blast/o	immature
blephar/o	eyelid
bronch/o; bronch/i	bronchus
bronchiol/o	bronchiole
bucc/o	cheek
burs/o	bursa; sac
calc/i	calcium
cardi/o	heart
carp/o	wrist bones
cec/o	cecum
celi/o	abdomen
cephal/o	head
cerebell/o	cerebellum
cerebr/o	cerebrum
cervic/o	cervix
cheil/o	lips
chol/e	bile; gall
cholangi/o	bile duct
cholecyst/o	gallbladder
choledoch/o	common bile duct
chondr/o	cartilage

ROOT	MEANING
chori/o	chorion
clavicul/o	clavicle; collarbone
coagul/o	clotting
coccyg/o	coccyx; tailbone
cochle/o	cochlea
col/o	colon
colon/o	colon
colp/o	vagina
coni/o	dust
conjunctiv/o	conjunctiva
cor/o	heart
corne/o	cornea
coron/o	heart
cortic/o	cortex
cost/o	rib
crani/o	cranium; skull
cry/o	cold
crypt/o	hidden
cut/o	skin
cutane/o	skin
cyan/o	blue; bluish
cyst/o	bladder; sac; urinary bladder
dacry/o	tears
dacryocyst/o	tear sac
dendr/o	branching
derm/o	skin
dermat/o	skin
dipl/o	two; double
dips/o	thirst
duoden/o	duodenum
electr/o	electricity
embry/o	embryo
encephal/o	brain
endocrin/o	endocrine
enter/o	intestines
eosin/o	rosy red; rosy
epididym/o	epididymis
epiglott/o	epiglottis
epis/o	vulva
esophag/o	esophagus
fasci/o	fascia; fibrous tissue
femor/o	femur; thighbone
fet/o; fet/i	fetus
fibr/o	fiber; fibrous tissue
fibul/o	fibula; outer lower leg bone

ROOT	MEANING
fund/o	fundus
gastr/o	stomach
gingiv/o	gums
glauc/o	silver; gray
gli/o	neuroglia; nerve cell
glomerul/o	glomerulus
gloss/o	tongue
gluc/o	glucose; sugar; sweet
glyc/o	glucose; sugar; sweet
gonad/o	sex glands
granul/o	granules
gravid/o	pregnancy
gyn/o	woman
gynec/o	woman
hem/o	blood
hemat/o	blood
hepat/o	liver
hidr/o	sweat
humer/o	humerus; upper arm bone
hydr/o	water; fluid
hyster/o	uterus
ile/o	ileum
ili/o	ilium; pelvic bone
immun/o	protection
ir/o	iris
irid/o	iris
is/o	equal
ischi/o	ischium; pelvic bone
jejun/o	jejunum
kal/i	potassium
kary/o	nucleus
kerat/o	cornea; horny tissue; hard
ket/o	ketone bodies
kyph/o	humpback
labyrinth/o	inner ear; labyrinth
lacrim/o	tears
lact/o	milk
lamin/o	lamina; thin flat plate or layer
lapar/o	abdominal wall
laryng/o	larynx
leiomy/o	smooth muscle
leuk/o	white
ligament/o	ligament
lingu/o	tongue
lip/o	fat

ROOT	MEANING
lith/o	stone
lord/o	swayback
lumb/o	lower back
lymph/o	lymph
lymphaden/o	lymph gland
lymphangi/o	lymph vessel
mamm/o	breast
mandibul/o	mandible; lower jawbone
mast/o	breast
maxill/o	maxilla; upper jawbone
meat/o	meatus; opening
melan/o	black
men/o	menses; menstruation
mening/o	meninges
metacarp/o	hand bones
metatars/o	foot bones
metr/i; metr/o	uterus
morph/o	form; shape
muc/o	mucus
my/o	muscle
myc/o	fungus
myel/o	bone marrow; spinal cord
myring/o	eardrum
nas/o	nose
nat/o	birth
natr/o	sodium
nephr/o	kidney
neur/o	nerve
noct/o	night
nucle/o	nucleus
nyctal/o	night
ocul/o	eye
olig/o	few; diminished
onych/o	nail
oophor/o	ovary
ophthalm/o	eye
opt/o	vision; eye
or/o	mouth
orch/o	testis; testicle
orchi/o	testis; testicle
orchid/o	testis; testicle
orth/o	straight
oste/o	bone
ot/o	ear

ROOT	MEANING
ovari/o	ovary
ox/i	oxygen
pachy/o	thick
palpebr/o	eyelid
pancreat/o	pancreas
par/o	bear; give birth to; labor; childbirth
part/o	bear; give birth to; labor; childbirth
patell/o	patella; kneecap
pector/o	chest
pelv/i	pelvis
perine/o	perineum
peritone/o	peritoneum
phac/o	lens
phag/o	to eat
phak/o	lens
phalang/o	finger and toe bones
pharyng/o	pharynx
phleb/o	vein
phot/o	light
phren/o	diaphragm
pil/o	hair
pleur/o	pleura
pneum/o	lung; air
poikil/o	varied; irregular
polyp/o	polyp
proct/o	rectum
prostat/o	prostate gland
pub/o	pubis; pelvic bone
pubi/o	pubis; pelvic bone
puerper/o	childbirth
pulmon/o	lungs
pupill/o	pupil
py/o	pus
pyel/o	renal pelvis
quadr/i	four
radi/o	radius; outer lower arm bone
rect/o	rectum
ren/o	kidney
retin/o	retina
rhabdomy/o	skeletal muscle; striated muscle
rhin/o	nose
rhytid/o	wrinkles
salping/o	fallopian tubes; oviducts

ROOT	MEANING
sarc/o	flesh
scapula/o	scapula; shoulder blade
scler/o	sclera; hard
scoli/o	crooked; bent
seb/o	sebum
semin/i	semen
sial/o	salivary gland; saliva
sigmoid/o	sigmoid colon
sinus/o	sinus
somat/o	body
sperm/o	sperm; spermatic cord
spermat/o	sperm; spermatic cord
spher/o	sphere; round
sphygm/o	pulse
spir/o	breathe; breath
splen/o	spleen
spondyl/o	vertebra; vertebral column
squam/o	scale
staped/o	stapes; middle ear bone
stern/o	sternum; breastbone
steth/o	chest
stomat/o	mouth
sud/o	sweat
sudor/o	sweat
tars/o	ankle bones
ten/o	tendon
tend/o	tendon
tendin/o	tendon
tenosynov/o	tendon sheath

ROOT	MEANING
test/o	testis; testicle
testicul/o	testis; testicle
thec/o	sheath
thorac/o	chest
thromb/o	clot; thrombus
thym/o	thymus gland
thyr/o	thyroid gland
thyroid/o	thyroid gland
tonsill/o	tonsils
toxic/o	poison
trache/o	trachea
trich/o	hair
tympan/o	eardrum
ungu/o	nail
ur/o	urine; urinary system
ureter/o	ureter
urethr/o	urethra
uter/o	uterus
uve/o	uvea
vagin/o	vagina
vas/o	vessel; vas deferens
ven/o	vein
ventricul/o	ventricle
vertebr/o	vertebra; vertebral column
vesic/o	urinary bladder
vitre/o	glassy; jelly-like
vulv/o	vulva
xanth/o	yellow
xer/o	dry

PREFIXES

PREFIX	MEANING
a-	no; not; without
ab-	away from
an-	no; not; without
ana-	no; not; without
ante-	before; forward
anti-	against
astr-	star
auto-	self
bi-	two; double; both
brady-	slow
carcin-	cancer; malignant

PREFIX	MEANING
contra-	against; opposite
dura-	hard
dys-	abnormal; painful; difficult
echo-	sound
ect-	outside; out
en-	within; in; inward
endo-	within; inner
epi-	above; upon
eso-	within; in; inward
eu-	same; normal
ex-	out; outward

PREFIX	MEANING
hemi-	half
hyper-	above; excessive
hypo-	deficient; below
infra-	below; inferior
inter-	between
intra-	within
iso-	same; equal
macro-	large
mal-	bad; poor; abnormal
meta-	change; after; beyond
micro-	small
mono-	one
multi-	many
neo-	new
non-	not
nulli-	none
oxy-	sharp; quick
pan-	all

PREFIX	MEANING
para-	beside; around
per-	through
peri-	around; surrounding
poly-	many; excessive
post-	after
pre-	before; in front of
presby-	old
primi-	first; one
retro-	backward; behind; upward
semi-	half
sub-	under; below; beneath
super-	above; over; excess
supra-	above; on top of
sym-	with; association
syn-	together; with; union
tachy-	fast
tri-	three
uni-	one

SUFFIXES

SUFFIX	MEANING
-ac	pertaining to
-al	pertaining to
-algia	pain
-ary	pertaining to
-asthenia	without feeling or sensation
-blast	immature; embryonic
-capnia	carbon dioxide
-cele	hernia; protrusion
-centesis	surgical puncture to remove fluid
-clasia	surgical breaking
-clasis	surgical breaking
-crine	to secrete
-crit	to separate
-cusia	hearing
-cusis	hearing
-cytosis	condition of cells
-desis	binding; fixation
-dynia	pain
-ectasis	stretching; dilatation
-ectomy	surgical removal; excision
-emesis	vomiting

SUFFIX	MEANING
-emia	blood condition
-gen	producing; forming
-genesis	producing; forming
-genic	producing; forming
-globin	protein
-globulin	protein
-gram	record; picture; x-ray film
-graph	instrument for recording
-graphy	process of recording
-ia	condition; abnormal condition
-iac	pertaining to
-iasis	condition; abnormal condition
-ic	pertaining to
-itis	inflammation
-kinesia	movement
-(o)logist	specialist
-(o)logy	study of
-lysis	destruction; breakdown
-lytic	destruction; breakdown
-malacia	softening
-megaly	enlarged; enlargement
-meter	instrument to measure

SUFFIX	MEANING
-metry	measuring; to measure
-oid	like; resembling
-oma	tumor
-opia	vision
-osis	condition; abnormal condition
-ous	pertaining to
-paresis	partial paralysis
-pathy	disease; illness
-penia	deficiency; decreased number
-pepsia	digestion
-pexy	surgical fixation
-phagia	eating; swallowing
-philia	attraction to
-phonia	sound; voice
-phoresis	carrying; transmission
-phoria	feeling; mental state
-plasty	surgical repair
-plegia	paralysis
-pnea	breathing
-poiesis	formation; production of
-ptosis	drooping; sagging
-ptysis	spitting up
-(r)rhagia	hemorrhage
-(r)rhaphy	suture of

SUFFIX	MEANING
-(r)rhea	discharge; flow
-(r)rhexis	rupture
-sclerosis	hardening
-scope	instrument for viewing
-scopy	visualization with a scope
-somnia	sleep
-stasis	control; stop; stopping or controlling
-stenosis	narrowing
-(o)stomy	creating a new or artificial opening
-therapy	treatment
-thorax	chest; pleural cavity
-tocia	labor; birth
-(o)tomy	incision into
-tonia	muscle tone
-tresia	opening
-tripsy	crushing
-trophy	growth; development
-tropia	to turn; turning
-tropin	stimulating effect of a hormone
-tropion	to turn; turning
-uria	urine; urination
-version	to turn

■ PART 2: MEANING TO WORD ELEMENT

WORD ROOTS

MEANING	ROOT
abdomen	abdomin/o; celi/o
abdominal wall	lapar/o
adenoid	adenoid/o
adrenal glands	adren/o; adrenal/o
air	pneum/o
alveolus	alveol/o
amnion	amni/o; amnion/o
aneurysm	aneurysm/o
ankle bones	tars/o
anus	an/o
appendix	append/o; appendic/o
arteriole	arteriol/o
artery	arter/o; arteri/o

MEANING	ROOT
base	bas/o
bear	par/o; part/o
bent	scoli/o
bile	bil/i; chol/e
bile duct	cholangi/o
birth	nat/o
bitter	acid/o
black	melan/o
bladder	cyst/o
blood	hem/o; hemat/o
blue	cyan/o
bluish	cyan/o
body	somat/o

MEANING	ROOT
bone	oste/o
bone marrow	myel/o
brain	encephal/o
branching	dendr/o
breast	mamm/o; mast/o
breastbone	stern/o
breath	spir/o
breathe	spir/o
bronchiole	bronchiol/o
bronchus	bronch/o; bronch/i
bursa	burs/o
calcium	calc/i
cartilage	chondr/o
cecum	cec/o
cerebellum	cerebell/o
cerebrum	cerebr/o
cervix	cervic/o
cheek	bucc/o
chest	pector/o; steth/o; thorac/o
childbirth	par/o; part/o; puerper/o
chorion	chori/o
clavicle	clavicul/o
clot	thromb/o
clotting	coagul/o
to clump	agglutin/o
coal	anthrac/o
coccyx	coccyg/o
cochlea	cochle/o
cold	cry/o
collarbone	clavicul/o
colon	col/o; colon/o
common bile duct	choledoch/o
conjunctiva	conjunctiv/o
cornea	corne/o; kerat/o
cortex	cortic/o
cranium	crani/o
crooked	scoli/o
diaphragm	phren/o
diminished	olig/o
double	dipl/o
dry	xer/o
duodenum	duoden/o
dust	coni/o
ear	ot/o
eardrum	myring/o; tympan/o

MEANING	ROOT
to eat	phag/o
electricity	electr/o
embryo	embry/o
endocrine	endocrin/o
epididymis	epididym/o
epiglottis	epiglott/o
equal	is/o
esophagus	esophag/o
extremities	acr/o
eye	ocul/o; ophthalm/o; opt/o
eyelid	blephar/o; palpebr/o
fallopian tubes	salping/o
fascia	fasci/o
fat	adip/o; lip/o
fatty, yellowish plaque	ather/o
femur	femor/o
fetus	fet/o; fet/i
few	olig/o
fiber	fibr/o
fibrous tissue	fasci/o; fibr/o
fibula	fibul/o
finger and toe bones	phalang/o
flesh	sarc/o
fluid	hydr/o
foot bones	metatars/o
form	morph/o
four	quadr/i
fundus	fund/o
fungus	myc/o
gall	bil/i; chol/e
gallbladder	cholecyst/o
give birth to	par/o; part/o
gland	aden/o
glans penis	balan/o
glassy	vitre/o
glomerulus	glomerul/o
glucose	gluc/o; glyc/o
granules	granul/o
gray	glauc/o
gums	gingiv/o
hair	pil/o; trich/o
hand bones	metacarp/o
hard	kerat/o; scler/o
head	cephal/o
hearing	acoust/o; audi/o

MEANING	ROOT
heart	cardi/o; cor/o; coron/o
hidden	crypt/o
horny tissue	kerat/o
humerus	humer/o
humpback	kyph/o
ileum	ile/o
ilium	ili/o
immature	blast/o
incomplete	atel/o
inner ear	labyrinth/o
intestines	enter/o
iris	ir/o; irid/o
irregular	poikil/o
ischium	ischi/o
jejunum	jejun/o
jelly-like	vitre/o
joint	arthr/o; articul/o
ketone bodies	ket/o
kidney	ren/o; nephr/o
kneecap	patell/o
labor	par/o; part/o
labyrinth	labyrinth/o
lamina	lamin/o
larynx	laryng/o
lens	phac/o; phak/o
ligament	ligament/o
light	phot/o
lips	cheil/o
liver	hepat/o
lower back	lumb/o
lower jawbone	mandibul/o
lung	pneum/o
lungs	pulmon/o
lymph	lymph/o
lymph gland	lymphaden/o
lymph vessel	lymphangi/o
male	andr/o
man	andr/o
mandible	mandibul/o
maxilla	maxill/o
meatus	meat/o
meninges	mening/o
menses	men/o
menstruation	men/o

MEANING	ROOT
middle ear bone	staped/o
milk	lact/o
mouth	or/o; stomat/o
mucus	muc/o
muscle	my/o
nail	onych/o; ungu/o
nerve	neur/o
nerve cell	gli/o
neuroglia	gli/o
night	noct/o; nyctal/o
nose	nas/o; rhin/o
nucleus	kary/o; nucle/o
opening	meat/o
outer lower arm bone	radi/o
outer lower leg bone	fibul/o
ovary	oophor/o; ovari/o
oviducts	salping/o
oxygen	ox/i
pancreas	pancreat/o
patella	patell/o
pelvic bone	ili/o; ischi/o; pubi/o; pub/o
pelvis	pelv/i
perineum	perine/o
peritoneum	peritone/o
pharynx	pharyng/o
pleura	pleur/o
poison	toxic/o
polyp	polyp/o
potassium	kal/i
pregnancy	gravid/o
prostate gland	prostat/o
protection	immun/o
pubis	pubi/o; pub/o
pulse	sphygm/o
pupil	pupill/o
pus	py/o
radius	radi/o
rectum	proct/o; rect/o
renal pelvis	pyel/o
retina	retin/o
rib	cost/o
rosy	eosin/o
rosy red	eosin/o
round	spher/o

MEANING	ROOT
sac	cyst/o; burs/o
saliva	sial/o
salivary gland	sial/o
scale	squam/o
scapula	scapula/o
sclera	scler/o
sebum	seb/o
semen	semin/i
sex glands	gonad/o
shape	morph/o
sheath	thec/o
shoulder blade	scapula/o
sigmoid colon	sigmoid/o
silver	glauc/o
sinus	sinus/o
skeletal muscle	rhabdomy/o
skin	cut/o; cutane/o; derm/o; dermat/o
skull	crani/o
smooth muscle	leiomy/o
sodium	natr/o
sound	acoust/o; audi/o; ech/o
sour	acid/o
sperm	sperm/o; spermat/o
spermatic cord	sperm/o; spermat/o
sphere	spher/o
spider	arachn/o
spinal cord	myel/o
spleen	splen/o
stapes	staped/o
sternum	stern/o
stiff	ankyl/o
stomach	gastr/o
stone	lith/o
straight	orth/o
striated muscle	rhabdomy/o
sugar	gluc/o; glyc/o
swayback	lord/o
sweat	hidr/o; sud/o; sudor/o
sweet	gluc/o; glyc/o
tailbone	coccyg/o
tear sac	dacryocyst/o
tears	dacry/o; lacrim/o

MEANING	ROOT
tendon	ten/o; tend/o; tendin/o
tendon sheath	tenosynov/o
testicle	orch/o; orchi/o; orchid/o; test/o; testicul/o
testis	orch/o; orchi/o; orchid/o; test/o; testicul/o
thick	pachy/o
thighbone	femor/o
thin flat plate or layer	lamin/o
thirst	dips/o
thrombus	thromb/o
thymus gland	thym/o
thyroid gland	thyr/o; thyroid/o
tongue	gloss/o; lingu/o
tonsils	tonsill/o
trachea	trache/o
two	dipl/o
upper arm bone	humer/o
upper jawbone	maxill/o
ureter	ureter/o
urethra	urethr/o
urinary bladder	vesic/o; cyst/o
urinary system	ur/o
urine	ur/o
uterus	hyster/o; metr/i; metr/o; uter/o
uvea	uve/o
vagina	colp/o; vagin/o
varied	poikil/o
vas deferens	vas/o
vein	phleb/o; ven/o
ventricle	ventricul/o
vertebra	spondyl/o; vertebr/o
vertebral column	spondyl/o; vertebr/o
vessel	angi/o; vas/o
vision	opt/o
vulva	epis/o; vulv/o
water	hydr/o
watery	aque/o
white	leuk/o
woman	gyn/o; gynec/o
wrinkles	rhytid/o
wrist bones	carp/o
yellow	xanth/o

PREFIXES

MEANING	PREFIX
abnormal	dys-; mal-
above; on top of; upon	supra-; epi-
above; over; excess; excessive	super-; hyper-
after	post-; meta-
against	anti-; contra-
all	pan-
around	para-; peri-
association	sym-
away from	ab-
backward	retro-
bad	mal-
before	ante-; pre-
behind	retro-
below	infra-; hypo-; sub-
beneath	sub-
beside	para-
between	inter-
beyond	meta-
both	bi-
cancer	carcin-
change	meta-
deficient	hypo-
difficult	dys-
double	bi-
equal	iso-
excessive	poly-; hyper-; super-
fast	tachy-
first	primi-
forward	ante-
half	hemi-; semi-
hard	dura-
in	en-; eso-
in front of	pre-
inferior	infra-
inner	endo-

MEANING	PREFIX
inward	en-; eso-
large	macro-
malignant	carcin-
many	multi-; poly-
new	neo-
no	a-; an-; ana-
none	nulli-
normal	eu-
not	a-; an-; ana-; non-
old	presby-
one	mono-; primi-; uni-
opposite	contra-
out	ect-; ex-
outside	ect-
outward	ex-
painful	dys-
poor	mal-
quick	oxy-
same	eu-; iso-
self	auto-
sharp	oxy-
slow	brady-
small	micro-
sound	echo-
star	astr-
surrounding	peri-
three	tri-
through	per-
together	syn-
two	bi-
under	sub-
union	syn-
upward	retro-
with	syn-; sym-
within	en-; eso-; endo-; intra-
without	a-; an-; ana-

SUFFIXES

MEANING	SUFFIX
abnormal condition	-ia; -iasis; -osis
attraction to	-philia
binding	-desis
birth	-tocia
blood condition	-emia
breakdown	-lysis; -lytic
breathing	-pnea
carbon dioxide	-capnia
carrying	-phoresis
chest	-thorax
condition	-ia; -iasis; -osis
condition of cells	-cytosis
control; controlling	-stasis
creating a new or artificial opening	-(o)stomy
crushing	-tripsy
decreased number	-penia
deficiency	-penia
destruction	-lysis; -lytic
development	-trophy
digestion	-pepsia
dilatation	-ectasis
discharge	-(r)rhea
disease	-pathy
drooping	-ptosis
eating	-phagia
embryonic	-blast
enlarged	-megaly
excision	-ectomy
feeling	-phoria
fixation	-desis
flow	-(r)rhea
formation	-poiesis
forming	-genesis; -genic; -gen
growth	-trophy
hardening	-sclerosis
hearing	-cusis; cusia
hemorrhage	-(r)rhagia
hernia	-cele
illness	-pathy
immature	-blast
incision into	-(o)tomy

MEANING	SUFFIX
inflammation	-itis
instrument for recording	-graph
instrument for viewing	-scope
instrument to measure	-meter
labor	-tocia
like	-oid
to measure; measuring	-metry
mental state	-phoria
movement	-kinesia
muscle tone	-tonia
narrowing	-stenosis
opening	-tresia
pain	-algia; -dynia
paralysis	-plegia
partial paralysis	-paresis
pertaining to	-ac; -al; -ary; -iac; -ic; -ous
picture	-gram
pleural cavity	-thorax
process of recording	-graphy
producing	-genesis; -genic; -gen
production of	-poiesis
protein	-globin; -globulin
protrusion	-cele
record	-gram
resembling	-oid
rupture	-(r)rhexis
sagging	-ptosis
to secrete	-crine
to separate	-crit
sleep	-somnia
softening	-malacia
sound	-phonia
specialist	-(o)logist
spitting up	-ptysis
stimulating effect of a hormone	-tropin
stop; stopping	-stasis
stretching	-ectasis
study of	-(o)logy

MEANING	SUFFIX
surgical breaking	-clasis; -clasia
surgical fixation	-pexy
surgical puncture to remove fluid	-centesis
surgical removal	-ectomy
surgical repair	-plasty
suture of	-(r)rhaphy
swallowing	-phagia
transmission	-phoresis
treatment	-therapy
tumor	-oma

MEANING	SUFFIX
to turn; turning	-tropia; -tropion; -version
urine; urination	-uria
vision	-opia
visualization with a scope	-scopy
voice	-phonia
vomiting	-emesis
without feeling or sensation	-asthenia
x-ray film	-gram

Appendix B

■ PARTIAL ANSWER KEY TO CHAPTER EXERCISES AND REVIEWS

CHAPTER 1 FOUNDATIONS OF MEDICAL TERMINOLOGY

Exercise 1-1

1. auto-; self
3. ab-; away from
5. intra-; within
7. ect-; outside; outer
9. hemi-; half

Exercise 1-2

1. b	5. i	9. e
3. j	7. a	11. g

Exercise 1-3

1. epi-	7. ex- (ect-)
3. ante-	9. iso-
5. inter-	11. brady-

Exercise 1-4

1. meta-; change; after; beyond
3. semi-; half
5. sub-; below; under
7. supra-; above; on top of
9. retro-; behind; backward

Exercise 1-5

1. c	5. b	9. j
3. d	7. f	

Exercise 1-6

1. supra-	5. tachy-	9. neo-
3. retro-	7. macro-	

Exercise 1-7

1. bi-; two
3. hyper-; above; excessive
5. hypo-; deficient; below
7. an-; no; not; without
9. contra-; against; opposite

Exercise 1-8

1. epi-; supra-	19. macro-
3. ante-; pre-	21. neo-
5. inter-	23. hyper- (super-)
7. ect-; ex-	25. contra- (anti-)
9. iso-	27. carcin-
11. brady-	29. dys-
13. supra- (epi-; super-)	31. a-; an-; ana-
15. retro-	33. uni-
17. tachy-	35. dec-
	37. bi-

Exercise 1-9

1. -crine; to secrete
3. -globulins; protein
5. -graph; instrument for recording
7. -(o)logist; specialist
9. -(o)logy; study

Exercise 1-10

1. h	5. g	9. e
3. a	7. f	11. c

Exercise 1-11

1. -cyte
3. -phagia
5. -ac; -al; -ar; -ary (-ous; -iac; -ic)
7. -iac; -ic (-ac; -al; -ar; -ary; -ous)

9. -gen; -genesis; -genic
11. -gram
13. -(o)logist
15. -crine
17. -phonia

Exercise 1-12

1. -scope; instrument for viewing
3. -version; to turn
5. -thorax; chest; pleural cavity
7. -phoria; feeling; mental state
9. -therapy; treatment

Exercise 1-13

| 1. b | 5. i | 9. f |
| 3. a | 7. c | 11. g |

Exercise 1-14

1. -pnea	9. -tocia
3. -thorax	11. -tresia
5. -phoria	13. -somnia
7. -trophy	15. -therapy

Exercise 1-15

1. -oma; tumor
3. -emia; blood condition
5. -malacia; softening
7. -algia; pain
9. -megaly; enlargement

Exercise 1-16

1. -emia	7. -algia; -dynia
3. -ia; -iasis; -osis	9. -oma
5. -cele	

Exercise 1-17

1. -paresis; slight paralysis
3. -(r)rhexis; rupture
5. -phobia; abnormal fear
7. -sclerosis; hardening
9. -pathy; disease

Exercise 1-18

1. m	7. k	11. h
3. a	9. n	13. d
5. f		

Exercise 1-19

1. -(r)rhage; -(r)rhagia	7. -algia; -dynia
3. -ptosis	9. -paresis
5. -itis	

Exercise 1-20

1. -centesis; surgical puncture
3. -(o)stomy; create a new opening
5. -(o)tomy; incision into
7. -pexy; surgical fixation
9. -ectasis; stretching; dilation
11. -sclerosis; hardening
13. -tripsy; crushing; friction

Exercise 1-21

1. -osis; -iasis; -ia	11. -cytosis
3. -desis	13. -stasis
5. -lysis; -lytic	15. -tripsy
7. -(r)rhage; -(r)rhagia	17. -pepsia
9. -cyte	19. -ptosis

Exercise 1-22

1. o	7. h	13. l
3. j	9. d	15. e
5. i	11. f	

Exercise 1-23

1. -plegia	9. -(r)rhexis
3. -graphy	11. -paresis
5. -poiesis	13. -(o)logist
7. -gram	

Exercise 1-24

1. e	7. c	13. h
3. j	9. d	15. k
5. f	11. g	

Exercise 1-25

1. arthritis	7. gastrectomy
3. arthropathy	9. cardiomegaly
5. dermatopathy	

Exercise 1-26

| 1. ampullae | 5. phalanges |
| 3. foramina | 7. thrombi |

Exercise 1-27

1. arthr/o = joint; no prefix; -algia = pain; joint pain
3. cardi/o = heart; no prefix; -pathy = disease; diseased heart (heart disease)
5. cardi/o = heart; endo- = within, inner; -itis = inflammation; inflammation of the inner lining of the heart

7. gastr/o = stomach; hemi- = half; -plasty = surgical repair; surgical repair of half of the stomach

9. gastr/o = stomach; hypo- = beneath, deficient; -ic = pertaining to; pertaining to beneath the stomach

11. oste/o = bone; no prefix; -pathy = disease; disease of bone

13. arthr/o = joint; poly- = many; -itis = inflammation; inflammation of many joints

15. dermat/o = skin; no prefix; -itis = inflammation; inflammation of the skin

Exercise 1-28

1. cardi/o = heart; no prefix; -pathy = disease; cardiopathy

3. gastr/o = stomach; no prefix; -algia = pain; gastralgia (Note: By convention, -dynia, which also means pain, is not used as the prefix for this term.)

5. cardi/o = heart; peri- = around; -ac = pertaining to; pericardiac

7. dermat/o = skin; no prefix; -plasty = surgical repair; dermatoplasty

9. hepat/o = liver; sub- = under; -ic = pertaining to; subhepatic

11. gastr/o = stomach; hypo- = below; -ic = pertaining to; hypogastric (Note: By convention, hypo- is the prefix used for this term.)

13. arthr/o = joint; poly- = many; -itis = inflammation; polyarthritis

15. cardi/o = heart; endo- = within; -itis = inflammation; endocarditis

Exercise 1-29

1. cell
3. tissue
5. front side; belly
7. pelvis
9. stomach

Exercise 1-30

1. abdomen/o; lapar/o; ceil/o
3. viscer/o
5. dors/o
7. later/o
9. nucle/o
11. chondr/o
13. lumb/o

Exercise 1-31

1. pertaining to the abdomen
3. pertaining to the navel
5. front
7. pertaining to the front side or belly
9. fat; fatty
11. pertaining to the skull

Exercise 1-32

1. Connective tissue connects and supports body structures. Epithelial tissue lines and covers body cavities, organs, and glands. Muscle tissue produces movement. Nervous tissue transmits nerve impulses.

3. liquid; adipose; fibrous; cartilage; solid (any order)

Exercise 1-33

1. ventral cavity
3. thoracic cavity
5. pelvic cavity
7. cranial cavity

Exercise 1-34

1. right hypochondriac region
3. left hypochondriac region
5. umbilical region
7. right inguinal region or right iliac region
9. left inguinal region or left iliac region

Exercise 1-35

1. sagittal
3. frontal
5. superficial
7. superior
9. epigastric

Exercise 1-36

1. posterior
3. cranial
5. ventral
7. supine
9. inferior

Exercise 1-37

1. anteroposterior; from front to back
3. left upper quadrant; left side, upper area of the abdomen
5. right lower quadrant; right side, lower area of the abdomen

Chapter Review

Case 1

1. no prefix; -(r)rhea = flow, discharge; loose, watery stools
3. a- = without; no suffix; without a fever
5. no prefix; -megaly = enlarged; enlarged liver
7. an- = without; -emia = blood condition; deficiency in the quantity or quality of blood
9. no prefix; -scopy = view with a scope; visualization with a scope through the abdominal wall
11. carcin- = cancerous; -oma = tumor; malignant tumor arising from a gland

13. hypo- = below, deficient; -emia = blood condition; deficient amount of albumin in the blood
15. sub- = beneath, below; -ous = pertaining to; pertaining to below or beneath the skin

Body Cavities, Planes, and Regions

17. coronal, frontal, horizontal, midsagittal, sagittal, transverse
19. abdominal cavity, pelvic cavity, thoracic cavity

CHAPTER 2 INTRODUCTION TO ICD-9-CM CODING

Exercise 2-1

1. ICD-9-CM (International Classification of Diseases, Ninth Revision, Clinical Modification) for medical diagnoses and procedures; Current Procedural Terminology (CPT) for physician and health care provider services and procedures
3. ICD-9-CM volume 1, the *Tabular List*, is a numeric list of diseases and conditions organized into specific chapters. ICD-9-CM volume 2, *Alphabetic Index of Diseases and Injuries*, is an alphabetic list of diseases and conditions to the codes in volume 1.
5. Nonessential modifiers are terms that apply to a specific disease or condition, and do not affect code selection.
7. encoder
9. category

Exercise 2-2

1. see; see category
3. *Not elsewhere classified* means that a specific condition or diagnosis does not have a separate or individual code.
5. *Not otherwise specified* means the same thing as unspecified; the diagnostic statement does not have enough information to select a more specific code.

Exercise 2-3

1. *First-listed diagnosis* applies to physician office coding and is the reason for the health care encounter. *Principal diagnosis* applies to hospital cases and is the reason, after study, that the patient received treatment in the hospital.
3. ICD-9-CM
5. Coding Clinic

Exercise 2-4

1. ulcer
3. burns
5. cancer
7. (residual) condition that remains after the acute phase of an illness or injury has been resolved
9. partial-thickness burn characterized by blistering

Exercise 2-5

1. Procedure Codes
3. Tabular List
5. main terms
7. Centers for Medicare and Medicaid Services
9. not elsewhere classified

Chapter Review

Short Answer

1. see; see also; see condition; see category
3. not elsewhere classified
5. parentheses
7. failed
9. first-listed

ICD-9-CM Coding Practice Sets

1. pain; 786.50
3. gastroenteritis; 003.0
5. arthritis; 714.0
7. hemorrhoids; 455.3
9. bronchitis; 491.1
11. esophagitis; 530.11
13. syndrome; 625.4
15. gastroenteritis; 558.9
17. replacement; 81.54 x2
19. hysterectomy; 68.41
21. repair; 53.11
23. tonsillectomy; 28.3
25. face; 86.82

CHAPTER 3 INTRODUCTION TO CURRENT PROCEDURAL TERMINOLOGY (CPT) CODING

Exercise 3-1

1. semicolon
3. triangle
5. plus sign
7. null zero; universal no

Exercise 3-2

1. E/M codes capture information about medical services related to evaluating health status, developing a plan of care, implementing the plan, evaluating the plan, and changing the plan of care as necessary.
3. Modifier -57 identifies that an E/M service resulted in the initial decision to perform surgery.

5. Available references include section and subsection guidelines; appendix C of the CPT manual; and *CPT Assistant,* a monthly publication with practical advice from coding specialists.
7. physical status
9. anatomical site

Exercise 3-3

1. answers vary
3. *surgical package*—term used in CPT to describe services that are included in a surgical or procedural intervention; *global surgery concept*—term used by Medicare insurance programs that describes services included in a surgical or procedural intervention
5. professional component
7. unbundling
9. medicine

Chapter Review

1. Current Procedural Terminology
3. Healthcare Common Procedure Coding System
5. Evaluation/Management
7. plus sign
9. anesthesia

CPT Coding Exercises

1. hysterectomy; 58150
3. cesarean; 59514
5. biopsy; 47000
7. dermabrasion; 15783
9. excision; 30110
11. x-ray; 71020
13. autopsy; 88020
15. tonsillectomy; 42825
17. mastectomy; 19303
19. colonoscopy; 45380
21. excision; 11400
23. excision; 21025
25. arthroscopy; 29874
27. circumcision; 54150
29. ultrasound; 76801

CHAPTER 4 INTEGUMENTARY SYSTEM

Exercise 4-1

1. melan/o = black; -cyte = cell; cell with melanin (literally, black cell)
3. kerat/o = horny tissue, hard; -tome = instrument for cutting; instrument for cutting hard tissue
5. dermat/o = skin; -(o)logy = study of; study of skin
7. derm/o = skin; epi- = above, on top of; -al = pertaining to; pertaining to above or on top of the skin
9. derm/o = skin; hypo- = below, under; -ic = pertaining to; pertaining to below the skin

Exercise 4-2

1. k
3. b
5. f
7. i
9. d
11. c

Exercise 4-3

1. epidermis
3. subcutaneous (adipose) layer
5. sweat gland
7. arrector pili muscle
9. (hair) shaft
11. lunula

Exercise 4-4

1. abrasion
3. acne vulgaris
5. contusion
7. furuncle
9. cellulitis

Exercise 4-5

1. albinism
3. carbuncle
5. furuncle
7. callus
9. alopecia
11. anhidrosis

Exercise 4-6

1. *Basal cell carcinoma* is a malignant or cancerous tumor of the skin. *Actinic keratosis* is a precancerous skin condition.
3. contusion; ecchymosis

Exercise 4-7

1. laceration
3. malignant melanoma
5. jaundice
7. petechia
9. pediculosis

Exercise 4-8

1. nevus
3. pallor
5. papule
7. nevi

Exercise 4-9

1. paronychia
3. pachyderma
5. onychomalacia
7. pilonidal cyst

Exercise 4-10

1. scabies
3. pruritus
5. urticaria
7. tinea cruris
9. vesicle

Exercise 4-11

1. tinea pedis
3. vitiligo
5. tinea corporis
7. pyoderma gangrenosum

Exercise 4-12

1. xeroderma
3. psoriasis
5. seborrheic keratosis
7. sebaceous cyst

Exercise 4-13

1. dermatoplasty
3. rhytidectomy
5. dermabrasion
7. debridement
9. Mohs surgery

Exercise 4-14

1. Botox blocks nerve impulses, temporarily paralyzing facial muscles associated with wrinkles. Collagen is a "filler" that temporarily reduces wrinkles.
3. Excisional biopsy is removal of the complete tumor or lesion. Incisional biopsy is removal of a portion of the tumor or lesion.
5. incision and drainage—cutting into a cyst and draining or suctioning the contents of the cyst

Exercise 4-15

1. inflammation of the skin caused by contact with an irritant; dermatitis; 692.83
3. an infected closed sac containing hair located in the sacrococcygeal area; cyst; 685.0
5. a purulent skin lesion characterized by irregular, blue-red ulcerations; pyoderma; 686.01
7. inflammatory skin disorder characterized by redness, itching, vesicles, weeping, oozing, and crusting; eczema; 686.8
9. fungal infection of the nails; onychomycosis; 110.1
11. lice infestation associated with the skin and hair; pediculosis; 132.0
13. precancerous skin condition related to excessive sunlight exposure; wart; 702.0
15. cancerous tumor of the basal cell layer of the epidermis occurring most often on areas exposed to the sun; carcinoma; 173.3
17. a cyst composed of sebum and epithelial debris; cyst; 706.2
19. fungal infection of the foot; athlete's; 110.4
21. partial or complete loss of hair; alopecia; 704.00
23. a viral infection characterized by painful skin eruptions that follow a nerve path; herpes; 053.9
25. chronic skin condition characterized by dry, silvery scales covering red lesions; psoriasis; 696.1

Exercise 4-16

1. use of extreme cold to freeze and destroy unwanted tissue; cryosurgery; 86.3
3. procedure to remove the contents of a cyst; incision; 86.04
5. surgical procedure for removing malignant skin growths in mapped layers that involves the removal of the visible and root portions of the malignancy; Mohs operation; 86.24
7. destruction of tissue by burning or drying the tissue with an electric current; destruction; 86.3
9. procedure of placing healthy skin on a lesion or site that is unable to regenerate skin, as in third-degree burns; graft; 86.61

Exercise 4-17

1. cryosurgery; 17000
3. incision; 10060
5. Mohs microscopic surgery; 17313
7. destruction; 17110
9. full-thickness graft; 15240
11. incision and drainage; 10080
13. excision; 15931

Chapter Review

Case 1

dermatitis, pruritus; dermatitis, pruritus; 692.9, 698.9

Case 2

psoriasis; psoriasis; 696.1

Case 3

cellulitis of forearm, positive staphylococcus; cellulitis, infection; 682.3, 041.10

Case 4

keloid scar; keloid; 701.4

Case 5

impetigo; impetigo; 684

Case 6

contact dermatitis due to detergents; dermatitis; 692.0

Case 7

actinic keratosis; keratosis; 702.0

Case 8

skin fissure of right leg, positive for streptococcus; fissure; 686.9

Case 9

cellulitis of lower leg; cellulitis; 682.6

Case 10

full-thickness burn of lower leg from knee to ankle; 945.34; excisional debridement of burn of lower leg and split-thickness skin graft; debridement, split-graft; 86.22, 86.69

Case 11

sebaceous cyst, sebaceous cyst; 706.2, 706.2; excision benign cyst of back, excision benign cyst of neck; excision, excision; 86.3, 86.3

Case 12

basal cell carcinoma, right upper anterior cheek and left forearm; 173.3, 173.6; wide excision of basal cell carcinoma right upper cheek and left forearm; excision, excision; 86.4, 86.4

Case 13

status post burns to the chest and abdomen with keloid scar formation; 701.4; removal of five (5) tissue expanders, excision of keloids with flap closure of resultant defects 41 cm total length; removal, excision; 86.05, 86.3

Case 14

ingrown toenail with cellulitis; 703.0, 681.11; avulsion of nail plate great right toenail with ablation of nail bed; excision; 86.23

Case 15

excisional debridement of burn lower leg and split-thickness skin graft; debridement, split grafts; 16025, 15100, 15101 ×19

Case 16

excision of benign cyst of back, excision of benign cyst of neck; excision, excision; 11406, 11423

Case 17

wide excision of basal cell carcinoma right upper cheek and left forearm; excision, excision; 11642, 12051, 11604, 12032

Case 18

removal of five (5) tissue expanders, excision of keloids with flap closure of resultant defects 41 cm total length; removal, tissue transfer; 11971, 14300

Case 19

avulsion of nail plate great right toenail with ablation of nail bed; avulsion; 11750

Medical Terminology Challenge

1. removal, excision, or amputation of body parts, growths, or harmful substances
3. pertaining to the ability to inhibit the growth of or destroy a living organism
5. type of anesthesia during which the patient retains a level of consciousness
7. type of anesthesia during which the patient is rendered unconscious
9. an anesthetic agent
11. pertaining to the nose and trachea
13. small node-like structure
15. having, containing, or displaying color
17. type of bacteria that occurs in chains, pairs, and clusters
19. pertaining to below the cuticle

CHAPTER 5
MUSCULOSKELETAL SYSTEM

Exercise 5-1

1. oste/o = bone; -cyte = cell; bone cell
3. clavicul/o = clavicle; -al = pertaining to; pertaining to the clavicle
5. oste/o = bone; -malacia = softening; softening of bone
7. cost/o = rib; vertebr/o = vertebra; -al = pertaining to; pertaining to ribs and vertebra
9. crani/o = skull; -al = pertaining to; pertaining to the skull
11. cost/o = root; inter- = between; -al = pertaining to; pertaining to between the ribs
13. lumb/o = lower back; sacr/o = sacrum; -al = pertaining to; pertaining to the lower back and sacrum
15. mandibul/o = mandible; sub- = beneath; -al = pertaining to; pertaining to beneath the mandible
17. clavicul/o = clavicle; supra- = above; -al = pertaining to; pertaining to above the clavicle
19. vertebr/o = vertebra; inter- = between; -al = pertaining to; pertaining to between the vertebra
21. articul/o = joint; sub- = below; -ar = pertaining to; pertaining to below a joint
23. patell/o = knee; supra- = above; -ar = pertaining to; pertaining to above the knee

Exercise 5-2

1. rectus abdominis
3. gastrocnemius
5. pectoralis major
7. Achilles tendon
9. hamstring muscles
11. quadriceps femoris
13. triceps
15. tibialis anterior

Exercise 5-3

1. abduction
3. flexion

Exercise 5-4

1. tendon
3. smooth (involuntary) muscle
5. cardiac muscle

Exercise 5-5

1. tarsals
3. calcaneus
5. phalanges
7. tibia
9. synovial fluid
11. xiphoid process
13. metacarpals
15. carpals
17. fossa

Exercise 5-6

1. diaphysis
3. epiphyseal line (plate)
5. yellow bone marrow
7. spongy bone
9. articular cartilage

Exercise 5-7

1. frontal bone, occipital bone, parietal bones, temporal bones
3. carpals, humerus, metacarpals, phalanges, radius, ulna
5. ilium, ischium, coccyx, pubis

Exercise 5-8

1. dystrophy
3. ganglion
5. contraction
7. fibroma
9. hypertrophy

Exercise 5-9

1. d
3. c
5. g
7. f
9. i
11. k

Exercise 5-10

1. dermatomyositis
3. polymyositis
5. tendinitis
7. tenosynovitis

Exercise 5-11

1. ganglionectomy
3. fasciotomy
5. tenosynovectomy

Exercise 5-12

1. laboratory test that measures blood levels of an enzyme associated with muscular dystrophy
3. suture of muscle tissue or muscle wound
5. suturing a tendon

Exercise 5-13

1. dislocation
3. Colles
5. open

Exercise 5-14

1. joint pain
3. inflammation of bursa
5. softening of cartilage
7. rheumatoid arthritis of the spine

Exercise 5-15

1. i
3. g
5. a
7. d
9. j

Exercise 5-16

1. kyphosis
3. lordosis
5. osteomalacia

Exercise 5-17

1. osteitis
3. spondylitis
5. osteochondritis
7. spur

Exercise 5-18

1. e
3. b
5. g
7. c
9. h

Exercise 5-19

1. D
3. D
5. D
7. P
9. D

Exercise 5-20

1. arthrocentesis
3. osteotomy
5. arthroscopy
7. arthroplasty
9. laminectomy

Exercise 5-21

1. incision into the skull
3. using an aspiration needle to remove a sample of bone marrow
5. nuclear medicine diagnostic imaging procedure of bone
7. x-ray picture of a joint
9. permanent joining of two or more vertebrae

Exercise 5-22

1. wasting of muscular tissue; atrophy; 728.2
3. autoimmune disease that affects the musculoskeletal system, involvement includes arthralgia, polyarthritis, joint weakness, tendon contracture, and joint erosion; lupus; 710.0
5. chronic, systemic inflammatory disease of the joints, especially the joints of the hands and feet; arthritis; 714.0
7. accumulation of synovial fluid in the knee joint; Baker; 727.51
9. inflammation of the bone and bone marrow; osteomyelitis; 730.05
11. inflammation and enlargement of the bursa of the joint of the great toe; bunion; 727.1
13. a cystic bone lesion associated with abnormal bone development during childhood; dysplasia; 733.29
15. shortening of the muscles on one side of the neck; torticollis; 723.5
17. softening of cartilage; chondromalacia; 733.92
19. fracture resulting from disease; fracture; 733.14
21. chronic bone disease of the adult skeleton characterized by hyperactivity of bone cells and the replacement of bone with a softened, enlarged osseous structure; Paget disease; 731.0
23. bony growth arising from the surface of the bone; spur; 726.73
25. rupture of the intervertebral disk, which protrudes between the vertebra and puts pressure on the spinal nerve root; herniation; 722.10
27. a type of loose body that resembles grains of rice; rice bodies; 718.17
29. immobility of a joint; ankylosis; 718.52

Exercise 5-23

1. process of recording muscle contraction when receiving electrical stimulation; electromyography; 93.08
3. tear usually associated with the anterior cruciate ligament of the knee; repair; 81.45
5. surgical removal of a bursa; bursectomy; 83.5
7. process of aligning fractured bones through manual manipulation or traction without making an incision into the skin; reduction; 79.06
9. noninvasive x-ray procedure that measures bone density; scan; 88.38
11. surgical replacement of the head of the femur and the acetabulum with synthetic components; replacement; 81.51
13. surgical alignment of fractured bones; reduction; 79.25
15. visualization of the internal structures of a joint using an endoscope; removal; 80.6
17. surgical fixation, binding, or immobilization of a joint; repair; 77.56
19. surgical puncture of a joint to withdraw fluid; arthrocentesis; 81.91
21. the cutting off of a limb or part of a limb; amputation; 84.02

Exercise 5-24

1. electromyography; 95860
3. excision; 25111
5. fasciectomy; 28062
7. repair; 27407
9. Colles fracture; 25605
11. osteoplasty; 27179
13. scan; 78306
15. diskectomy; 22222

Chapter Review

Case 1

compression fracture, C-5 due to a fall from ladder; fracture, fall, accident; 805.05, E881.0, E849.9

Case 2

fibrous dysplasia; dysplasia; 733.29

Case 3

gout; gout; 274.9

Case 4

rheumatoid arthritis; arthritis; 714.0

Case 5

plantar fasciitis; fasciitis; 728.71

Case 6

fibromyalgia; fibromyalgia; 729.1

Case 7

polymyalgia rheumatica; polymyalgia; 725.

Case 8

polymyositis; polymyositis; 710.4

Case 9

herniated disk L4–L5 right; 722.10; lumbar laminectomy and diskectomy L4–L5 right; laminectomy; 80.51

Case 10

bilateral hallux valgus corrected; 735.0; bilateral correction of hallux valgus with osteotomy; bunionectomy; 77.51, 77.51

Case 11

right intertrochanteric femoral fracture; 820.21; open reduction internal fixation of right intertrochanteric fracture with DePuy sliding screw; reduction; 79.35

Case 12

torn left medial meniscus; 836.0; arthroscopic partial medial meniscectomy; meniscectomy; 80.6

Case 13

osteoarthritis acromioclavicular joint right; 715.91; Mumford procedure right shoulder distal clavicle; Mumford operation; 77.81

Case 14

lumbar laminectomy and diskectomy L4–L5 right; laminectomy; 22630

Case 15

bilateral correction of hallux valgus with osteotomy; bunion repair; 28296-50

Case 16

open reduction internal fixation of right intertrochanteric fracture with DePuy sliding screw; fracture; 27244

Case 17

arthroscopic partial medial meniscectomy; arthroscopy; 29881

Case 18

Mumford procedure right shoulder distal clavicle; Mumford operation; 23120

Medical Terminology Challenge

1. surgical repair of a joint
3. pertaining to the iliac crest
5. muscles of the shoulder responsible for circular or rotating motions
7. from the front to the side

CHAPTER 6 CARDIOVASCULAR SYSTEM

Exercise 6-1

1. cardi/o = heart; -(o)logist = specialist; heart specialist
3. angi/o = vessel; -graphy = process of recording; recording a picture of blood vessels
5. electr/o = electricity; cardi/o = heart; -graphy = process of recording; recording the electrical activity of the heart
7. cardi/o = heart; -megaly = enlarged; enlarged heart
9. cardi/o = heart; -a = noun ending; brady- = slow; slow heart (rate)
11. cardi/o = heart; -(o)logy = study of; study of the heart
13. aneurysm/o = aneurysm; -ectomy = surgical removal; surgical removal of an aneurysm
15. steth/o = chest; -scope = instrument for viewing or examination; instrument for chest examination

Exercise 6-2

1. atrioventricular node; specialized cardiac muscle tissue located between the right atrium and right ventricle, conducts nerve impulses
3. mercury; reference used for blood pressure measurement
5. left coronary artery; a major coronary (heart) artery
7. right coronary artery; a major coronary (heart) artery

Exercise 6-3

1. right and left atrium (atria)
3. tricuspid valve
5. aortic valve
7. inferior vena cava
9. right and left pulmonary vein

Exercise 6-4

1. fibrillation
3. flutter
5. arrhythmia

Exercise 6-5

1. angina pectoris
3. atrioventricular canal defect
5. cardiomegaly
7. myocardial infarction

Exercise 6-6

1. ASD
3. myocardial infarction
5. mitral valve prolapse

Exercise 6-7

1. bundle branch block; interruption of the electrical impulse to the right or left bundle branches of the ventricles
3. hypertensive heart disease; heart disease caused by high blood pressure (hypertension)
5. premature atrial contraction; atrial contractions occurring before the expected time
7. rheumatic heart disease; heart disease caused by rheumatic fever
9. abdominal aortic aneurysm; dilation or bulging of the abdominal aorta

Exercise 6-8

1. aneurysm
3. bruits
5. hypertension
7. phlebitis

Exercise 6-9

1. inflammation of the blood vessels of the heart
3. hardening of the arteries
5. obstruction of any coronary artery
7. abnormally low blood pressure

Exercise 6-10

1. cardiopulmonary resuscitation; life support procedure with artificial respiration and external cardiac compression
3. electrocardiogram; graphic record of the electrical activity of the heart
5. transesophageal echocardiography; endoscopic and ultrasonic procedure for viewing the structures of the heart

Exercise 6-11

1. X
3. (no X)
5. (no X)

Exercise 6-12

1. P
3. D
5. D
7. P
9. D

Exercise 6-13

1. x-ray of an artery
3. surgical connection of two vessels
5. removal of the lining of an artery
7. ultrasound procedure used to evaluate blood flow through vessels within solid organs

Exercise 6-14

1. abnormal narrowing of the aorta; stenosis; 424.1
3. hardening and narrowing of the arteries due to deposits of fat and other debris; arteriosclerosis; 440.0
5. presence of a blood clot in the carotid artery; thrombosis; 433.10, 433.30
7. a sudden and immediate cessation of the pumping action of the heart; arrest; 427.5
9. enlarged heart and a condition characterized by impaired cardiac pumping resulting in an inadequate ejection of blood from the ventricles of the heart; cardiomegaly, failure; 428.0, 425.4
11. any abnormal condition of the arteries of the heart; disease; 414.00
13. heart disease caused by long-term high blood pressure; disease; 402.00
15. narrowing or obstruction of the leaflets of the mitral valve due to scarring or adhesions; stenosis; 394.2
17. abnormally low blood pressure due to decreased pressure on arterial walls; hypotension; 458.0
19. inflammation of the medium and small arteries; polyarteritis; 446.0
21. inflammation of a vein; phlebitis; 451.11

Exercise 6-15

1. a procedure for life support consisting of artificial respiration and manual external cardiac compression; resuscitation; 93.93

3. a nuclear medicine study of heart function while the heart is in motion; scan; 92.05

5. process of recording an image of blood vessels using a contrast medium to enhance the visualization of the location and internal structures of the vessels; angiography; 88.57

7. graphic record of the electrical activity and contractions of the heart; electrocardiogram; 89.52

9. surgical repair of a heart valve; valvuloplasty; 35.11

Exercise 6-16

1. a diagnostic procedure during which a catheter is guided into the heart through a blood vessel for the purpose of injecting a contrast medium to view and image the heart chambers and coronary arteries; catheterization; 93501

3. a method for visualizing direction and velocity of movement; Doppler echocardiography; 93307, 93325

5. process of recording the electoral activity and contractions of the heart; electrocardiography; 93224

7. ultrasound diagnostic procedure to evaluate and record the structures and motion of the heart; echocardiography; 93312

9. nuclear medicine imaging test that shows blood flow to heart muscle during exercise; stress test; 93015

11. graphic record of the electrical activity and contractions of the heart; electrocardiogram; 93000

13. surgical repair of a heart valve; valvuloplasty; 33400

Chapter Review

Case 1

unstable angina; angina; 411.1

Case 2

acute anterior wall myocardial infarction; infarction; 410.11

Case 3

paroxysmal atrial tachycardia; tachycardia; 427.0

Case 4

abdominal aortic aneurysm; aneurysm; 441.4

Case 5

annual physical exam, bruits, smoking; exam, bruit, smokers'; V70.0, 785.9, 305.1

Case 6

restless leg syndrome; restless leg syndrome; 333.94

Case 7

hypertension, controlled; hypertension; 401.9

Case 8

superficial thrombophlebitis; thrombophlebitis; 451.9

Case 9

acute pericarditis, resolving; pericarditis; 420.90

Case 10

right bundle branch block; block; 426.4

Case 11

right carotid artery stenosis; 433.10; right carotid endarterectomy; endarterectomy; 38.12, 00.40, 00.44

Case 12

abdominal aortic aneurysm; 441.4; aneurysmectomy of abdominal aortic aneurysm with Dacron replacement graft; aneurysmectomy; 38.44

Case 13

end-stage coronary artery disease; 414.00; coronary artery bypass grafting ×2; bypass; 36.12; per ICD-9-CM Tabular Code Also, cardiopulmonary bypass 39.61

Case 14

stenosis of the proximal left anterior descending coronary artery, stenosis of the diagonal branch of the LADA diagonal branch; 414.00; percutaneous transluminal coronary angioplasty of the left anterior descending and diagonal branch of the left anterior descending coronary artery; PTCA; 00.66, 00.41, 00.44

Case 15

protracted, high degree, atrial ventricular block status post inferior myocardial infarction; 426.10, 412; insertion dual-chamber cardiac pacemaker; implant; 37.83; per ICD-9-CM Tabular Code Also, any lead insertion; 37.71, 37.72

Case 16

right carotid endarterectomy; thromboendarterectomy; 35301

Case 17

aneurysmectomy of abdominal aortic aneurysm with Dacron replacement graft; aneurysm repair; 35081

Case 18

coronary artery bypass grafting ×2; coronary artery bypass graft; 33511

Case 19

PTCA; 92982-LD, 92984

Case 20

insertion dual-chamber cardiac pacemaker; insertion; 33213

Medical Terminology Challenge

1. from front to side
3. abnormal blowing sounds
5. difficult breathing
7. pertaining to the femur
9. below the clavicle
11. examination by touching
13. through the skin
15. narrowing of a vessel
17. beneath the sternum
19. through or across the heart

CHAPTER 7 BLOOD AND LYMPH

Exercise 7-1

1. hemat/o = blood; no prefix; -(o)logy = study of; study of blood
3. erythr/o = red; cyt/o = cell; no prefix; -penia = decrease; decrease in the number of red blood cells
5. leuk/o = white; no prefix; -emia = blood condition; condition of white blood (abnormal increase in white blood cells)
7. thromb/o = clot; no prefix; -osis = condition; having a clot or thrombus
9. lymph/o = lymph; angi/o = vessel; no prefix; -gram = record, picture; record of lymph vessels
11. myel/o = bone marrow; no prefix; -oma = tumor; tumor arising from bone marrow
13. sphere/o = round; cyt/o = cell; no prefix; -osis = condition; condition of round (red blood) cells
15. no root; an- = without; -emia = blood; without blood

17. adenoid/o = adenoids; no prefix; -ectomy = surgical removal; surgical removal of adenoids
19. poikil/o = varied, irregular; cyt/o = cell; no prefix; -osis = condition; condition of irregular (blood) cells
21. no root; macro- = large; -ctye = cell; large cell
23. lymph/o = lymph; no prefix; -oid = like, resembling; resembling lymph

Exercise 7-2

1. d
3. e
5. b
7. i
9. c

Exercise 7-3

1. agglutination
3. A antigen; Rh factor present
5. B antigen; no Rh factor
7. B antibody
9. A antibody

Exercise 7-4

1. h
3. a
5. c
7. i
9. b

Exercise 7-5

1. aplastic anemia
3. CML
5. anemia
7. erythrocytopenia

Exercise 7-6

1. acquired immune deficiency syndrome; syndrome of infections associated with the final stage of HIV infection
3. acute lymphocytic leukemia; malignant condition characterized by the replacement of normal bone marrow with immature lymphocytes
5. disseminated intravascular coagulation; generalized coagulation within blood vessels

Exercise 7-7

1. iron deficiency anemia
3. dyscrasia
5. granulocytosis
7. embolism

Exercise 7-8

1. rouleaux
3. thrombus
5. septicemia

Exercise 7-9

1. leukemia
3. lymphadenopathy
5. thrombocytopenia
7. polycythemia
9. tonsillitis
11. lymphoma

Exercise 7-10

1. diff
3. platelet aggregation
5. Hgb
7. prothrombin time

Exercise 7-11

1. red blood cell; red blood cell count—measures the number of red blood cells in a sample of blood
3. complete blood count—identifies the quantity and quality of the cellular components of blood
5. measures the amount of time required for platelets to aggregate and form a platelet plug
7. evaluates the quality of a fibrin clot and platelet function
9. surgical removal of the spleen

Exercise 7-12

1. inflammation of the tonsils; tonsillitis; 463
3. a condition characterized by a proliferation of mature appearing lymphocytes in the lymph nodes, spleen, bone marrow, and blood; leukemia; 205.10
5. anemia due to a vitamin B_{12} deficiency in the blood; anemia; 281.1
7. an increase in the number of erythrocytes in the blood; polycythemia; 289.6
9. deficiency of red blood cell production due to a disorder of the bone marrow; anemia; 284.09
11. hereditary bleeding disorder caused by a deficiency of coagulation factors in the blood in which the blood does not clot; hemophilia; 286.7
13. anemia due to the premature destruction of red blood cells; anemia; 283.19
15. hereditary form of hemolytic anemia characterized by crescent-shaped erythrocytes; anemia; 282.60

Exercise 7-13

1. withdrawal of a sample of bone marrow for microscopic examination or transplant usually performed with a biopsy needle or trocar; biopsy; 41.31
3. infusion of bone marrow from a donor to a recipient, autologous, the donor and recipient are the same person; transplant; 41.01

5. excision of lymph nodes; lymphadenectomy; 40.29
7. surgical removal of tissue by incision of the spleen for microscopic examination; biopsy; 41.33
9. administration of blood or components of blood to replace the loss of blood; transfusion; 99.05

Exercise 7-14

1. harvesting; 38230; report only once per day regardless of the quantity of bone marrow/stem cells manipulated
3. excision; 38525
5. lymphangiography; 75807
7. thromboplastin; 85730
9. splenorrhaphy; 38115

Chapter Review

Case 1

lymphadenopathy, splenomegaly, atypical lymphocytosis; lymphadenopathy, splenomegaly, lymphocytosis; 785.6, 789.2, 288.61

Case 2

iron deficiency anemia; anemia; 280.9

Case 3

malignant lymphoma, undifferentiated Burkitt type; lymphoma; 200.20

Case 4

pernicious anemia, hypogammaglobulinemia; anemia, hypogammaglobulinemia; 281.0, 279.00

Case 5

idiopathic thrombocytopenic purpura; purpura, 287.31

Case 6

relapsed acute myelocytic leukemia, severe pancytopenia due to bone marrow hypoplasia, secondary to chemotherapy; leukemia, pancytopenia, hypoplasia; 205.00, 284.1, 284.89, E933.1

Case 7

disseminated intravascular coagulation, ulcerative colitis, femoral artery thrombosis; coagulation, colitis, thrombosis; 286.6, 556.9, 444.22

Case 8

idiopathic thrombocytopenic purpura; 287.31; splenectomy, transfusion of platelets; splenectomy, transfusion; 41.5, 99.05

Case 9

Hodgkin disease; 201.90; bone marrow harvest; harvest; 41.91

Case 10

abscess, axillary lymph node; 683; incision and drainage lymph node abscess; incision and drainage; 40.0

Case 11

severe blood loss anemia due to uncontrolled bleeding, hemophilia A; 280.0, 286.0; blood transfusion; transfusion; 99.06

Case 12

ruptured spleen due to blunt trauma; 865.04, E819.9, E849.9; splenorrhaphy, partial splenectomy; repair; 41.95

Case 13

splenectomy, transfusion of platelets; splenectomy, transfusion; 38100, 36430

Case 14

bone marrow harvest; harvesting; 38230

Case 15

incision and drainage lymph node abscess; incision and drainage; 38305

Case 16

blood transfusion; transfusion; 36430

Case 17

splenorrhaphy, partial splenectomy; repair; 38115

Medical Terminology Challenge

1. X
3. (no X)
5. (no X)
7. (no X)
9. X

CHAPTER 8 RESPIRATORY SYSTEM

Exercise 8-1

1. pharyng/o = pharynx; no prefix; -itis = inflammation; inflammation of the pharynx
3. anthrac/o = coal; no prefix; -osis = condition; condition of coal in the lungs
5. no root; eu- = normal; -pnea = breathing; normal breathing
7. rhin/o = nose; no prefix; -(r)rhagia = hemorrhage; hemorrhage from the nose
9. alveol/o = alveolus; no prefix; -ar = pertaining to; pertaining to the alveolus
11. pneum/o = air; no prefix; -thorax = chest; air in the chest
13. hem/o = blood; no prefix; -ptysis = coughing up, spitting up; spitting up blood

Exercise 8-2

1. e
3. f
5. k
7. j
9. l
11. h

Exercise 8-3

1. nose
3. paranasal sinus
5. trachea
7. bronchus (bronchi)
9. alveolus (alveoli)

Exercise 8-4

1. dyspnea
3. rhonchi
5. hypocapnia
7. rales
9. aphonia

Exercise 8-5

1. rhinorrhea
3. hyperpnea
5. aspirate; aspiration
7. mucopurulent

Exercise 8-6

1. bronchiectasis
3. hemothorax
5. adenoiditis
7. hemoptysis

Exercise 8-7

1. emphysema
3. influenza
5. cystic fibrosis
7. COPD

Exercise 8-8

1. acute respiratory distress syndrome; adult respiratory distress syndrome—respiratory failure associated with a variety of acute conditions that directly or indirectly injure the lungs
3. incomplete expansion of the lungs
5. lung cancer
7. involuntary spasm of the bronchi
9. nosebleed

Exercise 8-9

1. pneumonoconiosis
3. nasopharyngitis
5. pleurisy; pleuritis
7. tracheostenosis

Exercise 8-10

1. obstructive sleep apnea—temporary absence of breathing during sleep due to repetitive pharyngeal collapse
3. pneumonia caused by the *Legionella pneumophila* bacteria
5. whooping cough, highly contagious respiratory disease
7. tuberculosis—contagious disease caused by a specific bacteria, pulmonary tuberculosis affects the lungs
9. heart failure caused by pulmonary disease
11. severe acute respiratory distress syndrome—syndrome caused by a coronavirus

Exercise 8-11

1. (a) diagnostic imaging test that shows cross-section images of the lungs; (b) nuclear medicine study to detect abnormalities related to air or blood flow to and from the lungs
3. (a) measuring the oxygen saturation of the blood; (b) measuring breathing or lung volumes

Exercise 8-12

1. CT scan
3. laryngoscopy
5. pulmonary function tests
7. thoracotomy

Exercise 8-13

1. (a) creation of a new opening for the trachea; (b) incision into the trachea
3. (a) surgical removal of a portion of the lung; (b) surgical removal of a lung

Exercise 8-14

1. laryngotracheotomy
3. laryngectomy
5. turbinectomy
7. laryngoplasty
9. septoplasty

Exercise 8-15

1. inflammation of the larynx and respiratory dysfunction that produces reduced air flow; laryngitis; 464.01
3. air or gas in the pleural cavity occurring secondary to parenchymal lung disease; pneumothorax; 512.8
5. acute inflammation of the lining membrane of any sinus; sinusitis; 461.1, 461.0
7. increase in size of the tonsils and adenoids; hypertrophy; 474.10
9. diffuse airway inflammation caused by a variety of stimuli that results in bronchoconstriction, bronchospasm, wheezing, and dyspnea; asthma; 493.10
11. respiratory failure associated with a variety of acute conditions that directly or indirectly injure the lung; syndrome; 518.5
13. difficulty breathing at night; dyspnea; 786.09
15. increased pressure in the arterioles and arteries that supply the lungs; hypertension; 416.0
17. chronic bronchitis characterized by airflow obstruction; bronchitis; 491.20
19. distention and destruction of alveolar walls causing decreased elasticity of the lungs; emphysema; 492.0

Exercise 8-16

1. a process of visualization of the bronchus used as treatment or surgical approach; bronchoscopy; 33.22
3. sinusotomy of the maxillary sinus with removal of the membrane lining of the maxillary cavity; Caldwell-Luc operation; 22.39
5. surgical repair of the nasal septum; septoplasty; 21.5
7. surgical removal of the larynx; hemilaryngectomy; 30.1
9. surgical removal of the tonsils and adenoid glands; tonsillectomy; 28.3
11. removal of fibrous material from the outer surface of an organ; decortications; 34.51
13. to regulate, restrain, correct, restore to normal a nosebleed; control; 21.03
15. surgical removal of the larynx; laryngectomy; 30.4

Exercise 8-17

1. thoracentesis; 32421
3. tracheostomy; 31600
5. laryngectomy; 31360
7. transplantation, extracorporeal circulation; 32853, 33960
9. excision; 30115
11. nuclear medicine; 78588
13. x-ray; 71020
15. oximetry; 94760

Chapter Review

Case 1

chronic sinusitis in the maxillary and frontal areas; sinusitis; 473.0, 473.1

Case 2

acute lower respiratory infection with pleurisy; infection, pleurisy; 519.8, 511.0

Case 3

laryngeal airway obstruction secondary to bilateral true vocal cord paralysis; obstruction, paralysis; 478.79, 478.33

Case 4

severe bronchospasm, status asthmaticus; asthma; 493.91; ICD-9-CM Tabular Excludes Note states that 519.11 diagnosis for bronchospasm should not be used with 493.91.

Case 5

spontaneous pneumothorax; pneumothorax; 512.8

Case 6

left lower pneumonia due to actinomycosis, acute bronchitis, chronic obstructive pulmonary disease, cor pulmonale; pneumonia, bronchitis, cor pulmonale; 039.1, 491.22, 416.9

Case 7

persistent cough, shortness of breath, abnormal chest x-ray; cough, shortness, abnormal; 786.2, 786.05, 793.1; Official Coding Guidelines states do not code unconfirmed diagnoses in the outpatient setting.

Case 8

nodule, left lung lower lobe, smoking; 518.89, 305.1; video-assisted thoracoscopy, left side, wedge resection biopsy left lower lobe times two, bronchoscopy right upper lobe with transbronchial biopsy times two; resection, biopsy; 32.20, 33.27

Case 9

maxillary sinusitis, obstruction of the natural ostia, ethmoiditis; 473.0, 478.19, 473.2; bilateral functional endoscopic sinus surgery, bilateral enlargement of the natural ostia and anterior ethmoidectomy; ethmoidectomy; 22.63, 22.63

Case 10

deviated nasal septum, chronic maxillary sinusitis, turbinate hypertrophy with nasal obstruction; 470, 473.0, 478.0, 478.19; septoplasty, bilateral submucous resection of the inferior turbinates; septoplasty, turbinectomy; 21.88, 21.69, 21.69

Case 11

left thoracic fibrinous hemothorax; 511.89; posterolateral thoracotomy with evacuation of loculated hemothorax; decortication; 34.51

Case 12

bronchogenic carcinoma, right upper lobe, occluded right upper lobe posterior and superior segments; 162.3, 518.89; flexible fiberoptic bronchoscopy with radiation catheter placement right upper lobe, placement of radiation beads; implantation; 92.27

Case 13

video-assisted thoracoscopy left side, wedge resection biopsy left lower lobe times two, bronchoscopy right upper lobe with transbronchial biopsy times two; thoracoscopy, bronchoscopy; 32657, 31628; report once regardless of how many biopsies.

Case 14

bilateral functional endoscopic sinus surgery, bilateral enlargement of the natural ostia and anterior ethmoidectomy; ethmoidectomy; 31254, 31254

Case 15

septoplasty, bilateral submucous resection of the inferior turbinates; septoplasty, turbinate; 30520, 30140, 30140

Case 16

posterolateral thoracotomy with evacuation of loculated hemothorax, decortication of fibrothorax, and insertion of two 36 French chest tubes; decortication; 32320

Case 17

flexible fiberoptic bronchoscopy with radiation catheter placement, right upper lobe, placement of radiation beads; bronchoscopy; 31643, 77761

Medical Terminology Challenge

1. presence of polyps
3. surgical removal of the ethmoid bone
5. within the trachea
7. maxillary sinus wall toward the midline of the face/body
9. removal of an endotracheal tube

CHAPTER 9 DIGESTIVE SYSTEM

Exercise 9-1

1. abdomin/o = abdomen; no prefix; -al = pertaining to; pertaining to the abdomen
3. bucc/o = cheek; no prefix; -al = pertaining to; pertaining to the cheek
5. ile/o = ileum; cec/o = cecum; no prefix; -al = pertaining to; pertaining to the ileum and cecum
7. peritone/o = peritoneum; no prefix; -al = pertaining to; pertaining to the peritoneum
9. proct/o = rectum; no prefix; -(o)logy = study of; study of the rectum
11. hepat/o = liver; bil/i = bile; no prefix; -ary = pertaining to; pertaining to the liver and bile (ducts)
13. no root; dys- = difficult, painful; -pepsia = digestion; difficult digestion
15. sial/o = salivary gland, saliva; lith/o = stone; no prefix; -iasis = condition; condition of salivary gland stones
17. col/o = colon; rect/o = rectum; no prefix; -al = pertaining to; pertaining to the colon and rectum
19. col/o = colon; hemi- = half; -ectomy = surgical removal; surgical removal of half of the colon
21. choledoch/o = common bile duct; lith/o = stone; no prefix; -iasis = condition; stones in the common bile duct

Exercise 9-2

1. mouth
3. esophagus
5. small intestine
7. anus
9. gallbladder

Exercise 9-3

1. common bile duct (pancreas, gallbladder)
3. small intestine
5. liver
7. gallbladder

Exercise 9-4

1. c
3. f
5. e
7. m
9. b
11. a
13. h

Exercise 9-5

1. ascites
3. eructation
5. dyspepsia
7. hematochezia
9. hematemesis

Exercise 9-6

1. diverticulum (diverticuli pl.)
3. aphthous stomatitis
5. Crohn disease
7. diarrhea
9. anorexia nervosa
11. cholelithiasis

Exercise 9-7

1. gallbladder; inflammation of the gallbladder
3. stomach, intestine; inflammation of the stomach and intestines (usually the small intestine)
5. duodenum; erosion of the lining of the duodenum

Exercise 9-8

1. ileus
3. IBS
5. Schatzki ring
7. intussusception

Exercise 9-9

1. hernia
3. herpetic stomatitis
5. gingivitis
7. pruritus ani
9. sialolithiasis

Exercise 9-10

1. occult blood test
3. cholangiography
5. small bowel follow-through

Exercise 9-11

1. bile ducts
3. bile ducts and pancreas
5. rectum
7. small intestine
9. esophagus, stomach, small intestine

Exercise 9-12

1. abdomen; incision into the abdominal cavity
3. gallbladder; surgical removal of the gallbladder
5. bile ducts; incision into the bile ducts to remove stones
7. esophagus, stomach; repairing the esophagus and stomach

Exercise 9-13

1. colostomy
3. abdominoplasty
5. bariatric surgery (gastric bypass; gastric banding)
7. appendectomy
9. gastrectomy

Exercise 9-14

1. nasogastric intubation
3. palatoplasty
5. total parenteral nutrition
7. laparoscopic adjustable gastric banding

Exercise 9-15

1. stomach, duodenum; creation of a new opening between the stomach and duodenum
3. tongue; suturing the tongue
5. ileum; creation of a new opening between the ileum and abdominal wall
7. uvula, soft palate, pharynx; surgical repair of the uvula, soft palate, and pharynx

Exercise 9-16

1. chronic gastritis with atrophy of the mucous membrane and destruction of the peptic glands; gastritis; 535.10
3. protrusion of an organ or part of an organ in the inguinal region; hernia; 550.92
5. ulceration of the mucous membrane of the duodenum with bleeding; ulcer; 532.60
7. inflammatory noninfectious ulcerated lesion of the lips, tongue, and mouth; stomatitis; 528.2
9. inflammation of the vermiform with perforation of the organ; appendicitis; 540.0
11. formation or presence of bile stones in the gallbladder with inflammation of the gallbladder; cholelithiasis; 574.00
13. inflammation and bleeding of the stomach due to alcoholism; gastritis, alcoholism; 535.31, 303.90
15. inflammation of the esophagus and moving backward of gastric contents into the esophagus, herniation of a portion of the stomach through the esophageal opening in the diaphragm; esophagitis, hernia; 530.11, 553.3
17. complete or partial interruption of the movement of the contents of the small or large intestine due to a knotting and twisting of the bowel; obstruction; 560.2
19. presence of white spots or patches on the mucous membrane of the tongue or cheek; leukoplakia; 528.6
21. presence of a large number of polyps in the large intestine; polyposis; 211.3
23. inflammation of the peritoneum; peritonitis; 567.21

Exercise 9-17

1. surgical repair of a hernia; herniorrhaphy; 53.12
3. surgical removal of the gallbladder; cholecystectomy, exploration; 51.23, 51.11
5. surgical removal of the gallbladder and removal of gallstones through an incision into the common bile duct; cholecystectomy, choledocholithotomy; 51.22, 51.41
7. surgical repair of an abnormal narrowing of a duct or canal of the esophagus; repair; 42.85
9. endoscopic visualization and examination of the esophagus, stomach, and duodenum with stomach biopsy; esophagogastroduodenoscopy; 45.16
11. excision of the pylorus and antrum and partial closure of the gastric end with end-to-end anastomosis of stomach and duodenum; gastrectomy; 43.6
13. process of removing liver tissue from living patients for microscopic diagnostic exam obtained through the skin; biopsy; 50.11
15. suture repair of a hernia; repair; 53.41
17. crushing of gallstones using ultrasound and shock waves; lithotripsy; 98.59
19. surgical division of postinflammatory or postoperative adhesions; lysis; 54.51

Exercise 9-18

1. excision; 43610
3. repair; 49561
5. dilation, esophagogastroduodenoscopies; 43450, 43235
7. cholangiopancreatography; 43260
9. ileostomy; 44312
11. incision and drainage; 42700
13. biopsy; 47000
15. laparoscopy; 49320

Chapter Review

Case 1

intestinal Hirschsprung disease, status post gastrostomy; disease, gastrostomy; 751.3, V44.1

Case 2

constricting lesion, lower sigmoid colon; lesion; 569.89

Case 3

bilateral inguinal hernias; hernia; 550.92

Case 4

gallbladder, hemorrhagic chronic cholecystitis with cholelithiasis; cholelithiasis; 574.10

Case 5

reflux esophagitis duodenitis, and hiatal hernia; esophagitis, duodenitis, hernia; 530.11, 535.60, 553.3

Case 6

abdominal pain, nausea, flatulence, change of bowel habits; pain, nausea, flatulence, change of; 789.00, 787.02, 787.3, 787.99

Case 7

adenomatous polyps splenic flexure, hyperplastic sigmoid polyp; polyp; 211.3

Case 8

cholecystitis, cholelithiasis and common duct stone; 574.70; cholecystectomy and common bile duct exploration; cholecystectomy, exploration; 51.22, 51.51

Case 9

foreign body in the upper esophagus; 935.1; upper esophagoscopy and removal of foreign body; removal; 98.02

Case 10

morbid obesity; 278.01; open Roux-en-Y gastric bypass; Roux-en-Y operation; 44.39

Case 11

diaphragmatic hernia with incarceration of the transverse colon; 553.3, 552.9; abdominal exploration with repair of hiatus paraesophageal-type hernia, partial colectomy transverse colon; repair, colectomy; 53.72, 45.74

Case 12

rectosigmoid colon cancer, umbilical hernia; 154.0, 553.1; exploratory laparotomy with low anterior resection with primary anastomosis of the colon, umbilical hernia repair; resection, anastomosis, repair; 48.63, 45.94, 53.49

Case 13

cholecystectomy and common bile duct exploration; cholecystectomy; 47610

Case 14

upper esophagoscopy and removal of foreign body; esophagoscopies; 43215

Case 15

open Roux-en-Y gastric bypass; Roux-en-Y procedure; 43846

Case 16

abdominal exploration with repair of hiatus paraesophageal-type hernia, partial colectomy transverse colon; repair, colectomy; 39502, 44140

Case 17

exploratory laparotomy with low anterior resection with primary anastomosis of the colon, umbilical hernia repair; excision, repair; 44140, 49585

Medical Terminology Challenge

1. surgical joining or connection between blood vessels or ducts
3. cricoid cartilage and pharynx
5. catheter placed into the bladder
7. pancreatic hormone
9. trapped
11. within the mouth
13. mucous membrane
15. inflammation of the parotid gland
17. pertaining to a serous membrane
19. face up

CHAPTER 10 ENDOCRINE SYSTEM

Exercise 10-1

1. cortic/o = cortex; no prefix; -al = pertaining to; pertaining to the cortex (of an organ)
3. endocrin/o = endocrine; no prefix; -(o)logist = specialist; endocrine specialist
5. thyroid/o = thyroid gland; eu- = normal; no suffix; normal thyroid
7. glyc/o = glucose; hyper- = excessive; -emia = blood condition; increased glucose in the blood
9. calc/i = calcium; hypo- = decreased; -emia = blood condition; decreased calcium in the blood
11. kal/i = potassium; hypo- = decreased; -emia = blood condition; decreased potassium in the blood
13. dips/o = thirst; poly- = many, excessive; -a = noun ending; excessive thirst
15. adrenal/o = adrenal gland; no prefix; -ectomy = surgical excision; surgical excision of the adrenal gland

Exercise 10-2

1. c
3. b
5. h
7. a

Exercise 10-3

1. pineal gland
3. thyroid gland
5. pancreas
7. ovaries
9. parathyroid gland

Exercise 10-4

1. c
3. g
5. a
7. d
9. c
11. h
13. j
15. c

Exercise 10-5

1. Addison disease
3. DM type 1
5. Hashimoto disease

Exercise 10-6

1. hypercalcemia
3. exophthalmos; exophthalmia
5. adrenomegaly
7. goiter
9. adrenalitis

Exercise 10-7

1. ketoacidosis
3. virilism
5. hypokalemia
7. pancreatitis
9. hyperthyroidism

Exercise 10-8

1. c
3. d
5. h
7. i
9. a
11. f

Exercise 10-9

1. no X
3. X
5. no X

Exercise 10-10

1. hyperplasia of the thyroid gland due to a lack of dietary iodine; goiter; 240.0
3. enlargement of the bones of the extremities and face due to excessive secretion of growth hormone; acromegaly; 253.0
5. absence of insulin production due to pancreatic beta-cell dysfunction or destruction; diabetes; 250.01
7. abnormal increase of cholesterol in the blood; hypercholesterolemia; 272.0
9. the most severe form of adult hypothyroidism, may lead to coma and death; myxedema; 244.9
11. an autoimmune disease in which the immune system produces antibodies that target thyroid cells; Hashimoto disease; 245.2
13. deficiency in the secretion of adrenal cortex hormones characterized by decreased functioning of the adrenal cortex; Addison; 255.41
15. inflammation of the joints in gout; arthritis; 274.0
17. abnormal decrease of calcium in the blood; hypocalcemia; 275.41
19. a congenital metabolic disorder inherited as an autosomal trait in which secretions of exocrine glands are abnormal; fibrosis; 277.00

Exercise 10-11

1. surgical removal of one or all of the parathyroid glands; parathyroidectomy; 06.81
3. any method in which the specimen for biopsy is removed by aspirating it through an appropriate needle or trocar that pierces the skin; biopsy; 06.11
5. surgical removal by thorascopic approach of the thymus; excision; 07.84

Exercise 10-12

1. needle biopsy; 60100
3. lobectomy; 60220
5. thyroidectomy; 60254
7. glucose; 82951

Chapter Review

Case 1

hyperglycemia; hyperglycemia; 790.29

Case 2

cold thyroid nodules; nodule; 241.0

Case 3

hyperthyroidism with a nodular goiter; hyperthyroidism; 242.30

Case 4

idiopathic hypopituitarism; hypopituitarism; 253.2

Case 5

adrenal virilism syndrome with hirsutism; virilism, hirsutism; 255.2, 704.1

Case 6

follicular carcinoma, both lobes of the thyroid; 193; total thyroidectomy with isthmusectomy, frozen section, and lymph node resection and frozen section; thyroidectomy; 06.4

Case 7

parathyroidectomy; 60500

Case 8

scan; 78000

Case 9

aspiration; 60100

Case 10

scanning, radioisotope; 78070

Case 11

excision; 60521

Case 12

excision; 61546

Case 13

total thyroidectomy with isthmusectomy, frozen section, and lymph node resection and frozen section; thyroidectomy; 60252

Medical Terminology Challenge

1. enlargement of the bones of the face and extremities; pituitary gland
3. insulin-dependent diabetes mellitus; pancreas
5. excessive production of cortisol; adrenal cortex
7. autoimmune disease affecting the thyroid gland; thyroid gland

CHAPTER 11 GENITOURINARY SYSTEM

Exercise 11-1

1. spermat/o = sperm; no prefix; -genesis = producing; producing sperm
3. no root; dys- = difficult, painful; -uria = urine; difficult urination
5. hemat/o = blood; no prefix; -uria = urine; blood in the urine
7. nephr/o = kidney; no prefix; -ptosis = sagging, drooping; sagging kidney
9. orchid/o = testes; no prefix; -itis = inflammation; inflammation of the testes

Exercise 11-2

1. (right) kidney
3. urinary bladder
5. adrenal medulla

Exercise 11-3

1. a	5. i	9. j
3. g	7. b	11. c

Exercise 11-4

1. diuretic
3. dysuria
5. nephroma
7. nephritis

Exercise 11-5

1. nephromegaly
3. nocturia
5. oliguria

Exercise 11-6

1. polyuria
3. ureterocele
5. pyelonephritis
7. urethrocystitis
9. uremia

Exercise 11-7

1. intravenous pyelography
3. voiding cystourethrography
5. urinary catheterization

Exercise 11-8

1. (a) recording the activity and condition of the urinary bladder and urethra during voiding (urination); (b) measuring and recording urinary bladder pressure during voiding
3. (a) color, turbidity, specific gravity, and pH; (b) presence of glucose, blood, protein, or other substances in the urine

Exercise 11-9

1. cystolithotomy
3. nephropexy
5. cystopexy
7. urethrostomy

Exercise 11-10

1. cystostomy
3. cystorrhaphy
5. meatotomy
7. nephrolithotomy
9. pyelolithotomy

Exercise 11-11

1. vas deferens
3. urethra
5. glans penis
7. scrotum
9. epididymis

Exercise 11-12

1. benign prostatic hypertrophy
3. phimosis
5. testicular carcinoma
7. cryptorchidism

Exercise 11-13

1. (a) absence of one or both testes; (b) absence or lack of sperm
3. (a) accumulation of fluid in the scrotum or spermatic cord; (b) enlarged, swollen, and twisted veins of the spermatic cord

Exercise 11-14

1. circumcision
3. prostate-specific antigen
5. vasectomy
7. orchidectomy

Exercise 11-15

1. inflammation and bleeding of the glomerulus of the kidneys; glomerulonephritis; 583.9
3. renal failure of sudden onset, such as from physical trauma, infection, inflammation, or toxicity; failure; 584.9
5. chronic inflammation of the epididymis; epididymitis; 604.90
7. a urinary calculus found in the renal pelvis and shaped like the antlers of a stag because it extends into multiple calices; calculus; 592.0
9. the passage of urine from the bladder back into a ureter; reflux; 593.70
11. infection of the urinary tract that can include the urethra, urinary bladder, and ureters; infection; 599.0, 041.4
13. accumulation of fluid in the scrotum or along the spermatic cord; hydrocele; 603.9
15. a developmental defect characterized by failure of one or both of the testes to descend into the scrotum; cryptorchidism; 752.51

Exercise 11-16

1. surgical fixation in the scrotum of an undescended testis; orchiopexy; 62.5, 62.5
3. exploration combined with biopsy to determine the type and extent of neoplasms, both deep and superficial; biopsy; 63.01
5. excision of a hydrocele; hydrocelectomy; 63.1
7. the physical restoration of a developmental anomaly in which the urethra opens inferior to its usual location; repair; 58.45
9. the removal of all or part of the prepuce or foreskin; circumcision; 64.0
11. performed through the skin, the removal and examination, usually microscopic, of tissue from the living body; biopsy; 55.23

13. any of various methods of surgical fixation of the urethrovesical junction area and the bladder neck to restore the neck to a high retropubic position; suspension; 57.89

15. cystourethrography in which radiographs are made before, during, and after urination; cystourethrogram; 87.76

Exercise 11-17

1. hypospadias; 54300
3. prostate; 52601
5. biopsy; 54865
7. circumcision; 54150
9. cystectomy; 51565
11. urography; 74400
13. urethrectomy; 53215
15. cystometrogram; 51725

Chapter Review

Case 1

urinary tract infection and pyuria; infection, pyuria; 599.0, 791.9

Case 2

enlarged prostate with bladder neck obstruction; enlarged, obstruction; 600.01, 596.0 per Use Additional Code note in ICD-9-CM Tabular

Case 3

enuresis; enuresis; 788.30

Case 4

polycystic kidney disease; disease; 753.12

Case 5

cystitis; cystitis; 595.9

Case 6

balanitis; balanitis; 607.1

Case 7

right kidney stone; 592.0; extracorporeal shock wave lithotripsy; lithotripsy; 98.51

Case 8

nephroptosis and hydronephrosis; 593.0, 591; nephropexy; 55.7

Case 9

left ureterolithiasis; 592.1; cystoscopy and left retrograde pyelogram, left ureteroscopic stone extraction with placement of a left double-J ureteral stent; pyelogram, removal, insertion; 87.74, 56.0, 59.8

Case 10

stress urinary incontinence; 625.6; cystoscopy and raised bladder neck suspension; repair; 59.79

Case 11

cryptorchidism; 752.51; bilateral orchiopexy; orchiopexy; 62.5, 62.5

Case 12

benign prostatic hypertrophy and bladder neck obstruction; 600.01, 596.0; cystourethroscopy and transurethral resection of the prostate; resection; 60.29

Case 13

extracorporeal shock wave lithotripsy of right kidney stone; lithotripsy; 50590

Case 14

nephropexy; nephropexy; 50400

Case 15

cystoscopy and left retrograde pyelogram, left ureteroscopic stone extraction with placement of a left double-J ureteral stent; removal, insertion; 52352, 52332; per National Correct Coding Initiative (NCCI) edits the pyelogram is not reported as a separate procedure

Case 16

cystoscopy and raised bladder neck suspension; urethropexy; 51840

Case 17

bilateral orchiopexy; orchiopexy; 54640, 54640

Case 18

cystourethroscopy and transurethral resection of the prostate; prostate; 52601

Medical Terminology Challenge

Case A

1. twisting of the testes and spermatic cord
3. removal of the left testicular appendix

5. face-up
7. to build a surface

Case B

1. malignant tumor arising from glandular tissue
3. projecting a radiographic image on a fluorescent screen
5. device for draining urine from the urinary bladder
7. section of the urethra toward the front

CHAPTER 12 FEMALE REPRODUCTIVE SYSTEM

Exercise 12-1

1. men/o = menses, menstruation; no prefix; -arche = beginning, onset; onset of menses
3. lapar/o = abdominal wall; no prefix; -(o)scopy = process of visualization with a scope; visualization through the abdominal wall with a scope
5. fibr/o = fibrous tissue; no prefix; -oid = like, resembling; resembling fibrous tissue
7. salping/o = fallopian tube; no prefix; -itis = inflammation; inflammation of the fallopian tubes
9. cervic/o = cervix; no prefix; -al = pertaining to; pertaining to the cervix

Exercise 12-2

1. uterus
3. vagina
5. fimbriae
7. myometrium
9. graafian follicle

Exercise 12-3

1. perineum
3. clitoris
5. lactation
7. menarche
9. Bartholin glands

Exercise 12-4

1. cervical carcinoma (cancer)
3. oligomenorrhea
5. menorrhagia
7. menometrorrhagia
9. premenstrual syndrome

Exercise 12-5

1. c
3. d
5. k
7. g
9. h
11. j

Exercise 12-6

1. mammography
3. tubal ligation
5. conization; cone biopsy
7. hysterosalpingography
9. uteropexy

Exercise 12-7

1. uterus
3. ovary

Exercise 12-8

1. part/o = give birth; ante- = before; -um = pertaining to; pertaining to giving birth
3. gravid/o = pregnancy; multi- = many; -a = noun ending; many pregnancies
5. gravid/o = pregnancy; nulli- = none; -a = noun ending; never having been pregnant
7. part/o = give birth; post- = after; -um = pertaining to; pertaining to after giving birth
9. par/o = give birth; primi- = first, one; -a = noun ending; first time giving birth
11. nat/o = birth; peri- = around; -al = pertaining to; pertaining to the time around birth

Exercise 12-9

1. umbilicus (umbilical cord)
3. fetus
5. amnion
7. chorion
9. amniotic sac (fetal membrane)

Exercise 12-10

1. Multigravida means many pregnancies; nulligravida means never having been pregnant.
3. Primigravida is a first pregnancy; primipara is a first childbirth.

Exercise 12-11

1. Chadwick sign
3. neonatal intensive care unit (NICU)
5. Braxton-Hicks contraction
7. lochia

Exercise 12-12

1. abortion
3. gestational diabetes
5. breech birth
7. hyperemesis gravidarum

Exercise 12-13

1. e   5. g   9. d
3. i   7. a

Exercise 12-14

1. amniocentesis   7. cerclage
3. episiotomy   9. cesarean section
5. pelvimetry

Exercise 12-15

1. general term that includes mastalgia, breast cysts, and nondescript lumpiness of the breast; disease; 610.1
3. inflammation of the vulva and vagina; vulvovaginitis, infection; 616.10, 041.4
5. forward displacement of the uterus; anteflexion; 621.6
7. caused by human papilloma virus infection or by an adenocarcinoma; carcinoma; 233.1
9. a cyst formed by the enlargement of a graafian follicle; cyst; 620.0
11. spontaneous abortion is commonly called a miscarriage; abortion; 634.91
13. a condition in which there is bloody discharge from the uterus but the loss of blood is usually less than in inevitable abortion and there is no dilatation of the cervix; abortion; 640.03
15. a cystic mass resembling a cluster of grapes that develops in place of a placenta and fetus; mole; 630
17. incision into the abdominal wall and uterus to deliver a baby; delivery; 652.31
19. premature separation of the placenta from the uterine wall; placenta; 641.20

Exercise 12-16

1. x-ray examination of the soft tissue of the breast; mammogram; 87.37, 87.37
3. surgical removal of the uterus, fallopian tubes, and ovaries; hysterectomy, salpingo-oophorectomy; 68.59, 65.61
5. widening of the cervical canal followed by scraping of the uterine lining; dilation and curettage, uterus; 69.09
7. incision through the abdominal wall and the uterus for extraction of the fetus; cesarean section; 74.1

9. surgical removal of the breast and surrounding tissue, allows the chest muscles that move the arm to be preserved; mastectomy; 85.43
11. percutaneous transabdominal puncture of the uterus to obtain amniotic fluid; amniocentesis; 75.1

Exercise 12-17

1. laparoscopy; 58670   7. insertion; 58300
3. sampling; 59015   9. cerclage; 59325
5. hysterectomy; 58150

Chapter Review

Case 1

menometrorrhagia; menometrorrhagia; 626.2

Case 2

hemorrhagic follicular cyst and chronic oophoritis; cyst, oophoritis; 620.0, 614.1

Case 3

endometriosis of the posterior uterine serosa and left fallopian tube, fibrous adhesions, adenomyosis of the uterus; endometriosis, adhesions, adenomyosis; 617.0, 617.2, 614.6, 617.0

Case 4

atrophic breasts with moderate fibrocystic breast changes and moderate ductal hyperplasia; atrophic, hyperplasia; 611.4, 610.1

Case 5

bilateral hypertrophy of the breasts with grade III ptosis; hypertrophy, ptosis; 611.1, 611.81

Case 6

cervical incompetence; cervical incompetence; 654.53

Case 7

cyclic pelvic pain, menorrhagia, endometriosis, uterine serosa; 625.9, 626.2, 617.0; diagnostic laparoscopy with biopsy, hysteroscopy with endometrial sampling; laparoscopy; 68.15

Case 8

ruptured left isthmic ectopic pregnancy; 633.10; laparoscopic left partial salpingectomy; salpingectomy; 66.69

Case 9

menometrorrhagia and cervical stenosis; 626.2, 622.4; diagnostic hysteroscopy and dilation and curettage of the uterus; dilation and curettage, uterus; 69.09

Case 10

class II cervical dysplasia, cervicitis; 622.12, 616.0; colposcopy with cervical biopsy; biopsy; 67.12

Case 11

high-grade papillary serous cancer of the endometrium; 182.0; total abdominal hysterectomy, bilateral salpingo-oophorectomy, pelvic lymphadenectomy with partial omentectomy; hysterectomy, salpingo-oophorectomy, lymphadenectomy, omentectomy; 68.49, 65.61, 40.3, 54.4

Case 12

intrauterine pregnancy at 40 weeks estimated gestational age, cephalopelvic disproportion, prolonged second-stage labor, fetal stress, and outcome of delivery; 653.41, 662.21, 656.81, V27.0; primary low transverse cesarean section; cesarean section; 74.1

Case 13

diagnostic laparoscopy with biopsy, hysteroscopy with endometrial sampling; hysteroscopy; 58558

Case 14

laparoscopic left partial salpingectomy; salpingectomy; 58661

Case 15

diagnostic hysteroscopy and dilation and curettage of the uterus; dilation and curettage; 58120

Case 16

colposcopy with cervical biopsy; colposcopy; 57455

Case 17

total abdominal hysterectomy, bilateral salpingo-oophorectomy, pelvic lymphadenectomy with partial omentectomy; hysterectomy; 58210

Case 18

primary low transverse cesarean section; cesarean delivery; 59514

Medical Terminology Challenge

1. both sides
3. surgical instrument for piercing the skin or the wall of a cavity
5. above the pubis
7. instrument for grasping and pulling
9. area between the vaginal opening and the anus
11. cutting or tying off with a suture or wire
13. suture technique that resembles a pursestring
15. controlling or stopping the flow of blood

CHAPTER 13 NERVOUS SYSTEM, EYE, AND EAR

Exercise 13-1

1. cerebr/o = brain; no prefix; -al = pertaining to; pertaining to the brain
3. neur/o = nerve; no prefix; -(o)logist = specialist; nerve specialist
5. neur/o = nerve; no prefix; surgeon (self explanatory); physician who operates on the nervous system
7. no root; hemi- = half; -plegia = paralysis; paralysis of one-half or one side
9. thec/o = sheath; intra- = within; -al = pertaining to; pertaining to within a sheath

Exercise 13-2

A. Neuron
1. cell body
3. axon
5. terminal end fibers
B. Brain and brain stem
1. cerebrum
3. midbrain
5. medulla oblongata
7. hypothalamus

Exercise 13-3

1. cerebral aneurysm
3. cerebrovascular accident
5. amyotrophic lateral sclerosis
7. glioma
9. hemiplegia

Exercise 13-4

1. (a) absence of a brain; (b) inflammation of the brain
3. (a) acute inflammation of several nerves of the peripheral nervous system; (b) genetic disorder

characterized by degeneration of cerebral neurons

5. (a) partial paralysis of one side of the body; (b) paralysis of one side of the body

Exercise 13-5

1. (a) slow-growth tumor of the meninges of the brain; (b) highly malignant tumor cells from embryonic neural tissue
3. (a) nerve pain; (b) any disease of nerves or nervous tissue
5. (a) fainting; loss of consciousness due to lack of blood supply to the brain; (b) temporary interruption of the blood supply to a portion of the brain, usually involves tissue death
7. (a) paralysis of the lower part of the body, including the legs; (b) paralysis of all four limbs

Exercise 13-6

1. b
3. g
5. a
7. f
9. e

Exercise 13-7

1. (blank)
3. (blank)
5. X
7. (blank)

Exercise 13-8

1. transcutaneous electrical nerve stimulation; pain-relief treatment
3. pneumoencephalography; recording an x-ray of the ventricles and other fluid-filled cavities of the central nervous system
5. cerebrospinal fluid analysis; laboratory analysis of cerebrospinal fluid

Exercise 13-9

1. ocul/o = eye; intra- = within; -ar = pertaining to; pertaining to within the eye
3. nas/o = nose; lacrim/o = tears; no prefix; -al = pertaining to; pertaining to the nose and tear duct
5. ophthalm/o = eye; no prefix; -(o)logy = study of; study of the eyes
7. corne/o = cornea; no prefix; -al = pertaining to; pertaining to the cornea
9. no root; hyper- = above, excessive; -opia = vision; excessive vision

Exercise 13-10

1. ciliary body (and muscle)
3. iris
5. cornea
7. sclera
9. optic nerve

Exercise 13-11

1. cataract
3. diplopia
5. glaucoma
7. chalazion
9. ectropion

Exercise 13-12

1. (a) inflammation of the eyelids; (b) drooping of the eyelids
3. (a) separation of the retina from the eyeball; (b) disease of the retina caused by uncontrolled diabetes mellitus

Exercise 13-13

1. hyperopia
3. nystagmus
5. myopia

Exercise 13-14

1. pterygium
3. trachoma
5. ophthalmia neonatorum

Exercise 13-15

1. (a) abnormal sensitivity to light; (b) damaged retina due to excessive exposure to light
3. (a) inflammation of the cornea; (b) inflammation of the sclera and cornea

Exercise 13-16

1. (blank)
3. (blank)
5. (blank)
7. (blank)
9. X

Exercise 13-17

1. eyelid
3. iris
5. eye
7. vitreous humor

Exercise 13-18

1. acoust/o = hearing; no prefix; -ic = pertaining to; pertaining to hearing
3. audi/o = hearing, sound; no prefix; -(o)logy = study of; study of hearing
5. cochle/o = cochlea; no prefix; -ar = pertaining to; pertaining to the cochlea

7. ot/o = ear; no prefix; -(o)logy = study of; study of the ear
9. tympan/o = eardrum; no prefix; -plasty = repair; repair of the eardrum
11. audi/o = hearing; no prefix; -metry = measuring; measuring hearing

Exercise 13-19

1. auricle (pinna)
3. tympanic membrane
5. incus
7. eustachian tube
9. cochlea

Exercise 13-20

1. acoustic neuroma
3. cholesteatoma
5. tinnitus
7. impacted cerumen

Exercise 13-21

1. (a) hearing loss caused by impaired transmission of sound waves; (b) hearing loss due to impaired or damaged auditory nerve cells
3. (a) fungal infection of the ear; (b) irregular ossification of the bones of the middle ear
5. (a) chronic inner ear disease with vertigo, tinnitus, nausea, vomiting; (b) inner ear infection or inflammation

Exercise 13-22

1. myringoplasty
3. otoplasty
5. audiogram
7. otoscopy

Exercise 13-23

1. a form characterized by dense localized infiltrations of lymphoid tissue that occur as a response to irritation; conjunctivitis; 372.02
3. inflammation of the meninges by either a bacterium or a virus; meningitis; 320.9
5. a form of macular degeneration occurring in persons over 40 years of age; degeneration; 362.50
7. separation of the retina from the choroid layer of the eye; detachment; 361.01
9. disease of the retina and its capillaries caused by long-standing and usually poorly controlled diabetes mellitus; retinopathy; 250.50, 362.04
11. inability of the eyes to gaze in the same direction because of weakness of the eye muscles; strabismus; 378.00
13. the most common kind of cataract, painless and of unknown cause, developing without any traumatic, ocular, systemic, or congenital disorder; cataract; 366.10

15. meningitis in piglets caused by streptococcus; meningitis; 320.2
17. severe weakening and wasting of various muscle groups due to loss of motor neuron; sclerosis; 335.20
19. recurring episodes of excessive or irregular electrical activity of the central nervous system and resistant to treatment with medication; epilepsy; 345.11

Exercise 13-24

1. drainage by cranial burr holes from collection of blood below the dura mater and above the arachnoid membrane; hematoma; 01.31
3. incision into the skull to provide access to the brain or to relieve intracranial pressure; clipping; 39.51
5. incision into the cranium; resection; 38.61
7. excision of the labyrinth of the ear and excision of the mastoid air cells or the mastoid process; labyrinthectomy, mastoidectomy; 20.79, 20.49
9. surgical repair or plastic surgery of the eyelid; repair; 08.34
11. removal of the crystalline lens and the anterior segment of the lens capsule and surgical implantation of a crystalline lens, usually done at the same time as cataract extraction; extraction, insertion; 13.59, 13.71
13. removal of a fragment of steel or iron from the eyeball by means of a powerful magnet; removal; 98.21
15. surgical implantation of an object partially or totally for prosthetic, therapeutic, or diagnostic purposes; implant; 20.96

Exercise 13-25

1. replacement; 62230
3. biopsy; 61576
5. evacuation; 61312
7. repair; 65286
9. keratotomy; 65771
11. otoplasty; 69300-69350; or 69300; 69300
13. cochlear device; 69930
15. labyrinthectomy; 69910

Chapter Review

Case 1

acute right otitis media and externa; otitis; 382.9, 380.10

Case 2

pterygium, right eye with limited inflammation; pterygium; 372.40

Case 3

chronic relapsing conjunctivitis; conjunctivitis; 372.10

Case 4

annual physical examination, status cortical petit mal epilepsy; examination, epilepsy; V70.0, 345.2

Case 5

quadriplegia, incomplete, fracture of the upper end of C-7, probable spinal cord compression or injury; quadriplegia, fracture; 344.04, 805.07

Case 6

arachnoid cyst and mild compression from the arachnoid cyst; cyst, compression; 348.0, 348.4

Case 7

acute vitreous hemorrhage, right eye; hemorrhage; 379.23

Case 8

aphakia, left eye; 379.31; anterior vitrectomy with implantation of anterior chamber intraocular lens; vitrectomy, insertion; 14.73, 13.70

Case 9

recurrent bilateral otitis media with persistent middle ear effusion; 381.4; bilateral myringotomy with tube insertion; myringotomy; 20.01, 20.01

Case 10

essential tremor; 333.1; placement of right internal pulse generator; implant; 86.96

Case 11

rhegmatogenous retinal detachment, left eye; 361.00; sclera buckle, left eye, cryotherapy, external drainage; buckling, sclera; cryotherapy; 14.49, 14.32

Case 12

corneal perforation left eye, intraocular foreign body left eye, possible corneal ulcer left eye; 871.6; pseudophakic penetrating keratoplasty left eye (patch graft), removal of intraocular foreign body left eye, injection of intravitreal antibiotics left eye; keratoplasty, removal, injection; 11.63, 12.02, 99.21

Case 13

anterior vitrectomy with implantation of anterior chamber intraocular lens; vitrectomy, implantation; 67010, 66985

Case 14

bilateral myringotomy with tube insertion; myringotomy; 69436-69450; or 69436; 69436

Case 15

placement of right internal pulse generator; insertion; 61885

Case 16

sclera buckle, left eye, cryotherapy, external drainage; scleral buckling operation; 67107

Case 17

pseudophakic penetrating keratoplasty left eye (patch graft), removal of intraocular foreign body left eye, injection of intravitreal antibiotics left eye; keratoplasty, removal; 65755, 65235; Per NCCI edits, the injection is a component/bundled of the keratoplasty and not separately coded.

Medical Terminology Challenge

1. both sides
3. holes drilled in the skull
5. paralysis on two sides
7. escape of fluid
9. within the vitreous humor
11. pertaining to a failure of development of a natural crystalline lens

CHAPTER 14 INFECTIOUS AND PARASITIC DISEASES

Exercise 14-1

1. jointed foot
3. inflammation of the intestines
5. round, clusterlike (structures)

Exercise 14-2

1. unicellular, living microorganisms, exhibit metabolic activity
3. round (round-shaped bacteria)
5. microorganisms that live in the human body; do not cause disease

7. organisms that live in a host and deprive the host of nutrients
9. spiral-shaped bacteria

Exercise 14-3

1. B	7. B	13. B
3. P	9. B	15. P
5. P	11. P	

Exercise 14-4

1. (blank)	5. X
3. X	7. (blank)

Exercise 14-5

1. (none)
3. histoplasmosis

Exercise 14-6

1. genital warts
3. genital herpes
5. syphilis

Exercise 14-7

1. chancre
3. gonorrhea
5. correct

Exercise 14-8

1. h	7. d
3. g	9. j
5. b	

Exercise 14-9

1. a chronic bacterial infection characterized by localized abscesses of the face and neck that produces a purulent discharge; actinomycosis; 039.3
3. a fungal infection caused by inhaling the spores of *Blastomyces dermatitidis*; blastomycosis; 116.0
5. inflammation of the vagina and bacteria infection; vaginitis; 099.53, 616.11
7. characterized by hepatomegaly, splenomegaly, lymphadenopathy, and bone marrow involvement; histoplasmosis; 115.90
9. a viral disease caused by the human papilloma virus; warts; 078.19

11. relating to or caused by herpes virus, the formation or development of an ulcer of the vulva; ulceration; 054.12

Exercise 14-10

1. screening (for); V75.8; examination (for); 90.92
3. screening (for); V73.3; examination (for); 90.59
5. vaccination; V06.4; vaccination; 99.45, 99.46, 99.47, 99.48

Exercise 14-11

1. culture; 87045
3. rubella; 86762
5. pinworms; 87172
7. vaccines; 90710, 90471
9. skin; 86580

Chapter Review

Case 1

examination (for); 90.59; screening (for) V74.8; actinomyces; 86602

Case 2

examination (for); 90.59, 91.42; screening (for) V73.88; infectious agent 87270; culture 87110

Case 3

examination (for); 90.92; screening (for) V74.8; culture 87045

Case 4

examination (for) 91.41; screening (for) V73.89; smear and stain 87207

Case 5

examination (for) 91.43; screening (for) V74.5; culture 87106; sensitivity study 87181

Medical Terminology Challenge

1. immunoglobulin produced in response to a disease-causing organism
3. pertaining to the study of cells
5. pertaining to the study of tissue
7. introduction of a substance into the body to produce an immune response
9. egg
11. condition that follows a disease or condition
13. study of poison or poisonous substances
15. substance used to induce immunity

CHAPTER 15 SYMPTOMS, SIGNS, AND ILL-DEFINED CONDITIONS

Exercise 15-1

1. mass, bleeding; 789.30, 569.3
3. hypertension; 401.9
5. fever, anemia, human immunodeficiency virus; 780.60, 285.9, 042
7. convulsions; 780.31

Exercise 15-2

1. evaluation and management; 99387
3. evaluation and management; 99215
5. CBC; 85025

Chapter Review

1. comprehensive preventative medicine exam, established patient; 99396; comprehensive preventative physical exam, bladder infection; V70.0, 595.9;

urinalysis with microscopy, CBC automated with differential; 81000, 85025
3. comprehensive history and physical exam, new patient; 99204; fever possible sepsis, hypercholesterolemia, hypertension controlled; 780.60, 272.0, 401.9

Medical Terminology Challenge

1. any irregular heart rhythm
3. general weakness and emaciation
5. electrocardiography (electrocardiogram); recording or record of the electrical activity of the heart
7. increased cholesterol in the blood
9. openings of the nose
11. irregular heart rate usually reported or felt by the patient
13. related to fainting
15. white blood cell (count); the number of white blood cells in a sample of blood

Index

Page numbers followed by f indicate figures and those followed by t indicate tables.